DISPATCHES FROM THE WAR ROOM

ALSO BY STANLEY B. GREENBERG

The Two Americas

The New Majority

Middle Class Dreams

Legitimating the Illegitimate

Race and State in Capitalist Development

Politics and Poverty

Hub —
You lived this moment
of change. Hopefully, lessons
to these times,

DISPATCHES

FROM THE

WAR ROOM

In the Trenches with
Five Extraordinary Leaders

STANLEY B. GREENBERG

To bold leaders

THOMAS DUNNE BOOKS
ST. MARTIN'S PRESS ✹ NEW YORK

THOMAS DUNNE BOOKS.
An imprint of St. Martin's Press.

DISPATCHES FROM THE WAR ROOM. Copyright © 2009 by Stanley B. Greenberg. All rights reserved. Printed in the United States of America. For information, address St. Martin's Press, 175 Fifth Avenue, New York, N.Y. 10010.

www.thomasdunnebooks.com
www.stmartins.com

Book design by Ruth Lee-Mui

Library of Congress Cataloging-in-Publication Data

Greenberg, Stanley B., 1945–
    Dispatches from the war room : in the trenches with five extraordinary leaders / Stanley B. Greenberg.—1st ed.
        p.   cm.
    ISBN-13: 978-0-312-35152-6
    ISBN-10: 0-312-35152-6
    1. Greenberg, Stanley B., 1945– 2. Political consultants—United States—Biography. 3. United States—Politics and government—1989– 4. World politics—1989– 5. Clinton, Bill, 1946– 6. Blair, Tony, 1953– 7. Barak, Ehud, 1942– 8. Sánchez de Lozada, Gonzalo. 9. Mandela, Nelson, 1918– 10. Political leadership—Case studies. I. Title.
    E840.8.G73A3 2009
    324.7—dc22

                                                                                        2008029884

ISBN-13: 978-0-312-35152-6
ISBN-10: 0-312-35152-6

First Edition: February 2009

10 9 8 7 6 5 4 3 2 1

*This book is dedicated to Rigby Maya Zentner,
Sadie Liberty Delicath, and Teo Issac Zentner,
our grandchildren*

CONTENTS

DISPATCHES FROM THE WAR ROOM

INTRODUCTION

I CONFESS. I'M a member of what the political reporter Joe Klein inelegantly calls the "pollster-consultant industrial complex." To its critics the members of this complex are ruining politics, robbing the political process of its romance and vigor, and leaving the populace stuck with overly cautious, cynical, mechanistic, and bland campaigns and politicians. The more spin, the less conviction and authenticity. The hot content in elections everywhere no longer is the election itself. The real excitement lies in the use of polls and focus groups to hunt down the elusive swing voter, pin him to the ground, and subject him to repetitive tests of "small, easily understandable ideas," a process painfully exposed in the British documentary *Election Unspun*. That the banal slogans "Your Family Better Off" and "Your Child Achieving More" could be championed by any of the major parties leaves viewers with this question: "How has British politics reached this desperate state of affairs where instead of great ideas we have meaningless trivialities?"[1]

Yes, I'm a "pollster," even if the word catches in my throat when people ask me what I do. I never write "pollster" on the immigration form lest I be refused admittance to the country. I write "businessman." Every nation wants businessmen.

So low is the repute in which the pollster is held that President George W. Bush—who has gotten *every* big decision wrong—feels he can reassure voters by saying, "We believe in principles, not polls or focus groups. We believe in doing what's right for America." Ask not what the pollster can do for his

1

country. It's a view shared by both sides of the aisle. Here's John Edwards, the straight-talking presidential candidate: "We don't need to be shifting and jiving to meet what the polls yesterday said or what the focus group said." And the pundits and politicians on the Sunday morning talk fests gain gravitas by taking their shots, too. "Too many Democrats are focus group leaders," observes Fareed Zakaria of *Newsweek*. Newt Gingrich, of all people, finishes the thought: "The country is sick of people who put their fingers in the air and figure out what position to take on the weekend."

The popular depiction of all this is richer, but no less demeaning of leaders who turn to consultants. For the most part, pollsters in *The West Wing* or in *The American President* are benign professionals who speak in numbers. "You're 10 points up"—the unstated "approval rating," part of the common language of the political class. "Eighty percent support an amendment prohibiting flag burning." "Gallup is saying 82 percent support immediate military action in response to Gaza." The pollster gives the hero not just a number, but a temptation, much like a drug dealer. If you take this position, you can be popular and therefore powerful; if you take it, you can head off a devastating thirty-second ad that ends your political career. When President Bartlet or President Shepherd refuses temptations it's because they have character, backbone, and idealism. They *believe* in something.

Hollywood's bad guys in the old political movies were corrupt party bosses worming their way into control over innocents who believed they were elected to do the citizenry's bidding. In today's political movies—*The War Room, Primary Colors, Wag the Dog*—the villain is the consultant, masterful and morally ambiguous, constantly testing the candidates' integrity with recommendations to run attack ads or take money from dubious sources in exchange for votes. The candidates often reject the advice, but inexorably the Rasputin-like consultant assumes an unseemly hidden control over the political leader who is supposed to be accountable to the citizenry.

In Britain, particularly during the Tony Blair years, the media made the term "spin doctor" a part of the language that requires no definition. Reporters and commentators routinely expect that the moment a candidate debate ends the "spin doctors" will rush to the "spin room" to tell journalists just how well their candidate did. The assumption that everything politicians say is "spin" makes a mockery of trust and authenticity. Not surprisingly, voters find it difficult to believe leaders will keep their promises or should be rewarded or reelected based on what they have actually accomplished.

Frank Luntz is perhaps the epitome of the modern *spinmeister*, now almost a parody of himself. In a segment of *The Daily Show* faux correspondent Samantha Bee described him as a man "who has made a brilliant career spraying perfume on dog turds" and asked Luntz to provide his take on several phrases:

BEE: *"Drilling for oil."*
LUNTZ: *"I would say responsible exploration for energy."*
BEE: *"Logging."*
LUNTZ: *"I would say healthy forests."*
BEE: *"Manipulation."*
LUNTZ: *"Explanation and education."*[2]

Then, there is me. In *The War Room*, I'm the short, bespectacled Jewish guy with bushy hair who speaks in numbers, never about issues or strategy. In *The American President* the fictional pollster modeled on me is a short, bespectacled Jewish nerd who speaks in numbers. In both cases my job is to help politicians amass power and win reelection.

But real-life depictions of me endow me with far greater powers. One Mexican publication labeled me "The Oracle of Delphi" and attributed to me the ability to accurately predict election day outcomes. I foretell if ambitious and insecure politicians will, on election day, win or lose everything they've worked their life to achieve. And because the media presume politicians are mere marionettes manipulated by their pollster puppet masters, being the successful pollster for prominent leaders multiplies the aura.

"Everybody wants to see the wizard responsible for the wins of Bill Clinton and Blair, Gerhard Schroeder and Thabo Mbeki," proclaimed one Italian newspaper. *The New Yorker* pegs me as the man who "for his part, has been quietly pursuing world domination." *The Akron Beacon Journal* is no less generous: "Meet Stan Greenberg, conducting the country's foreign policy." With my wizardry confirmed by electoral victories, the press assumes everything the elected leader does is the result of my clever handiwork. Britain's *The Guardian* credits me for stage-managing Al Gore's passionate kiss with his wife at the Democratic convention. Now I'm responsible when any candidate I advise kisses his wife.

Powerful is one thing, evil is quite another. When I asked to present our new poll results for Francesco Rutelli, the center-left candidate running against Silvio Berlusconi, I was shocked by the banks of television cameras and photographers and the hundreds of Italian and foreign journalists and politicians that gathered to hear me and my seasoned partner Jeremy Rosner. The correspondent for *Corriere della Sera*, Italy's equivalent of *The New York Times*, provided what amounted to color commentary: I was "sly Stanley Greenberg, consultant to the powerful all over the world" and "Rutelli's American guru." Jeremy fared worse. He was "all dressed in blue and with the evil air of some of those young CIA agents common in Bruce Willis movies." When it was over the "two Americans, Sly the Fox and Mr. Nasty" made their way into the day.

Why do I occupy this improbable niche of advising royalty, prime ministers, and presidents? I would like to think it is because of my writings on center-left politics, social democracy, and reclaiming the middle class. More likely, given the great uncertainties they face in the campaign ahead and the struggle to govern successfully, they simply feel more secure expanding their circle of advisors to include someone who was close to Bill Clinton, the vanquisher of the establishment's president in the most powerful country on earth.

But maybe they are giving in to their own fears and invite me to foreign capitals because I am the master of some "black art" and can show them the way to victory. I do muse of earlier times when kings, princes, and sultans found it useful to have Jewish advisors close at hand, albeit not too visible. They were uniquely literate and not of the society, especially skilled in financial matters frowned upon by the Christian and Muslim worlds. When I polled for Michael Häupl, mayor of Vienna in 2001, the anti-Semitic head of the Freedom Party, Jörg Haider, announced before his party convention, "Häupl has a strategist called Greenberg," eliciting giggles in the room. "He specially flew him in from the East Coast"—for Haider, read "East Coast" as New York City, the center of Jewish finance capital. "Dear friends, you have the choice on 25 March between spin-doctor Greenberg from the East Coast or the Viennese hearts." This was greeted by massive applause. But when Häupl spoke to his final rally of two thousand supporters jammed into the Hapsburgs' former stables, he finished with a warning to Haider: "His attacks against the East Coast and against our consultant Greenberg" and against the Jewish community at large are anti-Semitic. "This policy is against all of us."[3] In an instant, all the talk of the "black arts" is demystified and the need for a more sober assessment of our politics now all too clear.

This was a lot easier years ago when we were innocent enough to be excited about George Gallup's breakthrough. Finally, rigorously designed polls could give an ordinary citizen an equal voice on the issues of the day within the corridors of power. No longer would elected leaders have to make long journeys to the countryside to hear their constituents, pore over newspaper editorials to parse the electorate's mood, or have poorly paid staffers sort postcards and letters into "for" and "against" piles. The implication, of course, is that with more polls, leaders will have a better feel for people's thinking.

In the three decades up to the early 1970s in the United States there is considerable evidence that the new public opinion surveys did indeed influence leaders on major issues and played a role in the evolution of their thinking. It was, of course, a time when the nation held its politicians and elites in higher regard. Dwight Eisenhower, John and Robert Kennedy, Lyndon John-son, even Sam Rayburn, led during a time of changing attitudes on gender, race, and other issues and shifting ideologies. Although pollsters weren't then hanging out in the Oval Office and halls of Congress, politicians, less gerryman-dered and entrenched in their jobs, nonetheless anticipated, led, and aligned themselves in rough fashion with the emerging trends.

The last three decades have been different. Politicians have become less responsive to the public mood, a trend especially evident in the past decade's political polarization. Since the 1980s there has been a steadily widening ideological gap between the two major parties, producing partisan leaders and activists increasingly distant from the thinking of average Americans. Since the early 1990s the problem has been especially acute in the Republi-can Party, as its activists have grown ever more extreme and distant from independent voters. How else would it have been politically possible to pro-ceed with President Clinton's impeachment, the attempted privatization of Social Security, and the escalation of the Iraq War, actions that the American public intensely opposed? The looming chasm between the people and their leaders has resulted in historically low regard for both parties and a histori-cally low belief that political leaders are in tune with the people.

Is it possible politicians are turning to pollsters, consultants, and spin doc-tors not to better align themselves with shifting public sentiment, but to manage or even defy it, to avoid the public's ultimate sanctions on election day?[4]

The gap with the public may also be widening as the result of the dra-matic rise in income inequality over the last three decades, matched by a growing political role for business and the wealthy, who are two or three times more likely than low-income and middle-class voters to see their policy preferences reflected by Congress and the White House. On foreign policy questions, the views of globally oriented business leaders had the biggest im-pact, able to argue for less regulation and taxes and a massive bailout when the botom fell out. The views of the general public had almost no impact on policy. No wonder we have witnessed the doubling of the number of highly paid lobbyists in Washington since 2000.

The increasingly competitive twenty-four-hour news environment further widens the gap with the public and diminishes our politics. Coverage of polls even in the major newspapers and networks gravitates to the horse race and who's ahead, turning the polls themselves into news rather than covering is-sues and policy debates. In the United States, where the network evening news programs have lost half their audiences since 1980, cable networks use hastily crafted overnight tracking, automated phone and Internet polls to create cheap news content and battle for audience, a trend imitated in Britain and Israel. But erratic polls of uncertain quality create the appearances of volatility and voter fickleness and diminish the regard for voters themselves and destroy any chance the election becomes a defining battle over issues.[5]

V. O. Key, the inspired teacher and writer on politics and public opinion, tells us that "if democracy is to exist, the belief must be widespread that public opinion, at least in the long run, affects the course of public action." But some social scientists describe a contrary reality of where "most politicians are keenly motivated and amply skilled at evading electoral accountability for long periods." In today's world that is when the call goes out to the "pollster-consultant industrial complex."

Frank Luntz, the master of obscurantism, responded to the call and urged endangered Republican candidates in the 2006 elections to own the American flag and to "humanize, personalize and individualize their policies." On tax cuts mainly for those with the highest incomes, he declared: "Everyone must benefit—*particularly hardworking, overburdened American taxpayers*"; on spending cuts and Social Security privatization: "Stop talking about pain. Start talking about '*shared sacrifice*' and '*generational fairness.*'"

With the creation of a "war room" in the White House to win passage of the Clinton economic and health care plans, this all takes on the appearance of a "permanent campaign"—a critique raised by the media about Number 10 under Tony Blair and the prime minister's office under Ehud Barak. In this role, I helped "sell" the Clinton health care plan—a plan too "extreme" to win support among "centrist voters," according to critics—by helping politicians develop "crafted talk," infuse their communications with "alluring words," and use campaign and communication techniques to "simulate responsiveness."

Dick Morris, who as always takes everything to the level of the absurd, contends that a leader needs a popular majority not just on election day, but every day of his tenure in office. If a leader drops below 50 percent in the public opinion polls, "he is functionally out of office," says Morris. "A politician needs a permanent campaign to keep a permanent majority," and thus must keep a stable of consultants close at hand.[6] What an elixir that was for Karl Rove, according to Scott McClellan's insider account of the Bush White House. The politics of "manipulation of shades of truth, partial truths, twisting of the truth, and spin" that characterize campaigns "simply morphed into a different phase—governance." From his key seat in the West Wing, Rove put his "hands in just about everything" creating the ugly brew that provoked John McCain to vow, "If I'm elected president, the era of the permanent campaign will end."[7]

Are we witnessing a hostage situation—the centers of power seized by a professional elite who have turned high purpose into mere policies and leadership into a frenetic daily search for popularity? Is it possible that the techniques that I have mastered to make leaders more accountable to the people actually make it possible for political leaders to avoid accountability? What if my work permits "elected leaders" to grow arrogant and out of touch, even venal and unsympathetic to the common good without consequence? Put simply, does my work allow leaders to loosen their bond with people and diminish its purposefulness?

I take these questions seriously, which is why I decided to write these stories of five bold political leaders from my perspective as their pollster, helping them make their parties electable, fashion a governing strategy, and keep people with them as they advance their agenda and attempt to win a vote of confidence to carry on. This is not a conventional memoir or a conventional biographical account of these leaders. This is my account of what I do but also the story of my relationship with these leaders as they took their mission to the public in fraught times and battled to succeed. Because voters are judgmental and leaders ambitious, these stories are full of uncertainty; because I write about tumultuous times and leaders with ambitious agendas for change, these stories contain both drama and history. My role places me between people and these politicians and allows me to write these stories from a unique perspective. Because of what I do as a pollster and because I express my views strongly and in writing in the midst of these battles, these stories unfold in real time, with the information and advice leaders had at the time and the choices they made.

This book tells a story of five leaders—Bill Clinton, Nelson Mandela, Tony Blair, Ehud Barak, and Gonzalo Sánchez de Lozada—all presidents or prime ministers who won voters' support in formative elections, then used modern campaign techniques in their struggle to govern successfully. I am writing about them as leaders, but self-consciously from my vantage point, a perspective that may allow the reader to learn something new about their character and politics and the events and history in which they held the lead roles. In the process, the reader will see what I do as a pollster in real life and real time and how it affects society and people. It is not romanticized, and I wrote it for myself as well as the reader.

I worked for these leaders and write about them here because they are all reforming leaders who tried to make their parties electable by modernizing them and their countries and by battling against conservative forces to make them more equal and more united. I was attracted to these leaders, but also by the forces coming together at these particular times and the tumult that would likely produce elections that were about something. These were not political incumbents for reelection in happy times. That may give me a distorted vantage point on the larger world of elections, but I can live with that, as it shows what is possible through politics, not just the mundane and tawdry.

On the other hand these leaders turned to me not for my theorizing but because of my presumed skill in helping politicians win elections. Thus, the book is a real-life test of the proposition that both leadership and politics are diminished by the modern campaign methods I employ.

I take that opportunity to describe what I do behind that curtain at Oz.

What I do puts ordinary people into the story, but so did the times and the character of these leaders. These were desperate times in these countries when the citizenry longed for change and made great demands on politics. The expectation that some leader would touch people or win their confidence and bring about change is very much part of the sometimes unseemly struggle of politicians to rise above the many others who think they have such a claim. Thus, these leaders worked intently to build a special bond with people. Had they failed they would not have become leaders with the opportunity to govern and bring change. Nevertheless, most of them faltered or failed with consequences for their countries.

What is lost in the idealized view people have of the political consultants and the victory of their clients is how difficult it is to control the meaning of politics and define the choice in an election in a tumultuous period, how hard it is to actually act on your promises, and how hard it is to keep people with you. All these leaders sent expectations and hopes in their countries sky-high. They all struggled with a deep disillusionment that tested them personally and called into question their ability to succeed in their central political mission and in their own lives.

Each of these leaders developed his thinking, values, and political objectives over a lifetime and got the chance to sharpen and evolve those objectives at a moment of change in the country when a formative election changed the political fortunes of the parties and changed the public agenda. They were successful and changed the terms of debate precisely because they did not just ride the political tides. Rather, they constructed hard-hitting campaigns and war rooms and used polling advice to define the choice and the stakes and the type of leader the times demanded to make themselves indispensable to making the changes people were so desperate to see.

Once in power and up against the real world of forces conspiring against change, they struggled and faltered even as they worked intensely to engage people to carry forward their objectives, both the political project defined in the campaign and on election day and those that grew out of their life's work that governed many of the choices they made in office. These are all determined leaders with real goals who want both to educate people and win their support, perhaps even their affections. Some would succeed politically but at least two will find themselves prematurely out of office, one the result of an election, the other of violence.

While I am frequently frustrated and sometimes deeply at odds with these leaders on matters of principle, I have great respect for them, a respect undiminished by knowing them better. I know that is hard to believe, but in my work for them and in this book, I rely on a kind of self-conscious inno-cence to push aside the problematic and get to their main purpose in seeking to lead the country. I fully understand these are complicated people with complicated motives, ambitious, self-centered, and with more flaws than I want to know, but what other qualities would allow them to rise above the others with a claim to lead? For those who want to tell a critical story, they will find plenty of material here. But I also hope they will consider after read-ing these stories that politics can be filled with purpose and honor.

Whether what I do is filled with purpose and honor, and whether the "pollster-consultant industrial complex" elevates or diminishes leaders and politics, those conclusions I will leave to the unfolding account and the end.

In each of these accounts, I write about the main political project at the center of the campaign and the effort to carry forward the project in the after-math of the election when they are governing. That leaves out a lot, including the character of the leader, scandal and corruption, and other parts of their agenda that are central to the public's overall judgment about the leader. My filter is their purpose and project, affirmed in its own way by the voters in an election and how both the leaders and the public then navigate the way to a judgment.

Bill Clinton set out as his mission to renew the Democratic Party so it would be electable and so that it could, in turn, renew the country. The party of Franklin Roosevelt had lost the support of working people, the forgotten middle class who did not trust the Democrats to handle their tax dollars, make the country prosperous and secure, or to advance their values. My story begins with the election upheaval of the 1992 election when Clinton set out his economic plan and vision for expanded opportunity with a return to re-sponsibility and reformed government. The later battles over the budget and economic policies were, at their core, a fight for the Clinton presidency. It was also a battle over its meaning and mission.

Nelson Mandela led the African National Congress, the ANC, in South Africa's first democratic elections and hardly needed polls to know he was going to win. Yet he worked intently to become a democratic leader and head an inclusive, modern campaign that would touch people and form a govern-ment accountable to them—despite powerful forces in South Africa and among Africans that worked for a very different outcome. Reflecting a lifetime battle against racial domination, he rejected a campaign whose goal was to displace whites with blacks in government. Mandela embraced the banner, "A Better Life for All" and the struggle to make that real in a country truly desperate for a better life.

Tony Blair in 1994 became leader of a Labour Party that the public did not trust with anything important and that had failed to win an election in decades, even when the economy was crashing and the Conservatives were deeply hated. The 1992 defeat, the same year as Bill Clinton's victory, was a searing experience for the young leaders who would run and win in 1997 under the banner of "New Labour." That required relentless reassurance on values, taxes, and spending that allowed people to vote for an economy that worked for hardworking families and investment and reform of the public services, its main mission. This is a story about Blair's intense but uneven effort to advance that project in government and the even more intense struggle to keep the people with him, despite a breakdown in trust, later compounded by the Iraq War.

Ehud Barak, the new leader of Israel's Labor Party, was defined by history: heir to the assassinated Yitzhak Rabin, who had attempted to make peace with the Palestinians, and to David Ben-Gurion, Israel's first prime minister, who accepted the partition of Palestine to achieve statehood. But Barak was also heir to an elitist Labor Party out of touch with the waves of new immigrants and new social gaps and not trusted to negotiate with the Arabs. As Israel's most decorated soldier, Barak reassured on security, but he won dramatically because he promised to get Israel unstuck on the economy and social gaps and to break the embrace of the religious and settler extremists. With a very small window of opportunity and a fragile government, Barak threw himself completely into the task of achieving a historic peace with Syria, Lebanon, and the Palestinians and getting the Israeli public to contemplate issues never considered before.

Gonzalo Sánchez de Lozada is known to everyone in Bolivia as "Goni." Armed with the top economic portfolio during an economic crisis of biblical proportions, he brought Bolivia abruptly into the global economy, saved the nation's economy, and subsequently won the presidency. As Bolivia's leader he carried out vast reforms, including an innovative privatization of old industries that funded first-ever social insurance programs for the poor. In a period of rising popular unrest and opposition to globalization, Goni ran for the presidency again in 2002 and miraculously won as the leader who could "fix the crisis" and create jobs but more: not only to export the new natural gas reserves discovered by the privatized energy sector, but also to guarantee that all the revenue would fund education and restore pensions—a linkage that made him unique among market reformers. His weak government quickly expanded social insurance, until fiscal austerity and an indifferent U.S. government, and popular opposition to exporting gas into the global economy, engulfed Goni in violence and forced him from office.

These leaders sometimes risked everything for bold reforms and their opportunity and fate hinged on the character of the bond they built with people. Popular accounts belittle the politicians for such obsessions, aided and abetted by their stable of media advisors and pollsters. I wrote these stories, not because I thought the rejoinder or answers obvious, but because they are not, leaving us with exceedingly interesting leaders and politics.

1

BILL CLINTON
Act I

THE FIRST CALL comes from Frank Greer, a comrade in arms from my earliest battles battles who is doing the advertising for Bill Clinton's campaign for reelection as governor of Arkansas. Clinton wants me to join the campaign. He has just won the Democratic primary, but unimpressively. In the polls, he is barely ahead in the general election and if he loses this November, there is no tomorrow, no Bill Clinton campaign for president of the United States.[1]

Then Gloria Cabe, Clinton's campaign manager, calls. The governor has heard about my focus group work with Reagan Democrats, the disaffected middle-class voters angry with their own party for ignoring them. Working in suburban Detroit, I spotlighted their grievances and helped put them back on center stage. Will I come to Arkansas to work on the race? You will only be doing the focus groups because Dick Morris is doing the polling, she says.

Shit. Normally that would have stopped the conversation. Morris is the kind of slimy character that keeps me from calling myself a consultant. While I share as much information as possible in my work and invite discussion, I'm told he prefers to keep the process mysterious. He brings no discernible principles to politics that might set boundaries on his work. As one of the few consultants who cross the party divide, even to help design Jesse Helms's racist campaign against Harvey Gantt, he's a pariah among Democrats. That's before I get to the more basic problem that I almost never do focus groups alone without a more reliable representative survey of voters to confirm the findings. Focus groups with forty or sixty people are only slightly more reliable than anecdotes.

But we all know that Morris would be anathema in any national race. Frank and I have been talking about Clinton for many months. The chance to work on a presidential race for someone this intriguing is too compelling. With barely a pause, I accept Gloria's offer.

I don't know what Dardanelle, Arkansas, looks like. Our two-hour drive from Little Rock puts us there after dark and we go straight to a hotel whose small ballroom, usually host to local dances or Chamber of Commerce meetings, will tonight host two focus groups of voters—all people who voted for Bill Clinton in the past but who are uncertain whether he should have another term now. They are gathered at the end of the room in a circle on folding chairs with Marcia Hale, the former political director of the Democrats' congressional campaign committee who works for me now and will moderate the discussion. A bit closer to a city, they would gather in a more sterile conference-like room off a mall or an in office building, around a table, encouraged to speak their minds, but nothing is holding them back tonight anyway. I am usually behind a one-way mirror, looking for giveaway facial expressions and body language. But tonight I'm hidden behind an accordion room divider with Frank and Gloria, peeking out to get a feel for the back and forth and watching a closed-circuit TV, whispering lest our banter disturb the group.

On our way back to Little Rock, Gloria says Clinton wants to hear the results tonight. Tonight? It's going to be after midnight when we get back. I need time to look over my notes and digest what I've heard. Besides, I'm a morning person. I do some of my best work before the sun rises. But Gloria insists that we go straight to the mansion.

At the mansion Gloria leads me into the living room where people are seated on the sofa and in big comfortable chairs. Getting up to greet me, the governor and Hillary tell me how delighted they are to see me again. I sit down and catch my breath, all eyes on me as I start to panic, struggling to form coherent sentences. My lips are not moving. I gather up my nerve and say to Clinton, "I just can't do this now. I need some time and some sleep." To my relief he agrees and suggests we reassemble at 7 A.M., hardly his best time.

Back in my room at 1 A.M. I cover the bed with the postcards each participant wrote to the governor at the end of the group, telling him something he ought to be doing. Then I shuffle the papers into piles—doubts about Clinton, hopes for Clinton—trying to make sense of it all and jotting notes on what seem to be distinctive patterns. At least now I'll have something to say. Relieved, I move the papers to the floor and fall asleep.

At 7:45 A.M. the phone rings. Frank says the governor is waiting. Fuck, oh fuck, how did I sleep through the 6:30 wakeup call? Unshowered and unshaven I arrive at the mansion an hour late, much to the bemusement of Clinton's advisors. The governor, with unexpected time to wear off his morning puffiness, is as alert as he was last night and just as eager to hear what I learned. Thank God for that.

As I lay out the various responses I heard in the groups—that Clinton is too interested in national office and not focused on change in Arkansas—the governor engages one point after another, not resisting but drilling down to try to understand the nuances of the voters' thinking. Amid the discussion I couldn't help but think that here was a man who clearly loves campaigns, the battles, the courting of voters to create a special bond. He is also political to his bones: this is where he finds meaning and purpose in life. This isn't the conventional calculus of a politician running for office, but a person totally engaged with politics and life. And I'm hooked. What a joy to work with someone like this.

I propose that we run the campaign under the banner "Don't turn the clock back," though beginning with a series of positive, uplifting spots showing Clinton at work on Arkansas's problem. Frank embraces that idea, delighted that he will get to do some sunny commercials. But we draw opposition from Morris. He always wants to operate on the dark side and hungers to attack the opposition. He reminds me of the short guy in the mob movie who tries to prove he is the toughest and most loyal by jumping at the chance to do the hit, his look implying that the others lack the nerve to get the job done and thus do not the serve the boss well. When Clinton endorses the idea of starting positive, Morris is clearly disappointed the campaign will skip this first opportunity to kick the shit out of our opponent. I imagine he thinks winning through intimidation creates a kind of fear that greatly increases the power of the leader and perhaps, too, the power of the advisor.

Clinton's campaign wins the election with 57 percent of the vote.

GETTING THERE

How did I become part of the inner circle contemplating a race for the presidency of the United States? Clearly I passed some test in Bill Clinton's campaign for reelection as governor of Arkansas. That, coupled with my work bringing Reagan Democrats back to the party, according to Clinton's memoir, earned me an invitation. But as I thought about it, that was the shorthand for the longer story of my life that looks linear only upon looking back at it.[2]

My family was not political. More accurately, everybody was an FDR–Harry Truman Democrat like all Jews, except for the few socialists and communists. But with McCarthyism ascendant, our politics was repressed. My father, a brilliant man who had a deep understanding of numbers and physics, was a self-taught engineer without a college degree, the result of the family exhausting its money bringing relatives over from Russia. I was born in Philadelphia and lived there five years while my father took night classes, tried and failed at owning a series of grocery stores, and worked an assembly line at Westinghouse. In 1950 the family—my brother and I, my parents and grandparents—moved to Washington so my father could take an engineering job with the American Instrument Company, a manufacturer of precision instruments with many defense contracts that required a security clearance.

I grew up in many different neighborhoods of the segregated and very Southern Washington, beginning in an all-black, working-class neighborhood near the Tivoli Theater. I could jump the fence to get to school and my grandfather could walk to the Orthodox synagogue. Later we moved to a lower-middle-class, aspirant Jewish neighborhood called Riggs Park. Our house was right across the street from the temple that my parents, Sam and Yetta Greenberg, helped found. They became the presidents of the congregation and sisterhood and argued with the rabbi about everything. In the sixth grade, my mostly Jewish class was moved intact to an all-black school, as part of the city's desegregation plan after the Supreme Court's decision for Washington, D.C. I was pretty fearless, partly because I was short and fast and partly because my pals from my old black neighborhood protected me. I volunteered to be a school monitor and told a puny but even more fearless black kid not to piss on the boy's room floor and was surprised both by his swift punch and his teacher's lack of action. I danced with the only black girl in our class when she was left sitting alone and I helped raise funds to buy our black teacher a clock radio at the end of the school year. I was surprised when she broke into tears.

In high school, we moved to the suburbs where I attended Montgomery Blair High School. Only in my senior year did I begin to really read books and hang out with the so-called brainy kids from the more affluent neighborhoods. I thrived in an experimental class on American civilization that combined history, geography, and social sciences. I took to drama and school plays and was surprised with the rest of the college-bound crowd that our classmate Goldie Hawn opted to go to Broadway. My speech class introduced me to debate and earned me a "goodness, a very sharp mind" from the teacher. It was the first time I realized that maybe my older brother, the scholar and quarterback, hadn't gotten all the good genes.

As a high school senior my growing political awareness and a streak of teenage rebellion created an explosive relationship with my parents. I started attending a Unitarian church, I put a copy of Salvador Dali's *Last Supper* on my bedroom wall, and I threatened to join the pickets from my school in front of an all-white café next to the American Instruments building. The summer before going to college in 1963, I got a minimum wage job at one of American Instrument Company's factories in Laurel, Maryland, where nearly all the workers hailed from Appalachia, mostly West Virginia. It didn't take long for me to get in trouble when, during a lunch break, I asked my fellow workers whether they had ever considered forming a union. Somebody ratted and I got a stern lecture by the manager at the factory and then again that night at supper. When a contingent of civil rights marchers from New York City came right down Highway 1 in front of the factory, heading to the March on Washington, my white colleagues all lined up on the road to jeer them. I conspicuously remained behind with the small group of blacks who worked in the shipping department. That summer, I volunteered every night at the NAACP offices on U Street to prepare for the march and Martin Luther King.

In college, I quickly immersed myself in the Young Democrats at Miami University in little Oxford, Ohio, a membership that could endanger your security clearance in that part of America. I began writing a weekly newspaper column and helped organize a controversial program, called "Voices of Dissent," that brought speakers from polarized perspectives, including an editor of *National Review* and the head of the Communist Party in New York. That earned the displeasure both of the state legislature and the alumni association. Foolishly, I ran for president of the student body a year earlier than usual and lost to mainstream candidate Mike Oxley, who later became the chairman on the House Banking Committee and famous for the Sarbanes-Oxley bill that focused scrutiny on corporate governance. I led the protest over women's exclusion from off-campus housing, but also worked inside as a student senator to hold hearings and rewrite the university's by-laws on housing to grant equal rights to women. The protest was energizing, but the real victory was won in the process.

In the summer of 1964 I spent most of my waking hours working as a volunteer for the national Young Democrats in Washington, writing their position paper defending Lyndon Johnson's Vietnam War. I went as volunteer to the Democratic convention in Atlantic City, where I saw Robert Kennedy's stirring speech on the first night and then cheered Hubert Humphrey's selection as vice president.

The Young Democrats also brought me my first close brush with the world of the powerful. I was dating another volunteer whose close circle of friends included Beth Jenkins, daughter of the White House chief of staff, and Luci Johnson, the daughter of the first family. Implausible as it seems now we double-dated with a full Secret Service detail in tow and spent hours lounging on the couches in the Solarium atop the White House residence. Two years later I was picketing the White House in protest over the Vietnam War.

As a Harvard graduate student in 1968 I became heavily involved with a group of government department graduate students who, at the invitation of Robert Kennedy's presidential campaign, converted an American voting behavior project into a targeting and scheduling program for the campaign, processing the results of each primary and predicting in real time the types of counties where an RFK appearance would shift the most votes in the primaries to come. That work came to a crashing end the night of June 5 at the end of Sirhan Sirhan's .22 caliber pistol in the kitchen pantry of the Ambassador Hotel in Los Angeles. Too depressed and inattentive to carry on with the project, we left the computer center to dispose of our long trays of punch cards. Only after many extensions were we able to manage a final paper.[3]

For my generation, the choice between Eugene McCarthy and Robert Kennedy revealed your political heart. "Clean Gene's" antiwar campaign took with him the young, new suburban and professional classes, while the rougher-edged Robert Kennedy, increasingly attuned to injustice, appealed to both blacks and white blue-collar Catholics. Kennedy's death left the country to George Wallace's "law-and-order" campaign and Richard Nixon's "Southern strategy." The failed effort to unite the struggles for civil rights and for empowering workers left Democrats in the wilderness for more than two decades. I have spent most of my professional and political life in disparate settings and disparate ways trying to re-create a multiracial majority opposed to inequality and private excess and finding ways to build a society where equality and community mattered. I am not sure I understood what I was doing along the way, but I frequently pause to think about Robert Kennedy and what might have been.

I married very young to a fellow Miami graduate, Pam Russell, and to our surprise the union quickly produced twins at the beginning of my second year in graduate school. They were wonders in their own right, but they also likely kept me out of the draft, the consuming issue for the educated class in those years. To support my suddenly large family, I turned a part-time job at a start-up Cambridge research company into a full-time effort to live up to my billing to clients as an "expert" in the emerging field of survey research. It wasn't as audacious as it sounds since I did have some experience. My mentor in political science and senior year advisor at Miami, Herb Waltzer, had urged me to conduct a mail survey of students. That led, in turn, to a summer job before graduate school with Ithiel de sola Poole at MIT, using an unheard of new software that allowed me to personally analyze a survey on student housing using a freestanding computer terminal. Thus are "experts" born.

My work in opinion research soon began to accelerate. I headed a major project for Johnson's War on Poverty, to make sure the opinions of poor people played some role in a fifty-city evaluation of the anti-poverty program, and ultimately, I wrote a doctoral thesis under James Q. Wilson who taught me about civility and urban policy and pushed me to write my book about the politics of poor white, Latino, and African-American neighborhoods.[4] This all won me an offer of an assistant professorship at Yale after my third year, though I spent a good part of my first year visiting five poor neighborhoods, meeting and interviewing community leaders, trying to understand the history of the neighborhoods, particularly the origins of the people who had migrated there. I increasingly used in-depth interviews to understand how people lived and thought about their lives and to find patterns within all the complexity of their responses that might not be evident to the casual observer. I was greatly influenced by my Yale colleague Bob Lane and his in-depth work with working-class men in New Haven and the Italian communist Antonio Gramsci, who wrote about how working-class voters in Western democracies come to accept capitalism despite all its inequalities.

All the while I built a high barrier to keep separate my academic work at Yale and my political campaign work. I loved both and I think my work in both arenas benefited substantially from what I was doing in each. Few at Yale paid any attention in 1972 as I battled for McGovern delegates and ultimately headed up George McGovern's general election campaign in New Haven. I did, however, get the attention of local liberal Democrats who recruited me for the 1975 primary challenge to the New Haven mayor, a direct assault on the Democratic Party machine controlled by the party boss, Arthur Barbieri. Amid all this, Jonathan Greenberg was born in New Haven. Like his sisters, he, too, was a wonder, even absent the draft. Still, all the changes and pressures took a toll and my marriage was one victim.

As the scope of my academic work began to expand, I spent time in South Africa, Alabama, Israel, and Northern Ireland to research a book on the impact of capitalism and markets on race and ethnic relations. At the heart of the book was my struggle to understand the trade unionists that I came to know as they fashioned tactics and weapons, including discrimination, to help their members. These people were social democrats, sometimes spirited socialists, yet they were dividing their societies along ethnic or racial lines. Many were clearly racist, but even the racists within their world were working to lift up and secure something for their members.

The high barrier between academia and politics began to crumble with my marriage to Rosa DeLauro. As campaign manager for Chris Dodd's first Senate race in 1980, she enlisted me as the "volunteer" pollster and our basement was taken over by a dozen callers each night, Dodd hovering over them to listen for tidbits and taking a big chance on my talents. I later handed over the basement to Local 34 of the Federation of Hospital and University Employees Union, which used it in its successful organizing drive at Yale.

When I founded the company The Analysis Group, with three other academics—Kurt Schlichting, Peter Tuckel, and Joe Vitale—we worked with varying degrees of talent to frame, Sheetrock, and paint the basement as an office to provide modern campaign services to Connecticut.

The high barrier took a knock when I failed to get tenure at Yale. I wasn't surprised at the decision—my political activism made me something of a curiosity in the department—but my graduate students, who thought I was on a fast train to tenure, were shocked. They described my fate as being "Greenberged." No matter. I moved on in a matter of days, refusing to linger on things about which I could do nothing.

The high barrier was dealt a fatal blow by aftershocks of the political tumult that occurred in Michigan with the dramatic defection of progressive white United Auto Workers Union members in the working-class suburbs to Ronald Reagan in 1984. Ground zero was Macomb County, the most Catholic suburban county in America. The county that had given John Kennedy 63 percent of the vote in 1960 went 66 percent for Ronald Reagan in 1984. This was familiar territory because I had helped Bob Carr win back his congressional seat in the district in 1982 by overcoming some of these same forces. The Carr campaign was my first real effort as a pollster and when I met Frank Greer, who did Carr's advertising. I wasn't entirely surprised after the 1984 debacle to get a call from Rick Weiner, head of the Michigan Democratic Party, to come to a meeting with the political director of the UAW to work on the problem.

Unable to avail myself of the academic luxury of personally conducting in-depth interviews over a number of years, I chose a specialist in focus groups to head my company and introduced Democrats to a new way of listening to people and getting at the underlying problems. My report in 1985 was a scream of anguish from disaffected workers who, after hearing the moderator read a quote from Robert Kennedy about equal opportunity, shouted: "That's bullshit. No wonder they killed him." They were venomous, disillusioned with government and with Democratic special interests. There was too much "free spending" and "giveaways" to racial minorities. They had voted for Reagan and Wallace not because they had given up their ideals, but because they believed the Democratic Party had betrayed them. They still were hoping that the party would wake up and represent them. In the racially charged spirit of the times, they were looking for a government that would not "stomp on the average American white guy" and be for the "middle class" again.[5]

The storm that my report caused netted me an invitation to my first foray into Washington politics as a pollster. With the aid of Page Gardner, the top political advisor, at the Democratic Senatorial Campaign Committee, I parachuted into a group of some thirty operatives and pundits who had assembled in the large first-floor meeting room at the Democratic National Committee building to hear me repeat my presentation. When I was finished, the group sent a delegation upstairs to share what they had heard with Paul Kirk, the party chairman. Kirk hated my work. Racial tensions were already high and Jesse Jackson was threatening to run for the Democratic presidential nomination. Kirk later told reporters that he found my conclusion "inflammatory."[6]

Kirk shut the Democratic establishment's door in my face, but others were open to the idea that white workers had issues that should be heard and that Democrats should entertain a new political formula. Al From, the intense leader of the Democratic Leadership Council, a group of mostly Southern moderate Democrats, embraced me. While the members of the DLC were more concerned with bringing home white Baptists and building a white-black coalition in the South, they were also thinking about how the party could regain its footing nationally. They were attracted both by my lack of ties in the nation's capital as well as by my willingness to blunder along, saying the unthinkable without knowing who I was offending. It was the beginning of a close decade-long relationship with the DLC.

In 1988 I helped elect Joe Lieberman to the U.S. Senate in an upset victory over the popular Lowell Weicker. Joe, a close political friend in New Haven, ran as a crusading attorney general, fighting to win rebates from the big supermarket chains overcharging consumers, against a gas tax hike, and willing to talk about his faith. Lieberman's comfort with my Macomb County findings helped him carry the old blue-collar towns along the Naugatuck River, towns that other state Democratic candidates had been losing over the past decade.

With that upset victory, it now occurred to at least a few political observers that the professor might just be on to something that would help beat Republicans.

In late spring of 1991, when Clinton was formulating his plans for a presidential run, *The American Prospect* asked me to write a review essay on the wave of new books by prominent journalists that together chronicled the gloomy crisis of the Democratic Party.[7] The exercise was cathartic for me. Not only did it give me a place to crystallize conclusions from years of research but also a chance to assert my growing confidence that the Democrats, with the right candidate, could rebuild a national party grounded in middle-class values that could complete Robert Kennedy's mission.

With one exception, the various authors I reviewed believed the outlook for the Democrats was bleak. The party, they said, had become trapped by a "rights revolution" that seemed to put individualism and groups before community and showed an unseemly hostility to the military and family. That was a posture that Republicans were becoming increasingly skillful in attacking. Yet the first question I posed for Democrats in the review was whether all the angry voters had given up on the Democrats and embraced the Republicans. That answer, I said, is pretty clearly no. Despite the fumbling Jimmy Carter, the pinched and parsimonious Walter Mondale, and a Michael Dukakis unable to strangle his wife's murderer, I said, these Reagan Democrats check in year after to year to see if Democrats "get it yet."

The books make clear, I said, that the primary challenge for Democrats is to rediscover the forgotten middle class and to reinvent the party as one that puts the values and interests of the great majority of working people at the center of its politics. "Safety nets that protect only the poor," including welfare programs, are "bad politics," I said, but worse, demonstrably ineffective in alleviating poverty on their own and a "moral trap," asking those just above the poverty level to finance child care and health insurance benefits that they themselves lack. I considered that I might have crossed a line and might lose some of my liberal friends with this, but a growing band of left intellectuals urged me to move into this "no-go" area. I said that the party had to end its "moral agnosticism" about work and family and "defend the principle of reward for work and the social and moral worth of a strong family." The broad majority of the country hungers for leaders and for a party that honors work and recognizes the role of a middle class that carries the burdens of society.

I also noted that Reagan Democrats believed the Democratic Party had become blind to "middle-class America's deep frustration with the ascendancy of the wealthy and the corporations." Yes, the great majority think the middle is "squeezed," but less to pay for programs for the poor and more "to pay for tax breaks for the rich." Perhaps, I suggested, a party less tied to those interests would be able to better see reality.

I urged Democrats to "challenge the conservative hegemony" and define the Reagan-Bush years for what they were, unequal and self-indulgent, a time when "American leaders stood by while the notion of common citizenship gave way to private advantage, at the expense of the middle class." Democrats, I said, should run against this era, as Republicans ran in election after election against Jimmy Carter's pessimism.

Finally, I called on Democrats to defend social insurance programs, like Social Security, but with "a rationale for the government's role in society." Why wouldn't the country be distrustful and cynical about government when Democrats do not make the case for attacking problems collectively? The answer, I said, is "revitalizing politics and empowering Americans," particularly in health care where initiatives can address the vulnerabilities faced by the middle class.

The advice I offered in that review was yet to be seasoned by Bill Clinton's deep appreciation of Americans' skepticism about government and the need to change government in fundamental ways. He no doubt wrote some sharp comments in the margins of the draft of the article I sent him. My education would come later.

Clinton's journey to the 1992 presidential campaign began on August 19, 1946. He was born in the Julia Chester Hospital in Hope, Arkansas, to Virginia Blythe, a widow. His father, William Jefferson Blythe Jr., was killed at age twenty-eight in an auto accident as he drove from Chicago to Hope to fetch his pregnant wife and take her to their new home in Chicago. William Jefferson Blythe III was only four years old when his mother married the local Buick dealer in Hope, a fun-loving rascal named Roger Clinton.

What is clear among the twists and turns his early life took is that he is a man from humble origins and a man of the South who grew up in a world of contradictions between black and white, love and violence in his family, and Baptist churches and gambling parlors in Hot Springs. His beloved grandfather ran a grocery store in Hope and worked a second job as a night watchman at a sawmill. Race was the great divider in the South in those days, yet Clinton's grandfather treated his black customers no differently than his white ones. There was no "nigger talk" in his household and Bill was the only white child who played with black children. When Roger Clinton moved his family to Hot Springs, Bill found himself surrounded by diversity. While blacks and whites were segregated in the small town of 35,000, the hot springs for which it was named attracted visitors and retirees as well as gambling and other vices. There were Catholic churches—Bill went to a Catholic school for a time—as well as Greek Orthodox churches and synagogues alongside the Baptist churches where Bill went, mostly without his parents except at Easter.[8]

Although his family was not particularly political, Bill Clinton exhibited an early taste and talent for politics in high school when he campaigned intensely to win election as a senator at Boys State, the American Legion's national effort to build civic virtues among the young. Victory in that campaign carried him to Boys Nation in Washington, D.C., in 1963 where he distinguished himself from other Southern representatives by refusing to vote with them against civil rights and speaking of the "shame" that his state bore for its resistance to racial equality. Clinton's long stride carried him to the front row of a reception for Boys Nation delegates in the Rose Garden and the first handshake with President John F. Kennedy.[9]

After college at Georgetown and a year as a Rhodes Scholar at Oxford, Clinton arrived in New Haven in the summer of 1970 to attend Yale Law School at the same time I moved there to begin teaching political science. Amazingly, we never crossed paths. With a casual commitment to his classes, Clinton immediately volunteered to help the antiwar U.S. Senate candidate Joe Duffy win the Democratic primary, then agreed to coordinate Duffy's losing fall campaign in the 3rd Congressional District, including New Haven. Two years later, Clinton headed up the George McGovern primary campaign in the 3rd Congressional District. In the general election, I took over the New Haven campaign, while Clinton went to Texas as McGovern's state director, truly a fool's errand.

During the McGovern campaign, Clinton met with Arthur Barbieri, head of the entrenched local party machine in New Haven. Clinton proposed a deal: he would keep his eight hundred antiwar canvassers off the street if Barbieri supported the liberal McGovern. Barbieri offered to let Clinton make his case directly to the party meeting at a local Italian society. Bill brought Hillary Rodham, his fellow student and girlfriend at Yale, and after some initial taunts of "commie" and "fag," he carried the room.[10] Three years later, I would take a different approach when I helped the liberal reform candidate Frank Logue, aided by his chief of staff, Rosa DeLauro, defeat the incumbent mayor, a total surprise and near-fatal loss for the Barbieri machine.

From Hope to Oxford to New Haven, Clinton demonstrated an amazing ability to move comfortably in language, style, and bearing through very different worlds. He is as comfortable in a church pulpit as in a Wall Street conference room. And while his own life is full of contradictions, he is supremely talented at bringing combatants together to settle what no one else could before.

Clinton's first run for public office in 1974 was improbable. Six months after he and Hillary were married, the twenty-seven-year-old Arkansas law professor turned down an offer to join his new wife on the staff of the House Judiciary Committee as it began the Watergate inquiry and instead climbed into his 1970 Gremlin and set off to run for the House of Representatives. His quest took him from door-to-door, from cafés to country stores, across the most Republican, poorest, and whitest congressional district in Arkansas just two years after McGovern's crushing defeat barely left a Democrat standing. The Republican who held the seat, J. P. Hammerschmidt, clearly felt safe. A local Democrat could hope to win maybe a third of the vote in the district that had given Hubert Humphrey in 1968 and McGovern in 1972 barely a quarter. But Clinton began his political career with the question that I, too, was asking: how do you bring back the poorest and the powerless, the voters who should be Democrats, to their natural party? In Arkansas's mountain counties, where poor farmers eked out a living in the thin soil, the median income was only $2,000. But the hollows were rich in Baptist churches, one of Bill Clinton's favored venues.[11]

Clinton ran as a populist, a champion of the forgotten little man, battling against big, powerful private interests. He told the voters his economic advisors were the "small farmers, small businessmen, working people, retirees, and almost anyone you can imagine." Those advisors told him to go in relentless pursuit of tax relief for middle- and lower-middle-income people and to oppose at every turn gas tax increases while seeking higher taxes on corporations and closing loopholes that encouraged companies to invest abroad.

He combined his battle for the little people against the big corporations with passionate attacks on big federal bureaucracy and wasteful spending. Clinton called for breaking up the federal education bureaucracy, taking limousines away from federal bureaucrats, and relieving small business of government paperwork. And while they were at it they should balance the budget, too.

In the end Clinton lost with 48.5 percent of the vote. His biggest margins came from the bottom up, in the counties with the lowest income and education. George Wallace had carried four of the six counties in 1964.

Two years later Clinton tried again, making a run for attorney general. This time he had around him an aura of inevitability and swept the field, a feat he repeated two years later when he was elected governor with 63 percent of the vote.[12] He built his statewide standing battling the utilities, the symbol of big monopoly power in Arkansas.

Then came the shock, a surprise defeat in 1980 at the hands of Frank White. As governor, Clinton had proposed a 40 percent increase in school funding and a $1,200 a year increase in teachers' salaries, created a network of rural health clinics, and undertaken the first major road-building program in over a decade. To finance his ambitious investment program for Arkansas, Clinton proposed a penny increase in the gasoline tax and a tax on tags for cars and trucks, with the highest fees for the most expensive cars. But the legislature had other ideas and shifted the fee to passenger cars to be taxed by weight. With working and rural people driving older, heavier cars, Clinton's "car tax" became a tax on the little people, one they had the privilege of paying in person at the county revenue office on their birthday.[13]

It only dawned on Clinton late in the campaign that he might lose to White. Returning from a campaign trip he reported to friends that people felt betrayed, that "I kicked them when they were down." Sure enough, those people in the rural and poorest white and Wallace counties stopped his ascent abruptly in November 1980, a searing lesson for this very smart student of America.

Clinton also learned a lesson about the need for an aggressive and intense campaign. In his first run for the governor's office he had hired Dick Morris as pollster, described by Clinton as "a brilliant, abrasive character, brimming with ideas about politics and policy."[14] Morris was roundly despised by the campaign staff, but apparently provided Clinton with the creative tension on which the candidate thrived. In his campaign against White, though, Clinton gave in to pressure from his staff and replaced Morris with a more established national Democratic pollster. After his stinging defeat, Clinton would not be denied. When he set out to recapture the governor's mansion he had Morris back at his side. In his first ad, the candidate reminded people "my daddy never had to whip me twice for the same thing" and that he learned from his defeat that "you can't lead without listening."

Though more modest after his defeat, Clinton was no less a populist. He waged unrestrained class warfare, focused almost exclusively on the utility companies and their rate increases that kept jobs away from Arkansas and hurt people when they were down. When Governor White cut back on the monthly prescriptions for the elderly, Clinton ran an ad with the tagline, "Frank White. Soft on utilities. Tough on the elderly." Clinton advocated investment in education to spur economic growth, but there was no talk of a car tax or any new taxes. After winning easily with 55 percent of the vote, Clinton returned to his 1974 theme of investment and accountable government. He raised taxes for education, but this time it was accompanied by a mandated rise in measurable performance and competency tests for teachers, bitterly opposed by the Arkansas Education Association but supported by over 60 percent of the public. In 1984, the year of the Reagan landslide in the South and the defection of Catholics in suburban Detroit, Clinton won with 63 percent of the vote. His near fatal defeat at the hands of the humble voters of the South and his subsequent resurrection taught him a lesson with biblical force: Democrats could be redeemed only by struggling on behalf of the middle class. Government could be used to invest in people to create opportunity, but only if it is an accountable government, one that requires high standards and demands responsibility.[15]

After a decade of self-education that left him with a well-developed view of the path back for Democrats, Clinton became involved in 1985 with the creation of the Democratic Leadership Council, a group focused on cost-effective government, creative new ideas on social policy, and commitment to a strong national defense. Members of the DLC were sometimes referred to as New Democrats. But Clinton, in *My Life*, viewed Robert Kennedy as the first New Democrat. "He believed in civil rights for all and special privileges for none, in giving poor people a hand up rather than a handout; work was better than welfare."[16] Clinton, too, chose Kennedy over Eugene McCarthy in 1968 and was eager to follow this path.

AUDITIONING

When Clinton set his sights beyond Arkansas to the nation, he knew he would be confronting a sitting president still popular from his victory in the

Persian Gulf War and formidable enough to dissuade many prominent Democrats from running. But Clinton also believed George H. W. Bush was vulnerable. Unemployment in the summer of 1991 stood at 6.9 percent and was a leading indicator of widening economic distress. During the twelve years that Reagan and Bush held office, average income rose just 2.8 percent. Not 2.8 percent a year, just 2.8 percent. Total. But incomes for the wealthiest one percent rose nearly two thirds. While by most measurements the economy was in a modest recession, real people felt as if they were in a depression, one produced by exploding federal deficits, the failed savings and loans, the crash in real estate values, and waves of corporate downsizing and farm consolidation, even as Japan was buying up huge swathes of America.[17] Only one in four believed the "government is run for the benefit of all people, not for a few special interests looking out for themselves" and "can trust the government in Washington to do what is right."[18]

The Democratic Leadership Council's convention in Cleveland in May 1991 became an audition to see if any of the announced or potential candidates could make a compelling critique of the times and a strong case for beating Bush. It was the most important audience Clinton would face since his disastrously long nominating speech for Michael Dukakis at the Atlanta Democratic convention in 1988.[19]

He rose to the occasion in a speech, his last as DLC chairman, that opened the convention. I had read a number of drafts and edits, but wasn't in Cleveland with Clinton's team for the final drafts, which were done in the wee small hours before the day of the speech, so I was listening carefully to see how the text evolved. He began by asserting that he wanted to set a new course for the Democratic Party that would make possible "a new course for our country."[20] He lashed out at the Reagan era of the 1980s as a time that "glorified the pursuit of greed and self-interest," a time when "the CEOs of this country gave themselves pay raises" four times those of their employees. Then just as he had championed the forgotten little man when he first asked for their votes in a poor corner of north Arkansas, he now took the grievances of the middle class: "Middle income families' earnings declined for the first time in our memory, and not because we are lazy people. Working class families put in more hours at work and less time with their children." Yet he warned that the "very burdened middle class" had not turned to the Democrats in national elections because they did not trust the Democrats to "defend our national interests abroad, to put their values in our social policy at home or take their tax money and spend it with discipline."

To bring the middle class back, Clinton said, the party would have to offer a new political choice that offers opportunity for all, realized through a commitment to economic growth and a new investment agenda that recognizes that investment in people is the way to deal with global capitalism and the mobility of capital. In a big break with decades of Democratic orthodoxy, he also declared that "the government ought to help the middle class as well as the poor when they need it."

Where Clinton found his voice was his call on citizens to take responsibility. "Opportunity is not enough," he said. The country will only acknowledge "opportunity for all" if the party insists on "responsibility for all" as well. After investing in job training and child care, he said, "we should demand that everybody who can work go to work." The little secret, he told the crowd, is that "governments don't raise children, people do."

Finally, Clinton, once humbled by defeat for raising taxes on working people, called for the reinvention of government to push decisions down to the lowest possible level, "empowering people, increasing accountability, and treating our own citizens like they were our customers and our bosses." For Clinton, though not me yet, the commitment to changing government is what enables you to get your ticket stamped.

"We are not here to save the Democratic Party, we are here to save the United States of America," he concluded.

Clinton's passion, his rhetorical style, and the clarity of the mission he laid out in that speech brought the crowd to its feet thirteen times. The media wrote that he "dazzled the DLC delegates" and one pundit described it as "the best speech I've heard in ten years," better even than New York Governor Mario Cuomo's much heralded keynote speech to the Democratic convention in 1984.

Where did that speech come from? Like Cuomo, Clinton gave the speech of a decade and like him, he delivered a speech that reflected his maturing judgment about the political project that could take the Democratic Party to victory and change the country. Clinton had looked at many polls over the last few years. But much more important to the content and tenor of the speech was the campaigning he had done, getting pounded and getting elected every two years and developing a sense of people and the possibilities, leavened by his voracious readings on history and our times. While Cuomo likely sat alone in his study writing his speech, Clinton was no doubt on the phone to other governors, policy specialists, and some FOBs— the Friends of Bill. Doubtless he was still writing on his pad at the podium in Cleveland.

Pressed by the reporters who surrounded him after the speech about his presidential intentions, Clinton at first said, "I haven't given it a thought" and "I'm not running." But then he opened the door a crack: "If I change that position, I will have to do it only after some extensive conversations with people at home, because they are my employers."

In contrast to Clinton's stirring speech, none of the other potential candidates made much of an impression. Senator Paul Tsongas of Massachusetts came across as a liberal, focused on deficits and fiscal rectitude, subjects of little concern in DLC circles. Neither Mario Cuomo, the most formidable candidate in waiting, nor Jesse Jackson, who could become a problematic spoiler, was invited. Jackson chose to dramatize the slight by joining striking workers at a downtown rally.

Senator Al Gore, who if he chose to run would have had the potential to become a big obstacle in Clinton's way, was the final speaker. I had worked briefly with his advisors and even participated in a practice session for his speech. The practice didn't help. Gore buried his nose in his text and was wooden on the podium, a posture all too familiar to those who had watched him during his first run in 1988.[21]

Clinton's last DLC convention as chairman ended by adopting a platform that included, for the first time, a call for "higher taxes for wealthy persons," as well as "reducing the tax burden on moderate-income and middle-class families."[22] Clinton was advancing a middle-class tax cut before holding any presidential campaign meetings or doing any polls.

As the DLC convention ended Clinton studiously avoided Gloria Cabe's pressure to meet with Frank Greer and me about taking the first steps to launch the campaign. Two days later, trying again to corner him, Gloria went to the Excelsior Hotel in Little Rock where he was speaking to a large group at the Arkansas Industrial Development conference. She stood in the back of the auditorium trying to catch his eye, but he just kept taking questions. Finally she gave up and left. But as the conference meeting broke up Clinton did catch the eye of someone else: Paula Corbin, a state employee working at the convention, later to become known to the world as Paula Jones.

The group that would be at the core of a presidential campaign finally met a month later in the den at the governor's mansion. The Clintons, Gloria, Frank, and I were joined by Bruce Lindsey, Clinton's closest friend and lawyer, and Dave Watkins, Clinton's Arkansas ad man. There was much to discuss: the governor's commitment to serve out his term, what roles people would play, who would be available to join the campaign, what we would say to the press, how we would get the governor up to speed on serious policy issues, particularly defense, how we would let the big-money people know we were planning to run, and what kind of timetable we would need for deciding to run and announcing that decision. We also knew we had to commission research about Clinton himself, to find out before the media and our opponents if there were revelations that could kill his candidacy. Having survived a hostile Arkansas press and elections every two years in Arkansas, we weren't worried about a lurking financial scandal, but drugs, sex, and rock 'n' roll might be another matter.

The meeting laid out the first questions that any campaign has to ask itself: Why are you running for president? Who are you? Where will you take the country? What kind of leader will you be?

The answers to those questions lay mostly in Clinton's speeches, both the ones he had already given, particularly his DLC speech in Cleveland, and those he would give in the opening days of a campaign. But from this first moment he was determined to fashion a deliberative process that would intentionally bring together an array of strong-willed people with very different, sometimes clashing, perspectives, right into the inner sanctum. He was also thinking about the best uses for the extensive networks of family, roommates, friends, intellectuals, policy experts, elected officials, and party leaders—the FOBs—which formed concentric rings around the Clintons. Each FOB has his or her own private understanding about who Clinton is and what their relationship means. Certainly each of us in that first meeting believed that he or she represented the real Clinton, at least his better nature.

Despite our pressure, Clinton remained cautious, not even acknowledging to us that he had a process for deciding whether to run. It was my first experience watching him keeping all his options open to make sure all the issues have been examined, all the traps closed, and everybody on board. Maybe this produced better decisions, but close in, it was decidedly maddening as the final decision was delayed as long as humanly possible.

My job was to write two memos, one a plan for running, the other a plan if he did not. I relished writing the first, but could work up no enthusiasm for the second, mostly because I thought it was a fiction to maintain the illusion of indecision. So, completely confident he was running, on August 6, I wrote a memorandum to the governor, "Re: The Plan for Non-Candidacy." It began, "After careful reflection and wide-ranging discussion with all those concerned," followed by an inch of blank space and the one word, "NUTS."[23]

My wife had been elected to the Congress in 1990 in a grueling year-long election campaign with just 52 percent of the vote, and faced an almost certain ugly rematch with her hard-right opponent. To try to relax before she launched her campaign and I became embroiled in a presidential election we took a three-week holiday in Italy, ending on the Amalfi coast from where most of New Haven's Italian residents hail. I returned on August 30 and learned from Gloria that nothing had happened in those three weeks. No one had been hired; there was no organization and no announcement date. At Gloria's urging I sent the core group an alarmed memo.[24]

"This would-be campaign has a part-time, volunteer feel to it," I said.

"Critical up front activities have been stalled by the tentativeness, and we may, in the end, lose a month of organizational work.

"None of this weights very heavily now, but in February—when we are short of money and struggling to organize in 20 primary states—we will live with the consequences."[25]

The memo urged that the principal decision-making group begin meeting by phone every day for forty-five minutes to evaluate progress and make recommendations to Clinton, that the recruitment of staffers become a full-time activity for someone, that a short list of candidates for campaign manager be drawn up and vetted, that a strategizing group be formed to identify and study issues, and that we begin immediately to do the polling and research necessary to define our campaign before the media and the opposition can define us. Finally, I said, "we need a date to force the organization of other activities."

Clinton called me from south Arkansas at 7 A.M. on Labor Day to tell me voters were very enthusiastic about his running for president, and I learned from Mark Gearan, who had left the Democratic Governor's Association to become the campaign's one all-purpose employee, that Clinton had signed off on all the steps in my memo. In fact, he wanted to meet on it Thursday at the mansion in Little Rock—and we started improbably at 7 A.M. with Bruce and Gloria, Frank and I, and the Clintons and a few others watching but not commenting. We decided first to set up a long trip to Washington next week and, more importantly, we set October 2 as announcement day. And I was told to begin focus group research in New Hampshire, the first presidential campaign research to be commissioned by this "poll-driven" candidate.

Then came the real point of the meeting: an intense discussion of Clinton's "woman problem" that lasted at least an hour. Frank and I had pressed tirelessly for this meeting, and I steeled myself to ask the hard questions, but Hillary took charge. She said, of course it was a problem or else we wouldn't be discussing it and my diary of the meeting notes that both participated "vigorously and passionately" in the discussion. They assured us that this was not a problem now. I was so taken aback and uncomfortable that I never asked the right follow-up questions. At the end of the meeting, Clinton seemed depressed that this was all the media cared about. "They don't seem interested in what I believe in, what kind of person I am, where I want to take the country," he said.

I spent the next week working with Al From on the selection of people who would brief Clinton during his Washington trip. While not usually part of the pollster's brief, Clinton appreciated that my academic background and writings made me a good go-between to introduce him to other academics, policy experts in the think tanks, and the Congress. In the self-important world of Washington who ends up briefing sets off waves of speculation in the political class. Is this a signal about who will be secretary of state if Clinton wins? That he will continue U.S. policy toward Israel? That he is tilting right—or left? Since both Al From, one of the founders of the DLC, and I were tasked with organizing these sessions, I asked Clinton during a phone call what role he envisioned for From in the campaign. His response required some interpretation: I should treat From as a "confidant on message and issues," but "don't do a lot of insider political business with him." I presumed he meant that From should be deeply involved in strategy, but not in core meetings where Clinton wants people who are thinking only of him and his interests.

From and two of his smartest DLC colleagues, Elaine Kamarck and Bill Galston, emerged as a cadre eager to have Clinton run fully identified with the DLC and as the Southern conservative candidate. From wanted to use the dispute with Jesse Jackson to show the country that Clinton had the courage to fight the old Democratic special interests. I counseled Clinton against it. I had aligned with the DLC and applauded Galston and Kamarck's writing on most of the big issues, but I thought Clinton had the opportunity to go beyond his regional identity. "Both your friends and your [primary] opponents have an interest in defining you that way, but that may prove a trap, in effect deterring you from a more ambitious and national candidacy," I told him in a memo. The decision whether to be a Southern candidate or a national candidate has huge implications for which primary states a candidate contests and also how the candidate chooses and articulates the issues he wants to be at the heart of the campaign.[26]

On Friday, September 13, the Clintons' network of friends assembled around a set of tables arranged in a square in a large conference room at the Washington Court Hotel just blocks from the U.S. Capitol, chaired by Hillary and Mickey Kantor, a Los Angeles attorney with Southern roots and a longtime FOB. He told the group that Bill and Hillary wanted to hear from everyone during the two-day meeting and then introduced me to give the main presentation on the state of the country and the strategic issues facing the campaign. As I was preparing my remarks earlier I realized that we weren't playing make-believe anymore and I had drafted an eight-page outline that bordered on being an actual speech. Still, even with all those notes and with the ink barely dry on my piece in *The American Prospect*, I was nervous.[27] While I noted the honor that had been bestowed on us for having the opportunity to reshape America, I also emphasized the reality: a sitting president who, despite a recession, still had credibility on the economy and was, at the same time, deeply trusted to defend our country, the result of ousting Iraq from Kuwait. Together those factors gave George Bush the highest popularity rating since FDR. Then I added another obstacle: the Democratic Party—in crisis atop a failed coalition of voters.

To beat the most popular president in history, I reprised my article. Bill Galston followed me and made a case for an "insurgent campaign" built on a discontented middle class, but he also urged that Clinton be a candidate of the South, "securing the base and building out" to get his share of the blacks and suburban liberals.[28] He argued that Gore had "wimped out" and had he run a pro-defense, pro-South campaign for the presidency in 1988 he would have won. Before the issues sounding a national or a Southern candidacy could be fully aired, though, Carl Wagner, one of the participants, suffered an epileptic seizure, bringing the session to a sudden halt. Much of the next day's session was devoted not to the central questions of the campaign, but to the media's preoccupation with "the woman question."

As the second day of the meeting drew to a close Clinton went around the tables noting the points with which he agreed, including my point that the party needed to change the way citizens relate to government, but added his own interpretation: "less bureaucratic, more choice, more responsibility." With his face reddening, he closed the session with what seemed like a moral imperative for him: "Bush has never used the bully pulpit to attack the wealthy for screwing the workers."

The core group convened again Sunday night at Frank's office to do some back and forth with Clinton to prepare him for the next morning's Sperling Breakfast, a Washington institution in which journalists, hosted by the *Christian Science Monitor*'s Godfrey Sperling, question public figures. We decided to encourage a woman reporter to ask about "the woman question" so the Clintons could show how comfortable they were disposing of it.

Before Clinton joined us, I shared my amusement about the DLC cadre, a kind of communist cell, repeating the same mantra, "conservative, South, strong defense," and insinuating themselves into everything. Bruce Lindsey laughed and agreed, though he remarked, "They say the same about you." When Clinton joined us, he was tired but he had settled the big issue in his own mind: "Of course, we run nationally and contest Iowa." Now we knew where we were going.

Only a week away from the formal announcement of his candidacy Clinton squeezed his bulk into our firm's small windowless basement conference room in our Washington brownstone to hear the results of the first focus groups, the only research that had been done so far for the campaign. But before I made my presentation the group needed to settle a debate that had been dragging on by telephone for several weeks—where to make the announcement. Hillary had pressed hard for Little Rock High School, site of the confrontation between Governor Orval Faubus and the federal government over admitting nine black students. She called again during the meeting to underscore her seriousness. Announcing there, she said, would send a signal about Bill's commitment to education and being a "New South" governor. Frank Greer and Mark Gearan disagreed. An announcement at Little Rock High would only prompt the networks to get out the old tapes of the jeering white crowds and the 101st Airborne troops with the bayonets on their rifles. I added that the high school venue would emphasize the past and its "rights" agenda over the future and a new Democratic agenda. Since moving the office to Washington, my partner, Celinda Lake, gently suggested that maybe Clinton could do something at the high school the day after the speech, perhaps with daughter Chelsea. Clinton liked that idea, noting that he walked Chelsea to school every day he was in Arkansas. His response suggested that we might at least have some wiggle room on where to make the speech.

The presentation was interrupted a second time when Mark and I escorted Clinton up two flights to interview George Stephanopoulos, who had decided to leave his work for the Democratic House leader Richard Gephardt to work in the presidential campaign. Left alone in my office to talk, George, even shorter than me, was struck by Clinton as "bulky and butter-cheeked," like "an overgrown boy in his light summer suit. . . . Slow but not stately, almost lazy but loaded with self-confidence." Clinton ambled around my office, checking the books and photos, picking up a questionnaire or two, but then turned the half-hour interview into a "stream of consciousness" tour "across the political landscape of his mind," as George described it.[29]

With Clinton reengaged, we agreed that Frank would draft the announcement speech, drawing mostly on previous speeches, allowing everyone to concentrate on my analysis of the New Hampshire focus groups. I had welcomed the opportunity to go to Manchester to watch the group sessions, a kind of ritual for me at the beginning of a campaign. I needed to clear my head of all the insider strategizing and listen to people, unfiltered, but for the one-way viewing glass. The focus groups were done to test the ideas and themes that had been emerging in Clinton's speeches and our planning, a kind of gut check on what we might find in the first primary state Clinton would contest. There was nothing subtle about what emerged from the sessions: people were in deep distress about the economic crash in New Hampshire and they were breathless at the prospect of a candidate like Bill Clinton.

The starting point of my twenty-eight-page report—I have never written so much about so few people—was the "bleak mood" of New Hampshire voters. Clinton, who sometimes got Dick Morris's poll reports on a napkin, looked impressed as he leafed through it and read one voter's comments, New Hampshire's economy is "suffering bad, and it hasn't hit bottom yet," and another's, New Hampshire has "just totally gone to hell."[30] Even before hearing anything about Clinton, they were near desperate for a Democratic candidate who understands that "middle America" is suffering and "just not represented now."[31]

Given a one-paragraph biography of Clinton along with the other candidates, the participants were drawn up short. They just couldn't believe there was a Democrat talking about "individual responsibility" and "personal responsibility." The description brought cheers of "hear, hear," "yes," "I like that," and "I just think that's the basis of everything." When the biography was combined with extracts from Clinton's speeches about responsibility for both welfare and savings and loan cheats, the groups' responses became euphoric. "Got my vote" and "It sounds like the answer to everyone's prayers." Three quarters of the respondents left behind Clinton's biography with the phrase "putting welfare people to work" underlined as the single most important element of Clinton's distilled life.

On this simple gut check on Clinton's whole life, the answer I said is "Absolutely. There is an affinity between Bill Clinton and these voters."

DEFINING THE ELECTION: THE PROJECT

When I arrived in Little Rock on an overnight flight from Los Angeles, Frank Greer was berserk. Clinton had trouble the night before choosing between Frank's draft, pared down and sharpened by David Dreyer, the speechwriter for the House Majority Leader, and a completely different speech written by Bruce Reed, who joined the campaign from the DLC, where he was policy director. In the morning Clinton had started out working with Frank's rewrite draft, then decided it was shit, threw it out, and began writing himself in longhand. Late that afternoon Frank gathered up all Clinton's scribblings and we began reworking it, trying to create a single, coherent draft even as Clinton continued feverishly adding pages. Hillary brought us dinner as we worked late into the night. At 12:30 on the morning of the speech Clinton read our new draft, looked back at the original, then told us to go with the original, adding some good stuff from the subsequent drafts. Frank, Bruce, and I retired to what I considered the rec room, vacillating between panic, frustration, and laughing at our plight. Had he had time, Frank would have killed himself. Instead, we worked on the new draft until 3:30 A.M., when I had to get some rest. Bruce and Frank continued work until 6:30 A.M., the last minute for preparing a final copy for the wire services.

The chaotic speechwriting process was classic Clinton. He had invited all the FOBs to send him their ideas for the speech, providing them the opportunity, too, to claim ownership of the ideas and issues he adopted. He worked the phones late at night making calls to his friends to stimulate his own thinking. The process allowed him to consider conflicting perspectives, weigh downsides, and work through and refine his thinking. As sure as the sun will rise, Clinton will rig the process to create this not so ordered chaos.[32]

The resulting speech was an enormous success, delivered to thousands who gathered on the lawn in front of the Old State House. He closed with his purpose: "This is not just a campaign for the presidency—it is a campaign for the future, for the forgotten hardworking middle-class families of America who deserve a government that fights for them."[33]

After the announcement, some of the closest FOBs gathered in Bruce Lindsey's law office, excited but concerned about the lack of organization and fund-raising. I was given responsibility for hiring on a crash basis, aided by From and Gearan, and later joined by Eli Segal, a FOB of high standing who knew a lot more about head hunting. At the party that night at the mansion, Clinton was ebullient, although he told me that he was getting tired of being out there on his own.

From and I flew back together from Little Rock. While he complained that DLC folks and ideas were being excluded, I embraced Bill Galston's idea that Clinton should deliver three defining speeches to underscore the unity and clarity of his vision, to distinguish him from the rest of the field, and to position himself for a titanic battle of ideas with Mario Cuomo should Cuomo enter the race. Our earlier disagreements dissolved before that shared challenge. We formed a message group from the core campaign people, a group that now included George Stephanopoulos, joined sometimes by Harvard's Bob Reich, popular writer on economic affairs and Clinton's friend since Oxford; Will Marshall, the DLC's top policy thinker; and Sandy Berger, the Democrats' top foreign policy advisor and a FOB since the McGoueln campaign, to organize the addresses quickly and at a single venue, Georgetown University, a prestigious, but nonelitist setting. Meeting in my basement conference room, we all gravitated without much dispute toward the concept of responsibility under a larger theme of a "new covenant." We had to offer examples of irresponsibility as well as ways to challenge people with a new ethic of rights and responsibilities that could create hope in the country. The focus, I said in a memo summarizing the meeting, was to elevate Clinton's candidacy with "addresses that are bold, tough and inspirational."[34]

On Sunday night, the message group had a call with Clinton to get his input and go ahead. He was concerned that "personal responsibility" would not be big enough to carry the whole project. But with all of us united, he agreed to this being a "values speech." Still, he pressed us to read David Osborne's book *Reinventing Government* and include a large dose of policies to reform bureaucracies and find inventive solutions more responsive to citizens. On the Saturday morning before the speech, George called, "Oh God, Clinton wants to delay the speech. He is losing his voice and we are not intellectually ready."

The night before the first speech, the message group met at Greer's office for a six-hour session to refine the speech. With no time for sugarcoating, I told the group I hated the current draft for two reasons. First, it was scolding: "We lecture the middle class rather than honor it." Second, by toning down the populist rhetoric I thought it created an "imbalance" that had us "shooting the poor." From wanted a stronger attack on Congress and liberal special interests. Clinton accepted our points and a new draft came together that contained a stronger attack on Congress and corporations and allowed me to reintroduce the principle "no [tax] deductibility without responsibility." From wondered why Clinton was so shy of tackling Washington's powerful interests. Frank and I wondered why he hesitated before the corporate interests. Was he just personally averse to conflict or cautious before the citadels of power? He certainly spent a good part of each day with corporate lawyers and lobbyists and large donors.

For the first time, Clinton practiced with a TelePrompTer—and he was good. I left at 1:30 A.M. after the ninth draft.

As usual Clinton was penciling in changes just moments before Father Leo O'Donovan introduced him to an auditorium crowded with enthusiastic students. He began by lauding the American dream, admired all across the world, but "dying here at home," because our politics was failing us: "There's a hole in our politics where our sense of common purpose used to be," he said. The current Gilded Age, he said, is one that exalts "private gain over public obligation, special interest over the common good, wealth and fame over work and family." A Democratic Congress and two Republican presidents had "tripled the national debt" during a period of twelve years when middle-class Americans "have watched their economic interest ignored and their values literally ground into the ground."[35]

He then offered his "New Covenant," "a solemn agreement between the people and their government to provide opportunity for everybody, inspire responsibility throughout our society and restore a sense of community across our great nation. A new covenant to take government back from the powerful interests and the bureaucracy and give it back to the ordinary people of our country."

The starting point for change and creating the compact, he said, was not what Bill Clinton would promise to do, but "the responsibilities we owe to ourselves, to each other and to our country." The compact, he said, would tell corporate leaders at the top of the economic pyramid that "we will promote economic growth and the free market but we're not going to help you diminish the middle class and weaken our economy." While prepared to help business compete, raise training, and create incentives for investment here, "I expect the jetsetters and featherbedders of corporate America to know that if you sell your companies and your workers and your country down the river, you'll be called on the carpet." It is not right, he said, that CEOs make one hundred times what the average worker does while we fall behind Germany and Japan. That means a change in course: "There should be no more deductibility for irresponsibility."

But then came the unexpected for a Democrat: "To people on welfare, we're going to give you training and education and health care for yourself and your children, but if you can work you must go to work." Welfare "should be a second chance, not a way of life."

The new covenant, he said, should begin in Washington. "I want to literally revolutionize the federal government and fundamentally change its relationship to our people." There would be no more "top-down bureaucracy" telling people what to do. As for Congress, then under the control of the Democrats: "Congressional pay should not go up while the pay of working Americans is going down."

Finally he proposed to challenge every younger person, "to establish in this country a voluntary system of national service," a domestic GI Bill that allows all to go to college by giving something back in voluntary service or a portion of future income. That won the biggest applause of the speech.

Even as he concluded the first Georgetown speech, the second one, on issue number one, the economy, was much on our minds, particularly as New Hampshire voters were suffering through a virtual economic depression and Bush was suffering through a precipitous decline in popularity. Clinton had already told the message group that he wanted us to reach out to interesting people and for his economics to be "people-oriented." That meant education, training, and an investment budget to help Americans compete in the international economy.[36] The morning after the first speech, Clinton, George Stephanopoulos, and I flew to New York for a meeting at Goldman Sachs to hear their ideas for the economic speech.

As we sat in the conference room a touch more luxurious and bigger than mine, surrounded by investment bankers, I didn't hear Clinton throw out his Georgetown line about the "jetsetters and featherbedders of corporate America" and he touched only lightly on new taxes on the rich. The juxtaposition of the first Georgetown speech only a few hours earlier with the Goldman Sachs conference room gave me some appreciation for the conflicting pressures on the candidate. The bankers didn't shy away from attacking the "excesses" of Wall Street, but urged Clinton to tackle it through tougher enforcement. They offered inventive proposals using tax incentives and disincentives to create higher paid jobs, capital gains tax cuts, and IRAs for the middle class and tougher management of our trade relations with Japan. I don't recall any discussion about federal deficits. Descending in the elevator after the meeting, Clinton, his brain running full steam ahead, told me he wanted to move the economic speech on a faster track.

With a new sense of urgency I drafted an organizing memo for the message group that summarized the emerging approaches to the economy, narrowing it down to three. First, Clinton could be a pro-growth Democrat, or second, a Democrat who wants to see America "competing and winning," or finally, advancing the approach I preferred, Clinton could offer a "people-centered" economics that would contrast with Bush's policies to enrich the richest and the big corporations. I preferred it because it was more consistent with our political project and Clinton's history and I thought more likely to win voters for him as well. The last point I would soon test. And I preferred it because it was the best fit for the policies and values favored by the group, empowering people who want to work through education, training, middle-class tax relief, and incentives for creating jobs.[37]

A few days later Bob Kerrey, one of Clinton's primary opponents, gave an economic speech that received positive reviews. It angered Clinton, who thought Kerrey's speech offered nothing. "This guy's going to be elected on a war story, then jacking off the rest of his life," he told us. Then he said he wanted his own economic speech to be "much more hard-hitting" and to take on Kerrey directly, "no more of this bullshit."[38]

As we debated the content of the economics speech I was drafting our first real poll of New Hampshire voters—weeks after Clinton already gave his defining speech for the campaign. With the poll poised to field at 5 P.M. I got a call in the afternoon from Clinton, who had been carrying the draft questionnaire around with him for the past week. He hadn't had time to really look at it, but now he had "a few ideas," which stopped the presses and threw my office into chaos. Most changes I rejected because they would bias the survey against our opponents. But he wrote a serious revision of the "reinventing government" message, which I had to add to the survey while the phone callers sat on their hands for a couple of hours waiting. When late that night I reviewed the results for the half-done survey I found that Clinton's addition was testing very well indeed.

"He knows people," I wrote in my diary.

On November 19 the message group gathered to finish the economic speech, and I opened the session with an update on the New Hampshire poll. Over three quarters of primary voters thought the state was on the wrong track and over 60 percent in an unprompted question volunteered that the main problem was the economy, unemployment, or jobs.[39] For Clinton, who was in fifth place, getting only 6 percent of the vote, this near despair on the economy would provide a route to the top, I argued based on the survey. We tested nine versions of our economic message but it was Clinton's middle-class message that got the strongest response, giving us more confidence that Clinton's political project as laid out in the Cleveland speech would allow him to dominate. After all the candidates were described in the survey, Clinton doubled his vote and moved into the pack just below the top tier, not affected by his position on trade. The voters turned strongly to Clinton on two messages: a candidate insisting on responsibility for those at the top by denying deductibility for corporate irresponsibility and a candidate seeking to radically change government by cutting bureaucracy, making government more efficient, and giving people more choices, the latter added by Clinton in his last-minute edits.

When asked which one policy would improve the economy, a third of the voters said "make the wealthy and corporations pay their fair share of taxes," a quarter wanted to cut taxes for working people and the middle class, and 15 percent wanted to invest in education and job training. The message group had not even included deficit reduction as one of the policy options. Voters in New Hampshire were looking for a populist and people-centered economics.

When Clinton then turned to the speech, he scorned the current draft. "The country is in deep trouble and we're focused on the individual," he said dismissively and despite the poll. "The speech is thinking too small." America needs "massive public and private investment" and "massive commitment to education." He said the country needed to "reorganize society to compete." We were stilled by his comments this time, not sure he wasn't right. Clinton ordered the speech rewritten and gave us each our assignments: George and Stan, the new introduction; Rob Shapiro of the DLC, the new policies; and Bruce Reed to set up camp with Frank to work through the night. The draft reached Clinton at his hotel at 6 A.M. and for the next two hours he rewrote most of it before we hurriedly entered it in time for him to do a practice with a TelePrompTer at 10 A.M., not without further edits.

Back in the same hall at Georgetown, Clinton opened his speech with an inelegant call to arms: "A better life for all who will work for it—is what this campaign is about." Ugh, I thought. It sounded like something that Frank Greer and Clinton crunched together and shouldn't be repeated.[40]

But it got much better. He managed to bring together the concept of an empowering economics with his own desire to go beyond the individual in a sentence only he could craft: "We need a New Covenant for economic change, a new economics that empowers people, rewards work, and organizes America to compete and win again." He proposed immediate action to stimulate the economy and create work, but he rushed past those details to tell the audience that the real need was for a long-term national strategy. He devoted a quarter of the speech to laying out his specific plans to "empower every American with the education and training essential to get ahead." That took him into apprenticeships for high school graduates, a trust fund so all can finance college, adult education, and an expanded tax credit for the working poor. The last plank in his empowerment platform was a 10 percent cut in taxes for the middle class, paid for by those earning over $200,000—the populist economics favored by New Hampshire voters that the DLC had adopted as policy back in Cleveland.

He then gave equal time to leading a "revolution in government so it becomes an engine of opportunity again, not an obstacle to it." His signature policy commitment was a cut in federal bureaucracy—3 percent across the board, every year. He proposed to "cut the deficit drastically in five years in a dramatic budget reform," without making the complementary argument that a reduced deficit would facilitate growth. He also devoted a large portion of the speech to trade, calling for the development of a "national strategy to compete and win in the global economy."

"This is not just a campaign," Clinton said in closing and in tribute to the political project. "This is a crusade to restore the forgotten middle class, give economic power back to ordinary people, and recapture the American Dream."

The economics speech was followed by the third and final Georgetown speech on national security. Together the three addresses captured the attention of the media as well as voters. With the economy so bad, voters were looking for a leader with ideas. Alone among the candidates, Clinton saw his support rise nationally, doubling to 12 percent by the end of the year.[41]

While it was satisfying to Clinton and all of us to win this first phase of the primaries as the candidate of ideas, I also had to establish that these ideas would win over real voters in key states, particularly on our home field in the South where we would go soon after New Hampshire. At the heart of that inquiry were the focus groups I organized with African American voters in South Carolina and Georgia to confirm Clinton's affinity as well as something more important. The people who gathered around the table in the focus groups were a test of my life's work as well as Clinton's. The discussions were emotional and poignant, bringing me at times to tears as they voiced the shared values at the heart of the Clinton campaign, reminiscent of Robert Kennedy's original vision for bringing black and white workers together politically. They confirmed that I wasn't crazy when I said African American voters too were hungry for a politics centered on work and responsibility. That blacks as much as whites were hungry for a Democrat who will end welfare. The African American ministers understood that lesson every Sunday, but our African American political supporters were nervous about our direction, hectored by Jesse Jackson, who was still riding a "rights agenda," and Mario Cuomo, who still believed our policies would hurt the poor. But the liberals, I believed more strongly than ever, could not create a new majority because they patronized both black and white.

We were preparing for a major fight with Cuomo over the direction of the party and the country, testing Clinton's appeal in more focus groups in New Hampshire. I was in my upstairs study beginning to digest the results of the groups when the news came that Cuomo had announced he would not run for president. For all of our campaign bravado about wanting to take on Mario, I think we all suddenly breathed easier. It was as if you stood confronting a big bear in the center of the path and then it suddenly ambled off into the woods.

THE REAL WORLD TEST

The day after Christmas I began writing my memo on the latest New Hampshire survey to be presented at an all-day retreat in Little Rock the following weekend. I was energized because the survey was a huge strategic breakthrough, giving us a clear window into the downscale, mostly noncollege coalition that could carry Clinton to the top of the primary field. In Georgia, the New Covenant of individual responsibility and welfare reform was received like a revival meeting, but it did not do as well in New Hampshire where people were financially desperate and less religious. The message that elicited the strongest response in the New Hampshire survey focused on the excesses of the Reagan-Bush era that enriched the wealthy and politicians while the middle class declined. It promised to make the rich pay their fair share and to cut middle-class taxes by 10 percent. When we presented that message to the respondents Clinton's vote rose nearly 10 points and moved him to the head of the Democratic pack in New Hampshire, even with Cuomo still included in our polling. When asked to name the most important element of the message, far and away people recalled the 10 percent middle-class tax cut. The reinventing government message also tested well in the survey, particularly the part about politicians not getting pay raises—a nod to American voters' unrelieved suspicion of government and politicians. As a result I proposed that "elements of the radically changing government message should be incorporated into our middle-class message"—the synthesis of themes that Clinton had evolved over a lifetime.[42]

Paul Tsongas was running a tony campaign focused on economic issues, too, including a call for extensive deficit reduction to fix what he said was the main burden weighing on the economy. His plan, "A Call to Economic Arms," included bold action on energy and consumption taxes and entitlement reform that conventional politicians would not dare touch. He was running very well with the best-educated and upscale suburban voters nearest to Boston, but the survey projected Clinton's middle-class message would capture the undecided and pull away a quarter of the Tsongas and Kerrey voters and win noncollege voters across the board, particularly older noncollege women and seniors.[43]

The Little Rock retreat covered every base before the big test in New Hampshire, from fund-raising to opposition research. Rahm Emanuel, the finance director, reported that the campaign had $3.2 million on hand. Rahm had directed fund-raising for Chicago's Mayor Richard Daley, and he and I had bonded working on some of my first congressional races in Michigan. Together with David Wilhelm, I pushed to get Rahm, who we knew would suffer no fools when pursuing a goal, into the campaign. When Rahm in an earlier campaign failed to bond with another pollster, he sent him a dead fish, the kind of chutzpah required to put Clinton ahead of this crowded field when the fund-raising reports were made public a week later.

And Clinton said he was confident about how he would respond if the media or his opponents raised questions about his effort to avoid the draft and his Arkansas environmental record. He and Hillary were more concerned that our ads didn't hit the rich hard enough. Fearing Clinton's reaction, I had Frank tone down the ad copy, suppressed a laugh, and struggled not to make eye contact with him.[44]

For dinner, we took over most of Doe's, a Little Rock staple that lays out large slabs of beef and tamales to be consumed at rough wood tables. We were more confident than we deserved, already adding weight in rough proportion to Clinton's rise in the polls. Joe Klein of *New York* magazine circled the tables and interviewed the emerging powers.

On New Year's Day, Frank distributed to us all a one-minute economics spot that showed Clinton talking directly to the camera the entire time—a feat few politicians can pull off—about his economics program. Everybody liked it, including the Clintons, though Hillary and Chelsea thought he smiled inappropriately and looked pale. With public polls showing Clinton vying for the lead, he insisted the spot go up immediately, barely giving me time to launch a fast poll to establish a baseline so we could measure the ad's impact.[45]

The ad was broadcast for the first time a few days later. In front of an American flag, Clinton opened by telling New Hampshire voters they had a special role to play: "The people of New Hampshire know better than anyone—America's in trouble, our people are hurting." Then, in one sentence, he crystallized his whole argument and what had gone so badly wrong: "In the 80s, the middle class declined, poverty exploded, politicians in Washington raised their pay and pointed fingers, but no one took responsibility." The country needed a president with "a plan for change," he said, the national strategy he wanted at the center of his economics. It "starts with a tax cut for the middle class and asks the rich to pay their fair share again." Then it moved to "national health insurance, a major investment in education, training for our workers, tough trade laws, and no more tax breaks for our corporations to move our jobs overseas." He urged people to examine his six-page Plan for America's Future that had been distributed to libraries throughout the state. "Together, we can put government on the side of the forgotten middle class and restore the American dream," the ad concluded.[46]

On the January 17 daily morning conference call I reported that our two-week economics push had produced a surreal 13-point rise in Clinton's vote. He was now taking 33 percent of the vote and was decisively ahead of Tsongas, 5 points back, while Kerrey and Iowa senator Tom Harkin struggled far behind. Rarely are results this clear-cut and dramatic. New Hampshire voters had been waiting for Clinton and his middle-class vision. We all agreed that the campaign should stay on the offensive, particularly attacking Kerrey for his hockey spot, showing him defending the U.S. goal when we were arguing that America should be competing and winning on trade.

The discussion quickly turned to how to follow the economics ad. Clinton was reluctant to use the middle-class tax cut as the theme of the next ad, but a determined coalition of Greer, Greenberg, and James Carville persuaded him. I wasn't quite sure what was holding him back but I knew it was the most concrete economic offer for people in the polls and a key plank of the DLC program. But I also noted in my diary a "subtle shift in dynamics with Clinton looking for the last nod on decisions from Carville."[47] James and Paul Begala were the Southern, hard-edged wonder kids who used "health care as a right" of all Americans to engineer a surprise upset victory in last fall's special election to fill Pennsylvania's U.S. Senate seat. Frank, Mandy Grunwald, an associate in his media firm, and I lunched with them to see if the chemistry was right and I thought they were very attuned to our middle-class politics and urged them to join the campaign. In the end, they decided Clinton wanted the job much more than the other candidates and now they were getting his nod.

Then George Stephanopoulos stopped us: the *Star*, a tabloid newspaper, would have a story Monday naming five women involved with Clinton. What's more, the *New York Post* and Fox News, both owned by Rupert Murdoch, were going with similar stories. "Trash," Clinton said. George said our response would be a very tough "absolutely false." But James was worried that Clinton would get down when he needed to be up.[48]

That night I joined the Clinton motorcade up to a town meeting at Bedford, seven miles northwest of Manchester. It was bitterly cold and blustery with large mounds of snow framing every scene, yet Old Town Hall was crowded. Clinton was hoarse, but his emergence as the leader in a presidential race produced an electricity in the air that made even his stump speech delivered five times a day sound special. Then a woman asked Hillary, not Bill, whether fidelity in marriage should be a relevant issue for voters. She responded without embarrassment that their marriage was strong, that they supported each other, and that, while they've had issues, just like any other marriage, they should be allowed to enjoy a "realm of protection." Then she added, "Is anything about our marriage as important to the people of New Hampshire as whether or not they will have a chance to keep their own families together?" The crowd roared its approval. James and I watched in awe as Hillary triumphed in her first real battle.[49]

The reports about Clinton's relationship with Gennifer Flowers were quickly followed by new revelations about Clinton's dealings with his Arkansas draft board during the Vietnam War, disrupting what would have been a smooth takeoff on the economy and the middle-class message. The stories also disrupted our conference call routine as we all rushed to Manchester to figure out how Clinton would survive the tidal wave of bad news. The campaign would later become known for its "war room" in Little Rock, but the first war room was in Manchester's Days Inn, where we were joined by David Wilhelm and DeeDee Myers, our press secretary, very much in the line of fire. James Carville quickly became the driving force, pushing for any and all research and for rapid responses to media inquiries. This was no drill! None of us would have been there but for Clinton's response under attack, his sure-footed and open push-back against an intrusive and crazed media, and ultimately, making this a fight for the ordinary middle-class family.

I began polling every night but more important for my formulating my own advice were the groups we recruited to hold every night in Manchester. Marcia Hale turned on the evening news and each night James and I watched them react to the day's unfolding story. Nothing was more important to me than learning the first night that voters were determined to have an election that was about them, not one hijacked by the media. They liked the way that Clinton stood firm under the withering fire without becoming defensive or giving up.

The tabloids had little effect on Clinton's poll standing. But then *The Wall Street Journal* reported on an affidavit made public by Colonel Eugene Holmes, a highly decorated World War II veteran who had run the University of Arkansas's ROTC program. Holmes's affidavit accused Clinton of concealing his antiwar activities while attending Oxford and of deceptively applying to the Arkansas ROTC program to obtain a draft deferment when he had no intention of enrolling at the University of Arkansas or in the ROTC program.

On Sunday night at home in New Haven I braced myself for the call from my office when the interviewing finished, the tension only heightened by the calls every fifteen minutes from James and George. I knew in my gut the poll could be very bad and it was worse. After the amazing highs, this campaign could soon be all over, I thought, and called Carville, who had returned with a voiceless Clinton to the mansion in Little Rock for a weekend respite. "Meltdown!" I said without elaboration.

When Clinton's plane touched down in New Hampshire the next day the press was in a frenzy over the letter he had written to Colonel Holmes from Oxford, opposing the war and struggling to avoid the draft. Carville's instinct was to turn this final blow to our candidacy into an opportunity, confirmed by the ordinary voters in our nightly focus groups who read the letter in its entirely and saw the serious and anguished young man who wrote it. Clinton did the rest. Knowing that his lifelong goal was at stake, he gained new energy and purpose from the people who rallied to him. In Dover, he declared, "I'll tell you what the real character issue is, who really cares about you." The lumps he had taken in the campaign were nothing compared to what the families of New Hampshire had endured. His vow to stick with New Hampshire families "until the last dog dies" showed voters a real flesh-and-blood leader with the strength to fight for people.

Overtaking Tsongas was out of the question. But could we avoid calamity by possibly finishing second? When the early returns and exit polls showed us in a clear second, we rushed Clinton before the cameras and cheering supporters and he declared, "New Hampshire tonight has made Bill Clinton the comeback kid." And I never doubted that we won that day.[50]

A BIG PRICE

Clinton and Tsongas fell into a bitter war over integrity and ideas in New Hampshire. Tsongas ads charged that Clinton's middle-class tax cut was nothing but a gimmick and that Clinton would say whatever people wanted to hear. By contrast, Tsongas offered "straight answers" and wouldn't advocate any tax cut that would explode the federal deficit. "I'm not Santa Claus," he declared.[51]

From New Hampshire, Clinton flew directly to Atlanta and into the embrace of Governor Zell Miller, his strongest and most prominent supporter in the South. Miller ran interference for Clinton, telling the media that "Bill Clinton is too gracious to say this, but it's time to tell the truth." The truth, Miller said with some help from James and Paul, was that Paul Tsongas's program sounded a lot like the "trickle-down economics" of the 1980s that included a major hike in gas taxes, a cut in capital gains taxes for the wealthy, and reduced cost-of-living increases for Social Security recipients. Within days, Clinton took up the critique: "I am tired of what is cold-blooded being passed off as courageous," he declared. After New Hampshire we began using the phrase "people first, not corporations first."[52]

I rushed a survey into the field after New Hampshire—without getting Clinton's input—to see if Tsongas got a lift from his win and whether the public noticed our "comeback." I quickly heard from George: "No survey goes into the field until Clinton has seen it!" I groaned. James, George, and Frank had signed off but a presidential campaign was too fast-moving to wait for a back-and-forth on Clinton's edits. Dick Morris thrived off that kind of engagement but I did not and maybe Clinton wanted to reassert some control over us. When I caught up with Clinton that night at Chops in Buckhead outside Atlanta there was no sign of anger, but the next day I got his edits on a South Carolina survey. Each of the simulated debate exchanges that I took so much pride in crafting to be so fair and balanced that I imagined Tsongas himself would read it and see his words, had been rewritten to insure that the survey respondents would choose Clinton every time. As Gloria put it: "He always wants an A+."[53]

The campaign after New Hampshire was in trouble. Clinton quickly lost in Maine and South Dakota and polls showed us behind in Maryland, Colorado, and Minnesota, the states that, along with Georgia, would create the next wave. Even Georgia appeared to be slipping.[54] Clinton was angry at his campaign and at himself that he no longer was the candidate of change and ideas. With a pall descending, Clinton locked in on the middle-class tax cut as the source of his problems on trust, the economy, and ideas. Tsongas had become the candidate of the future and Clinton was raging. In a voice that Mark Miller, the embedded reporter for *Newsweek*, would describe as "raw with overuse," Clinton furiously told us that we had helped Tsongas "by running on this middle-class tax cut."[55] That the best-educated voters and editorial boards, particularly *The Atlanta Constitution*, were embracing Tsongas just confirmed his conclusion.[56] We sat silently waiting for the fury to pass, but also dumbstruck. Didn't he remember Gennifer Flowers and Colonel Holmes? We just didn't have time to dwell on the dynamics that focused his anger on the middle-class tax cut.

The Georgia primary loomed just days away to be followed a week later by the Florida primary. A disappointing finish in Georgia and a loss in Florida would effectively end Clinton's campaign. I figured that reiteration of James's contrast message—"people first versus corporations first"—coupled with overwhelming African American support would get us past the first test. On March 1 we caught up with Clinton at the Carter Center where we each offered our advice in turn. I sat directly across the table from him, reading and ticking off my key points: you're the front-runner in Georgia, act like it; we don't need to bring Tsongas down, don't be personal or petty, even though you hate his smugness; enjoy yourself; national strength is important in the South; be personal about the South; and, most importantly, take the opportunity to talk about ending welfare and about values and responsibility. James believed this was all a distraction—just too many messages. I told Clinton you should talk about being "imperfect." This was the South and the born-again are much more forgiving and trusting of those who have been tempted.

In back-to-back debates—one in Georgia, the other in Maryland—Clinton scored well. Minutes after the Georgia debate, he went on television and elaborated on his "imperfections," and seeing me afterward, he exclaimed, "When you guys let me go to church, I can think straight."[57] In Maryland, Clinton spoke powerfully about the Southern experience and about going up and down together, all of which was rebroadcast in Georgia. On the way to the post-debate party Clinton was ebullient, confident that he was back on message and on the attack.

On our conference call the day before the Georgia primary I told the group that we were dead-even in Florida and thus on the edge of life or death with a fateful week before us. Frank Greer raised the idea of pulling back from Florida instead of risking everything, but no one else agreed. We also were not unified on how to proceed. James Carville wanted to push everything through the filter of "trickle-down economics," the single-minded focus that had reversed our slide in Georgia and given us a strong lead. This was his signature approach to campaigns. I usually agree with James, but I argued even though time was desperately short, we had to take voters through a number of steps, starting with welfare, to educate them about Clinton's values. Clinton agreed with me,[58] but in a series of calls that day the debate became "something of a shouting match," I wrote in my diary, with Carville declaring, "My belief in a campaign is take one thing and drive it home as hard as you can."[59]

I returned to studying the dead-even Florida poll, which was proving a revelation for me on how not just to win Florida but to win decisively, and I began writing feverishly. About three quarters of Democratic primary voters and the undecided were noncollege graduates, values voters who were distrustful of Clinton and holding back. Our message turned a dead-even race into a 20-point rout, but only when it was infused with values. Clinton's commitment to creating jobs needed to be accompanied in equal measure by his opposition to welfare dependency. Only then did our economic contrast with "trickle-down economics" get heard. That meant our final advertising, including an ad that I wrote at the end of the memo, had to be "focused downscale and must associate with people at the values level." I concluded, "To put people first, we have to align with their values, too."[60]

It is always hard to focus on primary day as voters go the polls to decide your fate and there is nothing more to do about it, yet we dared not resolve how the campaign would close in Florida. Clinton signaled his support for my ad, but as we were talking, the first very encouraging exit polls came in from Georgia. A frenzied James Carville broke off from our meeting to call Clinton with the good news. The real tallies were even more spectacular: a two-to-one landslide in Georgia, with Colorado up for grabs, but Tsongas looking as if he would lose to former Governor Jerry Brown of California, surprisingly populist candidate, encouraged by our late anti-Tsongas ad. It was the best outcome we could hope for and the next day Kerrey canceled his schedule.[61] Suddenly we were all smart again because Clinton thought our anti-Tsongas ad in Colorado worked.

"Clinton now treats your research like a Bible," Mandy Grunwald told me. And Al From sent Clinton a memo weighing in on "the Greenberg/DLC message."[62]

Early the next day I received our Florida tracking poll results showing that we had surged into the lead, 40 to 24 percent, with big gains among the non-college, seniors, and those who want a president who "puts the middle class first."[63] But *The New York Times*, whose polls have great standing with the press, showed the race even and Tsongas walked into the trap, proclaiming that "Florida is the big test." With virtually no public polls since Georgia, we appeared to have a good chance of shattering expectations in Florida and Super Tuesday.[64]

Our growing anticipation of a Super Tuesday triumph was stopped short on a very late Sunday night call when George told us *The New York Times* was about to write a major story on the Whitewater land deal—opening a new front on the character and trust issue. When we got on the 9 A.M. call the next morning, Bill and Hillary went right to the new scandal. Hillary wanted to sue the *Times* for "the worst case of deliberate distortion" and "absolute arrogance in subverting the process."[65] I was sure she was right, though I was growing confident the voters would have the final say.

On Super Tuesday, my flight to Chicago was delayed by a snowstorm, and I rushed to catch up with Clinton downtown so we could prepare to take the results there, hoping they would propel Clinton into the next round of primaries in Illinois and Michigan. The early exit polls were stunning and consistent with our polls, which Bruce Lindsey had the good grace to point out. With my daughter Anna, who was finishing her first year of doctoral work at the University of Chicago, in tow, I caught up with Clinton to discuss his victory speech and some final comments as he was having makeup applied in his bedroom suite. On the way to the ballroom to watch the speech we had to pass through the hotel's back halls and kitchen, a journey that prompted both Frank Greer and me to blurt out in near unison, "I hate this. I just think of Robert Kennedy." The speech was good, not up to New Hampshire standards, but this time we really won.

When a clearly tired but relaxed and upbeat Clinton returned to the suite he put his arm around my shoulder and turned to Anna: "Who would have thought that this man would have taught me redemption?"[66]

Our overnight polls showed a big bounce for Clinton, a validation of Super Tuesday's results.[67]

On the Sunday before Super Tuesday, I finally returned a call from Doug Ross, the head of the DLC in Michigan, who had a big idea for addressing the character question. Why not have Clinton give the same speech to a white audience in suburban Macomb County one day and to a black church in Detroit the next? He could condemn the KKK leader David Duke and demand responsibility in both audiences.[68] I understood the implications immediately and so did everyone in the group when I raised it on the call that night. So, on the Thursday after Super Tuesday, I joined Clinton in the motorcade to Macomb County Community College. With Clinton and me alone in the backseat and the Secret Service in the front, the significance of this moment in my life did not escape me. Clinton was well aware of Macomb's history, that it was the home of Reagan Democrats, but I gave him a one-page memo and a short briefing, underscoring that the press would be there in force and understood the symbolic significance of this visit. The key point was that Democrats would have "a candidate who will stand up for the forgotten middle class, who understands their values, who believes in the work ethic and responsibility."[69] I told him he needed to emphasize to both audiences that "We're in this together." He then wrote out his own outline on both sides of a 5×7 card. Afterward, he handed it to me, not something he normally did, and I treated it like I caught Roger Maris's 61st home run ball.

Macomb County Community College educates the aspirant youth and those trying to find a step-up in mid-career in a white working-class suburb of Detroit. The student center of the gym had been reconfigured with a *Donahue*-style stage, rows of chairs on risers on all sides. Clinton worked his way around the front row amid the audience's applause and cheers. Then he came straight to the point and established his connection: Macomb, he said, is a "very famous county" because the "native Democrats" had turned to Republicans, not unlike the situation in his own state of Arkansas, because of shared grievances against a government that had little regard for "middle class effort and middle class values." He reminded them that the top one percent got 60 percent of the income gains, and "executives continue to raise their pay and their perks while workers get the shaft."[70]

Then he offered a new bargain based on "people-first economics." "I'll give you your values back, I'll restore the economic leadership, I'll help you build the middle class back, but you've got to do it with everybody in the country." Although he didn't say it explicitly, his call for a new unity of black and white essentially asked them to reclaim Robert Kennedy's Democratic Party.

Tom Edsall, who wrote the book *Chain Reaction* that said Democrats could never choose a leader who gave such a speech, and Ron Brownstein of the *Los Angeles Times*, who said that if they did the party would never be the same, were both there and in a festive mood. Brownstein added that my focus groups in Macomb and the New Jersey ones by famed conservative strategist Lee Atwater that gave America "Willie Horton," were "the most famous ever conducted"—a comment I managed to record in my diary. Clinton, in the holding room, pumped his fist in triumph. "God that was great!"[71]

After the speech I accompanied Clinton to a one-on-one meeting with Ron Brown, the chair of the Democratic National Committee. Brown startled us by declaring that the primaries were for all intents and purposes over and that he would treat Clinton as the nominee. I'm not sure what Clinton was thinking, but I thought, how appropriate that this be bracketed by Clinton's proposed compact in Macomb and the black church. Brown asked, "Who is your Tully?" Paul Tully was his political director with legendary knowledge of the political landscape. And then he asked whether he should be talking about fund-raising to the national finance chair Bob Farmer or Rahm Emanuel, which he pronounced, "ram." After some laugher, Bill said, "Stay with Ram."

The next morning Bill and Hillary headed to the Pleasant Grove Baptist Church in Detroit where more than two hundred African American parishioners were jammed in the pews, warmed up by a succession of ministers offering testimonials about Clinton. I arrived with Clinton, who was ushered off to a private meeting with the ministers. After several enthusiastic verses of "The Battle Hymn of the Republic," the Reverend O'Dell Jones, formerly of Arkansas, introduced Clinton as a man who came "from the bottom to lead the nation."[72]

That kind of welcome tapped Bill Clinton's soul more deeply than any Macomb student audience possibly could and he gave an inspired speech. While I, too, was lifted by the rising spirits, my soul was lifted in Macomb, a difference that I barely noted at the time. Clinton asked his audience to join "a new partnership to change the country" and told them about his visit the day before to white Macomb. "I offered them a deal," Clinton said, "a program that will restore the middle class, without regard to race. I told them, 'You have rewarded Ronald Reagan and George Bush, and they have punished you.'" That brought a chorus of "amens." Clinton then described the bargain he was offering these black congregants: "Today, I come here to challenge you to reach out your hands to them, for we have been divided for too long." Then he returned to the theme of responsibility, greeted with an even stronger wave of "amens."

"What I offer is a chance to give you the opportunity to assume responsibility that every American should assume for his or her own life,"[73] he said as the congregation rose, clapping and swaying to the muted tones of the organ and choir.

They, too, accepted the bargain that would restore the Democratic majority.

A CHILLY SPRING

The coming of spring in 1992 did little to lift the nation's dour mood. More than 80 percent of the population believed the country was on the wrong track. It was so off track that the Clinton campaign itself had become part of the problem, diminished by the media's obsession with scandal and by the attacks from various challengers on Clinton's "political" nature. After each primary victory the media would focus on the growing majority who believed Clinton "lacks the character and honesty to be president."[74]

The attacks took a big toll. Despite the hunger for change in the country, Clinton was running well behind Bush in a two-way contest in all our general election surveys from April up until the Democratic convention in July. When Ross Perot joined the race in June as an independent, Clinton ran third in all our surveys until Perot's withdrawal during the convention.[75]

After the New York primary, James, Mandy, and I pulled out of the primary effort to focus on the simple issue of rebuilding trust, what we called the "General Election Project," but that was quickly nicknamed the "Manhattan Project," because Mickey Kantor signed off on the project at our Manhattan hotel, and the scale and secrecy of the effort. Most of the intellectual and emotional energy of the campaign was directed toward the Manhattan Project rather than piling up victories in the remaining primaries. Ultimately, we decided that the answer lay in biography, beginning with Clinton's humble origins in Hope and building on his lifetime commitment to education, bettering himself, and raising up one of the poorest states in the nation. His biography showed a person who had gone beyond politics to become a leader with the conviction to battle for the average person. The key to having Clinton's project heard and understood was for voters to learn about his life.

But that was only a theory at that stage, a focal point to try to rally a flagging and dispirited campaign. James was demoralized and George gloomy. Clinton was down and frustrated, lacking confidence in his own campaign. My polls didn't help. Our message tests were flat.[76]

On June 4, I had finished editing a major survey to test the results of our latest brainstorming for the Manhattan Project and then hopped a flight to Little Rock. While I was airborne Susan Thomases, a new power center in the campaign, asked George to trash the survey, a notion he quickly rejected. But when I landed my pager went off, George demanding that I call him immediately. "Clinton pulled the poll," he told me. I couldn't believe it, so I called Joe Goode, head of the presidential work, in my office to confirm it. "George called me and said 'Pull it down.' What do I do, say 'no'?" Thomases had gone directly to Clinton, not only to kill the survey but to also dump the entire schedule that had emerged from the Manhattan Project meeting.

"George, I quit! I'm not working for her," I said, slamming down the phone.

I was beyond furious. I was in Little Rock for a convention-planning meeting at the mansion, but I refused to go. At Doe's that night, I refused to join the parade of people to Susan's table. Later she came over and sat next to me to try to persuade me on the research and the canceled schedule.

I arrived at the mansion at mid-afternoon to meet with Clinton. He was running late, delayed by satellite interviews and Mandy's meeting on town halls, giving me time to stew. When Clinton finally arrived we went into the governor's study to discuss the situation. Clinton began by asking for some trivial changes in the questionnaire. No problem, I said, but quickly added that "I am angry with you. You're destroying your own campaign with second-guessing and lack of confidence and allowing people to circumvent the process." Then I said some unrepeatable things about Susan Thomases. I ended by telling Clinton that I would not accept any process that produced chaos.

Clinton could see how angry I was. "I have complete confidence in you," he said. "The polling has been very accurate and the theme and issue side has been very good. To be honest, I have never allowed anybody to do a survey, as you have, without my involvement and sign-off. Dick Morris was my alter ego, and I wouldn't let him conduct a survey without my seeing it." I'm not going to touch that, I thought. Even with the roller coaster in mood, I cherished my relationship with him and relished the struggle to win and shape this new compact, but it was less personal and shaped more by our overlapping and evolving political projects. For me, that produced the deepest possible bond outside my family and closest friends. But Clinton admittedly wanted an almost private relationship with a pollster with special powers/talents away from the rest of the campaign team where he could develop confidence in his own path to success. All I wanted now was continuing intense discussion and feedback and I didn't want to labor under the burden of a Clinton sign-off on everything I did.

"Fine," he said. Then he told me he was desperately in need of rest, and indeed, his eyes started to close on me.

Were they open when he made the deal with me?

THE PLAN

With the campaign still without a powerful message for the general election, I briefed Clinton a few weeks later at his suite at the Washington Court Hotel on the results of our latest polling. Clinton drew on a treasure trove of messages and I had distilled three of them to test: "reinventing government," "for the middle class, not the elites," and "investing in people." Each of the themes, I explained, got a very positive reaction. Yet at the end of the survey Clinton picked up only 4 points and still lagged behind Bush and Perot, held down by doubts about trust and honesty. Clinton was troubled by the results. What chance did he have to get an audience with such negative perceptions? The meeting ended early when Clinton took a call from Perot, who wanted to negotiate one-on-one debates, without Bush, because he was convinced that James Baker, the White House chief of staff, had a wire to reporters' earpieces.[77]

I got up at 5 A.M. Sunday to work on a new survey and began to see how these distinct themes could work in combination and tell a story. We didn't have to choose after all. Half the respondents for the new survey would be hit first with a message that government is failing, thus creating the credibility to use government and to invest in people. The other half of the sample would hear the argument in reverse order. I was conscious, reflected in my diary entry, that I had joined David Osborne's critique of bureaucratic government and advocacy of innovation with Bob Reich's case for bold investment in human capital to achieve national greatness.

When I talked to Clinton later that morning he had gone beyond being upset about the trust and honesty issue to being upset that we hadn't been able to move the dial. We were in last place and some polls were barely giving us the 25 percent threshold for federal matching funds, so movement was becoming critical. Nevertheless, we spent the rest of the conversation talking about Jesse Jackson's demand for a role in the convention after being denied one at the Democratic Leadership Conference meeting in Cleveland. The clash between Clinton and Jackson had escalated when Clinton faulted the rapper Sister Souljah for her racist and violent lyrics in front of Jackson at the

Rainbow Coalition meeting in Washington on June 15. Al From finally got his national conflagration with the Democrats' special interests, which I welcomed at that point before facing the whole country. Clinton drew a firm line that Jackson would have no significant role at the convention, which was no doubt popular with the public, but would create mayhem in Democratic circles. My liberal friends had warned me of an impending apocalypse.

Because of the urgency of the campaign settling on a message, we did the new national survey over just two nights, and the results were stunning. They were more exciting than winning the last primary in California, and I spent the flight coming back writing the memo, arguing with James who did not appreciate the significance of first attacking government before telling people how you want to use it. I presented the results to Clinton with George, Paul, and James in his study at the mansion in Little Rock, though it began rockily. Clinton, distracted, wanted to talk about the leaks to the press, declaring, "I wish I had a wire attached to all of you." This was his way of saying I'm fed up with all of you, but no one took the bait. I got right to my memo, winging it without a paper copy, but this "People-First Profile" was seared into my brain.[78] The message began with the bold assertion that government had failed the average person while taking care of the wealthy. Worse still, the middle class had worked harder to pay for a government that had done little about the economy or health care. The answer? Bill Clinton, a man of humble origins who worked for what he got and who believes "we need a government that puts people first again," a man who proposes a national economic strategy that invests in our own people—in welfare reform, education, vocational training, and health care.

After hearing that profile, as well as messages from Bush and Perot, respondents were asked to vote again and Clinton moved into a tie for the lead. After an attack on Bush for economic policies that favored the few, Clinton surged into the lead. The "people first" message, combining themes of government failure and government initiatives for the middle class, proved twice as powerful as any message we had tested in the past.[79] Clinton took a certain satisfaction that the DLC folks consumed with revolutionizing government, and the middle-class populists consumed with using government, would be forced to work together under this umbrella.

Clinton seemed immediately comfortable with the message, something that had not happened before. My presentation and the discussion about it ended just half an hour before Clinton was scheduled to appear on Larry King's show, but he rehearsed questions and answers using the theme as he prepared. On the air he played the theme as if he had been living it all his life, which in fact he had been. Each question turned into a "people first" response. After the show, Clinton pulled me into the men's room to get my reaction to a number of things and told me he felt really good about the show, thanked me, and said, "If I can see the light at the end of the tunnel, I can get focused."

With the new clarity of the "people first" theme, I gave Harold Ickes, a tough-talking FOB with a unique understanding of New York City politics who was running the convention, the go-ahead to use the slogan on all the convention posters, even though Clinton kept mulling it over, wondering from time to time if it was "big enough." He was right to pose that question, but "people first" now distilled in the two words first crafted by Frank the whole political project and would set up the choice with George Bush.[80]

As we were developing the story and message of the campaign, others were working on the policies. We received the economic plan from Bob Boorstin, manic veteran of the presidential campaign and in charge of speech-writing, and Gene Sperling, a former Cuomo policy advisor with an economic bent. With twenty-four-hour days, they had two weeks to bring together Clinton's proposals into a plan, kicked off by a half-day meeting that Clinton convened with his closest policy advisors and a group of investment bankers that included Bob Rubin, Roger Altman, Barrie Wigmore, and Ken Brody. The group agreed that the focus of an economic plan would be on three broad policies: deficit reduction, investment in education and health care, and liberalized trade. Some pressed harder for cutting deficits while others preferred a stronger tilt toward investments, but that was precisely the kind of difference and tension that delighted Clinton. I was delighted that "People First" became the title, the lead, and organizing principle. Even better was the fact that we got our plan out before Perot released his.

The first page of the plan declared: "Our national economic strategy puts people first by investing more than $50 billion each year for the next four years while cutting the deficit in half." Suddenly we were giving equal attention to a deficit that had barely figured in our past discussions, even when battling Tsongas, who made deficit reduction a keystone of his campaign.[81]

When the plan was revealed publicly at the end of June, there were some questions about the economic assumptions and reality of the budget cuts, but that was more than offset by the fact that for the first time a national candidate had laid out a full plan and budget, with year-by-year projections over five years.[82] It committed the Clinton presidency to "the most dramatic economic growth program since the Second World War," including a national investment in lifetime learning and in developing the "world's best communication, transportation and environmental systems." It promised to end welfare as we know it and to achieve middle-class tax fairness. It offered the middle class and working people a choice between a children's tax credit and "a significant reduction in their income tax rates." It promised to provide affordable health care for all by "radically controlling costs," it aimed to revolutionize government by cutting 100,000 federal jobs, and it would open up world markets, starting with a free trade agreement with Mexico. To pay for the combination of investments and deficit reduction, the plan would save $300 billion by cutting spending in ways that were not specified, by closing tax loopholes and by raising taxes on the wealthiest and eliminating deductions for excessive CEO pay.[83]

Nowhere did the plan mention the number of jobs that would be created if it were implemented. I pressed Gene Sperling relentlessly for a number so I could test which elements of the economic plan were most important for voters. While a succession of economists demurred, one labor economist finally projected that a normal recovery would produce eight million, the exact number I had used as a placeholder and soon to become a central pledge for Bill Clinton.

THE WAR ROOM

Just before the gavel came down to open the third night of the Democratic convention in New York City, James, Mandy, and I were huddled in the den of the Clintons' expansive suite on the fourteenth floor of the InterContinental hotel waiting for a private meeting with Hillary. When she joined us, followed by Bill ten minutes later, I told them that we were soaring, up 10 points in a day, the combined result of the economic plan, saying no to Jesse Jackson, and, more than anything, the selection of Al Gore as running mate. Gore's choice presented the nation with a powerful image of two families from a new generation of the South eager to lead. But that was only the preamble to what I really needed to say. "We are in great danger," I said, exposed to attacks from our opponents, who were coming while we were unprepared. Nothing was in place. James jumped in behind me to complain that all the efforts to create a war room had been thwarted by those who felt threatened by a centralized campaign.

James's vision was for a single war room that would house all the key campaign people, the opposition researchers, policy people, and news monitors, everything geared toward fast analysis and near instant response. Hillary stopped him with a wave of her hand. "James, we want you to take over this campaign. Just put down on paper whatever you want and we will announce it to the campaign before we leave New York."

As we filed out she stopped us for a moment to tell us how much she appreciated what we had done to make it possible. "We are deeply in your debt," she said. Later I met James for a drink in the bar before heading over to watch Clinton's formal nomination—and we needed it. We had a lot of campaign meetings in our lives and many with the Clintons, but in a matter of

With James Carville in the war room in Clinton's Little Rock headquarters, overseen by Ricki Seidman, liberal activist and former legal director of People for the American Way, and Bob Boorstin. [David Burnett, Contact Press Images]

minutes, they empowered us to take over Clinton's national presidential campaign. And now we had to do it.[84]

One of the first tasks for the war room was to simplify what we would present to voters as the "choice" in this election. For James, this was the filter through which everything must pass; for me, it was the underlying meaning of the election. To do that I wrote a question that asked respondents to listen to a series of choices that "some people use to describe the main difference between George Bush and Bill Clinton." Two that I tested were "Bill Clinton is the future and George Bush is the past" and "Bill Clinton is strong and George Bush is weak." After each, people were asked whether this was a real difference or not and if it made you more likely to vote for Bill Clinton. After three surveys the choice that rose to the top—"Bill Clinton is change and George Bush is more of the same"—was believed to be a "real" difference by two thirds and for them, two thirds said the difference made them more likely to vote for Clinton.[85]

Soon James had scribbled on the white board in the war room:

Change vs. more of the same
"The economy, stupid"
Don't forget health care

THE IRRATIONAL ENDGAME

Within minutes of the end of the second presidential debate in Richmond two and a half weeks before the election I could sense that voters were resolving their doubts, ruling out candidates and getting comfortable with their choice for president. Clinton did well and held on to his 43 percent of the vote. Perot made some gains among the undecideds and headed toward 20 percent, while Bush, who had been caught looking at his watch in the midst of the debate, drew some Republicans back to the fold and was polling about 37 percent. With our lead settling in at 6 or 7 points we were positioned for a big Electoral College win. Our dinners were spent reworking the political map. If we won Wisconsin and Michigan, where we had double-digit leads in late October, we didn't need to carry any Southern states nor Ohio or New Jersey. We knew Perot's very volatile vote could have a big impact on which states we would carry. Our goal was to get Perot voters to break for us, but they still saw Clinton as an untrustworthy politician.[86] We believed we could partly overcome that by returning to our New Covenant themes in the closing ten days: a tough responsibility message, challenging student audiences, crowds, and business. But inexplicably Clinton would not go there, preferring a more literal approach. He just kept repeating before audiences his opponents' attack on trust, prompting a frustrated James Carville to ban the "t-word" from the war room.

The endgame in presidential campaigns brings out all sorts of irrationalities, starting with the media polls. Many are criminally bad. Some are done in one night with no time for callbacks and thus over-represent people who are easily reached by phone, often seniors. They are not carefully weighted and, as a result, show wide swings in voter preference that the media interpret wrongly as voter fickleness. And they usually ask the respondent only for whom they will vote without any prior questions that build trust. With people reluctant to tell a stranger for whom they will vote without being warmed up, many of the media polls report an inflated number of undecided voters. Worst of all, a poll that shows a result sharply different from all the others gets media attention because the difference is "news" when it is likely the result of normal sampling fluctuations or careless polling practices.

The media coverage and the suspect polls tend to make campaigns paranoid. On Sunday, October 25, the *New York Times*, CNN, and ABC polls all showed some drop. I had already cautioned the campaign to expect that as the normal post-debate settling that would not change the race. Nonetheless, I spent most of that day pushing back the panic. Even Clinton was shaken and got the hotel operator to break in on one of my calls.

We started our national tracking poll and most of our state polls that night. When the national calling was finished in California at midnight East Coast time my office began crunching the data so I would have numbers when I met James for breakfast at 6:30, our morning routine. George and James were too keyed up to sleep that night and even I, for all my so-called confidence, noted in my diary that "I am in near dread of the numbers."

There was no need to worry. The numbers were fine and stable nationally and in the thirteen states in which we had the first half of our two-night polls. Clinton even made gains on some key attributes.[87] That day we decided to run a spot validating Clinton's economic plan as the best way to limit Perot's gains, getting voters focused at the end on the main reason for change and for choosing Bill Clinton. With Perot on three networks explaining why he hired private investigators to look into the Bush family, I wondered if perhaps "trust" would be the big decider after all. I went back to the hotel exhausted but pleased that things were under control, a perception that George and James did not share. When Clinton called me late that night he described our situation as "perilous."[88]

That night, a week before the election, we learned that the Bush campaign was putting 100 percent of its media buy, every penny, behind a single negative ad attacking Clinton's record in Arkansas. The ad was over-the-top, depicting Arkansas as a barren place, closing with a buzzard on a tree in the midst of a windswept plain. This took voters to the obvious conclusion that Clinton, failed governor of a small state, was unprepared for the awesome responsibilities of being the president of the United States.

We had read the script in our nightly focus groups, as soon as we learned about it, and Frank worked through the night and produced an effective counter ad. Yet with time to consider the team decided not to respond to the attack, a position that required unbelievable unity and firmness in the face of Clinton's desperation to defend his record. We gathered around the speakerphone in George's office to listen to Bill and Hillary calling in with their traveling party, all exhausted and on edge. Though it violated every Dick Morris instinct to leave the attack unaddressed, the campaign team was determined to finish on our terms and not on the defensive on "trust." Our focus groups over the last two nights had confirmed that the Bush ad was overly sensational and it fell to me, apparently the only calm person in the group, to make the case to Clinton against a response.

"It goes against everything I believe," Clinton shouted over the phone. "I did that once and was beaten in 1980, and I've never allowed that to happen since. I am very worried about this." Nevertheless, he reluctantly acceded to our judgment. "All right. I'm not saying I agree, but you guys do what you think is right."

The overnight polls on Wednesday morning were a little closer. Our lead was down to 5 points with diminished but still strong leads in California and Minnesota and closer in Georgia. George and James were deeply worried that the race was collapsing and only became more upset when an angry Clinton called, this time about a Perot ad attacking him.

"They are attacking my character and we must attack Perot's character," Clinton said. "We need to take a meat ax to his brain, cut his head open." He wanted a fast response with "red meat and passion, no more pussy ads." Even as he was demanding that we get a new ad out, Clinton was writing the spot himself, defending his record.

Amid all the angst I retreated to my corner of the war room to study the data and grew less and less worried. There had been no drop in the Clinton vote and Bush's gain had come in the deep red states where Bush was merely enlarging his majorities. I talked with Clinton that night, my confidence buttressed by some strong state polls. Sounding marginally reassured, he laughed and reminded me of his glorious second-place finish in New Hampshire. "You know, this time I can't get credit for second place," he said. "I can't run up there and claim victory for second place."

Thursday morning was our last chance to change the advertising traffic. We decided to stand pat and stick to our economy message.[89] Half of our ad buy was devoted to attacking Bush on the economy and half to the spot validating our economic plan. That spot opened with Clinton working at a desk as the narrator intoned: "Endorsed by over 600 economists, including 10 Nobel Prize winners, as the best hope for reviving the nation's economy." The names of the economists began scrolling down the screen. "More than 400 of America's most respected business leaders say the Clinton plan will create jobs. A panel of independent experts convened by *Time* magazine concludes that Clinton's plan has the best solutions to our economic problems. And now, even the author of Ross Perot's plan has endorsed Bill Clinton for president. Let's get our economy moving again."

By Friday morning I was able to tell James at breakfast that our tracking polls once again showed us with a 7-point lead.[90] At the war room meeting immediately after breakfast everybody understood the meaning of the numbers when I laid them out for the jammed room. When CNN came in a short while later with a one-point difference in the race, everyone ignored it.

On Saturday morning I got on a conference call with George, James, and Clinton to work out the remainder of the schedule. Afterward, I was about to leave to fly back to Connecticut where my wife was campaigning to hold her seat in a tough race when Rahm Emanuel charged into the war room with the news that Wisconsin was getting tighter based on a poll in Les Aspin's congressional district. Reluctantly, I changed my travel plans to remain in Little Rock to try to keep things steady. A worried Clinton called when ABC showed the race at only 3 points, but other polls were higher. When my office finished the national poll later in the day, we were still 7 points up.

"Yes!" I wrote in my diary.

Later we went to the mansion to review a cut of a thirty-minute final film and afterward hung out in the kitchen to fix the Sunday schedule that had Clinton at a black church, even though we were promised a white one. I was very self-conscious about how we had to complete Robert Kennedy's project. The scheduler said that was Clinton's wish. Then, Hillary came downstairs carrying her clothes for the final campaign swing. Before heading for Cincinnati to join her husband she gave me a big hug "for doing such a spectacular job" and then hugged George and James. While the three of us were eating dinner James got a call from Mary Matalin, his future wife, who was his counterpart in the Bush campaign organization. After he hung up he only said that her mood was down. "They must have some bad numbers." George was then paged and looked up, "He really wants a black church."

At my computer in the corner of the war room in Clinton's Little Rock headquarters as Election Day approached. [David Burnett, Contact Press Images]

On Sunday in an act of penance for spoiling my plans to return to Connecticut, Rahm arranged a private plane to take me to New Haven and dinner with Rosa, some London friends there to campaign for her, and the core campaign staff before returning me to Little Rock late that night.[91]

On election eve we had an emotional war room meeting with Clinton participating by phone. The room was packed with cameras and people and George and James gave emotional, tearful speeches. You could feel the growing pressure in the room, almost bursting the walls. I noted in my diary that "what we were about to accomplish overwhelmed everybody."[92]

ELECTION

Election day was chaotic in the war room. Well-wishers and media people overran the offices and no one could do any real work, except for a small group tucked away in a nearby room to monitor the networks' reporting of exit polls. The first wave of polls at about 10:30 A.M. was breathtaking and another round at noon seemed to set us on a course for an unimaginable double-digit victory. The FBI must have seen the exit polls because they evacuated the building for a bomb sweep at noon, leaving James, George, and me to the eerie silence, except for some unanswered phones and a call on my cell from Bruce from the plane to get results for Clinton.[93]

The real results came in around 6 P.M., led by Georgia and Michigan, and virtually every announcement on the TV brought cheers. We broke for dinner, then went to a commotion-filled bar-and-grill restaurant located off the lobby of the Camelot, to join the FOBs, big donors, and war room crew to wait for Clinton and watch the results and projections. The actual results were not nearly as good as the exit polls had indicated. Clinton was running much closer to the expected margins, and both Texas and Florida looked as if they would break against us. Surprisingly Perot seemed to be doing much better than we had expected. Both James and I thought his support would drop to the mid-teens by election day, the historic pattern for third-party candidates.

When the votes were all counted the result was an impressive accomplishment for Clinton and our team. Clinton had 43 percent, Bush was at 37 percent, and Perot had 19 percent, almost exactly what we had been projecting for the last week. It was the first Democratic win since 1976 and the largest margin and Electoral College majority since 1964, when the Johnson landslide wiped out most records. Amid the "landslide" exit polls and triumphalism we did not dwell on what it meant that a majority of the voters had cast their ballots for someone other than Clinton with one in five voting for a lunatic. The election also failed to bring many new Democrats to the Congress, and in fact, when all was said and done, Democrats lost a net nine seats in the House. But none of that mattered at the moment. We had engineered a breathtaking comeback from the dead, with a special candidate, to a historic result.

Late that night we joined thousands of others jammed onto the lawn in front of the Old State House where Clinton had announced for president, its portico now surrounded by a stage more appropriate to a rock concert. The surrounding streets were crowded with satellite trucks, their extended antennas ready to beam images of the new president to audiences around the world. It was a very cold night, but the war room team was pumped, warmed by hugs and what seemed like permanent grins.

Bill and Hillary came onstage glowing and holding hands, waving to the crowd. Knowing that the television anchors and pundits would begin talking before his speech was even half complete, Clinton opened with the meaning of the election: ". . . to restore growth to our country and opportunity to our people, to empower our own people so that they can take more responsibility for their own lives, to face problems too long ignored, from AIDS to the environment, to the conversion of our economy from a defense to a domestic economic giant." The economy I thought barely more important than AIDS and the environment, I noted in my head. And then he added "perhaps most important of all," the goal of uniting the country "to bring our people together as never before so that our diversity can be a source of strength." He was making crystal-clear why he had gone to Macomb County and Detroit, the work of his life, to knock down the racial barriers. As I listened I was suddenly struck by the thought that I didn't know what he was going to say, the first time that had happened in a long while. The authority granted in New York at the Democratic convention had been unceremoniously revoked. I also noted that not once did he utter the words "middle class." But I let the thought pass quickly, crowded out by Clinton's nod to us. He thanked "my brilliant, aggressive, unconventional but always winning campaign staff, they were unbelievable."

After the speech, around 1 A.M. I walked back to the hotel with James and Mandy, still a little amazed that we did not suffer a fatal crash in one of the many tests along the way, but also a little unsettled. James, though, was just fine.

The next day I had my first opportunity to discuss the results with Clinton. After the new leader of the free world told a press conference of America's peaceful intentions, he told me that he should have attacked Perot, evidence that he was already thinking about the meaning of that big bloc of Perot voters. Hillary invited the campaign staff to a party Thursday night, but I had to decline on the grounds that I had to get back to Washington for a party for my staff, which had worked through every night for many months. Clinton then put his arm around me again and said, "Stan, I am the leader of the free world and you need to get your priorities right."[94]

Thursday morning I was up early to write a memo urging the new administration to establish a strategic center in the White House and to set priorities so that issues elevated in the campaign, especially economic and welfare reform, as well as the reinvention of government and a cleansing of politics, would not be lost.[95] I shared the memo with George so he could incorporate it into his proposal for organizing the White House, though for the most part that morning we were all hanging out in George's office waiting to pounce on the special issue of *Newsweek*, which had embedded a team in the campaign to observe how we worked. They had agreed not to publish their observations until after the election.

I had a last meeting with Clinton that afternoon before running to the airport to party with my staff. He began by thanking me profusely for helping him stay on message, but added that "I still should have attacked Perot." He said he was relieved we did not carry Florida or Texas, which would have raised expectations enormously. He seemed weighed down by those expectations. "By April, I expect to be the most popular president or a bum," he said. His lids were beginning to droop, so I wasn't sure how far I should go, but I did give him the memo I had drafted that morning. He scanned it quickly, and then said, yes, "the administration must be an extension of the campaign." He told me he wanted a war room in the White House and then added, "I want a more racially diverse inner core," sending a signal about his priorities and the character of the presidency.

That ended the meeting and we walked into the kitchen to see Hillary. We had a good laugh about his picture in *The New York Times*. I handed her a copy of my memo, but she was more interested in the *Newsweek*, which she promptly swiped. Only late that night, after returning to Washington and attending our staff party, did I have a chance in bed to read the *Newsweek* coverage of the war room operation.

"Ode to the war room and message group," I wrote in my diary that night.

2

BILL CLINTON

Act II

THE WORD "CONFIDENTIAL," stamped ominously at the top of each of the six copies of my memo on the national post-election survey, brought home the new formality of working with President-elect Bill Clinton. And rightly so. My survey showed that voters took the election seriously because they thought it was important to their lives. They had, I said, suspended "their feelings of distrust and cynicism" and allowed themselves "to opt for hope."[1] Every new president enjoys at least a brief honeymoon with voters, but in our case the voters associated Bill Clinton with hope, change, getting things done, and a concern for people and the economy.

The election had been totally about the economy: over half said their priority when voting was the economy and jobs. Less than 20 percent identified the budget deficits, Perot's central issue, as a priority and only about 5 percent chose health care or welfare reform. Less than two weeks after the election I felt compelled to remind Clinton and his transition leaders that "Perot voters, by two to one, say address the economy before the deficit."

At least for an instant on election day, Clinton advanced the political project that he had laid out in Cleveland: the great majority of voters saw him as a "new kind of Democrat" who won by a wide margin among "middle-of-the-road" voters. The Democratic Party was now defined by Clinton and Al Gore, not by Ted Kennedy, "liberals," or the "Democrats in Congress." Clinton was preferred to Bush on the economy, but perhaps as importantly on "rewarding hard work" and even on "personal responsibility" and handling taxes.

This was "a sea change and an extraordinary opening for a new Democratic Party, with plans to use government to achieve broad goals for the country," I said, alluding to the argument I developed in *The American Prospect*. While he did not carry Macomb County, he made drastic inroads with Reagan Democrats—nearly two thirds of them leaving the Republicans to help Clinton carry Michigan.

While the election revealed the vast political changes and the post-election goodwill toward Clinton, some things did not change very much. In an election that produced a revolt against politics, over 60 percent afterward viewed Clinton as "too much of a politician." The problem of trust endured, almost undiminished.

Clinton's victory was the product of a collapse in confidence in Republicans. Voters disillusioned with that party were drawn to Perot, who they saw as better than Clinton on the economy and standing up for American jobs. Perot voters were libertarian in instinct, disproportionably white, younger, blue-collar, and noncollege men who were deeply distrustful of politics and government. Thus, "the new Clinton majority is still in-waiting," I wrote. Perot had given defecting Republicans a place to pause, but the election would only "prove historic and re-aligning," as happened when Nixon worked to incorporate the Wallace voters after the 1968 election and when Robert Kennedy appealed to them before, I wrote, if we accepted the challenge of bringing Perot voters into our coalition. That was our highest political priority.[2]

LIKE A LASER

Clinton had committed to focus on the economy "like a laser," and he did. A month after the election Alan Greenspan, chairman of the Federal Reserve and the most powerful economic policymaker in the country, flew to Little Rock to brief the president-elect. Instead of a one-hour meeting, Clinton and Greenspan huddled privately for nearly three hours. According to Greenspan's account of the meeting, Clinton matched Richard Nixon in sheer intelligence and far surpassed all the previous presidents for grasping complex economic issues. He was eager to enlist Greenspan and the Fed to help initiate an economic recovery that created jobs. For his part, Greenspan focused on what he considered the most important economic issue confronting the nation: the huge and looming federal deficit that kept long-term interest rates stubbornly high. While the Fed sets short-term interest rates, Wall Street's bond traders drive the direction and magnitude of long-term rates. If they see the threat of inflation rising over the ten- to thirty-year span of most bond issues, they will bid up rates as protection. They believed that high deficits led to high inflation and their concern was palpable in the market as the budget deficit estimates kept climbing. Only a credible budget and deficit reduction program would persuade them to reduce long-term rates, Greenspan told Clinton, but the big payoff would come in new housing, expanding businesses, and new jobs, as well as rising stock values by the late 1990s—if Clinton did not already appreciate the primacy of addressing the deficit.[3]

A week later Clinton began announcing his choices for leadership positions in his administration and it did not go unnoticed that the first choices he announced involved his economics team. Lloyd Bentsen, the dignified chairman of the Senate Finance Committee, would be the new treasury secretary. Goldman Sachs's Bob Rubin, razor-sharp, self-deprecating, and soft-spoken, would chair the National Economics Council, a newly created office in the White House that would coordinate the actions of the many agencies that had roles in determining economic policy. And Leon Panetta, the former chairman of the House Budget Committee, would be the director of the Office of Management and Budget. Those choices sent a powerful signal that Clinton was rising above politics in his focus on the economy. None of the three had played any but the most minor roles in Clinton's campaign.

The rest of the economic team was equally impressive in the scope of their experience and brilliance. Roger Altman, chairman of the Blackstone Investment Group, was named deputy treasury secretary; Larry Summers, the youngest tenured professor of economics ever at Harvard and former chief economist at the World Bank, would serve as undersecretary of the treasury for international affairs. Alice Rivlin, the humorless deficit hawk who ran the Congressional Budget Office, would serve as Panetta's deputy. Robert Reich, an economics professor who had become close friends with Clinton during their time as Rhodes Scholars in Oxford, was named labor secretary, and Laura Tyson, an economics professor at the University of California, Berkeley, was appointed to head the Council of Economic Advisors, which would include Professor Alan Blinder of Princeton and Joseph Stiglitz, a Nobel Prize–winning economist. Clearly the new president had his priorities right. He gained additional credence with a two-day economic summit in Little Rock that brought together prominent businesspeople and economists.[4] A striking 70 percent of the public approved his handling of the transition.[5]

While the business and economic elites gathered in Little Rock, I gathered some ordinary voters in Atlanta and Fort Lee, New Jersey, so I could step back and listen to their thinking about the election and their understanding of Clinton's economic plans and commitments. It quickly became apparent that people gave Clinton a wide birth when it came to keeping any specific pledge. The bigger worry was that Clinton—so inexperienced, and a typical politician himself—wouldn't be strong enough to break the gridlock on the economy in Washington. After years of being ignored, the voters wanted re-sults. They knew Clinton had a plan and some knew about the promised eight million jobs, though not any of the specifics. They would support him as long as they were confident he had a long-term strategy and that everybody would share in the sacrifices. No one mentioned the "middle-class tax cut" and certainly no one expected it, George Stephanopoulos and I noted behind the glass in Fort Lee. For all my self-confidence, this was the first time I had elected a president and I was figuring it out as I went along, too. These very wise citizens were telling us don't be literal about the promises. Act for the whole country. In Atlanta, one of the skeptical Perot voters said, "I hope he will reach down, pull up his bootstraps, and bring us all up with him," but then added: "It's like Ross said on election night—we're all in this together and we've got to work with our leaders."[6]

The first meeting of the economic team had the formality of a cabinet meet-ing. The team members, as well as Al Gore, Hillary, and George, gathered around the dining room table of the governor's mansion on January 7, 1993, just two weeks before the inauguration and six weeks before Clinton would present his budget and economic plan to the country. It started with a de-pressing litany of economic problems. The deficit was climbing toward $360 billion and would probably rise to more than $500 billion by the end of the century. Unemployment was nearly 8 percent and only modest growth could be expected in the next year. A deficit reduction program that hobbled gov-ernment spending might even be enough to push the country into recession before the 1994 election. Any gains that the new administration would make would be longer term: less federal borrowing that freed up savings, and raised productivity and living standards. The entire team acknowledged that our audience was the Federal Reserve and bond traders, a realization that prompted a half-angry whispered exclamation from Clinton: "You mean the success of the program and my reelection hinges on the Federal Reserve and a bunch of fucking bond traders?"[7] Just an hour into the meeting Clinton was convinced: deficit reduction, he said, was a "threshold issue." Only George and Gene Sperling realized at that point how much the economic priorities had changed since the beginning of the campaign.

   The meeting went on for six hours as Clinton wrestled with the idea of setting an official target for deficit reduction, something Rubin pressed him to do. He took some solace from the optimists, including Larry Summers and Lloyd Bentsen, who argued that the bond traders were demanding a very high "inflation premium" in the form of high long-term interest rates, a pre-mium that could fall sharply and quickly if Wall Street was convinced that Clinton was serious. They also believed that Greenspan might cooperate with lower short-term rates to try to keep growth alive amid the reduced government spending that deficit reduction would require. In any case, Gore argued the country would rally to a president who acted boldly, a course affirmed by Clinton when he aligned himself with the deficit hawks at the meeting's close.[8]

A week later Gene Sperling laid out the bad news for the political and campaign staff: to meet Clinton's goal of reducing the deficit by half while the deficit was rising we would have to cut $240 billion out of our spending plans, including reducing investments from $50 billion to $20 billion or perhaps even $16 billion a year. New investments were only possible with ugly new cuts or taxes. What stood out to me were the delayed cost-of-living increases for seniors and various gas and energy taxes, almost all of which would fall heavily on the middle class.

The room was dumbstruck and quickly overwhelmed Gene with hostile questions.

"When did the deficit become the main goal?" asked David Wilhelm, who had recently become chair of the DNC.

"Where is the economic growth?" demanded Al From.

The discussion continued among the weakened political advisors over a late dinner at Doe's. I was badly in need of red meat and I became increasingly angry. "Why did we run?" I asked, pounding the table. "The presidency has been hijacked." At that point I viewed Clinton as the victim.[9]

The economic team met the next day at the mansion and accepted the inevitable death of the middle-class tax cut. And perhaps more consequential, Clinton, in a pre-inaugural interview, committed to cutting the deficit to $145 billion.[10] That was exactly half the deficit at the time his plan was released. Now, with deficit much higher, his commitment would require Clinton to submit a very austere budget indeed.[11]

How austere? According to Greenspan he told Bentsen and Panetta in mid-January that Clinton had two basic choices: "a package of spending programs that would fulfill some of his campaign promises, or he could opt for a deficit-cutting plan. There was no in-between."[12] I don't know whether they shared that conclusion with Clinton, though he would instinctively resist the idea that he couldn't bring his talents to bear to keep some of his investments.

About the same time Paul Begala and I attended a weekend retreat of Dick Gephardt's House Message Board, where we were asked to present on the "message objectives" of the Clinton administration. I began ironically. "I confess, I'm here this morning with no ideas," I told the group of House leaders, though I wasn't at all certain this was ironic. While I had not noticed Clinton's pre-inaugural interview, I was well aware that deficits were supplanting investments in the administration's priorities. I wondered if the political project that got us here was being supplanted, too. I did present our post-election poll findings and reminded them that Clinton had centered his campaign on "rediscovering the middle class" and that he is a new kind of Democrat, focused on such issues as welfare reform, budget discipline, and revolutionizing government. That Clinton had dropped references to the middle class and embraced old congressional leaders more than reform provoked me to reassert the goals. When I got to the economic plan, the highest priority for the country, I emphasized that Clinton was committed "to *both* investment and deficit reduction." Clinton had already moved to a different place, but I presumed the conclusion could still be contested or that he could be rescued from his captors, so I asserted: "On this, he will not yield because it is central to his whole identity. Investment-led growth is a precondition for deficit reduction."[13]

The inaugural festivities were just beginning on the eve of Clinton's presidency as I drafted a letter to the new president. "I write to you as you travel from Monticello, the last leg of an extraordinary journey that has changed all our lives and that, hopefully, is about to change America." I noted how exhilarated we all were to have a chance to make a difference, but I also told him that there was "a sense of foreboding" among his political advisors: "There is a broad feeling among the advisors that 'we have lost our focus' and 'strayed from the economic mission and core values' that should infuse this Presidency." While almost everyone else in America believed the transition was going well, I said, "we think you share our view of the chaotic reality in the most unvarnished way: Your own advisors are uncertain about our direction and commitments—particularly to economic growth, middle class values and re-inventing government."

Not fully grasping that Clinton had decided that big deficit reductions were the key to everything else, I wrote, "You would think from watching the news that cutting the budget deficit in half was our only goal." I reminded him that the public remained focused on growth, job creation, and rising incomes, a plan that would begin with investment. Once again the president that everyone thought was so poll-driven had never polled on his new central premise, that deficit reduction was the heart of a successful economic policy. With our thinking shaped by the intense year-long campaign, I warned Clinton that "our fate is in the hands of middle class voters," not the elites who were seeking deficit reduction and entitlement cuts that would hurt the middle class.

Writing on behalf of his other advisors, I urged him to bring a message that is "optimistic, uplifting and future-oriented, distant from the grim deficit discussion in Little Rock. People need to know that the specifics are part of a strategy and that all share in the sacrifice." If he was going to ask for tax increases, I said, then he had to show that things had changed in Washington, just as we had premised in our campaign's message: reform government first so that it can more active for people. "There must be immediate evidence of budget discipline, spending reductions and management changes, visible abolishing of perks, and introduction of political reforms," all things that had gone by the wayside as the president-elect rushed to embrace Washington. What had happened, I wondered, to the signature policies of the campaign: "What about two-year welfare—the closest thing to a read my lips?"

I also objected on behalf of the advisors to his plans to issue a flurry of executive orders on abortion in his first week in office. "The first week has all the makings of a group-driven agenda," I said, fearful that we were in danger of tipping back to the liberalism that drove away mainstream America. "We are opposed to moving on abortion, gays in the military and other subjects in the first days and weeks," I said. Rather, "our first week must be focused on the economy, 'like a laser.'"

I closed the memo with a personal aside, noting that I had finished writing at 6:45 A.M. after attending the "Re-Union" on the Mall and the festivities at the Lincoln Memorial. A formation of military jets had flown over and as they climbed into the sky I told him I had turned to Rosa and said, "Those are our planes now," half mocking. But I added that it underscored "the awesome power that has been handed us." That emboldened me, and I added that "you should know I am haunted by the 'Re-Union' theme that makes diversity and unity our mission." Earlier, I had voiced my objections to Rahm, who headed up the inaugural's organizing committee and who looked at me like I wanted to challenge some higher power. And now after the nation's most accomplished saxophonists took over the Lincoln Memorial stage and rocked the place, I took my objections to the top, knowing this was untimely and unwelcome. The "combination of the artistry" and the "array of communities ringing bells celebrated our diversity" but missed much of America. "Diversity is a powerful and ennobling concept, but only if it is genuinely broad and inclusive and only if it lifts us up as a nation for some purpose," such as the ones that animated in our run for the presidency, like restoring the covenant between people and government. I had not yet acknowledged that for Clinton and the first couple, unity—erasing America's racial divide—was their primary reason for being here.

POLLSTER TO THE PRESIDENT

The Saturday after the inauguration Mack McLarty, Clinton's new chief of staff, called a White House retreat on the budget at Blair House, home for visiting heads of state directly across Pennsylvania Avenue. This was the first meeting of the White House staff, political advisors, and some of the economic team to develop a shared strategy for the budget—the five-year program of new investments, spending cuts, and new taxes, the policies and priorities that would form the Clinton administration's plan for the economy. Congressional approval of a budget is a matter of life and death. Despite those stakes and Mack's hope that the Andrew Jackson–era setting would quiet things, the simmering dispute was very much in evidence. The political advisors assumed that key budget issues were still open for debate or that Clinton would reopen them as he had in the past. The economic advisors assumed that the key issues were settled, and they were much more right than we realized. What made the whole thing surreal was the fact that three quarters of the country said they agreed with Clinton's policies and goals.[14] But which set of competing goals, I wondered.

The economic advisors were likely puzzled by my report on survey results that began the meeting since the president had already embraced a tough deficit target. I reported that four times as many people identified the slow economy as the main problem than identified budget deficits, and if forced to choose, by a two-to-one margin they would stimulate the economy rather than reduce the deficit. While 80 percent thought it would be a "big accomplishment" to reduce the deficit, only a third would try to eliminate it or cut it in half—the goal the president had locked himself into without consulting any polls. It looked to me as if we were solving the wrong problem with the wrong solution, at least from the perspective of the people who had elected Clinton president.

None of that mattered, of course, since the decisions had been made. But it would matter because President Clinton's budget had to win majority support in the U.S. House and Senate and we were on weak ground. The president was elected with 43 percent of the vote and a Perot-like insurgency remained alive. We were proposing to raise taxes while the country believed it was in recession. A stimulus- and investment-led package would win over 70 percent support; one centered on deficit reduction would take us down to a whole new level, leading me to read the finding, word for word, to the group: "A serious deficit reduction program" achieved with "major spending cuts and new taxes" failed to win majority support in my survey; we lost a third of Democrats on our economic plan. While voters were open to a broad range of spending cuts and increased taxes, particularly on the wealthy, they balked at energy taxes or large gas tax hikes that fell heavily on the middle class. It would be hard to generate a wind at our backs unless the plan was "growth-led and motivated—and unless people think the burdens are shared broadly and fairly," I concluded, fearful these people were casually putting the president at risk.

On Wednesday the 27th, I met with President Clinton in the Oval Office for the first time, just the two of us, and I was very conscious of how precious these fifteen minutes alone with him were and the signal it sent in the White House world where power is completely derivative. I was supposed to be the seasoned advisor, but in truth, when Betty Currie, Clinton's Oval Office secretary, shut the door behind me, I felt my breath being sucked out of me. I struggled for words. Clinton's obvious comfort and graciousness, even though he took the oath of office only a week earlier, made it easier. He puttered around the office at first, delighting in telling me which furniture, paintings, and sculptures he had kept or brought in. He was particularly proud of his desk, used by President Kennedy and memorialized in a picture of little John John crawling underneath. He showed me the small private office as well, but then, as if an alarm went off saying, you'd better get serious, he urged me with a long, extended arm and open hand to sit on the sofa, right at the end close to his big armchair, so we were virtually knee-to-knee. The second armchair, reserved for the vice president, was empty.

I took a deep breath and opened my briefcase, trying not to look like a geek, my papers stacked precariously on my knees. The president was poised

Presenting poll findings to Clinton in the Oval Office during one of his 15-minute one-on-one meetings. [Author's collection]

to snatch them before I could present them properly. I wasn't sure whether he was more interested in my polling or the economic team's budget numbers.

"Mr. President, the purpose of these meetings is to keep you honest, in touch with what is going on in the country. I'm going to tell you where you stand, unvarnished." In my experience, I have never paid a price for frankness. "I have no agenda," I said, which wasn't entirely true. I felt an obligation to keep his mandate and the vision he articulated in the campaign alive, and I presumed that's why he agreed to a weekly fifteen-minute meeting. I confirmed that understanding by pointing out that we both wanted to make sure ordinary people were heard in the Oval Office over the din of other voices. "The bottom-line goal is to figure out how we can take the public with us."[15]

Before designing the White House polling program, I had a post-election breakfast with Richard Wirthlin, pollster to President Reagan. He told me he polled monthly on a national basis and on specific issues as needed, including in-depth projects on qualities of leadership in which he identified target audiences for the Reagan administration to reach. Most important were the fifteen minutes he had each week with the president, one-on-one, religiously protected, and his briefing of the chief of staff and senior staff. In a memo to Clinton I had proposed we try to build on the Wirthlin model, adding my brand of focus groups and outreach to historians and social scientists. I said that I wanted to play a role as part of a strategic group, not on my own, "to ensure discipline and continued attention to political goals."[16]

Speaking from a detailed outline in that first meeting. I began bravely with his high personal poll standing, the support for his overall program and direction, and support for the first lady taking on health care. There was no one else present to witness me suck up, but people out there were really rooting for him to succeed. Our polls did not yet reflect the troubled nomination of Zoë Baird to be attorney general before "Nannygate" scuttled her chances. Nor were they tarnished at this point by the controversy over gays in the military or the leaks from the economics team about possible energy taxes and cuts in Social Security cost-of-living increases, all of which served to drive away the middle class.[17]

Then I turned to the economy and the economic plan and handed him the bound book of graphs, so he could see the results and policy preferences more clearly. The president thumbed through the whole book in what seemed like a few seconds and his expression said "just test me." I later learned from Bob Rubin to never, ever give Bill Clinton a book of data or graphs. He will simply rush ahead, draw his own conclusions before you present yours, and you lose control of the meeting. Give him the report page by page and control the meeting. If only I had gotten investment advice from Bob.

"Above all," I said, thinking about those people in the Fort Lee focus groups, "voters are watching to see whether you move immediately and boldly to address the economy." I understood the importance of getting this right and with the time to study the data and write a clarifying memo, I underlined the key sentences to present to him. I told him that people were watching him closely and hopefully, pleased to have a president who cared about ordinary people, but they were "fearful that the rich and special interests will capture you" and they would be forgotten. The citizens of this country had "their fingers crossed." They had never really expected a middle-class tax cut, I said, but the opposite, a middle-class tax hike, could easily be seen as a "betrayal."[18] The challenge and perhaps the paradox, I said, was that there was no majority for a deficit-centered economic plan and just over a third for a tax increase if the purpose was simply to reduce the deficit. The country wanted more than what the green eyeshade people were offering. I looked up to see his reaction since I knew he was not about to settle for such a crimped vision for his presidency.

"I understand all that, but what do you think I should be doing?" Clinton replied, primed, as always, to act. He clearly was avoiding showing a reaction to my dire finding, leaving it unclear to me whether he was with the green eyeshade people focused only on the deficits.

To my growing frustration, Clinton had not asked for advice in these last three months as my thinking had evolved along with that of the voters. They weren't ticking off a checklist of pledges from "Putting People First." They wanted to put their trust in a leader who would keep them in mind, focus on the economy "like a laser," and act boldly in the country's interests. So I surprised myself and maybe Clinton, too. "I'm with Bentsen," though taking the treasury secretary's thinking far beyond the deficit. "Go long," I said. "The country will support a bold program—a major stimulus, serious investment, serious deficit reduction, broad tax increase." I knew as I offered that course of action, James was with me but not Paul.

To make such a bold course feasible, I proposed that Clinton take other actions, numbering my recommendations for emphasis. "First, you need to lead with reform, cleaning house, starting at home in the executive branch, major reforms showing immediately that you can be trusted with the money. Second, voters must hear that you are big and bold when taxing the wealthy. They must hear that all are contributing." Finally, I told him he needed to "take some action on middle class tax relief components, maybe phasing in the child tax credit or triggered by reaching some GNP growth targets."

I was way out of my league on the policy, but at least I offered him a way forward that would enable him to preserve his political project, combining the reform with government activism that won him middle-class support in elections over two decades and in the 1992 upheaval. It would take his economic focus beyond the literalism of the campaign plan and show that he had the space to be bold. I had not planned to use my precious fifteen minutes to elaborate my own plan of action, as I had hoped the core strategy group would have done that. But there was no strategy group.

I was invited together with Paul and Mandy Grunwald to open a weekend retreat at Camp David, the storied presidential enclave in Maryland's Catoctin Mountains. Since I was only staying Saturday, I was driven up, avoiding the buses that transported the cabinet and White House staff for two days of bonding. When I was a kid, my father drove us on this same route, jammed in our Studebaker for the two-hour drive every summer weekend to picnic, swim in the public pool, go on the giant slide, and reach for the brass rings from the carousel, little aware of President Eisenhower's new nearby retreat.

Just before I was to speak to this one-time gathering of the new government in the big family room of Laurel Lodge, Clinton grabbed my arm and said, "We've lost track of why we ran." Few of the people at the retreat had worked in or advised the campaign and my goal in any case was to build a common understanding of the mission.

To get their attention and to get back to the mission, I paid tribute in my introduction to former New Jersey governor Jim Florio, who passed a brave budget but lost the legislature and the mansion after his unexplained tax hike produced a voter revolt. Are you thinking about the president's interests? I wanted to ask, hoping the president was paying attention, too. Then I told the group that the people who elected Bill Clinton "want change; they want it to be big and bold; break the gridlock; get movement on the economy starting with stimulus; and don't forget the ordinary people and [don't] give in to the special interests."[19]

After we spoke, the president pulled Paul, Mandy, and I into a side room to say that he wanted us to get involved on a daily basis to give the White House strategic direction. That felt like an immense hug after weeks of what I perceived as unexplained estrangement. Then Hillary asked the three of us to write a communications plan that would introduce the economic plan and to fax it that night to Camp David. That meant I had to rush back to Washington, skipping the visit to the Camp David store to load up on the mugs and T-shirts I had promised my wife.

THE ECONOMIC PLAN

Over the next two and a half weeks the president presided over a series of almost daily meetings, some lasting all day and described by all the participants except the president as excruciating, to get the economic plan ready for the State of the Union speech.[20] To meet the deficit goal, they had to find spending cuts, but the president agonized over every one and Howard Paster, the congressional liaison, reminded us that each program or pet project eliminated might cost a vote in Congress. Whenever the group flagged in its resolve, Bob Rubin and Lloyd Bentsen assured them that Alan Greenspan likely would respond to $140 billion in deficit reduction next year and $500 billion over five with lower short-term interest rates to reduce the risk of an economic slump. When Paul asked Clinton why he was listening to the elite economists obsessed with the deficit, the president defended them. "We can't do anything for people unless we reduce the deficit." Bob Reich got nowhere in trying to scale back the deficit goals to allow more investment. While the president never wavered on the $27 billion in tax credits for the working poor, the funds for welfare reform—training, day care, and health care—were zeroed out, pushing it far down on the administration agenda and the public's consciousness.[21]

I wasn't in those meetings because I had staked out a different role. However brave the plan being shaped in the meetings, the president in remarkably short order had lost the confidence of the country and political class, and my task was to figure out a strategy to take them with us on February 17 in the State of the Union Address—or the plan would be lost. To concentrate their minds, I sent a memo to the president, vice president, and first lady, using the understated subtitle, "New Kind-of-Democrat?" I could see the president reading it. When asked "what have you heard recently about Bill Clinton," almost 60 percent volunteered "gays in the military," followed by taxes on the middle class. That produced a stunning 12-point drop in those who believed "Clinton can be trusted to defend America," exceeded by the 17-point jump in those who said Clinton is "too ready to raise taxes." Plotted in graphic terms, Clinton's image moved into a tight cluster with "liberals," "Congressional Democrats," and "Ted Kennedy," a place we did not want to go. The greatest disillusionment came with Perot voters, who were neither pro-gay nor pro-taxes. Among them Clinton crashed over 20 points on "fights for the middle class."[22] That was an unimaginable result for a president just weeks into his term with a bold agenda. James Carville warned about the "risk of a failed presidency" and the need to reorganize a White House in which nobody seemed to be in charge.[23]

Once the main points of the economic plan had been hammered out I fielded a full survey, mainly as a simulation of the public battle ahead and a search for the best arguments to fight it, which I presented to Clinton a week before the speech. Respondents were read a long description of Clinton's economic program. The good news was that 64 percent favored the plan; the bad news was that a bare plurality thought it would help their family. The good news was that the best reason people found to support it were the investments. The bad news was that those investments were being slashed out of the plan. Only 10 percent mentioned the reduced deficits as something good about the plan.

After we attacked the plan as the Republicans would, support dropped sharply and a majority no longer backed it. After this simulated debate, "strong opponents" to the plan outnumbered "strong proponents" by two to one and more people than not wanted their member of Congress to vote against it. We only began to reclaim lost ground in the survey when we focused on cutbacks in government perks (ahhh, reinventing government first!), more on the investment in people, and when we underscored that everybody contributes.[24]

My response to these findings was to press for more reform and more investment—both in the actual budget and our message—but I was uncertain whether Clinton was still committed to them, which troubled me. But with deficit reduction now the centerpiece in reality and investments almost meager, should I have stepped back and explored a wholly different tack to the economic plan? After all, this was a progressive budget—hiking taxes for the rich and giving tax credits to the working poor—and in reducing deficits, we showed that the president could be trusted with the purse strings and would likely increase the prospects for economic growth. But to settle for just budget austerity was antithetical to everything we had done to elect the president and to what Clinton himself was trying to achieve. I believed the country still wanted that and I fought even harder for that vision.

Many of the people working in the White House, including some speechwriters and virtually all of the economics team, had never lived through the process of drafting a major speech with Bill Clinton. Those of us from the campaign knew the drill: early drafts discarded, multiple drafts, multiple points of entry, competing and unresolved views in the room, issues closed and reopened, all-night sessions entering edits and merging drafts, long handwritten pages from Clinton, practice sessions just hours before the event, and further edits just minutes before delivery. It was a process that, however chaotic, produced speeches that set Clinton apart from the rest of the political world.

The process had begun weeks before the scheduled speech, but I knew most of that was mere foreplay. As part of the process, we organized research to see how people reacted to a video of him personally making his best economic arguments in a town meeting, their reactions registered on a dial meter that allowed us to watch their averaged responses shoot up, down, or hold at a high level. On the Saturday morning four days before the speech, I met with the president in the Oval Office, along with David Dreyer, now part of the White House communications team, and speechwriter David Kuznet, a skilled wordsmith out of the union movement, who were drafting the address. I told the president that the results of the town meeting research were "extraordinarily positive," confirming for Clinton that he could bring the country with him if given the chance. When people see you on that screen, I said, "they transcend their own cynicism and just believe you try for people." I underscored the opportunity by reading out loud a few postcards that people addressed to the president and wrote after watching him: "I am counting on you to assist me in making my dreams come true," and one that I marked with a double star: "Do something that will make the people say, 'Wow.' Something that we can believe."[25]

Two nights before the State of the Union speech, we decided that the president should give a short Oval Office address to get out all the bad news on taxes, including the abandonment of the middle-class tax cut. We hoped that would free the press two nights later to report on "our bold economic plan." The TV speech began by recalling the previous twelve years when "the middle class was less important than keeping taxes low on the wealthy" and when deficits "roared out of control." You need to know, the president told millions of viewers, "I've worked harder than I've ever worked in my life" not to ask more from those "who gave the most in the 1980s," though not successfully. But with those with the most paying the most, "for the first time in more than a decade, we're all in this together."[26]

The speech was not a great success, though it clearly achieved its main objective. Headlines the next morning read, "Clinton Plans Broad Tax." The president did not seem comfortable speaking into a camera from behind the desk with an audience of just the technical people and a few anxious aides. Many in and outside the economics team viewed it as divisive and too partisan; Mack told the president that it was judgmental and antibusiness. "I don't think that's what you believe," he said. The next day's 83-point drop in the stock market did not help, strengthening the case for those who wanted to tone down the rhetoric about the wealthy and business.[27] I remember thinking to myself, how do these so-called analysts decide whether it was the rhetoric about the wealthy or the higher taxes they would pay that produced the drop?

But no one had time to dwell on that speech as we plunged into the final frenzy of drafting a State of the Union speech that would provide the "Wow." Everyone pounced on each draft off the press and contributed to the chaos, even as David Dreyer and Bob Boorstin tried to enter the changes. Gene

Sperling represented the economic team, although Gore weighed in from time to time and Rubin wrote a crisp description of the plan that Clinton agreed would be incorporated in its entirety. My own edits were wide-ranging, but I repeatedly attempted to write in "jobs" as the goal of the plan and to insert the phrase "we're all in this together" to keep a focus on the new social cohesion after years of individualism and greed.[28]

The day of the speech, the Roosevelt Room was reserved for those working on the speech. The president was usually not there, instead rewriting sections on his own. By late morning we got the word that he was unhappy with the draft. It sounded like a list of programs and big spending. That prompted Hillary to take us through the speech page by page, slashing parts and designating people, including me, to write new segments. Rubin was upset about the "class-laden" language and raised the issue with Hillary, who escorted him to the Roosevelt Room so Rubin could oversee Paul Begala editing the parts he didn't like. In mid-afternoon about a dozen of us regrouped in the small White House theater in the basement for a practice session with Clinton reading from a TelePrompTer. He was very workmanlike, trying sections, sometimes rewriting, raising policy issues, sometimes speaking extemporaneously, while the speechwriters struggled desperately to capture the new material on their laptops. What does the army detail in charge of White House communications make of this? I asked myself. Its mission is to have the loaded disk at the U.S. Capitol by 9 P.M. and failure is not an option. But with each run-through, Clinton removed more and more of the spending cuts. At the end we huddled with Clinton and he agreed to restore the cuts to rural electrification and told us to find more. He left the theater just twenty minutes before he was to be at the other end of the Mall. George Stephanopoulos, Mandy Grunwald, and I rushed to the Roosevelt Room and struggled to get in the last edits and find more spending cuts before George dashed off with the disk.

I went to an office in the Old Executive Office Building that had been turned into a kind of war room for watching the president on a big TV, with an open phone line to Dayton, Ohio, where a group of voters would respond to this address, second by second. We also had an open line to George, who would watch the speech on a small TV in a cloakroom just off the House floor, listening for signs of how the speech was being received. We all knew that a State of the Union is normally watched by over half of the American people.[29]

As Bill Clinton stood at the podium to present what may have been the most important speech of his career up to that point, few television commentators missed the fact that Alan Greenspan was sitting next to Hillary, an implicit endorsement of what the president would present to the nation. Clinton noted in his speech that ordinarily a State of the Union address would tackle a full range of issues and challenges. But, he said, "these are not ordinary times." Instead, he said, it was a time to focus, unite, and act on one thing: the economy. "Together, we must make our economy thrive once again."

He began by recalling President Reagan standing in the same place twelve years earlier, asking the audience to visualize the deficit, a stack of thousand-dollar bills towering sixty-seven miles into sky. Today, Clinton said, that stack would reach two hundred miles further. It was the most important problem facing the country and solving it would change the economy for the better. In choosing that image and metaphor, Clinton—but not his political advisors—made a huge personal transition, no longer talking about the twelve years of a Reagan era that made keeping taxes lower for the wealthy more important than fairness to the middle class. Instead, he sought to avoid assigning blame. "There is plenty of blame to go around in both branches of the Government and both parties," he said.

"Tonight I present you a comprehensive plan to set our Nation on that new course," he said, beginning with a $30 billion economic stimulus that he urged Congress to pass quickly to create jobs and guarantee a strong recovery. "And there's no recovery worth its salt that doesn't put the American people back to work," he added, pausing for the applause. There's my line, I beamed, surviving all those drafts and edits. Then he made the central case for shifting from consumption to investment by "investing in our people, their jobs, and their incomes over the long term," although the amount of the budget devoted to this purpose had been drastically cut back. He described the plan, word for word, as crafted by Rubin: "It is an investment program designed to increase public and private investment in areas critical to our economic future. And it has a deficit reduction program that will increase the savings available for the private sector to invest, will lower interest rates, will decrease the percentage of the Federal budget claimed by interest payments, and decrease the risk of financial market disruptions that could adversely affect our economy."

Even more than me, Rubin must have felt the exhilaration of the president actually using his words. The difference, Rubin later told me, was that his words got "zero applause" in the chamber.

"By expanding the refundable earned-income tax credits, we will make history," Clinton told the audience. That was his passion and revealed his values: "We will reward the work of millions of working poor Americans by realizing the principle that if you work 40 hours a week and you've got a child in the house, you will no longer be in poverty." That was historic because the budget actually funded that goal after surviving all the pressures to cut it back.

He also promised to "offer a plan to end welfare as we know it later this year," not mentioning that the budget did not fund that goal.

"To revolutionize government, we have to ensure that we live within our means," he said, listing the 25 percent cut in White House staff and the cut of 100,000 federal bureaucrats. But then he challenged the chamber with one of his last edits: "I recommend that we make 150 specific cuts, as you know, and that all those who say we could cut more be as specific as I have been." He also began ad-libbing at that point, leaving me struggling to relate the scores I was getting over the phone from Dayton with the words in the "final" text. I took solace that the House minority leader, Bob Michel, who would be delivering the televised post-speech response, also was frantically flipping pages to find the text.

Then Clinton got to the core of the economic plan: reducing the deficit. Only by achieving that goal, he said, would the nation have the money "to invest in jobs and education and the future of this country." People would also benefit through reduced costs of borrowing for businesses and for families with mortgages and college loans.

He said simply that the nation pay for the plan "fairly" by "asking the most of those who benefited the most in the past, and by asking more Americans to contribute today so that all of us can prosper tomorrow." Again, he avoided mentioning that those uneven benefits had been established by design by his predecessors. And "to middle class Americans who have paid a great deal for the last twelve years and from whom I ask a contribution tonight, I say again as I did on Monday night: You're not going it alone anymore." Except for one other technical reference, that was the only mention of the middle class in the speech. The phrase "We're all in this together" was used not to talk about obligations on taxes but on the need for both parties to address the deficit, the new mission.

"There is so much good, so much possibility, so much excitement in our nation," he concluded. "If we act boldly, as leaders should, our legacy will be one of progress and prosperity."

Everyone in the chamber rose to their feet, applauding what they knew was indeed a new beginning.[30]

We were as high as a kite. You need not have been in the House chamber to know that here was a larger-than-life figure speaking of enormous changes and dominating, at least for that night, the national political class assembled for the nation to watch. The speech worked as a speech and the plan came together as a plan, even if it was not exactly the plan on which we had run. And our immediate post-election survey of just the fifty people in Dayton showed breathtaking shifts in opinion about both Clinton and the plan. The

Presenting the results of my research after the president's Joint Session Address to the Congress on February 17 in the solarium atop the White House residence. From left to right around the table: Clinton's mother, Virginia Kelley; the President; me; Jonathan Prince; Paul Begala; and Dee Dee Myers. Bruce Lindsey has his back to the president and the young man on the sofa is David Leavy, Dee Dee's deputy. [The White House]

CNN polls released that night showed 79 percent support, higher than even my simulation. It was a remarkable result considering that the president had just proposed a broad tax increase.

We were asked to join the president and the family in the Solarium atop the residence to celebrate the night. The Solarium is every president's favorite room because it feels like a real den with built-in comfortable areas for lounging. You come up into the hexagonal room using a ramp, as if President Calvin Coolidge knew the requirements of the Americans with Disabilities Act, and take in the big picture windows on three sides, facing south for the sun and the view of the monuments. That is why the Nixons called it the "California Room." I sat next to the president at the glass table to share topline results from Dayton and the networks, as bowled over as the voters. We all laughed about the young army guys tested as never before and I shared my story of making out as a young college student in this room. That got his attention. Two days after the speech, Alan Greenspan, testifying before the Senate Banking Committee, described the plan as "serious" and "plausible," a very big embrace by a man who chose his words carefully and who embodied the conservative economic establishment.

While different cabinet members fanned out to different parts of the country, Bob Rubin got the thankless job of going to the floor of the New York Stock Exchange and having dinner with a small group of CEOs. It was an ugly encounter. Stock prices had not followed the optimistic lead of long-term interest rates. Rubin reported back the next day: "Mr. President, you're seen as antibusiness. You're seen as punishing the rich." The wealthy believed they were being blamed for the greed of the past twelve years. They were particularly angered by the line "We're all in this together." Rubin was reinforcing a point he had been making for some time: "the class-laden language," the use of the word "rich," implies there is "something wrong with being successful financially." More importantly, this "polarizing rhetoric" could "undermine business confidence in President Clinton and his policies" and without that, he said, we will not get the private investments necessary for a strong economy. Then, venturing outside his expertise with apology, Rubin said he did not think the politics worked well, either. "Middle-class people don't respond well to disparagement of economic success," he said.[31]

It was very difficult to win these arguments with Rubin. He spoke softly and reasonably and listened to the political advisors. Clearly he was a person of good values, tolerant, concerned with the poor, and championing policies, like the earned income tax credit, which we expanded despite the deficit. He also embraced a progressive budget with a big increase in the top tax rate and corporate income tax, even accepting a "millionaire's surtax" and barring corporations from deducting high CEO pay. He just did not want the president to talk about taxing the rich, which I believed put the president at grave risk. If we did not define the plan, then our opponents would, starting with the tax increase. If we did not talk about "why," then we would lose the chance to make an argument that associated Clinton with middle America, as President Reagan did with great force. At stake were the Perot voters, intensely antielitist, who were judging our work. I wanted to shake Bob because this kind of "liberalism," so rare in the business community, is exactly the politics that had lost so many Democrats in the middle and blocked Democrats from creating a real majority.

And Clinton is too big to shake.

DOSE OF REALITY

We all gathered with the economic team on the Saturday morning after the State of the Union to rework the national communication effort and presidential schedule and review the congressional strategy. Howard Paster began with his assessment of the probability of passing the plan: 85 percent in the House and 50–50 in the Senate. 50–50? That was when grim reality intruded on my naive belief that a Democratic Congress would, in the end, have to support its president on his signature policy, when defeat would mean the virtual death of his presidency and put the Democrats back in the wilderness for another couple of decades. But the Clinton budget would have to get through the Senate Finance Committee. With eleven Democrats and ten Republicans, any maverick Democrat on the committee could defeat the plan and it was a committee of conservative mavericks, chaired by Pat Moynihan. Those mavericks had a lot of support in both chambers from many of the freshmen members elected with a lot of Perot voters and those members were focused on cutting the deficit with much deeper spending cuts and fewer tax increases.

The political advisors, joined by Al From, wanted the president to go to the country to rally support for the plan and put pressure on Congress, raising the prospects that individual members would support us. Paster believed in cultivating the key powers in the Congress, the caucuses, and swing voters and believed, probably accurately, that the political advisors were dangerous. We would be goring the ox of the Democratic establishment we depended on for votes. He won every argument. That was why the political reform agenda in the State of the Union was so modest.[32]

That afternoon I met with the president in the Oval Office to report on reactions to the State of the Union, a moment in which to revel and pander. The results were breathtaking. The gains were personal, taking his personal rating beyond what we had measured to that point. His job approval jumped 10 points and on handling the deficits and the economy, it was up even more. Most important for the task ahead, two thirds favored his economic program. When we asked the open-ended question why people like the plan, one in five said because it was "balanced," "everybody contributes"; another 15 percent because of the long-term investments, and a like number because of the economic stimulus. That changed the political calculus: before the speech, more voters said they would be less likely to vote for a member of Congress who supported the plan, but afterward, many more said more likely, a swing of more than 15 points.[33]

The Perot voters—always the reference point—were discriminating in their response. Clinton's personal favorability did not improve even a point, but his job performance jumped over 15. Two thirds supported his economic program.

"Mr. President, you touched people," I told him. After watching the State of the Union, people in Dayton were asked to "tell him anything you want" on postcards. The cards, I said, contained many grateful messages: "Thank you," "Good luck," and "God Bless you." With the cards in piles on the couch next to me by type of response, I began handing them to him. He seemed to inhale them.

Mr. President,

I'm very impressed with your ideas. Not sure how long term it would be to start seeing results. I agree we need health care for all not just the wealthy. I'm willing to pay more to help our country. Overall, I'm very impressed.

Help the hard working lower & middle class people to break even and begin to see the daylight! Spread the wealth to the working people and not just among the already wealthy! Listen to the working people and stop "money" from running the government. Get the crooks out of government!

I hope that what was said in the President address is not a lot of hot air and tickling the American people's ears. Since you talk the talk, I hope you walk the walk.

I enjoyed the speech tonight. It was great to hear things most of us have felt for a long time. A great change is needed and you *are* the man to do it. Good luck and my prayers are with you in this troubled time.[34]

Watching Clinton studying the cards I was conscious of my role empowering people and delivering their mail to the Oval Office. Would their messages linger as long as Rubin's and Paster's?

White House counsel Bernard Nussbaum interrupting my weekly meeting with President Clinton at his desk in the Oval Office to let him know that one of the president's nominees had been confirmed. [Author's collection]

TOWARD "MELTDOWN II"

In the first formal step in the process, the House on March 18 passed a budget accepting the broad outlines of the program, setting overall levels of spending and revenue collection for the five-year program, followed by the Senate a week later. The real votes on the economic plan would not come for months when each body would pass its version of the detailed budget known as budget reconciliation and then again after a joint House-Senate conference worked out the differences to the final version, which is voted on by each chamber. The economic team was satisfied with those first steps. The projected deficit reduction over five years was actually higher than that proposed by the president, producing a lot of self-congratulation by Alice Rivlin, Lloyd Bentsen, and Leon Panetta. The charts prepared by OMB also showed the new estimate on investments—only $1 billion in year one and $6 billion in year two—the product of "spending caps" required by the previous budget deal three years ago, cutting out $100 billion of Clinton's investments, without the White House rising up in arms. The original "Putting People First" program proposed $50 billion a year of future-oriented investments, which was almost halved in the plan that went to the Congress. At this rate, the American people would see no investments for three years.

That reality prompted a crisis meeting with the president on April 7. Clearly Clinton had no hint of what had been lost in the Congress. Now he was angry, his red face glaring as he slammed his fist on the table, giving vent to his feeling of being let down by his team and losing purpose: "We have just gone too far. We're losing our soul." We all felt as if we had disappointed the president, but hardly anyone, including Reich, believed it was intentional. I was less charitable. They wouldn't have been so nonchalant if they suddenly discovered a $100 billion loss in deficit reduction, at that point the plan's first purpose.[35]

Whatever our suspicions and whatever solace we took in Clinton's anger about "losing our soul," you could not escape the reality of the investments being zeroed out. This was a time to regroup. How do we keep people with Clinton for this deficit reduction plan financed primarily by broad tax increases, and attacked every day by our own moderate supporters for offering too few spending cuts and too many taxes? Wasn't this the time for a new Manhattan Project that would clear away all the old thinking and figure out how to sell the deficit reduction as the source of all good? Clinton was angry and frustrated and asking, "What is the plan?" He, too, was reluctant to accept the diminished investments and wanted his political advisors to move first and acknowledge the new reality.

The economic stimulus to jump-start the economy and the most understandable and popular economic lever was cut in half after the president's speech to just $16 billion and near insignificance when it passed the House. Worse, it became a magnet for every congressman's pet project. The political advisors and Al From repeatedly lobbied the president to exclude them, but mysterious forces kept putting them back in. Robert Byrd, chair of the Senate Appropriations Committee and someone with more than a passing experience with pork, took ownership and promised to pass the stimulus package without changes on the floor so it could go right to the president for signature. But the venerable Byrd couldn't stop a filibuster started by two moderate Democrats who were later joined and led by a unified Republican opposition. Round-the-clock sessions over the next four weeks failed to break the filibuster and Clinton was forced to abandon the stimulus, defeated by Washington pork and gridlock.[36]

The spectacle in the Congress produced a near crash in judgments about our work, I told the president in the Oval Office on April 16, which would make it only harder to win. Rattling off the numbers was my shorthand method for expressing frustration, without having to use words. The number of people enthusiastic about the plan was only half of what it was a month earlier. Opposition was spreading and intensifying. One of the most vociferous opponents was Ross Perot, who denounced the plan and met with the freshmen Republicans to bolster the opposition.[37]

I used one of my late April meetings with the president to preview our study of Perot voters conducted for the Democratic Leadership Council and scheduled for presentation at the DLC's New Orleans conference at the end of the month. The most dramatic finding was a hypothetical presidential 1996 contest. While there was solace in Clinton winning with 40 percent of the vote, the president had not expanded his support or eroded Perot's bloc in the six months since the election. In fact, the Perot bloc had grown to a quarter. This bloc of younger, noncollege, and male voters was "self-consciously independent, critical, [have a] show me" attitude, was an "enduring force," and would not be easily moved, I said. [38] They were open to Bill Clinton, I later told the DLC, "but only if he changes government first," hardly evident in the spectacle in Washington. He must be "oppositional and challenging" to government and the big interests: "A re-inventing government agenda is virtually a pre-requisite for reassuring and reaching the Perot bloc."[39]

Clinton's job approval ratings at one hundred days were widely reported as the lowest at the same point for any twentieth-century president.[40] The assault on the budget and stimulus, as it turned out, was the least of the administration's problems.

The disastrous month prompted me to pen a memo to the president. I called it "Manhattan II," recalling an earlier memo that also reflected "the collective thinking of your political advisors." I said we needed to "pause, regroup, and [take] strong steps to move in a different direction," back toward the "agenda and values that drove the campaign." Our highest priority, the memo argued, was reassuring people that Bill Clinton really was a "new kind-of-Democrat." In a sentence carefully vetted by my colleagues, I wrote, "Bill Clinton was not sent to Washington to put gays in the military, open our borders to all HIV positive immigrants, create abortion on demand and cut the deficit by taxing the middle class." Certainly we needed successes on our economic measures in the Congress to restore confidence that we could break the gridlock, but our activist agenda must be "relentlessly balanced by attempts to reassure on our commitment to middle class values." That meant prioritizing in this order: welfare reform, reinventing government, family responsibility, crime and National Service, and a higher-profile set of activities as "commander-in-chief." We were seeking to revitalize the larger project and his presidency; yet again, the deficit was not mentioned as a point of departure.[41]

"I know what's wrong," the president responded with exasperation. "Give me a strategy. Give me a plan with, one, two and three."[42]

On May 5 the political advisors held a strategy meeting in the Roosevelt Room with the president and vice president to focus on rebuilding public trust and support, though undermined by a certain unreality. The context, the president made clear, was an out-of-control Congress: "These people, these bastards, are trying to take all our investments," he said, punctuating his remark with his fist. The meeting's agenda was driven by our collective memo on "the economic campaign," fashioned over weeks of daily meetings, requiring "a new discipline and focus over this entire month." The plan presumed a month devoted to the economy that would make it "a high cause" and that would send the president "aggressively campaigning for his economic program" outside Washington. The public debate was all about more spending cuts, but we needed to recapture the program of the State of the Union, a program that was balanced between investment and spending reductions, honest, fair in that it asked everyone to contribute, and that took America in a new direction toward jobs, growth, and a stronger America. Still, the plan took no account of the budget's lost investment focus and made no mention of deficit reduction.[43] But much more important than our strategy meeting was the meeting the next day when the eleven Democrats on the Senate Finance Committee met with the Clinton and Gore. They did not have the eleven votes to move the budget. Kent Conrad of North Dakota was clear about his opposition to the new tax on carbon emissions, called the BTU tax: "I won't cut the throats of my people." David Boren of Oklahoma was even more negative and would spend the next month attacking the plan and developing an alternative with the Republicans. Nevertheless, Pat Moynihan promised to get the votes for passage "because, Mr. President, your presidency is on the line. If you get this, you are a strong president. If this fails, you are a weak president."[44]

Despite our efforts to focus national attention on the economy we were thwarted by more sensational news: the troubled nomination of Lani Guinier—the "quota queen," according to *The Wall Street Journal*'s editorial page—to be assistant attorney general for civil rights; the president's so-called $200 haircut with Christophe at the L.A. airport, and the firing of the White House travel office staff in favor of a Little Rock travel agency.

Clinton was having trouble holding moderates in the House. Dave McCurdy of Oklahoma announced that he would vote no, making him the center of White House lobbying. With the bells ringing in the chamber signaling the start of voting on May 27, McCurdy and a handful of moderates were promised privately that the Senate would eliminate the BTU tax and cut the energy tax, accept entitlement cuts, and create a White House friendlier to the conservatives, which won over four of them. The ever-polite Dick Gephardt, who as House Majority Leader had just persuaded two hundred Democrats to walk the plank for the BTU tax, uttered some expletives, but with the vote count stuck on the board two short of the majority, he found the votes he needed. At 8:44 that night, we won the first life-or-death vote, 219 to 213.[45]

That we squeaked by in the House where our chance of passage according to Paster had been 85 percent cast a pall over our hopes for final passage, worsened by Clinton's meltdown in May. The Senate loomed forebodingly, perhaps signaling a further weakening of the president. In June, the LAX haircut was far and away the biggest top-of-mind news. That may have seemed trivial compared to what was happening in Bosnia, but the perception that Clinton was "out of touch" jumped 10 points, breaching his special relationship with the middle class and making him much more vulnerable to the attacks in the Congress. Two thirds of those surveyed said Clinton is "too ready to raise taxes." For the first time, I wrote in a memo to the president the day of the vote, Clinton's fall was personal, not based on performance. That, I said, made the outlook much more dangerous, raising the possibility of further declines. Overstating my case and wearing out my welcome, I wrote, "the Clinton Presidency is in grave danger four months after inauguration," as the public's mood turned bleaker. "Clinton voters are demoralized," and the rest of the country had "polarized against us," particularly the Perot bloc, I said. In response to a question we asked for the first time, a stunning 55 percent of the public agreed that the president is "over his head."

"The White House is gaining all the stature of a county court house," I wrote. "We look parochial, small, and overwhelmed."

Two days later the president announced the appointment of David Gergen as counselor to the president, leaving George with responsibility for communications. By going to someone with experience with Republican presidents, Clinton sent a big signal and put a new perspective at the table. The campaign cadre in the White House was demoralized but James and I knew that George was getting the job with the office next to the Oval Office, a move that greatly enhanced his policy and political role, something we had recommended a month earlier.

A NEW CHOICE

On virtually every question, Clinton's standing and policy support dropped further in early June. Just 44 percent supported our economic plan and we faced a 20-point drop in people thinking it was "fair to people like you" and "helps the national economy," the two most important props for a plan that promised higher taxes.[46]

But Clinton was in no mood to sink further into depression and when I met with him I offered a memo that teed-up the choices before the White House, each weighted toward the positions favored by the political advisors. Choice one, I said, was deficit reduction versus economic growth. In practice the administration had already opted for the first, but I hoped the political advisors' rationale could change that. Focusing on the deficit, I said, "plays to our weakness, empowers the deficit hawks and fails to give the middle class Americans a compelling enough rationale for supporting the plan." That must have left him frustrated, though he didn't say it. Is Stan so stuck that he doesn't understand the economic plan is now a deficit reduction plan? Doesn't he know this is a false choice? Deficit reduction is supposed to produce economic growth. The second choice, I said, was between "non-populist" and "populist." "In our view, the administration's silence on populist themes and the middle class was the single biggest error since the State of the Union, allowing most Americans to believe they will be stuck with 'the biggest tax increase in history.'"

The third choice I presented was between a "legislative focus" and a "real world focus." The focus on the legislative process had allowed the Democratic senators to define our message and plan and prevented the president from mobilizing support in the country.[47]

While preparing that memo, I also wrote a scrupulously balanced message survey to test each of the choices so that I would command some authority in the intense internal deliberations. I presented the deficit reduction option as a genuinely bold move with economic consequences—"lower interest rates" and "more job-creating investment"—and found, amazingly, that it tested as strong as our economic growth message with investments.[48] That had never been true before and that stopped me. After listening for months to leaders herald the virtues of deficit reduction and less spending, people began to shift their thinking. But I also asked myself, had we all accepted deficit reduction as the purpose and argued the economic virtues, would we have gotten here sooner?

I presented that result to the president first for his peace of mind and in the hope that it would provide common ground for unifying the various factions in the administration. Mandy accused me of becoming a "pod person" right out of *The Invasion of the Body Snatchers,* planted by deficit hawks to undermine good order. But my survey results forced me to think totally differently about the mission.

The day after the meeting with the president, I wrote another memo underscoring how critical the next two weeks would be as we defined our plan, a definition we would have to live with for the next three and a half years. I proposed a new and simplified core message about "putting our house in order" through courageous deficit reduction resulting in a strong economy, with no mention of investment. That would be for a later day. "Our future growth," I wrote, "depends on these bold steps to put our house in order." But I emphasized that it would have to be achieved fairly, a theme that had disappeared from our narrative over the past months, but was now embraced by the president. I proposed a simple formulation, consistent with the new method and not yet tested:

> Every $10 devoted to deficit reduction
> $5 comes from spending cuts
> $4 comes from taxes on the wealthy (over $100,000)
> $1 comes from everybody else[49]

Sometimes a message comes at the right time and works and within a day Gene Sperling had rewritten the "Reconciliation Message" for the economic team and communications staff.[50]

With the energy tax unceremoniously buried by Bentsen on a Sunday morning talk show, and key senators saying no gas tax greater than five cents, David Boren agreed to allow the plan out of the Finance Committee, producing a 49 to 49 vote on the floor, with the vice president breaking the tie. The economic plan then went to conference negotiations aimed at producing a single overall budget bill that would face a near simultaneous vote in both bodies before the summer recess. At the White House we, too, went into "conference mode" and emerged with a memo to the president emphasizing that we needed to firmly establish that "this plan is good for the economy and that it is fair."[51]

Before leaving for the G-7 meetings in Tokyo, Clinton called a special meeting in the Solarium in the middle of the July 4th weekend to settle all the outstanding issues before the conference committee began deliberations. The political advisors feared that people believed Clinton's economic plan was now seen as a tax plan. Earlier, I had supported the plan's broad tax increases and energy tax as essential to acting boldly. But now we knew that the small gas tax would raise only $15 billion over five years. For that small amount, we would surrender the ability to say the financially pressed middle class had been spared and we would make all the Democrats in Congress vulnerable to attack on taxes. Worse, if the White House took no clear position on the differing tax options being floated, the news for the next month would be dominated by taxes. Worse yet, people would assume that the White House was really for the bigger broad energy tax. As an alternative, I presented "the bold zero option."[52]

Gore argued for an energy tax but wanted the form left open so the administration wasn't seen as killing the BTU tax, the country's first tax on carbon, and Rubin believed that the credibility of the package required an energy tax of some kind to spread the sacrifice. Knowing how difficult the conference negotiations would be, Paster told us that he needed every chip, including an energy tax. "This isn't an election," he said with some vehemence. Finally breaking with the political advisors, James Carville came out for a nickel gas tax: "We have to be for something."

As the meeting ended Hillary said, "This isn't working," meaning both the organization of the White House and the narrative for telling the country what the economic plan was about. She wanted a war room to get people coordinated and moving, and her rising passion excited the president, whose wave of anger ended with a demand to meet every day and get it done—and don't wait for his return from Asia. A lot of chastened people made their way down the ramp.[53] George was particularly gloomy because he believed the vice president would continue to lobby for the carbon tax and Paster would keep all his chips—and the news would be taxes all the time. I was not gloomy because Rubin offered his private plane to drop me in New Haven in time to make July 4th. Maybe I've been unfair to all those who got rich in the 1980s?

In mid-July, Laura Tyson, Alan Blinder, and Joseph Stiglitz of the Council of Economic Advisors drafted a memo that got everyone's attention: the short-term economic outlook had deteriorated since January. Growth in the first quarter had been negative and they warned that the emerging economic policy might worsen rather than offset the problem: the stimulus package was dead and Congress was bent on front-loading the deficit reduction. The plan would produce a "fiscal contraction" for the critical year ahead and they proposed delaying taxes, particularly the gas tax, to prevent an economic slowdown.[54] This produced a full meeting of the economics team, but the economists were no more successful than the political advisors in moving Bentsen or the team off the $500 billion dollar goal, where symbolic values had transcended economic merits. They were accepting the short-term economic risks, which could easily have included Democrats losing control of the Congress.[55]

THE VOTE

On July 29, the House and Senate conference negotiators finally agreed on a 4.3 cents per gallon gas tax increase, the last outstanding issue for the economic plan. Nonetheless, Boren came out against the plan on *Face the Nation* the next Sunday morning. We would be going to the finish line with no votes to spare.

Just days before the two houses of Congress were to vote on the economic plan Clinton delivered a final Oval Office address to win public support. "For at least 20 years, middle-class incomes have been nearly stagnant," he said, the victims of "politics of abandonment—cutting taxes on the well-off and asking nothing of them in return either, while raising taxes on the middle class to pay for more of the same government, instead of investing in our jobs and our future." But the middle class is back, he said. "No more something for nothing. We're all in this together." In Dayton, Ohio, fifty people dialed their meters and Clinton's support among the Perot voters jumped almost 10 points.

Then the president imitated Perot, bringing out a chart to show how big those deficits would grow if his plan wasn't approved. One of the first benefits of his plan, he said, would be economic growth that would create eight million jobs. Further, the plan would be guided by fairness: "Those who have the most contribute the most," he said. Finally, he said he had worked to "ensure the lowest possible tax on the middle class," a 4.3 cents a gallon increase in the gas tax, "no more than $3 a month in new taxes." At that the Perot voters turned their dials down 20 points, more than wiping out all earlier gains. To prove the plan's fairness Clinton pulled up another chart titled "A Fair and Balanced Plan." Right over the pie chart was my offering: "Every $10 in deficit reduction comes from $5 in spending cuts, $4 in taxes from the wealthy and $1 in taxes from the middle class." In Dayton the Perot voters spun their dials 10 points in our favor, but not quite as quickly. After reading my chart to the country, Clinton simply said, "This plan is fair. It's balanced. And it will work."[56]

The goal of the speech was to shift the momentum before the congressional vote and we conducted a fast-and-dirty, eight-hundred-sample one-night survey to give us ammunition for dealing with the news media. For the first time, we leaked to the media a memo addressed to the chairman of the DNC with our poll findings: voters favored the economic plan by a considerable margin, 48 to 41 percent; by an even larger margin, they thought the plan was "fair" to people like themselves. The speech produced nearly a 10-point drop in the percentage thinking the middle class would bear the main burden.[57] We also conducted a fuller poll over the next two nights to give us a more reliable reading on the impact. The gains it showed were real, albeit modest, as support for the plan rose and worries about taxes dropped on the eve of the vote.[58] It left me with a deep sense of satisfaction that we could learn and regroup and bring people with us when we remembered the values that got us here and acted in the long-term interest of the country.

The economic program went to the House floor with the leadership sure of only 180 votes. We needed 218 to win. Strong lobbying against the plan from the Republicans, Perot, and the Christian right who wanted to see Clinton fail, hurt our cause. At 5:50 P.M. we heard from the floor that we did not yet have sufficient votes to win. That prompted a discussion in the Oval Office about whether we should pull the bill with all the uncertainties that would create. Then at 7 P.M. David Bonior called to say he believed we had the necessary votes. Balloting began at 9:55 P.M. and fifteen minutes later we were behind 211 to 212. The last votes trickled in. "No" from Ray Thornton of Arkansas, the president's congressman and "that prick," as my wife described him. "Yea" from Pat Williams of Montana and then another "yea" from Pennsylvania's Marjorie Margolies-Mezvinsky, one of the most vulnerable freshmen members. The final tally: 218 for, 216 against. The Democrats on the floor burst into cheers while the Republicans chanted, "Bye, bye, Marjorie." In the Oval Office it was all hugs, concluding with all of us crowded around the president's desk while he picked James Carville's pocket, the one most likely to pay the "millionaire's surtax."[59]

Even as we were sweating the House vote, Bob Kerrey had called the president the morning of the vote to tell him he would vote against the plan when it came before the Senate. Kerrey said the economic plan did not address entitlements or any of the long-term economic problems and the higher taxes threatened to put the economy in recession. Clinton and Kerrey had a complicated relationship formed by their very different responses to Vietnam and their competing baby-boomer claims to the presidency. Clinton ignored Kerrey's reasoning and simply responded: "If you want to bring this presidency down, then go ahead." Kerrey resented Clinton's attempt to shift the blame to him and suddenly they were yelling at one another. "Fuck you," said Clinton, perhaps a first for him and almost certainly the first time Kerrey had heard that from a sitting president.

President Clinton with my wife, Rosa DeLauro (on the left) and my parents, Yetta and Sam Greenberg and myself (on the right) in the Oval Office after the President's Saturday radio address. [Author's collection]

The celebration of the House vote was short-lived with the Senate vote looming. Kerrey agreed to come over the afternoon of the vote and spent some time alone with Clinton on the Truman Balcony. Later he called the president. "Mr. President, I'm going to vote for it. This vote's for free." Of course, nothing is free and Kerrey delivered a patronizing attack on the Senate floor, announcing, "I will vote for a bill which challenges America too little." Then the Senate called the roll of one hundred names and the tally emerged: a 50–50 tie. Gore cast his vote and the victory, however narrow, was ours.

George, James, and I joined Rosa for a very late dinner and private celebration at Bice that night. While we were eating, somebody in the restaurant sent over drinks. It took us a minute to realize they were from Senator Kerrey, who lived in the building and often sat at a front table. We acknowledged the gift with a modest tip of our wineglasses and paused for some uncomfortable small talk.

THE AGENDA

Someone in the White House got a pirated, photocopied version of Bob Woodward's new book, *The Agenda*, late on the night of Saturday, June 4, while most of us were in Chicago to celebrate Rahm Emanuel's marriage to

Amy Rule the next day. Instead of staying up all night partying, we spent much of the night reviewing the book and preparing to do damage control when Woodward appeared the next night on *60 Minutes*. George was with Clinton in Europe where Clinton would commemorate the D-Day landings in Normandy, but we knew that Clinton and the first lady would be steaming about Woodward's depiction of the sausage making in the White House and the less-than-flattering accounts of Clinton's temper and Hillary's strength. I checked first on my exposure. Did it read as if I was self-promoting at the president's expense? I did only one interview with Woodward on the Solarium meeting and took a follow-up call from him, but gave him no documents. Nevertheless, I appeared early in the book and many of my memos were included.

The next night Mike Wallace opened the segment on *60 Minutes* with Woodward at his computer while Wallace examined the boxes of audiotapes from Woodward's many interviews with White House staff and FOBs. "You paint a picture of disorder, disarray at the White House," Wallace said to Woodward. "You repeatedly use the word 'chaos.'"

"It's a word used by the people who were there," said Woodward.

"Chaos?" Wallace asks again.

"Chaos. Absolute chaos at many crucial times."[60]

Naturally chaos was the theme in the news media the next morning. Under the headline "Absolute Chaos" *Newsday* wrote, "The White House staff under President Bill Clinton was so often out of control during his first year in office—and the president unwilling or unable to impose direction—that those running the country frequently functioned in near-total disorder."[61]

I have since interviewed Woodward about his depiction of the administration. Looking back from the vantage point of 2007 and the Bush administration's decision to go to war in Iraq, Woodward expressed some regrets, although not about the use of the word "chaos." "It was chaos," Woodward told me. "You would agree it was chaos."

But then he added that chaos was only part of his account in the book and the other "is a fully, an incredibly engaged leader." In light of what we now know of George Bush, you can see "the sense of drive and commitment Clinton put into this, the hands on . . . forming the economic plan, which I think in retrospect looks quite commendable. So I should have been more of, 'hey, look, yes, there's this side and there's that side.' It's not emphasized enough."

Then he observed, "Turns out, I think, this plan was the crown jewel of the Clinton administration, wasn't it?" If the White House had admitted the chaos but explained the deliberative process that produced the new economic policy, Woodward said, everything would have looked different. "One of the things I found among political figures, leaders, consultants, pollsters, senators, presidents, and so forth, they don't know when they've won," he said. "And you won this."[62]

THE ELECTION OF 1994

In the fall of 1994 Clinton was on the campaign trail trying to help the party hang on to its increasingly tenuous majority in Congress.

"You sent me to Washington to reverse a dozen years of failed policies that brought higher taxes on the middle class, lower taxes on the wealthy, higher unemployment, reduced investment in our people and less ability to compete and win in the global economy," Clinton reminded voters in rally after rally. "Now, if I had told you then not only what I would try to do, but if I told you on Election Night . . . that we would have cut our deficit by over $250 billion; eliminated over 100 government programs outright; raised income taxes on the wealthiest 1.2 percent of our people; cut taxes for 15 million working families; made 90 percent of our small businesses eligible for a tax cut; produced 4.3 million new jobs . . . if I had told you that on November 8th, you would have thought that I slipped a gasket." The crowd laughed. "Wouldn't you?" The laughter turned to applause.[63]

One of my weekly fifteen-minute meetings with the president took place on Air Force One that fall. It was the first time I had flown on the big jet since this was the first campaign since Clinton's election. Air Force One is better than the White House anyday, and nobody I know is cool about it. You check the manifest—your name really is there—and then you head up the stairs hurried enough to look important. You do not look back to wave to the cameras. The fact that the "football" containing the nuclear war plans travels with you, along with a "situation room" in case the "leader of the free world" needs to deal with a crisis while in the air lends a macho air to everything. Nobody wears seat belts and everyone uses their cell phones when the plane is taking off. I no longer believe the flight attendants on commercial flights when they announce "FAA rules require you turn off your cell phones . . ." What I really want to do is say "On Air Force One . . ." but that would be just too obnoxious. Actually, I much prefer to pick up the heavy phone, get the operator, and ask the officer to place a call to Rosa and then my parents. I imagine the look on my father's face when he answers the phone and is told "Mr. Greenberg, you have a call from Air Force One."[64] My reverie was interrupted shortly after takeoff when an officer leaned over my seat and said, "Sir, the president would like to see you."[65]

I had to tell the president that the numbers were not good and that nothing seemed to budge the people's growing contempt for Congress and the Democrats. Clinton clearly was unhappy that people did not know of our accomplishments, that the media was much more interested in "Travelgate" and "Troopergate," "Whitewater," and Paula Jones, than the real hard work of government, that his own White House was failing to communicate effectively, that the political advisors offered him only problems, not solutions. I made some ironic comment about maybe we needed to present them a longer "litany" of accomplishments—his main response to not getting heard—but he was in no mood for irony. It only made him angrier. Clinton was very attuned to people and when two thirds of the country said things were "off track" and his approval rating had dropped to historic lows, he knew deep trouble loomed. He had lived that chapter before.

He was also frustrated by the difficulty of getting credit from the public for the boldness of his plan and the risks he took, such as the front-loaded deficit reduction program that he knew would almost certainly slow growth in the short term. That was a critical, brave choice, done knowingly although the president clearly believed he could educate the public about the necessity of it. While unemployment was down to near 6 percent over the year, GDP growth was uneven and running at only 2.3 percent in the three months before the election. There was virtually no income growth in all of 1994 and it was even negative in one quarter and stuck at just .3 percent in the quarter of the election.[66] So, the president, like virtually every leader who makes tough choices, wanted credit for the indicators when people were only willing to give him credit for improvements in their lives. In the year after the economic plan's passage, voters continued to see an economy in bad shape, little deficit reduction, and most obviously, higher taxes. Using the gas tax as a cudgel and millions of campaign dollars, Republicans battered Democrats for passing "the biggest tax increase in history," an impression allowed to deepen as the White House mostly went silent on questions of distribution until the 1994 campaign's last weeks. The president's lowest job approval ratings before the election came on "handling taxes" and the highest word association with "Democrats" was "taxes." [67]

From the outset in 1994, the whole White House was immersed in tracking all the economic indicators, at least as closely as Alan Greenspan and the Fed. Everyone knew the stakes. There were no illusions about the voters themselves. During the first half of the year two thirds described the economy in pessimistic terms. In June, when I asked people in groups to respond to just the word "economy," I got back a caution that ran deep: "frozen in time," "inching along," "fragile," "scary," "bad, bad." Thus, I began with a first principle: "The discussion of economic progress must always acknowledge that most people are not feeling the change and that progress is not good enough." I soon realized that Clinton, who never settled for less than an A for effort, just wouldn't say it.[68]

We spent a number of weeks trying to fashion an economic message and mission statement and wanted to focus on the economic "facts" and where Clinton wanted to take the country rather than getting into definitions about what constituted "progress." But Clinton's entire persona demanded that he convince, cajole, and educate voters about progress. When he did a prime-time news conference in August, our Dayton dialers responded positively when he declared, "the central mission of this administration, renewing the American Dream, requires us to restore economic growth." But when the president asserted that "we are making progress," the dials turned down 15 points in a matter of seconds.[69]

Late that summer I returned to the survey exercises that had helped us define the choice in 1992 and struggled into October to get a choice that could make some headway against the powerful negative currents confronting us. The exercise was easy on the Republican side: 'The Democrats support *big government and higher taxes*. The Republicans want *small government and lower taxes*." But with the unveiling of Newt Gingrich's *Contract with America*, we were able to create a powerful choice: "The Democrats want to *go forward* to address the problems of ordinary people. The Republicans want to *go back* to the Reagan policies of tax cuts for the wealthy paid for by cuts in Medicare." The phrase "not going back to 'Reagan'" was included for only half the respondents, as an experiment so that I could see its added impact. Those who heard the choice with the Reagan references gave the Democrats a significantly larger lead at the end of the survey.[70]

But there remained substantial forces pushing people to vote for change—the year-long battle and tragic failure to achieve health care reform, "gays in the military," various scandals, including Paula Jones's sexual harassment suit, and the disastrous initial defeat of the president's crime bill by the House Democrats to close the Congress. All year I had commented on the fact that the Democratic thermometer rating had slipped below the Republicans, something that had not happened in an off-year election since 1966. Attitudes toward the hated Congress and the Democratic Party were aligning as the country seemed to be brewing for a rebellion. When asked what comes to mind when you hear the word "Congress," the results were ugly: "farce"; "scandal a week"; "country club"; "an American politburo"; "overpaid"; "money grubbing"; "puppets"; "thieves"; "fat cats."[71]

Six months before the 1994 off-year elections I wrote a memo for the eyes of the president and first lady only: "The administration, the Democrats in Congress and the party face a disaster in November unless we move urgently to change the mood of the country," I said. "The drama of the Bill Clinton Presidency must be about ordinary people and what Bill Clinton is fighting for to make sure they have better lives." I presented this assessment to them alone in the residence to underscore how dire our situation was and to tee-up the recommendation of the political advisors that Leon Panetta assume the position of chief of staff. A month later, I followed with a more broadly circulated memo in which I punctuated my point by saying "it is not out of the question that we lose the Senate and at least 30 seats in the House."[72]

Doubtful that any of what I said would survive the bleak currents, I proposed a bold reordering of priorities to shake things up: pull back from the current health care bill and announce support in an Oval Office address for a moderate bipartisan leadership bill, which I described as "non-bureaucratic," with "responsible checks on spending," phased in with protections for small business and "universal (with trigger)"—and challenge the Senate Republican leader to support it. Then, I proposed really changing the game by demanding action on welfare reform before the end of Congress. That would be "the most dramatic step Congress could take," I wrote, and "the Clinton promise that matters most to voters and will capture the public's attention." I followed that with a memo to the House and Senate leadership and a proposed meeting with Speaker Tom Foley, but so many were already invested in the existing agenda and fearful that welfare reform would blow up the black caucus that my proposal died for lack of a second.[73]

Before the president's Middle East trip, the first lady, also doubtful, that our overall strategy could survive the currents, gave Dick Morris a call to get his view of the political situation, and he ended up conducting a survey in late October. The focus of the survey tested people's reactions to Clinton's accomplishments, essentially the same exercise we had been conducting in most months since the beginning of the year. But in Morris's version the president was allowed to embellish each accomplishment, if we are to believe Morris's account. After reading each accomplishment, Morris reported a plaintive Clinton refrain: "of course, nobody knows we did this" or "the newspapers never printed that we got this one done." Morris briefed them over the phone: yes, Clinton was in "deep, deep trouble." Voters did not believe that deficits were smaller, or that jobs and exports were rising. With the economy so central to their lives, "you'll never convince them otherwise. Never. It's a total waste of money to try,"[74] Morris said.

Morris returned to the 1994 campaign in the final days, much as he did in 1980 in Arkansas after a period of exile. I knew nothing about his poll, of course, but I was aware of Clinton's discomfort with our closing choice, going forward for ordinary people versus going back to Reagan policies. I queried James, who also couldn't figure out why we couldn't get the president to seize the moment. It turned out that Morris, a Republican consultant, was telling him the *Contract with America* was popular and "class warfare" unproductive, mostly confirming Clinton's own instincts. It was the beginning of a new phase in the Clinton presidency and project.

The 1994 election was indeed an earthquake. The Democrats lost fifty-four seats and control of the House and eight Senate seats and the majority there, too. It ended four decades of Democratic rule and changed the terrain on which Bill Clinton could use his great talents. In the end the Republicans only got 52 percent of the vote and a twenty-six-seat majority and would create an embittered, polarized politics to hold it. Their most enduring political triumph was their two-to-one support among Perot voters that allowed Republicans to battle back toward parity. Nonetheless, voters remained invested in Bill Clinton. The "protest voters" we found in a post-election survey for the DLC were sending a message much more about "politics as usual" than about Bill Clinton. Two thirds of the 1994 voters said "no, I have not given up on Clinton" and "I'm still hopeful that Clinton can succeed."[75]

The meetings after the election were tense but it never crossed my mind that I wouldn't be there to plan the comeback. Clinton and I had been joined at the hip and weathered many ups and downs. I simply presumed I was too central to our shared political project. Not only did I not entertain the thought that I might no longer be a part of the team, I went on vacation at Thanksgiving. Only when I got back in December did I learn from Harold Ickes and other friends in the White House that Clinton was particularly unhappy with me, most evident in the fifteen-minute meetings that no longer happened. Clinton was clearly pained by the election and hated that so many good Democrats lost their seats because of him. Clinton also had an unseen advisor telling him he was ill served. I was seen as too much in the press and too committed to big-government health care and, as reported by Morris, Clinton told him "Stan wouldn't tell me what to do."[76] I, too, was pained by the 1994 debacle, but had a more complicated analysis. Clinton called me at Christmas supposedly to clear the air but never got to a real conversation. I continued to poll and played my normal role in the drafting of the State of the Union, but Clinton worked on his own draft in the residence with what we now know was Morris's draft. Over the next months, my role grew increasingly marginal and Harold finally let me know my White House role would end. This all happened in slow motion without any final meeting with the president. By this point, frankly, I was as worried about my company's finances as my White House role. The solution in the end was Clintonesque. Senator Christopher Dodd, who took a big chance on my novice polling skills fifteen years earlier, became DNC chair and with that came a polling contract that allowed me to continue to poll on a large scale for the Democrats in the White House through the 1996 election.

I initially resented the lack of loyalty and the fact that the personal relationship had been broken without even an opportunity to talk about what had happened. But that soon gave way to my discomfort at being marginalized in the White House. Even the Secret Service looked at me differently. When the president told a group of Texas donors that "you'll be surprised but I thought I raised your taxes too much," I knew the breach was more fundamental.[77]

True to my nature, I had thrown myself into the 1994 campaign trying to figure out a way to minimize the losses. But then I wound up owning the results, too. "Elections have consequences," James Carville observed, and a good portion of the political team left after 1994. It is also my nature to not dwell on things I can't do anything about and I was ready to move on.

ASSESSING THE CLINTON MISSION

In his address to the Cleveland convention in 1991, Clinton laid out his big project: to renew the Democratic Party as the precondition for renewing America. The party had lost the support of those who were the victims of the Reagan-Bush years, the hardworking middle class, who did not trust the Democrats to manage the economy and defense or to advance middle-class interests and values. The path he set was to expand opportunity again but with a return to responsibility and a revolution in government.

Today, Clinton must look back at the political challenge posed in Cleveland with some satisfaction. The "Gingrich Revolution" quickly alienated the country. And while the economy slowed significantly to barely one percent growth in the first two quarters of 1995, with no further drops in the unemployment rate over the whole year, prayers and patience produced robust growth in the presidential election year that was sustained beyond the election, bringing unusually low unemployment, sharp reductions in poverty, and rising incomes for all by the late 1990s. With the Oklahoma City bombing, Clinton found his voice as president. With the government shutdown and the contest with Gingrich on Medicare and education, Clinton crystallized his role as defender of social insurance and investment. And with welfare reform and the balanced budget, he showed by his moderation an ability to change government. The result was a renewed Democratic Party, competitive in any presidential election over two full decades—no small piece of history.

The Democrats, however, have failed up until the elections of 2006 and 2008 to build a new majority in the country. Our modern game of politics has mostly been contested around the fifty-yard line, in a volatile new period that has been shaped by the choices Clinton made.

Clinton's politics is, in the end, grounded in Hope and Hot Springs, Arkansas, with all the contradictions that shaped his lifelong personal quest to unite black and white and erase America's biggest historic divide. He carried that and his classless quality with him in his first steps into politics at Boys Nation and in his first steps to create the new Clinton administration. My consciousness was shaped by Robert Kennedy's appeal to black and white in tumultuous times and the later effort to unite white Catholics and blacks in metropolitan Detroit so that the country could assail inequality and injustice. The inequalities of the Reagan era were the defining backdrop for my new Democratic politics. Clinton's focus, on the other hand, was the clash of white and black Baptists of the South, but also their intertwined lives that left them both at odds and mutually dependent. For him, the villains are the latter-day white supremacists of the Old South who incited fear of "Negro rule," and the modern ones like Lee Atwater who used images of escaped black convict Willie Horton to create fear and keep white and black from coming together to vote for change. Our projects overlapped and brought us together but they are not the same and that had consequences that were not clear to me at the time.

It pains me that Clinton failed to bring middle-class America back to the Democrats. They worked more hours in the 1990s than in previous decades. Income gains for the noncollege-educated and blue-collar workers were modest, except for a couple of years at the end of the decade. Clinton's economic plan, with up-front tax credits for the working poor, by contrast, brought dramatic drops in poverty among African Americans and Hispanics, just as he hoped.

The white noncollege voters led the revolt in 1994, angry about taxes, the weak economy and stagnant incomes, guns and gays, welfare and the Democratic Congress. This revolt was not hard to explain. Afterward, Clinton no longer elevated the aggrieved "middle," choosing instead to educate the country about the new prosperity that would allow everyone to cross into the twenty-first century. It is not clear he was ever comfortable with the "class project." The near derailment of the Clinton presidency by the venomous politics around Monica Lewinsky and the impeachment alienated these middle-class voters, evident in the accelerating flight of the white noncollege voter in the 1998 off-year elections and affirmed in the next two presidential elections. Al Gore and John Kerry barely won 40 percent of those voters. The Perot voters—the prize—broke two to one for the Republicans in 1996, and by 2000, effectively reintegrated into George Bush's Republican Party. Those were the white voters Obama struggled to win over in 2008.[78]

However, the project at Clinton's core—addressing the differences that have kept America divided—did not end in failure. I have no doubt that he viewed the whole effort to reclaim the middle class, victimized by the first Bush, as wholly consistent with his underlying project to reconcile those who are not reconciled, reflected in the politics he forged in 1974 and in his decade as governor, reflected in the streams of black and white Arkansas volunteers who rushed to join his national effort. The theme of division and unity was not one we explored as an alternative way to run for the presidency. Indeed, I never tested it in a survey because Clinton knew what the result would be. Before there was a Clinton presidency, such a choice would have been quickly caricatured as old-style, group-based cultural liberalism. Indeed, when he and Hillary wanted to announce his candidacy at Little Rock High, when I listened to him on election night 1992, when he requested a more diverse core group afterward and a cabinet that "looks like America," and when he elevated "gays in the military" to issue status, I was sure voters could not distinguish his policies from those of a traditional permissive liberalism. At that moment in the early 1990s, his personal mission clashed with the political project showcased in the campaign, though he stuck with it, despite the polls and the consequences. In my period in the Clinton White House, I watched him fashion an economic plan focused on long-term benefits. But the president was unmovable on ensuring that low-income Americans, heavily minority, make gains in the short term—a combination that produced predictable consequences in 1994.

Clinton's starting point was the African American community where he clearly was most grounded and which protected him in time of trouble. He could speak about the need for responsibility, as he did with the African American ministers in Memphis in 1993 and in Detroit in 1992, allowing him to lead a national discussion about affirmative action, allowing him to beat back the conservative assault on it and reiterate the continuing national mission to "close the gap between the ideals" in our revolution and our Constitution "and the reality of our daily lives." Clinton realized, perhaps more than anyone, that ending welfare and demanding personal responsibility removed "rights" and "entitlements" from the debate, fundamentally changing the conversation. He carried those principles into his opposition to California's Proposition 187, the conservative attack on illegal immigration, and worked visibly to strip the anti-immigrant provisions out of welfare reform. The role of the first lady, though controversial at one level, also sent a powerful message about the role of women. Despite the high political price Clinton paid for advocating "gays in the military," a large majority of Americans today favor the policy.

After his reelection in 1996, Clinton was clearer still about his personal project, declaring in his State of the Union address: "For any one of us to succeed we must succeed as one America." When his term was ending and he was lecturing Democrats on their mission in the next century, he reaffirmed the need "to build one America at home," but one encompassing the new reality: "to make strength of our diversity so that the other nations can be inspired to overcome their own ethnic and religious tensions."[79]

Clinton's biggest accomplishment was building the consensus against discrimination and for tolerance and building the presumption for a modern America in which diversity is a strength. That has allowed Democrats to emerge as the natural party of young people, virtually all racial and immigrant minorities, the best-educated women, the most cosmopolitan and global regions, and increasingly, suburban America.[80] Democrats may or may not be able to move the battle beyond the fifty-yard line with this alone, but Clinton's project.

That is how I closed the first full draft of my memoir on Bill Clinton that I turned into the publisher in the summer of 2007, reasonably confident Hillary Clinton would blow back the "boys" in the Democratic primary, but not at all certain she was electable in the November contest against the Republican nominee. She carried a lot of scars from the "Clinton wars" of old and the specter of a woman president of the United States threatened to the tilt the balance of forces against men in relationships and families all through society. But Barack Obama ended such speculation when he marshaled the forces of change in the country and the Democratic Party and swept the Iowa caucuses. Suddenly the two historic prospects were joined in a titanic clash for the presidency—and just as suddenly, Bill Clinton was cast in the ironic role of saving one and destroying the other.

With Senator Clinton facing near certain humiliation in the New Hampshire primary just days away, Tony Blair and I met in a Jerusalem hotel and shook our heads at the likely result. But it is never wise to underestimate the Clintons, seared by the 1980 defeat for reelection as Arkansas governor, the near derailment by sex and draft scandals in the 1992 presidential primary and the 1994 defeat of the Democratic Congress. They were determined to halt Obama's powerful momentum, a huge task in a presidential campaign when the media and elites have turned against you and become enamored with the young Obama. Hillary and Bill showed a steely resolve to win at all costs, an ambition that would not be squelched by an unfair and unelected media, an ambition that translated into a visible determination to persuade every last voter. It was all predicated on an egoism that the country would tolerate in few leaders, but had come to accept and even expect of Bill Clinton, who had fulfilled mythic roles for the country.

Losing was just not an option and it fell to Bill Clinton the unenviable task of bringing down the young candidate of hope and change, the first African American with a chance to be elected president of the United States.

Though I was not unhappy to see Hillary lose, I had a different reaction to the position of the former president and wanted to call him. I had just finished writing this chapter and felt I understood how fraught was this role and hard to play without tragic results. His default choice at every point in life was to knock down racial barriers and reconcile black and white. As president, he fought for policies that raised people out of poverty and his economy raised African American living standards faster than any other group but Hispanics. When he placed his post-presidential office in Harlem, his popularity with African Americans hit such unheard of heights that he became widely described as the nation's "first black president." For these reasons, only Clinton had the standing to blow back Obama's momentum, and I am sure he convinced himself it was something he had to do for Hillary, and the right thing to do. He came to lead the camp in the campaign that felt Obama had to be attacked, as he had in 1992 with Ross Perot.

The press part was easy. The Clintons have resented the role of the media since the tabloids put Gennifer Flowers on a national stage and hounded him and Hillary in the campaign and White House. Clinton accused the press of giving Obama a free ride, failing to examine his inexperience and record and asking Hillary the tougher questions in debates. Having himself fought back Republican attacks in 1992 on his inexperience and foreign policy credentials, Clinton convinced himself that Obama was not up to the job that his wife was clearly qualified for, implying that only McCain and Hillary crossed the commander-in-chief threshold. Trying to push back this powerful tide, he had to find the words and outbursts to diminish Obama without seeming to demean the young black hope. Sometimes he overreached, as when he said "Give me a break, this whole thing [on their Iraq differences] is the biggest fairy tale I've every heard"—in a tone that surprised a number of African American leaders.

At the outset of the primary, both Hillary Clinton and Obama understood that their allure was in not running as "firsts" but transcending the limits of identity politics, something the former president made seem plausible. She rejected Mark Penn's advice that she highlight Obama's "lack of American roots," Penn disdaining Obama's vision of a "diverse, multicultural" America. "Save it for 2050." That would have meant denying her husband's greatest legacy.

But to stop her slide and fight back to win almost half the primary vote, Clinton embraced identity politics, which put both Bill and Hillary on treacherous ground where it is easy to take a fall. Bill told the congregation of the

Temple of Praise Baptist Church in Washington, DC, "Now God works in mysterious ways. All my life, I have wanted to vote for a woman. And all my life, I have wanted to vote for an African-American. I wonder why God gave us this dilemma?" I am sure he was expressing genuine wonderment at the dilemma and he told many, many African American audiences he understood their pride in having Obama reach such a peak. Yet it was also self-interested and perhaps cynical, as most everyone I know believed and yet I've observed Clinton's political brain churn and I know he has already worked out the consistency of his idealism and realism. With women forming almost 60 percent of the primary electorate everywhere, Clinton observed, "I think it would be just as much change, and some people think more, to have the first woman president as to have the first African American president." Essentially, he was putting one identity ahead of another.

Nonetheless, he was convinced based on his entire life that he could persuade South Carolina's African American voters to stick with Hillary Clinton. They didn't. And when he compared Obama's win in South Carolina to Jesse Jackson's wins there in earlier races, it seemed as if he were consigning Obama to a more marginal black candidacy. In what seemed like a "big lie" to Clinton, the highest ranking African American Congressman, Jim Clyburn, warned that these attempts to "denigrate" Obama "is angering African America voters" and "trying to send some kind of signal on race."[81] It was an implication he bitterly denied, instead accusing the Obama campaign of playing the "race card" on him. When an Obama supporter who was also a former Democratic party chair in South Carolina said Clinton's tactics were "reminiscent of Lee Atwater," Clinton exploded. I was disturbed by his South Carolina comments and fearful he would take himself down along with Hillary and Obama, but I also reacted to the Lee Atwater charge. It was because of such racially divisive politics that Clinton traveled to Macomb County and Detroit to reclaim Robert Kennedy's mantle and project. So, nothing was more certain to enrage him and with his finger wagging ominously, he exclaimed to CNN reporter Jessica Yellin, "Shame on you."

The media and pundits focused on the outbursts of anger and finger pointing, the injudicious comments and tongue-lashing of reporters. It was all part of an "abiding anger" and "mood changes," according to Todd Purdham's *Vanity Fair* piece, that are the consequence of aging, guilt, and major heart surgery that often brings a postpartum-like depression. People who have undergone the surgery wind up "never really being the same again," Purdum wrote.

That is nonsense, of course. Anybody who worked in the heart of the Clinton White House can tell you that the waves of anger—"like Mount Vesuvius erupting," according to David Gergen—happened frequently, at least every morning, and "within minutes, you were back to work." During the primaries in 1992 as he lost voters' trust, Clinton grew depressed and was angry at his campaign over many months. And with few voters giving him credit for his accomplishments and defeat looming in the 1994 off-year elections, he insisted on finishing each campaign stop with a litany of successes to win voters over, not unlike the litany of "real facts" his office released the day after the *Vanity Fair* piece to remind people of the 1,300,000 lives he had saved in his post-presidency.[82]

The one thing I have learned in working with Clinton close up is that he is passionate, engaged, intriguing, complicated, maddening and paradoxical: his reach for the high points can leave him very low; his strengths are simultaneously his weaknesses; his self-centeredness and ambition are inseparable from his idealism. You just can't just wish away the dark stuff without making him antiseptic or ahistorical or deny him the skills and personality that allowed him to emerge from the pack and become one of the defining leaders of the times.

That was on display to the world when he spoke at the 2008 Democratic Convention in Denver, and declared, like his wife and 18 million of her supporters, "I'm here first to support Barack Obama." Marshalling everything he learned in his eight years as president and his good work since in America and across the globe, he declared, "Barack Obama is the man for the job." Then, moved deftly to his own territory, closing to thunderous applause, "Barack Obama will lead us away from the division and fear of the last eight years back to unity and hope."

Obama and Clinton met at Clinton's Harlem office and Clinton campaigned for Obama in key battleground states, but the two men never addressed publicly or symbolically what kept this past Democratic president and the future one from fully embracing. The charge Clinton played the "race card" gnawed at their shared politics, denying Clinton's whole life mission and presidency and the new forces that propelled Obama to the top. It is unimaginable that they will not find a way to embrace because it is still true that Bill Clinton changed American and its politics and made possible the election of the first African American president with his own call for hope and unity.[83]

3

NELSON MANDELA

HOW DO YOU begin a conversation with a mythic figure who has spent twenty-seven years in prison? Nelson Mandela's lifelong struggle to lift the smothering blanket of apartheid from South Africa is so fundamental to everything I have done as an adult that I felt as if I was about to meet my maker. Frank Greer and I had traveled to South Africa in June 1993, five months after Bill Clinton's inauguration, to work with the African National Congress and Mandela in the first democratic elections in South Africa. We had already met with the leaders of the election campaign to outline the basics of our working relationship and we were now to breakfast with Mandela before leading a campaign workshop for eighty ANC campaign organizers. I may have been working for Bill Clinton, at that point the most powerful man in the world, yet I still felt somehow unworthy to be here, as if I had not done enough to justify this meeting.

When Mandela entered the room, tall, erect, and almost regal in bearing, he grasped our hands in both of his in greeting, but it was evident he had something else other than pleasantries on his mind. He sat down at a table set for eight and gathered the campaign leaders around him. He made no effort to stifle his voice and he spoke sternly.

"How could you schedule the meeting with the shop stewards and workers committee in Pietersburg," he said. He had traveled to the rural north to rally African support for national elections, but the workers at a factory had appealed to Mandela to intercede on their behalf in a local dispute. After all, the Congress of South African Trade Unions, COSATU, had been the closest of allies in the struggle to liberate South Africa from white rule and would be a powerful force in the upcoming election. But Mandela apparently had refused their entreaties, although certainly with great empathy. Now, though, he was vehement. "I am no substitute for the workers organizing themselves and doing the hard work with the employer. It is not the job of the president of a country to be drawn into such a fight."

Of course, Mandela was not the president of the country. Yet here he was self-conscious about his own role as leader, as educator of people in their duties and responsibilities.

His acolytes called him "Madiba," a clan name that traces to an eighteenth-century chief and used universally by black South Africans as a term of respect and affection. "Black" is inclusive of all African language groups but also mixed-race Coloureds and Asians. He was the son of a chief who ruled a tiny poor village in the Transkei, the largest tribal area in early-twentieth-century South Africa. Born in 1918, Mandela grew up in an ordinary kraal, a grouping of huts, under the care of one of his father's four wives. He was educated by missionaries and, after his father's death, lived in the royal residence of the regent of his tribe. From his father, Mandela learned sternness, stubbornness, and a sense of fairness. From the regent, he learned an appreciation for wise counsel that drew tribesmen from all over the area, and an appreciation for fine clothes.[1] At our first meeting, Mandela wore a business suit instinctively, not at all like *Shawshank*'s newly released ex-convicts and their ill-fitting suits.

After his brief lecture Mandela once again turned his attention to us, apologizing for being inattentive. He was deeply respectful, almost as if he were the one honored to be meeting us. As waiters hovered around the breakfast table eager to be near Madiba, he asked them to pay more attention to his guests. "The gentlemen need more coffee." I knew we were being vetted here at breakfast and in the workshop and I wondered just how much Mandela understood of what we did and how we did it. I needn't have worried.

Frank and I were the kickoff speakers for the strategy workshop. We mounted a small stage, while Mandela eagerly took his place in the front row. While the participants had attended other such workshops over the last few years, the reality of an imminent campaign kept them focused on what Frank and I had to say. My remarks were aimed at defining the election through the choices of issues and leaders and what the times required. That is always so much harder than you think it will be. They presumed issues came organically out of the history of the ANC and its charter through elaborate deliberations. But a campaign can't champion every issue. At the very least polling can help it decide which issues matter the most. Further, what issues the campaign embraces and the battle lines it draws determine who gets mobilized and who can be persuaded to support the campaign. Embracing an issue or a purpose would allow the ANC to be the master of its own fate, not just be buffeted by the explosive dynamic in the country. Would the ANC get to define the victory ahead? Our goal was a message that crisply embodied all of that. To make the point, I peppered my talk with references to our exploits in Clinton's campaign—"the economy, stupid," and "people first"—to emphasize how the tyranny of message can impose order on the inherent disorder of a campaign.

When we finished, Mandela raised his hand to ask the first question: "Mr. Greer and Mr. Greenberg, in your vast experience with modern campaigns and President Clinton, is it better to have a low building with functions spread out across a few big floors or to have a tall building with functions on each of many floors?"

I was taken aback. Clearly Mandela was willing to get deeply into the weeds. Only later did I discover that, despite his determination to lead a modern, effective campaign, that the ANC had already bought and occupied the old Shell House, a twelve-story office tower that was the visual opposite of the squat, two-story building that housed the Clinton campaign and war room in Little Rock.

He told Frank not to apologize for telling him about the basics of political campaigns. Learning how to do a campaign right was part of Mandela's own personal transition as a leader, and learning so self-consciously and visibly was a way of bringing his party with him. And he, like Clinton, exhibited an intense interest in the polling and trying to understand what people were thinking and how to bring them with you on the journey. As part of his own journey and to the horror of his staff, he suggested that he would oversee the research himself.[2]

How the Americans would work with the ANC wasn't at all clear until two nights before, when Frank and I sat down for a private dinner with the Elections Commission, the ANC's leadership body charged with running the campaign. Around the large table was a virtual hall of fame of antiapartheid civic activists. Like so many others in the internal resistance, Popo Molefe, the chair, became active in the black consciousness student associations and the Soweto uprisings of 1976. "Terror" Lekota, nicknamed for his football skills, not his resistance efforts, had been imprisoned on Robben Island in Capetown along with Mandela and, when released, became publicity secretary for the United Democratic Front (UDF), the internal resistance movement. Both Popo and Terror were sentenced to ten years in jail for treason in 1985.

Pallo Jordan was the most prominent intellectual on the team. Raised in an academic family, he had studied at the best universities in South Africa and Britain, and took up major information roles in the ANC while publishing widely and regularly clashing with South Africa's Soviet-aligned scholars. He drew easily on history and Hegel, but was also political and practical, finishing his points with a distinctive, raspy laugh.

I hadn't known Gill Marcus before meeting with the ANC leadership but she is hard to miss. A very tall white woman, typically clad in an African-printed caftan, she was in charge of media and advertising for the campaign. She had done communications for the ANC in exile and returned immediately to South Africa in that role as soon as the ban on the ANC was lifted.

Coordinating everything was Ketso Gordhan, a UDF organizer, who was raised in a successful Indian family in Natal. He organized and managed the incredibly diverse set of interests that participated in the ANC's first policy conference. Intense, very smart, and good-natured, he nevertheless did not suffer fools.

All of those talents were desperately needed to bring order out of the chaos that was the ANC, a polyglot organization of exiled leaders, some 40,000 guerrilla fighters, the former Robben Island prisoners, and the vast network of allied civic groups and unions. The ANC was held together more by the immediate mission than organization or ideology. ANC headquarters had only notional management and no presence on the ground. It was an organization that an internal memo described as lacking "enterprise, creativity and initiative," content with "populist rhetoric and cliché." Out of this, Mandela said, would have to come "a strong and well-oiled task force."[3]

These focused quick studies were ready to exploit or learn on a crash basis from any country, organization, or expert who would offer help, including the American and European pollsters, media experts, and fund-raisers who arrived in waves. There was absolutely no hesitation to use foreigners. After all, the ANC had depended on foreign powers and support for survival during the thirty years that it was banned. They even welcomed Americans, despite the fact that the apartheid government that had repressed the ANC was often seen as allied with the West while the ANC drew support from South African communists and the Soviet bloc. I assumed that all the returning ANC white exiles were communists and occasionally wondered if the Secret Service would take my White House pass away.

But the ANC's struggle from the beginning was inspired by Western democratic traditions from both Britain and the United States, in addition to developments in the African American community. The AME Zion church, the dominant Baptist convention in the segregated South, sent missionaries to minister to black South Africans. From the late nineteenth century, Africans attended black colleges in the United States, creating a parallel life for Booker T. Washington's ideas of self-help and industrial education and W. E. B. DuBois's ideas about civic equality. The ANC's first president was sent to Oberlin College by American missionaries and returned to build industrial schools for the Zulus modeled on Alabama's Tuskegee University.[4] And the most promising African students including Mandela attended South Africa's University of Fort Hare, whose professors were educated at places like Lincoln University in Pennsylvania.

Marcus Garvey and the "Back to Africa" movement in the United States produced a millennial reaction in the South Africa of Mandela's youth and its most enduring impact was felt among the peasants of the Transkei where Mandela was reared. "Large numbers of uneducated Africans now came to regard the voice of America as that of a mighty race of black people overseas," a contemporary historian wrote, with motor cars and airplanes and weapons of war. They were convinced a "black fleet" from America was sailing to speed the liberation of black South Africa. The ANC in its early days in the 1920s embraced Garvey's call, "Africa for the Africans," with the Cape branch naming its office Liberty Hall, the name of the general assembly at the Garveyite center in New York City.[5]

At roughly the same time and on parallel tracks, the American civil rights movement struggled to overturn state-sanctioned racial segregation as the ANC turned to nonviolent defiance campaigns and boycotts to stop the new apartheid laws in the 1950s and 1960s. Robert Kennedy went to South Africa in 1966 and spoke of two countries struggling to overcome a history of racial injustice. His speeches there, regarded by many as the best he ever made, honored the Nobel Laureates Martin Luther King Jr. and Albert Luthuli, the banned head of the ANC. Kennedy was mobbed on the campuses, in central Johannesburg, and in Soweto.[6]

To the discomfort of the ANC's older leaders, Stokely Carmichael, Malcolm X, Eldridge Cleaver, and the American black power movement had an electrifying effect on the black consciousness movement and among black student associations that fed the revolts of the late 1960s and 1970s.[7] A decade later, a broad swath of American civil society, from religious groups, to city councils, to civil rights organizations, mobilized to pressure the U.S. Congress to impose sanctions on South Africa and override President Reagan's veto, a move that built strong bonds with America in the final phase of the struggle against apartheid.

How Frank and I would work for the ANC was not at first clear when we sat down for the private dinner with its Elections Commission and election team. Our trip was sponsored by the National Democratic Institute for International Affairs in Washington, and Pat Keefer, NDI's representative in South Africa, was there to enforce their mandate: the ANC could only have a bipartisan

American team and would receive only four economy-class round-trip tickets during the entire campaign, the same benefits that were being provided to the other parties.

Ketso Gordhan was having none of that. The ANC, he said, didn't want to have any Republicans on the team and it wanted a much closer relationship with the American team than four round-trips could provide. Frank and I were on the spot, very much intent on joining the ANC effort, but concerned about violating the NDI rules and undermining Pat. Without having to huddle, Frank and I let slip that we would work for the ANC pro bono if the party would cover business-class travel and survey costs. The deal was done. While we toasted our new partnership Pat did not join in and later told us that we left her "on the dance floor without a partner."

Why was I asked to work with the ANC on its campaign? In other places, that question is sometimes difficult to answer, but not in the case of the ANC. In my previous life as an academic I helped create the Southern African Research Program at Yale. My work on poverty and race relations eventually took me to South Africa as a Guggenheim Fellow and I was hooked. I lived there for almost a year in 1973 and 1974 when the park benches and bathrooms all had "Whites Only" signs. I traveled to South Africa often after that, sometimes staying for months while working on various books, including the impenetrable 489-page, inelegantly titled *Race and State in Capitalist Development* that argued against many "liberal" economists and business-people, as well as President Reagan and Britain's prime minister Margaret Thatcher, that "constructive engagement" by multinational companies helped entrench whites in power. When Congress considered the issue of sanctions and divestment I testified before the House Foreign Affairs Committee that "every step toward incorporation has been accompanied by yet more elaborate controls over the great majority of the population." Businesses, I said, have been responsive to change not when compelled by some "economic logic," but when facing "sustained opposition from the black community in South Africa."[8]

When the book came out in 1980, I was working for the Rockefeller Foundation–funded Commission on U.S. Policy Toward Southern Africa. I traveled to South Africa to meet academics and others who might contribute to the commission's work and accepted an invitation from a South African friend and academic to speak one evening in his living room with a small group of his colleagues from Stellenbosch University. I talked about the book and answered questions about the implications for divestment. It was a mistake. My talk was covertly recorded for South Africa's security branch. The very next day, I got an urgent call from the commission. Apparently, the South African ambassador to Washington was flying up to New York to meet with Franklin Thomas—head of the commission as well as the Ford

Foundation—to lodge a formal complaint about my comments. None of the members of the commission, including CEOs of Xerox and Cummins Engine, among others, would be granted visas for the planned trip if I were to accompany them. In a moment of great bravery in the foundation world, we reached an accommodation on my departure and return to Yale.

Mandela was intensely loyal to those who supported the ANC when the party was in the wilderness, even if it meant embracing Libya's Muammar Qaddafi and Fidel Castro on the same trip that he visited with George H. W. Bush and British prime minister John Major. I assumed reaching for me was a modest nod to my modest contribution to the antiapartheid struggle. But it wasn't even a nod. Rather, early in 1993 as the ANC was planning its campaign, Popo Molefe and Terror Lekota flashed a copy of *Newsweek*'s special election issue on Clinton's 1992 victory and the whiz kids who got him there. "We would like to work with these people," Popo told Pat Keefer of the NDI. Keefer thumbed through the issue. "Yes," she said, "we do know them. . . . Something could be worked out."[9]

So it all was very simple: Frank and I were the guys who put Clinton in the White House and, as Ketso said, "We are all pretty impressed with the Clinton campaign."

After the Mandela breakfast and the workshop, Frank and I had dinner with the union team from COSATU that would be working on the election. Usually such affairs are just a check-the-box meeting with unions that lack the energy to organize anybody. But in South Africa the independent unions were the real thing. For more than a decade, they were virtually the only legal multiracial organization in the country. Their battle-tested organizers created a movement with some 800,000 members, and their parallel campaign team was at the dinner to make sure the ANC was ready for prime time. Gratifyingly, they had read my book.

I had been in Durban in 1973 during the strikes there, interviewing employers and union officials for the book. After a year of strikes, the government had been forced to legalize the unions and the black National Union of Mineworkers emerged as the largest in the country and joined in the mid-1980s with other unions to create COSATU, the multiracial Congress of South African Trade Unions, allied with the UDF.[10]

Much to my delight the COSATU team included Marcel Golding, the deputy general secretary of the Mineworkers. During the 1992 Clinton campaign, Halton Cheadle, one of my closest friends and a constitutional lawyer advising the ANC, asked whether Marcel could come to Little Rock to learn about organizing a U.S. presidential campaign and he had wound up in the war room. Someone was thinking ahead.

Marcel and the other unionists recalled a piece that I had written two decades earlier that appeared in a publication allied with the new unions, and
my last book on South Africa published five years earlier.[11] Those works
cleared away many barriers between us and now they were not subtle in their
demands: did I think the ANC campaign would be real? They were eager to
take over key functions and clearly were fearful that the ANC would lose
sight of its socialist principles.

I spent an entire day on that first trip for the ANC listening to presentations
by the three impressive groups that were helping the ANC with focus groups
and polls. Blacks may have been denied the right to vote but they had the
right to be polled. The government financed polling among the blacks in the
mid-1980s, as civic unrest threatened to undermine the government's latest
efforts at political separation.[12]

The perverse history of South Africa had multiplied every obstacle to
polling. The half-century effort to create separate tribal nations, called African homelands, meant surveys had to be translated into nine languages and
reach into nine very different provinces. The apartheid labor system, when it
worked, pushed an artificially large African population to remote impoverished areas without basic services. When it broke down, it left large popula-
tions in sprawling, un-serviced squatter areas around all the metropolitan
centers. Research companies, more interested in consumers than voters,
rarely surveyed beyond the metropolitan areas. A bare handful of Africans
had phones and interviews had to be conducted face-to-face unless you
were in rural KwaZulu-Natal where bloody clashes between the ethnic
Zulu Inkatha Party and the ANC had created "no-go zones" for politics and
polling.

The ANC commissioned its own focus groups and polls starting in late
1992 with a team headed by a former dissertation student of mine, Craig
Charney, who assembled a serious group of academic researchers. A second
group was put together by a nonprofit firm that conducted surveys for unions
and other antiapartheid groups. A third group coalesced around Research
Surveys, the largest commercial survey research company in the country.
The head of the company, Jannie Hofmeyr, had developed "Conversion Modeling," a way to sort consumers and voters into "loyalists" or "winnables" to be
either mobilized or converted. Tony Trew, a soft-spoken mathematics professor who stretched his portfolio into political theory and linguistics, took over
as coordinator of all the ANC's research efforts.

While I did not quite realize it on that first visit, my role was to arbitrate
the flood of good advice from different sources and respond after the groups
had presented. As Pallo Jordan pointed out, I was "a complete outsider" of

high reputation, working "as scientifically as possible," "the closest thing" the ANC had to an objective observer. I immediately used that objectivity to criticize the flood of surveys and pile of printouts that were devoid of any testing of strategy and message. For me, it was second nature that a leader, party, or campaign evolve its message and direction, understanding how real people react to it—if only to figure out how to bring them with you. But I clearly violated a taboo. Many in the campaign were fiercely opposed to such a test. Some thought it was a slide into PR that would simplify and dilute the ANC's mission. Others thought the people ought to get with the program and simply follow the party. I argued that real people were a precondition for popularizing the ANC's mission and, fortunately, Ketso and Pallo went with me.[13]

Everything about the situation told me I needed to be in South Africa. But my colleagues in Washington weren't convinced. Most of them thought I was mad. I was, after all, the president's pollster. We were in the middle of the fight of our lives to pass his budget and economic plan and we were about to launch the initiatives to win passage of the North American Free Trade Agreement (NAFTA) and his plan for national health insurance. In the months before South Africa's election we reached our high point with the president's State of the Union message in January 1994 and our low point with "Trooper-gate" and "Travelgate" and Congress's successful effort to destroy our plans for health care.

Nevertheless, I worked out a modus operandi. Beginning in June I flew to South Africa monthly, then every two weeks after the New Year. The routine was to take the direct seventeen-hour New York–to–Johannesburg flight, leaving on Thursday night and arriving Friday afternoon. I would work furiously through the weekend, then leave Sunday night to arrive at JFK by 6 A.M. and be back in the White House by 9 A.M. They hardly missed me.

TORTURED ROAD

During my ride on the Clinton roller coaster, from the first days of joining the campaign in Little Rock right through the election, only the most conse-quential events in South Africa broke through despite my long history there. They were all compressed in time beginning in 1990 when President F. W. de Klerk announced the lifting of the ban against the ANC, the Pan-Africanist Congress, and the South African Communist Party. Then came Mandela's release from prison, greeted by euphoric crowds at Cape Town's city hall. His-tory continued to unfold through headlines, each more amazing than the last: liberation figures returned from exile; apartheid laws were repealed; the state of emergency was lifted; and the ANC suspended the armed struggle.[14]

The ANC hoped to move as quickly as possible to form an interim government and then elections of a new assembly to draft a new constitution. But the National Party was in no hurry. De Klerk needed to bring along the white community, which comprised about 20 percent of the electorate, and believed he could make an alliance with the surviving African homeland leaders in traditional rural areas, who might control over a quarter of the electorate, and win over Coloureds and Indians—the other official racial designations—representing another 10 percent. Clearly he had no intention of losing power.[15]

The negotiations dragged on for years with more breakdowns than breakthroughs. The ANC struggled to dampen discord and unite its diverse membership. The party's first national conference had to be delayed six months into 1991 and still became a forum for discontent. The ANC quieted the discontent and put pressure on the government through "rolling mass action."[16] Ultimately de Klerk agreed to a new parliamentary government by majority rule with no formal protection for whites.

Over those three years more than one hundred people died each month in the political violence, almost all involving Inkatha-ANC battles in KwaZulu-Natal that spilled over into Johannesburg. Mangosuthu Buthelezi, the Inkatha founder and leader, was using the weapons available to him to put himself and Zulus center stage in the grand negotiations between de Klerk and Mandela that would shape South Africa's future. Buthelezi had legitimacy and real support, but he also had a secret alliance with elements within the security forces that financed the Inkatha Freedom Party and trained death squads. In some of the worst violence, Zulu migrant workers living in hostels in the Johannesburg area used traditional weapons to hack to death some thirty ANC supporters in Sobekeng. A couple of months later, armed gangs rampaged through a commuter train departing from Soweto, killing twenty-six.[17]

Mandela had warned from the earliest days of his negotiations with de Klerk, about a "Third Force," a secret, semi-official operation within the security establishment that was fostering Inkatha-on-ANC violence. De Klerk denied it, but Mandela thought his passivity unconscionable. While Mandela spoke of de Klerk as "a man of integrity" when he was released, their relationship turned very cold. When in June 1992, two hundred Inkatha hostel dwellers rampaged through a squatter settlement at Boipatong, a shaken Mandela went to the site of the massacre and addressed de Klerk: "I can no longer explain to our people why we continue to talk to a regime that is murdering our people and conducting war against us."[18]

Nonetheless, Mandela and de Klerk came together at crisis points to move things forward. In the fall of 1992, the ANC and National Party settled the many outstanding issues and agreed that the election would be held some-time in 1994.

The April 1993 assassination of Chris Hani, the charismatic popular leader of the South African Communist Party, by a Polish anticommunist immi-grant, galvanized the NP and ANC to set a firm date and bring the tortured process to a conclusion. Hani's death also allowed Mandela to rise above the tumult. Amid expectations of widespread violence, Mandela spoke on televi-sion of a "white man, full of prejudice and hate" who "committed a deed so foul that our whole nation now teeters on the brink of disaster. But then he addressed a woman of Afrikaner origin who alerted the police and risked her life so that we may know, and bring to justice, the assassin." He reached out "to every single South African, black and white," and called on them "to stand together against those who, from any quarter, wish to destroy what Chris Hani gave his life for—the freedom of all of us." Hundreds of thou-sands joined the rallies and the funeral that, with the aid of ANC marshals, heeded Mandela's call to remain peaceful.[19]

The ANC immediately announced the resumption of negotiations. With Mandela and de Klerk scheduled to travel to the United States to meet with President Clinton and to jointly receive the Liberty Medal in Philadelphia on July 4, they announced a formal election date of April 27, 1994. The agreement called for the dissolution of the old parliament and for the cre-ation of an all-party transitional executive to oversee the country during the campaign period and the Independent Electoral Commission to oversee the election.

For de Klerk and Mandela, however, it was a cold peace. In December, they were both awarded the Nobel Prize, a tribute to the role they played together in a historic transformation. That day Mandela said, "This is a time to speak of what is best for our country." But within a month Mandela ac-cused de Klerk of "allowing violence to continue among Africans, in which men, women and children are being slaughtered."[20]

Long before I joined the campaign, the ANC leaders heard the research team's grim conclusion: the people were in an ugly mood, shaped by the vio-lence and tangled negotiations. Their lives had not changed for the better and the researchers characterized their feelings in bleak terms: "crushed expecta-tions," "disempowered," "despondency." In the groups, people always started the clock with Mandela's release from prison, the moment when the new his-tory began, "but nothing good has emanated from the release." They were conscious of their hopes and how those hopes had led to their low mood: "we expected too much, we expected things to change too soon." The poverty and struggle for work just carried on as before, but with the added political violence and rising crime. A Soweto woman observed: "We are drowning in our own blood. That is why it does not rain any more."[21]

These attitudes translated into very modest poll numbers for the ANC in the large number of public polls in the first half of 1993, with most reporting that the ANC would be hard pressed to garner more than 50 percent of the vote. There was no white support for the party and the Coloured and Asian voters had defected to the National Party, despite it being the party of apartheid. Among Africans, who comprised 76 percent of the potential vote, the ANC had stronger support, but it still ranged unimpressively between 60 and 70 percent. That would drop further, while the undecided rose to a quarter of the vote. Craig Charney and the academic researchers suggested it was not inconceivable that African turnout could fall below 50 percent. A progressive journal produced a special issue with the title, "Can the ANC Win?" The editors wrote, "Formidable hurdles still separate the ANC from the kind of victory it needs to deliver on even a fraction of its promises."[22]

By the fall, the campaign's own large-scale polls, by then incorporating many of my questions, largely confirmed the earlier results: almost three quarters of Africans and two thirds of whites thought things were "going wrong" in the country. To produce a victory that would cement the legitimacy of the ANC in the first democratic elections after centuries of racial oppression and a half century of apartheid, the party needed to generate enthusiasm and near universal participation among Africans and needed to emerge as the only party able to win support across all black groups. Neither of those goals was evident in the numbers.[23]

Certainly the poll numbers were far short of what the ANC needed to dominate a unity government in which cabinet ministries would be allocated based on the percentage of the vote. With Africans jammed in rural areas, a vote under 60 percent nationally would leave the opposition in control of the main commercial centers of the Western Cape, including Cape Town, the Johannesburg-Pretoria complex, and KwaZulu-Natal, including Durban. Whites, Coloureds, or Zulus dominated those areas. To get anywhere near 60 percent, the ANC needed 85 percent support among Africans and nearly as high a turnout number. No poll indicated anything approaching those numbers.

More difficult than the numbers was the deepening sense among Africans that Mandela himself and the exile leaders were disconnected from life in the African community and perhaps could not be counted on to make life better. The militants who had agreed to suspend armed struggle were disgruntled about the rush of concessions, the silence on land or economic change, and what they thought was an ANC that was disappearing into a world of cocktail parties. Winnie Mandela, estranged from her husband, described the negotiations as a meeting of the "the elites of the oppressed and the oppressors," without regard for the people.[24]

While the election team was prepared to believe the accuracy of those polls, they did not get a happy response from Mandela or his colleagues, who had spent a lifetime getting to that point and sternly counseled patience. Unknown to me at the time, the election team in September persuaded Mandela to observe a focus group in Durban. He sat behind the one-way window and saw how a group of ordinary ANC supporters from the township talked with such great frustration about the current state of things.[25] And like virtually every group we held in this period, people talked of their pessimism and about the remoteness of ANC leaders, even Madiba. It got Mandela's attention, who always learned from his engagement with people. With the election date set and the big constitutional issues about to be settled, the ANC had to rethink how it related to its supporters and to voters.

PEOPLE'S FORUM

At the end of September, campaign leaders from all the regions came to Johannesburg to discuss and ratify the decision for the allied parties, including the Communist Party and COSATU, to run under the banner and symbols of the ANC. Mandela's picture would be featured on the ballot and Mandela would reach beyond the ANC's traditional supporters during the campaign.

Frank Greer and I spent what seemed like a whole day locked in a room at Shell House, sitting around a long table with the communications team debating for hours how to reverse the rapid downward spiral. Among the participants was a new player, Joel Netshitendze (pronounce as fast as you can and impossibly,"Net-shit-ten-zee"), the young editor of the ANC's journal, *Mayibuye*. He was trained as an economist and spoke sharply and rapidly using bursts of eloquent English and a contagious laugh that won him considerable respect in ANC circles. He was also now Mandela's principal speechwriter, and the key to making the campaign work. While engaged and civil, he was deeply skeptical about the idea of consultants—people who advise but are not part of the political project—and of the value of American campaign techniques for South Africa. That put up a big barrier for Frank and one a bit smaller for me because of my history in South Africa.

While we were apologetic about drawing on American examples, both Frank and I mentioned the Clinton campaign's use of town meetings to reach people and underscored that Clinton was a leader who listened. It had become the signature method for distinguishing him from the "born-with-a-silver-foot-in-his-mouth" George H. W. Bush. It was part of our rescue effort in the New Hampshire primary where the presidential debate in town hall format, probably the final defining moment in the 1992 election campaign, set Clinton off from Bush and Ross Perot. We suggested that this was a way for the ANC to connect in a new manner with its own people.

The ANC was holding large gatherings, but they were as likely to drive voters away as bring them closer. Large crowds gathered to listen to hear Mandela and a coterie of national and local luminaries who would gather on a high stage and drone on for up to four hours, Hugo Chávez style. Pallo Jordan reminded us that these meetings were pretty alien from ANC tradition and political culture, which required broad consultation among the members, even general meetings if the conditions allowed, where all views were heard before a consensus could emerge. That reflected Mandela's own youthful experience with the tribal elders: people traveled long distances to assemble together and all could speak before a consensual decision was reached. Pallo pointed us in particular to the campaign for the Congress of the People in 1955 that wrote the "Freedom Charter," the ANC's guiding statement of principles. It invited some two hundred organizations to hold meetings and sent out circulars in the townships and villages, asking people for their suggestions: "If you make the laws, what would you do? How would you set about making South Africa a happy place for all the people who live in it?"[26]

Before we left the room, we developed a radically new way for the ANC to relate to its supporters, and we knew immediately the campaign had something special. Mandela would be entirely alone on the stage. Gill Marcus was assigned to keep all the other leaders from massing behind him in their natural urge to bask in Mandela's reflected power and legitimacy. Mandela would not make a speech. Instead, the campaign would construct a separate stage equal in height where any ordinary person could climb the stairs and ask any question of Madiba. The team from the advertising agency, Hunt Lascaris, got the picture, loved it, and came up with the name "People's Forum."

The first forum was held on November 6 in Uitenhage and by the end of the month Mandela was doing three a day. Before each meeting, the ANC published open letters in newspaper ads, inviting readers to attend the People's Forums, where they could "give us your views on jobs, affirmative action, crime, security, language and culture. Tell us where you stand." Included in the ad was a clip-out coupon to send in a question for Mandela and the ANC.[27] At the end of two months, the ANC published a series of ads, thanking the people who attended the People's Forums.

The forums were wildly popular and most popular accounts wrongly said they were "directly borrowed from the Clinton campaign." They were part of a similar process of leaders, not manipulating but connecting with people.

For Clinton, the town meeting brought out his character and underscored real differences on how he would use government. In South Africa, the People's Forum was an antidote to a party hierarchy that thought voters should sit quietly and listen, but the campaign team, comprised mostly of those in the civic protests rather than exile organizations, understood what was going on. The People's Forum with Mandela not only addressed the building frustrations, they were leveling and symbolic of a new relationship between the leaders and the people and tilted the balance to the latter. They became the main vehicle for communication in the campaign for the next five months. Mandela was energized by the encounters and clearly listened to people and their issues. By the end he had conferred with an estimated 2.5 million people.[28] The blending of traditions enabled a liberation movement to find its own route to becoming a political party.

THE SMALL MATTER OF THE PAC

Mandela was fixated on the PAC, the Pan-Africanist Congress, which was getting one percent of the national vote and 2 percent among Africans in our first polls. Sometimes the vote was too small to be visible at the bottom of our graphs, but that was where Mandela's eyes focused. When Ketso Gordhan came back from a meeting with Mandela, he reported, "He wants to know more about the PAC." We would have to look harder.

The PAC was the only other party with standing in the antiapartheid struggle and thus a majority of Africans viewed it favorably; about one in ten African voters said the PAC would be their second choice in the election and another 5 percent considered voting for the party. Those numbers were always higher in the Eastern Cape where the black consciousness movement was historically strong. The PAC attacked the ANC for "selling out" and boycotted the negotiations for most of this period, a strategy that made the PAC the only legitimate outlet for the younger, most disaffected voters in the townships. The PAC had internal problems and its leaders were not prominent, but it was a party unembarrassed to talk about socialism and the need to expropriate white land for Africans.

The election team pressed for focus groups among PAC supporters before the end of the year, organized in the Eastern Cape. That was followed by a special survey of the Eastern Cape to see whether the PAC had potential for future gains.

This was deeply personal for Mandela. While he was nearly always inclusive and forgiving, he was intent on smashing the PAC, reducing it to historical insignificance.

When whites formed the Union of South Africa in 1913, the ANC formed to petition white and British authorities to protect African rights. But the whites in 1948 elected the National Party, which enacted draconian laws to force everyone into racial and language groups, ban sex between all race groups, eliminate mixed living areas, channel Africans into separate language groups, and ban leaders and organizations and bar almost all protests. Under that burden petitioning seemed almost quaint. It was a formative political period for Mandela, who joined together in 1949 with Walter Sisulu, Oliver Tambo, and others to form the Youth League of the ANC, which transformed the ANC into a mass and militant organization. It pushed the ANC into popular confrontations, including boycotts and passive resistance and a more prominent role for African leaders, scorning reliance on Indians, Coloureds, and white communist allies. It was a turning point for South Africa, the ANC, and Mandela. The young Mandela was very much part of this "Africanist" impulse, with some Youth Leaguers believing that only Africans could rule a future South Africa.[29]

But the young Mandela and Tambo were more interested in the militancy of the Youth League than its nationalism and soon broke with the Africanists. Indeed, the first big mass action for the new ANC leadership was the Defiance Campaign, a joint call of the ANC and South African Indian Congress in 1952 to engage in nonviolent noncooperation. Mandela, the new national organizer, told his biggest audience ever that the unity of black people—Africans, Coloureds, and Indians—"would make history."[30]

When the government moved to suppress the growing resistance, the ANC decided to formalize its principles and goals and launched a process that brought three thousand delegates, mostly African, but also three hundred and twenty Indians, two hundred and thirty Coloureds, and one hundred and twelve whites, to adopt the Freedom Charter. It declared that "South Africa belongs to all who live in it, black and white, and that no government can justly claim authority unless it is based on the will of the people" enjoying "equal rights and opportunities." Even then, the charter gave serious attention to minority rights, stating that "all national groups and races" have "equal status in the bodies of the state," with protection against "insults to their race and national pride" and "equal rights to use their own language."

The Africanists bitterly opposed the charter. They fought its core principles and nearly blocked it from being accepted at a special conference in 1956. They offered a counter-set of principles that asserted Africans' exclusive "ownership rights." No less fervent than the ANC charter, their publication asserted, "The African people have an inalienable claim on every inch of African soil."[31]

The dispute reached a climax in 1958 after the Africanists led an insurgency that sought to topple the executive of the Transvaal Congress, with

Mandela himself the target, at a time when Mandela was immobilized by the treason trial. In the wake of that bitter, near physical confrontation, the ANC expelled the Africanists, who a year later formed their own competing movement, the Pan-Africanist Congress.[32]

With little organization and support, the PAC launched an anti-pass campaign but the police overreacted and massacred close to seventy demonstrators at Sharpeville, putting the international spotlight on the PAC. For the new African states, it was the PAC that was seen as the leading force for change. So when Mandela surreptitiously traveled outside South Africa for the first time, he found the ANC's multiracialism oddly out of step with the winds sweeping Africa.[33]

That is why Mandela's 1964 opening statement from the dock in Rivonia during his trial for his role in launching the armed resistance after the ANC was banned was so impressive. The ANC consciously chose sabotage solely of property, not terrorism, so lives would not be lost, and because "it offered the best hope for future race relations." Mandela reminded the judges that he spoke as an admirer of "the Magna Carta, the Petition of Rights and the Bill of Rights." With these convictions, he said, "I have fought against white domination, and have fought against black domination." For that ideal, he told the court, "I am prepared to die."[34]

Sentenced to a life of hard labor, Mandela found his core convictions challenged by each generation of new militants, especially the black consciousness movement of the 1970s that produced a wave of new inmates at Robben Island, as hostile to the ANC's multiracialism as to the government's apartheid's policies. There were violent clashes between ANC inmates and black consciousness activists who allied with the PAC.[35]

Mandela came to the conclusion in prison that neither the ANC nor the government could achieve their goals through military means. Over five years he engaged in direct discussions with white government leaders, including two years of secret talks kept from his prison mates and exile leaders. Both the UDF activists and freedom fighters would have been alarmed had they known that in 1989 Mandela wrote President P. W. Botha, with the support of the ANC in exile, lamenting the escalation that was raising "the specter of two hostile camps . . . slaughtering one another."[36]

The PAC boycotted the negotiations with de Klerk to hold elections and when it joined the campaign, advocated expropriating white land without compensation and organized menacing rallies, with chants of "one settler, one bullet."[37]

So when Mandela asked again about the PAC, my "one percent response" settled many scores and guarded he thought against a destructive black nationalism that could ruin everything he was battling to create.

FROM "NOW IS THE TIME" TO "A BETTER LIFE FOR ALL"

We all assembled again in November for two days of meetings at a conference center outside Johannesburg listening to many pollsters drone on about the state of the race. My job was to say what it all meant. Timidly, I asked the group, "How committed are you to 'Now Is the Time'?" That was the slogan on all our posters, sometimes combined with "Freedom" and "Justice." Banners with "Now Is the Time" formed the backdrop for all the rallies.

"Why do you ask?" Joel Netshitendze asked, clearly irritated, as he turned around in his chair three rows in front of me. As the de facto communications director for the campaign and editor of the principal organ of the ANC, he owned the collective effort to define the election in this powerful and simple way. He was not at all sure he wanted to grant that Frank and I could ask such a question. "Now Is the Time" was very popular with the ANC activists and had been taken up as a chant, identical in the Zulu and Xhosa languages, that animated the rallies. It had not been tested in research, but that was not my issue. When PR people create a slogan detached from anything, it can trivialize politics and I am almost embarrassed to test such slogans. But if a slogan captures the moment it can give meaning to an election. "Now Is the Time" seemed to me to tell the whole history of repression and black exclusion and to define the vote as an act of liberation. Earlier in the year, the ANC's election committee described the election as a "continuation of the contest between apartheid and democracy," and the election itself as a "liberating event to black communities." Most importantly, the campaign said, "it is not about setting up government."[38]

When Craig Charney had presented the research earlier to an election workshop, and described the weak showing among Coloureds, one activist stood up, dismissive, declaring, "We are the liberators"—with the implication that Coloureds would have to vote for the ANC in a "liberation election."

I recalled, together with Frank, that every campaign evolves and crystallizes its message and, indeed, its slogan. (Clinton's "People First" came after many false starts, only weeks before the Democratic convention.) Then I said, "I want you to consider that the phrase means exactly what it says: 'Africans are going to seize power; after years of powerlessness, they are going to take control of government.'" As I spoke to the roomful of people who had spent a lifetime fighting apartheid, I asked myself: *Who is this white American to be raising this issue?* I was nervous and began each point with an apology for speaking out of school.

"The Coloured and Indian communities, not just your committed activists, are listening to what you are saying," I continued, "and there are a lot of African voters who are holding back, too. Why is that? What is missing for them?" Now I was really taking a risk. " 'Now is the time' is an election about apartheid, about the past. Maybe people want something more, about the future; indeed, about what you will do with government."

Frank and Joel, chain smokers, retired to the outside to continue the fight. Joel was heatedly opposed to our critique. They continued the debate through the next break, although Joel agreed that the slogan should be put before a set of focus groups being held that night with African voters. Frank worked hurriedly to come up with some alternatives, drawing heavily on his recent campaigns for the U.S. Senate: "A better day," "A better future," "Together, a better future," and "A better life for all."

That night, we sat with Joel and about ten others behind the glass watching a group of African voters talk about their lives, then the election, and finally, the slogans. I wanted to kiss them. "Now Is the Time" was okay but did not light up the room. For sure, it was about power and freedom, for themselves, but after more than three years of frustration, the slogan did nothing to dispel the despondency. Putting the final nail in the coffin of apartheid was not enough. Will our lives really change? Will a new government bring an end to the violence? But "A Better Life for All" and the other slogans about the future lifted the spirits in the room. It was as if someone gave them permission to hope for something better.

Joel laughed and nodded to the Americans. Clearly, Africans wanted something more from this election and the new government, and when we conducted the same exercise with Coloureds in Cape Town, they went even further: maybe the ANC would be inclusive, for all communities; maybe it could control its own supporters and wanted peace; maybe it could unify the country. Out of the exercise I gained a mandate to explore the choices in a survey, but only if I committed to come back and personally make the case to each of the regional campaigns that they would have to give up "Now Is the Time" and accept some soft American campaign slogan.[39]

As we were having our first debates about the slogan, the "New National Party" had retained Saatchi & Saatchi, masterminds of the successful Conservative campaigns in Britain, and was already presenting itself as a new moderate party, able to bring "peace and prosperity," a home for all "God-fearing" South Africans led by "the man who abolished apartheid." De Klerk told a National Party rally that the ANC was a "dangerous" party with "dangerous economic policies" that "cheers the violence and intimidation."[40]

Then, on the fourth anniversary of Mandela's release from prison, February 2, 1994, the ANC held a solemn commemoration with Mandela and other former political prisoners lighting a "torch of freedom." De Klerk once again seized the moment to take credit for "the death of apartheid" and the NP ran a full-page ad highlighting the ceremonies: "Today, Mr. Nelson Mandela honors President de Klerk with a 'Flame of Freedom.'" Angry beyond words, the ANC put up a simple poster with a picture of all the past National Party presidents and just one line: "These people want you to vote for them." A follow-up depicted Mandela as a boxer, knocking out apartheid and exclaiming, "I did it."[41]

"Apartheid is a trap," I wrote the campaign team. "The NP wants to debate this issue because one in five Africans believed the NP has changed and ended apartheid," which was the NP's most convincing argument for the election. A majority of Coloured voters in the Cape no doubt agreed. Engaging this issue would leave us mired in the past, while the NP would be free to attack the ANC as dangerous to everyone's future. The NP was creating a choice that would produce the best electoral result for them.

I proposed that we attack the NP not for their historic wrongs, but for their current policies that left millions unemployed and without housing, and imposed a new value-added tax on food and lavished money on educating whites. That attack would lead voters to shut out the NP and to look to the ANC for the better life it could bring.[42]

With growing conviction about the strategic consequences and the need to put people at the center of the campaign, I pushed past my uncertain legitimacy and wrote: "This election is about making life better for people—not theoretical or abstract things," like apartheid.

When I returned to South Africa in December 1993, I found no resistance among the campaign team to the idea that the ANC must move from apartheid to a better life. These folks were so smart and skilled that I sometimes forgot that nobody could do any of this lawfully until now. Once they heard the strategic rationale, saw the supportive research, and watched the impact on people's mood, they moved. Ketso's quick, analytic mind consigned "Now Is the Time" to the campaign's "mobilization phase." For Pallo, the debate over "tactical" things like slogans brought home the need for the campaign to move to "an inclusive South African nationalism." He knew then that "the future . . . is where we want to go."

As the outside authority with objective data but also with the right political leanings and some knowledge of the history and terrain, I had the job of presenting this strategic turn to people in the different levels of the campaign. The team watched with some amusement to see if I would crash or carry the room of activists, a process repeated many times over the next few months as the campaign used Frank and I to build a new consensus.

One of the biggest tests we faced was in the Western Cape, where a majority of the population was Coloured and only a fifth African. The ANC leadership in the Western Cape was decidedly Africanist and believed Coloured voters should follow its lead.[43] In my presentation of the poll results I did not get into a complicated discussion about the ANC's evolving strategy. Instead I used my full White House reputation to convince the Western Cape ANC leaders that the poll numbers were real and that the campaign could not succeed without focusing on the Coloureds. We all agreed that the Coloured undecided voters were the key to the election here, but we also knew that among them de Klerk was three times more trusted than Mandela.[44]

A month after my presentation in Cape Town, the Africanists' local leadership was defeated in party elections and a new campaign team emerged, with UDF Coloured leaders and COSATU playing a much larger role. The NP immediately struck back, contrasting its own "constructive" approach with an ANC that "disrupts schooling," "breaks houses down," and "intimidates people." One poster simply declared: "ANC stands for African, not Coloured."[45]

THE PLEDGES

Well before I joined the campaign, the policy and economic team had taken over the nineteenth floor of Shell House, energized by the mix of young and old activists, intellectuals, those tutored in exile and those tutored in the UDF resistance at home, including Ketso. The Freedom Charter, with its commitment to both nationalization and private enterprise, had to catch up quickly to the market and global economy, which would have a lot to say about the ANC's economic course and policies to transform South Africa. It had to confront an economy and state finances whose condition was dire, bordering on default.

In the fall, Frank and I had asked a number of times for an outline of the policies and commitments the ANC could take into the election. Each time Ketso replied, "Soon, soon. They're coming." As it turned out, the ANC was sorting out much more than the pledges to put on a pledge card.[46]

From a distance, the apartheid regime looked set for a generation. But close up de Klerk must have known the truth. Over half the African population lived in poverty and 30 percent of the active workforce was unemployed. Short-term borrowing during the rising unrest had pushed the government perilously close to default, even as it raised pay for white civil servants to keep them on board. Capital flight from South Africa reached 5 percent of the economy in 1993 and the budget deficit rose sometimes to over 10 percent of the GDP. Any new government would face massive economic and fiscal problems.[47]

The average income of whites then was 9.5 times that of Africans, who owned almost no property and were educated in the Bantu Education System and thus had few skills.[48]

Mandela earlier had proposed that the ANC drop nationalization from its program, but drew little support. At the big policy conference that finally took place in May 1992 the party deferred to Mandela by smartly reinterpreting the ANC's economic slogan, "growth through redistribution," as two separate and parallel goals. With intense courting by the IMF, World Bank, and South African business and a lot of self-education, Mandela by 1993 persuaded the National Executive Committee, the ANC's governing body, to drop mention of nationalization.[49]

But COSATU was on a different track and continued to view "redistribution" as the route to "growth." It produced its own plan with a big role for government investment in housing, education, health, electrification, and roads.

To maintain the election pact, COSATU got the job of drafting what was called the Reconstruction and Development Program, the RDP, which was negotiated through six versions over the course of the fall as Frank and I kept asking "Where's the plan?" In a grand compromise, the ANC recommitted to redistribution as an economic strategy, but also reaffirmed the importance of fiscal orthodoxy: not raising taxes and not raising government spending as a proportion of the economy. It would expand public sector investment by re-channeling state revenues. With no mention of nationalization and a due respect for markets, the RDP got the private nod of the World Bank and IMF. With the renewed commitment to addressing inequality and poverty and prioritizing public investment and reconstructing the economy, COSATU enthusiastically signed off.[50]

The ANC's promises for the election were certainly not derived from a poll, but as Tony and Ketso began passing Frank and me lists of policies that were part of the RDP, we pushed back to make sure these were the pledges that would hold up under expert scrutiny and partisan attack. Were they affordable? Could they really be achieved? With the need to focus on a few pledges, I tried to identify which were the most credible with the public and, more importantly, revealed a bigger story about the ANC's priorities and values. And if you heard this whole list of pledges, I asked in a survey, would you think of the ANC as a serious party, ready to govern?

Mandela accepted that the election must be about the change, "the better life" that achieving power would bring. With the final draft of the RDP in hand, Pallo observed, it became "the meat on the bones of that slogan."

At the very end of January, the ANC launched its election manifesto and kicked off the campaign. A smiling Nelson Mandela traveled on a fourteen-car "freedom train" jammed with supporters that took him from the Johannesburg railway station to a cavernous hall just a mile away on the edge of Soweto where an invitation-only crowd of dignitaries, businesspeople, and diplomats awaited him. He wore a dashiki and stood on stage under a large arch of green, black, and gold balloons, the ANC's colors, and a huge banner proclaiming "A Better Life for All." Mandela told the crowds, "The ANC is ready to govern." He began with "the ANC's vision of a South Africa in which people live in peace and with equal opportunities, the ideals which sustained me during my 27 years in prison." Those were big things but they were also the low-hanging fruit from the end of apartheid. So today, he said, we come with an ambitious plan for reconstruction and development, where we reach much higher. "Democracy means more than just the vote," he added as a way of explaining the new moment. "It must be measured by the quality of life of ordinary people."

With Clinton I could watch his thoughts develop as he edited and re-edited multiple versions of a speech to capture and embrace key concepts. I was not privy to Mandela's speech-crafting process, but however he did it, it worked. He had struck precisely the right chord.

He held up the fourteen-page manifesto titled "A Better Life for All" and declared "The millions of people without jobs will be at the top of the ANC government agenda." With seven million copies of the manifesto in print, the ANC pledged to create over five years 2.5 million jobs, build a million homes with loans, underwrite public buildings, electrify 2.5 million, provide free health care to all children up to six years of age, provide ten years free education, and clean drinking water for all.[51]

With the ANC also committed to reducing taxes for the poorest, one journalist observed, "fiscal logic appeared to be seduced by undiluted idealism." Yet the campaign and Mandela believed they had laid out achievable goals. Looking back on the campaign, one academic observer noted that the proposals had the "merit of being simple, vivid and seemingly plausible," with enough detail to "appear fairly pragmatic," but also buttressed with "a battery of highly technocratic policy studies."[52] COSATU joined with the ANC because they thought this was real. And despite being seared by the experience of the Clinton budget, Frank and I did, too.

HOLDING BACK AND BREAKING THROUGH

On March 3, less than two months before the election, I was back at Research Surveys' focus group facility in an upscale Johannesburg neighborhood where many of the nicer houses had been converted into offices. Research Surveys had sent out minibuses to recruit people at bus stops and railway stations who met our key criteria, usually arranging a later meeting time or, sometimes, just sweeping them right up. I was a bit disconcerted, but learned that it was not the least bit unusual for Africans to find themselves in offices like this working in janitorial or clerical jobs or to be taken to a worksite in a minivan.

I had asked to bring together first a group of Sotho-speaking women who were undecided in their vote, with less than a Standard 8 education, meaning most maintained strong rural ties and were not literate; and a second group of older Zulu-speaking men, not migrant workers, who were also undecided. Focus groups anywhere need to be homogenous so people feel free to speak, interact, and develop their thinking, and with so many imposed divisions along race, language, urbanism, class, and gender lines, this rule in South Africa became an imperative. The groups were conducted in the people's first language, while Tony and some other members of the ANC research or communications team observed behind a one-way glass. As with almost all the African groups, there was a simultaneous translation into English, with a full English transcript from tape two days later.

I needed to have these voters in my head to crystallize my thinking for the meetings over the next two days on how to get the large number of undecided who were still holding back to break for the ANC. I sat right up against the window with my writing pad to capture the words and body language and exchanges, writing down as much of the conversation as possible, underlining some things, but also writing bracketed side notes to myself on my real-time thoughts and ideas.

These Sotho and Zulu undecided voters recruited here from the townships would speak that night for the larger group of undecideds who had been confounding us everywhere since February. In the Western Cape, we were making no progress with the Cape Coloured undecided, unlike the NP whose scare tactics were paying dividends. When we conducted an experiment and asked African respondents in the Eastern Cape to cast their votes in a "secret" ballot box, we discovered a hidden vote of 5 percent for the NP and 9 for the PAC that did not register when the interviewer asked face-to-face. The ANC vote among Africans was stuck in KwaZulu-Natal and the Johannesburg-Pretoria area—which brought me to these groups.

I did not know what to expect because focus groups in the United States with undecided voters late in the campaign usually sweep up the least engaged and socially connected, the least informed and least partisan. They are people who lack a framework for sorting out all the information and making a political choice. Focus group moderators hate these late undecided groups because it is so tough to get a conversation going. And here we were talking to mostly rural, nonliterate African women, the largest of the groups holding back. It could have been a grim evening.

But the undecided African voters were following the election very closely and had a very distinct framework in their heads for sifting through the political claims. Before the moderator could even ask a question, they began talking to one another. "What are the elections going to be for us?" asked one. "Is it going to make life better?" said another. I nearly cheered out loud. It was as if I had recruited them specifically to make my point. When the moderator asked, "What about the ANC?," they responded with a question that betrayed their fear of being hopeful: the ANC was "making promises they want to follow, but will they be able to fulfill them?" Their own discussion developed, without prompting, much along the lines of the ANC plan: "the ANC is promising jobs," "free education for 10 years," "building houses and removing the squatter camps," "better life, no apartheid."[53] One of the Zulu men in the later group repeated the ANC's distilled message: "Jobs, peace, and freedom," and then asked, as if part of the slogan itself, "Will they keep their promises?" If they do, there will be "years of waiting."

I wrote a bracketed note to myself, "Very articulate—politically." If these voters were holding back on making a commitment, they had their reasons. The elites ought to be compelled to listen to these people so they could learn some of their wisdom.

They were undecided about the ANC because they desperately wanted to believe these plans to make a better life, but their earlier hopes had been eroded by four years of turmoil and disappointing, out-of-touch political leaders.

They were not undecided because they were considering supporting other parties, like the PAC, whom they knew very well. They were just about "land, take back the land" and "drive the whites to the sea." The Zulu men, living and working in the Johannesburg area, were extremely disturbed, even embarrassed by Inkatha, the Inkatha Freedom Party. It "says nothing, only fights." It was bringing "the racism of the National Party into our ranks"; it was "just for the Zulu." And so, one of the men concluded for the group, "We don't listen to them."

They completely got what the "New National Party" was about. Indeed, they were amused by its "T-shirts and boxes of groceries"; if you agreed to be their agent, "they'll buy you a car." But as one very articulate woman put it, "Don't listen, don't read, don't want to hear anything." If they have so much to offer, "Why didn't they do it before?"

We tested attacks on the National Party, euphemistically called the proposed "contrast" phase of the campaign: its education policies (three times as much for each white student) and its management of the economy and jobs (five million unemployed). The attacks produced a deeply clarifying re-sponse: "It's time now for our children to have the best education for all the years. We've suffered 48 years." The attack on the NP's present performance led to a judgment about a half century. And it also led people on their own to say it would be different under the ANC: "The ANC is going to create jobs."

In my bracketed notes to myself during this "contrast" exercise, I noted the women started using the word "We," identifying with the ANC. They even became protective of it. Then I wrote, "Creating positives off negatives"; "Negative produces positive"; and "Running against the NP clarifies the elec-tion." These women were more likely to view the ANC's commitments as real when presented as the alternative to what the National Party would do. And I wrote in a big box in the middle of the page: "We've Had Enough of the National Party."

The very artificial focus group setting was a haven for them, allowing the women to have a discussion with other women, suppressed in a real world of capricious violence. "Everybody is scared" and "I'm confused because we don't know what's going to happen." You want to travel but "many of the taxis belong to the Inkatha." Even in the family, you have to be careful: "With all this, I can't even tell my child who I'm going to vote for." The same was true for the Zulu men who were nearly suppressing the election: "I'm not thinking about it." They spoke of not "belonging to any party" and "not knowing anything," because such things could get you killed.

But then the moderator read a statement by Mandela calling for "no more finger-pointing, let's all take responsibility" to end the violence, and all the heads began to shake, some participants almost crying. "We are all God's chil-dren"; "Right"; "Violence will not help, enough"; "Zulu and Xhosa must come together." The same Mandela statement unlocked the Zulu men, too. While some were cynical about his motives, most of the group embraced the "coming together" that would "give peace a chance." Two of the men said "makes me have hope."

Again, my bracketed comment: "Extraordinary debate—Politically so-phisticated." These undecided, illiterate voters were acutely conscious of their political history and the possibilities of the moment, suppressed by the violence and the skepticism over whether change could happen. Their reac-tion to a closing radio ad, "Magic," produced such a hopeful response that I wrote in brackets: "Must finish with positive."

THE PLAN

Suddenly the plan became crystal-clear to me. I was up long before dawn, furiously typing a memo to Mandela, the election team, and the advertising agency.[54] Yes, I said, we are on the right track with our "better life message," and optimism is up in the polls with over three quarters now saying things will get better after the election. The People's Forums are showing the ANC as "more for the people" and "in touch." The RDP and pledges are showing up in gains on having good ideas and good plans, countering some of the NP's advantage on experience.

To realize all of this, I proposed, after some long calls to Frank back in the States, a three-phase campaign for the remaining two months—a consolidation phase centered on the seriousness of the plan, a contrast phase with sharp attacks on the NP, and a closing reassurance phase that would allow people to put aside their doubts and skepticism and vote their hopes.

To make the plan as credible as possible, I said, we needed to focus in on a few commitments where the public's priorities are very clear and pretty uniform across groups: a public works program to create 2.5 million jobs (cited by 60 percent as the strongest element) and ten years of free and quality education by over 40 percent, followed among Africans by building one million houses and among Coloureds and Indians by removing the VAT on basic foodstuffs.

Gill, Joel, Ketso, Pallo, and Tony took the ideas and sat down with a dozen-strong team from the advertising agency at the agency's offices in Sandton to work through the concepts and various executions. By mid-March, the ANC would run a series of full-page print ads, with the words "OUR PLAN" on what seemed like a book jacket, next to the picture of a brick that symbolized the small houses it would build. Across the top on another ad was the banner headline, "GETTING SOUTH AFRICA BACK TO WORK." "We will create 2.5 million jobs over the next ten years through a national public works programme"—"people will be employed in public works to build houses, roads, schools and clinics; to provide electrification and telephones; to lay pipes for water and sewage." Another had the banner headline, "MAKING EDUCATION FREE AND EQUAL FOR ALL," noting that nine million could not read or write.[55]

Based on the focus groups, I did not believe voters would rally to our plan until we attacked the National Party on the economy and education. The contrast phase, which would begin in the third week of March, should start with the economy, "the NP's weakest point." We were, in fact, doing something very ordinary in democracy, making the party in power accountable, in this case, making the NP "responsible for the conditions in South Africa by saddling them with their immediate record." Attack one was the five million people the NP left unemployed, a charge found believable by over 80 percent of Africans. Attack two was the three times as much the NP spends on each white student, found believable by three quarters of Africans, but more importantly by almost half of Coloureds and Indians. Attack three was the NP-imposed VAT on basic foodstuffs.

"Rather than going back to the evils of apartheid," Joel said, "we have to show that, even now, under the new transformed de Klerk, policies still discriminate against black people." When people drew that conclusion, they stopped listening to them, bringing their role to an end.

Radio allowed us the greatest penetration with our attacks on the NP.[56] One ad opened with the sound of a ticking clock, then a voice: "Take a minute to look at the National Party's economic record. Five million people have no jobs. South Africa's standard of living has fallen every year since 1974. The National Party—the same economic policies that have kept average income of blacks six times less than that of whites." The ticking stopped and an alarm sounded, followed by music and again the voice: "It's time we had a government that gets our economy moving. The ANC has a plan to give people the training and skills they need. To create through a National Public Work Programme alone, 2.5 million jobs over 10 years." And the obvious conclusion, "The National Party had their chance. It's time for a change."[57]

Mandela was an important voice of the message, but even when he registered to vote and paused for the cameras, he said it was "to bring an end to apartheid," not to achieve any of these goals. Frank and I proposed the team create a "traveling representative of the central campaign who is deeply steeped in the strategic thinking and message of the campaign." In the 1992 Clinton campaign, that was Paul Begala. In South Africa it would be Marcel Golding, already familiar with the war room. Marcel ended up writing virtually all of Mandela's speeches on the road and inherited the job of answering Mandela's query after finishing each event: "How did I do? Did I hit the points we wanted to make?"[58]

In the campaign's final phase, I wrote, we "must end positive and hopeful," but that required reassurance about how the ANC would govern. People were holding back because of "worries about violence; worries that the ANC is too powerful and will trample on people's rights; and worries that the ANC will stand up only for its supporters." Nothing in the campaign's "crime program" communicated "firmness" or left voters any more reassured.[59]

On the other hand, Mandela's statement on "no finger-pointing" on the violence and the ANC taking more responsibility brought a strong, emotional response, confirmed by the 80 percent in the survey who found it reassuring. With the Inkatha and security forces playing such a vicious role, it wasn't easy for Mandela to say, but he knew that only he could do it.

The election team later met with Mandela to discuss my memo, which he embraced. Tony Trew called right afterward and said the president wanted Frank and me to draft a set of talking points for the national and local candidates based on it.[60] That call was a rush because we usually had to divine his thinking and because he had just signed off on the entire concept of how to conclude the election. We wrote out the talking points along with a suggestion from Frank that all candidates and party speakers carry a copy of the ANC plan with them at all times, a la Chairman Mao's *Little Red Book*.

THE FUNERALS IN KWAZULU

Up until the beginning of March, a number of key actors had refused to join the election, with violent consequences that affected the perceptions of the ANC and undermined confidence in the country's future. The violence created a level of tension and sense of personal vulnerability, all out of proportion to the closeness of the election itself.

Intransigent white nationalists, some forming paramilitary groups, staged protests in Bloemfontein and Newcastle at the end of February, demanding a separate white homeland. At a Cape Town rally, the head of the AWB (in English, Afrikaner Resistance Movement) claimed to have sixty thousand "Soldiers of God" ready to fight for their goal. More troubling was the growing alliance with intransigent homeland chiefs threatening to bar their citizens from participating in the election. On March 11, just a week after our strategy meetings, a thousand white armed commandos of the AWB rampaged through the streets of the Bophuthatswana homeland, firing wildly, in support of the chief. They were routed by the mutinous homeland defense force, but more than forty people died in the clashes while the country watched live on television the humiliating retreat and execution of some commandos. A South African Defence Force of fifteen hundred restored order and the next day the homeland was abolished.[61]

Mandela's patient determination and spirit was continually tested by the funerals in KwaZulu. Less than a week before the strategy meeting, the entire village of Mahehle crowded into a tent to bury the fifteen young people who, while preparing for voter education work, were slaughtered by an Inkatha band armed with automatic rifles and knives. Walter Sisulu, Mandela's partner in the Youth League and now deputy vice president, told the assembled, "When I look at these boxes here, my strength leaves me." In February and March, there were five massacres in KwaZulu, taking the lives of 350 people, almost all ANC supporters. Those lives took on a new meaning when an independent commission concluded that rogue police generals were financing, arming, and training Inkatha fighters. Joel, clearly angry, wrote a "reassurance" radio ad that aired decrying the National Party's responsibility for the lack of peace.[62]

Some sixty thousand mostly Zulu ANC supporters marched peacefully through downtown Durban on the last Friday in March in support of the elections that Buthelezi was insisting be delayed. But just days later, on March 28, exactly a month before the election, a demonstration by Inkatha supporters, displaying traditional weapons of spears and clubs, spun out of control and turned Johannesburg's downtown streets and towering office towers into a war zone that cost fifty-three lives. Peaceful demonstrations at the library gardens broke out in shooting, perhaps provoked by unidentified sharpshooters; the Zulu demonstrators began firing pistols and sawed-off shotguns; police fired at anybody with a weapon. A band of chanting demonstrators were circling Shell House when shooting erupted, leaving eleven Inkatha demonstrators dead, apparently shot by an ANC security guard on the first floor who feared an assault on the building.[63]

I was distraught watching the news on the assault on Shell House and couldn't reach anybody there by phone. But Tony Trew sent an e-mail with an attached note apologizing for not sending further comments on the recent survey, as promised on the phone the day before, "but today has been a terrible day and a sad one. You will know the news by now—we've had almost an hour of intermittent gunfire around the building this morning: eventually our security returned fire on a group firing into the building, killing eight people." He expressed frustration that the police did nothing to protect the building before the shooting. "Only then did the police act to disperse the marchers and cordon off the building." But now he understood the scope of this. "The police said there were at one point forty-six locations with shooting exchanges in the central business district." He then matter-of-factly proceeded to confirm the conference call on the poll for 8 P.M. South African time the next day.[64]

"I watched with horror the picture of the carnage outside Shell House," I wrote in my return note, which would become the introduction to my poll memo. "That you can still concentrate on the work at hand is testimony to your commitment. I pray for your well-being." Frank and I were calling each other feverishly and on the conference call we offered to drop everything and fly immediately to South Africa to work day-to-day on the campaign, uncertain at that point if we would have to rethink the campaign plan. That seemed more urgent than the two Democratic senators who were filibustering President Clinton's economic package at that time.

The poll I reported on was actually a breath of fresh air after so many months of failure to break through or change the mood. That probably explained why they wanted to do the conference call. The poll went into the field following the full media effort but before the latest wave of violence showed, as I wrote in my memo, "It is hard to imagine a more positive result on the main themes of the media campaign. The ANC is scoring well above its vote in all groups on 'good ideas about the economy and jobs,' 'good plans for the future,' and 'will make life better,'" that last up 7 points overall. The contrast-negative ads were working as planned, driving the ANC's thermometer score up while driving both the National Party and Inkatha down. The attacks could just have easily driven everybody down.

But what would happen next now that downtown Johannesburg was a war zone and some were accusing the ANC of an unprovoked attack on the demonstrators? I wrote, "You are in a much better position to judge reactions," but from my point of view, on the other side of the globe and immersed in the data, I expected African voters "to rally to the ANC." But I added that the ANC will almost certainly look "ever more dangerous" to white, Coloured, and Asian communities and the violence would "stall the growing optimism that furthered the mobilization of the African vote."[65]

Two days later, Tony wrote to urge us to stay put, noting that "we were all deeply moved" by the offer, but a lot was going on—steps to contain the violence, meetings with the Zulu king, and possible mediation, none of which was yet in the news—that made any "considered changes in direction" impractical for the moment. What the campaign needed more than anything was to figure out how best to raise the "reassurance theme," given what had happened.

I responded later that day, again apologetic, self-conscious that I was more than an ocean away and that my words might be "inappropriate given the unfolding situation in South Africa." People were dying and I was uncomfortable advising on how to best to advance our political goals. Though I was confident Mandela's instinctive response would be right, I urged that he "personally show his deep sorrow about the loss of life" and "call on all the institutions of the country to commit to achieving a peaceful election." He must continue to be optimistic about the election and the chance for a better life. And most important, "with the ANC only four weeks away from assuming the leadership of the country, [it] must assume responsibility of controlling events and its own supporters." With emotions high and the conviction that Inkatha provoked the violence, this was advice many would find hard to swallow. After consulting with Frank, I drafted a statement for Mandela, with two key lines: "Responsibility begins with me and every person" and "The ANC will assume responsibility for bringing peace to our country and a better life for all."[66]

The government, under tremendous pressure from the ANC, declared a state of emergency in KwaZulu-Natal on April 1 to contain the violence and prepare for elections, despite Buthelezi's threat of a civil war if the elections proceeded. In the week following the emergency, at least one hundred people were killed, mostly in ANC strongholds, and thirty thousand fully armed Inkatha supporters staged a defiant demonstration that showed the police were incapable of disarming them.[67]

When I arrived at Shell House about a week later, I saw new security measures, starting with the guards who circled my rental car, passing a large mirror underneath and inspecting the trunk before I could drive down into the basement garage. Upstairs, the seventh floor was abuzz as usual, but on the lower floors windows were still blown out from the shooting. Meetings there felt like a real war room.

An ANC print ad launched at the beginning of the reassurance phase in the closing two weeks proclaimed, "Above all, an ANC government will take responsibility for bringing peace to South Africa. Now, more than ever, it is time to accept that it is the responsibility of every South African—every individual and every group, including the ANC—to ensure that we put an end to the violence."[68]

DEBATE

Twelve days before the election Mandela and de Klerk were scheduled to debate face-to-face on national television. While Mandela trusted his skills, the campaign team, freely using Clinton's debate materials, set up a mock U.S. presidential-style debate camp complete with set, role players, video playback, and critique, thick debate books, opposition research, and props. Gill Marcus played the role of the moderator-journalist and Allister Sparks, a liberal journalist and unrelenting critic of the National Party, played de Klerk.

Mandela joined us for a discussion of the debate strategy in a classroom setting. Sick with the flu, he sat unsmiling in a small desk at the front of the classroom, clearly wishing he were somewhere else. This was the man who didn't even rehearse his speech at the dock in the Rivonia Trial and now he was being forced to put himself into the hands of these "handlers" for two days, the longest period I would have with Mandela.

Ketso began by explaining the format of the debate and the rules, then outlined the opening statement and main points we were trying to achieve, all reflecting the campaign's established strategy. The debate book, which had undergone multiple drafts, called for Mandela to claim moral standing at the start by talking about the deep sacrifices people had made to reach this point. That standing, we said, allowed Mandela to define what the election was all about: "a moment to improve lives." Only the ANC, with its "plan to build a better life for all" and commitment to "uniting the nation" could achieve that goal. Our strategy, Ketso explained, was to "create moments," memorable exchanges with de Klerk. The opening page of the debate book bore a stern reminder: "Uncontrolled anger and personal attacks on de Klerk loses the debate."

Then we moved quickly into the first full mock debate. Sparks was brilliant as de Klerk. He wasn't a complicated politician nor was his message hard to divine. He looked like an American football fullback and his presentation reflected his appearance: he just barreled ahead without fanfare, grinding it out a yard at a time.

"We ourselves took the initiative to end apartheid, opened up the political process in every sense, and learned from our mistakes," Sparks/de Klerk proclaimed in his opening statement. "I can tell you, there will never again be apartheid on an inch of South African soil. The National Party opened its heart and doors to everybody. And now with the future at stake, we have the immense experience in government and know how to make a good economy, the envy of Africa." The ANC, he said, was still consumed with the politics of protest and destruction and was mesmerized by discredited ideologies.

"Mr. Mandela, how many communists on your list?" Sparks demanded, pointing his finger at Mandela. "These are dangerous people with a hidden agenda. It is your own supporters who are responsible for the crisis in education and the violence, this very day." Sparks portrayed a commanding figure on the stage while Mandela sat silently and stiffly.[69]

Mandela's opening was scattered and defensive. The split screen showed him slumping and inattentive, his eyes wandering rather than looking at the reporter or de Klerk. He mistakenly dignified de Klerk's charge that the ANC is "untrustworthy" by defensively repeating the attack. And he attacked de Klerk for the "Third Force" but didn't take it anywhere. He arrogantly asserted that the ANC could govern with or without the National Party and defended mass action, blaming Inkatha for the violence. My notes reflected the tenor of his performance: "The opposite of reassurance." Sparks slaughtered him.

A review of the video clips was painful, but at least Mandela no longer doubted the value of the exercise. He quickly engaged and I could see the wheels turning behind those eyes, driven by the prospect of a hanging—being dominated and patronized by de Klerk before the whole country. For the first time, I was struck by the fact that he was seventy-six years old. While smart and alert and wise, his speech was plodding and he was not quick in response. No amount of training would make him a boxer again. He barely got started with his opening statement before being put off his stride when the gong signaled that his time was up. And while Mandela was truly charismatic, that charisma was derived from his whole life, that moment in history and his personal relationship with the audience, not from the eloquence of his words or delivery. His attacks were aimed correctly, but under the unrelenting attention of the camera, he looked and sounded hectoring. As I sat there watching his response framed by the TV and debate format, he looked stiff, dour, and old.

In his postmortem, Frank urged Mandela to smile, which would make him look "radiant" on TV. But Mandela thought it made him look "foolish." And if he was going to speak so s-l-o-w-l-y, Frank said, it would be best to "put your conclusions up front."[70]

At the end of the sessions, Pallo and I had the job of summarizing the good, the bad, and the ugly. I started by saying that he couldn't confine the historic choice just to the opening statement; Mandela would have to keep coming back to it. I also said it was important for Mandela to look big, not small, to come across as "presidential." That meant he could not be constantly attacking de Klerk. It was clear, even with Sparks as the stand-in, that Mandela hated de Klerk for his lack of courage and honesty in dealing with the "rogue" security forces, the thousands of dead ANC supporters, the brutality, the funerals, and his effrontery and self-congratulation on claiming credit for ending apartheid. I understood his response, but our purpose was bigger. Thus, the debate team's mantra to Mandela was to avoid being too negative and too personal; that would negate the hopefulness for the campaign's close and diminish him as a leader. Finally, I said, you need to use this rare moment to look into the camera and reassure people that you regret the loss of life and without finger-pointing, tell your own supporters and the country, "We must all take responsibility to end the violence and bring peace."[71]

After the session, Tony and I stayed behind to rewrite the opening statement. I didn't even think about the significance of that: just how was I going to cut the length in half? Tony delivered it to Mandela at home and found him sitting up in bed under the sheets in a night coat, with the massive debate prep book propped against his knees, studying. The rest of us gathered for dinner to indulge my need for Mozambican prawns.

On the morning of the debate we held another mock debate and Mandela was much better, going on the offensive, hitting de Klerk for forty-six years of no progress, failing to contain the "Third Force," and the racism of his current campaign. Sparks was again good, red-baiting all the way, which Mandela trumped well: "This has nothing to do with people's lives. They want jobs and peace and freedom."

Around midday, Marcel, Frank, and I accompanied Mandela in a sweater to the debate site at the Johannesburg Civic Theatre so that he could get comfortable with the chair and table, the placement of cameras, and positioning of his table next to de Klerk's. I used the occasion to recite the campaign mantra, noting how hard that would be in such close proximity to de Klerk. Mandela left to go home to nap and to prepare on his own.

Doing a walk-through with Mandela at the debate site before he went home for rest and preparation. [Author's collection]

When Mandela returned that evening, he was every inch the president, fitted out in a well-tailored suit, tall and erect. While Frank and I sat with him in a small green room off the stage I started to raise some issues, but Mandela cut me off, almost abruptly. He was a listener and learner during the prep but now he had arrived at some self-understanding, some clarity about what he was doing that night, and he was not entertaining discussion.

Despite his concentration on the debate that was just twenty minutes away and perhaps because of it, Mandela turned to Frank, not for media advice but to ask about his family. Frank responded, "I have a daughter three years old and my wife's expecting." Mandela, touched, said, "It must be tough being away from them with such a young child." Frank quickly responded that no, no, there is nothing more important than this. Mandela asked Frank for a picture of his daughter. "I'd like to write her a message about where you were when she was three years old."

Then he walked on stage and ripped out de Klerk's heart.

Frank and I took two of the twenty-five seats that the ANC had been allocated for the debate, even though in every other campaign we watched the debate on TV in a war-room-like setting—the only place you can really judge what is happening. But this time, we knew we had to be there. Mandela began by elevating this "historic election when many South Africans will claim, reclaim their hopes for a better life." What could be better? He thanked the "work and struggle of so many people who made the democracy a reality" and the "good work that inspired me every day during those twenty-seven years of my prison life."

From that point on, Mandela was totally on the offensive, hostile and disparaging, in some ways more pointed—some in the press said, "pedantic"—because he spoke so slowly: "Mr. de Klerk is not putting it accurately"; "He is less than candid"; "Obviously, Mr. de Klerk was not listening."

Mandela was at de Klerk mercilessly for "Third Force" activity, for distorting the official commission reports, for being "very, very stubborn" about "the involvement of senior police officials in this violence. This is the truth. That is the total picture." The press commented on the hostility of the exchanges, particularly Mandela "wagging his finger." De Klerk held his ground, hitting the ANC for promises it could not fund and the violence it could not control, while taking credit for bringing the changes that made this choice possible. At that, Mandela spoke for the ages, not the campaign. We are here because "of the suffering of the masses of the people, supported by the international community. It is them who came out to the streets, called strikes, boycotts, who were shot and killed by the racist security police of the National Party, who threw us in jail, who turned our lives into nightmares."

Watching Mandela hammer de Klerk stirred me deeply. The man deserved everything Mandela was dishing out. But I should have been watching on television where I could be more dispassionate.

Then Mandela suddenly shifted gears and changed the perception that everyone would take away from the debate. After attacking de Klerk one more time he paused for effect: "But we are saying let us work together for reconciliation and nation building," saying each word ever so slowly. Then he reached out his hand. "I am proud to hold your hand for us to grow solid together. Let us work together to end division and suspicion."

After being lectured for an hour, one reporter observed, de Klerk could not mount much of a smile but had no choice but to accept the gesture.[72]

Afterward, Mandela celebrated with the debate team, all relieved it was over, barely conscious that Mandela had just executed his own debate strategy, including the final moment. Amidst a lot of picture taking, he said to Frank and me with a mischievous smile: "I realized that you were going to be angry with me for being so mean to Mr. de Klerk, so I decided to reach out for his hand."

FINAL ACT

Mandela launched the final week of the campaign in the toughest place to reassure people about the prospect for peace, making a series of campaign

The debate prep team, myself and Gill Marcus to the left of Mandela and Marcel Golding and Frank Greer to the right, congratulating Mandela on his aggressive debate with de Klerk. [Author's collection]

visits to Natal where Buthelzi continued to boycott the election and threatened violence on election day. I learned later that the campaign had official reports that arms were being stockpiled and five thousand Inkatha supporters were training in a Natal game reserve. When Mandela spoke to ten thousand supporters at Umlazi stadium, the site of violence just a few weeks earlier, he used the moment to praise the Zulu monarch, an ally of Buthelezi, for his attempts to bring peace. One day later, the papers reported a meeting of Buthelezi, Mandela, de Klerk, and Cyril Ramaphosa, the skilled and articulate former leader of the Mineworkers Union who stood with Mandela when released and ANC's negotiator for all important things.

And on April 19, less than a week before the election, with ballots already printed, Buthelezi called off the boycott and immediately launched his campaign, bringing a rapid end to the violence that had cost 14,000 lives since Mandela's release. It also brought a change in mood and widespread cries of joy all across the country, with Zulu nationalists thrusting spears and clubs in the air and Bishop Desmond Tutu doing the comparable thing for him: "We have a God of surprises, who performs miracles all the time."[73] As one reporter observed, "the killing fields of Natal" were silent but for politicians on the hustings.

The ANC's Natal campaign and the team of pollsters were confident of an

ANC victory in KwaZulu-Natal. The real level of support was somewhat of a mystery, however, because violence kept the poll takers away and no one quite knew how many people lived in the rural areas of KwaZulu where the IFP was based. With no poll showing Inkatha ahead, including those of the state research institute and state broadcasting corporation, all observers expected the ANC to be the lead party when the votes were counted.[74]

When I went to the final election rally in Mitchell's Plain, the large Coloured home-owning area on the rim of Cape Town, I quickly discovered the big gap between the best-laid plans and the execution on the ground. Supporters were gathered in a big tent, and the defrocked Rev. Allan Boesak, whose highly publicised extramarital affairs and high lifestyle made him unpopular among Coloureds, was leading off the program. "What you've been fighting for, what you've been working for, what you've been suffering for is coming true next week," he proclaimed, undeterred by a faltering sound system. "We will be free next week! Mandela will be president next week! And the ANC will win the Western Cape next week." I paced around the tent and called Frank on my cell phone. For all our good work, the ANC's most prominent leader in the Western Cape had closed the campaign with "Now is the time."[75]

With our polls showing a shot at a third of the vote, I accepted an over-under bet with my friend and sociologist Wilmot James: a case of South African wine of our choice if the ANC captured 30 percent of the vote.[76]

On the Tuesday before the election, Mandela visited the floor of the stock exchange where the all-white traders stopped their work for fifteen minutes. That raised eyebrows among the ANC left-wing supporters, but it was an important symbolic step in the path to governance. "I am interested in economic stability in this country," Mandela told them. "Mass action was the weapon of people who had no vote" and that would end on election day. The traders' questions revealed their skepticism of the Reconstruction and Development Programme commitments that involved so much government. I'm sure Mandela wanted to say to them, you did not mind big government under the apartheid regime, but he resisted. The program was based on "sound market principles" and included "not a single sentence about nationalization."[77]

On the eve of the election, an America reporter spoke with an African woman in Alexandria township, itself surrounded by Johannesburg's wealthy northern suburbs, who told him of her hopes for a "real toilet" and "clean water." She was one of 350,000 people crammed into this square kilometer of houses and shacks, with many living in medieval squalor, walled off from the wealthy Sandton suburb, where the election team held its meetings with the advertising agency, and far from the trading floor of the stock exchange. She paid a lot of attention to the pledges for a better life, which was why the ANC's chief economist assured the reporter that a new government could finance its commitments and Pallo Jordan told him the pledges were a compact that could not be broken: "The price of failure would be a curse to South Africa."[78]

I went with the election team to the stadium for the remarkably festive final rally in the Johannesburg-Pretoria area. The ANC was in full color and showing the incredible diversity of clubs, union branches, mineworkers, football teams, police units, and dance troupes, all with flags and banners, marching with rhythmic clapping, making their way slowly to join the sixty thousand in the stadium under very blue skies. I watched in awe for hours, walking through the stands, taking photos of people completely un-self-conscious in their joy in the coming election. It was a long way from the despondency of those first focus groups.

Mandela arrived in a red shirt, visible sitting among the section of children, clapping along with music so loud that it was unrecognizable beyond the beat. His introduction brought waves of cheering but also volleys of gunshots that seemed to fade off into the vast open sky. Mandela looked grave and put aside his comments on unity, waiting for the firing to cease. "It is clear that criminality, even among members of the African National Congress, is deep-seated," he bellowed, clearly angry. "If I find out the people who are firing these guns, I have no alternative but to expel them from the organization. We do not want them!"[79]

The crowd and all of us soon returned to the festive mood, but did not easily forget Mandela's insistence on responsibility even when joining his own people in a celebration of freedom.

Sunday was the last day for campaigning and the morning calm was interrupted at 9:50 by a car bomb set off next to the regional offices of the ANC. The blast killed nine people, including an ANC candidate, and wounded almost a hundred. The two-hundred-pound bomb, the largest yet set off in South Africa, blew out windows in the nearby office building, including at Shell House. According to the police, it was almost surely the work of extremist whites, who were the only ones still outside the process.[80]

I was not at Shell House that morning. Frank and I were traveling with Mandela and the election team in his motorcade for a series of events in Durban, including the final rally of the campaign—100,000 gathered in a large flat sports ground, far larger than the ten thousand gathered for Buthelezi and Inkatha. Mandela told the crowd to be calm and "don't concentrate on the violent activities of those who want to disrupt these elections." Without apparent irony he told them to leave it to the "security forces."

The crowd had gathered up to five hours before we arrived and it appeared to be a sea of heads undulating with the music, a South African version of the waves that sweep across crowds in U.S. sports events. To get a feel for the mood and scale of it, I stupidly walked into the crowd that was pressed up against the protective fence and found myself lifted and powerless to control my course. I imagined the minor story the next day: U.S. pollster crushed, unnoticed by the exuberant crowd.

Mandela was standing on the high stage, fist raised, together with Walter Sisulu from their Youth League days, as well as Zuma, head of the Natal and KwaZulu campaign. "Now, we must work together for our country," Mandela told the crowd in English, simultaneously translated into Zulu. "The enemy of peace is also poverty, illiteracy, and hopelessness," he said, making clear one last time that his agenda went beyond the vote on Monday.

I stared up at Mandela from just a few feet in front of the high stage, taking photos, barely distracted by the some one hundred people hanging from every inch of the high tower of scaffolding that was meant for the loudspeakers and the large green, black, and gold banner, "A Better Life for All."[81]

ELECTION

When Frank and I met at the war room Monday morning for an election planning meeting, the joy and satisfaction of the day before gave way to the reality of some 23 million people going to vote, most for the first time, at nine thousand polling places, many never used for that purpose before. The bomb the day before had smashed the windows on the upper floors, making the threat of violent disruption much more immediate and real. In the next few hours, a car bomb even bigger than the one before would kill ten people standing at a taxi rank for Africans just outside Johannesburg. That bombing brought a pall over the war room because it was clear Sunday's bomb had not been an isolated event. Later that evening, three white youths rushed off in a car after throwing a bomb into a café in an African area in Pretoria, killing two more.[82]

The rectangular conference room on the seventh floor of Shell House, surrounded by offices and open workspaces, was jammed with perhaps twenty-five people. It had begun as a center for election work, but had evolved into the operations center for the ANC. With the transitional national governing body in recess and its authority transferred to the Independent Electoral Commission, the war room was the deliberative body for issues affecting the legitimacy of the election, in informal partnership with the National Party. I tried to keep my head down, lest anyone notice that Frank and I were here

Large crowd hanging on scaffolding and listening to Mandela at final ANC rally of the campaign, with banner "A Better Life for All." [Author's collection]

but nobody seemed to doubt our role, as we were the only ones who had weathered such storms before.

Ketso laid out the structure: Madiba was communicating directly through Cyril Ramaphosa, who had built up trust with all parties in the negotiations, and Thabo Mbeki, the ANC's chief diplomat in exile and second to Mandela in the leadership. Thabo and others were at the communications center of the IEC, a makeshift conference center with fourteen direct phone lines to the regions; Gill and Pallo were at the ANC's press center at the Carlton Hotel; the lawyers and health personnel were with us at Shell House, and two helicopters and an airplane were on standby.

The last agenda item was the question of declaring victory. Frank and I argued for Saturday night, two days after the balloting, when most of the votes would be counted, but well before the results would be official, which could be a week later. I argued that it was important to create a moment in which Mandela had total attention and could articulate the meaning of this victory, rather than leaving it to fate and the pundits. Most others presumed we should wait for the official final tally.

With the threat of more violence, Mandela, de Klerk, Buthelezi, and the head of the South African Defence Force made a joint statement assuring the people of a safe election, despite the right-wing violence.[83]

Everyone gathered at 4 P.M. for a meeting on the security situation. There had been nine bombing incidents and a threat of attacks on international observers, but there was a break in the case. A high-level police delegation met with Madiba. They were ready to arrest twenty-nine people clearly involved in the bombings, all with "Third Force" and right-wing affiliations, but also Inkatha, Buthelezi's Zulu party. People in the room were wary of the police arresting any Inkatha members.

I have sat through meetings on the eve of elections elsewhere, including the last war room meeting when James Carville and George Stephanopoulos gave their final speeches, but that all seems so trivial now that I was here in a country on a precipice.

Faced with such crucial issues, it was hard to concentrate on the mundane work of the election, but Tony had requisitioned volunteer computer people to work with me on a system for receiving the vote tallies and interpreting the results. We were starting from scratch. There was no vote history, no census, nothing. When the voting was done, the ballot boxes would be transported from over nine thousand polling places to nine hundred counting stations from which ANC agents on the scene would report the tally to me.

For the record, in the bottom corner of my notepad, I wrote a column of numbers: 59, 24, 6, 2, and 2, my election eve prediction for the ANC, NP, IFP, and then perhaps the PAC.

Day One, Tuesday

Voting began on Tuesday, April 26, 1994, in South Africa, a day reserved for the infirm, handicapped, and elderly, creating a poignant start for the election that those of us in the war room nearly missed. The long march to this moment and the right-wing attempt to thwart it created a steely resolve to vote. As one reporter wrote, "They came from squatter settlements and thatched huts. Some walked and some crawled. The sick and lame came on crutches. Others were pushed in wheelbarrows. Some cried, others laughed." In a country whose history was so turbulent, a calm settled over the polling places.[84] It all took on a biblical quality, as if the moment had finally arrived, and the people just came in the millions.

The special voting day was, in effect, a trial run for the real election, when many more people would vote over two days. Except for the calm at the polling places, all the signs were ominous. At the 4 P.M. war room meeting Ketso reviewed the mess. An untold number of polling places did not open, including six hundred in the Transkei where no voting equipment was delivered. The situation in the Western Transvaal, including large homeland areas, was described as "totally chaotic." IFP stickers that had to be placed on each ballot were not available in many polling places. In theory, that could disqualify those ballots or Buthelezi could contest the election. In rural KwaZulu, the polling places were under control of Buthelezi's officials, not the Independent Electoral Commission, and security was provided by his KwaZulu police force. When the IEC monitors went into the area earlier to locate possible sites for polling stations, two of the schools were burned down. So on the first day, the ANC branch there sent the war room a report already declaring "that elections in this region North of Tugela River are not free and fair" and warning that the IEC and security forces had lost control.[85]

Our people at the Independent Electoral Commission were pressing it to get control of what were being called the "pirate polling stations." Buthelezi decried the chaos elsewhere in the country and called for a two- or three-day extension of the voting, which the IEC rejected.

He would have a case for contesting if voting went forward without IFP stickers placed on each ballot. Ketso declared word must go out to all agents: "No IFP stickers, no voting." But would the IEC have the capacity to distribute the stickers to nine thousand polling places?

There were a dozen bomb scares that day, but only one bomb. It knocked down an electric pylon, the signature target of the right-wing groups.

As the momentous day ended, I was asked to outline what a Mandela victory speech would look like.

Day Two, Wednesday

Wednesday was the first day the whole country could vote. Mandela voted that morning in a high school polling place in Inanda, near the grave of John Dube, founder of the ANC. That Mandela cast his vote in KwaZulu-Natal sent a signal about the ANC's unique aspiration to lead all sections of the country.

At the early morning meeting, people were pessimistic about the Independent Electoral Commission, even though the judge who headed it said they had worked through the night to fix the problems from the first day of special voting. We decided to disperse to various parts of the Johannesburg-Pretoria area to observe the vote and then reassemble before noon to share notes. I went with Gill and her driver, joined by my wife, Rosa DeLauro, who had traveled many times with me to South Africa and could not stay away during the election. We went to Soweto, visiting polling place after polling place, mostly in schools but also community centers. As early as it was, the lines were already long, very long, stretching down the streets and around the block, people speaking quietly. Even the babies, held tightly to their mother's backs with blankets, seemed quiet. While the long lines seemed not to be moving at all, the voting in the polling places was proceeding at a steady and unhurried pace. Nobody appeared worried about the lines; they were savoring the whole experience. To our fright, the moderator stopped the voting to show the white observers—and indeed, all the international observers—how they were checking voting cards and checking hands with an ultraviolet light to reveal the telltale ink of multiple voting; they showed us the ballot, IFP sticker attached, on which people placed a mark by any party, and the cardboard voting booth that allowed people to mark the ballot in private before putting it in the box, with its seal. At each polling station, we looked back at the lines and the story was the same everywhere: calm reigned.

But back at Shell House for the 11:30 meeting we found that a lot of things were conspiring to break the calm and test voters' patience. Overnight, the police had raided a KwaZulu training camp and seized weapons and documents. That morning a white man had parked a white Peugeot just outside the international departures hall at Jan Smuts Airport. The explosion after he fled caused much damage and injured eighteen people.

Ketso and Frank came back from the East Rand, an industrial area east of Johannesburg where there were no ballot papers and no IFP stickers at many polling places in the African areas, even as all the white, Coloured, and Asian areas were up and running. That deepened the sense that the IEC had allowed the old apartheid order to be replicated in the organization of the vote. Mandela went on television to declare that "It is clear to me that there has been massive sabotage."[86] When we reassembled at 2 P.M., there still were no ballots in the East Rand and the military was warning of potential violence. Somebody reported a rumor of people in Alexandria burning down a polling station, but a check quickly concluded it was false. More sinister were reports that in the Northern Transvaal, where the white Conservative Party was in control, that no ballots had been delivered to the post offices, the polling stations for the large former African homelands. "Those niggers are going to burn things down," Pallo warned, articulating as only he could the worries of the war room. The IEC was busily printing two million new ballots.

That afternoon, the police arrested thirty-one members of the Afrikaner resistance elite unit, including two police officers, strongly suspected of involvement in the wave of right-wing bombings. But at that point, the right-wing violence seemed the least of the problems. The reports from ANC people in northern KwaZulu-Natal read more like appeals to the world by prisoners behind enemy lines. The ANC party agents and IEC monitors fled the polling stations with the arrival of armed Inkatha youth, and later the head of the ANC in the province saw his house burn down.[87]

There was such an overload of problems that the 7 P.M. meeting became an urgent search for reliable information on the extent of the problem to enable us to develop an action plan. Voting would end the next day. Ketso dispatched the helicopter to the East Rand for an update and the leader in Transkei was scheduled to give us a report by 8:30 that evening. With the Natal problem still not picked up by the national press, the ANC needed a national person—Cyril Ramaphosa, as it turned out—to travel there and report back on how serious were the issues.

Day Three, Thursday

At 6:30 A.M. on the last day of voting Cyril's report from Natal prompted us to discuss at some length how to send up urgent alarms without the ANC itself crossing the line and looking like it was disputing the result. But the main focus was how to get the voting extended an extra day in the old homelands, particularly in the Transkei and the rural homelands in the north, areas where we expected the ANC vote would top 90 percent. If we got it wrong, a lot of votes could be lost. The South African Defence Force was being deployed in KwaZulu-Natal.

The world grew excited about the dramatic aerial shots of the maze of voters twisting all through the fields waiting at polling places all over South Africa, but in the war room, we grew alarmed, lest those voters start to head home. We used Radio Transkei to plead with people and dispatched Winnie Mandela and others to walk the lines and persuade people to stay and vote. Ketso redeployed his forces in the most dramatic way I have seen in a campaign, moving seventy buses and "loud hailers" from the Eastern Transvaal sixty-four miles to the north and commandeering a hundred taxis from the Pretoria-Johannesburg area, sending them up to the Northern Transvaal to move people to working polling stations.

Finally, at 3:30 P.M., the IEC declared that while it was satisfied with the overall voting situation, balloting would be extended a day in the ex-homeland areas with the counting to start on Saturday.

That afternoon Rosa and I commandeered Gill's car and driver and headed west and north, traveling in a ring around the metropolitan area to visit a string of polling places in more remote areas. The polling places were in schools or community centers, always in a brick compound, most surrounded by fields. As it turned out, there were real people in those motionless conga lines, but they were as calm as they had been the day before. Rosa, a member of the U.S. Congress and an accomplished campaigner, began to work the line to see if the frustration was growing. She asked a young man who had been in the line for over twenty-four hours why he was staying. "If I will be able to vote and come out into this field and be killed, at least I will have voted once in my life," he told her through a translator. Rosa hugged him, then teared up as she told me the story. Those are the moments when you have to suspend all the cynicism that keeps you from understanding why all these people have come.

My wife, Congresswoman Rosa DeLauro, greeting voters who waited in long queues over night to cast their first vote. [Author's collection]

The Natal complaint had been formalized on ANC national stationery. It reviewed the efforts to gain redress, but also stated in clear legal context: "we wish to put it on record that the ANC has received extensive reports of violations of the electoral laws, regulations, and code of conduct."[88] The leaders of the Natal ANC were angry and drove up to Johannesburg at 2 A.M. to attend the press conference later in the morning where the complaint would be announced.

At as I settled in for that evening's meeting, I noted at the top of my pad "Too tired to take notes." There was much pressure from the Independent Electoral Commission on the ANC to declare the election "free and fair," something we clearly did not believe. The good news was that the monitoring division of the IEC, led by a strong lawyer, Peter Harris, had waged "a palace revolt," as one reporter called it, and with the help of the Defence Force got ballots and equipment distributed in the Transkei and then took charge of voting nationally.[89]

Day Four, Friday

Well before dawn on Friday morning Rosa and I were driven to a small airport where we joined Gill on a small private plane for a lightning inspection of key towns in the remote Venda homeland. We spread out and went to a number of the polling places, which were open but with no voters, just monitors and workers waiting for someone to arrive. But no one came. Where were the voters? Didn't they learn of the extra day? Did they give up and go home? We then tried another approach, each of us canvassing the stores on the block of buildings, the clinic, the bus stop, the water tap, the men sitting on stumps. We could not find a single person who had not voted. Venda was calm, too.

We flew back for a meeting with Mandela, my first with him personally since the election began. The war room moved en masse up to the eleventh floor board room, situated between Mandela's office and a matching one for Oliver Tambo, who died soon after his return from exile. There was a side table for the coffee and a desk at the end of the room, where Mandela put his papers. Maybe fifteen of us took up seats around the much bigger conference table in a quieter setting to lay out the grim reality in Natal and lay out the plan of action for Madiba, who had already spoken out in anger about the process. Ketso convened the session by reviewing the state of the voting process around the country, quickly turning to the unresolved question of KwaZulu-Natal, where the expulsion of the monitors, "pirate" polling stations, and complete Inkatha control threatened to make a mockery of the election. As usual, Ketso described the situation rapidly without adornment, and then yielded to others, each of whom, including me, elaborated on some aspect of the problem. The consensus began to build toward taking action. There was some talk of the rising anger of our own supporters in Natal who believed, with my support, that only such a grand theft could deny the ANC a victory in KwaZulu-Natal. As each person spoke, Mandela circled the table, thinking. Barely noticed by others, he took up the coffeepot and my eyes followed him as he went around offering to pour coffee for each person, an offer I accepted. Such a simple gesture but, I thought, a measure of his thoughtfulness and courtesy that made him even larger in scale.

Mandela had said nothing during the discussion. Then he brought the room to a full stop. "Tell the comrades to cancel the press conference. We will not do anything to make the election illegitimate. The ANC will not say the election is not 'free and fair.' Prepare our people in Natal and the Western Cape to lose." In a stroke, he had dissolved the consensus and asked us to educate the ANC activists as we were about to count the ballots. As if waving a wand, he made everybody seem small for not thinking bigger, including me, who should have known better than to get caught up in the war room hothouse. He embraced and thanked each of us as he departed, without any further discussion of the issue, leaving it to Ketso to sort out who would tell the Natal comrades to brace for a loss.

They demanded and got a meeting later in the day with Mandela in that same room to express their anger over the decision and to reverse it, but Mandela would not change his mind.

Mandela held a press conference in which he noted the problems that nearly left millions unable to vote and said "the irregularities" were being investigated, but that he believed the voting would be judged "free and fair."

Mandela's calm quickly gave way to reality in the war room, where everyone gathered for the 9 P.M. meeting, including Thabo Mbeki, pipe in hand, and all of Mandela's personal team. With the polling places closed, everybody was there for Cyril's reports on the "total chaos" at the IEC center, where there was "no security and nobody in charge." He said straight out, "The whole counting machinery has collapsed" and estimated it would take four or five days before the counting could even begin. His report had a cataclysmic feel, tempered by the fact that at least the IEC was no longer saying, "everything's fine." The rules provided that no counting could begin before "reconciliation"—matching each ballot box with a polling station and matching the number of ballots with the number of voters there—yet the lawyers were reporting that "There is too much chaos to reconcile."

De Klerk, Mandela, and the chair of the IEC met. Cyril Ramaphosa noted that the judge had "lost confidence in the directors at the management level and is shivering. He fears the whole thing will collapse." The solution described by Cyril was to have the suspended Transitional Executive Council, the TEC—the earlier working partnership of the NP and ANC—to move in to supervise the process. Stop all the counting, then reconcile and begin counting again, with results becoming known from Saturday to Tuesday. "If they fail in this," Cyril concluded, "the country faces disaster."

The room exploded, though slowly as each person elaborated on his or her objection to the solution. The Transitional Executive taking over would be viewed as an "ANC–National Party takeover of the counties process." It would be better to bring in people from "civil society, businesspeople" with management background, one of the legal team recommended. Others believed that solution would create an opening for the Inkatha to say the election was rigged. Pallo backed that position and urged that the administrators resign and put Peter Harris and his lawyers, who earlier took over the monitoring, in charge. An increasingly intense discussion produced a decision, summarized for impact by Thabo: "The TEC must withdraw any staff support and the ANC must communicate it is opposed to any TEC involvement." My notes say Thabo wanted to strangle Cyril.[90]

The war room then focused on mobilizing everyone's networks of skilled people. For his part, Ketso formed hit squads to troubleshoot and go into different counting stations. They pressed the IEC to move on some basic things:

Meeting of the greatly expanded campaign team in the war room of the ANC headquarters in Shell House in the final days of balloting for the 1994 election. Starting on front, left-hand side and going around the table: Azar Cachalia, Geraldine Fraser-Moleketi, Marcel Golding, Carl Niehaus, Joel Netshitendze, Gill Marcus, Thabo Mbeki, Sydney Mufamdi, Essop Pahad, Jabu Moleketi, Ian Robertson, Tony Trew, Ketso Gordhan, and my coffee cup, papers and phone. [Author's collection]

secure the counting sites, make sure the workers were paid, and take the disputed boxes in Natal to the central counting area in Durban.

THE COUNT

I moved over to the ANC's media center, set up in a ballroom, with the press in the middle and the election team working out of a series of partitioned offices along the side. The hotel was buzzing with international press, NGOs, and ANC people, mostly aglow from the grandeur of the voting, though the massive problems in administration were becoming a growing part of the story. Awed by what they witnessed at the polling, journalists described the election problems as "snafus" and "snags," a counting process with "considerable early confusion," "almost comically glitch-ridden," dominated more by Murphy's Law than malice.[91] The counting was starting a day late and slowly, though Tony Trew and I were set up with our team, modem and phone lines and computers, waiting for calls from the counting stations that bypassed the official process at the IEC. But like every other campaign, the results came in unidentified, scribbled on the back of a napkin from a reporter on the scene or a secret call from an ANC worker to Ketso.

By Sunday morning, after counting overnight, the IEC reported results for 8 percent of the total registered voting population, with the ANC starting the day at 54 percent. But in our cluttered workspace we had many more tallies, though they were still too few and too scattered to allow me to discern any patterns. I kept staring at the fragments, acutely aware that I had pushed hard for the ANC to take control early of the interpretation of the election results. There were no results from KwaZulu-Natal because all the ballot boxes had to be shipped to the Durban Exposition Centre where the two parties, at war for the last four years, faced each other in the counting process. By Sunday afternoon the disputed ballot boxes had been segregated from the others, allowing the counting to begin only from a few rural KwaZulu polling stations that put Inkatha in the lead. The count was slowed by protesting unpaid counters and bomb scares.[92]

Even though we didn't know when victory would come, Tony gave me a draft of Mandela's victory night speech and asked whether I wanted to add anything. I wrote sections of President Clinton's State of the Union and health care addresses but somehow this was more personal and weighed heavily on me. I escaped out of the hotel to a café and concentrated on the front part, rewriting sections to state clearly what the election was about. In any case, Tony told me that Mandela's instruction to him was that a "better life for all" must be the main theme and, above all, all the parties joining the unity government had an "obligation" to get behind the Reconstruction and

Development Programme and the pledges. I did not notice amidst the madness over the voting that two days ago Mandela, when asked skeptically about his ability to implement his plan, including a million new houses, responded that he would raise taxes before cutting back the plan: this "is the minimum policy which we have to address the basic needs of the people. It is inconceivable that any time we will cut down on that policy."[93]

By Sunday afternoon, I felt fairly confident enough about the contours of the election, the scale of the win and support in key groups, to brief the team and prepare talking points for Cyril, who was to hold a press briefing at 5 P.M. I was entirely on my own; everyone seemed prepared to let me take the fall if I got it wrong. For his part, Cyril was happy to claim a landslide victory based on my reputation as Clinton's pollster.

My memo projected that the national vote would give the ANC 58 percent of the vote and that it would rise higher as the African rural vote came in; that the ANC would win the Northern Cape, only possible because the ANC was close to winning half of the Coloured vote there; that the ANC would win the industrial heartland of the Johannesburg-Pretoria area with around 60 percent of the vote; that the ANC would win almost 95 percent of the African vote in the Northern Transvaal, the former homeland, and finally, that the PAC had "no support base anywhere in the country." With the slow count and no projections from any of the broadcast media, the press reported Cyril's prediction of an "overwhelming victory," based on tallies from ANC observers, "analyzed by the organization's American pollster, Stanley Greenberg," noting, "Greenberg is also President Clinton's pollster."[94]

The ANC in effect conceded the Western Cape to the National Party, with Sunday morning returns showing the National Party with 54 percent and the ANC at 34 percent, both a point above what each would ultimately get.[95] The ANC result was strong enough for me to call Wilmot to ask him to select the wine, a case of 1986 Meerlust, a vintage some believe to be the best South African wine of the last half century.

On Monday, defying all pre-election polls and the deep presumption within the ANC and myself, Inkatha was ahead in the count in KwaZulu-Natal, which we believed could only have been produced by a rigged election. In a few days the press reports would be full of accounts of serious irregularities, disputed boxes, and near chaos in the Durban counting station where the votes were tallied. What I did not know was that on Monday, the ANC—no doubt with Mandela's strong hand—allowed the 112 disputed ballot boxes from Zululand to be counted, giving the IFP an absolute majority of 51 percent in the region and 11 percent nationally.[96]

A year or so later, Buthelezi was overheard to say, "At the end of the day, we all go with what was in Dr. Greenberg's poll."[97]

VICTORY NIGHT

A very hoarse Nelson Mandela declared an end to the journey with this call: "We ask you all to join us. Let's get South Africa working because we must together, without delay, begin to build a better life for all South Africans."

It was a joyous room at the Carlton Hotel in downtown Johannesburg that had just heard Thabo Mbeki announce with a broad smile, "Ladies and gentlemen, I present to you State President Nelson Mandela." The sound of it was glorious to anyone who knew that just five years ago these people were prisoners or terrorists, saboteurs, "enemies of the state." After his speech, Mandela danced on the stage, no doubt joined by millions as they learned the news. A choir, joined by everyone in the room, sang "Nkosi Sikelel' iAfrika:" "God Bless Africa."

There was no history of such victory nights for most South Africans. But with half the vote counted, the ANC vote stood at 63 percent and the ANC win was inescapable.

Rosa and I were pressed up against the rope cordon, guarded by an intimidating ANC security detail that was intent on defending the stage for Mandela. We stood next to Coretta Scott King, with her own security contingent from Atlanta that was pressing the guards to let Mrs. King join Mandela on stage. My immediate reaction amid the crush was, "that's nervy." I noted that Walter Sisulu was not on stage. But Mbeki was a bigger man than me. When Mandela told the crowd, "You can loudly proclaim from the rooftops: we are free at last," Mbeki acknowledged Mrs. King and corrected Mandela with the full quote, "Free at last, free at last. Thank God Almighty, we are free at last."

Mandela gave more than a victory speech, evidence that his mind had already begun to turn to the mandate and his obligation to the "ordinary, humble people" who had voted to "reclaim this country as your own." In the prepared text, he held out "a hand of friendship to the leaders of all parties . . . to join us in working together to tackle the problems we face as a nation." But on stage Mandela added an obligation not in the speech text: "If there any attempts to undermine the programme, there will be tensions in the government of national unity. Nobody will be allowed to participate in the government of national unity to oppose the programme."[98] Mandela showed as much passion for the program as for the freedom just won and had already started to educate and cajole his government, not yet formed.

Mandela's dance on the stage gave the room permission to celebrate and for the team to let up, to no longer worry that if you lost your focus, it would all go badly wrong. In fact, the troubled counting process would go on for a week and produce what a European Union report described as "an approximate

Celebrating after Mandela declared victory on May 2 (left to right) with Marcel Golding, Ketso Gordhan, and Tony Trew. [Author's collection]

result."[99] But that night we got to hug and drink, with a sense of triumph that you only get in an election campaign—even in this one, where the choice of president was known from the beginning. What was contested was the meaning of the election and whether these parties—shaped by the decades of racial domination and managed tribal conflict—could allow an election in which every citizen could vote. The answer was in the lines more than the process, which is why I was desperate to get out of the hotel to be among people on their night.

At 2 A.M. Gill Marcus and her driver, Rosa and I jumped into Gill's car, decorated with ANC posters and flags, and headed to Soweto—to Jabavu Stadium and Orlando, where much of this history began. It was mad, three white people and an African driver, but Gill could go anywhere, particularly that night, as the celebration and dancing followed us on our slow drive. When the car stopped, people draped themselves over the hood and windshield, but slid off and jumped up and down with fists raised when we opened the windows to share the excitement. The crowds had thinned somewhat, but some would continue to celebrate long after we had passed.

Almost six months later, in October 1994, Nelson Mandela came to the United States for the first time as president of South Africa and was hosted by President Clinton and the first lady, only the second state dinner of the Clinton presidency. Unwilling to throw a tantrum to get an invitation to the dinner, Rosa and I attended the concert afterward featuring Whitney Houston under a tent in the Rose Garden. The mood followed Mandela wherever he traveled and that night Whitney Houston reached for something special. After the last song, all the guests remained standing at their seats while President Clinton and President Mandela made their way up the center aisle, much as if they were in a wedding, except that they stopped frequently to greet people along the way. The president said a warm hello as he passed and when Mandela reached us, he lit up and reached for the president, grabbing him literally by the collar, "Bill, Bill. This man elected me president of South Africa." Always ready for such a moment and facing a very difficult congressional election in only a month, the president came back and put his very large arm around my shoulders and said, "Apparently, he did a better job for you than he's doing for me."

THE MANDATE

When Mandela has arrived at a conclusion in his own mind, he becomes brutally single-minded, and in all his public addresses in the week after the election, he began lecturing on the character of the mandate. "The people of South Africa have spoken in these elections. They want change," he reminded those about to assume power. The cornerstone of that change was the Reconstruction and Development Programme, the RDP. And while still "fully committed to the spirit of a government of national unity," he warned at the grand parade preceding his inauguration, "we are determined to initiate and bring about the change that our mandate from the people demands." By the next day standing atop the hill of the Union Buildings in Pretoria, he began his inaugural address with the common obligation "to produce an actual South African reality that will reinforce humanity's belief in justice, strengthen its confidence in the nobility of the human soul and sustain all our hopes for a glorious life for all."[100] With my work in America in turmoil, I chose not to go back to South Africa with the White House delegation just a week after the victory night, but those words nevertheless were a wonderful birthday present for me. This victory was special and personal for Rosa and me and I selfishly didn't want to be part of the big crowd of "beautiful people" rushing to be in Pretoria.

Each year thereafter, South Africa celebrated Freedom Day on April 27, the anniversary of the country's first free elections. And each year, Mandela spoke with increasing urgency of that election's mandate. "The ultimate goal of a better life has yet to be realized," he said in 1995, acknowledging the freedoms won, but cautioning that South Africa must "strive to do better, and even better." By 1997, he was reminding voters of the mandate in the very first sentence: "three years since we made a pledge to work together as a nation to bring a better life for all."[101]

Some social scientists, schooled in the old South Africa, looked at the results of South Africa's first election and saw a "racial census" or "a liberation election," that had little to do with "issues" or a "mandate."[102] But in a racially and ethnically charged environment, the ANC was one of the few parties that sought and won votes across all groups. Immediately after the elections, three quarters of the voters and large majorities of Coloureds and Asians believed the ANC was the one party that looked after all in South Africa, not just one group. Mandela led the only major party that ran on a broad set of issues, rather than group rights. The mandate Mandela embraced reflected the overriding priorities shared by all groups for the new government: unemployment and jobs, housing, education, lack of water, crime, and peace.

Going from "liberation" to a "better life" was critical to the ANC's mobilizing its own party's supporters and reaching out to others during the election. But as Mandela clearly understood, it created the mandate that would weigh on the new government and entitle ordinary citizens to demand accountability.[103]

REALITY

The new government faced daunting challenges of poverty, lack of basic services—from water to housing—unemployment, and a staggering inequality in income, wealth, and investment in human capital. It took over a nation whose priorities were a hangover from the apartheid era, saddled with a bloated civil service with guaranteed jobs and an uncertain capacity and will to implement bold new programs. It inherited a declining economy and incomes, weighed down by a massive and growing debt load and interest payments, capital flight, and protected industries. The pledge of the RDP was to restore the fiscal stability in government, while simultaneously reordering priorities and investing boldly in new ways.[104]

From the vantage point of the financial markets, South Africa's position was fragile, to say the least. Mandela and Mbeki were forced to affirm the primacy of austerity and appoint a National Party finance minister, retain the head of their Federal Reserve, and make austerity official ANC policy, even if meant delayed RDP targets. The results were high interest rates and a constrictive economic policy for nearly the whole of the ANC's first term in office. The first budget raised the proportion of the budget for education, health, and housing by barely a percentage point each.[105]

Under the old regime, the government had total responsibility for building African houses outside the homelands. Under the new regime, no houses were built for two years. Yet the government did move almost immediately to expand access to water, electricity, health care clinics, and schools. With the government working visibly to shift direction, over 70 percent of whites and Coloureds and 80 percent of Africans believed the country was headed in the right direction.[106]

The government appointed a former head of COSATU, the trade union congress, as the cabinet minister responsible for meeting RDP targets, but the super-agency proved redundant and came into conflict on economic priorities. Within two years, the government, at the direction of deputy president Thabo Mbeki and effective prime minister, adopted a new strategy, GEAR (Growth, Employment, and Redistribution), to formally prioritize economic growth, achieved by stringent deficit reduction and sharp tariff cuts, privatization, and moderated wage increases, combined with increased infrastructure investment and further shifts of spending to social needs. COSATU attacked the program as an abandonment of the RDP.[107]

The government succeeded in sharply reducing the deficit to below 3 percent by the end of the five-year term and the economy grew modestly, around 2.5 percent, after years of decline. As pledged in the RDP, public investment did not rise as a percentage of the economy. All of this won the ANC government great respect in financial circles and allowed a more expansive policy in the ANC's second term. The ordinary voters, however, did not understand that fulfilling the election compact depended on satisfying financial markets, a constituency that did not have a vote in that first election.

FOUR YEARS

At the end of 1997, the public was in an ugly mood. According to the polls, the ANC's support had dropped to around 53 percent. With Mandela announcing in the summer of 1996 that he would not seek a second term as president, deputy president Thabo Mbeki carried the burden of the government's uneven performance, without Mandela's common touch and authority.[108] Whites, Coloureds, and Asians were dispirited. The National Party was faltering, without a political home or much hope. Voters were feeling detached from the centers of power and pulling back from all the national parties, with one in four not supporting any party.

At the outset of 1998, almost four years after the first election and just over a year before the second, the research team organized focus groups to make sure we understood this disengagement before giving any thought to how we would go back to voters for a renewed mandate. The campaign was managed by Roshene Singh and a new Elections Commission, the ANC's campaign committee for the next election, the old team having been swept up into government.[109] Roshene was responsible for the vast voter education effort in the first election that achieved a nearly universal vote and took over the campaign for the local elections, winning under the banner "Better Life for All—Make It Happen Where You Live." Roshene is a short, tough woman who speaks in short, pointed bursts, with a dry sense of humor and sensitive bullshit meter. Like her husband, Ketso, she knows how to get things done.

Early in 1998 we held focus groups in Johannesburg and Cape Town, among rural Africans in Pietersburg and in Nelspruit near Kruger National Park and Umtata in the Transkei. I was not at those sessions, though I attended others a few months later. It didn't matter. We were virtual at that point, with Tony Trew and others sending me e-mails with their verbatim notes and observations during the groups and a transcript of the discussion a few days later. What came through was the eloquence of these ordinary Africans and these would soon capture the attention of the "rich and powerful." They spoke of a distant ANC political class, expressed metaphorically, multiplying the power of their observations. "Today, their stomachs are full so they are no longer near us," a Cape Town woman observed about the ANC politicians, affirmed by a simple man in Johannesburg: "Our Premiers and Councilors—they live well but look at the people on the ground. [We] had hope they will lead us well, but they have forgotten us—the very people who have elected them." Others jumped in to underscore the point:

> It is like a man who marries a woman: he promises to do everything for this woman. When he fails, who suffers?
> The government promised a lot of things. He promised us houses, free education but none of those things are fulfilled.
> These councilors are there to eat money.
> They have the best food and give us leftovers.

The people "up there see the change" because they do well, "but we down here, things are still the same," an unemployed man recounted. They couldn't even throw the ANC out because they were halfway through their meal: "These people came to power with empty stomachs. Now their stomachs are half full; so now, if we bring another person with an empty stomach, we'll be poor forever."

Put simply, the poor were hungry because the political class had filled its stomachs, leaving little for the poor to eat. How else could we explain why the ANC walked away from its promises to the people and left so many lives unchanged? That left them feeling used and abandoned. "If they cared for us, they could reduce their salaries and give to the poor." Another concluded, "So, the best thing is for me not to vote at all, because they are getting richer and I am poorer. When it rains, I don't know where to go because I do not have a house."

The violence of crime and lawlessness was closing in on their lives, making the abandonment that much more poignant: "The government has no law"; "A man who raped a little girl, got bail and came back and killed the little girl"; "People are scared because the police do not protect them." The ANC politicians off in a world of their own failed even to protect them.

In March 1998, with the public polls showing further erosion of ANC support, the campaign commissioned its first genuine national poll—1,300 interviews in all regions and all groups.[110] The results concentrated the mind: the ANC was at 50 percent, a red line few thought would ever be crossed, and among Coloureds and Asians, support dropped to embarrassing levels.

I received the survey results and graphs in New York just as I departed for Johannesburg on April 19. It didn't take a close reading to figure out that we were in dangerous new territory. At dinner that night Roshene and Ketso weren't surprised and told me to be totally frank the next day with the Elections Commission. I spent most of the night studying the data and preparing my notes.

Focused on the struggle to govern successfully since the first election, few had paid much attention to election preparations. But this meeting of the campaign committee back in the war room brought out the top advisors to the president and deputy president, key members of the national executive, joined by a sizable portion of the 1994 team, including Gill Marcus and Pallo Jordan. I sat in the middle along the long side of the table with Tony at my side and Roshene sitting at the end corner. Still, I knew I was on my own. My unstated instructions: use your reputation and position as an objective outsider to grab them and shake them.

"This is a very disturbing poll," I said, making eye contact around the table, picking up a mix of reactions that were not yet clearly formed. "Unless we change the dynamic developing in the country, the ANC risks a low turnout and disappointing performance, including defeats in key regions. . . . It risks a racially polarized and dispiriting election result." With half of the citizenry believing things were getting worse in the country, there was no reason to assume this was the bottom.[111]

In almost all areas important to Africans, they believed conditions were getting "decidedly worse and believe the government is doing a poor job." In some areas, like jobs, that judgment approached near unanimity. The conclusion had a special power, I said, because they also believed the ANC government was distant from the people. Then, focusing closely on my notes to now avoid making eye contact, I noted that people were drawing ugly conclusions from news stories about ANC politicians taking gifts and bribes. Drawing directly from the focus group results and feeling an obligation to these people to speak to power, I said, "There is poignancy in the perception of a government that does little about poverty and starvation, but is at the same time wasting money, driving in fancy cars, and 'no longer live here.'"

The problem facing the ANC was not the defection of supporters to other parties but an alienation and disengagement that could take a third of Africans out of the electorate and a racial polarization that could undermine the ANC's "moral authority." As I moved the problem to this more elemental level, I was conscious that being seen as an objective outsider alone did not provide me the space to make this assertion. I had also to be seen as committed to the ANC's political project. Being objective and committed are often at odds but my life and this role required it—tested as never before.

While I had been told before the meeting that those attending needed to hear what I was saying, most were silent during the very tense session. Some strongly disputed the accuracy of the findings and some even attacked the methodology. Many in the room just could not accept that the change from a white to all-race government did not matter. They were like the journalist Allister Sparks, who looked down from the press gallery of the National Assembly and saw the rainbow diversity on the floor and wrote that "what is before me now cannot possibly be real. The change is too great." For all that had been undone, they could not believe that what had been done had not touched people. They knew that a rural African woman used to walk twelve kilometers every day to get water and wood, but now walks only a hundred meters and has a television.

They also believed that the ANC government had made brave decisions about public finances and a crippled economy that was nearly finished off as we were meeting by the Thai financial crisis, which prompted panicky investors to withdraw a billion dollars from South Africa and send the South African stock market down 40 percent.[112] There was not a lot of patience with my critique of their stewardship, which Mandela declared unapologetically had brought "economic successes."

Are you saying we should not be talking about our accomplishments? they asked. My heart stopped, as Clinton had asked that very same question and my answer contributed to my departure from the White House. But I carried on. I am sure you should, I replied, but more as a work in progress, not a finished product. And while I was not quite sure of the formulation, I knew the ANC must find some way to "acknowledge the lack of progress" or obstacles to progress. In democratic countries, leaders of governing parties conventionally give voice to their frustrated ambitions and incomplete control over government, but here, our supporters believed the ANC's election by definition would bring popular and total control over the formerly strong white government. Well, we needed to "step outside the government and freely express frustration and anger that things have not improved." Looking around the room, it seemed like I was speaking a foreign political language. But they could not be this voice, I concluded, if the ANC political class was seen as "corrupt and distant and out of touch"; we would get an audience "only by dramatically shifting the ANC downward."

As a start, Joel said it was critical that I present these findings to the deputy president, who would be the candidate for president next year. I flew to Cape Town for a one-on-one meeting, with Joel observing. Unlike the Shell House meeting, Mbeki listened without pushing back, poker-faced, but apparently taking the results seriously. He still seemed the diplomat who chooses his words, an intelligent man who engages and thinks through issues in a complex way. I had no idea what he made of me or the research or the whole idea of engaging with the public. There was no indication he wanted to be as deeply involved as Mandela was. Using the voters' own metaphors, I told him that they see the politicians on a "gravy train," while the people were being left behind, with empty stomachs.

I raised the question, not addressed at Shell House, about what role he would play as the campaign became more formal. In his function as the de facto prime minister, he was seen as a doer and manager, but not a person of the people. In focus groups, people spoke of him as "high-class" and "because he doesn't reach grassroots levels, he's always at the top." I did not share with him some of the graphic metaphors people used to describe him. However, there would come a moment when he would have the stage alone and people would listen to him in new ways. The campaign needed to figure out the role that only he could play.

Back in Johannesburg I had a breakfast meeting with Mandela at his house with Tony Trew, Melissa Levin overseeing the research from inside, and Jannie Hofmeyr, who was again fielding all the surveys. We were standing having coffee and cake when Mandela came down, tending to his grandchildren and appearing in no hurry to get down to business. He was interested in what each of us was doing, particularly Melissa, the youngest in the group. But suddenly, he said okay and we sat down in the living room, with Jannie and I together on the couch. Mandela pulled up a chair right in front of us, no more than three feet away, either to focus his attention or because he couldn't hear. Because of his manners and mission, I didn't have any worry that he wouldn't listen or understand the metaphors and plea of the people in those groups. I started with the 50 percent red line we had crossed, the third of Africans who were detached and alienated, the corruption and hunger, and the grim possibility of a low-turnout election, which would leave the ANC with diminished "moral authority." Mandela was disturbed and did not dispute the reality or mask his distress. He asked Jannie if he agreed. Then, rather than drawing a wise conclusion as he usually does, he simply said, "We have much to do."

Between the earlier meeting at Shell House and that later session, we accomplished what Roshene had intended. We had shaken up the complacency, dislodged the funds necessary to run a real election, brought on an ad agency, and concluded a contract with me, the first since I started working with the ANC five years earlier.

CHANGE

No one in the new campaign team and certainly not Mandela nor Mbeki was confused about what we were facing. Voters who had grown despondent after four years of stalled negotiations and violence after Mandela's release were now becoming disengaged after four more years without change and they would no longer settle for slogans or sleight-of-hand. They wanted the real thing: better lives.

By the time we met at Shell House, 1.3 million more people in rural areas were able to get clean water within a short walk from their homes; by the summer, 2.5 million people had gained access to clean water since the ANC came to office. Electrification would reach two million additional homes that year, with 400,000 homes added in 1997 alone. In 1994, health care was made free for pregnant women and young children, followed by universal access to primary care. The government added five hundred new health clinics serving five million additional people by end of 1998; eight million children were now being immunized and five million were in school nutrition programs.

Housing was very much a work in progress. The impasse in the first two years was broken and construction of subsided cheap housing began, picking up momentum in 1997. By mid-1998, 400,000 subsidized cheap houses were built or under construction, with another 700,000 planned by the end of 2000. Altogether there would be housing for five million people, just under half of what was needed.[113]

Jobs and unemployment were an entirely different matter. While the government employed 240,000 people in road and public works, those efforts were swamped by the transformations taking place in the economy. All the new jobs in the formal sector were more than offset by sharp job losses in the gold mines, manufacturing, and government through 1999. A million new jobs had been created in the informal sector, but they were low-paid and marginal and swamped by the millions of women in the former impoverished rural homelands now part of the labor force. At the same time, the country witnessed a dramatic rise in black businesspeople, managers, and profession-als forming the new middle class.[114]

I have polled in many of the most affluent countries in the world, but no-where else do people read the material world so accurately, and in such a nuanced way, as if there were no media or leaders to influence their conclu-sions. In our first survey in March 1998, people by large margins believed electricity, access to water, and health services were getting better, not worse. They were almost evenly divided on whether housing was improving, par-ticularly with the program gaining momentum only a year earlier. But over 80 percent said jobs and employment were worsening and over 70 percent thought crime rates were getting worse. While many ANC politicians com-plained that people did not know of their good work, the public seemed to get it just right.

When I tested the facts about progress in the May and June focus groups, some of which I observed, people responded initially with a kind of cynicism I thought reserved for the mature democracies. They are "saying this now . . . because elections are nearer," said one person. "It's a campaign strategy," said another. "Now that we are nearing the elections, they are building hospitals." Some comments went straight to Mbeki: "He's preparing our minds so that we can look at him." These African voters understood the concept of spin.

The facts about progress did not add up to a big conclusion because voters were not willing to renegotiate downward their vision of a better life. They did not deny the facts. They were as articulate in focus groups as cabinet ministers with the press in rattling off how their children could now get free health service or go to a formerly all-white school, how you could get promo-tions at work or how the rural areas had adult education and water from a tap. They noted, almost matter-of-factly, "people are now equal," "black and white earn the same salary according to qualification." They were not "ha-rassed" for the pass book all Africans carried to show they were legally in the area and "no longer have to use the back door." They could "build squatter camps where they want"; "there was no more segregation," no "no entry" signs for blacks; "we are able to swim together at the beach and public toilets are open to all." But "all those things are natural," things that happen in a normal society, "so I don't think there's a change."

That could not be the end of the story, because people had no money and no shelter, while the politicians had both.

In the fall, with the polls showing some progress, albeit not on the impor-tant things, I laid out a range of options at a strategic meeting of the election team at Shell House.[115] I was not at all certain if any of my ideas would work.

I had watched too many people through the one-way glass as they angrily dismissed, minimized, or explained away almost everything we put before them. I introduced the concept of the ANC "trying" or "struggling" to make progress against the resistance of the old order. I also raised the possibility of putting all this in a "future-past" framework, where progress on employment becomes a future commitment, something to get done with a new plan. Maybe Mbeki could emerge as the voice of the ANC's acknowledgment of the reality and frustration and new commitments.

The action points to test in the next survey and discuss with the advertising agency were straightforward: a listening campaign that began in September with members of parliament going back to the villages; an initiative against corruption; a "Not Enough" theme articulated by Mbeki; and a jobs plan, which would take the form of a "Jobs Summit" in October.

But for the first time I wasn't certain if the points were real or for appearance. Would a listening campaign really change how MPs governed? Would a jobs summit really lead to policy changes that could create jobs? What I did know was that the government was working feverishly to make progress on the key promises and that was a good enough reason to struggle to develop a strategy for the election.

AIDS made its entry into South Africa at virtually the same time as South Africa's first democratic elections in 1994, surely the devil's perverse revenge. In 1996, Mbeki took charge of the government-wide task force to address the problem, though he was sidetracked by hopes for a South African–developed "miracle cure" that wouldn't bankrupt the country. But with the surge of the infection rate in 1997, the government moved legislation that allowed South Africa to suspend patents and import low-priced generic drugs when facing a health emergency. That led thirty-nine pharmaceutical companies to sue, with the support of the U.S. government, which threatened sanctions. While I was not then working for President Clinton, I heard the entreaties of a good friend, Chuck Blitz, who asked that I call Vice President Gore. Gore's chief of staff assured me that mine was not the first call he had received on the issue and hinted that it would be sorted out. Eventually, the U.S. companies, facing a public relations disaster, offered drugs at deep discounts to South Africa.[116]

In October 1998, the government flew flags at half-staff for the 360,000 lives lost to AIDS and Mbeki spoke live on television for the first time, awakened, he said, by "the groans of wasted lives," by the weight of "small and big coffins" carried to "many graveyards." For the first time, the deputy president spoke to the whole country of abstention from sex or using a condom and to "spread the message of prevention."[117]

I was aware that the media and anti-AIDS organizations were critical of this late effort at public education and even later effort to mobilize the country's health resources or fund use of AZT, even for pregnant women. In January 1999, Bill Harris—close friend, leader on children's issues, and town crier on outrageous things—traveled to South Africa on a fact-finding mission and warned me that the AIDS epidemic was so great it threatened the economy. While I raised the issue with the campaign team and my friends in the president's office, there was a clear reluctance to see AIDS emerge as an issue. I presumed South Africa, like the United States and others, would be tardy but ultimately would be forced to mobilize its resources to tackle the disease, though here confounded by the crushing demands on government resources and capacity. The government was meeting their commitment to build clinics and provide free health care for mothers and children, but now they faced needs that could take up three quarters of all health care spending.

I did not get the significance of the silence around the issue. Mandela himself had not spoken to his own country directly and when he spoke at Davos, Switzerland, on the AIDS epidemic in 1997, it was analytical, focused on the colonial inheritance, inequality, and poverty, without any mention of AIDS as a sexually transmitted disease. One close observer reported that Mandela could not imagine an elder leader speaking of sexual matters in a public forum, though after the election he would visit an AIDS clinic, acknowledge a son lost to the disease, and declare, "We have wasted time."

After the election, Mbeki would take a different turn. He would deny the connection between HIV and AIDS and thus the role of sexual transmission in the growing health crisis. He would question the value of AZT and "western medical models" and the implication that Africans are "germ carriers, and human beings of a lower order that cannot subject its passions to reason."[118]

The silence of the leaders before the election was reflected in the silence of the ordinary citizens, even as the crisis grew. We conducted dozens of focus groups over the year beginning in February 1998 and at the outset of each group the moderator would ask what was going right and wrong in the country and what were people's feelings about the ANC. I attended some of the groups and listened closely for new signs of anguish, and while tens of thousands of people died from AIDS during this period, a word search of the transcripts and my handwritten notes showed only three mentions of the subject.[119] AIDS was surely an issue but it would not become an election issue in the year ahead.

With growing frequency at the end of 1998, people in groups began to see and talk about the construction of houses; sometimes to complain about them being too small or lacking a big enough yard, but they could see them with their own eyes and see the impact on the impoverished areas around them. A house seems transforming in the way other changes are not: "I also have faith in them as we see the houses." The most fortunate who got a house talked about the revival of their spirits. "Sometimes I feel angry, but I understand that and moved to a house and I'm working," one person observed. "So I feel I could see a bright future."

NEW NARRATIVE

At the beginning of January 1999, I presented for the research team to the greatly expanded election group at Shell House, including Mbeki's principal people. A rising delivery of services produced an almost one-to-one shift in perceptions of progress, what I described as a "breakthrough" on housing, schools, and health. Six months earlier, barely a third thought housing was getting better—now, over a half thought that; on schools 40 percent saw progress, now 56 percent did. I reminded the room of what I labeled last April as "the most dispiriting result"—Africans divided evenly on whether South Africa was making progress under the Mandela government. But at the New Year, South Africa's summer, there was an abrupt shift of judgment, with voters by two to one saying life was improving.[120]

In most countries when you get that kind of shift of judgment, it sweeps everything else along. But that wasn't the case with South Africa's discerning and demanding population. On what I described as the "basics"—the "big three of jobs, crime and corruption"—you have made less than "no progress," I told them. With over 80 percent already thinking the job situation was worse, it could hardly go lower, though we did hit an "astonishing" 90 percent who disapproved of the government's performance. There was a sharp rise to over 80 percent disapproving on crime and almost as high on corruption. Thus, the ANC's vote crept above the 50 percent red line, but not by much.[121]

But what was most exciting about the survey was the voters' openness to narratives that explained the emerging reality and to reassurances that the ANC understood the problems. The strongest testing description of the reality was one describing the fight for change against the odds, a four-year battle to make the government work for all, a battle that had finally brought changes that 70 percent of Africans could see. Like other leaders I have known very well, ANC politicians were reluctant to admit they hadn't been able to keep all their promises, but when they did in the survey, the progress they had achieved persuaded 80 percent to say they were more likely to vote for the ANC.[122]

A few days later I wrote a memo for the elections team and ad agency to crystallize the narrative that would frame the campaign to the end—capturing the idea of change and struggle, progress in believable areas, acknowledging the difficulties, and implicitly calling on people to "strengthen [the ANC's] hand in the fight to bring change" and a better life.[123]

FIGHTING FOR CHANGE

The ANC has fought to create a government that will make life better for all. The ANC ended apartheid laws but it has fought a 4-year battle to change the civil service and make it work for everyone. Progress has been difficult, but now changes are happening. 3 million people with new taps for water. Schools getting better. And finally, the ANC broke the logjam and nearly a million houses are being built. The ANC—fighting for a better life.

With the ad agency hovering, desperate for us to settle on our approach and produce slogans and scripts, we organized focus groups over the next week with the disengaged and swing voters to play out the new narrative. From somewhere in the world and during the launch of Ehud Barak's campaign in Israel, I read through all the transcripts and sent a somewhat tardy e-mail on February 3. The new narrative "lifted the voters out of the negativism that characterized the groups at the front end," I said. It was believable, "creating hope for the future, without being too arrogant and without over-promising." The slogan, "fighting for change to make a better life for all," said to people that positive things had happened but that even more could happen to bring a "brighter future."[124]

It was clear in the groups that the "breakthrough on housing . . . is legitimating our entire message," I said. Only with that real change in life would voters listen to a narrative that explained what they had lived through and reengage their hopes.

The most important finding, I wrote, is how "open" and "non cynical" voters were about the reassurances, particularly when the new leader, Thabo Mbeki, showed he understood what was happening in their lives and acknowledged that "enough has not happened." I concluded, "If we run the right campaign, the ANC can make important gains in the next few months."

The reassurance ads were a critical turn for the campaign and for Mbeki, yet the draft scripts did not capture the moment and did not use Mbeki. To get it right, Melissa and I wrote the sixty-second radio scripts that Roshene and Gill then took to Mbeki to see whether he was prepared to become the voice of this amended contract. Amazingly, the bureaucratic hurdles fell away. The campaign closed with Mbeki's reassurance on crime and jobs and his new plans to make progress, the final element of the new narrative.[125]

When I heard Mbeki's reassuring words on the radio, I felt very satisfied that we created a narrative that explained the progress and brought people back, and to hear the next president give voice to my words. But I didn't know Mbeki in the way I came to know Mandela, whose thinking was impacted by research and who tried to change what the ANC actually did. I just wasn't close enough to know whether the campaign was formative for him and whether he would crack down on crime and corruption and work to create jobs.

ELECTION AGAIN

On June 2, 1999, 16 million people voted in South Africa's second democratic election. With the memories of the chaos five years earlier, Melissa took me to the Independent Electoral Commission's now professional operation in a large conference center at Midrand, the elegantly named new city halfway between Pretoria and Johannesburg. There, the IEC had banks of PCs networked to tally the results as ballots were counted around the country, while the various parties each had marked off areas to monitor results and phones to call in results to their campaign headquarters. With the experience of the local elections behind us and peace in KwaZulu-Natal, everybody seemed pretty confident the systems would not fail.

We drove to Gallagher Estate where the ANC would take results. Melissa, Tony, and I had a room with computers to monitor the tallies, using a form we created to monitor turnout and where the ANC vote stood in comparison to 1994 and local elections in between. We were up all night, struggling to get in enough results from key areas to be revealing about the meaning of this election, to be shared with Mbeki. Apparently, I again had that role. By morning, 61 percent of the ballots were counted, compared to just 8 percent five years earlier.

We sat down with Mbeki and his team of advisors, thinking less of the tumult and excitement of the first election and more of the dire mood a year ago. Almost a third were disengaged, the vote had dropped below a 50 percent red line, few had any hope for a better life, and Mbeki was himself a distant figure. But in this election he found a popular touch and his popularity rose and he spoke frankly about where the ANC fell short, which allowed people to trust him to lead. I told him that the ANC was currently getting 64 percent of the vote, but rising, "likely pushing close to two-thirds."[126] Even more important, given the alienation and threatened disengagement, 87 percent voted, "an extraordinary figure" that allowed the ANC to maintain its unique standing to address the tasks ahead. The ANC was building up large majorities with Coloured voters in the Northern Cape, Gauteng, and nonmetro areas of the Western Cape, making the ANC, even more than last time, the only truly national and multiracial party.

Mbeki was appreciative. He shook my hand and passed my working paper to Joel to begin to prepare his remarks. A thousand supporters were gathered in the big hall as Mbeki entered, the big screens for results on all the walls showing the new president in traditional African garb. He began by acknowledging the people "in their millions and without hesitation" who have "renewed the mandate"; the people, "both black and white," who have affirmed "our vision of a non-racial society." They "have directed us to move forward faster" with our program "so that a goal of a better life for all is achieved sooner rather than later." Mbeki interpreted the voters' new instructions: "radically to improve the safety and security of all our people" and to "continue to develop into a modern and internationally competitive economy" that "grows at higher rates, that it creates new jobs."

The press reported that a radiant Mbeki joined his wife on the dance floor.[127]

AN INNOCENT LETTER

In Mandela's final State of the Nation address to the final session of South Africa's first democratic parliament, he began by reading the letters of a "notorious prisoner," written ten years ago to President Botha, as Mandela describes him, "the head of the apartheid state." He began there so no one would miss the long road traveled to that moment. The prisoner warned the president of "the specter of a South Africa split into two hostile camps: black on one side . . . and white on the other, slaughtering one another." The humble prisoner reiterated the ANC's nonnegotiable demand for "majority rule in a unitary state," but combined with the "structural guarantees that majority rule will not mean domination of the white minority by black." Today, he said, we take so much for granted, as the difficult struggle for "equality, the right to vote in free and fair elections and freedom of speech" are "now mere footnotes of history."

South Africa, caught up "in a momentous process of change," had "no time to pause," not even "for farewells." Even though we had traveled so far together, "The long walk is not over. The prize of a better life is yet to be won." This remains, he declared, "our founding pact" and, thankfully, it "has become a national passion."

When I read the draft of the speech, I set it down and became quiet. I wanted to maintain a perspective on Mandela's journey and his attempt to create a final compact binding on the new generation of leaders that began with people just wanting something simple, a better life. I could also see Mandela, mischievous to the end, using the innocent letter of the notorious prisoner to chide leaders black and white to assume responsibility and "build the country of our dreams!"[128]

4

TONY BLAIR

Act I

THE COMING BRITISH election in 1992 seemed to promise something that the Labour Party had not savored for more than two decades: victory at the polls. Britain had slipped into a deep recession and unemployment stood at 14 percent. The Conservatives, under Prime Minister John Major, were extremely unpopular having imposed a per-head "poll tax" so hated that it produced rioting in London. Opinion polls on April 1 showed a clear lead for Labour under Neil Kinnock. Yet when the votes were cast just a few days later, on April 9, Labour lost, and lost badly, at least in part the result of an effective Conservative ad campaign warning voters that Labour planned a "tax bombshell"—sharply higher taxes to fund its myriad of promised programs and spending. The lesson was clear: Labour could not be trusted with serious things.[1]

The defeat was shattering for the party. Kinnock resigned the leadership position, giving way to John Smith. The blow was felt particularly hard by two of Labour's rising young stars, Gordon Brown and Tony Blair. Brown and Blair were known as energetic modernizers—"two bright tyros" whose potential "was soon spotted as exceptional"—and impatient with the pace of change in the party.[2] Inseparable, the two had shared an office and risen quickly in the House of Commons; by the time they were in their mid-thirties they took the top opposition cabinet roles—formally dubbed "shadow" positions—that daily faced off against their opposites in the ruling party. Brown was the shadow chancellor, the second most powerful post after Smith. The shadow chancellor commands the most time in the House of

Commons debating the chancellor, who, because he is responsible for the Treasury and the budget, holds the second most powerful position in government after the prime minister. Brown's unhappy task within the party was to wring out of Labour its penchant for spending and taxes while formally abandoning the shadow budget that both he and Blair believed had cost Labour the election. Brown imposed a discipline that permitted spending only "as resources allow." That meant only economic growth would permit higher spending, not new taxes.[3]

Blair, who had recently moved from shadow employment secretary to shadow home secretary, responsible for law and order, wrote a pained assessment of the party. Despite the modest changes, "the public was insufficiently sure of the new Labour Party to put it into government." He used the term "New Labour" for the first time. Like all his publications and speeches, he wrote the article himself, choosing his words carefully to get the meaning right through three or four drafts. While the pain of the election was fresh, he put down his marker: the party must "intensify the process of change if Labour is to be electable again." It was a political mission strongly reminiscent of the one Clinton staked out a year earlier at the outset with his Cleveland Democratic Leadership Council speech.[4]

Still unsettled about Labour's frustrating defeat, Brown and Blair watched keenly as another young modernizer, Bill Clinton, fought his way to the White House later that year. Eager to learn and use the lessons that propelled Clinton to the presidency, Brown and Blair flew to Washington just after the New Year. In four exhilarating days, they met with Clinton's campaign and economic advisors and other Washington luminaries. They balanced meetings with economists like Larry Summers of the World Bank and Federal Reserve Chief Alan Greenspan with populist Paul Begala and polemicist Sidney Blumenthal. I, along with Al From and Elaine Kamarck, met Blair for tea at the British embassy. "He looked like a kid," Elaine said later, though he also was "very courteous, very humble, very focused," which is the way I have found him to be ever since. He wanted to hear as much as possible about how Clinton won and he took furious notes about everything as we recounted how smart we had been.[5]

Even as Blair listened to our account of Clinton's victory, the Labour Party fell into a big public brawl over the meaning of Clinton's victory and what the party's response should be. John Prescott, a Labour stalwart, did not have much regard for the "Beautiful People" who wanted to take over the party of workers and warned that the party would not rediscover its voters or its soul through media wizardry and show business techniques designed to appeal to the metropolitan middle class rather than the unions. That was all the handiwork of pollsters, he said, the new "high priests" of politics. And John Smith, angry with Blair and Brown for making their pilgrimage to Washington, was dismissive. "All this Clintonisation business, it's just upsetting everyone" and dividing the party.[6]

But Blair was energized and unapologetic about the association with Clinton, a winner at a time when Labour's biggest challenge was becoming electable. Winning was important, of course, but Blair's visit was also about mission and his return to London marked what may have been an important turning point in his thinking. You could run for the middle ground without sacrificing the base; you do not have to lose on "tax," and, most importantly, the left can speak without apology about social issues, particularly crime and community.

"I think it's important that we are tough on crime and tough on the causes of crime, too," Blair told BBC's Radio 4 the night he returned from America. That was language that came from Blair and Brown, not the Clinton people. When in mid-February a two-year-old, James Bulger, was murdered by two ten-year-olds, Blair, as shadow home secretary, became the voice of the nation's anguish, produced by those "hammer blows struck against the sleeping conscience of the country." The answer, he said, did not lie just in legislation. "If we do not learn and then teach the value of what is right and what is wrong, then the result is simply moral chaos," he said. The individual would find his worth in community, a "communitarian" theme that was empowered by Clinton's victory. "It's a bargain—we give opportunity, we demand responsibility," Blair wrote in the *Sun* in March. "There is no excuse for crime. None."[7]

To tilt the balance in Labour's internal debate, Philip Gould, polling advisor to the party and an earlier observer of our Little Rock war room, asked a group of Clinton advisors to come to London for a presentation to a large gathering of pundits, journalists, public relations professionals, and party and union leaders. I accepted as much to squeeze in a holiday before Clinton's inauguration as to preach the gospel.

I shared the stage with Paul Begala and Elaine for the one-day conference on "Clinton Economics"—so named to permit a truce and allow all sides to attend. The audience was a mix of the curious and the hostile come to hear about another failed left party that was now triumphant. Few wanted to show any fascination with Clinton's allegedly "superficial" approach to policy or his campaign methods. Prescott was sitting up front, his expression dour and his arms crossed. Neil Kinnock sat in the back, but was among the few to speak up during the course of the day: "Winning is better than losing," he said, adding, "Unfortunately, I wasn't able to convince everyone else in the Labour Party."

I tried to win over the room by thanking the victorious Tories for our being there, using the popular name for the Conservatives. By rehearsing their tax scare campaign against Kinnock last year and then exporting it to the colonies, Clinton and the Democrats were able to expose and discredit it. "There is a certain justice in our being here," I declared, to the warm applause of the audience, reformers and traditionalists alike. My critique of my own party, "an elitist and suburban party with contempt for working Americans," got less applause. I was free to say publicly what many attending the forum reserved only for private conversation. I explained that Clinton centered his campaign on the broadly defined "middle class," promoting its economic interests and respecting its values, including toughness on crime, a work ethic, and welfare reform, ideas that won support with the poor and working class as well. That brought no applause. Such assertions were drawing less applause in Little Rock, too, only increasing my determination to state them. All of us on the panel challenged the strong presumptions in the room that "Clintonism" was "mere symbolism."[8]

After the session, I went over to Prescott, who was still in his seat, to remind him that Senator Chris Dodd, his Irish soul-mate and closest buddy in America, had brought him to Rosa's and my house in New Haven to change clothes. To my surprise, Prescott was very warm, almost winking at me as if to say, "Don't take all this too seriously, lad. We will sort it out." Afterward, Gould took Paul and me to meet with John Smith at his parliamentary office. Smith was polite enough and thanked us for sharing our experience, but there was no sense of a shared political project.

It turned out that Philip had already sent a memo to Smith—quickly buried—that outlined the lessons of the Clinton campaign and called for a "unified decision-making structure; a rapid-response capacity; the development of a war room where all the campaign functions are included." He called for the party to build "a new relationship of trust with the British electorate" by launching a transparent process for change: "Labour has not changed until it announces that it has changed," he said, citing the Democrats for labeling themselves "New Democrats." In a published article in January, he had urged Labour to "emulate Clinton's success in discarding the Democrats' image 'as the party of the poor and of the past' by forging 'a populism of the centre rather than the left'" and identifying with "the working middle class."[9]

Philip had read my *American Prospect* articles.[10]

THE HAPLESS TORIES

Prime Minister John Major's government could not have started off more wrong-footed in its relations with Bill Clinton. Major apologized for the ads attacking Clinton on taxes—developed by his party's British media advisors for the Republican presidential campaign. That was no doubt difficult to explain. But that was just the start of the accelerating downhill slide for Major and his party.

From virtually its first day in June 1992, Major's Conservative government became a nonstop soap opera, riddled with greed, hypocrisy, and incompetence. Major could hang on for up to five years as long as he kept his majority in the House of Commons. Usually a leader would find a good patch and call early elections by going to the queen to ask that the Parliament be dissolved. The resulting campaign often lasted only a matter of weeks. But under Major things were such a mess that the Conservatives could not dare call for elections.

Major was constantly teetering on the edge, forced to turn each issue into a "no-confidence" vote and mini-drama in the Commons, where defeat would mean new elections. He repeatedly was saved by only a handful of votes even as he expressed disdain for his own caucus. Little wonder that over 80 percent of the country viewed the Tories as "divided." After shamelessly warning the electorate about Labour's alleged "tax bombshell," the Tories proceeded in their budget to raise the national insurance contribution, reduce tax allowances for couples and mortgage holders, extend the VAT to fuel and power, and impose new taxes on insurance premiums and travel. Three quarters of the country concluded that they had been misled on taxes.

The party of probity and tradition was wracked by scandals that became cumulatively known as "Tory sleaze." By June 1996, nine members of the government had resigned amidst sex scandals and lurid affairs. Nearly as many resigned over financial irregularities. Under Major, "privatization" of the big utilities turned into higher bills for consumers, layoffs, and breathtaking increases in executive pay, share options, and bonuses.

All that paled before the unraveling of the Tories' central economic policy, formally linking the pound to European currencies through the Exchange Rate Mechanism, the ERM. On "Black Wednesday," just months after Major's 1992 election victory, exchange rates plummeted, forcing up interest rates from 10 to 15 percent in just hours. With variable mortgages the norm, real people felt the increases immediately in the form of punishing increases in housing payments. After a day of frantic efforts to save the pound, a shaken and pale chancellor faced the cameras to announce the cancellation of the government's economic policy. The party of economic competence had been humiliated and Labour moved into a 20-point lead on handling the economy.[11]

The Tories also slowed spending on the National Health Service and schools, roads and public transport, all of which created drama as cameras focused on rows of elderly patients on gurneys filling hospital hallways, waiting to be attended. "Conservatives continuing to undermine the NHS" soon emerged as the top reason that people gave up on the Tories, 20 points higher than the next best reason.[12]

THE THANKLESS TASK OF CHANGING OLD LABOUR

John Smith may have been loath to divide his party publicly over Clinton or reform, but he did take important steps to reduce the proportion of union delegates, end the union bloc vote, and create a one-man, one-vote system that increased the role of individual members. How far he could have carried his reforms is anyone's guess. Smith died suddenly of a heart attack on May 12, 1994.

Smith was genuinely mourned, but that didn't stop speculation about the leadership contest. Blair emerged quickly as the front-runner, although it was expected that he would be challenged not only by the old guard, but also by Brown, who everyone presumed thought it was his turn. After a series of tense meetings between the two—meetings whose specifics are contested to this day—Brown withdrew in favor of Blair on the condition that Brown would have wide latitude on the economy and domestic issues and the next claim on leadership. In the party election in July, Blair won almost 60 percent of the vote across the MPs, party and trade union members, while John Prescott won as deputy leader with Blair's support.[13]

With the Tories so hopeless, Labour surged ahead and maintained a breathtaking 20-point lead for a good year.[14]

But Blair understood that this was make-believe because Labour's position was much more dire than the Democrats' had ever been. Labour had not won a parliamentary majority or chosen a prime minister in over two decades. The party gained ascendancy in the wake of the ravages of World War II when the country threw out Winston Churchill and gave Labour a huge majority in Parliament as well as a mandate to create the National Health Service, and to nationalize public utilities and the iron and steel industry, the heart of the industrial economy. Old and New Labour leaders look back on that period as Democrats look back on the New Deal, but it was downhill from there.

The deep economic problems of the 1970s brought out all of Labour's unresolved ugly contradictions. The "Trotskyite" left and trade unions took control of the party at many levels and produced a program that rejected a mixed economy and the European Union. When the last government entrusted to Labour tried to restrain inflation and wage increases, the trade unions scorned the Labour prime minister and called strikes that blacked out areas from London to Scotland and left rubbish piled up in city streets. The winter of 1978–79, the "Winter of Discontent" recalled from Shakespeare's *Richard III*, ensured Margaret Thatcher's landslide victory in 1979. Within two years, a sizable bloc of "moderate" Labour MPs broke away to form the new Liberal Democratic Party. When Britain fell into the deepest recession since the Great Depression, the citizenry could not bear to turn back to Labour to manage the country's economic affairs. By the early 1980s Labour was calling for confiscatory high tax rates, public ownership of the big industries, and unilateral nuclear disarmament. One senior party leader described the 1983 party manifesto as "the longest suicide note in history."

The party's election of Neil Kinnock as Labour leader after the 1983 debacle kicked off a decade of reforms. He bravely expelled the Trotskyist "militant tendency" and he began a multiyear policy review in 1989 that showed a party looking for innovative ways to work with the market. And he appointed Blair shadow opposition employment secretary, who quickly let it be known that Labour would not bring back the old union protections. Nonetheless, Kinnock did not dare try to repeal Clause IV in Labour's constitution, adopted in 1918, that committed the party to nationalization of major industries.[15]

Clause IV had a mythic quality. Drafted in 1917 and adopted in 1918, the clause elaborated on Labour's commitment to socialism rather than liberal reform. It set the goal of securing for workers "the full fruits of their industry . . . upon the basis of the common ownership of the means of production, distribution and exchange." It essentially affirmed Labour's socialist identity, even as successive Labour governments in practice learned to live with markets and advance all sorts of liberal reforms.[16]

Blair knew that Labour's modernization and poll lead were fragile and surprised and unnerved his inner circle when he told them he intended to challenge Clause IV. At the very end of a speech to the first party conference over which he presided, Blair called for a debate on the party's first principles, to launch a process that would rewrite Clause IV. Blair's advisors had good reason to be nervous because two days later the conference attendees, with strong union backing, approved a resolution rejecting any change in the clause.

Blair's defeat at his first party conference revealed how thin the support was for his brand of reform. The defeat strengthened his resolve to change the party. With the new year of 1995, Blair cleared his schedule to attend constituency meetings every week, all with the single-minded goal of changing Clause IV.

The most challenging and revealing part of the effort was writing a new Clause IV to substitute for the old. Blair rejected a version given him by his policy unit, headed by David Miliband, and wrote a substitute himself in his cumbersome style. The Labour Party, it said, believed "by the strength of our common endeavor we achieve more than we achieve alone, so as to create for each of us the means to realize our true potential." He accepted another clause, written and pushed by Peter Hyman, a member of the policy unit with populist sensibilities, that said "a community in which power, wealth and opportunity are in the hands of the many not the few." It closed in Blair's hand: "where the rights we enjoy reflect the duties we owe, and where we live together, freely, in a spirit of solidarity, tolerance and respect."

Blair called for a referendum among the some 300,000 party members and union members from over 150 local parties and created his first real campaign organization. On April 29, almost two thirds of the ballots were cast for the new Clause IV, driven by the 90 percent support among the members in the local constituency parties.

Some commentators viewed Blair's success in changing Clause IV as akin to Clinton's Sister Souljah Moment, when he showed he could stand up to Jesse Jackson and the special interests in his own party. Certainly I had discussed that moment with the Blair people. But altering Clause IV was more than symbolic. Blair's bold challenge to the unions and the fact that he helped bring into the party tens of thousands of new members demonstrated to the country that Blair was strong enough to change his own party. Unfortunately, Philip Gould believed it also revealed a party organization not yet ready for prime time.[17]

Before Smith died and Blair won leadership of the party I had met with Blair and Brown separately in America. In November 1993, Blair, still a relatively unknown opposition MP with responsibility for crime and justice, came to the United States to meet New York mayor Rudy Giuliani and inspect the landmark policing and "zero tolerance" methods that had radically reduced crime in New York City. Sidney Blumenthal organized a small dinner for Blair at his house in Washington. When Sidney toasted Blair as "the next leader of the Labour Party and prime minister," everyone thought Sidney was just being a gracious host. Most of the discussion was about American, not British, politics, but that suited Blair just fine. I was still polling for Clinton, who had won passage of his economic plan only after a troubled fight with his own party, had launched NAFTA and health care, but had offered no initiatives on welfare reform and crime. Was he governing as a "New Democrat"?

Blair—very tall and fit with a perpetual smile—sat immediately to my right. He seemed delighted to be there and engaged immediately to get me to expound on what was really happening. I could not resist making comparisons with the president, as they seemed like blood brothers, youthful and energetic, a passion for politics, comfortable with the same language—"opportunity," "responsibility," "community"—and sharing the challenge of making their own parties listen to them and to the people in order to become electable again. Blair showed the passion for the project, but he seemed uncommonly polite and respectful and exhibited no sign of Clinton's explosive anger. Yet unlike Clinton, he seemed to relish the prospect of confrontation with the unions, which suggested to me that Blair's politeness had another side.

He talked at length with Rosa about the Congress, knowing that if the Clinton project got buried in Speaker Tom Foley's Democratic Congress it would be noticed across the Atlantic. Blair wanted to hear that Clinton would do well in the elections of 1994 and 1996. Without seeming at all impatient with the pleasantries, he focused intently on the question of whether Clinton the New Democrat would succeed.

I assumed he was a completely secular politician, and he gave me no reason to think otherwise. He was a lawyer and professional, much like the new class of Democrats being elected in the suburbs. At one point the thought occurred to me that Blair seemed like a Bill Clinton without all the complexity. I did not share that conclusion with the dinner table. And, of course, things are never what they seem.[17]

Then in early 1994, Gordon Brown came to my office in the Washington brownstone, escorted by a young officer at the British embassy, Jonathan Powell, who had made it his mission to build close relations with the "New Democrats." As shadow chancellor, Brown had taken up one mission with messianic zeal—to make Labour electable by making sure it was trusted on the budget, spending, taxes, and managing a stable economy. With that mission, Brown looked to me like Alan Ameche, an American fullback who would grind out five yards each time toward the goal, carrying a bunch of defenders with him.

Brown came straight to the point. "I've read your article and I can't agree with you on one point: voters will not trust the 'left' if they are making the case for more government." While he had watched from the hall and been stirred by Mario Cuomo's eloquent 1984 keynote address about America as "a tale of two cities," he had read everything America's new Democrats had been producing, and was loaded down with a pile of policy reports from the DLC as well as his impressions from his meetings with Bob Reich, Larry Summers, and Alan Greenspan. He was smart and had already processed and settled the battles on reform that we were still working through on the way to being electable.

POLLSTER IDOL

After Blair became leader of the party, Philip Gould began to tempt me with glimpses of their surveys showing Labour way ahead, even though the Major government did not need to call an election for three years. With the approval of the White House and the Democratic National Committee we created a "foreign exchange program." Philip traveled to some focus groups in Los Angeles in early February 1995 to see if Clinton was still breathing after the November 1994 massacre. I was to reciprocate by observing groups in Britain.

But Philip wanted much more than that and my departure from the White House in the spring of 1995 allowed me to oblige.[18] He wanted me to take over the national strategic research for the Labour Party and work directly with Blair as part of his team. I agreed to a three-day visit, starting May 15, for me to meet people and offer my thinking and for them to get comfortable with the idea of a "Clintonista" in their midst. The trip took on the quality of a reality TV contest for "pollster idol." First I would observe one night of groups with Conservative Party defectors and then a second, with defectors from the Liberal Democrats. I would examine a new national poll in raw form without crosstabs and a raft of new public polls, then pull it all together and make a knock-your-socks-off presentation on Wednesday morning to Blair and the team, who would decide if they wanted to make me a member. It would be a test of my ability to discern patterns that others did not see and to understand the significance that others overlooked.

The first focus group was held in the living room of a two-story house in Edgware with Philip moderating. It was a far cry from the sterile conference rooms with one-way mirrors used for focus groups in malls or office buildings in the United States. I spread out my papers on a table, intent on looking as if I were Mr. Gould's deaf-mute assistant. I didn't want the group to hear my American English. As I observed the people I took nearly verbatim notes, underlining phrases that captured some emotion and writing things to remember on the side of the page. What was most striking that night was that these Conservative "switchers," as they are called in Britain—voters who have supported the Tories in election after election, but intended now to vote for Labour—were completely self-conscious about who they were and their potential role. They knew they were the backbone of the Tories. They had kept nearly the whole south of Britain anchored in the Conservative world. When the Tories became the party of "aspiration," home ownership, and low taxes under Margaret Thatcher, voters in that area gave over half of their votes to the Tories. But Labour was now ahead by about 20 points in the polls nationally, and that could only happen if a lot of these voters walked away from that history.[19]

People required few words to show they were done with the Tories. The Tories had not just failed, they had betrayed these constituents: "They let us down—made a hash of it."[20] The economy was the heart of the indictment. People were in obvious pain. These aspirant Tory voters, who respected Thatcher for allowing millions of council house tenants to buy their property, now faced "negative equity," houses worth less than the purchase price. They were in a trap. They shared war stories and the horror of people they knew personally losing their homes. They focused on the health service as the number one symbol for all public services, summarized even more simply: "disgusting" and a "disgrace." They spoke of a Britain in which "everything is crumbling" and people were "on your own." The Tories, you ask? "They had their chance," with a sense of finality.

Philip moderated in the same frenetic and blustery way he spoke in meetings or when he was trying to persuade someone. It was not the moderator style to which I was accustomed, but it engaged the people, who shared their sense of betrayal. Philip probed and argued, but in ways that left them amused. One would certainly learn more with a less intrusive style, but these groups were as much about Philip as the voters in the room. This was his way of bouncing his ideas off real people, who in turn affected his thinking. It also enabled him to use their examples in the discussions with the Blair team. It was one of the ways Philip gained authority in the intra-party debates.[21]

For the most part the switchers said this time they would "give Labour a go. They can't make more of a hash of it, can they?"

I was surprised Philip introduced me as his American collaborator observing the elections here and in other countries and said, "Stan, do you have any questions you want to ask?" Sometimes an outsider can bring an honesty that an insider will not elicit. I tried an exercise I used once in Joe Lieberman's race for the U.S. Senate. Imagine it is election day and you are behind the curtain and about to mark the ballot for Labour and you hesitate, I asked. What's holding you back? Your mind recalls all those horrors, the strikes, the garbage in the streets, the taxes. Can you go through with it? They went silent.[22]

I also visited BMP, Labour's ad agency, where Philip had gathered people from the agency, the party, and the Blair team to hear my firsthand account of the Clinton campaign. For all my great virtues, that was really why I was there. We did not know in the spring of 1995 whether Clinton offered a successful model for governing. But for them, the Clinton campaign was transcendent, taking the Democrats to victory after decades of defeat. The New

Democrats won in 1992 and Labour, insufficiently reformed and modernized, lost. At this point, they were ready to transport the full set from the war room and just get on with it. When the party moved from its old Gothic quarters to Millbank Tower, an ugly 1960s modern frame-and-glass office building, the open first floor above the ground level had been reserved for a new flexible, fast-moving, media-oriented campaign with the war room somewhere in the middle. The organizational chart for the real war room in Little Rock was posted on a column in case anyone missed the point.

Finally Philip escorted me into Westminster, properly the Palace of Westminster, to my first presentation to Blair. I paused to gawk at Westminster Hall, its remarkable wood-beam ceiling extending unsupported for nearly a football field, built by the Normans. In Congress the leadership offices are more splendid than the public places, but the opposite is true in Britain. Nonetheless, it was still a bit intimidating. With Blair was his team: Alastair Campbell, the very sharp, tough former political editor of the pro-Labour *Mirror,* now in constant combat with the media on behalf of his boss; Peter Mandelson, the original head of Labour communication, now an MP and abrasive, but a master organizer of modern campaigns, and Jonathan Powell, formerly of the embassy in Washington, and now Blair's chief of staff. Anji Hunter was the intimidating woman at the desk guarding the office, but she was the only one among them who went back with Blair to university days and clearly had her last word after we left.

Nobody referred to Blair as "Blair," just "'Tony," a familiarity I resisted, referring to him as the "Leader" to everyone's amusement. I never dropped the formality with him in person or in my memos. On the other hand, Blair greeted me warmly and asked about Rosa and how the president was doing, expressing confidence that he would bounce back. The U.S. presidential election would be held the next year, well in advance of the British election. It would send a signal about the success of their shared political project. The Gingrich Congress had already overreached and I mentioned how the president mourned for the nation after the Oklahoma City bombing a month ago. I said he seemed now to be in a new place. His poll ratings were up.

I wrote a five-page outline to be sure my first presentation was tight and intriguing. But it really wasn't that complicated. My most important observation was the simplest: the so-called switchers know they are switchers and, compared to elsewhere, "lack tentativeness," which I said raised my confidence that the lead Labour held was real and durable. I had probably said enough, but I carried on. The lead was "situated in three powerful, inter-related dynamics." First, voters said they had had "enough of the Tories and this will be a 'change election'"; second, voters saw a declining Britain, "the erosion of everything that matters to everyday people"; and third, they wanted "New Labour" to be real, that is, not a risk. If we could advance those points in a mutually reinforcing way, I said, we would lock in the vote. The biggest challenge, I said, was that last point, as it had been with Clinton. It would be much tougher in Britain, though, given Labour's history.

The first strategic task was "reassurance"—on the trade unions, taxes, and on focusing on serious issues. With the Clause IV battle just won, Blair had established that he would challenge the unions. He showed the reality of New Labour's moderation even though a third of the switchers in Labour's poll still worried a lot about union power. "Voters need relentless reassurance," I repeated relentlessly. On taxes, over 40 percent thought Labour would raise taxes on the rich, but would eventually wind up raising them on everyone. Voters were worried "they will be fooled." With Labour's uncertain credibility, I urged "a relentless focus on the Conservative tax betrayal," keeping the Tories on the defensive on their historic issue.

I ended with a broader conclusion that pointed to their larger purpose. Labour was emerging with a "classless quality," being "for everyone" with a critical double meaning: first, Labour was not for the special interests and the unions, and second, it was for the "everyday, ordinary person." That was fully in line with the new Clause IV commitment to a "community in which power, wealth and opportunity are in the hands of the many not the few," written well before I arrived. With over three quarters saying the Conservatives represent only one class, Labour could be for people "in a more elevated way, to lead the nation," I concluded.[23]

I did not know the results of the postmortem of my performance, but suddenly the fax floodgates burst open with page after page of memos. I figured I was hired, even though there was no signing ceremony and no fee schedule. Had I been Dick Morris, I would have written, "This was the turning point for Tony Blair, as he will soon change Labour as Bill Clinton changed the Democratic Party." In fact, the Conservative *Daily Mail* would later write that I "persuaded the modernizers to dump Labour's traditional tax, crime and welfare policies and its socialist ideology to lure back working class voters who defected to Margaret Thatcher."[24] The only problem with that account was that Blair had already changed Labour.

UNFINISHED CHOICE

Philip sent me his draft "confidential" plan for the campaign, titled "The Unfinished Revolution" and immodestly subtitled "Winning Power, Sustaining Power, Transforming Britain." Philip used urgent rhetoric to push the team to build the kind of machine and political project that had sustained the Tories in the last century. He urged "renewal versus decline" as the "central strategic focus," but also offered three "key secondary messages": first, "people versus privilege," which would encompass "opportunity, aspiration, and potential"; second, "community versus social disintegration," which led to "rights, responsibility and duty"; and third, "extremism versus moderation," which encompassed the attack on privatization and sleaze.

I was exasperated and said so in my marginal comments on the document. It was too fragmented, not a message at all. Labour was for everything. There was no core message, and I wrote, "But what is the philosophy underlying it?" They were searching for a defining choice, certain only that economy must be at the center of it.

From my very first meeting, I realized everybody was jittery about the economy. It would be the biggest factor in the election, it was mostly beyond their control, and it was genuinely recovering. Unemployment had dropped from near 11 percent to around 8 percent. Pessimism was receding and the Tories remained plausible on this issue. Gordon Brown's initials were much in evidence on these rounds of memos.[25] I was less jittery about the economy because I had watched so many incumbents trumpet an improving economy and rising living standards and get no credit from voters. Just ask former presidents Bush and de Klerk and, indeed, President Clinton in 1994.

Philip dumped on me all of Labour's focus group research on the economy, mostly a grab bag of voter preferences and indicators that was less than useful. Looking at the same data, Philip had produced a seventeen-page memo laying out the different options, but lacked any focus: "the economic message must include *decline versus renewal* as the central divide, and reward for hard work as a crucial promise, linking to our wider fairness and privilege messages. Investment, education and long-termism are also central." Each concept doubtless had a powerful patron. Philip knew his list of choices was too encompassing but he was too close to the players to force a choice. I was too innocent to know who was championing what and just stumbled into the debates. Philip readily acceded when I said the campaign desperately needed a message poll with the authority to delineate the choices.

Struck by the similarities I had heard among the British focus groups and the long-ago New Hampshire groups that had spoken of "the forgotten middle class," I began drafting a full message survey at the end of July.[26] My starting point: "The Labour Party seeks to put hard working families back at the center of civic life in Britain." This was not an American imposition. The sentiment and words pervaded the British focus groups, a desire among ordinary people living through hard times to be recognized by those with power.

Before the message survey fielded, my office ran some statistical models using regression analysis that specifies the unique impact of various attitudes and beliefs, as well as which ones have the greatest ability to shift the vote, which I presented to Blair personally on July 21. I wondered what his tolerance was for regression analysis. Strategically, we knew we wanted it to be a "change election," but we knew more: the cry for change was closely correlated with the feeling that the Tories "don't care about the ordinary person" and are "on the side of the rich and powerful." Change meant getting rid of a government that had failed ordinary people. And the strongest predictor of contempt for the Tories was the belief that the Tories did not govern "for all Britain." While I had battled to defend such a finding in America, at least here the data would win out, I thought. We were edging toward a definition of the election.

To my amazement, Philip incorporated all my firm's computer runs into an unwieldy PowerPoint presentation for Blair before he left for summer holiday.

"Tony likes it a lot and is on board for the general direction," Philip told me. Philip was recommending that the party conference be organized around the choice: Labour "governing for all the people" versus the Conservatives, "betraying the people."[27] At least he got it half right.

When Blair returned from holiday in September, however, he had to be persuaded all over again. That always happens when a political leader is left alone to think, read, and talk to normal people. In a long memo, Philip wrote, "Governing for all the people is Labour's central value," full of beneficial double meanings: both for opportunity and "a more cohesive society," both for "equality" to bring in the left and "inclusiveness and national message" to bring in the center. I thought Philip's formulation failed to go big enough. It made no explicit reference to the idea of "community," which I sensed had special importance for Blair and I wrote repeatedly in the memo's margins.[28]

The message survey fielded using door-to-door interviews over an entire month. The most important exercise in the message survey was the full pages of choices for defining the election. By far the strongest reaction came from the "populist" option: *Labour works for all the people. The Conservatives work for the privileged few.* More than 60 percent described that choice as real and half said it made them more likely to vote Labour. It was a stunning 10 points stronger than the next definition: that Labour "will renew Britain" and the Conservatives let "Britain decline," a premise on which Philip earlier had staked his life. It was also 15 points stronger than a recycled choice from the Clinton campaign that I tested on a lark: "Change versus more of the same." Now the message was emerging more clearly.[29]

Blair, however, had his own ideas. He told Philip he wanted to organize the conference speech around the theme "One Nation," an idea the team universally opposed as too abstract. But Blair would not let go of it. Philip rushed the concept into focus groups and got a quick and decisive reading: "None of the one-nation themes worked because they are not addressing a problem that people thinks need solving."[30]

Blair would take the first cut at the speech.

"ONE NATION"

The prime minister's speech to the annual Labour Party conference at the beginning of October is his most important each year. Certainly it is the one to which he and his teams devote the greatest amount of time. The hope is to achieve an enduring impact, much as U.S. presidents attempt to do in their acceptance speeches at party conventions and in their State of the Union addresses. In Blair's first conference speech he had combatively called on his party to keep changing and opened up the debate on Clause IV. As he prepared for his next conference speech many hoped that this time he would beat up the Tories instead of his own party, give the activists something to cheer for, and provide a window into New Labour's vision.

The conference was in Brighton, a faded holiday resort where the delegates had to dodge the panhandlers, beggars, and winos, and compete with the "fringe meetings" where the unreconstructed activists and trade unionists still hung out. A good week earlier, Blair began to work alone over the weekend at a friend's estate, outlining the argument and getting gut reactions from Alastair Campbell, then working long stretches on his pad, pages and notes strewn at his feet. By the time the team took over a floor of the main hotel for most of a week to prepare for Tuesday's midday speech, previous drafts were scrapped as "hopeless." At the hotel Blair edited in bed, and then turned it over to Alastair, Philip, and Peter Hyman to write or edit sections on the computers. At one point Alastair reported that Blair "had panic in his eyes," although they had a big laugh about that later.[31] The tension in the air was heightened by the high security, including the clearing and lockdown of the convention center, standard fare since the IRA bombing attempt on Margaret Thatcher in Brighton eleven years ago. I had not been part of that process in the first year because of the fear that copious faxing would risk leaks.

Blair received a euphoric reception from the conference attendees on Tuesday, a far cry from the 50.5 percent who voted to humiliate him on Clause IV a year earlier. It was a united party, growing comfortable with the pink backdrop and banners proclaiming, "New Labour. New Britain." The hall was united by hatred of the Tories, a hatred Blair articulated well: "the most discredited and dishonorable Government in living memory." Later in the speech, he declared flatly, "I love my country." Pause. "And I hate what the Tories have done to it."

He quickly moved on to crafting an alternative Labour offer. For too long, Labour had spoken of a socialism expressed through nationalization and consumed with economics and politics, he said. But that obscured socialism's essential meaning: "It is a moral purpose to life; a set of values." It represented, he said, "a belief in society, in cooperation, in achieving together what we are unable to achieve alone." He grounded those beliefs without apology in Christianity's simple truths: "I am worth no more than anyone else. I am my brother's keeper. I will not walk by on the other side." He affirmed the basic principles of his politics: we are "members of the same family, same community, the same human race." His eloquence was winning over the hall.

While Labour sought unity through community, the Tories had left a country divided—"a class system—unequal and antiquated"; "a social fabric tattered and torn." His ire rose: "Look at the wreckage of our broken society," he said, most evident in the drugs and violence that denied the country a sense of community. The answer was not more government, he said, but a strong family. Labour "cannot be morally neutral about the family. It is the foundation of any decent society. Behind strong communities lie strong families," he said, returning to the certitude of his formative political period.

"We created the National Health Service. We will save it."

Some journalists may have been put off or amused by the religious allusions, but Blair was making a moral critique of Tory social divisions and offering a "socialist" vision that brought the delegates to their feet. They were allowed to be euphoric about Blair, even the party. He won them over by acknowledging, "It has been hard, I know." But he said he understood that without returning the party to its values, they could not change the country.

"I want us to be a young country again," Blair said, "a nation for all the people, built by the people. Old divisions cast out. A new spirit in the nation. Working together. Unity. Solidarity. Partnership. One Britain." He put his Christian values at the heart of his "one nation" speech: "Where your child in distress is my child, your parent ill and in pain is my parent, your friend unemployed or helpless is my friend; your neighbor my neighbor."

The journalists were uncertain whether to declare a nation with shared values "spin" or "vision."

At the close, Blair derided the Tories for their claim to the Union Jack. "It is no good waving the fabric of our flag when you have spent sixteen years tearing apart the fabric of our nation, tearing apart the bonds that tie communities together and make us a united kingdom," he said. With that primal indictment, he promised the children and families of Britain that "I will do all I can do to get the Tories out." It was, more than ever before, a mission.[32]

It was an eloquent speech that spoke of Blair's vision and values, posing a powerful choice but one mostly divorced from those being hammered out in his campaign. With the delegates so enthusiastic and the journalists suspending their skepticism to praise the speech's authenticity, the Blair team quickly declared it immensely important, though only after the fact.[33] If only the O.J. verdict had not come in right before the evening news.[34]

STRUGGLING TO SQUARE THE CIRCLE

I was mostly nervous that my car would get bogged down in traffic and make me late for my 7:30 A.M. meeting with Blair at his home. I never knew when to expect congestion as English property owners over centuries have retained a right to block boulevards or highways at their will, forcing the traffic elsewhere. With a regular "black taxi" I would have been confident the driver would create his own mazelike route to miraculously pitch up at the doorstep on time, but my driver had his map book open on the front seat. At least that gave me time to rehearse my presentation, spread out on the backseat. We were making our way to Islington, an inner borough in north London where middle-class professionals began gentrifying homes in the 1960s, though the shops on the commercial roads were nothing to write home about and there were plenty of poorer and tough areas, too. Blair's house at One Crescent Circle was a tall four-story on a quiet street with no evident security, no media, and no guard on the walkway up to the front door. I imagined my driver had gotten it wrong. I walked up the stairs and rang the bell. Philip opened the door with a flourish, pleased with himself for getting the meeting organized at home, where the discussion would be protected.[35]

Not really. As Tony greeted me, he apologized for needing to help the kids get ready for school. Cherie, Blair's wife, came out to apologize, too, as she maneuvered the kids toward the door and stuffed her legal papers into a briefcase. That the Blairs' house apparently was more Tory than Labour went right past me. It all seemed so normal. Wasn't that the way every professional, two-career, two-barrister family lived everywhere in the world? And wasn't that the way any of them would react if a pollster arrived at the door at 7:30?

I waited in the front living room, comfortable with high ceilings, while the Blairs busied themselves in the kitchen. He soon joined us, holding a collection of mugs for the coffee and tea. From the first moment there, I felt completely at ease.

But we had a problem, a big problem, despite the success of the party conference. That was why I was there. The conference speech had focused on "One Nation" and social divisions and had barely mentioned our recommendation about "Working for all the people." Blair was in a different place, but given Labour's history and the improving economy, we did not have the luxury of just discarding our most powerful definition of the election. With the need to resolve this tension so important, I had written a memo, underlined, accompanied by graphs, which I handed to him. Unlike President Clinton, Blair stayed with me, graph by graph.

Voter ratings of the economy were rising. Major's standing was improving. Both the Liberal Democrats and Conservatives were winning back some of their defectors. While Labour was much more trusted than the Conservatives on managing the economy, it was still the Tories' strongest area. "Who to turn to on the economy," according to our regression analysis, was the strongest predictor of the vote, which could readily go against us if the recovery became more robust. "Conservatives can look at this chart with some encouragement," I pointed out with a glint to concentrate his mind on the risk in his current choice.

With over half the country believing Labour would raise taxes, "I could construct a campaign that is waged on their terrain," I told him, pointing to a striking graph that showed the Conservatives' definition of the election as credible as our own. Labour's vote was 10 points above the percentage identifying with Labour, and we were certain to lose altitude at some point.

That is why we had to pay attention to the choice that had the most power for us, I said, dwelling on that likely slide. But I revised the choice to incorporate my earlier thoughts about "community" and Blair's conference speech. I chose my words carefully and put them in bold italics in the memo: *"The Labour Party and Tony Blair will capture the imagination of the British public if they keep building the central contrast—a Labour Party prepared to represent the whole nation and a Conservative Party that aspires to aid only the richest and most powerful."* Labour representing all the people was elevated as the "whole nation," consistent with Blair's patriotic formulation a month earlier. Tories were singled out for promoting the powerful, but this was a different indictment than his attack on the Tories for tearing apart the social fabric. He clearly understood the populist element and said he agreed, but he did not take the point further.

I used all the tools available to me, including the presentation for the first time of the Voter Choice Scale—combining eight questions that enabled us to display separate color bars for our base, the "loyalists" and "supporters," and the voters we might lose, the "conditional" and "vulnerable." These erodible voters were significant because they leaned Tory on tax and the economy, but tilted back because the Tories only worked for the rich and powerful; they responded strongly to the populist attacks.[36]

To leaven the results and curry some favor, I presented a regression analysis that showed that feelings about John Major were not very important to the vote. This election was all about how people felt about the Tories, which was mostly contempt. But it was different on our side, where attitudes toward Blair were as important as feelings about Labour in predicting the vote. It was very un-British, more like U.S. presidential. His personal standing was a critical part of Labour's lead in the race at that point.

I was beginning to realize that I didn't really know Tony Blair. The likenesses to Clinton were too simple. The common language of "opportunity," "responsibility," and "community" had allowed me to presume I knew much more than I did about his political mission. Why was he so uncomfortable bringing inequality and fairness into his indictment of the Tories' dissolution of society? I assumed this was the conventional push-back as in Clinton land, but maybe there was more to it.

THE PERSON

That Tony Blair was focused, decent and polite, well-mannered, hardworking, self-confident, enthusiastic, and ambitious, that he honored self-reliance and aspiration, was unsurprising, given his father, Leo. That he was religious, motivated by a morality that sorts good and evil, also was not surprising, given his mother, Hazel. That he had a passion for social justice and assuredness about his convictions that took him into the Labour Party was harder to explain, even on reflection, though his university years seemed unusually formative, I learned years later.

Tony was raised in a prosperous home, as his father moved from a university lectureship first in Australia, then at Durham in Scotland before joining the bar and building a successful practice near Newcastle, increasingly liked and respected in his community. In Newcastle he was chair of the local Conservative Association with ambitions to sit in Parliament. A severe stroke abruptly ended that. Hazel devoted herself to Leo's recovery, all witnessed by the three children. She later nursed the youngest daughter through a form of rheumatoid arthritis. Tony credits Hazel with his religious faith and remembers her good manners, kindness, lack of malice, and commitment to others.[37]

Tony Blair lived a protected life in private schools and, until university, showed little intellectual, social, or political interest. At Fettes, where discipline was unbearably tight, Blair was active, likable, and enthusiastic, joined sports and drama and was an exuberant performer in more and more roles, where he took care with the words, timing, and presentation. But he was restless, questioning of every rule and antiestablishment. His growing defiance nearly got him expelled before he left early for Oxford. That was more about drinking, curfews, and long hair than drugs, and the coarseness of the times and seemed not to involve politics.[38]

He arrived at St. John's College at Oxford in 1972 where he studied law, diligently but without great distinction. He was active in football, soccer for U.S. readers, and social gatherings, grew very long hair, smoked, but not marijuana, and drank, but not in excess. While seen as a leader in his social groups, he took no part in the Oxford Union, the debating societies, the anti-war demonstrations, or the political clubs. He did not carry on with the theater at Oxford, instead participating in small revues for his college, performing Monty Python–like characters of his own creation.[39]

He spent a growing amount of time in late-night philosophical conversations with his closest group of friends, mostly left and far left in their thinking and critical of the politicians of the day, more interested in Marx and Engels and Gramsci and Habermas. In the group was Peter Thomson, an Australian priest with a social mission. He was taking classes at Oxford and built a lifetime bond with Blair, rekindled in the years before Blair became prime minister.

They discussed John Macmurray, a professor of moral philosophy almost forgotten until Blair called attention to his importance to his thinking. In unusually accessible English, Macmurray seemed to answer what must have been a troubling question for this enthusiastic Oxford student: how can individual ambition be realized in society? This was a "powerful influence on me," Blair remembered, "because it seemed to make sense of the need to involve the individual in society without the individual being subsumed in society." Others in the group described Blair as "fired up" by this idea, allowing him to settle on the importance of "community" if the individual is to prosper.[40] It was almost as if he found a way to respect his father's example on aspiration, consistent with his new thinking about society.

The group, with Thomson at the center, spent a lot of their time on Christianity, which led Blair, an indifferent congregant over most of his life, to start attending chapel. After extended and private conversations with the chaplain, Blair decided to be confirmed in the Church of England. While the rest of Britain was growing secular, Blair was becoming seriously religious, though in his own private way. The chaplain described him as "full of vitality, warm and politically aware" and excited about discovering God. His faith reinforced his desire to do practical things and work toward a good society. He became aware of his mother's struggle with cancer only in her final days as she met with each of the children in turn. Her death affected him deeply and people began to witness a new focus and sense of purpose.[41]

In September of 1975, at age twenty-two, Blair left Oxford to study for the bar and a few months later joined the Labour Party, believing that it was the only vehicle for his Christian social approach and for working to achieve an impact. With limited contacts in London, he was fortunate to land a position in the chambers of Derry Irvine, who had good relations with the Labour Party. Blair decided to specialize in employment law, representing individuals against corporations, and to work on issues that had practical effect, all the while building good contacts with the trade unions. With a passion for social justice, he became active in the Chelsea branch of the Labour Party and aligned himself against the militants. He even acted as counsel to the party when it sought to expel them.[42]

He also met Cherie Booth in the competition to secure a position in Irvine's chambers. It was an extraordinary match. She was a kind of phenomenon, at age twenty-one one of the top law students in the entire country. She took a different route there. Her father was a famous actor on a comedy series and a cult figure for the left, but he was also a philanderer and drunk who abandoned his family, leaving her mother and Cherie in Liverpool to struggle for support, working fish-and-chips and the like. She went to Catholic schools and, upon arriving at the London School of Economics, decided on the law. Unlike Blair, she won top honors. She studied for the bar at the same time and competed for a place in Irvine's chambers. Deciding she would lose out to Blair, she moved on. But they dated and, after a long engagement, married in 1980. They shared a lot, including the importance of faith, wanting a large family, and a deep passion for the Labour Party. They both tried to find seats for which they could run. Blair used his skills to win over the local party and ran successfully and fortuitously in Sedgefield in northern England in 1983, after losing earlier in a by-election for a seat in the Tory heartland. At age thirty, he was the youngest Labour MP and perhaps the one with shortest tenure in the Labour Party, having joined just eight years earlier. In January 1984, they had their first child.[43]

Also elected in the 1983 Tory landslide was thirty-two-year-old Gordon Brown, the new member from Dunfermline East, just outside Glasgow in Scotland where the Labour Party still had a pulse. Unlike the new member from Sedgefield, Brown had been a member of the Labour Party, probably since birth, but certainly from the age of twelve when he was first sighted canvassing in a by-election in Kinross and West Pertshire. Brown is a son of a Presbyterian minister, the Reverend John Brown, whose parents and grandparents were tenant farmers during the high unemployment of the 1920s and 1930s. Their parish was on the outskirts of Glasgow, the industrial heartland of Scotland, where unemployment and poverty were high. Brown and his brothers were instilled with a Calvinist faith in hard work, self-reliance, and self-improvement. At age twelve, he and his brothers created a local newspaper with the banner header, "Scotland's Only Newspaper in Aid of the Families from Hunger Campaign," understanding early that having Victorian values of hard work was no guarantee against misfortune.

Gordon was something of a prodigy and was catapulted to Edinburgh University at age sixteen, full of problems by his own account. But to his friends he was sociable and a leader, consumed with sports, "ferociously bright" but never a "swot." On arriving at university, he lost sight in one eye permanently due to a detached retina, but he was soon active as a pamphleteer against the university administration, forcing divestment from South Africa. He was elected student rector in 1972, a position he created over the administration's objections.

He spent the early 1970s teaching at university and actively considered running for a parliamentary seat in 1974 at just age twenty-three, a period of ferment for the thirty thousand Scottish coal miners in the pits of Fife near Brown's home. He did run for Parliament in 1979, losing in Edinburgh South, but in the meantime joined the Transport and General Workers' Union—the largest union in Scotland and "the machine" in many of these constituencies—and fortuitously became active in union education. Labour was challenged there by the growth of the Scottish nationalists, the Trotskyite militants, and the Social Democratic Party breakaway from Labour. When the newly drawn seat at Dunfermline East became available at the eleventh hour in 1983, encompassing Brown's home in Fife, the coalfields, as well as the north coast, the TGWU stood with him. He won election at age thirty-two, going to Westminster to confront Thatcherism at its height and the Labour Party at its nadir.[44]

Blair and Brown ended up sharing a small windowless office with their desks facing each other, Brown's mountain of papers spilling over into their shared space. They were variously described as "joined at the hip" or "the brothers." Within seven months Blair became the party's spokesman on the City, London's Wall Street, and moved to the front benches faster than anyone ever had before him. The front benches literally are for those with any kind of shadow cabinet position or spokesperson on an issue. Within two years Brown was appointed frontbench spokesperson on trade and industry. After the 1987 defeat, he was appointed assistant to the Treasury shadow secretary, an appointment that moved him into the shadow cabinet at age thirty-six, the fastest rise in anyone's memory. Brown was an aggressive debater and keen critic of the Tories. In June 1984, Brown posed a question to the Social Security minister: "Will the Honorable Lady comment on the fact that Britain still has the most unequal distribution of wealth in Europe and that it has the least successful economy?"[45] His leading role challenging the Tories' economic policies and his finely honed debating skills helped him rank first in 1988 in balloting among Labour MPs, an informal queue for leadership in the party. Blair, who was appointed shadow employment secretary, was rising rapidly, too, and ranked fifth.

In 1985, Neil Kinnock brought in Peter Mandelson, a researcher for a weekend news show, to direct party communications and campaigns, a concept foreign to most Labour politicians, but not to Blair and Brown. They endorsed, embraced, and fully exploited Mandelson's talents, Brown already familiar with the role of such methods in the United States. With Brown the senior figure, the three men formed a troika with a passion to change the party. They knew their quest to win over voters required new methods of listening and communicating. For the first time focus groups became part of the Labour Party tool chest, with Brown making the most demands on Gould. In the 1987 election campaign, Mandelson got Kinnock to abandon the red flag as Labour's symbol in favor of a red rose.[46]

At the end of January 1993, inspired by his trip to the United States and by the "crime issue," itself unconventional for the European left, Blair gained a new clarity on community and a new certitude about social action. At the risk of stating the near obvious, he said crime arose because of "our disintegration as a community." Crime "is quintessentially a problem that the individual cannot tackle alone"; it "demands that communities work as communities and fight it." That philosophically disqualified the Tories, and thus enlarged the political landscape open to Labour because the core inner-city poor voters, not just middle-class England, looked to sort it out.[47]

In the foreword to a book published for the Christian Socialist Movement, Blair boldly declared that above all Christianity "is about the union between the individual and community, the belief that we are not stranded in helpless isolation, but owe a duty both to others and to ourselves and are, in a profound sense, dependent on each other to succeed." He said a society dominated by "acquisitiveness and consumption" or "selfishness or even individualism" could not succeed. His foreword gave a religious, though not necessarily evangelic, cast to his political project. "Religion, whether practiced by Anglicans or Catholics, places a duty, an imperative on us to reach our better self and to care about creating a better community to live in," he wrote. Christianity is also judgmental, he said. "There is right and wrong. There is good and bad." And when we look at our society, "we should not hesitate to make such judgments," giving his words and his mission a new force.[48]

Blair also realized along the way that his role as shadow home secretary, more than Gordon's as shadow chancellor, offered the larger stage to address the nation. For the first time, Blair emerged at the top of the balloting for the shadow cabinet.

So why during the whole process in 1995 to frame the election and the choice did we not even test Blair's "One Nation" concept, captured in his closing sentence in Clause IV, "where the rights we enjoy reflect the duties we owe, and where we live together, freely, in a spirit of solidarity, tolerance and respect"? Nobody asked for and I never wrote for our survey, "The Tories divide Britain. Labour will create One Britain. Is that the real difference? If so, does it motivate you to vote Labour?"

With Philip and Alastair providing ungainly lists of message options, it did not occur to me three months into the job that they had left off something so fundamental. Blair's article on Christian socialism was not one of the pieces that came over the fax. Why was it not on the list? First and foremost, they just didn't believe it was an effective message. I never heard a real voter longing for unity and deploring division, other than for scorning the Tories "who can't stop bickering." "One Nation" was so abstract that it left voters mostly puzzled as to what it was about and thinking Blair was disconnected from their lives, maybe "a bit smarmy."[49] Around 40 percent thought Blair was a "person you can really trust" when I started, but that had dropped to a third after the party conference.

Maybe they thought that "One Nation" was too remote to get buy-in from Brown, not to mention the rest of the shadow cabinet. Brown was formally named head of election strategy the night before the conference and the previous summer he had told David Frost, "Fairness will be the theme, indeed, the agenda of a Tony Blair administration." In his conference speech, Brown attacked the Tories: "The only connections they care about are the City connections"; "the only network they want to preserve is the old boys' network and the only train they will run on schedule is the gravy train."[50] In this parliamentary system and this deal for governance, Blair would share the stage. He was not running to be president.

But the political advisors, like the political class, social elites, and the media in Britain, were fully secular and averse to all that talk of social morality and certainly not of God. When Blair was interviewed later in the campaign about his faith, Alastair warned him that this would bring "nothing but trouble." This is not like America; British People "hate it." And when the stories proved unfriendly, Blair promised Alastair he would "never do it again."

But Blair's religious views were "very well formed" and he attended church every week, he told me many years later, "which was pretty unusual for any aspiring political leader, I suppose."[51] If he got time during the campaign, he was more likely to read theology than politics.

But for me, Blair was totally political, not unlike Clinton, consumed with how to make his project electorally successful. But what was his project?

SETTLING THE ECONOMIC NARRATIVE

Fairness.

One Nation.

Opportunity.

And then add into the mix an improving economy.

Suddenly my mission at the New Year became to develop an economic narrative that all could champion. The choice of narrative tells voters what problem Labour seeks to solve, its approach and values and the types of people it honors and welcomes. With the economy the main reason to vote against the Tories and for Labour, I was given the green light to sort it out over the next four weeks and fielded two surveys, observed groups, joined back-and-forth talks with Philip and David Miliband, and met with Blair twice. He and Brown had evolved their own thinking and, since November, David and Philip had been struggling to find a synthesis that was not just a diminished compromise. By the close of this intense period, I would offer just such a synthesis. Now, could I get the leaders to see that?

I wrote a memo to Blair right after I got the January survey data in order to gain his attention. Labour had 49 percent of the vote, but that could fall to 43 if we lost older voters to the Conservatives and a lot of younger voters who were just not that committed to politics. We were facing growing confidence in the economy and improving living standards. Our advantage over the Tories on managing the economy was only 10 points, half as large as our lead in the election. With managing the economy the best predictor of the vote in the regressions, our lead was certain to drop in the months ahead, unless we could frame the narrative right.

These results dramatically highlighted the importance of getting to a solution, if Blair and then Brown were open to it. Labour's commitment to "One Nation" could have "extraordinary power," I wrote, as it contains "the public's greatest aspiration for Labour" but also the Conservatives' "principal vulnerability." The Tories had created a "divided, two-tier Britain." What animated this critique and defined "two-tier," I pointed out, was the Tories' support for the rich and powerful and their uncaring attitude toward ordinary citizens.[52]

At the end of January, I flew to London and went immediately to Watford, a town to the northwest in Outer London for one focus group with Liberal Democratic defectors and a second with Conservatives. Philip moderated and I again played the role of mute assistant. Both groups dismissed Major: "prat," "wimp," "no balls."

I wrote detailed notes on a pad, bracketing and circling the growing number of expressions about "change." At the end of the first group I wrote: "Anti-Tory. Determined." After the second: "Determined to get rid of Conservatives." They even made the turn: "Give those Labour boys a chance for a change."

What drove this mood more than anything else in this so-called period of economic recovery was the pain the Tories had caused people and how deeply vulnerable they felt. When Philip described a two-tier Britain, with hardworking families doing their part, it opened a floodgate: "brought us down," "we are struggling beyond belief," "we have no holidays," "damning our children to second class education." When the discussion turned to the National Health Service, the people in the room seemed overwhelmed. The hospital was "appalling," you can wait five years for operations, father is terminally ill and "the home is lost," my mother-in-law had cancer treatment, "atrocious treatment," "I had two heart attacks, a year ago for open heart surgery and no bed, nearly died." That is what they wanted the election to be about.[53]

Listening to people each night, I became a virtual missionary on the political and moral necessity of getting Blair to make this pain and indictment the centerpiece of his economic narrative.

In the focus groups, Philip showed a video of Blair's speech on a "stakeholder economy" in which he tried to give greater concreteness to his "One Nation" ideas.[54] The group glazed over. "Sounds good," "heard it all before," "sincere, aren't they all," "hopeful, but wishful thinking," "brilliant, nothing new." I watched them just staring through it. "Not listening," I wrote on my pad, Blair offering an aloof vision of the economy that did not explain their pain or show them how to vote for change.[55]

While I was home, Brown did an end run and came to see me in my Washington brownstone office to make his case on the economic narrative, accompanied not by Jonathan Powell like last time but Ed Balls, his closest economic and political advisor. Though Philip and I had begun meeting with Brown in his parliamentary office, he did not get the full polls or memos with my unfettered views. I shared first my thoughts and polls on what was happening in U.S. politics; Brown was getting the economic story direct from Reich, Summers and, Greenspan. But then he strongly pressed his case for an "on your side, hardworking families" economic message, for which I was more than sympathetic.

My philosophy for dealing with the Blair-Brown "marriage" was to keep my head down. While I was part of the Blair team, I had met Brown before Blair independently and his team in turn believed I had an independent status.

I knew Brown to be smart on center-left politics and wasn't entirely sure he wasn't right on some key issues. I also knew the power of this unique collaboration and I thought my detachment from the battle gave me some cachet to communicate effectively with Brown.

I met with Blair and the team at his parliamentary office and told him the groups and surveys were getting us close to an effective economic message, though I asked for a few more days to write a narrative and Philip and I agreed to take our hands to separate memos. Philip set out in his memo on March 3 with a barely disguised exasperation about what "convergence" must achieve: a *central economic argument* that you agree on," one that is not "rarefied" and "above people's heads"; a "real, concrete populist offer" that shows how people are "better off, their lives improved under Labour." In a gambit to spread the pain equally, Philip proposed to take off the table "modernisation," "stakeholding," and "opportunity." Then he passed the ball to me: "Stan will be writing a follow-up note to this in the next few days.[56]

With the detachment of a few days in America, I finally worked through a simple formulation and choice, "a shared perspective, which contrasts powerfully with the Tories'." It was not a compromise that diminished Blair's and Brown's points of principle, but a "powerful economic message rooted in these ideas." I laid it out in a box, with the headline in boldface caps: "LABOUR'S ECONOMIC MESSAGE." It offered a choice, bringing together much of the last six months' work, starting with the simplified description of the Conservatives: *Tory economics: Two-tier Britain.*" That was defined simply and in populist terms: "for the privileged, all they can get," capturing everything people were thinking about privatization, greed, and sleaze. For everyone else "a second class NHS and schools, low investment in industry, skills and infrastructure" and "higher taxes." The result: "national economic decline," "life harder for working people," and an economy "you dare not depend on."

The contrast was with *Labour economics: One Nation Britain,*" further elaborated in the subtitle, "Where everyone has the opportunity and tools to prosper." I was pleased with myself, having joined "One Nation" and "opportunity" in a way that I thought was real. That meant: "quality schools and Health Service, modernization of industry, infrastructure, technology and skill training, taxes down for hard working people"—indeed, any set of policies they championed, but always with the purpose of creating "One Nation," where all have "the opportunity and tools to prosper." The result was "national renewal, greater prosperity for people, an economy you can trust"—a happy ending, contrasted starkly with the nightmare people were living.

In the memo, I played out the kinds of symmetric choices that flow easily out of that economic message: "Tory economics says to the most privileged, take all you can get; Labour economics said, "we are One Nation where everyone must have the opportunity and tools to succeed." Tory economics meant second-class health service and schools, while Labour's economics meant quality schools and heath service; low investment versus high investment; high taxes versus lower taxes; "national economic decline" versus "national renewal."

"The breakdown of community and cohesion are strongly implied—though not explicitly presented," I wrote in my last bullet point for Blair. What I offered was this: "The aspiration to One Britain will allow the leader to elaborate on his hopes for the country and communicate his values," inviting him to use this choice as a vehicle to elaborate his core beliefs.[57] I lingered on that sentence, wanting him to know that I understood what he wanted to achieve.

A week later I met with him to make the case personally with a powerful new survey buttressing the recommendations. I began our characterization of the economy by noting that while the Tories thought it was so good, real people were working harder with no rise in living standards, the NHS and schools were faltering, and wealth was more a result of "windfall" than real growth. That was the reality for more than 80 percent. While a growing number accepted the Tory claim that the economy was strong, it was a grudging and soulless agreement, with only 15 percent saying "there is a great deal of truth" in it. "Mr. Leader," I said, "we have a message," an assertion I underlined and marked with double asterisks in my presentation notes. "There is no reason to be shy about our description of this economy."

The strongest critique of "Tory economics" said, "The British economy is not working for hardworking families. They face negative equity. Their taxes have gone up 22 times. They are working more for less, while the wealthiest few are making windfall profits." That was the meaning of "two tier" when you got to the economy. The message was stronger still when you added that the Tories were running down the NHS and schools. The strongest positive by far said, "New Labour has a vision for a better Britain. It will build up the economy and industry and capacities of people. It will build up the schools and hospitals. Britain deserves better." Almost 60 percent said they were more likely to vote Labour after hearing our economic message.

"We're there. It is settled," I said, waiting to see if there was any push-back before going on to discuss Europe.[58]

I also described a fascinating change in the race, even though I knew this could make my job much harder. Labour still led the Conservatives by 20 points, a lead that had been stable for two years, but over the last two polls the pattern of support had shifted sharply, producing a "class collapse," as I described it for Blair. Amazingly, Labour had taken the lead among professionals, self-employed, the upper-income and supervisory employees; the gains were almost as strong with white-collar, office, and skilled workers. And while Labour had monumental leads with "blue collar and unskilled workers and the poor and those on public assistance," the lead had fallen off 10 points since the beginning of the year. Blair had his own measure of success and transcending class was one of them. For some in the team like Peter Mandelson and Anji Hunter, that was more important than maximizing his vote—and I wasn't at all sure Blair wouldn't prefer such a classless outcome as well.

Settled?

Only two months later I wrote a note to Blair, unhappy with our progress on the message. Mostly I was upset because the Leader had slipped back into his default position. I wrote: "This is not about overcoming divisions and uniting the country"; "this is about a Labour vision that says the country should work for everyone, not just the privileged few." I tried to get him back to the message, almost invoking a contract, "That is the core promise of the one nation idea, and we seem to be losing it."[59]

With Blair about to write his 1996 conference speech, his last and most important before the election the following year, Philip urged me to review all of Blair's interviews and write him a note. To my surprise, "I am impressed that all the material seems to advance a single narrative" but the message was still diffuse. "We accuse the Tories of failure, hurting people, causing damage, messing up, being a threat to their families, lying and betraying and of getting the fundamentals wrong." And the message was "moving too many steps away from people."[60]

In his conference speech at the Winter Gardens in Blackpool, Blair did not mention "hardworking families." But he managed to get there in his own way, making clear this was a speech about the future, an "era of extraordinary, revolutionary change" that required his priorities to be "education, education, and education." The Tories were content with a "30-30-40" economy, in which 30 percent "do very well; 30 percent just getting by and 40 percent struggling or worse." It was Blair's fairly benign picture of an unequal or two-tier Britain. Regardless, he posed his new or revised first question: "How do we create, in Britain, a new age of achievement in which all of the people not just a few can share?" And he answered with "the choice" for the electorate: "For all the people. Or for a few." Sadly, the country could not turn to the Tories to make the right choice. He called them "the most feckless, irresponsible and incompetent managers of the British economy in our history." Blair relished talking about the "Tory economy": "Sure the few at the top have become wealthy under the Tories, but they have put up the taxes of ordinary families in Britain by the largest amount in peacetime in history." He enjoyed using the new choice to deny them being the party of enterprise and ambition: "When the Tories talk about the spirit of enterprise they mean a few self-made millionaires." With their convictions, they "run a country where a few winners take all, rather than all of us as winners and see what happens— huge costs of unemployment, crime, social decay. Higher taxes to pay for it." And then he asked, taking it back to his first question: "What kind of world is it where the best education, the best jobs, the best skills, are available only to the few?" Sure some will succeed, but was that the kind of world in which we can take pride? "That, Mr. Major, is the real moral question we face." He had finally redefined "two-tier Britain" in his expansive, nondivisive moral terms. I listened and cheered because the moral content and his turn to a question made this choice so much more powerful.

Then he proudly unfurled the label "New Labour"—"a party open and in touch," attracting new members and new voters who know it is the party of the future.

"Britain can do better. Britain can do better than this."

"I say to the Tories: Enough is enough."

"Enough. Be done. Be gone."

In our October survey after the conference, the public picked two attributes that best described Labour: "for the future" and "for people like me." For the Tories, it was, first and foremost, "for the rich," and then, "divided."[61]

People were clearly listening to Blair and drawing the conclusions that set up the strongest possible choice.

THE PLEDGES: THE POPULIST OFFER

To build confidence in the party's readiness to govern and Blair's leadership, the team approved the idea of writing an early manifesto—goals for change and responsible budgeting—that Blair and the shadow cabinet could take to the conference and then to a vote of the full membership for approval before the end of the year. In the tradition of Clause IV, this was intended to show a party careful in its spending commitments, with a leader able to dominate his own party and regain some of the lost trust.[62]

Paralleling this effort was an attempt to define five pledges that would form the heart of a contract with the public, described by Peter Hyman, the driving force behind it, as "an offer" to the voters that was "concrete, tangible and populist to match [the] Tories," who would pledge to cut taxes. The Tories' contract was much easier to write. Each of Labour's pledges reflected the real priorities in the manifesto, but distilled to be real, understandable, and credible. Philip's focus groups in May and June were devoted almost entirely to testing the various policies, finding words that made each understandable with outcomes that mattered most to people in their lives. I opted out of the pledge process because it was so closely linked to the debates in the shadow cabinet over priorities and in the endless meetings in Blair's office.[63]

Joined by the whole shadow cabinet, Blair released *New Life for Britain* at a July 4 press conference, with the pledges buried in the back and nearly lost.[64] Peter Hyman battled to relaunch them, aided by Margaret McDonagh, now head of the campaign, who urged that they be printed on a wallet-size card, like the ones she had seen in California listing the benefits of a yes vote for a ballot initiative there.

The first four pledges emerged right away, both from the policy process and the strong response in the groups.

Pledge one: "Cut class size to 30 or under for 5 to 7 year olds, using the money Conservatives reserve to fund students opting out of public schools."

Pledge two: "Fast track punishment for persistent young offenders by halving the time from arrest to sentencing." That Labour included being tough on crime with juveniles in its top two pledges was a surprise for a left party and a key reassurance.

Pledge three: "Cut NHS waiting lists by treating an extra 100,000 patients in a first step by releasing 100 million pounds saved from NHS red tape."

The pledges on schools and the NHS fast became the most important as our polls in the fall showed that Tories' undermining of the NHS and schools fueled the biggest doubt about them and provided the best reason to vote against them.[65] The more relentless we were on reassurance of Labour's prudence and mainstream values, the angrier voters grew with the Tories on public service cuts. They now believed there was a safe way to restore public service spending, and investment in the NHS was now the campaign's number one pledge for voters.

Pledge four: "Remove 250,000 under 25-year olds from benefit and into work by using money from a windfall levy on the privatized utilities." That was Brown's signature policy to address youth unemployment but in the context of welfare reform, financed by a tax on the imprudent.[66]

Gould tested a pledge on Labour not raising income taxes but Brown wanted to wait until much closer to the election to announce such a change. With the economic recovery ever more robust, Philip wanted a pledge that was reassuring about Labour and the economy, which Ed Balls happily drafted.

Pledge Five: "Labour will set tough rules for government spending and borrowing; ensure low inflation; strengthen the economy so that interest rates are as low as possible."[67] With the economy issue number one, Labour's offer was not a plan but merely economic stability, after years of Labour and Tory boom and bust.

"The pledges worked better than anything else I have ever tested in politics,"

Gould wrote. "Nothing else came close." Both media and academic critics later described the pledges as "trivial, poll-tested commitments." But they missed the point: the concreteness of the pledges made the policy changes more real to voters. Each was shorthand for a bigger set of changes and commitments. A government that focused on smaller class size for the youngest pupils and on reduced waiting lists in hospitals as its first priorities had a larger set of policy changes for the public services. The commitment to keep interest rates as low as possible was the leading indicator for a bigger set of economic policies and priorities. Brown had already pledged that a Labour chancellor would be governed by a "Golden Rule," borrowing only to finance public investment, not consumption. Together, these pledges gave the public something tangible by which to measure a new government's work.[68]

Confidence in the economy was growing and in November, the Tories tried to take advantage of the economic gains and rerun their "tax bombshell" campaign, charging that Labour would have to raise taxes by £1,200 a year for the average family to pay for the party's plans. But this time Millbank went to war, launching a shadow cabinet rebuttal, followed by a Labour charge that Conservatives had raised taxes twenty-two times since 1992. Unlike previous elections, voters were actually growing less worried that Labour would raise taxes.[69]

In early January 1997, Blair and Brown, ever nervous that worries about economic stability could shift voters away, met in Islington to decide finally that Labour would not raise income tax rates, even for the richest taxpayers. Blair and his people had long wanted to make this commitment but Brown held up the decision, possibly to keep open the option or more likely to avoid it leaking to the press before he did. At the end of January and on the eve of an election campaign not yet called, Brown began a series of speeches to lay out the red lines that would take tax and spending issues and management of the economy off the table. "Because we want to encourage work, and after 22 tax rises since 1992, which have hit hard-working families," Brown began, "I want to make clear that a Labour government will not increase the basic rate of income tax." Taxes were off the table—a pledge tested in no poll of mine. And in the next speech, he announced that as chancellor, he would accept the Conservatives' proposed spending levels for the next two years. In short, Labour would bar itself from spending any more than the Tories. I was blown away at the boldness of this ultimate reassurance and the ability to pull it off as a surprise. Spending was off the table.[70]

Hurriedly, the campaign reprinted the pledge cards with a new Pledge five: "No rise in income tax rates; cut VAT on heating to 5 percent; and keep inflation and interest rates as low as possible."

Labour's five top pledges on a pledge card handed out in the 1997 campaign, modeled after a card that Margaret McDonagh saw used in California for a statewide referendum when she volunteered and worked in the 1992 Clinton campaign.

THE ELECTION

On March 17, 1997, John Major announced that Parliament's work would end in three days, though not adjourn formally for three weeks, followed by elections on May 1. He was using every available device to extend the campaign half again as long as the norm since 1960. The Conservative government that had hung on for the full five years in hopes the economy would save it from the sleaze and divisions wanted to stretch out the campaign to the maximum possible in hopes that Blair's inexperience or Labour's demons would drag them down or that the sheer tedium would demoralize the already alienated electorate.

Major's announcement was like the firing of a starter's pistol, the runners training for so long and so over-ready. Blair went to a south London school with Cherie while Brown and Peter Mandelson assembled all the campaign staff to declare that this was what we have prepared for. Rupert Murdoch was waiting for the shot and the reliably Conservative *Sun* newspaper, read by one in five, immediately endorsed Labour, describing the Tories as "tired, divided and rudderless."[71]

With presidential campaigns in America lasting more than a year, forty-five days seemed pretty civilized to me, but nobody else thought so, certainly not the voters, who were quickly bored with it all. Before Parliament was even dissolved and before the most intense campaigning, people wrote, "Bored with it!"; "Two-sided slogging match"; "I'm sick of it"; "On too long—centuries." And the campaign had barely started.[72] Fortunately, I could not be there for the first two weeks of slogging, but was for three of the last four, taking breaks in London from South Africa where I was working with the ANC on the local elections.

Millbank had the feel of a twenty-four-hour operation, with a full staff monitoring the media through the night, ready for Brown's 7 A.M. war room meeting, previewing the 8:30 A.M. daily press conference of the leaders, and talking through the issue of the day for the campaign. Distinctive for Britain were the press conferences that the three parties held each morning that together drove most of the campaign news, after which the leaders set off in their "battle buses" to solicit marginal constituencies. Philip and I were always in transit to focus groups somewhere in the Greater London area, organized every night except Saturday.

Philip obsessed about the campaign going all wrong as it did in 1992 and wanted to speak directly with the voters as they were finally making up their minds. Frankly, there is no substitute for that interaction if you are in a life-or-death campaign. Every night I watched Philip moderate the groups of switchers, sometimes a group we had met with three weeks earlier who now got a beer and discussed the campaign as if they were part of our team. I sat off to the side, writing notes on their degree of certainty; reactions to the news, which we watched with them live or on tape each night; the advertising; and the developing conclusions about Blair and Major, Labour and the Conservatives, circling the observations I wanted to recall. Philip and I would talk about the results in the train or car, and he would write a note to the campaign and one to Blair that same night, usually calling Alastair, sometimes Blair, along the way. Sometimes he handed me the mobile phone to speak directly with Blair, which I found awkward, as I would rather wait and distill all the research coming in, not seize on the one or two people who said Blair "got a bit flustered" or that "he had the energy and the drive" for the job. But Blair certainly seemed to have a high tolerance for such reports.[73]

This was mostly therapy. The voters in the groups were not undecided and were not struggling with their vote. I wrote down their first names and next to each how firm was their vote: "Won't go back to Tories"; "Absolutely can't stand this government"; "anti-Tory vote"; "Just waiting for a new government." There were a couple of patches where the campaign was on the defensive, but much stronger was the deepening impression over the forty-five days that Blair was "passionate," "inspires confidence," "strong personality," "definitely strong leader." At the same time, there was growing confidence, with a little help from advertising, on the pledges and that Labour's priority for government was sorting out the schools and hospitals.

Power in the war room gravitated to the crush of desks at the center, where Margaret McDonagh and Philip, Mandelson, Peter Hyman, David Hill, and Charlie Whelan, Brown's press person could be found. Blair and his aides, including Derry Irvine, Blair's mentor in the law, had offices upstairs. The polling team took over a row of tables projecting into the room from the back, including Karl Agne and Greenberg Research's computer, both flown over lock, stock, and barrel from Washington to create an on-site tracking program. Until then, the agile, super-fast modern campaign conducted each survey with long face-to-face interviews, taking a full month, which I described as "cumbersome and inflexible." It was hard to believe. "This may be New Labour," I challenged Philip, "but how can you aspire to create the Aeroflot of polling operations?"[74] By May, we were conducting three national polls a week.

The Tories were staking everything on the economy. In February, the Conservatives dumped their old ad campaign that failed to raise doubts about Blair and one week after announcing elections, launched their new campaign, "Britain Is Booming. Don't Let Labour Blow It." With unemployment dropping sharply to 6.2 percent, the lowest since 1990, they put all their chips on this strategy.[75]

Everyone was very twitchy, but me. The Tories had finally focused firmly on the economy and the definition of the election, but if I had learned anything in all my work, "Britain is booming," would offend people who were working damned hard to make it and did not give the Conservatives a bit of credit for the recovery. Ad agencies and the press loved this kind of boldness, but I thought their ad would drive voters to us. In the groups, people looked up, "booming?" "Are you serious?" Clearly it was to our favor that the Tory billboards communicated that the current government believed things were good enough, that they were okay with this "boom and bust" economy.[76]

With Brown's reassuring speeches on the economy, the polls could not have been stronger at the outset of the campaign. Labour had pushed its lead on taxes to over 10 points and comparable numbers of voters expected the Conservatives and Labour to raise income taxes. Labour had a modest lead on managing the economy, a pretty extraordinary start, given the state of the economy.[77]

I began writing my "on-site" memos from the war room with Karl Agne crunching data overnight, aided by the Washington office operating five hours earlier. That enabled me to report on the poll at the 7 A.M. war room meeting. There was not much sleep time in between the focus groups and the meeting, but I had to establish my authority, even though I had done no prior U.K. election. On the other hand, nobody here had ever won a national election. Our surveys showed Labour with a lower vote and margin than the media polls, because we reported the undecided vote and did not allocate them to the parties. I believed the undecided were hang-dog Tories waiting to go home and young voters waiting to stay home. Labour's vote settled down by mid-April, two weeks before the election, to 46 percent, with the Conservatives near 30 percent. The media polls were still reporting a higher Labour vote than us, but down, too. People began to hover not around the power tables at the center but the polling tables on the side. The confidence in the economy had broken through at least for traditional Conservative voters—perhaps the audience for those ads—some of whom pulled back from Labour. Based on a poll finished eight days before the election, I wrote that the race "has changed," with Labour's vote dropping to 45 percent. It had "plateaued at a somewhat lower level," choosing my words very carefully, "and that is likely to move to lower plateau in the days ahead." But I emphasized, realizing panic was close, that this was "not the first sign of a collapsing Labour lead." Blair and Labour remained popular, with the lost vote entirely the product of Conservative consolidation.[78]

The final poll completed three days before the election showed Labour with 43 percent, and I projected a 43 to 31 percent Labour win, both numbers exactly right, noted by Philip in his diary. When a *Guardian*/ICM poll showed Labour at 43 percent—even though the media polls on average showed Labour with 47 percent—the war room grew even more tense, and I wrote to reassure: while the vote had eased down, "there is no change in the structure of the race and no evidence of new erosion."[79]

Derry Irvine had become my best friend. He asked how big the majority would be—how many more seats than all the other parties would Labour get—and with no experience on how a national percentage would translate the contest in each constituency, I said, simply, "massive." With the "class collapse," I fully expected Labour's lead of over 10 points to spread pretty evenly across the country, making possible surprisingly large gains in seats. But what did I know? According to Philip, Derry asked repeatedly, "But is Greenberg's track record any good?"

Blair, too, phoned Philip, concerned about the changing race. Philip told Blair that Stan Greenberg was "confident of a landslide."

"This is not a landslide country," Blair shot back, nervous about the result.[80]

On election day, May 1, Millbank emptied out, sending off volunteers to work in the "marginal" seats. I accepted an invitation to have lunch with Clive Hollick at his office at the *Express* newspaper building. He was an appointed member of the House of Lords and longtime financial backer of the Labour Party and "New Labour" institutions, a fan of the Clinton Democrats and America and head of United News and Media group, and we became fast friends at Millbank. I was caught off guard when he asked whether it made sense to form with Philip a London-based strategic research company, which we would in the coming months.

About 2 P.M. Philip got the first "leaks" of the exit polls, and we were indeed headed toward a double-digit win, making it all very real for the first time. Nobody was more interested than James Carville and George Stephanopoulos, who felt they owned a piece of this because of the Tories' meddling in 1992. With the polls closing at 10 P.M., I got to the war room around 9 P.M. to watch the returns on the television sets perched around the floor. There was almost nobody there, except Paul Begala of all people, soon joined by Philip and his family at 9:30. At just seconds after 10:01, all the channels were on with over-the-top graphics, competing to display the scale of the Labour "landslide," amazingly an unprecedented 179-seat margin. But with the ballots counted by hand in each of the 659 seats, it wasn't until after midnight that we got to see what it meant in real seats. Britain has the wonderful tradition that I was watching for the first time requiring every candidate in a constituency, sometimes numbering ten or more, to stand together side by side behind the moderator as he or she reads the results for each party in alphabetical order. So, one hundred Conservative MPs, including a growing number of senior cabinet ministers, had to stand emotionless, listening to the humiliating count, as the cameras zoomed in looking for any cracks in their expression. At around 1:30 A.M., Blair, too, got to stand together with the other candidates in the safe Labour Sedgefield constituency in the north of Britain, only then accepting the scale of the win but still struggling not to sound too triumphant.[81]

The swing from Conservatives to Labour of 10.3 points (drop in the Tory percent and rise in Labour's) was the largest since 1945 after the war; the 179-seat shift was the largest for any party since the 1930s and biggest in the history of the Labour Party. Was it now safe to call this a "massive" victory? The Conservative vote fell to 31 percent, its lowest since the beginning of the modern party system in 1832. They lost virtually every seat in Scotland and Wales and every major city north of London and gave up large parts of Outer London and across the south of England.[82] The commentators were competing over which historical referent could most powerfully capture the scale of the Tories' humiliation.

Philip and his family and those remaining in the war room were going to make their way over to Royal Festival Hall on the South Bank to join what would grow to a thousand activists, Labour politicians, and entertainment and business celebrities to greet Blair when he finally made his entry at 5 A.M. The festivities did not end until sunup at seven. Blair told the crowd the scale of the majority imposed a "special sort of responsibility on us"—elected "as New Labour and we will govern as New Labour." And then, as if he embraced my first day's memo on the last day, "We were elected because . . . we represent the whole of this nation and we will govern for the whole of this nation." Then he uttered the words, "We will speak up for that decent hard-working majority of the British people whose voice has been silent for too long in our political life." I felt like he was speaking directly to me, but lest I thought the debate resolved, he quickly declared that "we will build a nation united with common purpose," reflected in "the great thing about tonight's victory— support from all walks of life, all classes of people from every corner of our country." The country was "uniting to put the divisions of the past behind us . . . uniting at last as one nation."[83]

It must be an election-night pill taken by presidents and prime ministers. The pill provides relief from the divisiveness and high emotions of the campaign and feeds the hope that one's partisan mandate can become a national one, with broad support. But for Blair as for Clinton, there was more to it than that—a way to break out of the constraints imposed by the campaign's definition.

Near exhaustion, I decided not to join them for the festivities, but instead to join my friends Philip Kremen and Wendy Braverman, Labour supporters through thick and thin who turned over their mews house to me during the campaign. Philip Gould, too, quickly agreed that was for the best. He was happy to avoid any media frenzy in the morning about the "Clintonistas" behind the win. When reporters inquired later about my role, he responded half accurately, "No. Greenberg is in South Africa with the ANC." But I was outed in *The New York Times* a week before the election when Rosa and I went to a Blair rally, sitting inconspicuously in the crowd, only to be greeted by Maureen Dowd in the row in front of us. How sweet.

"The candidate for New Labour, the 43-year-old Oxford-educated lawyer with the impressive lawyer wife, has saxophones and a rock anthem and TV stars at rallies, rapid response in the imitation War Room," and "for extra verisimilitude," she wrote, "Stan Greenberg, President Clinton's old pollster, who is now working with Mr. Blair, was on the scene."[84]

I got to Philip and Wendy's near 2 A.M., in time to see what was everybody's favorite result that night, the defeat of Michael Portillo, the flamboyant Thatcherite, Euro-skeptic, and ambitious self-promoter taken down by the very young starstruck "Twigg, Stephen, Labour Party," in the safe Enfield Southgate seat, not so far from Edgware/Watford. I remembered little after that, though it is reported by those in attendance that I fell deeply asleep in an overstuffed chair in front of the TV, my hands locked around a wineglass, later nudged from my grip.

In the morning, the newspapers were not nuanced with their headlines: "Landslide Victory for Labour"; "Blair's Britain Is Born"; "Massacre"; "Buried: The Worst Tory Defeat This Century."[85]

At around noon I went over to Number 10 Downing Street, among the first to join a couple of hundred of Millbank's finest, including Margaret and Philip, who had been alerted that Blair was leaving Buckingham Palace to make the short drive up the Mall to Whitehall.[86] Despite the headlines, we were numb and still resisting the full scope of the victory less than twenty-four hours after the polls closed. But we were allowed this one time past the big gates to Downing Street, and pressed up against the barriers on each side of the short block, cheering madly "Tone-ee, Tone-ee!" when Blair and Cherie got out to walk up Downing Street and stand with their three young kids in front of the door, the number 10 clearly marked.

When you lose, the pundits quickly root out what went wrong and identify the stupid people who showed such bad judgment. When you win, especially on a historic scale, the pundits speak of the wondrous campaign and the brilliant team at the top. With all the excitement, who really has time to dwell on the 6-point drop in turnout to 72 percent, the lowest level since 1935? If you dwell on that, you discover the pull-back came not with demoralized Tories, but in the strongest Labour areas, among Labour's working-class supporters and trade union members. That the Conservatives ended up with fewer "very strong" identifiers was no great surprise, but so did Labour, creating a large bloc, over 40 percent, with a weak or no party identity.[87] Tony Blair, the "radical," may have achieved exactly what he intended, smashing the old party patterns linked to the outdated industrial order, and he took a lot of satisfaction in it. The project, however, left a lot of traditional Labour supporters less engaged and wondering where they fit in the new politics.[88]

President Clinton arrived in London to considerable excitement just four weeks after the May 1 triumph to address the cabinet and then hold a joint press conference with Blair in the garden where the two leaders affirmed areas of mutual interest and bond by offering competing "Third Way" riffs. Blair: "This is a new era" that "calls for a new-generation leadership," that "prefers reason to doctrine" and "practical results"—"the radical center of politics." Clinton: "Our first task must always be to expand opportunity for our own citizens, to expect them to behave in a responsible manner, and to recognize that we have to maintain a community." While Blair spoke more quickly because he was nervous and Clinton more slowly because he's from Arkansas, they seemed like kindred spirits. According to Alastair, "Blair really felt Clinton was someone on his wavelength," with both needing to affirm the boldness of their project against both the skeptics and forces of reaction. If we share so much, Clinton pointed out, "I'm still looking for my 179-seat majority."[89]

When Blair spoke to the first party conference after the election in the fall, he made that shared mission his organizing principle, an obligation to be great modernizers, "not just a better government than the Tories but one of the great, radical, reforming Governments of our history"—a step above what Clinton might have achieved in government. He called on his party to be "united behind our mission to modernize our country." But there was no mention of governing "for the whole of this nation" or the "decent hard-working majority of the British people," a result also interchangeable with the Clinton example, though I didn't pause to take note of it.[90]

President Clinton more than reciprocated the Number 10 meeting with a black-tie state dinner at the White House in February, requiring Blair to commandeer a Concorde to escort the cabinet, political advisors, and "Third Way" luminaries to Washington to stand in the receiving line with Harrison Ford and Barbra Streisand and join two days of meetings on strengthening their shared project.[91] Rosa and I did the receiving line, not the meetings, as I was kind of the odd man out: I was not part of the new regime in the Clinton White House and not so enamored of the "Third Way" now so fashionable. Those of us who won elections under that banner understood much of the language was too remote, that real people do not inhabit the "center," and that modernization without concrete gains for the middle class loses meaning for voters. That left me bemused and not angry and indeed he and Cherie greeted Rosa and me very warmly, Cherie reaching over for Rosa's scarf and asking where she got it. Rosa replied with a wide smile, Georgina Von Etzdorf, right at the front the Burlington Arcade next to the Royal Academy in

London. Cherie, with a considerable appreciation for British clothiers, looked as if she wanted to put her head back and laugh, but she held herself erect and proper.

DELIVERING

With Blair and Brown acutely conscious of Labour's grim history on the economy, delivery came quickly after the election. On May 6, the new chancellor, Gordon Brown, announced to everyone's surprise that the Bank of England would be independent, able to set interest rates free of political interference, and the Treasury would be reorganized to implement the "Golden Rule" and tightly control spending. The markets applauded, sending interest rates down much as they had for Clinton in his first year. Unemployment fell from 5.4 percent to almost 3.5 percent by the end of 1999. The swift and radical moves on the economy would be the most enduring impression of New Labour.[92]

In July, Brown announced that his first budget would include an additional £3 billion for the NHS and schools to reduce class sizes He announced plans for a "windfall" profits tax on privatized utilities to pay for a "New Deal" to move young people from welfare to work. Parliament repealed the VAT on fuel and enacted a law banning all handguns in Great Britain.

On August 31 of that first summer, Princess Diana died in a tragic car accident in Paris. As with President Clinton and the Oklahoma City bombing, Blair found a voice that spoke for a nation moved by her death, expressed through the flowers and notes that covered the gates at Buckingham Place and, even more, the gates at Kensington Palace where Diana lived.

In September referenda, Scottish voters supported the creation of a Scottish Parliament, and the Welsh by a narrow margin voted to create a Welsh Assembly. London residents also voted by referendum to restore local government, dismissed by Thatcher years earlier, and to elect a mayor for the first time. All parties in Northern Ireland agreed to peace talks and, in an unprecedented meeting, Blair met with Gerry Adams of Sinn Fein, the political wing of the IRA.

I returned to Britain in the third week of September for my first meeting with the prime minister at Number 10. On May 2, I had stood outside the gate cheering, but this time I went up to the officer and said, "Good morning, Stan Greenberg to see the prime minister." He ran his finger down the list and on to the second page and then said, "Okay mate." I went quickly through the small security building to have my briefcase X-rayed and then up Downing Street, trying not to be self-conscious. I rang the bell at Number 10 and the door opened immediately, a well-tailored gentleman greeting me and calling down to the prime minister's office. One of the civil service staff fetched me and took me to Blair's office—a very small nondescript office with a fireplace, directly off the back foyer. He seemed a little embarrassed with even these trappings and probably had not noticed the place seemed a touch run-down. The paintings and sculpture certainly were noteworthy for those better schooled than I, but the paint was faded and the lights more government issue than elegant. Jonathan told me he would soon move to better offices, though for the time being Blair would have to lead without the intimidating advantage of an Oval Office.

The country was euphoric about its new leaders and the direction of the country, providing poll results that were more embarrassing than the trappings. In this "not-a-landslide country," almost 60 percent said they wanted to vote Labour; almost two thirds had a favorable view of the Labour Party and almost three quarters of Blair, seen by almost 90 percent as a "strong leader"—a result noted gleefully by Alistair in his diary when I called in a day earlier. Two thirds thought the government was "keeping its promises."[93]

While the public and the media presume politicians quickly discard their campaign promises, Blair was consumed with fulfilling the contract and

With Tony Blair in his first Downing Street office. [Author's collection]

disproving the history of Labour failure in government. Though his popular-ity clearly transcended headway on those specific commitments, for him this was a matter of honor and how one won the right to continue. The very first survey in September, worked together with Philip, was devoted to how to measure whether the government was keeping its promises in each policy area. I used a series of two-part questions: Is the government "trying to keep its promises" in that area or not? Is the government "making progress" or not? While large majorities believed the Blair government was trying to honor its pledges, the public was very discriminating right from the outset about what was happening. The government got high marks on raising school standards and giving Britain a strong voice in Europe; fairly good marks on crime, creat-ing jobs for young people, and "keeping taxes low for hardworking people"; and it got modest marks on the NHS, with many saying, "too early to tell." This was about people's lives and they did not let the "honeymoon" get in the way of their discerning judgments.[94]

Blair spoke to a pulsating hall at the Labour Party conference and re-minded them that "what people give, the people can take away." Like the frenzied work of the first half year, the speech was focused on the "contract with the British people—we are honoring—the promises already kept." Con-fident that they were honoring the contract, he called on the conference for more modernization and reform, particularly of the NHS. We must not just "save the NHS but make it better. The money will be there. I promise you that. This year. Every year"—a not very subtle recognition that the election freed people more than anything else to hope for gains in the health service. But the bargain was "in return, I want reform."[95]

Early in 1998, I put up a warning flag for the NHS, which was the voters' "number one criteria for evaluating success of this government." In meetings with both Blair and Brown, I noted that only a third thought Labour was "trying and making progress"; there was almost a 10-point jump in people saying the government was not trying to keep its promises.[96]

In Brown's second budget in March, he moved ahead with a commitment to create the working families tax credit, modeled after the earned income tax credit in America to shift benefits to low-income workers. Britain signed the European "Social Charter" scorned by Thatcher and introduced the min-imum wage. In July, Brown's spending review found £30 billion additional funds for the NHS to be disbursed, starting in April of the following year.[97]

I flew up to Manchester and then drove on to Blackpool for Blair's confer-ence speech at the very end of September 1998. Blair's speech was not his most exciting, his modernizing project a touch out of step in this hall with chandeliers and two levels of opera-house-like boxes that had hosted a ball-room dancing festival since 1920. "This year, we meet in more mature and sober reflection," he began. He calibrated the moment: "We have pride in what we have done, yet the wisdom to accept there is much more to do." Waiting lists had been rising year after year, and now, "month by month they are falling." Last year after each of these, he pronounced, "A pledge made," but this time he was more cautious: "A pledge being kept." He then reviewed the progress in policy area after policy area, recalling Mario Cuomo's quip: "We campaign in poetry, but we govern in prose." I worried that the delivery would be too uneven and the focus on modernizing Britain too remote to keep people with us. The speech was more a progress report than a statement of a higher purpose, describing Labour's mission merely "to modernize for a purpose; to build a Britain strong and prosperous."[98]

After the speech and after Blair had done a press availability, he and Cherie held a small reception at the hotel for their family and closest friends and the Blair team involved in the speech, maybe fifteen people. He came over immediately upon seeing me, and I said some positive things rehearsed in my head. From politicians as diverse as Rosa to Mandela, I've learned this is not a moment for nuance. I got his attention with my frustration with the Democrats in the Congress and the White House for not making the Republican overreach on Monica Lewinsky a political issue in the November elections. Blair's instincts were to go for the jugular, though I assured him that the Republicans wouldn't have the nerve to impeach the president.

At the outset of 1999, the prime minister asked his closest policy advisors to draw up estimates of the progress they could expect in key policy areas by December 2000, six months before a possible election. Economic stability was on track. In education, they were close to meeting the goals for class size in primary schools, but not more broadly. The "New Deal" would take more than the promised 250,000 kids into employment. But health was "different from the others," David Miliband wrote. There was a paltry number of new doctors and nurses. He urged "a narrative not just a list" to show the progress that would come in years eight to ten. Peter Hyman was much more skeptical. "We have convinced ourselves that we have allocated historic sums of money. We have not. Over at the Parliament the money going into education and health is not a quantum leap." London was so underfunded that only a "Clause IV-style jolt to the system" will make a difference.[99]

Blair studied all the papers on delivery and came away pessimistic. He warned, "either we really step up delivery; or we will find the conclusion is: . . . competent Government, but disappointing on public service delivery." Specifically he worried that the boost to the NHS and schools would not be felt in the coming year. He wanted a series of big speeches to make them part of a "big picture vision of modernizing Britain for the 21st century," but then he was not at all sure the delivery would be real. "I repeat, again, for the umpteenth time," Blair wrote later, "should we end up in mid-June with schools and hospitals facing cuts, we are in serious difficulty."[100]

I met with the prime minister at Number 10 before his summer break with findings that would elevate his anxiety. He was in a bigger office, with a set of couches and coffee table, as well as his desk and small conference table, looking out on the gardens. I sat on one couch, directly across from him, each of us with printed bound graphs from the latest poll. Jonathan, Alastair, Peter Hyman, Sally Morgan, new Blair's political secretary, and Philip were there, each with their copies. Unlike President Clinton, Blair dwelled on each graph as I talked about the results, without paging ahead. Alastair had already paged through his. When I met Gordon, he would be impatient to get through them to discuss the implications and what we do.

The poll did show some fundamentals right. Labour maintained a 20-point lead, unchanged from February 1998 and stronger than the 1997 landslide election. Almost three quarters saw Blair as strong, in control of his party and good in a crisis; two thirds said he was on the side of the people. On the schools, almost 60 percent thought Labour was trying to keep its promises. And on inflation and interest rates, the core of the economy, two thirds said the government was both trying to keep its promises and making progress.

Then I turned to the NHS and the result was a "bombshell." The NHS graph was nearly the opposite of the economy and I placed the two graphs back to back. Barely half thought the government was trying to meet its commitment and only a third thought it was trying and making progress, down from almost half when Brown had released £40 billion in the spending review last summer. The public not only doubted the reality of the government's work, it was beginning to think it was all spin on the policy most important to judging the government. Under half of the electorate thought this very moral man was "a person you can really trust," down almost 15 points from the past summer. Blair was dropping more than Labour and the team stared at the graph nervously.

I could not do anything about the reality of delivery, but I could address narrative, what Blair called "strategy." The truth was he was being heard. The public thought he was "trying to modernize Britain" and "prepare it for the 21st century." Those were at the top of the list of things they thought he was trying to do, but at the bottom of the public's own priorities. Hardly anyone thought Blair was consumed with "making Britain both fair and prosperous" and "governing for all the people." There was "no fairness project, no advocacy" for people that would allow them to interpret his valiant efforts, even if they fell short. He needed a new narrative, as he had indicated, not a report card on delivery at the conference coming up at the end of September in

Bournemouth, the one resort on the south coast where one might get decent weather.[101]

FORCES OF CONSERVATISM

I was impressed by Blair's speech at the conference. Right at the top he defined his project anew: "A New Britain where the extraordinary talent of the British people is liberated from the forces of conservatism that so long have held them back, to create a model twenty-first-century nation, based not on privilege, class or background, but on the equal worth of all." He associated the Conservatives with these forces, creating perhaps his most powerful and moral critique: "The country has run far too long on the talents of the few, when the genius of the many lies uncared for, and ignored." Such a worldview made Britain a poorer nation. "Every person liberated to fulfill their potential adds to our wealth." In this conflict and choice, "true equality; equal worth, an equal chance for fulfillment, equal access to knowledge and opportunity." He confounded the conservatives by affirming, "The class war is over, but the struggle for true equality has just begun." That was the case I had tried to make with "two-tier Britain," but he had gone beyond it.

The struggle for change and progress against the "forces of conservatism" was not just against the Conservatives, he noted. It was against the forces in the nation everywhere that would deny progress, not exempting his own party: "there were forces of conservatism who said changing Clause IV would destroy the Labour Party when in truth it was critical to our renewal." He talked explicitly about "the old elite, establishments" in the professions and in the "senior parts of Government" and talked about the teachers who must come on board if there was to be reform.

He spent a little time on the progress made—like devolution, Bank of England independence, working families' tax credit, minimum wage, and the struggle to replace failing schools and reduce class size and deliver change in the NHS—but always in the context of the conservative forces, particularly the Tories, who continued to battle to stop the progress. In education, the stakes were so high: here "a failed education is a life sentence on a child." Yet "the forces of conservatism, the elite, have held us back for too long," calling on the three thousand in the hall to join the struggle for progress.

He tempered that urgency with a nod to the time frame: "In ten years we will have transformed our schools. And our NHS, too." I am sure nobody heard him.[102]

But commentators immediately understood both the power and implications of this speech, many pushing back hard. Conservative-aligned media who enjoyed Blair's attack on Old Labour suddenly found themselves in the

crosshairs and realized that his "Third Way" politics could be intensely partisan and philosophically anti-Tory; often content to say Blair "stole our clothes,"
they were finding that Blair drew fundamental distinctions, not just attacking the hapless Tories for incompetence.[103] The Murdoch papers did not like
it. The public service unions were not happy.

The divisions were evident in the family and friends reception afterward.
Alastair reminded the press that this was also a critique of Labour and Jonathan was wavering. Peter Mandelson was not and cornered Blair when he arrived: the speech was divisive, "tactically foolish," offended former Tory
voters, and gave up new territory. It would alienate business, who we had told
were welcome in our big tent.[104] I told Blair, on the other hand, that I was
impressed, which might not have been reassuring, though Philip supported
me. He really had found his voice fighting for modernization to liberate the
many. As with no other leader I've worked for, Blair was in a continuous
struggle not just to find the right words but to define his main political project, and I thought he just had a breakthrough that could bring peace of
mind.

Philip followed up with an urgent note a couple of days later. He urged the
prime minister to "not be deflected or unnerved" by the opposition. It had
been a speech that showed "he stands for something." Nonetheless, Alastair
and Blair, worried about the political impact a few days after the speech, did
some interviews to reassure that he was not attacking all Tories and wanted
the support of "One-Nation Tories."[105]

A couple of weeks later, I sent the prime minister a memo marked "urgent" and entitled "The New Strategic World: Opportunities for Hegemony." New Labour in 1997, like Clinton in 1992, was elected because you
offered "change from the Tories and change from Old Labour." "We got our
energy from not being either, which meant advancing the concept of 'Third
Way'" but that positioning was "necessarily backward looking" and historically specific. But real people live in the present and future. "The speech at
Bournemouth was so important because it promised a new Labour project
motivated by a passion to liberate every individual to realize their potential
and by a struggle against the forces of conservatism that stifle opportunity,
except for the privileged few." This took the reform and modernizing project to a new place, but most important, it was not about past battles, it was
about current ones, with forces struggling to stop us from expanding opportunity. There was a new choice: "Conservatism creates opportunity only
for the privileged few"; a progressive Labour Party is committed to creating
"opportunity for all, based on their equal worth." This was not theoretical
and obscure; it was a battle for real things—"improved employment for everyone, gaining the learning and skills necessary to succeed, having decent

health care"—that made Labour relevant and in-touch. "If we get this right, new Labour has the opportunity for hegemony."[106]

The prime minister found the memo "brilliant," in Philip's characterization. David Miliband called it "really very powerful indeed": moving us from "triangulation" against both Old Labour and the Tories to a "bipolarity" against the Tories, which "is immensely challenging but right."[107]

CRISIS

The flu epidemic struck over the Christmas holidays, swamping hospitals and turning the new year of 2000 into an unending set of horror stories about the National Health Service. Newspapers reported dangerous shortages of intensive care beds. By one account in London a mere ten extra patients would touch off "mayhem," while other papers reported on patients shuttled around the country to find a bed. The "crisis" became highly personalized when the papers wrote of one woman whose cancer operation was canceled four times before she was told the tumor was inoperable. When the Labour spokesman described the ten-year "turnaround" plan, one of the leading Sunday papers editorialized the unhealthy truth: "In a decade, another 250,000 people will have died from cancer when they could have survived."[108]

As the crisis grew, Blair, in an interview on the BBC's *Breakfast with Frost*, said he wanted spending on the NHS to rise "to the average of the European Union—it is too low at the moment." That simple statement—raising health care spending from around 7 percent of GNP to over 9 percent, probably up to £10 billion a year for some time—was incendiary because it had not been settled with the chancellor.[109]

With the budget to be presented in mid-March, it was not clear whether Brown would accept such a radical departure from spending discipline. This was probably one of the occasions when Jonathan heard them yelling through Blair's office door, and I got the job of persuading Brown, drawing on the credibility of my research, outsider status, and friendship with Bob Shrum, one of Brown's closest advisors since they met in 1996. While I had worked earlier with Shrum on Senator Dodd's reelection campaign and on President Clinton's health care plan, I had not worked seriously with him as a media consultant until Ehud Barak's campaign in Israel but we forged a close bond there. He urged me to let Brown get to increased investments without being publicly pressured.[110]

On the mid-February trip, my meeting with Brown at the Treasury had the highest priority. "Labour is on the edge of major electoral trouble," I told him. Above all was the widespread discontent with its performance on the NHS. There were alarming numbers but they might be just a foretaste of a crisis to come. That barely 20 percent said we were trying to keep our promises and making progress on the NHS swamped everything else we were doing. The nightmarish stories in January took away something fundamental, pushing up perceptions of Labour as "out of touch" and "arrogant." With possible elections a little more than a year away, a large majority saw the "New Labour project as losing steam." We would only be heard if the party committed to a new "bold" course: "Labour has to commit itself to substantial new resources, committed over a series of years to a measurable goal" and ask "to be held accountable."[111]

It was a sobering meeting with Brown's team, and I got an e-mail afterward from Philip: "I understand the GB presentation broke through with him, and they are considering big bold NHS initiatives." While the Blair team was not at all sure Brown would commit the money, Shrum told me on the side that Brown already had planned on doing that as part of his budget process. Regardless, a few days later, Philip went further: "Your poll has broken through in a serious way. GB's [Gordon Brown] strategy document has been rewritten around the poll." Perhaps with Shrum's help, he began the March strategy document with "Standing up for Britain—working hard for Britain's hard-working families." Philip wrote, "GB has decided, I hope, that we're such a lot of wankers that only he can sort out the health service which is fine by me. If he gets behind it, it will happen."[112]

They arranged for me to come back to meet with Brown and his team, and then with Blair, four days before the chancellor was to present the budget in the House of Commons. At 9:30 A.M. I met with Brown. At two that afternoon I presented the results to Margaret McDonagh, who had become the general secretary of the party, and Greg Cook, head of research who everyone turns to on any constituency matter. In between, they arranged that I meet with Blair at his House of Commons office at 12:30, right after question time when the leader of the opposition Tories and other members can ask pointed questions. The poll results were so grim, I was hoping that the hostile questions might distract him.

MR. BURNS OF WEST CHELMSFORD: *"Does the Prime Minister agree that the incidence of beggars in the street caused by economic migration to this country is an affront?"*
MR. WILLIAM HAGUE, *leader of the opposition: "Yesterday, the Prime Minister's press secretary said that the Government has increased taxes. In that new spirit of honesty, will the Prime Minister admit that Labour's promises on taxes at the election were a total, barefaced election lie?"*
THE PRIME MINISTER: *"I certainly will not. . . . For the first two years, the Government's duty was to cut the huge deficit that we inherited."*

MR. HAGUE: *"What is moral about breaking every promise on taxation, and delivering worse public services at the same time? Let's have an answer now: does the Prime Minister admit that he has broken all those promises?"*
THE PRIME MINISTER: *"We know Tory morality: tax cuts for a few at the top, and boom and bust for the rest of us."*
MADAM SPEAKER: *"Order. I will have order in the House, on both sides."*[113]

I watched it on the television in his office, along with Alastair and the team. We were soon joined by the prime minister, who looked harried. "I understand I am going to enjoy this even less," he said. There was no discussion about America, even though Al Gore had put away the nomination with his wins in the Super Tuesday presidential primaries. We went straight to the matter at hand, and it was hard to find adjectives up to the scale of the problem, beginning with "Labour faces a profound political crisis." While the Tories were too bankrupt to benefit directly, I said, Labour's supporters were shifting to the Liberal Democrats, fragmenting to the nationalists and smaller parties, rapidly losing enthusiasm for Labour, and, perhaps worse, the number saying "I will not vote" had doubled to nearly 20 percent in just a month. We had lost 8 points off our margin, and in a simulated campaign with the Tories attacking us for broken promises, a failed NHS, and asylum seekers, our lead fell to just 6 points.

This government and the public came away from 1997 with a profoundly different understanding of the electoral compact. In the last campaign and since 1994, I said, you have engaged in relentless reassurance on spending and taxes and liberated people to support new investment in the public services, particularly the NHS. The steps you took to take those worries off the table—the tax pledge and no spending increases for two years—ironically allowed people more and more at the campaign's close to say they were voting to fund health care and schools, without fear that a Labour government would go too far. But your promised austerity deprived you of the resources to meet their expectations. You and Gordon "viewed those as serial projects." Put the economy and public finances in order first and then in years to come there will be resources to invest, presume fiscal austerity and investment would happen in parallel at the same time. Certainly people never thought they would have to wait four years or even ten for delivery, which is a lifetime when you are talking about losing lives or a generation.

Did we mislead people and contribute to the anger, I was asking Blair and myself. He was clearly impatient with my musings about the past and Brown was even less interested.

As a consequence, I said, we faced a real breach of trust. The public was asking "Is Blair real?" All the talk of being "a bit of a showman," "spin," and "slimy," I said amid Blair's spin doctors, "have reemerged full force." The people were talking about being "betrayed" by someone who was "out of touch"; we were headed toward only 40 percent or less who thought Blair was a "person you can really trust."

As a result, I said, we are up against a wall built of deep skepticism; basically, "show me the money." When you condition investment on "reform," the voters don't take it seriously because they think you lied about the investments over the last three years. Their ears perk up only when you are clear that there will be an immediate infusion of money, £20 billion this year; then, they are open to a five-year sustained commitment to invest £100 billion; and they want something concrete, lots more nurses and doctors. This is back to basics.[114]

On March 21, 2000, the chancellor presented his budget in the House of Commons. Based on the government's success in moving from deficits to surplus, he announced not only more spending in the coming year for the NHS, but committed to higher levels of spending for four years. "We have decided that from now until 2004 the NHS will grow by twice" the rate it did under the Tories—"by 6.1 percent a year over and above inflation, by far the largest sustained increase in the NHS funding of any period in the fifty year history of the Health Service." This was a real increase in health spending of over one third, and of course, "more resources must mean more reform and modernization." And so to close, "We have been prudent for a purpose: a stronger fairer Britain. And I commend this Budget to the House."[115]

In a break with precedent, the prime minister also spoke in the Commons on the budget the next day to show the public that this new commitment was real and that both the prime minister and chancellor were personally invested in making it happen.[116]

The 2000 crisis over delivery after the great hopes of 1997 produced a loss of trust that would never be regained. It was like a compact had been shattered and the parties to it could not afford to figure out a new basis for working together. It was possible to win back these votes, but on a very different basis. The commentary about "spin" and "spin-doctoring" was almost comical for the media, but the years of overselling the scale of public investment as people lived the reality of the NHS, exposed by the winter flu epidemic, made lack of authenticity and manipulation an inescapable part of the Blair world.

The crisis exposed the thinness of Labour's program for reform, elevated by "Third Way" rhetoric but barely developed in the 1997 manifesto and providing little guide for government.[117] The decision to move from austerity to sustained investment after three years meant Labour would have to run in the coming year pretty crudely on spending: year-on-year spending increases for education and health versus the Conservatives, who were intent on tax cuts that would put the investment at risk. Reform would have to await another day.

As a consequence of this period of crisis, the Labour government would always be playing catch-up—on the investments that did not happen in the first three years, on the reforms put off until after 2001 when other events would delay them further, and on trust, once betrayed, always questioned.

With so little space for reform, the prime minister was unsettled with the emerging choice for the election, which sounded very Old Labour. "We need to get right back to first principles in explaining the nature of our politics," Blair wrote in a memo to his core people—"the values of opportunity, responsibility, community, one nation values." As for "working hard for hard-working families"—the centerpiece of the politics most of us were championing—that was fine, but "it is a campaign theme—it does not express value or belief." Use it in the campaign as a tagline but "do not confuse that with persuading people of the nature of our politics."[118]

Blair's memo set off a lot of discussion in Number 10 about why the "New Labour" language seemed abstract to the public, though I was impatient: because it *was* abstract and disconnected from a political project that matters to people. Shrum, Alastair, Philip, and I had dinner to address the problem and unite the Brown and Blair camps. "Our formulation is abstract" and "people just don't know what we are trying to do," I wrote in the follow-up note for the group to Blair and Brown. "The solution to trust, we believe, lies in conviction." To that end, Alastair, Shrum, and Philip agreed that "we must go back to the Bournemouth speech," back to the reference to the negative pull of the "forces of conservatism" that Blair crafted and that embodied his convictions, even if the language needed to be changed to be less off-putting.[119]

All of Blair's and Brown's senior advisors participated in a two-day retreat held at TBWA, the ad agency for the next campaign. We broke into pairs—one from each camp, including Shrum and myself—to write fifty-word mission statements, to be synthesized by the group at the end. Alastair and Ed Miliband, brother of David and Brown policy advisor, arrived at "We exist for the middle class." Philip's summary note began, "There was a general consensus towards many not the few in some form as our basic guiding principle," though we found new ways to express it. Blair had few allies in his closest circle.[120]

Reacting to all of our work, Blair tried his hand at a message: "We stand for traditional British values—fairness, obligations to others, creative talent, but have the courage to apply them in a new way for a new world." To achieve that—the means—"we need to make Britain work not just for the top ten percent but for all the people," inserting the "not just" so they would know

we're "not chucking them out," he later told me. "I just don't believe the problem with Britain is the few at the top." But even with the amendment, he
worried that moving toward "middle and lower class families" might take us
"back to old class-based politics," "not attacking aspiration but encouraging
opportunity."[121] The tacking back and forth was not indecision; it was a near
total discomfort with the political project that united his advisors.

On June 1, I made my first trip to Chequers, the prime minister's country
residence, a place much more intimidating than Camp David. The
sixteenth-century grand brick Tudor home on a country estate reminded me
why it takes so long for the many to catch up with the few. I met with Blair
and Philip in a small wood-paneled study on the ground floor to help Blair
embrace a strategy to reverse the continuing slide of his and Labour's standing and a deepening public pessimism. Our model, which took account of
voter disengagement and reduced turnout, put Labour ahead by only 42 to 31
percent over the Tories. Blair was unsettled and wanted fewer graphs on the
depth of the problem and more solutions, but he remained uncomfortable
with the solutions, too.[122]

I reviewed how all the messages fared in a national survey, and I was not at
all sure he would be happy with our results. The strongest-testing mission
statement: "We are working to change Britain so that in a modern and uncertain world, hardworking people, not just the few, have the opportunity to
make a better life." Without the phrase "not the few," the statement was 15
points weaker. He did not respond but he probably thought I was offering
him a pact with the devil to ensure his reelection. I later asked why he hadn't
fired us. "You were giving me the right advice for an election. It's just that I
was choosing not to take it," he responded.[123]

I also shared a narrative that worked for the African National Congress in
its second election, which the ANC had just won. I had offered this framework earlier as a curiosity and a hypothesis, but now I was more adamant.
Thabo Mbeki's message "on progress" only got heard when he began the narrative with changes that people believed really happened, like providing water and electricity. In our case, it would be primary schools. Then, Mbeki
talked about the great difficulty of bringing change against the old apartheid
forces and regretting that it had not been fast enough. In our case, it was the
"forces of conservatism." But despite that, Mbeki was able to highlight a
critical area where people were beginning to see progress, housing. Maybe for
us, it would be the NHS. And finally Mbeki's narrative addressed the most
pressing unfinished issue, employment, with a serious plan for future action.

In the latest survey, we tested the concept with promising results, suggest-
ing British voters, too, were hungry for an explanation of what had happened
and looking for a way to say, "give 'em another go." "The strongest formulation

of our mission combines a description of progress made combined with a new programmatic offer," particularly strong when the future offer is bold changes in education. This formulation had power because we were saying "this is a work in progress," with much more to come; it did not sound "self-satisfied or static." Indeed, it sounded like we, too, were "impatient with the progress," even as we educated the voters on what had been done.[124] While Clinton and the ANC's top leaders resisted this narrative, Blair really believed "an old fashioned establishment" was blocking change and was very receptive.

That closed the session on an actionable, optimistic note. While Philip carried on with a thirty-minute private meeting with the prime minister, Cherie and I sat at a small dining area while she, unprompted, told me how difficult Gordon had been and how she heard Tony personally on the phone beg the chancellor for more health spending. She was either unconcerned about her feelings becoming more widely known, I thought, or fully confident of my loyalties in the Blair camp. Afterward, the boys walked out to the large flat upper lawn at the back of the estate and kicked around a soccer ball until the Brown people and policy advisors arrived for the second meeting. After passing up a chance to head the ball back and lamely kicking it to the prime minister, I thought, "I am very blessed." I also felt guilty that I couldn't find a solution that worked for Blair.

The second meeting was held upstairs in the grand dining room—large enough for us to have carried on with our football—this time kicked off by Blair and Brown, who made opening statements that did not exactly lead to a bonding around the table. When Clinton and Gore sat across from each other in a meeting, you did not have to figure out who had ultimate authority, but I was struck by the lack of any such presumption in this meeting. I presented the latest survey, which reinforced the sense of uncertainty in this interregnum, the sense that we had not settled fundamental things. And the leaders' summary statements didn't help either as each repeated and embellished his point of view, making their gulf look even wider. The surroundings were extraordinary but I would have been happy to see the meeting end. I did not think we would be adjourning to the upper lawn.[125]

The day after the meeting, Brown launched a "class war," according to the press, attacking Oxford University for denying a place to a star female graduate from a state school in Newcastle who was forced to settle for Harvard.

A week after the meeting, Blair, still on paternity leave taking care of one-month old Leo at Chequers and obsessing on his politics, wrote his own speech for the Women's Institute that became as consuming for him as a party conference address. Unfortunately, it was poorly received. The not-so-friendly audience responded with heckling and slow handclapping.[126] Lance

Price wrote in his diary, "it's a total mish-mash of New Labour jargon mixed up with John Major–style pleas for old-fashioned values." Blair's take on a "big tent" that would be open to many conservative voters. The prime minister's mood was hardly helped by calls from Philip about his "grumpy" and "worst ever" groups and the voter that thought opposition leader William Hague would be a "better Prime Minister." Nonetheless, Blair uncharacteristically instructed his senior aides that "the big tent will be our approach" and "everybody should get on board."

Bob Shrum convinced me only a month before the Republican and Democratic conventions that I should take over the national polling for the Gore campaign, which meant I could not get to London to present Labour's poll results before the August holiday. But given the results, that was a blessing and I wrote a long e-mail with the graphs so Philip could spoil Blair's holiday.[127]

Gore, in his acceptance speech, comfortably called on the Democratic convention and the country: "Together, let's make sure that our prosperity enriches not just the few, but all working families"—one part Gore, one part Shrum, and one part Greenberg.[128] For this key line tested in my research, I directly expropriated Blair's "not just" formulation for precisely the same reasons that Blair used it and closed with an inclusive populist appeal "for all Americans," though Gore actually preferred Shrum's "people versus the powerful."[129] The impact on the convention was electric and allowed Gore to erase George W. Bush's big lead in the polls.

If things were not difficult enough back in Britain at the beginning of September, truck drivers protested the rise in petrol prices by blockading the entrance to the Channel Tunnel, creating massive traffic jams that spread to oil terminals and refineries. The standoff lasted almost two weeks, leading to panic buying and widespread shortages, with escalating threats to use the police to clear protesters. Despite the U.S. election campaign, I went to Britain to meet with the prime minister, observe focus groups, and provide input on the conference speech, rewritten to address those events. It was frustrating because in the focus groups people were finally talking about real effort and delivery. And while they thought the government was doing the right thing with the protesters, "they resent the arrogance, the certitude, and the seeming indifference to 'public opinion,'" I wrote in an e-mail. "We dare not give a speech that fails to acknowledge error and that fails to show some humility." It seems Blair got the balance right at the conference in Brighton, but a month afterward a breathtaking 60 percent said Labour was "getting too arrogant and out of touch." Labour's lead dropped to just 6 points.[130]

BEYOND THE DARKNESS

"I think we have good reason to believe that we have a breakthrough with people that will put us well ahead," I wrote to the team at the outset of 2001. In fact, the pre-Christmas survey already showed significant gains that were confirmed by the one at the end of January. Labour was making big inroads on managing the economy and on "keeping interest rates low and stable," reflecting real change in the economy at the end of 2000 and first quarter of 2001—lower interest rates, unemployment falling to 3 percent, and a spurt in consumer confidence. The belief that Labour was keeping its promises on "rebuilding the NHS" surged along with the real surge in investment to over 50 percent, though I warned them not to get carried away: nobody in the groups mentioned actual improvement, just that Labour was putting "more money in the NHS," "more cash for NHS." They were simply following the money with a hard realism.

A full 60 percent of the public had moved to the modest threshold judgment that "Labour has done a good enough job to give them another go," yet a comparable number with the same intensity said, "Labour promised much but has not delivered." This was a very qualified joyless vote, and enthusiasm would actually go down in the campaign ahead.[131]

The Tories had reached almost parity with Labour on taxes the past September, perhaps reflecting their high-profile "tax guarantee"—taxes would decline as a proportion of national income under a Conservative government, and "there will be no escape clauses, no fudging" that commitment. But as the new money actually began flowing into the public services, voters thought the "tax guarantee" might threaten the investments. In December, the Tories described £8 billion in tax cuts paid for by cutting waste, but Brown exposed the unfunded "black hole" that would mean "deep cuts" in investments for health and education.[132]

Labour moved to a 10-point lead on taxes at the New Year, a lead that rose inexorably through the following months to almost a 25-point Labour advantage on the eve of the campaign.[133]

I flew to London after the New Year, the U.S. presidential election having been decided by the Supreme Court on December 12. Margaret organized a presentation at Millbank on the U.S. election, which was not at all cathartic, and I had dinner with Brown to talk about the British campaign. He took one big lesson from the Gore-Bush election: Gore should have run on the strength of the economy, without apology, and even more important, he should have blasted Bush for putting the economy at risk. I wondered to myself what Gordon and Shrum talked about. I tried to explain that the U.S. economy had slowed, Bush was not very risky, continuity was two-edged, and that

Gore viscerally would not embrace Clinton's economy, but Brown was impatient and I rushed to a close. Waving aside my economic message for Britain, Brown asserted our whole message and campaign should end with a "boom and bust," what would put these economic gains at risk.[134] The plan was to have a short four-week campaign that began and ended with the economy with public services sandwiched in between.[135]

I met with Blair at his Number 10 office on January 25, five days after Bush's inauguration. This was a campaign and leader growing confident and engaged, though Blair seemed on a mission to convince the electorate that they should be excited about casting this vote. He later winced when I called the mood "joyless" and headed toward yet lower turnout, an unacceptable result for him. When we all stood up to leave his office, he talked positively about his recent conversations with President Bush and the plan to see him in the next month, and I responded, "I don't envy you that." I remember his look and half smile as he said, "Had you done your job, I wouldn't have to do all this."

On April 2, Blair announced that because of the outbreak of foot-and-mouth disease that had created no-go areas in the countryside the local elections would be postponed to June 7, almost certainly meaning the national elections would be delayed as well. This was depressing for a campaign poised at the starting gate. In this election, my desk as well as Shrum's were among those clustered at the center of Millbank's large open floor, forming the war room.

"This is a manifesto with big ambition for Britain—a mission for reform of public services," Blair declared on May 6, surrounded by nearly all the cabinet. But most of the bold signature ideas were screened out in the process and the press was skeptical. Hugo Young, the respected columnist, wrote that it "sounds exceedingly boring."[136] The policies and the politics of the campaign centered on investment, not reform. The strongest messages being tested by the campaign were straightforward, with Labour committed to "significant and sustained investment in the NHS, education and transport." The Conservatives "make a different choice." They would cut taxes and "cut back our new investments." While Brown and his team were visibly nervous about taxes, Shrum and I were moving to a shared conviction that every time the Tories talked about tax cuts, voters heard cuts in spending for public services.[137]

Blair was not at all comfortable with either the public's grudging support or our asking voters to choose based on public investment that lacked a modernizing character. I may have provoked him with my observation about the choice: "The voters have a diminished investment in Labour because the electoral choice is becoming merely instrumental, without any real sense that Labour (or Blair) is motivated by conviction, a commitment to some historic or ideological project, or that Labour politicians really are fighting for them."

Rising to the challenge, Blair on April 21 wrote a fifteen-page memo—
what he called "the most important note I will have written since becoming
leader"—on his vision for the election: "There is a great danger that this coming campaign fails to arouse, enthuse and inspire in the way necessary not
just to win but win with enhanced power and authority." The alternative was
to use Thatcherism to highlight our difference: it brought "serious failure:
economic instability"; "under-investment in public services; social division;
and isolationism." I really liked where he was going, underlining madly.
"These failures were not accidental," Blair wrote. "They derive from the limits of the Thatcherite philosophy and values. The intense individualism, the
belief that Government was only an obstacle not a help, the contempt for
much of the public services—in short, the refusal to accept the role of society
in helping the individual succeed." But what this era required now were "values of community, mutual responsibility, opportunity for all, solidarity between people within a nation and between nations." Reaching back to
Bournemouth, this is an era that needs "New Labour" to liberate "the human
potential, economically and as citizens."

The campaign's billboard and newspaper advertising would begin with
the economy as Brown understood it, translated brilliantly by the ad agency
into billboards for new movies. There was "Economic Disaster II" starring the
smug shadow chancellor, Michael Portillo, as "Mr. Boom" and the opposition
leader, William Hague, as "Mr. Bust," an epic that would be "coming to a
home, school, and business near you." But the billboard that got the most attention, going up about ten days before the election, showed Hague with
earrings and a wig, looking painfully like Margaret Thatcher: "Be afraid. Be
very afraid." Just days before the election, Blair delivered the critique of
"Thatcherism" personally at the Ex-Servicemen's Club in Birmingham: he
accused Hague of wanting "to go back to the 1980s" and accused the Thatcher
and Major government of underinvesting in the public services "as a matter of
ideology."[138]

With diminished enthusiasm, in the final week I proposed that we be sim-
pler and bolder, worry less about the philosophic choice and show "we have a
passion for investment in the public services."[139] The campaign would finish
not on the economy, but by carrying a banner crafted by Shrum: "Schools
and Hospitals First."

On June 7, 2001, the voters of Britain produced an unimaginable result: a
second consecutive landslide for Labour. The party lost only six seats and the
Tories gained just one, their vote rising only a single point to 33 percent. The
167-seat majority left commentators dumbstruck. The Conservatives had not
even begun the process of eroding Labour's majority and becoming electable

Discussing a draft statement, as Bob Shrum edits at the center table in the 2001 Labour Party war room in Millbank Tower. [credit: unknown]

again. Labour's vote dropped 2.4 points, not insignificantly to 42 percent, but the votes lost moved left, not right, to the Liberal Democrats, who won one in ten Labour supporters, particularly in industrial, mining, and inner-city seats, as well as in the best-educated trendy areas and university seats.

The big story of the election, however, was the successive crash in turnout on an unimaginable scale. In 1997, turnout dropped 7.5 points to 71.5 percent, a historic low. In the latest election it fell to 59.4 percent, a further 12-point drop, the lowest voter turnout since 1918, when Britain moved to a universal franchise. On election night, the nearly 13 million viewers for election specials in 1997 dropped almost in half, as people chose a good night's sleep over watching returns.[140]

This new disengagement from the political process was most pronounced in strong Labour seats and with unskilled manual laborers, men without a university education, and the younger blue-collar workers.[141]

On election day, I went out to a London inner-city seat to canvass and encourage people in these lower-income council houses to vote, thinking my American accent might be enough of a curiosity to get them to go to the polls. Everyone told me they already had voted. I used the afternoon to make some final edits on an op-ed piece for The Washington Post entitled "The Death of Thatcherism."

At 1:30 A.M. Blair lined up with the other candidates in his Sedgefield constituency to listen to the results amid a less celebratory mood, which carried over to the flight back from Teesside Airport. This time I was present for the early morning victory celebration, not at Royal Festival Hall, but in a back lot behind Millbank Tower. I was elated with the majority and clapped like a fool, though Blair's speech lacked not just triumphalism, but any sense of victory. Later, when he stood in front of Number 10, there was a somber we-got-the-lesson tone: "It is a mandate for reform and for investment in the future and it is also very clearly an instruction to deliver."[142]

5

TONY BLAIR
Act II

9/11

TONY BLAIR SAT in his suite at the Grand Hotel in Brighton, laboring over a speech that would unveil before a less-than-welcoming Trade Union Congress some of Blair's most contentious reforms for his new term. He never gave the speech.

First he was interrupted by an aide who told him that a plane had crashed into New York's World Trade Center. The prime minister continued working on his speech. But at 2 P.M. British time he was interrupted yet again: a second plane had struck the second tower. Blair immediately put his speech aside and joined Campbell and others watching the events unfold on TV.

At 2:45 a third plane crashed into the Pentagon, and at 3:28 he watched the second tower collapse. Like everyone else watching around the world, Blair knew he was seeing an unprecedented attack on America, more menacing because of the scale of the carnage and the uncertainty of its scope and maker. Within a half hour he went before the delegates, his speech discarded. Apparently shaken, according to press reports, he told them "there have been the most terrible, shocking events in the United States of America in the last hours," alerting the delegates and soon the nation to the unfolding horror in real time. "I am afraid we can only imagine the terror and carnage there and the many innocent people who have lost their lives." And then, with unusual clarity, he concluded: "This mass terrorism is the new evil in our world," defining the event, much as he did with Princess Diana's death, for Britain and the world.[1]

The delegates sat shocked, breaking into applause as he left the hall to catch a train, considered the fastest and safest means to London. He placed a round of calls to the key security and intelligence agencies, but spent most of the train ride thinking through the implications of the attack. The government moved to address the risk of an attack in Britain, including banning all flights over London, and to learn more about Osama bin Laden and al-Qaeda, immediately identified as the likely perpetrator.

With the White House scrambling and Bush unaccounted for as he flew from airbase to airbase, Blair was worried about a possible public panic and made a second statement, this time in front of the door at Number 10. "We've offered President Bush and the American people our solidarity, our profound sympathy, and our prayers." The reassurance he offered was the clarity of the choice: "This is not a battle between the United States of America and terrorism, but between the free and democratic world and terrorism." And Blair was clear about how it would all turn out: "We, like them, will not rest until this evil is driven from our world." When he reached Vladimir Putin, Gerhard Schroeder, and Jacques Chirac, Blair later recalled, all understood immediately that it was a "terrible act against humanity, not just against America."[2]

The next day, the biggest concern at Number 10 was how Bush would respond to the attack and how to build the closest possible relationship with him, as the war on terrorism became the mission of his presidency and perhaps Blair's new term. Bush called near noon that day, his first call to a foreign leader. Blair informed Bush of the worries that America would act precipitately and Bush reassured him as they talked about how to use the United Nations and NATO to marshal the global outrage. Blair immediately sat down and wrote out his thinking, typed up as a five-page memorandum, and then faxed it to the White House.[3]

I flew to London a week after 9/11. I met with Charles Clarke, the new head of the Labour Party, at his office in the Parliament and that night observed focus groups in Isleworth, followed by two days of meetings. This was all planned before the attack to advance the conference speech, but the prime minister apparently placed a higher priority on his visits to Berlin and Paris to organize international support before he went to America.

Starting in Paris on the morning of September 20, Blair flew to New York to attend the memorial service with Bill Clinton and Kofi Annan for the British victims at the St. Thomas Church, on Fifth Avenue near "Ground Zero." They then flew to Andrews Air Force Base outside Washington and were taken by a motorcade of black limousines to the White House to join Bush in the Blue Room for a private reception. Bush pulled Blair aside and said, "The job at hand is al-Qaeda and the Taliban. Iraq we keep for another day." Blair and the British assumed Bush meant the discussion, not the act. Bush delivered an address to a joint session of Congress that evening, and, unlike his predecessor, Bill Clinton, he was not in the family theater rewriting the speech with aides. The speech had been long put to bed and the press briefed on the red line it would draw: "Either you are with us, or you are with the terrorists."

Over dinner, the British were briefed on the planning for the attack on Afghanistan. At the conclusion, Blair accompanied Bush in his car in the motorcade to the U.S. Capitol and joined the first lady in the gallery overlooking the House chamber. During the speech, he looked up to Blair, saying, "I'm so honored the British Prime Minister has crossed the ocean to show his unity with America."[4]

Tony Blair was the most esteemed political leader in America, indeed within a few months, more esteemed than the president.[5] Blair was embarrassed when I shared the findings with him, though not uninterested.

I took the train to Brighton on October 1, a day before Blair was scheduled to speak at Labour's annual conference, this time shortened out of respect for the lives lost and the serious task ahead. Blair knew this was the speech of his life for a world fundamentally changed. Unlike any other conference address, his aides held back as Blair wrote draft after draft from Saturday. My London office had secured me an all-areas pass, enabling me to avoid the long lines back into the hall after the security sweep and to meet up with the team behind the stage before sitting in a section reserved for visitors in the first few rows. Blair was introduced by John Prescott, who spoke of a leader seen in new ways who had mounted a higher stage. They applauded him, but differently from in the past, and then got almost quiet.

Blair was not shy in signifying what happened in America just three weeks earlier: "The millennium" for all the fanfare was "only a moment in time"; 9/11 "marked a turning point in history" with humankind facing new choices. The British families of the victims he saw in the church near Ground Zero, "hands clutching photos of sons and daughters, wives and husbands," trying to preserve hope, did not want revenge, he said. "They want something better in memory of their loved ones," and Blair took on the task in their name: "out of the shadows of this evil should emerge lasting good . . . "[6]

"Be in no doubt: bin Laden and his people organized this atrocity and were given succor by the Taliban regime," itself unspeakably repressive. "Whatever the dangers of the action we take, the dangers of inaction are far, far greater," he proclaimed to sustained applause in the hall.

But "let there be no moral ambiguity about this," he continued. Britain's actions would be "proportionate" and "targeted" but the perpetrators "have no moral inhibition on the slaughter of the innocent. If they could have murdered not 7,000 but 70,000 does anyone doubt they would have done so and rejoiced in it?" The hall did not have to answer. "There is no compromise possible with such people"; "just a choice: defeat it or be defeated by it. And defeat it we must." Journalists instinctively on their guard could already feel that this was "almost certainly the most powerful speech of his career." Blair was able to "synthesize" anger into a "constructive, focused force for good," barely evident in George Bush's call to arms.[7]

And "amidst all the talk of war and action, there is another dimension appearing," a dimension that allowed Blair to spotlight one of his core principles. "There is a coming together. The power of community is asserting itself."

He reminded the hall of Kosovo: "We won, the refugees went home, the policies of ethnic cleansing were reversed and one of the great dictators of the last century will see justice in this century." He recalled Kosovo, not just because of the just result, but because it was so formative in his thinking about the international community and humanitarian intervention.[8] Faced with what the United Nations called an "imminent human catastrophe," NATO decided to launch an intensive bombing campaign, but it was so prolonged, produced so many civilian casualties and refugees—all on CNN and the BBC—that Serbian leader Slobodan Milosevic came to believe he could outlast the international community. Despairing at Easter 1999, Blair came to believe in turn that only visible military escalation and the credible threat of ground forces could force Milosevic to surrender, producing a major rift with the Clinton administration and heated personal encounters with Clinton, constrained from action in Kosovo by a hostile Congress that was trying to impeach him and perhaps by some ambivalence about the moral imperatives. While Clinton insisted that Kosovo be based more narrowly on "security" needs, Blair addressed the Economic Club of Chicago and argued for a radical change in international rules, and later in Europe characterized the conflict—unfashionably at the time—as "good against evil" and "democracy against tyranny," language more suited to the Bush era.[9]

The determination of the world's nations to act together now against this evil, Blair believed, perhaps innocently, changed the moral equation. "I tell you if Rwanda happened again today as it did in 1993, when a million people were slaughtered in cold blood, we would have a moral duty to act there also . . .

"The critics will say: but how can the world be a community? Nations act in their own self interest." Yes, they do, but only as a community can they address terrorism, climate change, or world trade. At this moment of tragedy and threat, maybe people could understand the principle that has guided him. "It is that our self-interest and our mutual interests are today inextricably woven together."

This global moment, unlike the political moments we have struggled with, liberated Blair to think about how "the power of community" combines with "justice." "If globalization works only for the benefit of the few, then it will fail and will deserve to fail," Blair affirmed. Then he proceeded seamlessly to the choice his political campaigns had just struggled with: "If we follow the principles that have served us so well at home—that power, wealth and opportunity must be in the hands of the many, not the few, then we will be a force for good."

My jaw dropped. September 11, terrorism, and the new global imperative allowed him to accept for nations what previously he could not for his own nation.

Hugo Young noticed, too.[10] "It sounded like the speech he had been trying to make for a long time, a summation of what his public life might be for. The Taliban did him a favour, allowing him to get it out." This was "the most truthful, heartful, least manufactured speech he has given"; "it came from deep inside him, with words, I guess, that nobody else had to write," in contrast with Mr. Bush. It came from a place where his faith had settled questions of good and evil, defined the moral struggle that gave him in these three weeks since the towers fell on 9/11 a new certainty about his mission.

The "power of community" took him to his agenda for the country, a Britain not isolated but leading in Europe, thus ready to have Britain join the Euro Zone and "have the courage of argument, to ask the British people for their consent in this Parliament."

Labour's "values" informed that choice as did the continuing struggle for change in Britain. "The governing idea of modern social democracy is community," and thus "the test of any decent society is not the contentment of the wealthy and strong, but the commitment to the poor and weak," a "two-tier Britain" he previously declined to put central in his project.

"For decades there has been chronic under-investment in British public services," creating "our historic mission" to put that right, now moving comfortably to the choice he resisted so assiduously in the election. That was the meaning of the "historic shift" in the June 7 election: "investment to provide quality public services for all, comprehensively defeated short-term tax cuts for the few." He just formulated that choice more clearly than his advisors ever did, freed of all the reservations and angst. And while some leaders might reach out to unite all political parties at this moment of great threat to the nation and the world, Blair instead crystallized the partisan choice in moral terms. September 11 had made clear he must oppose the Conservative approach that "would be contrary to the very basis of community."

"For those people who lost their lives on September 11 and those that mourn them," Blair concluded, "now is the time for the strength to build that community. Let that be their memorial."

Afterward, the delegates filed out as if they were leaving church, not a conference, except for the standing ovation at the close. I went over to wait for him at the reception for the family and the team and I sensed even more than usual an immediate recognition, though with his broad smile held back by the seriousness of it all. Blair was not a hugging type, as far as I knew, but we managed a half hug. I thanked him for speaking to America, finding myself reacting as an American, someone who experienced 9/11 in Washington, with my family there and in lower Manhattan, vulnerable in ways we did not appreciate. When Bush went missing on 9/11, the members of Congress, including my wife, assembled on the steps of the U.S. Capitol, the likely target of the plane that went down in Pennsylvania, and sang "God Bless America" to show that our leaders were very much in charge. I was not alone in asking, Why can't Blair be our president right now?

Others were at his elbow and I promised him a note.

On October 7, the United States, with the support of Britain and the NATO allies, began military operations against al-Qaeda and the Taliban. I wrote Blair a letter immediately after the conference but held it, "not wanting it to land there at some especially difficult moment."

While the rest of the world was ready for Blair to rush through that stuff for home consumption, "I paid close attention to the whole speech, particularly themes like 'power of community' that bear vitally on the New Labour project," I wrote. By highlighting "the themes you wove through your speech," hopefully you "will give them life—outside and beyond the immediate conflict." What he did at Brighton was give force to the idea of "solidarity": "faced with new threats, the country and people want to come together, build loyalty and mutual responsibility." We now understood that "unity" was something special in the face of an enemy. "Community creates a sense of capacity and sense of possibility" and "by acting together, we move from the realm of individual interest to moral power, derived from community." Such a community "facilitates the many, not just the few, gaining opportunity and a better life."[11]

I felt Blair had finally found peace of mind, and I wrote the note to specify what he said in political terms and to get his nod for this new contract. I felt such relief, after years of relitigation of the project. Jonathan observed that Blair "would sometimes be a bit of a flippertygibbet about things" and change his mind, and Alastair spoke of his brooding and "struggle to find a rhythm," and I, too, was frustrated by his not being willing to accept many of my solutions, that attempted to accommodate his views. He was also very political and tactical about how to win voters, encouraged by some of the people closest to him, producing a lot of second-guessing. But for all that, I was so deeply fond of him and his decency and respectful of his extraordinary talents that mostly I was upset with myself for not being able to reach a settled place. But 9/11 changed him, as "if a rod had been inserted in his spine," Sally Morgan, a political advisor, observed from inside Number 10. So much rubble that cluttered the route from his personal faith to his political project was suddenly cleared away, as he told me later, that "there was a complete alignment between my view of the world and my view of the country, the values that I had and the politics."[12] "Community" now had a meaning and power that allowed him to bring people with him as he sought to remake society, consistent with his values and mine.

IRAQ

Blair arrived at Bush's ranch in Crawford, Texas, on April 4, 2002, for a two-day visit to discuss Iraq, an obsession of many in the Bush team, particularly Vice President Dick Cheney and his neoconservative allies in the administration. At that point Bush seemed set on resorting to military force to remove Saddam. But Blair was there to talk about Iraq because he wanted to be talking about Iraq. Five years previously and less than six months after his 1997 victory, Blair warned, "It is absolutely essential that Saddam backs down on this or that he be made to back down."[13] It was easy to imagine that Bush and Blair would find a shared language of "right" and "wrong," even if the two men came to these words and principles from very different religious and partisan traditions. Bush later described Blair to the world as someone "who does not need a focus group to convince him of the difference between right and wrong." It was good they left Philip in London. He did bring Alastair, whose secularism and atheism were a constant curiosity for Bush, who found he could pray with Blair.[14]

Blair was open to moving against Iraq, but he believed that working both for a broad coalition under a U.N. mandate and for progress on the Israeli-Palestinian front would make it much more likely the Iraq policy would succeed and that he, Blair, could win support from his own party. What mattered to the Bush people was that Blair would be with them; the rest was mere detail. "I explained to the Prime Minister that the policy of my government is the removal of Saddam," the president commented almost matter-of-factly at their joint conference. Blair danced around that but put down an equally strong assertion on Iraq's weapons of mass destruction: "You cannot have a situation in which he [Saddam Hussein] carries on being in breach of U.N. resolutions and refusing to allow us to assess whether and how he is developing these weapons of mass destruction." Blair added that how to proceed "is a matter that is open for us." The president, however, misspoke with a purpose: "Maybe I should be a little less direct and be a little more nuanced, and say we support regime change."[15]

While Blair believed he did not commit Britain in Crawford to support military action, Bush, no doubt, sized him up and saw what many heard when Blair reported back to the cabinet meeting that there was, as Robin Cook describes, "an implicit guarantee that Britain was committed to join the U.S. military action."[16]

My views of George Bush had been earned in close-up battle, so I did not take as realistic Alastair's and Blair's observations that this was a surprisingly savvy, canny politician. I assumed I was being spun to further build the bonds with Washington; in any case, they knew any nuance would be lost in translation. I gave Blair a lot of room on Iraq, as I was cautious as an American advisor getting into foreign policy and national security issues, unless invited or unless central to our political project; indeed with President Clinton, I avoided those issues in my polling and walled off the corridors of the National Security Council so the president, with rocky relations with the military, could not be accused of poll-testing command decisions. Dick Morris put up no such barriers in his time.

Nonetheless, I did not trust George Bush and his political team. They were deeply ideological, ruthless partisans, America-centric and arrogant, edging toward the lawless, so the pending marriage had me nervous. When I asked Philip why, he was very circumspect but repeatedly came back to the importance of the British strengthening Colin Powell's position in the inner circle to keep the internationalist impulse alive and that not all issues were settled with Bush. But perhaps more important was Blair's analysis of the Bush inner circle where things were black and white: you were either with them totally, or you were not; there was no space or respect for gray. If you wanted to influence the course of American policy, you had to be with them 100 percent.

The price of being with the Americans 100 percent, Robin Cook warned, would mean a dramatic break with Europe and the end of Blair's efforts to take Britain into the Euro Zone and lead in Europe. You could not battle with Europe for the first part of the year and then convince British voters in the next to vote in a referendum to give up sovereignty to Europe.[17]

The head of the British Secret Intelligence Service reported in July that the Americans were moving perceptibly to a new place, according to a memo summarizing a joint MI6-CIA meeting on Iraq: "military action was now seen as inevitable." The memo concluded, "Bush wanted to remove Saddam, through military action, justified by the conjunction of terrorism and WMD. But the intelligence and facts were being fixed around the policy."[18]

Blair fell to new lows in August 2002, just as he needed to rally the citizenry to do challenging things. He was crashing on the things he needed most, including "trust," while hitting historic highs on being "arrogant and out of touch."[19] He was not too out of touch to know that only a third supported military action, though we asked no questions on Iraq that year and he sought no polling guidance on how best to bring people with him on Iraq or humanitarian interventions, seeing the clarity of purpose and moral outcome as the message.

In this period, Blair shared with only his closest advisors *Le Grand Stratégie*, as he called it, to announce his intention to serve out his two terms, but not to "fight an election." The advisors were mostly not enthusiastic but he would not be put off and forced a meeting and discussions over a couple of months on all facets of the choice, according to Alastair's account. I was not privy to these discussions, but I can imagine that he wanted to get the decision of going to war together with George Bush out of an electoral context.[20]

Bush, too, saw his standing drop 5 points in August in the public polls as congressional Democrats moved into a 4-point lead in the congressional vote. With off-year elections looming, the Bush White House was pretty unapologetic about timing the Iraq vote for political purposes: "From a marketing point of view, you don't introduce new products in August"—a time of year when everyone is still on holiday, both in the literal and figurative sense. They rushed the Iraq resolution to the Congress for September to divide the Democrats and shift the focus back to the war on terrorism in Congress's last month.[21]

Blair returned to Camp David on September 7, a few days before Bush was to address the United Nations General Assembly, to try to win support for a broad coalition and a U.N. resolution. Both were opposed by Vice President Cheney and Secretary of Defense Donald Rumsfeld. Blair won Bush's commitment to such a resolution, though the line only made it into Bush's speech on delivery. According to a close aide, Blair was passionate about exhausting all nonmilitary options before going to war. But if war came, he would commit British troops to fight alongside the Americans. Responding to reporters' questions, the two men affirmed their commitment to addressing the grave threat, and Bush declared, without qualification, "Saddam Hussein possesses weapons of mass destruction." Afterward Bush commented to Alastair and the others, "I don't want it on the record, but your guy's got balls." Bush knew at that point that Blair would be with him no matter what happened. Alastair wrote in his diary that "Blair had a real sense of certainty about [Iraq]" and that Britain couldn't let Bush go alone.[22]

But the Bush people played to type. While giving Blair enough rope to build European and Security Council support, they did everything possible to make his job more difficult. Bush had already withdrawn from the Kyoto treaty on climate change and the nuclear anti-proliferation treaty and had frozen any U.S. effort to promote an Israeli-Palestinian peace. Now the administration was putting intense pressure on its allies to exempt U.S. soldiers in Bosnia from the new international court, threatening to undermine both U.N. peacekeeping and the court, both of which Blair strongly supported. In late September, Bush declared a new national security doctrine, asserting the right to strike preemptively at regimes that acquired weapons of mass destruction—in my view, the polar opposite of what Blair believed in.[23]

When the Iraq resolution came before the Congress, I was conflicted, which surprised many of my friends. I was determined not to repeat my mistake before the Gulf War in 1991 when, along with most Democrats, I opposed the resolution, even though that had been a clear case of aggression under international law, justifying the use of military force. The nation watched attentively the sober debate in the Congress and I attended some of it personally, sitting in the family gallery, watching my wife cast her first vote in Congress—against the war. But at the time, I commented to her after listening to Steve Solarz of New York, "I'm not at all sure he isn't right." So, I was determined not to be a knee-jerk opponent. People I trusted, from Sandy Berger to Tony Blair, were convinced that Iraq had weapons of mass destruction, and at the very least a war criminal would end up on trial for his crimes. On the other hand, James Carville, my partner in Democracy Corps, which provides strategic research for U.S. progressives and many things, was deeply opposed to the war from the beginning—a fact he reminds me of all too often. Before the vote in Congress, James and I sent a painfully confused memo because I insisted on offering message advice to both the Democratic opponents and proponents of the war.[24]

At the same time people I trusted in the Israeli intelligence community were pretty confident Iraq would descend into a Lebanon-style internecine conflict, producing more instability and terrorism requiring years of occupation costing hundreds of billions of dollars. I deeply resented the Rove White House crudely using the war against Democrats, but I thought it was more cynical than that. I came to believe as I was writing *The Two Americas* that the administration preferred to act unilaterally to demonstrate American power with "shock-and-awe" to polarize our politics. That would be disastrous for Blair and it would be disastrous for Iraq and the world. I supported my wife in voting no.

The Authorization for Use of Military Force Against Iraq Resolution of 2002 passed the Congress and was signed into law by the president on October 16. It authorized use of the armed forces as "necessary and appropriate," without U.N. support, showing official contempt for Blair's efforts to give the war an international character.

I attended a private reception at Number 10 with Blair on a pleasant fall afternoon when we were able to stand about in the garden. While it was a social occasion, Blair and I had a lot to talk about, mostly about America. I was not very optimistic about the Democrats' chances in the upcoming elections and resented Bush for timing the resolution for maximum partisan polarization, unlike his father, who had waited for the new Congress. I was annoyed at the Democrats for being wimps and failing to challenge Bush's budget and tax cuts, indeed, his entire economic philosophy. But since we were talking about America, I ventured some insights. President Bush's unilateralism was ideological. He wanted the effort at the United Nations to visibly fail. The war was meant to demonstrate American exceptionalism and American power to try to recapture the "Reaganism" of the post–Cold War era. What I didn't say, but was thinking, "How could you support this man who has done more than Margaret Thatcher to undermine the idea of 'community'?" I ventured further in another area where I was deeply involved. Bush and his Middle East advisors viewed the whole history of James Baker and Clinton shuttle diplomacy as humiliating for America and saw the Palestinians and PLO leader Yasser Arafat as part of the terrorist world. They had no interest in any peace process. While there were areas of disagreement in the White House, Israel and Palestine was not one of them. Their strategy for the next presidential election was to achieve a new Republican era, including cementing Evangelicals and Jews over Israel, eroding Jewish financial support for Democrats, and winning over Jewish voters in Florida—all predicated on Bush's uncritical embrace of hard-line Israeli prime minister Ariel Sharon. There was not a chance they would do anything real on the Israeli-Palestinian issue. I am sure Blair thought I had been drinking the Democratic Kool-Aid, but I had to say it.[25]

On November 5, 2002, the Republicans won back control of the U.S. Senate, giving them control of all branches of the federal government—Congress, the Supreme Court, and the executive branch. The victory strengthened their mandate for Iraq and sent a signal to the world about America's new posture.

On November 8, the Security Council unanimously adopted U.N. Resolution 1441, warning Iraq of serious consequences if it did not comply with U.N. resolutions, allow full inspections, and destroy all WMD. The Bush administration believed this was all the sanction it needed, but Blair made the case at the White House at the end of January that he needed a second resolution specifically authorizing force if he was to carry his own Labour government with him. Bush supported his efforts against Cheney's advice, though Blair was way out on a limb, dependent on his ability to persuade France and Germany and a majority of the Security Council, which somehow Blair thought he could achieve. The first part of the year left Europe bitterly divided and Blair resentful of the reemergent Franco-German axis.[26]

I met with Blair at Number 10 on January 16, with the polls showing him losing the country. The graph lines for "the country is on the wrong track" and "New Labour is losing steam" both shot up, literally off the chart; the lines trusting Blair shot down off the chart to under a third. Regard for Bush went even lower.[27] We asked our first questions on military action in Iraq with a likely debate in the Commons just months away. Only a third supported Blair at that point. The country was split down the middle on whether Blair was acting out of conviction or just being a "poodle" of the United States. A large majority were opposed to military action if there was no U.N. resolution authorizing force.

On February 15 somewhere between one and two million demonstrators descended on London, protesting the specter of an Iraq war. Blair lost further ground in the country and the crash became political. While Iraq was the precipitating issue, those disappointed in Labour mentioned in equal measure "crime and asylum," "Iraq," and "overpromising on public services and spin," even as Blair lost his domestic focus, and as the prime minister roamed the world and the Houses of Parliament lobbying for support for an unpopular war.[28] With confidence in his principles and superhuman effort, he had moved support for the war in Britain to just over 40 percent.[29]

I spent a good part of a week in the run-up to the Commons vote in an intense meeting at Number 10. Blair was taking the most difficult television interviews in order to move the country and his Labour supporters. President Bush helped with an announcement that in April, as soon as Mahmoud Abbas was installed as president of the Palestinian Authority, he would publish a new "road map" for Israeli-Palestinian talks.[30]

On March 18, Blair gave two major speeches, the most important and impassioned to the Labour MPs and then to the Commons. "This is not the time to falter," he declared. "This is the time to show that we will confront the tyrannies and dictatorships and terrorists who put our way of life at risk, to show at the moment a decision that we have the courage to do the right thing." With the support of the Conservatives, there was no doubt about winning the vote; the issue was, did he lose over 150 Labour MPs—in effect, losing his majority, winning only because of Conservative support? Blair implied he would resign if that happened. In the end, Blair got just enough support, losing 139 Labour MPs, one third of the parliamentary Labour Party, and two cabinet resignations, most prominently, Robin Cook.[31]

Bush followed the balloting and cheered the results. That was a kind of turning point for me, however. I found myself silently applauding each defecting MP. I felt disloyal, yet most everyone in the team "had severe moments of doubt," about the Iraq decision and according to one author, even Cherie later wrote, "there were times when I faltered." No one had taken the Kool Aid for Bush and his policies, and when Prescott would later injudiciously tell a group, "President Bush is crap," Blair paused and responded, "Your standing in the Party will go up ten points."

So they gave me a pass on Iraq and Bush. Did I consider resigning? No. I did not question Blair's motivation and his political project transcended this war.[32]

The Iraq War began on March 20. Just three weeks later, the U.S. military toppled the giant statue of Saddam Hussein and on May 1, Bush declared "Mission Accomplished," though no WMD had yet been found and the anarchy and looting seemed to prestage a greater chaos. British public support for the war jumped immediately with the advent of hostilities, holding until July, when the public turned on the war and the country's leaders.[33]

On May 29, the BBC aired a report that Blair and Campbell had "sexed-up" the intelligence dossier in September to win support for the war, producing a ferocious battle between Number 10 and the BBC. I was present for some of those meetings. Alastair resented the BBC's biased and smug reporting and wanted an official repudiation of the story. If the story was allowed to stand it would leave the prime minister presumed guilty of the worst kind of public deception. All the parties testified to a parliamentary investigation, with David Kelly, the government's leading expert on Iraq's arms, acknowledging he was the source for the story, though denying key parts of it.[34]

We polled in June. For the first time in what seemed like a century, Labour and the Conservatives were tied in a future election contest, beginning a year-long period during which Labour barely matched or actually trailed the Tories. The turn against Labour was focused on Blair. If it was any consolation, Bush's popularity was even lower, which I took perverse pleasure in sharing with the team at the end of June. The prime minister had paid a heavy price for his decision. Our graphs showed what I called "The Labour Gap," people who still identified with Labour but who would not vote for Blair or vote at all.[35]

On July 9 I had my first meeting with Blair since the war began. He looked grayer and a little weary. Jonathan and Alastair were impatient with the Americans' aimless, so far futile search for WMD, and listening to Blair, I told other skeptical observers, "He certainly believes they are going to be found."[36] The advisors were also hoping that with Labour's lead lost Blair would begin to focus on the political rubble at home, though he clearly was putting his money down on WMDs and success at stability in Iraq to change the probabilities. With Philip's and Jeremy Rosner's help, we tested some messages incorporating the war, but for Blair, a successful conclusion to the unfinished war was the message.

We did not have time to speak about Blair's address to a joint session of the U.S. Congress, a rare and special honor bestowed for his extraordinary role in support of America since 9/11. I promised him to write a note on my thoughts.

I took about five days because it was a minefield, and I did not really know what he was trying to get out of the address. "The challenge," I wrote in my e-mail to Blair, via Jonathan, would be to construct a speech that "advances your vision for global affairs" that also helped him and Labour at home and maybe the Democrats sitting in the hall, while being "supportive of President Bush and his efforts." I tried to get him to factor in his politics and mine, explicit as possible, up front about my multiple loyalties. It was important to get both "Democrats and Republicans united and standing together, applauding what the two countries have achieved" and I urged him to speak about 9/11 before Iraq. I suggested he go back to his first messages from the British people, speaking for American sensibilities: "first, that we are not alone and second, that people appreciate the cost we bear for freedom." On Iraq, "you should begin with the armed forces that are there now," the "young generation whose idealism and patriotism took them to Iraq."

Most of my note was devoted to various ways for him to gently and indirectly associate himself with "internationalism." "I do not know how far you can go, consistent with your beliefs," I wrote, but "I think it is very important from a UK and Labour Party perspective." I suggested various indirect devices: "nothing would make me happier than to see [Saddam] on trial in the Hague"; reference to other conflicts, like Afghanistan and Kosovo, where the U.N. and NATO were seen to have played a positive role: "Anything you say that raises the legitimacy of the U.N. and NATO—including a possible role in Iraq—will suggest a commitment to internationalism, absent right now in DC."

My biggest idea I also thought was the most obvious, to come back to "your vision of community"—the post 9/11 conference speech—that allowed him to speak again about "the meaning of community, how we depend on each other and achieve more." Whether or not he made any connection to immediate events, that would lay the basis for mutual dependence and an international role in the future. It was a way, I hoped, to nudge Bush back into the world by simply recalling what Blair stood for.[37]

On the 17th, I opted to watch him deliver the address in person from the family gallery overlooking the House floor, where I could see him and my wife and feel the dynamics in the chamber. Rosa was in the leadership delegation that met him off the floor and, to the surprise of the others, got a full hug. Blair worked on the speech on the plane, and I had no idea what he was going to say. He began by thanking Congress for bestowing upon him the Congressional Gold Medal. "But you, like me, know who the real heroes are: those brave service men and women, yours and ours, who fought the war and risk their lives still." Democrat and Republican alike were on their feet in an instant, applauding. And that was the last of my advice that he heeded, realizing at each decision point that it was a speech to strengthen his bond with the president and, to some extent, the Republicans. Right in the first few paragraphs, "let me express my gratitude to President Bush" for his leadership and more, bringing the Republican side of the chamber quickly to their feet, the Democrats rising respectfully. The speech was full of cues that would get the attention of the right: "never a time when the power of America was so necessary or so misunderstood"; the "political culture of Europe is inevitably rightly based on compromise," but "I don't believe you can compromise with this new form of terrorism." Rather than legitimizing the United Nations, he called for it to be "reformed"; rather than offering an opening to a disaffected Europe, he told the chamber, "never forget, many European nations supported our action," listing the countries of the new Europe. All agreed when he said the greatest risk to the world were states with weapons of mass destruction coming together with the terrorists. But then he went further: "I say we know the Taliban supported al Qaeda. We know Iraq under Saddam gave haven to and supported terrorists," eliding the two and allowing the audience to infer Iraq's connection to 9/11. I sat back in my seat, defeated.

He offered very few cues for those who wanted a more internationalist course: "let us start preferring a coalition and acting alone if we have to, not the other way around"; "America must listen as well as lead," though quickly qualified, "members of Congress, don't ever apologize for your values." Blair also mentioned global challenges, like climate change and the Israeli-Palestinian conflict, though without any specific challenge to the United States.

He never used the word "community." The value that he spoke about with passion in his address was "freedom" and the importance of promoting democracy and giving people the choice to be "free," values deep in the American experience and embraced by all our traditions, though at this moment central to Bush's policy toward the world. Blair used the word "free" or "freedom" twenty-four times. Thus, in his close, he declared: "You are not going to be alone," alas something I suggested, but in a different context. "We will be with you in this fight for liberty."[38]

After he made his way up the center aisle, acknowledging the enthusiastic well-wishers, I went to meet my wife as she left the Democratic cloakroom. Rahm Emanuel—my friend and colleague from the Clinton campaign, now in Congress—came out first and immediately said, "Took care of his business. Not a sliver of light between him and the president," holding up his half finger to make the point. Blair felt he had gone as far as he could have gone, but it left me feeling like a member of some sect that still believed the "power of community" animated our work.

After the speech, Blair flew to Asia and halfway there learned the terrible news that David Kelly was dead—unused to the public spotlight, he went to the woods and committed suicide.[39] An indecent British tabloid asked of Number 10, "Proud of Yourselves?" The death put a pall over Number 10 and the BBC, a crushing dose of reality, what one author described as "an extraordinary blow to an already exhausted prime minister." There was a media frenzy and an inquiry under Lord Hutton to report on culpability. By one judgment, "Blair's office ceased during the long hot summer of 2003 to operate as an effective centre of government."[40]

The public polls showed Labour's numbers turning down again in September, not helped by the long-put-off decision to bring President Bush to Britain in November. I was in London for the visit and security was unbelievably tight to keep demonstrators away.[41] Philip and I had meetings in the House of Commons with the heads of the campaign, Gordon and his team at Treasury, and a meeting with the full political and communications team in the Cabinet Room at Number 10. There was a lot of gallows humor around the table. The Conservatives were gaining on every issue. Two findings pushed them back in their chairs. We had long taken comfort with the idea that no matter how Labour screwed up, the Tories still couldn't connect with half the country. That was no longer true. Only a third now ruled out voting for them. At the same time, we were rapidly losing Labour's voters, vividly displayed in a graph. My follow-up memo in early December was entitled, "Overcoming Tory Consolidation and Labour Demoralization."[42]

There were reports that in early November, John Prescott, the deputy leader, hosted a meeting with the prime minister and chancellor, with Blair agreeing to stand down before the next general election in 2005 and Brown to be supportive of the government initiatives over the next year. I treated those stories like the years of headlines, "New Breakthrough in Middle East Peace Talks"—I'll pay attention when it really happens. Unknown to me, Prescott really did host a meeting at his official residence, Admiralty House, where, unlike previous meetings where the two shouted at each other, the two reached an understanding that Blair would depart before the next election, as would be reported by Prescott in his memoir. Bob Shrum would later tell me of the promise, but I decided to spend no time sorting out what was real.[43]

On January 28, 2004, Lord Hutton issued his 750-page report on the intelligence leading up to Britain's participation in the Iraq War. The report exonerated Blair and Alastair of "sexing up" the intelligence findings, but it was nevertheless an embarrassment, greatly diminishing the credibility of the evidence of a threat from Iraq that was the justification for going to war.[44]

We later learned that after Brown presented the budget to the Commons on March 17, he and Blair spoke alone. The prime minister apparently was convinced he could not win back the public's trust and "can't get through on Iraq."[45] Blair proposed that he announce his decision to retire after the Easter recess in the beginning of May. Brown preferred that he wait until later in the year in order not to kick off a long leadership contest.[46] In his own head, Blair had crossed some line, a conclusion likely shared with Jonathan, Alastair, and Philip, though I knew nothing about it.

Our March poll probably reinforced Blair's thinking. The Tories continued to gain ground, emerging ahead on many issues, including tax and restoring trust in government. The negativity about Blair was unchanged. And most dramatically, the poll showed the previously hapless Conservatives taking a 3-point lead in the race.[47]

When Jeremy and I finished presenting those results in the Cabinet Room, I asked if the team wanted to see some of the ads running in the building U.S. presidential campaign. Jonathan, always a keen follower of U.S. politics, leaned over my shoulder, and the group, happy for an escape from the barbarians at the gate, crowded around my laptop. I really enjoyed these attacks on Bush and took unseemly pleasure in them. The "Misleader" ad came up first on the screen: "George Bush is spending 87 billion dollars more in Iraq. What is his plan for taking care of America?" That was followed by a powerful ad that won first place in a MoveOn competition, "Bush in 30 Seconds." It showed a series of children working in adult jobs, washing dishes, cleaning floors, and on an assembly line, followed by a text on screen: "Guess who's going to pay off President Bush's $1 trillion deficit?" Smiles.

Then, I pressed play for "Polygraph." "Ladies and gentlemen, President George W. Bush," the announcer started, as the lines traced by a polygraph tracked across the screen. In the background you could hear Bush's statements: "Saddam Hussein had an advanced nuclear weapons development program." "Saddam Hussein recently sought significant quantities of uranium from Africa." "Saddam Hussein aids and protects terrorists, including members of al-Qaeda." With each statement, the polygraph needle jumped wildly.

The ad closed with a simple text message on the screen: "Americans are dying—for the truth." Nervous laughs; not such a good escape after all.

The ads I showed the Blair team came in part from my work with MoveOn.org, what had become the largest antiwar group in the country focused on the coming presidential election. With my advice and a group of insurgent consultants, MoveOn had prepared the ads to shine a bright light on President Bush's request for $87 billion for rebuilding and continuing military operations in Iraq, clear evidence that Iraq was not going to be the quick and costless operation the president had promised. The $87 billion was a symbol of deception and bad priorities. I also began to work with ACT, a new outside organization that was allowed to take large contributions to fund a media campaign independent of the Democratic primary candidates. While the candidates battled for the nomination, ACT would air ads intended to put Bush on the defensive. I was intensely opposed to the war and thought it now possible to bring down George Bush on it.[48]

I was not alone. After John Kerry emerged as the effective nominee on Super Tuesday in March, he also emerged with a small lead over George Bush for the general election. A growing majority said the country was off track and Bush's approval fell to 50 percent for the first time since 9/11. For the first time since the Iraq War began, a significant majority said it "is not worth the cost of U.S. lives and dollars."[49]

On April 14, the president stood with Prime Minister Ariel Sharon in the Cross Hall in the White House to make a formal statement endorsing Sharon's plan for unilateral withdrawal from Gaza. Bush began well: "These are historic and courageous actions." That was something with which Tony Blair would doubtless agree. But then the president launched into a completely one-sided and unprecedented series of assertions. "The Palestinian people must insist on change" and a new leadership. That kind of advice likely was received more warmly with Jewish voters in Miami and with Likud voters in Israel than in Ramallah. He announced America's support for Israel's position on the "right of return" of Palestinians and recognition of the "realities on the ground," including Israeli annexation of large settlement areas around Jerusalem.[50]

Two days later I watched on TV a visibly uncomfortable Tony Blair stand with the president, this time in the Rose Garden, and describe the president's actions as furthering the "road map." I was embarrassed for him. Wasn't this the final evidence of the scam? The peace process was Bush's one nod to internationalism in this whole venture, but it was a fraud. I wanted to shake him. "That fuckwit Bush has taken down every leader who has allied with him. Break free," I nearly shouted to him through the TV.

The war pushed even deeper into the public consciousness on May 1 with the publication of photos of Iraqi prisoners being humiliated by American military personnel in the Abu Ghraib prison, scene of some of Saddam Hussein's worst abuses against his citizenry. Day after day, the images of stacked bodies and hooded prisoners ratcheted down the moral authority of the United States and the war's higher democratic and moral purpose. When the Red Cross informed the British government that its soldiers, too, had abused Iraqi prisoners, Blair apologized, which was far more than Don Rumsfeld could manage. But Blair's apology was barely noticed amidst the cacophony of headlines, full of revulsion—"A New Monster in Chief," "Floundering in a Moral Swamp," "Catastrophe," "Bush Praises a 'Courageous' Rumsfeld."[51]

Jeremy and I went to London on May 5 and 6 for a full round of meetings that included Number 10, the party leaders, Brown and his full team at the Treasury, and the ad agency. Philip asked me to think of it as one of those times to just go back, look at the old data, and see if you can find some new ways to come out of a dark period.

As a prelude to doing that, we posed the question: How willing is Blair to acknowledge problems or mistakes?

This is often a precondition to be heard by voters, but the question was left unanswered.

Philip rarely shared what was going on in Blair's innermost circle, but on May 15, Prescott hinted in an interview that there could be a change of leadership soon. That Blair had crossed a line was now more generally known, causing great alarm among his close supporters. Philip speculated, based on close observation rather than Blair's words, that he was deeply affected by Abu Ghraib and for the first time contemplated that the Iraq War might have been a mistake.

Over the past month since telling Brown of his intention not to run, Blair was wracked by the decision, but also by problems with one of his children. He stopped reading the press, according to some in the team who later described him as "demoralized" and "very despondent." Cherie would write, he "suffered a crisis of confidence." Even as key members of Blair's and Brown's teams met about the transition, the pressure from Brown "sucked his energy."[52]

Philip asked in June that I conduct a "special poll on trust," to be shared only with the prime minister and Jonathan.

On July 10, Andrew Marr, the highly reputable political editor for the BBC, reported that an announcement by Blair on his possible retirement was imminent.[53]

As only outsiders can, Jeremy and I ignored all of that and did some of our most inventive work, trying to figure out a strategy that would enable us to look at trust, Iraq, acknowledging mistakes, ways to distance from Bush, and to go beyond left orthodoxy on immigration and asylum. It was a complex experimental design to see what combination could move the vote and judgments about Blair. The survey finished on July 14 along with a regular Labour Party survey, no doubt circulated in raw form at Number 10.

On July 20, I presented the results of our Labour polling, but not the "special poll," to Brown's team. This was the first time in many years that we had not shared the full result with Brown and I felt odd about it, but these were personal questions about Blair. My report of Labour's new 3-point lead quieted the meeting, Brown making no observations.

A day later, I presented all the results to Blair in the Cabinet Room, with two hours blocked out. For the first time in a long while, I was in good spirits and presenting with a real sense of possibility, and not just because Labour had moved back into a lead and Blair's approval rating was up 7 points, though all that helped. I was sitting on one side of the long table, my back to the windows. Blair sat directly across from me with his full crew in attendance. Everyone struggled to read the PowerPoint projected on a screen from an earlier century, askew at the far end of the table that was long enough to accommodate the whole cabinet. With more than a passing interest in the survey, we did not pause to talk about the presidential election. British voters responded to the message "chance for a better life" and actually began to be dislodged from their torpor when Blair showed his frustration with the pace of public service change, stood up to Europe on the constitution and asylum, and differed with Bush on climate change. We did not even mention Iraq, but independence in any area got the attention of Labour's disengaged voters, and they moved back to Blair at the end of the survey. This was actionable, I thought, and I clearly had Blair's attention. All deferred to him and he almost breathed out, seeming to say, "Thank God, we're not dead." He rephrased some of the findings, wanting to listen to them again, and said, there is a great deal that is interesting here, and then the others engaged.[54]

I was intrigued when Philip asked my office to prepare a version of the slides for him to present to Alan Milburn, one of Blair's favorite reformers, who had clashed with Brown before leaving the government.

Only later did I learn that a few days before our Number 10 presentation, Blair had changed his mind and planned to announce that he would run for an unprecedented third term, though not a fourth term.[55] After the August holiday, Blair announced that Alan Milburn would head the next Labour Party campaign, a brief public announcement that in effect brought a difficult private period to a close.

With the Kerry campaign faltering badly in August 2004, I once again broke my pledge never to do another presidential campaign. I started after Labor

Day, and James Carville and I had one mission: get John Kerry to speak with clarity on Iraq after being tied up in knots over his vote for the war and his vote against the $87 billion to fund its continuation. We pressed for a major speech on Iraq, with James threatening to pour a can of oil all over his body and immolate himself if Kerry wouldn't do it.

"Iraq is the window through which people view Bush's performance on foreign policy and the war on terrorism," I wrote in a memo to the campaign. But Kerry would not be heard on the dominant issues of the election unless he could say, "I would not cast the same vote knowing what I know today." In some sense, I was trying to get Kerry to do what Blair would not, though Kerry really did regret the vote, even if he preferred blaming Bush for deceiving him. That acknowledgment finally freed Kerry to speak about Bush's series of bad decisions: "He failed to tell the truth about the rationale for going to war . . . rushing to war without letting weapons inspectors finish their work. He went without a broad coalition of allies."[56] Consumed with the campaign, I did not even think about what Blair might be thinking when he listened to Kerry's speech.

On September 27, I went to Brighton for the party conference, arriving the day before Blair's speech. My room was part of Number 10's bloc for the first time. I read a draft and came down in my Yale gym clothes, apparently tighter and shorter than the British norm as I learned when Pat McFadden, the prime minister's political secretary, waved over folks to marvel at my attire. At one point, the call went out mysteriously that Tony wanted to see people in his room, but I held back, not having played that role before. Blair's speech centered on "Britain's hard-working families" and for the first time he spoke personally about the hospital porters, the office cleaners, the dinner ladies, at the school canteen—"the workers who we too often see right through, walk straight past, take for granted." They motivated our agenda. "So, here are ten things a future Labour third term can do for Britain's hard-working families," centered on making a better life. He spoke of it as a national purpose, not just a tagline.

On the other hand, the speech was full of tortured talk about apologizing on Iraq or acknowledging mistakes. Though he agonized about it, he simply could not go there. He accepted why I recommended it, disagreed, and then said that Britain had to "stand with the Iraqi people until the job is done."[57]

I saw him after the speech at the reception, pleased that he took half the advice and thinking that it would be tacky to mention that the message would not really work without the acknowledgment of mistakes and learning and showing independence from Bush in some area. He's clearly doesn't believe in it, so let it go. In any case, with the U.S. presidential race very close—

Bush ahead by 49 to 46 percent in our Democracy Corps polls finished the day before—that was what he wanted to discuss.[58]

I followed the voting on November 2 in the Kerry headquarters in Washington, all the pollsters and media people jammed into a single room. Earlier, I shared a tiny room at the edge of the war room with Joe Lockhart, Clinton's spokesman at the end of his second term, but we were all evicted to make room for the lawyers and voting monitors. The exit polls were good and we were high. Philip called every hour, and I read down the states, which he then read to Blair and Jonathan. As the polls closed in a few states in the East, Philip called one last time before Tony went to bed. I didn't see how we could lose.

Of course, we did. The exit polls had been very wrong. The curtains came down in the early morning. We all stood in a windowless room, listening on the speakerphone to the Ohio headquarters slowly coming to the conclusion there were not enough contested ballots to win. Who would call Kerry?

ENDGAME

In mid-December, I flew to London, intent on ironing out the details of the proposed polling program for the upcoming campaign with an election presumably in May. My first meeting was with Matt Carter, the general secretary of the party. He took me up to the small conference room, closed the door, and then laid aside my draft proposal. Before I could speak, he said, "You know how much we value the work you do for the party." Pause. "I'm not sure why this job has fallen to me," implying he had no hand in it. "Mark Penn has been conducting polls for Number 10, and Tony wants the polling program split between the two of you."

I paused. Penn? This isn't really happening, I thought.

"No," I said, my breath draining out of me, "I won't be doing that. The Labour Party deserves better than that," speaking more quietly than I wanted to.

"I understand, but give it some thought. This is really what Tony wants."

It felt like I had been punched in the stomach. Philip was the last person I expected to show such disloyalty and Penn the last person I would expect Blair to turn to. Unwilling to even think about Blair, I decided to take a slow walk back to my flat through St. James's and Green Parks. Philip was afraid to meet with me alone and asked Sally Morgan—Philip now a lord and she a baroness—to meet at the House of Lords, where they escorted me to a bar café used by the members. Sally told me that during the period of Blair's deepest doubts, President Clinton and Hillary, too, called repeatedly to urge Blair to run again, pointing out how Al Gore had failed to protect the Clinton Legacy. They also pushed for Blair to use Mark Penn to help find a way out. They pushed for him in lots of places. But it did surprise me that Blair agreed and had conducted a series of polls, according to Sally, that were not even shared with Philip, a completely implausible notion in the inner circle. Philip added that Penn supported the war and his polling was on Iraq. While I did not know when Penn began, as early as May, Philip was deleting all the Iraq message batteries that we drafted for our surveys. After one such exchange, I responded testily in an e-mail: "We should talk about Iraq and more. Won't go away." Apparently, Penn was not so sympathetic to the idea of Blair acknowledging disappointments, frustrations, and mistakes on the war or other issues. It isn't something leaders love to do.[59] In any case, Penn may have been more in step with Blair's thinking on these issues, though I wasn't going to even open that window at this point.

I should have noticed the telltale signs of Penn in the conference speech—"if you're a young married couple trying to buy a house," "if you're trying to balance home and family life," "modern life is being perpetually stressed out," "and more choice for mums at home and at work." They were the building blocks for Penn to let Blair know that "soccer moms"—married women with children—were why Kerry lost and the way Blair would win. He would chase that chimera and press to make "mums" Blair's highest target, even though two thirds of the lost Labour voters were neither married nor had children at home.

Philip said that if Kerry had won, he might have been able to get the decision reversed, but he was working closely with Penn, becoming secretive. He moved as much of the research there as possible before the election and Penn's company took over his business without a financial payout after the election.

Sally and Jonathan later told me that I was actually "fired," but somehow nobody ever did it, and I ended up taking over the polling in the marginal districts and the daily tracking, watching it all from a dysfunctional new war room. The Penn people were grouped at one set of long tables and my people at another, a touch further away from the cluster of tables at the center. It was a daily humiliating experience, but I decided I had too much invested in "New Labour" to walk away, even though we were working without any funding at the end.

Right before Blair called the election, I warned that Labour looked like the "insiders" to a citizenry ready to cast "protest votes" on Iraq, taxes, and immigration. With Penn's encouragement, Blair had stopped talking of "hardworking families," but the Conservative leader had not. Our last poll in over one hundred marginal seats in mid-March showed Labour with only a one-point lead, which would mean Labour losing over fifty seats, wilting its majority by over a hundred, leaving the party with perhaps only a fifty-seat majority. This was a shocking scenario that brought perspiration to many brows. Penn's national polls had Labour with landslide leads, but our look at the public polls at the beginning of April showed Labour slipping in all of them to just 37 percent and holding only a 4-point lead. My e-mail to Blair about that led Philip to erupt in the war room, shouting at Sam Weston, my field lieutenant in the campaign, "Tell Stan these e-mails to Tony are wrong and very destructive." While Sam would later go on to describe war room encounters as completely uncomfortable and frustrating, watching the way the campaign was being run and not being able to do anything about it, my mood had evolved to contempt and diffidence, allowing me to concentrate on the sparse data available to me. On April 5, Blair called the election for May 5, beginning with a satisfaction rating of only 34 percent according to media polls. No prime minister had won reelection with so low a number.[60]

In the real lead-up to the election, Blair negotiated with Brown to get him reengaged, particularly as the campaign had to be launched on the economy, still the most compelling reason to keep Labour in power. They worked out yet another arrangement that brought Brown back to lead the campaign and allowed Blair and Brown to campaign together for the week, wholly on the economy. The effort reversed the earlier slide in the polls. The Brown people, which now included Bob Shrum, occupied space on the other side of the headquarters away from the war room, and they welcomed me as a refugee. I did the early morning meetings, edited the daily tracking memos written by the team in Washington, and then got out of the headquarters as soon as I could. I worked out in the afternoon and, at night, attended groups and wrote e-mails directly to Blair, becoming a kind of toothache about what should be done differently. In the last week, I saw Blair at the early morning meeting where he always greeted me with a smile and handshake and was solicitous of my views, but it didn't change anything. We never met to discuss my "firing," an emerging pattern I didn't take time to think about. With days left, we combined all the polls from the last two weeks of tracking to get a big enough database to look at the bloc of marginal seats. Labour had only a one-point lead, portending a difficult election night in those seats.[61]

Election night in the war room was very tense when Philip announced the first leaked exit polls, a majority of under one hundred. At 10:01, the BBC showed Labour winning, but only by 3 points, projecting a Labour majority of just sixty-six seats. The room fell into stunned silence, broken by Philip's loud protestation that this was too low and would not stand. The unstated goal of the campaign was a hundred-seat majority, but now the worry was that it could fall to fifty, a margin that would allow twenty-five defecting members to stall the government's reforms. While each channel was using different graphics to illustrate the scale of the shift, the room broke up into small groups, sharing rumors about the count in different areas. As the vote count went on past 2 A.M. there were rumors of a "hung Parliament." Labour would be the largest party but would not have an overall majority, a possibility Greg Cook quietly confirmed. Exhausted, we sat in our places, as if in a plane encountering sudden turbulence, wearing seat belts, powerless and afraid to say anything, not knowing how bad it will get and how long it will last. That is how Sam Weston, my field lieutenant in the war room, described it. I was more than a little angry that Labour's ascendancy had been put in jeopardy, but I joined the hush, rooting silently for a real majority. At 4:30 A.M. the BBC declared that Labour had won a majority and when it climbed over thirty seats at 5:15 the Tories conceded defeat. The media was reporting that Labour had won but "with a drastically reduced majority."[62]

At about 5 A.M. we all abandoned the war room and headquarters and walked past Westminster and up Whitehall to Trafalgar Square and the National Portrait Gallery to hear Blair, victorious in his Sedgefield constituency, declare, "the British people wanted to return a Labour government but with a reduced majority"—because of Iraq, unstated but understood by all. Blair promised to respond "sensibly" and "wisely," an acknowledgment of learning after the fact.[63]

I watched the speech with the war room staff and activists looking down from an escalator stopped for the night, and afterward I walked out onto Trafalgar Square with Sam and nodded to Alastair. The streets were empty at 7 A.M. except for the few tired warriors and the pigeons. I took a black taxi back to the flat and packed up without sleeping, caught an 11 A.M. flight to JFK and finally home to Connecticut. I was quietly angry that Labour's unassailable majority had been lost but felt content that we had tried our best for Blair and Labour. But I also knew this chapter was done.

Labour's vote in the end dropped 6 points to just 36 percent in Britain (not including Northern Ireland) and the disengaged electorate mostly stayed as disengaged as it was four years earlier when turnout crashed. The Liberal Democrats raised their vote by almost 4 points to 23 percent and gained eleven additional seats; the Conservatives picked up an impressive thirty-three seats but raised their percentage of the vote by only a half a point, still stuck at 33 percent. The swing against Labour was greatest among younger voters, with all the gains on the left to the Liberal Democrats; a massive defection in safe Labour seats, rising with ethnic diversity; and a big swing against Labour with blue-collar voters, Britain's "hard-working families," with the gains going equally to the Conservatives and Liberal Democrats. With anti-immigrant and anti-Europe sentiment strong, the Conservatives came back in the Southeast and came close to winning a lot more; they made their biggest vote gain and nearly as big a gain in seats in the Outer London upscale suburbs where "New Labour" was at risk.[64]

The election left Labour with a reduced majority of sixty-six seats and more importantly a historically low vote and the country with a historically low turnout, symbolizing Labour's diminished position in society.[65] It had to hold its ground in the face of strong winds of discontent, but to the end four in ten voters identified with Labour—and just a 2-point improvement would have enabled Labour to hold eighteen more seats and achieve a hundred-seat majority. What kind of campaign you run matters and this one made some wrong choices for the times and the leader.[66]

LEARNING FROM THE REAL WAR ROOM

Two weeks after the election, I wrote three memos to Blair and Brown to explain the voting patterns and dynamics in the election and their implication for future strategy. I knew, of course, that I would not be part of that strategy unless Brown succeeded to Number 10. I wrote the memos partly for closure, but more to put on paper in an inescapable way my outrage at the polling and the banal strategy that followed from it that put Blair and Labour at risk. Jeremy and the whole Labour team joined in the cathartic analysis that we felt morally compelled to write.

I thought carefully about my characterization but decided not to qualify it: "The research program was unprofessional and lacking in methodological rigor, though it asserted a scientific certainty; it was erratic but rigid at the same time; it was biased, self-deluding and overly optimistic; it lacked both transparency and accountability." Even as I was writing I was thinking, as I had during the campaign, how can such quality people have any patience with this kind of work?

Penn's errant polling methods had produced landslide predictions all along, giving way in the last week to a roller coaster: first Labour crashed, then it surged back. One could only divine the cause because Penn's firm "provided none of the information normally delivered by a professional research organization," I wrote. The lack of transparency allowed findings to be "packaged in scientific surety that should never have been reported with anything but the greatest qualifications."

The biggest problem was that the campaign fixated on winning over some Americanized target group. Without any evidence, Penn touted that "soccer moms" were the key swing group in the 2004 U.S. elections. In Britain that group became "married mums." The problem was that three quarters of the "lapsed Labour voters" in the marginal seats did not have kids at home. Penn set the campaign on a course that missed most of its key targets and would not adapt. So, "during the campaign, we successfully raised Labour's support with women with children at home" but "that came at a price" among older voters and pensioners and men under forty-five who were not stirred by yet one more initiative on breast cancer screening and childhood obesity. "It was as if creating an American-style gender gap was something to emulate, when Democrats in the U.S. have had so much difficulty winning nationally." I concluded that this mindless, fixed theory had "consequences": "a reduced Labour vote share and a reduced parliamentary majority."

"It had a theory of the race and only sought information that allowed it to elaborate its plan or deepen support with its pre-defined target audiences," I wrote. Accordingly, "it only conducted focus groups with mums and dads, and when groups were finally held with older voters, they were so hostile the campaign decided not to do them again." And to keep the campaign on its predetermined course, "the national surveys were riddled with questions whose biased wording seemed to get the reports to a preferred conclusion." In short, the tests were rigged.

The rigidity meant that Labour lost its ability to do what I do: listen to people and learn. The research program was totally at odds with "war room thinking." "The successful and winning campaigns we've experienced are focused, disciplined, sensitive to all kinds of information, and anxious to jump on any sign of a strategy going awry or not proving effective enough," I wrote. In a campaign, bad news "concentrates the mind."

"The result was a surprisingly rigid and conservative campaign, unwilling to risk expanding on the economic narrative or taking the gamble of really offering people a hopeful vision for the future."[67]

WINNING AND LOSING THE VOTER

Blair set out to make Labour electable and he certainly did that on a historic scale. After the hospital crisis of 2000 when hopes crashed against the reality of limited investment, he lost the public trust, which was pushed even further away by the Iraq War. What support he had was grudging. Nonetheless, some 40 percent of voters continued to identify with Labour at the end and Blair changed the terms of debate, with the Tories accepting the expanded public investment while putting their tax cuts and small government on hold. The current Conservative leader, David Cameron, declared he was "heir to the Blair legacy."[68]

Key to Labour's electability was the "relentless reassurance" that Blair and Brown advanced instinctively that I underscored in my first meeting, but the pledge to limit spending and new taxes constrained what Labour could actually do with its mandate. As a result some of the most respected columnist-critics, from the late Hugo Young to Peter Riddell, grew disillusioned as Blair failed to be brave, radical, and bold before so many challenges they prioritized.

Riddell never accepted "New Labour's" first task, "relentless reassurance," believing Labour created its own straitjacket.[69] But he did not live through the searing 1992 Labour defeat when tax worries wiped out years of change, nor did he have access to our research leading up to 1997 that showed tax worries still close to the surface.

While Blair is not content with merely a social democratic legacy, Labour nonetheless produced ten years of uninterrupted economic growth, indifferent to the downturns elsewhere, full employment with targeted initiatives that eliminated both youth and long-term unemployment. Unlike the United States, where incomes stagnated since 1999, Britain's economy saw real income increases of around 2 percent every year for nearly all, aided by the new minimum wage. With focused tax credits and programs, they cut poverty rates for children by almost 20 percent and even more for pensioners, falling every year since 1999. They reversed two decades of accelerating inequality, actually reducing inequality in the last few years, like few other countries in that period.[70]

Despite the slow start, health care spending increased by 7.4 percent a year above inflation in the second term, more than double the rate for the whole history of the NHS. NHS spending doubled. Reducing waiting lists was Labour's most important pledge, which worsened in Labour's first two years. That is all history. The number waiting six months for an operation dropped from over 350,000 in 1997 to almost zero a decade later.[71] In the eighteen years before Labour was elected, education spending rose only 1.4 percent a year, producing one of the most unequal education systems in the developed world. Labour tripled the rate of increase, doubling spending overall for the decade. It established a goal of 50 percent getting advanced education and a radically new funding scheme to make it possible.[72]

For sure, there are big outstanding issues: the persistence of wealth inequality and a not very mobile society has become less mobile; school achievement is still very unequal, immigration continues without a social contract that would allow broad acceptance, and all sectors of society know Britain needs to move to bold new levels of action on global warming.[73] How government-financed health care and education become more flexible and responsive to the times remain challenges. No doubt those will figure centrally in the political project for Blair's Labour successors, especially Gordon Brown.

But Blair lost the voters that he sought to bring with him on his journey that will forever characterize his leadership. He lost them first because of the sense of betrayal and lost trust, stripping him of his power to convince voters and other leaders to follow. He never recovered the public's trust after Labour's first three years brought almost no new investment in public services, the most important promise of the election, and after he cajoled the country to join Bush at war and then no weapons of mass destruction were found.

Blair lost the voters as voters: one in five withdrew completely. He smashed the old class-based politics rooted in the industrial order but failed to substitute a new political choice or mission that affected people's lives. As a result many working-class voters simply disengaged. For me, that was one of the biggest disappointments in all this work. No amount of tactics or targeting could bring them back without a political project.

Blair was, for many years, relentlessly unsettled about that project, as he tried to navigate the intersection of his faith and politics—something I was barely conscious of at the time and something his secular team was reluctant to acknowledge. Only recently I asked him about his very private meetings with the religious study group before his first election, and he told me it was to keep him honest: "The important thing the whole time to me was to make sure that the preoccupation with winning an election after four election defeats wasn't misaligned with what I was trying to do." That struggle with misalignment ended with 9/11, when his deep sense of right and wrong fully infused his role as national and global leader. For a time, that gave him peace of mind about his political project, rooted now in the "power of community." But Blair told me he had to make a fundamental moral and strategic choice: the engagement against these new evil forces would only happen if Britain fully aligned with the United States under George Bush, who scorned his view of community, whether within or between nations. In effect, it required a pact with the devil. Bush's willingness to go to the United Nations and to advance an Israeli-Palestinian peace were the measure of Blair's ability to move Bush closer to his principles. Blair worked mightily to convince Britons he was right, but the risk to his majority was a measure of his alignment of politics with his values.[74]

Blair contemplated well before the crash after Iraq not running for reelection and taking his work outside of the electoral context. When Iraq looked broken, along with the public trust, he was depressed and prepared to pass the torch to Brown. My work in this critical period showed him a road back, but he didn't take it. It required acknowledgment of mistakes and independence from Bush, both of which I now understand conflicted with his surety about his course. Better to hope for catching some fairy dust from Clinton land. The turn to the chimera of "married mums" was mere tactics to win reelection so he would be able to carry on his unfinished work on reform and terrorism, with Labour's purpose even more undefined and the voters even more unsettled about the meaning of Tony Blair.

For all that, I still admire him.

6

EHUD BARAK

MY FIRST ENCOUNTER with the Barak world came round-about. Ehud Barak, Israel's most decorated soldier, had just been elected leader of the Labor Party and someone from his campaign called my office to ask if I would come to meet with them. I was in the Philippines at the time and the caller told my office, No, it couldn't wait until I returned to the United States. Okay. On Wednesday, July 30, 1997, I flew overnight on Philippines Airways, sixteen hours from Manila to Frankfurt. Blessedly, it was first class, so I slept okay. But then I had to rush to catch a Lufthansa flight to Tel Aviv, arriving at 3 P.M. on Thursday. Just five hours later, I was on a long flight to Brussels. Sabena lost my luggage. I then hopped an early commuter flight to the City of London Airport to make a meeting. At 6:30 that night I caught up with my luggage at Heathrow and flew eight hours from London to JFK, landing at 9 P.M. Friday. Fortunately I was awake enough to spot the driver holding the "Greenburg" sign, my ticket for a two-hour drive and a midnight homecoming in New Haven.

"Should I heat up some pasta?" Rosa asked.

And the meeting jammed into my five-hour state visit to Israel?

I remember nothing. They tell me that we had lunch at the Olympia Restaurant on the water at the Tel Aviv port where they conducted a preliminary interview. Doron Cohen, Barak's brother-in-law and closest advisor, listened and watched closely to determine if Ehud would be impressed. Also there was Boris Krasny, an Israeli political consultant and unpaid advisor to the campaign, who was casting a net to capture the world's famous consultants. Apparently he asked me if I thought my earlier writings on Israel and South

Africa could become an issue in a future Barak campaign, something a potential competitor had kindly shared with him. No wonder I have blocked out this meeting. Not a problem, I said, apparently reassuring them. The lunch must have ended on a friendly note, though it is hard to imagine why it wasn't our last encounter.

My next contact with Barak world took place in Florence. My family and some close friends had taken over a farmhouse in Tuscany for a couple of weeks in August when I got a call on my cell phone. A team of Barak people would like to see me—and no, it could not wait until September. I was beginning to learn what it means to put so many Jews together in such a small place. Everything is urgent. Barak's military background combined urgency and an intense focus on completing missions. He had dispatched a team to Florence: Doron and Boris, along with Moshe Gaon, the young, fast-talking, and implausibily redheaded communications director and campaign strategist. Nobody in my family was happy about this sudden blot across the Tuscan sun, but I persuaded some, including my wife, that it was an opportunity to shop for yet more leather in Florence. To this day, she remembers the raspberry- and beige-colored suede suits, for which she salutes the Israelis.

I arranged the restaurant for an extended dinner meeting, and nothing about the mission dulled anyone's enthusiasm for the pasta and the wine. But this was serious business and Doron was direct. Ehud wanted me involved in his campaign. Boris tried to make the offer sound more tentative so he could retain negotiating room on price later, but to no avail. This was a mission, not a negotiation. Barak was elected head of the Labor Party on June 3. Three weeks later he flew to London with his team to meet Tony Blair, who himself had won an election only two months earlier. In that meeting at Number 10, Blair was enthusiastic about my role with New Labour and urged Barak to meet as well with Philip Gould, Alastair Campbell, and Peter Mandelson.

I allowed myself to believe that Barak wanted Stan Greenberg at the heart of his campaign because of my ideas about modernizing center-left parties, my books about social and political transformation, my role as a famed strategist, or my academic experience in Israel. But that had nothing to do with anything. It was all about winning.

The Barak team, itself fairly inexperienced in electoral politics, had just won a Labor Party primary, depending on the traditional politicians. They experienced an organization whose political intelligence had all the credibility of "Egyptian army reports," as they described it to me—phantom armies, phantom supporters, about 10 percent efficiency in information. In London, they visited the command center at Millbank Tower, Labour's attempt to replicate the war room that the Clinton team had first built in Little Rock in 1992. They knew then that there was a professional way to run a campaign.

They saw a campaign that used information, moved fast, and communicated with message discipline. They were awed. From that point, Barak nagged his team to get the organization charts from the Blair and Clinton campaigns pinned up on the wall, just as the New Labour team had taped up the war room plan from Little Rock.

Barak understood that he was facing a tough campaign against Benjamin Netanyahu, a charismatic and ruthless leader, masterful on TV, who was advised by the American media consultant Arthur Finkelstein. The Israeli press swooned over Finkelstein, conjuring up a force with near magical powers—"a rare mixture of genius and magician, the guru with no compare," a man with unseen power and influence, "a modern day Rasputin." They said he held court at the King David Hotel where ministers came to see him to win his support for policies.[1] And I thought, Hmmm, so what is so bad about that?

Finkelstein worked for Netanyahu in his first campaign and was there when Netanyahu, leader of Likud, shocked the left and defeated the Labor Party prime minister Shimon Peres.[2]

Many months later, Barak asked Philip Gould and me to organize a weekend workshop in London so his campaign people could hear from people who played key roles in the Clinton and Blair campaigns. We met on the top floor of the Express Building, with vistas of the Thames and St. Paul's Cathedral. James Carville sent a how-to video and Bob Shrum a video of Finkelstein's best attack ads. They also watched the movie *The War Room*, about the Clinton campaign, and traveled to Millbank for a tour of Labour's war room, where they observed the open floor plan with desks jammed together in the middle forming the central command, the media monitoring, opposition, and policy research areas.

After everybody flew back home from the workshops, Doron and I dined together. It was the night before the elections in Germany that brought Gerhard Schroeder and the Social Democrats back to power. I was to fly there early the next morning and Doron was surprised that I was so calm. I assured him the Social Democrats would win handily, probably taking 41 percent to the Christian Democrats' 35 percent, my estimate based on our last poll there. As it turned out, it was one of those rare times you actually get the result right to the point—indeed, the Social Democrats won 40.9 percent of the vote and the Christian Democrats came in second with 35.2 percent—but Doron picked up the phone and called Ehud. "Ehud, get this guy working. I don't know whether he's a magician or coincidence or professional. He told me the results and it came out exactly the way he told. Treat this guy seriously."[3]

So why was Barak's team in Florence? For Barak, the military man, it was simple: "Clinton won, and then Blair won." That the same people who elected

Clinton helped Blair meant that "they know how to win in a different environment."

That is why we were lunching in Florence and why at the end of the vacation, I was on a plane from Rome to Tel Aviv.

RABIN'S WAY

The flight from abroad always comes in from the west and across the Mediterranean, with only sea below. Soon, after a voice breaks the silence, "We are preparing for our final descent to Ben-Gurion Airport," the shoreline and land rush at you. We flew right over the Dan Hotel, though that morning it was just part of the built-up shore that introduced the vast plain of low white buildings that is Tel Aviv. I have never lost the sense of surprise at all that is there at the edge the desert and the edge of a map I know more from the Bible than history. When the plane touched down, the passengers no longer broke into song, singing "Ha Tikva," as they did in my memories decades ago.

In Florence, Doron had asked whether I would do this race.

Would I do this race? Are you serious? I would pay you to do this race. This is probably the most over-explained "yes" in my life, from Tony Blair and Bill Clinton to Sam and Yetta Greenberg, my parents and presidents of the synagogue and sisterhood, respectively, to Rabbi Halperin, who never understood why such a promising student would choose baseball over post–bar mitzvah classes.

I first met Ehud Barak in Doron's law offices, a sterile, businesslike setting where all of us, except Barak, were gathered in a conference room talking through different ways to run the race. Barak came in late in the day, making an unheroic entrance. I just couldn't associate the Barak I was looking at with the Barak I had been reading about. It was simple for Carville when he first met Barak. He could not take his eyes off his hands. How many guys had he killed, strangled, come up from behind and cut their throat?

He was thinking of the Barak who led a commando unit into the heart of Beirut, landing his rubber raft on the beach and, disguised as a woman, brunette wig and all, stormed an apartment building and killed three members of Black September who were thought to be responsible for the 1972 Munich massacre of the Israeli Olympic team. Barak took part in the Entebbe raid that sent two Israeli Boeing-707 jet aircraft, commandos, and a few transport planes streaking across the African night, rescuing 105 hostages in Uganda and landing them safely in Kenya, where Barak waited.

My starting point was different. All my life, I had sorted the world into tall and short people. That Barak is short—five foot six, just an inch taller than me—was very disconcerting. He was stocky and well built, with almost no neck, not like me. More like a fire hydrant. He was wearing a sport jacket, very starched white shirt, and tie, his new uniform after leaving the Israeli Defense Forces, the IDF, three years earlier. Nonetheless, I was sitting next to the most decorated soldier in the history of the state of Israel—in U.S. terms, a soldier who achieved the unimaginable, five Congressional Medals of Honor.

And he was listening. One close observer of Barak noted that he takes one of two tacks in such situations: if he thinks you are worth educating, "he talks intently," but if he decides you can educate him, "he listens intently."[4]

Everyone describes Barak as incredibly smart, indeed brilliant, analytical, though that quickly gives way to characterizations as arrogant and dictatorial. He graduated in mathematics from Hebrew University and engineering from Stanford, focusing on systems analysis. Since he is usually the smartest guy in the room, he does more educating than listening. Once he has worked out a solution, he is usually confident of what is the right path, even in new territory where he might be better served learning from others. But none of that was apparent to me now as he listened without any interjections. The others in the room were also observing intently, to see how long he would defer and whether I was a candidate to be Barak's "guru," somebody he would listen to.[5]

In Israel in my experience, nobody defers to anybody. They all think they are the smartest person in the room. It is a country full of Jews. I did not know yet from my own experience that Barak was uniquely the smartest and uniquely Jewish.

Barak is also a concert-quality classical pianist, lest you think he is only smart and kills people in the night, though the piano is more his private passion to relieve the tension. I have only heard him play for a few seconds, but the effect was overwhelming as the music filled the room and Barak, eyes closed, seemed in a trance. He spends many hours at the piano right by the entrance at his home in Kochav Yair, a small community of ranch houses north of Tel Aviv, abutting the West Bank, and housing many of Israel's most prominent IDF generals. He likely did the same in the prime minister's residence, with its Steinway in the living room. He is a perfectionist and very self-critical. He hated when the prime minister surprised him and insisted that he play at his own retirement dinner at the prime minister's residence. Shrum was successful in getting him to play before cameras for a potential TV ad, but Barak immediately noted the missed notes and refused to let the imperfect performance air.

His hobby is clocks, which he disassembles and reassembles. He has a famous memory for detail, which was invaluable in his previous profession. In my presentations, he would get a mischievous smile when I presented the thermometer score for each political figure, perhaps as many as ten different people asked in a given poll. The average score could range from zero, meaning very cool, to 100, very warm, with 50 the midpoint. In his first survey, Barak's thermometer was 56.5 degrees. Even after a period of many years, Barak remembers everyone's thermometer for every period, with all the ups and downs. He always noted where his score fell short of his own personal standard. It was a measure of performance in the political world where he was still feeling his way. He was surprised that Netanyahu retained support at 53.4 and that Ariel Sharon was even higher at 57.8 degrees.

He did not have a lot of regard for politicians, and politicians did not have a lot of regard for him. These feelings were no doubt nurtured in Barak's long period as an army officer and, eventually, army chief of staff, where his relations with Israel's top elected leaders, except Rabin, were cool at best. Even when he became prime minister, he eschewed the identity of a politician, telling one reporter, "I don't feel like a politician, even now! When someone approaches me and uses the word—in Hebrew, it's *politikai*—I have to pass a tenth of a second to realize that I am one of them!"[6]

Barak had surveyed the strange political terrain that is Israel and was trying to put together an "operation" that would succeed in achieving its goal. Indeed, his closest people, many of whom had served with him in the elite military unit Sayeret Matkal, freely moved between the words "campaign" and "operation." "The unit" was known for its daring, dangerous, intensely planned secret missions behind enemy lines. Its members, not surprisingly, were intensely loyal to each other and isolated from others. Barak joined the unit as a young soldier, changing his name from Brog to Barak, which means "lightning." By all accounts, he was remarkably brave, self-confident, and cool under pressure and came to lead it.

In time, I came to understand how Barak approaches politics, though had I understood it earlier, I might have advised him better, perhaps avoiding tragedy. He was only interested in battles for big goals, for himself and Israel. Army chief of staff. Prime minister. A comprehensive peace with all of Israel's enemies. He would show uncommon resolve in pursuit of such goals. He simply wasn't interested in lesser missions with limited goals. On the important mission, however, he devoted his entire capacity for analytical thinking, systems analysis and modeling, attention to vast detail, and developing a plan of action. He focused on the current mission, pushing away any distractions. Doron described him simply as a "one-mission guy."

Barak believed that only with careful planning and minimizing risk at each step can one contemplate the daring. He once told me a story about his time training with a French commando unit—a story he has shared with more than one reporter—when he had to scale cliffs in the French Alps. He was impressed with the "very careful planning and very careful behavior," emphasizing each aspect. They understand "when you are walking very close to the cliff, you have to behave in a very risk-averse way." And then, as if laying out one of his own missions, he said you need preparation, self-discipline, and the skill to operate under the toughest conditions. He concluded that you can be daring, "walk very close to the cliff—if you make sure that every step is stable."[7]

Our first meeting was part of the intelligence process for his mission.

I do not remember asking him, as I do almost all other candidates: What is the mission? Why should voters choose you to lead the country? This is the question that trips up first-time candidates, but also experienced ones, like Ted Kennedy in 1980. It simply didn't occur to me that Barak would be confused about his mission.

His mission was much more Zionist and patriotic than socialist and political. His parents were active in Zionist youth movements in Poland and Lithuania in the 1930s and came to Israel infused with socialist ideals to help build up a modest kibbutz, where Ehud was born in 1942 and reared. He shared in the collective experience, sleeping and eating with the other children. Life was austere. They were trying to survive, and so was the new Jewish state. "Our ideology was in our deeds," a fellow kibbutznik observed. "Ehud was brought up to contribute, in the kibbutz and in the IDF."[8]

When Israel faced a surprise attack in the 1973 war, Barak flew back from Stanford to take charge of a tank unit. A close childhood friend from the kibbutz describes crossing the Suez under heavy Egyptian artillery fire, when suddenly a tank came up on the left, with Ehud riding on top of it. They stopped and embraced atop Ehud's tank, and Ehud said, "Since Bar Kokhba," leader of the Jewish revolt against the Romans, "the nation of Israel has never been in such a dangerous risk of its survival." It was, his friend said, "things you only hear from Hollywood."[9]

He seamlessly interlaced his observations about contemporary events with comparisons to past trials of the Jewish people and supported his conclusions with references to Talmudic scholars.[10] With one set of grandparents murdered at Treblinka, he came to politics from a close reading of Jewish history and intense Jewish nationalism.

The most important mission, Barak believed, was getting Israel back to "Rabin's way." Leader of Israel's triumphant military in the 1967 Six Day War, Rabin was the only previous army chief of staff to become prime minister. Rabin personally monitored Barak's operations behind enemy lines, fearful the young lieutenant would get into difficulties and cause Israel problems. Rabin, much more cautious and pessimistic than Barak, valued his boldness and attention to detail. When Rabin became prime minister, he first passed over Barak but then promoted him to be chief of staff and, more importantly, coaxed him out of retirement from the military to enter politics and become a minister in Rabin's government. Just months later, Rabin was assassinated.

Rabin was a military man who believed the Arabs would only make peace when they concluded Israel could not be defeated. He was a reluctant dove who only reluctantly shook Yasser Arafat's hand when signing the Oslo Accords on the White House lawn.[11] That is why a majority trusted him to make this peace—the first to recognize the Palestinians as a people, concede land, and create a process to settle the "final status" issues, including Jerusalem.

Barak opposed the Oslo Accords, much to Rabin's dismay. Fearing it conceded too much early in the process and undermined Israel's leverage for the final talks, Barak alone in the cabinet abstained. For Barak, that conflict only underscored what they shared. Rabin "was the most hawkish and centrist in his own party," Barak observed. "Quite similar to my position."[12]

Rabin was shot down by an extremist settler who thought Rabin was "giving everything to the Arabs"—an assassin whose hatred many said had been fanned by Likud—politicians, including Netanyahu, who described the Oslo Accords in apocalyptic terms. Shimon Peres succeeded Rabin as prime minister after the assassination but lost the 1995 election to Netanyahu, sinking the left into despair. With Netanyahu's victory, it seemed like Rabin's murderers had won the day. That, more than anything else, motivated those at the core of the campaign.

Barak challenged Peres for leadership of the Labor Party, promising to carry Rabin's fallen banner in the battle against Likud. When Barak declared his candidacy for party chair, he underscored his life as a soldier, his strength and moderation. He declared that Rabin was "my commander, my mentor, my friend."[13] He declared that only a military man and hawk, a moderate, could defeat Netanyahu. Rabin's widow, Leah, exalted in Barak's elevation to leader of the party: "Starting tomorrow, Mr. Netanyahu will finally have an opposition. We'll have an intelligent, moral opposition leading in one direct way: toward peace."[14]

Enough said for the mission.

ISRAEL'S FIRST QUESTIONS

In our first survey right at the beginning of September, voters preferred Barak to Netanyahu by a wide margin, 48 to 40 percent, but that would vanish under pressure of events and the close scrutiny of the public. In an Israeli campaign, I learned, you are always facing political calamity. The very precariousness of the Netanyahu government created a sense of an imminent election, even though it could be years coming.

That produced an intensity evident in the crush to get started. Within two weeks of meeting in Florence, we were already working through issues that most campaigns do not get to for six months.[15]

We organized focus groups to make sure I really understood the Israeli mood and how people were judging potential leaders. While the group sessions were conducted in Hebrew, I watched people closely, zooming in on a particular man or woman, watching the body language and hands, how seriously they took the discussion. A focus group could not be a more artificial setting, yet the people I was watching treated it as very real. They were earnest, boisterous, talking over each other. Their seriousness about the issues communicated an attitude: "And why hasn't somebody asked me sooner—before the politicians made such a mess of the country?" And what "a big mess": "it's like we're digging a hole in the ground"; "I feel like a time bomb." They could not decide whether the economy was in recession or depression; they just knew the country was "headed for economic ruin." At the same time, "there can be a war between brothers."

Presiding over this stuck and divided country was "Bibi" Netanyahu, somebody "who doesn't break under pressure" and "manages to pull himself out of every trap." But they did not trust him: he's "a snake and has no integrity." He presided over a government at war with itself and therefore unable to move the country in any direction or make things better for people. His leadership style, marked by cabinet clashes and resignations, exacerbated the division in society rather than attended to the nation's needs. With support from the ultra-Orthodox Jews and settlers, Netanyahu had provoked violent conflicts with the Palestinians, dashing the hopes of peace that came with the Oslo Accords.

In Israel, the most fundamental questions of Israelis' existence and character, things Americans settled at the time of our Civil War, remained unresolved. They were not debating prescription drug coverage for seniors or what kind of tax cut would be best. This was about people being blown up in markets, bus stations, and nightclubs; it was about the existence and acceptance of the nation; it was about how Palestinians and Jews end their war; it was about whether this was a theocracy or secular democracy or something in between. Politics was about the country's borders, its frontiers and destiny. It was about biblical lands. It was about who was allowed to be Jewish, who was a citizen, whether the Arab minority is a fifth column or equal citizens. In Israel, you debated who was selling out the country to Israel's enemies—in short, who was the "traitor."

There were times in the South Africa campaign when electoral politics took on this intensity and scope but not every day. Here, as a Jew, I had permission to join the argument, and I confess an exhilaration in this politics without limits, though of course I had the luxury of flying away for more normal climes.

On September 4, five days after my first meeting with Barak and two days into calling for our first poll, three suicide bombers from the Martyrs Brigade of Hamas set off their explosives one after the other in Jerusalem's Rehov Ben-Yehuda, the most popular pedestrian shopping promenade. They struck in sight of each other at 3:10 in the afternoon when the boutiques and cafés were jammed, leaving four dead, eight severely wounded, and 180 rushed off to hospitals. A day later, Israel lost eleven commandos in a botched raid in Lebanon. That was my abrupt, but still protected, introduction to Israel's violent reality. Five weeks earlier, as I headed on vacation, two suicide bombers with attaché cases, also in sight of each other, also affiliated with Hamas, blew up the crowded Mahane Yehuda vegetable market in Jerusalem, killing fifteen Israelis and wounding some 150.[16]

During the first two nights of my survey, "peace" was the number one problem people wanted the government to address, followed closely by "security." But on the last night of the survey, security dominated everything.

The bloody, violent events produced a vicious politics, stripped of normal limits, that deepened the divisions on the most basic things. Rather than rallying around the government, Barak attacked it for the grudging and stalled peace process that had left the country vulnerable. The government countered, calling on Labor politicians to "hang their heads in shame and stay silent" because the Oslo Accords were responsible for the terrorism. Labor came back angrily: "Stop hiding behind Peres's apron strings and Rabin's grave."[17]

No wonder people here longed for normality.

In our first survey, over 60 percent of the country believed "Israel now needs a prime minister who will pursue Rabin's policies and show his kind of leadership" and those voters instinctively believed that was Barak. For many voters—and I think for Barak himself—this meant he would take risks for peace. But at this early point, being in the Rabin tradition also meant that Barak was patriotic and strong, trusted, effective, able to unify the country and make progress for a nation weary of Netanyahu's soap-opera government.

But owning the Rabin tradition would not be enough. Rabin himself never broke through the big left-right, secular-religious, rich-poor blocs to create a majority. For all the public angst about Netanyahu, a majority of Israelis would find it difficult to vote for a Labor prime minister. While the Labor Party had once been hegemonic—creating the Jewish state and forming the government in its first three decades of existence—it lost its fervor for nation building when faced with the new waves of poorer oriental Jews from North Africa and the Middle East. These new generations of Israelis resented the Ashkenazi elites and their own second-class status and turned to other movements and parties. With the election of Likud leader Menachem Begin in 1977, the right emerged ascendant, drawing on the least prosperous and least European blocs of voters. While Rabin became prime minister, he did not win with a majority of Jewish voters. He depended on the support of the Arab parties, who agreed to give him a working majority in the Knesset, Israel's parliament. The new immigrant Russian voters, growing from nothing to 15 percent of the electorate in just a decade after the opening of the Soviet Union, distrusted Labor as too socialistic and too pro-Arab.

That history was reproduced in our first poll, showing why Barak was concerned with Labor's electability. When I posed the question like I first asked for Clinton and Blair—"Do you think the Labor Party under Barak should be thought of as a party changing for the better or should it be thought of as just the same old Labor Party?"—only 40 percent thought we were Israel's version of "New Labor."[18] And while Barak may have held a lead over Netanyahu for prime minister, the same was not true for Labor and the left in a prospective election for the Knesset. That vote would happen at the same time as the election of a prime minister, but even at that low point for Netanyahu, the left was only running even with the right and religious parties.[19]

To upend the current balance and emerge electable, I wrote in our first report, the campaign would have "to create something new that changes the old rules that creates new openings and allows for new kinds of political formations."[20] The starting point for the Barak campaign, therefore, was the reassurance that Barak understood the history that pushed so many of the voters away, the history that no previous Labor leader had been willing to revisit.

The most important reassurance in that first survey was on security— Barak acknowledging that the Labor Party in the past made peace its number one priority but now Labor "will put security first." Absent that reassurance, a majority presumed Barak would be forced to listen to his "left-wing and Arab allies" and be "too willing to compromise" with Israel's enemies. A third of Barak's own weak supporters presumed that Barak would agree to divide Jerusalem.

Almost as important as the reassurances on the security issue was Barak's acknowledgment of Labor's history of arrogance toward the Sephardim and many later immigrants.[21] And Barak could hardly wait for the results of the first poll to start addressing those big historic questions. Within three weeks, he organized the Labor Party's convention in Netivot, a poorer development town in the Negev. It is predominantly Sephardic, with families displaced a long time ago from Morocco and Tunisia. To the surprise and consternation of many Labor politicians, Barak apologized to the Sephardic community for Labor's failure to take up their cause in the same ways it took up the cause of Europe's displaced Jewish survivors after statehood.[22]

Facing these issues seemed like bad manners in the Labor establishment, many of whom questioned the apology, but it was the price of entry, the reassurance that allowed those voters to at least listen to him. Clinton and Blair faced down the opponents in their own parties to make their case, but they were political modernizers and relished the battle for change, which defined them as leaders and their political project for the country. I assumed Barak battled in the same tradition, but he was barely a politician and even less a modernizer. Barak took up the task of change and reassurance with a vengeance, not because he had a lot of interest in changing his own party, but because he had knocked down a major barrier between him and his much bigger goal.

Despite the dream résumé, Ehud Barak was not a great candidate. He came to politics with a well-established reputation as ambitious and arrogant, someone who did not suffer fools, and who was not at all sensitive to people. Indeed, press accounts of Barak used the words "brusque" and "high-handed style."

When I arrived in Israel for my first visit, Barak was in the middle of firing half the staff of the Labor Party in order to erase a looming budget deficit. The employees protested, draping the building in black flags. It was a small event, but ordinary people watched Barak closely. In the focus groups, they started with "just like he fired that thirty; he might fire millions." He "tries to conquer his goal," perhaps "like Stalin." They saw him as a careerist: "He wants a chair, a desk and an office." In this, he seemed "just like Bibi." One person concluded, ruefully, "He'll disappoint me like Bibi."

To take people with you on a big mission as political leader does require, I believe, some kind of bond with people. In our first survey, about two thirds of voters described Barak as "patriotic," "strong," and "trustworthy" and as somebody who "will get things done," but less than half said he "cares about people like me." In a later survey, only 40 percent chose Barak over Netanyahu as "being on your side."[23]

Was this remoteness from people just the other side of "strength"? Ronald Reagan always scored dismally on caring about people, but that was an integral part of his leadership appeal—strong military and unwavering convictions. And this was Israel. But our statistical modeling called regression analysis surprised me: which candidate was on your side was as important as which would make Israel secure and stop terrorism in predicting how people would vote.[24] So, I noted in my first memo: if Barak wants to be a political leader, not just a security man, he needs to combine his leadership strength "with some sense that he wants to govern on behalf of people."[25]

IF I WAS A PALESTINIAN

On March 6, 1998, nearly four months after the first set of strategy meetings, Barak appeared on an obscure cable channel show, *Personal Encounters*, and was asked what he would be doing if he had been born a Palestinian. Not knowing to avoid hypothetical questions at all costs, he replied: "If I was the right age, at some stage I would have entered one of the terror organizations and have fought from there, and later certainly have tried to influence from within the political system." Later in the interview, Barak was unequivocal in his condemnation of terrorism, but none of that mattered when the clip appeared as a flash on Channel 2 news.[26] In a near perfect storm, the government announced on that very day that it had uncovered a terrorist cell, arresting five Hamas members responsible for the two Jerusalem bombings that had killed twenty-one Israelis the previous year. A few days later, one of the terrorists told the court in his defense that Barak himself had said "he would be a soldier in Hamas or Fatah or Hisbullah."[27]

The political pundits were derisive and merciless. Columnists in every national daily described Barak, variously, as "gone," "crashing," "a loser," sure to be "haunted" in any future campaign. One paper described him as "just the latest general to be parachuted into politics without a parachute."[28] Likud politicians went further: nobody with such views could "represent a Zionist party in the state of Israel." When Barak spoke in the Knesset without apology, one Likud member shouted, "You're the copywriter for terrorist organizations."[29]

Ehud was combative. On the first day of the storm, he asked reporters, "What did you expect me to say in response to this question? That if I were a young Palestinian, I would become a third-grade teacher?"[30] Indeed, both inside and outside the campaign, privately and publicly, he insisted that it was not a big deal and that the storm would pass. He was partially right but only because Israeli voters take their responsibility more seriously than the pundits and politicians.

Moshe was on the phone wanting to know how quickly we could organize focus groups. "Houston, we have a problem." Or more accurately: "We're fucked," as Moshe put it. The campaign fully understood the nerve Ehud had touched and that political death was near at hand. Barak, however, was unmoved. Maybe, we thought, results from focus groups might sway him. That set in motion frenzied efforts to recruit focus groups, which we held before the end of the month in Rishon Le Zion, Ramat Gan, and Ramat Hasharon.[31] This is a hotspot for the Sephardim and the more traditionally religious, who we expected had learned more than they wanted to know about Ehud Barak in the last few weeks.

Here is my frame of reference: how do you think American voters would react if a candidate for president, caught off guard, responded, "If I were born a Muslim in Saudi Arabia, I would likely have joined al-Qaeda before going into politics." I doubt we would have conducted focus groups before writing his obituary.

Barak's comments about growing up a terrorist led voters to a fundamental reassessment about Ehud Barak as a leader, but in a focused and measured way that left Barak breathing, though barely. The voters did not simply mimic the pundits and politicians. Unlike the Likud politicians, they still thought Barak was a patriot who hated terrorism. They thought Barak was surprised by the question or that it was a terrible slip of the tongue. Many described Barak as honest, speaking a truth about Palestinian aspirations that even Israelis sometimes acknowledged. I searched the transcripts for comments contesting the actual observation, with its underlying equivalence of claims and methods, without success.

But politicians in Israel cannot make such slips or be so honest. People may die as a result. As one woman noted, "you can be honest in other fields but not on something like this." A group of Sephardic women acknowledged Barak's empathy and honesty, with one woman observing, "I think that deep inside I am not angry at him because had I been a Palestinian, I would have fought for my land," though she quickly added, "but since he is the one who wishes to be a prime minister, he has to be more careful. I think that it is going to haunt him." The other side is always listening. "What scares me is the message that the Palestinian side is getting," one of the men observed. A leader who can say such a thing exposes the people to danger and fails in his first obligation as a leader.

Two weeks later, I delivered the news to Ehud personally and in a memo, my first test of the bounds of frankness for Israel and Barak.[32] I was not even close to the edge, as it turned out. The good news: voters were not finished with his service to Israel and did not think he is soft on terrorism. The bad news: inexperience had produced the impermissible and that inexperience had consequences: two thirds believed Barak was "too inexperienced and new to be Prime Minister." We trailed Netanyahu by 7 points, almost a 20-point swing in the race.

But the political collapse paled before the strategic collapse. Barak's comments had undermined the foundations of his candidacy. The themes we were building, the reassurances on security, the attacks on Netanyahu, and the choices we wanted to pose, all lost their force. Voters were not listening to Barak, even though they were still desperate for change. Against all odds, we had made Netanyahu look good, or at least competent at getting out of traps. That Netanyahu was a "magician" had become a positive conclusion about his leadership.

Barak entered the wilderness. Nine months would pass before voters re-opened their minds to his qualities and mission. But even amidst the rubble, voters wanted us to understand the basis for their new judgments. At the end of each of those rushed focus groups, I asked people to write a postcard to Ehud Barak. They responded respectfully and personally. I marveled at the underlying generosity given what had happened.

To Barak,

I think you are a serious man with a great military record. You did a lot for the state of Israel and still have a lot to give. But you have to try and control the things that you are saying. I was hurt by what you said about what you would do had you been a Palestinian. It undermined the trust in you, but you still have time to prove otherwise.

––––––––––––

To Barak,

I would like to express the feelings of a simple citizen. I have a lot of respect for you as an army man with a lot of experience. I am sorry but I feel that politics is not the right place for you. You are arrogant and have miserable slips of the tongue.

I focused on the last cards in which the writers urged Barak to use time to gain more experience and wisdom, "no disrespect for what you have done." And concluded, "You are you, but I hope that you will turn into a leader, like Rabin in 10 years from now."

THE POLITICAL WILDERNESS AND UNITY PROJECT

Now we had to think in wholly new ways. The previous fall, when Barak had been the perfect profile and running 10 points ahead of the reviled incumbent prime minister, we had thought we only had to knock down the barriers to Labor and voters would rush to our candidate and agenda. Barak would draw red lines he wouldn't cross, but now less than a third of voters believed he wouldn't compromise his red lines.[33] We had to think about new dividing lines and big questions. Maybe Rabin was not the only way for us. Maybe Israel could have an election in which new issues were primary, not just terrorism, security, and peace.

The public, if not the politicians, had been focused on the rising division over religion.[34] From Israel's founding, there was always a tension between the Zionist and Orthodox religious parties. Many Orthodox parties reject the idea of a Jewish secular state. Nonetheless, Ben-Gurion and generations of Labor leaders kept religious parties in coalition to expand their Knesset majority but also to maintain the Jewish character of their nationalist project. But now, Shas, the party of the haredim—the ultra-Orthodox Jews, mostly from the shtetls of Eastern Europe—was playing a much bigger role. Only with its support did the Netanyahu government survive. In exchange Shas got its way most dramatically on funding for its separate education system. To the public, it seemed little more than organized blackmail. I looked at the issue for the first time in our March survey. Despite the preoccupation with Barak's empathy for terrorists, it was hard not to notice the simmering anger: that "Netanyahu gives in to the demands of the orthodox" at the "expense of everybody else" raised more doubts than virtually all other potential attacks.[35]

As the public watched this spectacle, the High Court of Justice took up the incendiary issue of yeshiva students being exempted from military service. The position of the haredim morphed from paradox to outrage for voters when you got to the question of the IDF, where universal service has made the army the primary agent of acculturation, citizenship, and national unity. Ben-Gurion himself as defense minister had created the exemption for four hundred special students, though at a time when protecting Torah study seemed like a noble act for a people struggling to survive. But now, virtually all the haredim used the yeshiva exemption to get out of military service.[36] People asked, How can it be that the ultra-Orthodox control the government yet won't defend the country?

After conferring with the diverse factions of his party, Barak introduced a bill in May that would restore the limited exemption for outstanding students, in effect, requiring that yeshiva students be drafted. The bill was defeated two months later, but not easily and only after the defection of some Russian members of Netanyahu's coalition and only after Netanyahu went personally to the Knesset to save it.[37] Later in the year, the High Court would rule unanimously that the Defense Ministry could not exempt yeshiva students and gave the Knesset a year to resolve the question.

As I soon discovered, the politicians only touch these religious prerogatives with greatest reluctance because they raise so many underlying and unresolved issues about a Jewish, yet secular and democratic, state. In a virtual compact, the major Zionist parties declined to join the issue.

I proposed that Barak break the compact and, more than that, use the issue as the center point of a much larger argument, critique, and choice. I was fully aware of the sensitivities on the issue but felt it was my role to press the point when the evidence was so strong and also where I felt the elites were losing touch with strong popular currents.

We had been in the wilderness for five months, but finally we were on the verge of developing an integrated message about "unity" that could capture the attention of voters, at least in my polls.[38] It began with a core critique of the Netanyahu government: it is so dominated by the extremist settler and Orthodox parties that it was at an impasse on every problem. Its fractiousness explained its inability to make progress. What the country longed for, I wrote in the fall, was a "government that works for all, not just the extremist groups." They wanted unity, not the special interest politics of the ultra-Orthodox and settlers.[39]

This was a framework that provided a platform for each issue. Because the government was captive of the extremists, it first and foremost could not manage the economy for all: it had produced "more and more Israelis without work," raising serious doubts for three quarters of the voters. Because it was forced to overspend on the settlements and haredim education, the Netanyahu government could not fully fund education for all, raising doubts for two thirds of voters. Because it was captive of the extremists, it could not move forward with its own peace agreements. And most important, it was not a government that could hope to unify the country. The aspiration for unity was an aspiration for a government that would address normal problems and work for the whole country.

Our "unity message" defeated Netanyahu's best message by 10 points and at the end of the survey, after people had heard this simulated campaign around unity, Barak moved miraculously into a tie with Netanyahu for first place.

But this path out of the wilderness was only evident in our surveys and certainly not to the politicians who had picked up the scent of death. With Barak going from "conquering hero to walking wounded," a queue of politicians warned that Barak would have to reverse his poll fortunes by the end of the year or face a challenge.[40] A raft of high-visibility "center" party candidates emerged to compete for the change voters. By the end of the year the emerging field had driven us down to only a quarter of the vote and fourth place in my own polling.[41] I had a theory about how to win, but the rest of the world only saw a failing campaign about to lose its claim to lead the challenge against Netanyahu.

JAMES CARVILLE AND
THE POLITICAL WILDERNESS

At the outset of Barak's time in the wilderness, Doron Cohen asked me if I thought James Carville would consider working for Barak. I was very surprised. James? A Cajun to the core, Catholic, profane, explosive, and outrageous, whose English is barely understandable in America? James has never set foot in Israel or contemplated it, except as a not very humble pilgrim. More to the point, James got paid a lot for what he does, a lot more than me. James had an operating formula for these matters: "the higher the literacy rate in a country, the less you get paid." Well, this is the most literate country in the world. But what they liked most about him was his offensive, take-no-prisoners politics.

I said I would ask. Why not? And then, I was even more surprised. James loved the idea of working for Barak and coming to Israel, though for the moment we only agreed to monthly meetings, usually at a Manhattan hotel.

Boris Krasny had been working for more than a year to get Bob Shrum hired to do media consulting because he had beaten Arthur Finklestein in the United States and because he considered him the best. Barak and Shrum met and talked at a small dinner in 1997 and Moshe Gaon liked his tough advice on Barak's Palestinian terrorist remark. Boris, with my support, simply wore everybody down and Shrum came aboard. Jim Gerstein, an American active in progressive Jewish groups and living in Israel, became our liaison translator and close collaborator in the team.

Israelis take political consultants more seriously than any other country in which I have worked. In most places, consultants are a fascination of the political class and media, but in Israel ordinary voters pay a lot of attention. They think strong leaders have strong campaigns, with world-class advisors; they follow stories about Finkelstein and Greenberg like they follow stories about pop stars and Hollywood icons. Earlier, when I asked voters to write postcards to Barak, they wrote about his political inexperience that could put Israelis gravely at risk, but they also freely offered campaign advice.

Mr. Barak:

Allow me to give you several pieces of advice. You have to work on your charisma and appearance with media consultants.

Mr. Barak:

Based on your failing attempts to express yourself, take someone like Finkelstein who will help you to become prime minister.

When Barak and Netanyahu faced off in the Knesset for the first time in eight months to debate the implementation of the peace agreements, the high point, according to the press, was their exchange of their media advisors' telephone numbers.[42] Barak spoke of Netanyahu's isolation, reading the list of leaders who would not take his calls: Arafat, Clinton, Albright, Mubarak, Israel's president Ezer Weitzman. Then Barak gave out Finkelstein's New York phone number as the only person who would take Netanyahu's call. But Netanyahu retorted with Greenberg's area code, chiding Barak: "I don't know how much this guy Greenberg is familiar with Israel politics, I can tell MK [Member of Knesset]. Barak: If your speech today is a result of his advice, you had better improve fast."

So I should not have been surprised that the campaign decided the three American advisors should have a coming out in Tel Aviv—just before the New Year. If we could not get our poll numbers up, at least we could tell the country, the media, the disgruntled Labor MKs and the auditioning candidates in the wings, "don't mess with Barak."

In near unison, James, Shrum, and I said it was a terrible idea. It made the election about the consultants and process rather than the candidate and issues. Invariably, the consultants would be portrayed as all-powerful and the candidate diminished and manipulated. Doron and Moshe waved aside our objections. First of all, Ehud wasn't the least bit concerned about being overshadowed. His ego was very secure. The purpose of the trip, Doron wrote in an e-mail, was "massive media coverage with the message: we have the best team in the world working with us, here we are, ready to win; and the world experts say Barak is going to win." This would give a "moral boost in our camp"—and, he did not say, to all the people who said Bibi was a magician and has Finkelstein. It would send signals "to Bibi and the public about seriousness, professionalism and preparation," but it also would be a message to other independent candidates: "Don't even think about putting [your] team on the court against this team."[43]

Tal Silberstein was now the campaign manager. He is an explosive, young, gifted organizer who abandoned a conventional career to found a million-person peace and social justice organization after Rabin's assassination. He pressed us for an answer. We said yes and he promptly leaked it to the press.

On December 15, four days before our unveiling, James and I met with Barak and Doron at the New York Palace Hotel to discuss what the campaign was trying to achieve. At the end of the meeting, Doron leaned over toward James and me and said, "A final thing." Pause. "Is there anything in your past that Ehud should know about, something that could prove embarrassing, if it came out under all media pressure next week?"

James and I both were taken aback with the directness of the question, as if there was something they already suspected. James responded first and he mumbled something about an early campaign in Louisiana where he was attacked for something. I was unable to make sense of what James was saying because I was panicking. My whole life flashed before me. What part of this did I want to talk about with a prospective future prime minister of Israel? I quickly pushed aside confessing my deep aversion to going into synagogue. There were some real issues here, things I said and wrote during my academic career that nearly became public controversies when I started working for Bill Clinton. I had repressed the issue in my first meeting with the Barak campaign.

A few years ago, the *Forward*, the Jewish weekly in New York, wrote a story that I was anti-Zionist. They quoted a former student of mine who said that in my course on Israel, I was highly critical of Israel's invasion of Lebanon. The article produced a flurry of protests from Democratic congressmen. And when the story would not go away, I asked the political director of the American Israel Public Affairs Committee—AIPAC—to intercede to arrange an interview with the reporter, which produced a kind of truce. He wrote that Greenberg identified with the Mapam movement, which became a socialist party, but at least the party was always Zionist, not with Matzpen, which was a Trotskyist splinter. He concluded that Clinton was surely the only presidential candidate with a close advisor who had read Ber Borochov, a founding Labor Zionist.[44]

Barak just listened impatiently. He didn't seem amused.

The other issue was more worrisome because it was full of nuanced academic distinctions that get caricatured in the political world. I wrote a book that looked at the way the Histadrut, the general workers' union in Israel, used ethnic distinctions to advance the position of Jewish labor. It was part of a book that dealt with a number of countries, including South Africa.[45] Simply dealing with Israel and South Africa in the same book leaves you subject to the charge that you are equating Zionism and racism. There is no such discussion in the book, but is Greenberg part of that U.N. crowd that is always condemning Israel?

Ehud cut me off, waving his hand dismissively. "I don't care about any of that. I thought you were going to tell me that you lost some big election somewhere."

I was at peace. With that one dismissive gesture, the prospective prime minister of Israel absolved me of my sins.

It was so politically steamy in Israel you could feel the tension in the air. Netanyahu had just frozen any further implementation of agreements with the Palestinians. By coincidence, President Clinton was in Israel, but the main event was his speech to the Palestinian National Council, with a backdrop of Israeli and Palestinian flags, reflecting his frozen relations with Netanyahu. The prestigious finance minister resigned while we were there and talk of elections grew more insistent and, indeed in one week, the government no longer fought a bill to dissolve the Knesset.

Our team was trailed by a mob of reporters and, together with Barak, we did a long interview on the top-rated television news show, as well as interviews with key journalists; a reception with academics, business leaders, and political junkies; and a large workshop with communications and PR professionals. We had a private, icy dinner with Shimon Peres, who advised Barak to run on a campaign of "open borders" with the Arab states. When we left, James looked at me. "He wants us to lose." We met in Jerusalem with a closed caucus of Labor MKs and got their attention, after which James got a tour of the Old City and the Western Wall. Wherever he went James got superstar treatment, as the press marveled at this tall thin figure, head shaved, distinctive brow: "Svengali," the presumed leader of "Barak's spin doctors." His polo shirt was a step up from his usual T-shirt. James sounded like someone still learning and listening but he was on message: the country seemed to want to change and was frustrated with the failed government.[46]

The unveiling of the American consultants was a media success. The journalists wrote about a new kind of Labor Party, the one Barak wanted to present: "lean, focused, aggressive, professional and speaking in one voice." And "by showing off his fancy new team of consultants, Barak . . . signaled a clear message to his party colleagues—a message of 'I know what I'm doing and you will do what I tell you because otherwise you will just get in the way of my victory.'"[47]

For others in the media, it was just more material for the ironic treatment in popular culture of leaders who seemed more political than national and who seemed ever more entangled in Israel's tight embrace with America. One episode of the popular TV show *Hartzufim*, which regularly portrayed politicians as life-size puppets, presented Netanyahu and Barak in a debate, wearing earphones to listen to their American consultants. The debate began with Israeli topics but slid into American ones, like Bill Clinton's impeachment.[48]

CALLING NEW ELECTIONS

Faced with near certain defeat in a no-confidence vote at year's end, Netanyahu brushed aside all these distractions and focused only on Arafat and the Palestinians and Barak's approach, which is "to give, to give, and to give, to give without any second thought."[49] That is why Arafat "wants a change of government" that will allow him to establish a Palestinian state, "which will be a launching pad for terrorist operations."[50] The choice: Netanyahu's way or Arafat's.

Barak did not accept the choice, decrying Netanyahu's speech as more an "incitement" to violence than a real choice for the country. Barak pushed back as he rose to his feet: "Knesset Speaker, assembled MKs: No one can lecture me about Israel's security." He promised to restore trust, beginning with separation from the Palestinians and "clear red lines on security," starting with "a united Jerusalem under our sovereignty that will remain Israel's capital forever—period."[51] But Barak's passion was reserved for the Israeli people, who watched the spectacle with despair, yearning for a new direction and leadership. He noted the silences in Netanyahu's long farewell: no mention of "the collapse of the education system," the "250,000 Israelis who are unemployed," or the "300,000 children living below the poverty line." The people tire of a government that survives by "systematic surrender to the extremists," of a government "both incapable and unwilling to work for the good of the entire Israeli people." Barak committed to work for "a united Israel that serves all the people." That was a competing choice for the country.

With the new year, the deadlocked campaign became ugly. The Netanyahu campaign began with the unnuanced charge that Barak was guilty of dereliction of duty and was a traitor. Likud launched a poster campaign that pictured Barak with the words "runs away," alluding to false allegations that Barak had abandoned his dying soldiers killed in a training exercise gone badly wrong. Another poster proclaimed, "Barak runs away from responsibility," alluding to his remark about being a Palestinian terrorist.[52]

The ugliness and intensity was brought home to me when burglars entered my office brownstone in D.C. through a rooftop vent, circumvented the alarm, and spent some part of the night looking at files, targeting offices with materials from international campaigns, and left with the backup computer tapes from a locked safe in the basement. Our office manager arrived early, walked into the mess, and called the police, whose detectives quickly concluded it was the work of "professionals," perhaps with international connections. They called the FBI. In Israel, the leading daily immediately ran big banner headline, "Israeli Watergate," and an ugly campaign got uglier, with finger-pointing by Labor and Likud spokesmen. The media in both countries were taken aback by this turn, a little in awe of how "bitter and volatile" the campaign's early stage had become and how the break-in threatened "to inject new venom."[53]

Over the month, there were break-ins at the homes of three of Barak's top campaign people, including Tal Silberstein.

This all became much more ominous a week later when our offices were attacked a second time. This time, the burglars scaled the roof and broke through a second-story window, disabling a new and significantly upgraded alarm system that was designed to deal precisely with movement and secure that space. The intruders left behind some blood and footprints, but importantly, targeted financial records and Israeli files, which disappeared with the burglars. Our office manager arrived at 6:45 A.M. and made the pained call to the police. They arrived with three mobile crime scene vans and the full FBI fingerprinting and investigative team and began interviewing potential suspects, all current and former employees. In Israel, the blatant double burglary produced, one reporter observed, "a bizarre mirror-image guessing game of motives and intentions."[54] The prime minister told Army Radio, "There is a bad smell here of a deliberate provocation, this is theater of the absurd." In Israel, a consensus developed that this operation involved graduates of the Mossad or the Special Forces, costing a great deal of money.[55]

The immediate consequence was a whole new level of security in our lives, giving the campaign in Washington an Israeli feel. Alarm systems were supplemented by twenty-four-hour security guards in the building. All our files and transmissions related to Israel were encrypted. For three months, I had security guards in our D.C. house, including a detail that took over the basement apartment. A former commando, Barak grilled me on the new security arrangements, though he actually laughed and shared a "we-know-all-about-it" look with Doron when I told him about the guards. "There is no security guard who can't be bribed," he said, no doubt reflecting on past exploits in Beirut and North Africa. When he said it, it seemed so obvious. And for the record, Netanyahu, too, had served in Sayeret Matkal and was schooled in commando operations.

I was spooked by the second break-in. First, I was embarrassed that the intruders had been able to brush aside our new security system. We looked like we were not serious. Even now I am perplexed by the bravado of the second attack. What were they looking for, what was so important that justified the risk?

I never doubted—nor does the FBI—that it was an Israeli operation. I never doubted that it was the work of somebody affiliated with the Netanyahu campaign, mainly because I cannot imagine our own campaign taking such a risk for a few days of publicity. The chief FBI agent on the case found no evidence implicating either of the campaigns. Absent evidence, the agent had an operative formula: which campaign benefits from the publicity? Using this formula, they concluded that I did not break into my own offices: too much negative publicity and damage to my reputation. The jury was out on the campaigns, however. When I heard their operative theory for sorting the case, I commented, "I guess the Democrats were responsible for the Watergate break-in." The agent wasn't into irony.

THE RELUCTANT ECONOMY

Because the mood was so negative, we tried to begin our focus groups on an upbeat note: "Are there some events that make you happy, make you laugh or may be something to be proud of?" our moderator asked. People wanted none of that: how could we be speaking of happiness when they felt so much anger—about the social gaps, and divisions, the broken peace and insecurity. On the economy, they searched for the right descriptive: "shattering," "regressing," "there's no economy," "catastrophic."[56]

But here was the problem: those voting on the economy, not security, were voting for Netanyahu over Barak by over a 20-point margin. Likud was the party that had watched out for the social and economic needs of the workers. I urged the campaign "to take ownership of the economy" and for it to become "an overriding preoccupation of the campaign." Yet in the same January memos, I was perplexed that our response was so mechanical, so rhetorical and muted. The campaign had no economic plan and none in the works. I could not even figure out what was Labor's or Barak's philosophy about the economy.[57]

The Labor leaders just couldn't get themselves to take the economy seriously. Peres ran for reelection in 1996 following a year of 7 percent growth, yet lost, because of terrorist bombs and worries that Peres would give too much to the Palestinians, trumping the economy. The overlearned lesson for Labor politicians was that voters, no matter what they say months before an election in a poll, will ultimately cast their vote on peace and security

Fortunately for us Netanyahu fell captive to what I called the *Treasury Secretary–Ministry of Finance–Chancellor of the Exchequer Syndrome.* In 1998, the economy stopped growing and in the first quarter of 1999, unemployment rose to nearly 9 percent. But the government beat back many strikes and internal battles to cut the budget deficit in half and bring inflation down to single digits, the lowest rate in three decades.[58] Despite the weakening economy, Netanyahu was proud of his government's economic performance. Grabbing on to snippets of good news, he said in various venues, "unemployment is shrinking," "economic growth is gaining," and finally, "we're performing an economic miracle here."[59] I've heard that before.

With the growing gap between the real economy and Netanyahu's rhetoric, Barak moved to an almost double-digit lead on who would "improve the economy." Only the Russian immigrant voters remained confident in Netanyahu on the economy, yet they were still desperate for a leader who would make the economy a priority.

Our growing advantage on the economy finally persuaded Barak to focus on the plan. He pushed the team of economists and business leaders to think about a concrete economic offer, not just a promise of sound management. James and I reminded Ehud of Clinton's promise of eight million jobs, the most remembered commitment in his successful campaign. Barak, never to be outdone on a daring goal, sought to raise our jobs commitment from 250,000 to 400,000.[60] The economic team and researchers accepted 300,000, a commitment that Barak was determined to keep.

THE RELUCTANT CULTURE WAR

Without much help from the political class, people had turned their concern with extremism into a much deeper critique of Israel's ascendant political culture. The government was losing "authority" because the political culture tolerated the appeal of "every group, ethnic, religious or other," people declared in groups. The conclusion: "there are no [public] values anymore." Ordinary Israelis were not thinking beyond the self to community, society, and nation. Worse, the leaders "are actually riding on this trend and are becoming representatives of certain parts of society—behaving more like heads of tribes rather than heads of state." "Political culture" had given way to a "tribal culture."[61]

For the very secular Russian immigrant voters, this political culture was produced by a society that married religion and state power. That produced Russian marriages that were deemed illegitimate by the government, and war dead who could not be buried with the other Jewish soldiers. They believed they were "treated like half-people."

These feelings about Israel's political culture gained new force with each new battle in the culture war. Court decisions that gave new legitimacy to

Reform and Conservative Judaism were met by a hail of invective. Rabbi Ovadia Yosef attacked the High Court of Justice as "wanton and wicked" and as "unclean copulators," and his son described the president of the court as a "Jew-hater" and "anti-Semitic." Ignoring appeals by the country's president to cancel a demonstration, 250,000 black-cloaked haredim marched through Jerusalem, challenging the secular authorities.[62]

The Barak candidacy was brought back from the dead by his willingness to challenge the privileges of the ultra-Orthodox, starting with draft exemptions for yeshiva students. Our first billboards started with "Barak is fighting for Israel," proudly, Israel's blue and white, and in parallel, "Netanyahu gives in to the haredim and extremist settlers." In effect, Barak was for the nation; Netanyahu for the extremists and small groups. That meant sharp differences in priorities, evident in the billboards that followed: "Money for the university, not the yeshivot" and "Support the unemployed, not the Settlements."

I mostly lost the battle to keep that choice center stage. When the theme was unveiled in billboards, the Labor Party politicians fanned out to convince the various groups that Labor didn't really mean it. Some, including his very wise, close advisors like Isaac "Bougie" Herzog, son of Chaim Herzog, sixth president of Israel, described the message as "divisive." How can you be the candidate of unity if you are attacking the Orthodox? Do the Americans really understand Israeli society? One particularly scornful journalist, briefed from inside, warned, "By the time Carville and his friends understand that Barak cannot afford to give up on the vote of a single hesitating yeshiva student or settler disappointed by Netanyahu, the Likud will have managed to steal 'national unity' from under their noses and to nail Barak with the slogan 'divisive.' "[63]

Soon the billboards turned to mush: we oppose all "extremes," which disembodied the extremism that people felt.[64]

I asked that James and I meet with Ehud alone at his home, which we did one Saturday morning. James made it clear that there were not very many successful campaigns that decide to go with a new message and purpose three months before the election. We sat around Barak's small dining room table off the kitchen and laid out the power of the choice. We had been building this choice for almost ten months; it was the issue on which we had the biggest advantage over Netanyahu and the best chance to break open the Russian immigrant community.

Ehud listened, without comment and without arguing back. I argued one more time, as if the Labor politicians were in the room: it is the current special interest political culture that is divisive; only when you have the courage to assail it can you emerge as the candidate of unity.

The shift of resources from the yeshivas and settlements to employment and education was by far the campaign's most popular policy initiative. The strongest choice we tested up to that point was "Netanyahu gives in to the orthodox. Barak will fight for all." Voters wanted a united Israel, an inclusive concept, I wrote in a memo, "that is genuinely seeking to represent and advance the needs of all the people."[65]

Barak just listened, did not say yes or no. He thanked James and me for coming. It was all very pleasant.

When we got into the car, James immediately blurted: "It's done, finished. There's no way he's going forward with this message. Put a nail in it."

I was depressed. We had a powerful message that was beginning to capture the rising sentiment, and only just recently, Barak had moved into a small lead in the race.

We got back to the hotel and locked ourselves in the room for the day, joined by Moshe, Tal, and Rafi Barzilay, a colleague of Tal's from the Dor Shalom—the Peace Generation—days. We called down for food because we were not coming out of the room until we had a new, big concept, an alternative framework for the campaign. To clear the slate, I went back to the transcripts of the very first focus groups of the campaign: "the country is going down," "stumbling in all fields," a "mess, a big mess, a whole mess," "we're stuck." And "stuck" began to emerge as our organizing idea. In fact, we had been tracking an attack on Netanyahu, centered on his "divided and failed government" that was at "an impasse on almost every problem." The consequence that bothered people the most was the unemployed 230,000. We began to chant the words, "stuck, stuck, stuck," which sounds even better in Hebrew, *"takua, takua, takua."* To this day, Cajun James Carville can be prompted to blurt out, staccato style: "ta-KOO-uh, ta-KOO-uh, ta-KOO-uh."

We tested the message in emergency focus groups over the next few nights and, by the last day in February, we had a new draft message box. "Stuck" became the central critique rather than the country being captive of the haredim and extremist settlers, and the campaign and candidate were relieved. Netanyahu being captive to the haredim was still present in the message framework, but now as an explanation for why the Netanyahu government was stuck. There was relief that getting Israel unstuck would be the primary rationale for our campaign, rather than reducing the influence of the haredim.

But Israel was too profoundly divided on the religion question for the issue to go away. In mid-March, Shas's leader, Aryeh Deri, was convicted of bribery, aggravated fraud, and breach of trust, which led to a further round of attacks on the secular judges by the haredim rabbis: "for them the Torah is like a thorn in their eyes"; "when the judge spoke hate bubbled from his throat."[66] With less than a month to the election, our surveys showed that the imbalance in education—three times more spent for haredim education as for all of Israel's universities—was without question the strongest attack and correcting the imbalance was our most popular policy.[67]

We were drawn back to the issue, not just opportunistically, but because successful campaigns are rooted in their times. It had suited the political class in Israel to leave the issue unresolved, but by putting the ultra-Orthodox and the religiously nationalist settlers at the center of his government, Netanyahu made it hard for the political class to suppress voters' focus on this issue. I introduced the issue wherever I could with Moshe's and Tal's backing, knowing that underlying "stuck" was voter anger at the extremist politics polluting the country's culture. Touching on that anger could shatter coalitions and build Barak's vote and our Knesset majority, which was by no means assured.

THE EXISTENTIAL QUESTIONS ABOUT ISRAEL'S ENEMIES

Existential questions have hung over Israel's elections from the beginning: Which leader can best deal with Israel's "enemies"? Is this the right moment to consider peace? Is this the moment to achieve an accommodation with the Arab countries and the Palestinians?

When Netanyahu launched the campaign against Barak with Arafat, he gave his answer. By attacking Netanyahu for the impasse on peace and by saying he would lead in Rabin's way, Barak was saying he would be a hawkish dove in the tradition of Ben-Gurion. The public's conclusion would tell us who they trusted on peace and security, but also whether they felt comfortable enough to take up the "normal" issues.

Voters had little doubt Barak would pursue peace. They were not sure he wouldn't go too far and trust the Arabs too much. At the launch of the campaign in the new year, Netanyahu enjoyed more than a 10-point lead on "making Israel secure" and a 24-point and growing lead on stopping terrorism. With Netanyahu making Arafat the central issue, almost half the electorate said Barak was too willing to listen to the left. When we presented voters at the outset of 1999 with our red lines and security plan, over 60 percent said Barak would compromise anyway. "In short," I wrote, "Barak has a security problem," undiminished by our reassurances.[68]

This was a period of relative calm, as the Palestinian Authority, perhaps with Hamas's reluctant cooperation, was uncharacteristically cracking down on the suicide bombers. But Lebanon would not go away. It gripped the country from late February when six soldiers and elite officers were killed in action, compared to twenty-four losses from the entire previous year. A gloom fell over the country, while the widows maintained vigil outside the prime minister's house.[69]

Barak was deeply anguished over the loss of some of his closest comrades in the military and the sixteen-year operation. He declared that, if elected prime minister, he would remove IDF troops from Lebanon within one year. We never polled this commitment, but Ehud believed he could arrive at a settlement with Syria, making the withdrawal possible. The public was uncertain about such a deadline for withdrawal, but Barak embraced the commitment ever more strongly. It was our first pledge in our list of pledges, underscoring that Barak would take steps for peace.

But the violence in Lebanon and Barak's pledge increased concerns about Barak on security. We were less trusted than Netanyahu on security, trailing him by over 20 points among the Russians. In mid-April, two weeks before the television advertising was to begin, I drafted and tested Netanyahu's best security attack and, sadly, it was potent: "Barak actually said, 'If I was a Palestinian youth, I would have joined a terrorist organization.' No wonder Arafat has said he wants Barak to win. But Israel dare not have a leader ready to compromise with Jerusalem."[70]

So what might people see or learn at this point that would allow them to ignore the Netanyahu attacks that proved so devastating to Peres's reelection three years earlier? By the numbers, the survey said the strongest reassurance was our team of ex-generals, repeating our commitment that "Jerusalem will remain undivided and the perpetual capital of Israel."[71] But the focus groups told a different story. After people saw a clip of Barak empathizing with terrorists, they went silent, asking themselves, "What makes Barak tick? Can we trust him?" But present to them Barak's biography, his life story as Israel's number one soldier, and perceptions changed. While Barak thought it looked like too much self-promotion, what voters saw was someone who was strong and honest, a man who was followed and who would inspire patriotism.[72]

Our goal was for Barak to cross a threshold of credibility on security. But Barak had a different goal. For Barak and his army comrades, it was unimaginable that Bibi, his subordinate in the unit, could be more trusted. Their goal was to win resoundingly on the security issue.

THE VERY MAD ADVERTISING PERIOD

The TV advertising period in Israel begins three weeks before the election and is the mad by-product of an electoral system that allows any party that can convince 1.6 percent of voters to support it to win two seats in the

Knesset. Each was entitled to a proportionate share of the free, allocated television time. To make it all even more bewildering, all the ads were aired in sequence, forming a sixty-minute block each night on the two state channels. Before the rest of the world even dreamed of such a concept, Israel had turned political advertising into a nightly reality show. While Labor and Likud had the largest segments of each night's show, they shared it with a cacophony of thirty-one parties, each working intensively to be as creative or as outrageous as possible to get noticed. The lead Russian party, the Israel B'Aliyah party, hammered home the "Shas control" to drive up its vote.[73]

In order to produce advertising that could break through and define the race, the campaign took over an office building and media center, equipped with studios, editing, makeup and green rooms, offices, and small meeting rooms. It was surrounded by fences and secured to protect Barak from the unknown and our advertising from any rogue Netanyahu commandos. It was the only building in which your briefcase was searched going in and out. The whole scene had the feel of a movie set, where young, eager assistants rush by in the halls, doing something important. Does it really take all these people to produce ten minutes of ads each night?

In this crazed advertising period, life was organized in frantic twenty-four-hour cycles, beginning when the first advertising block was aired at 6 P.M. on April 26. We studied our opponents' ads to learn their strategy and to detect any smaller party that might break through the clutter. We sensed our own ads were successful, but that was all anecdotal. Everyone waited around for the "real" data, gleaned from the four focus groups we conducted each night with swing voters.

We were also conducting national tracking polls, three times a week, so that we could know if any of it mattered.[74] The survey was conducted by callers at phone banks in Tel Aviv and Haifa, the results wired to our offices in Washington, seven hours earlier on the clock, which then worked in a frenzy to call the top-line results to me in the conference room at maybe 11:30 P.M. Sometimes Ehud was there, but usually I called him. In Washington, our people worked overnight to process the whole survey, with demographic breakouts and analysis trends, and sent the encrypted print files to the campaign, which delivered the book to me at my hotel room before sunup.

Every night was a struggle to arrive at a clear decision on what ads to run and what new ads to produce overnight, which had to be at the government Office of the Comptroller by 7 A.M. Somehow, the group moved to a conclusion, just as James and I left before midnight to get a late dinner and cool down. Shrum stayed all night to fight off all the forces of the night—the candidate, Labor politicians who said we must air some message or include some key endorsement or lose some particular group of voters, and even the creative team with some new idea. Shrum was a rock and sometimes we didn't see him until the next afternoon.

The first night of ads was an earthquake, though we only realized it over three or four days. Everything, eighteen months of work, came down to one two-minute-long spot, which began with Ehud Barak, "the son of immigrants," who "turned into the soldier with more decorations for his courage and strength than any other soldier in our history." The screen filled with black-and-white still photos of a Sabena airliner and Barak there dressed in mechanic's clothes, leading the operation that freed the hostages and killed the terrorists. "He penetrated Beirut and brought justice" to those who killed Israel's athletes in Munich. Munich gave way to Entebbe, with photos of the plane on the tarmac. It was a great day then when "Ehud Barak, the number one soldier in the state of Israel, was appointed Chief of Staff." Lest there be any doubt about what made Barak tick, for him, "fighting terror, daring operations and protecting our security, are not just words . . . but a way of life."

This first ad did not stop there, however, moving immediately to the larger framework for the election: "With the same determination, he will bring a change to Israel." Had we not made that linkage and only addressed his biography, we risked accepting Netanyahu's framework for the election: who is better on security? But our goal was to free people for economic and social change and their hopes for peace.

The ad, now a full-color film of Israelis at work and school, set out "Barak's plan: 300,000 new jobs with proper wages in the next four years," with pictures of people at work; "Free education from age three, and free entry into university."

Only Barak could bring these changes because "only Barak has the courage to give equal treatment to all and not submit to blackmail." That meant new priorities and choices: "money for education, instead of money for new settlements"; "jobs and not preferential treatment for Haredim." Only Barak could shatter the culture of particularism that undermines Israel's unity. "Only Barak has the courage to fight for the future of the state, which he has fought for his whole life."

The narrator concluded: "Ehud Barak. Patriot. Family Man. Number 1 soldier. Fighter for change in Israel."

The ads over the next couple of nights underscored the centrality of the economy. Netanyahu was depicted as self-satisfied with an economy that left 203,000 unemployed, and the ad concluded, memorably, with Bob's close: "If one hundred thousand Israelis lost their jobs, why should he keep his?"

Our other key ad tried to settle the Jerusalem question. It ran a press interview by Ehud Olmert, then the Likud mayor of Jerusalem: "I have no doubt that Ehud Barak is committed to the unity and wholeness of Jerusalem, the capital of Israel." That must have caused a lot of pain in the Netanyahu camp, allowing Barak to affirm personally in his ad: Jerusalem, "united, under our sovereignty, eternal capital of Jerusalem, period."

Netanyahu opened his campaign with a singular message: Barak will make Jerusalem capital of a Palestinian state. From Day Three until the end, it was a campaign about Arafat and a broadcast campaign that would be unimaginable elsewhere in the world. The Likud ad depicted Arafat marking off the days on a chalkboard as the narrator says, "There's someone who finds it very important that Barak get elected. He knows that Barak will give in." On Day Four, Likud ran the ad we had been anticipating, Barak talking about "if I had been Palestinian . . . ," with the narrator concluding, "Deep inside, something's wrong here. A man like this cannot be Prime Minister."

In an instant on that first night, everything crystallized for the wavering voters. They all shifted toward Barak. I have only witnessed such moments once or twice in my life in which suddenly the voters reach a new conclusion that aligns everything else in an instant. In the two nights before the television broadcast, we trailed Netanyahu by 3 points in the multicandidate first ballot and were tied in the runoff among Jewish voters. In the two nights of polling after the broadcast, we took an astonishing 10-point lead in the multicandidate race and in the head-to-head runoff with Netanyahu. We were now winning the Russians by 15 points and fully expected to get 90 percent of the Arab vote. The election was over!

When the office called me with the results, I didn't believe them. It was some bizarre sample or a computer or programming error. I asked my office to go back over everything. The political world simply doesn't change so much in one night. I reluctantly gave the results to Moshe and Tal, Bob and James, with caveats and an oath of secrecy, though James wagered that they were correct.

We immediately conducted another poll over the next two nights. Identical results. Astoundingly, we were now more trusted than Netanyahu on security. A breathtaking 60 percent of the country now saw Barak as strong and as having what it takes to be prime minister; 70 percent felt that he could be trusted to protect Israel's security. It was a long way from the political wilderness, even two months earlier, when barely half the country thought these things. Their comfort with Barak as a leader allowed people to act on their deep frustration with the country's impasse and divisions and to vote for change.[75]

With the end in sight, the memory of Rabin's murder—for many in the campaign the only reason they were there—began to be felt. It exploded in the campaign when an independent media consultant who worked earlier for Barak showed up with an emotional ad on the Rabin assassination, with visuals of Likud politicians making hateful and provocative statements before Rabin is struck dead. Many of the Labor politicians and others wanted to run the ad on the last night. But we decided no, but only after we all crammed into the room for a long and emotional debate with Barak there.

A couple of weeks before the election, Leah Rabin invited the American consultants up to her Tel Aviv apartment for a Shabbat meal to thank us for what we were doing. The walls were full of memorabilia of Yitzhak Rabin's moments, and we were honored to be there. After pouring our tea and circulating with cookies, she said, "I just want you to know how deeply grateful I am that you have made such a personal commitment to Ehud's election." The public polls now showed Barak ahead, and there was a sense of impending victory, though people dared not acknowledge it. "I'm not sure it could have happened without what you have done." She had a much less complicated view of our mission and the work of those many months. "You know that Bibi is guilty of the murder of my husband." She said it matter-of-factly, without elaboration. She was a determined and confident widow on the last mile of a journey for justice and I wondered how I got the chance in my life to help bring about such an end.

It was a reminder that the goal of taking the country back to "Rabin's way" had a special standing. All the rest was just tactics.

ELECTION DAY

At 10:01 P.M. Monday, May 17, just a second after the polls closed across Israel, Channels One and Two flashed their graphics with the exit poll results—Ehud Barak's red vertical bar improbably towering over Benjamin Netanyahu's blue one. The "magician" had defied the odds so many times before, but now the weight of the economy and scandal, a bitterly divided government and society, an endless war in Lebanon, and failed peace with the Palestinians left him with few tricks. Across Israel, people held their breath, remembering that four years earlier the networks had declared Shimon Peres the winner, only to see their joy wiped away by the late military ballots. Could it really be true that the nightmare was over?

In Barak's suite atop the Dan Hotel overlooking the Mediterranean, satisfaction quickly turned to the task of declaring and defining the victory. And in as few seconds as it took the news channels to declare victory, I knew this story would not turn out as we imagined. I took a few moments for myself, standing in front of the television to relish our graphic victory, insulated from the commentators and pundits, who were blessedly carrying on in Hebrew.

Watching the main Israeli TV networks in the hotel rooms taken over by Barak, and taking down vote tallies right after the polls closed, with Jim Gerstein on the phone translating. [Author's collection]

Somehow the Lord had the vision to banish all those words from my consciousness soon after my bar mitzvah, turning all that TV punditry for this one night into babble.

We gathered around a dining room–like table, while Ehud took congratulatory calls from various world leaders. We congratulated ourselves. I took pictures of everyone with Ehud and also of Ehud while he was speaking with President Clinton. The president must have been as joyous about the result as all of us at the table. "Mr. President," Barak shouted as if trying get heard across the ocean, "I also look forward to working together." Ehud's English always seemed louder than his Hebrew.

But this self-congratulatory moment soon gave way to exasperation among my comrades who had gathered in the passageway. "Can you believe that," someone blurted out. There, unannounced—but no doubt at Barak's invitation—was Eitan Haber, longtime aide to Yitzhak Rabin who had given the final tribute at the Rabin funeral, remembered for holding the blood-stained paper of song lyrics from that ill-fated peace rally. Now he was here with a full draft speech of his own. Shrum was standing there, not at all calmly, holding his draft—the one that had been circulated, discussed, and translated earlier in the day. With tempers rising and a growing crowd of

With Barak in his suite on election night after taking a congratulatory call from President Clinton, but before Barak spoke to supporters at the hotel and in Rabin Square. [Author's collection]

would-be editors, Barak ordered that only four people, including Haber and Shrum, join him in a closed room to hammer out the speech draft.

There was no way the two drafts could be easily merged. Barak hurriedly cut and pasted the two drafts, with Shrum adjourning to his computer afterward in a mostly futile effort to reclaim some of the campaign's themes. That the campaign manager and communications director were excluded from this effort to fashion the campaign's final statement was not a good sign. Moshe headed home as a result, but a call from Barak brought him back.

We were poised to go downstairs to the ballroom where thousands of campaign workers were gathering. The music was blaring, the stage had been carefully set, backdrop and all, "One Israel." But across Tel Aviv, jubilant citizens were just picking themselves up and making their way to Rabin Square, the spot where Yitzhak Rabin had been murdered and so many hopes had been wiped out. The streets were clogged with cars, bicycles, and people on foot, making their way, spontaneously, to the celebration. Over 100,000 were gathered there, banners waving, cars honking, drummers whipping up the crowd into different chants, "Bibi go home," "We want peace." Others chanted, "Just not Shas"—fearing somehow Shas could end up back in government.[76]

In Barak's suite, we marveled at the wave of spontaneous joy, but it was also confounding and, initially, the room said, No, Barak should stay away. There were security concerns and, originally, Barak was to helicopter to the north to show this is a national victory. We all understood the symbolism and power of affirming our victory at that spot. While Barak had surely promised to lead in Rabin's way, his election was about much more than the peace process. In the public mind, the square was owned by the "peace camp" and by secular, cosmopolitan, and leftist Israel. The campaign worked from the moment of Ehud's candidacy to show that Labor was not old Labor and cared about a different Israel. Tal, shouting, not speaking, said "No way," after hearing about the chants of "Just not Shas." This was a betrayal. "Our new voters aren't in that square."

Shrum and I were in a different place. "You created this moment. You have to go." And Ehud agreed. I would later make my own pilgrimage there together with Jim Gerstein and Dahlia Scheindlin, just milling in the crowd and breathing in the moment.

Barak went first to the ballroom.[77] "I pay tribute to the hundreds of thousands" who voted and gave us this victory. An unexceptional beginning, but then the night's second big signal that Barak was already rewriting this chapter before it even closed and the first clue as to what ended up on the cutting room floor. No mention of the economy. No mention of education. And while the campaign had spoken pointedly, shifting the country's attention and resources away from the extremist settlers and the haredim, represented by Shas, Barak was gracious, and why not, I thought. "We extend a courageous hand to all, to the secular and the religious, to those from an Ashkenazi or a Sephardi background, to those who emigrated from the former Soviet Union, from Ethiopia, to the Arabs, the Bedouins, the Sirkhasians, the Druze, everyone. Everyone is part of Israel."

Barak then asked the ballroom crowd to quiet itself and listen for a moment. "There are hundreds of thousands of people waiting for us in Rabin Square," and he had something serious to say. "There is a very special person who has a very special role in this event, not with us this evening. He was our commander, he was my commander. He led me into politics. He was our guide, Yitzhak Rabin." For Barak there was no doubt about the meaning of this victory. "If Yitzhak is looking down on us from heaven, [he] knows that we together will fulfill his legacy." This was no rhetorical flourish for election night. He told the room and later those in the square, "in the coming months and certainly in the coming few years, we will be faced by what will definitely be among the most difficult and fateful decisions of the whole history of the country." He declared, I won't flinch, and surely he meant it. Like any ordinary Jew, he can only still wonder whether he has really figured out God's intentions.

The Barak campaign and war room team on the balcony off Barak's suite overlooking the Mediterranean the day after the election. Moshe Gaon is on the phone in the middle, next to Tal Silberstein with a beer. The small sign says, "Bob, Stan, and James: We all Jews and we all love you." [Author's collection]

"Let us hope that our efforts will be blessed. As the ancient Jewish prayer says, may the Lord protect us, may the Lord give us peace, may this be His will."[78]

Shrum and I soon had the chance to compete with Barak's calling upon Rabin's legacy and the Lord's blessings. Two days after the election, on May 19, the campaign convened a large breakfast briefing in the ballroom at the Dan Hotel, attended by a few hundred Israeli and foreign reporters, activists, and campaign aides from all parties. Interest in the miracle and the "American advisors" was intense. We must have seemed arrogant and impressed with ourselves. *The Washington Post* described us as giving ourselves, and the candidate, a "pat on the back."[79]

I began by reminding the assembled, "things were very bleak for a very long time."[80] We were supposed to lose.

Looking out on this very intent audience, I was conscious of being an American and not lecturing Israelis about the meaning of things, when the stakes here were so high. What struck me that morning after a year and a half of battle was that Israelis longed for Israel to be normal. Could they live normal lives, like other people, and debate issues, like the economy, poverty and education, pensions? Normal things. That's all they wanted.

Standing with Bob Shrum, speaking at post-election conference at Dan Hotel about Barak's victory two days earlier. [Author's collection]

We conducted a survey on election night and the night after to understand why people voted the way they did. About half of Barak voters said "peace" was the reason, but almost as many said the "economy" and social issues, like "poverty." For the Russian immigrants and Sephardic voters who supported Barak, economic and social issues were much more important than peace—the reason they could move to Barak.[81]

In Tel Aviv that morning, I said, we opened up a new socioeconomic landscape for Labor, "maybe the most important new element of this Barak campaign, victory and mandate. We must never forget what happened here." An unelectable Labor Party that was a "caricature of a leftist party, out of touch and that scared a majority of the country, ran unrelentingly on the economy, education, and shifting priorities away from the haredim." The ability to vote the whole range of one's emotions and needs allowed Barak to make historic gains among the Sephardim and win the Russians and win an absolute majority of the country.

That evening, Ehud summoned Bob and me to his suite at the Dan for some thanks and celebration before we left the country on a midnight El Al flight.[82] He was still using the hotel for post-election meetings, and the security detail of three men still guarded the way the moment one got off the elevator. While it seemed like any other night, I suspected the detail was now connected to a much more elaborate network of guards on rooftops, nearby commando units, helicopters overhead, and satellites protecting the new leader.

Barak had a bottle of 150-year-old brandy somebody had given him that he wanted to share with us, along with some cigars. I really have no taste for either, but it was hard not to be one of the boys. I drank the successive glasses of brandy, with the desired effect. We were all pretty numb, but that did not stop me from offering one piece of unsolicited advice. "You've got to decide what's practical, but you can't form a government with Shas." That would repudiate our entire social and civil agenda and leave our supporters bewildered. Shrum added, "You shouldn't get yourself in a situation where Shas has you over a barrel." And in a position to hold up all your new money for education and everything else you want to do.

Ehud barely listened. Maybe it was the brandy. But as we were walking to the door, Ehud put his arms around the two of us, hugging us tight, and reflected out loud, "Someday, there will be people in this land who won't even know your names but will be alive because of what you have done here."

Ehud had no doubt about his mission and mandate. To be honest, I thought, who am I to be second-guessing the prime minister of Israel and the history he wants to make and the lives he wants to save?

For the moment, we were swept up in a great sense of hopefulness that pervaded the country. At Ben-Gurion Airport, the security guards and interrogators escorted Bob and me to the front of the line, dispensing with the usual questions. On the peaceful flight to New York, the El Al pilot of the 747 came down and thanked me.

Before the election, Barak had found it difficult each year to join the annual memorials for the slain prime minister because he felt that the murderer had somehow won. That all changed for Barak with his first memorial as prime minister. Facing a field of tombstones on Mount Herzl, as well as the grave for Rabin, he concluded, "Yitzhak," and whispered, "Only one who has been bereft of his closest friends can understand us."[83]

For Barak, winning election as prime minister of Israel was about much more than the power and trappings or the programs and pledges. Certainly every one of Israel's leaders paused for such reflection. In reaching back with intimacy to Rabin but also Ben-Gurion, Barak placed himself in a "chain of generations" of Israeli leaders who made bold and patriotic choices.[84] Barak described Ben-Gurion as "the greatest Jew of this millennium." "I don't know what the people want," Barak would quote Ben-Gurion as saying, "but I know what is needed by the people of Israel."[85]

Ben-Gurion helped create the association of Jewish unions, the Histadrut, to lead the settler community under the British mandate and eventually the world Zionist movement. He was determined to declare statehood, even as many others, facing the isolation of Palestinian Jewry and the imminent march of the Arab armies, hesitated. That is the history that all Israelis own. But for Barak, Ben-Gurion's example also encompassed a comparable willfulness to strike a bold and durable compromise for the Jewish state. In 1937, Ben-Gurion spoke in uncompromising terms before the Zionist Congress, "The integrity of the homeland and our full right to the homeland is engraved . . . on our heart." Yet within two years, he accepted "a Jewish state in a part of Palestine" rather than holding out for the whole of it, producing intense opposition and dividing his own party. He engaged in a multiyear battle, where, as one author observed, "he carried the Palestine Zionists to a new position."[86]

Barak believed Israel faced existential threats, not just the terrorists who struck at Israel's markets, cafés, and buses, but the autocratic regimes in Iraq and Iran who were developing weapons of mass destruction, the technology and missiles to produce a much greater terror. He was deeply conscious of the calendar—the presidential elections that would bring the Clinton presidency to an end and the worsening health of Syria's Hafezal-Assad and Arafat that could remove legitimate partners. Barak believed, like Rabin, that he must act quickly to settle the conflict with the Syrians and Palestinians and achieve peace with the Arab world. And Barak believed in his bones that if he reached accords with Israel's historic enemies and the Palestinians, requiring the "most difficult and fateful decisions of the whole history of the country," he could carry the citizenry to a new position.[87]

FORMING A GOVERNMENT

With only forty-five days to form a government out of a very fragmented Knesset, Barak faced a fateful decision. The voters took out their wrath on Netanyahu and the Likud Party, which collapsed to just nineteen seats in the 120-seat Knesset. But they only gave One Israel, Barak's renamed Labor Party, twenty-six seats, down one seat from the last election. Even with the left Meretz Party and the new Center Party, Barak still held only a third of the Knesset, twenty seats short of the sixty-one necessary to form a government. The ultra-Orthodox rallied to Shas, which remarkably doubled its seats to seventeen, complemented by the smaller United Torah Judaism's seats. Secular voters rallied to a new secular party, Shinui, and Natan Sharansky's Israel B'Aliyah Party, with about five seats each. They, along with Meretz, ran on a virulently anti-Shas platform.

What a mess.

Barak had two unsatisfying choices. First, he could form a government with Likud, precariously supported by a hodgepodge of smaller parties. Netanyahu's abrupt resignation after the election left Ariel Sharon in charge and unity government seemed possible, but only if Barak prioritized the economic and social changes and moved cautiously on making peace with the Syrians and Palestinians. Alternatively, he could form a government with Shas and a different hodgepodge of smaller parties. With Shas prepared to make peace with Israel's enemies following a religious imperative to save lives, Barak would have the space to pursue negotiations, even withdraw troops from Lebanon. But that choice would mean no draft of yeshiva students, and likely no shift of resources away from the religious schools to public education.

In our survey a week after the election the citizenry was very clear about its choice. A large majority of the country, including three quarters of the Russians, were vehement in their objection to including Shas in any government.[88]

Barak was taking his own counsel at that point, not consulting with his former political team, either Israeli or American. I believed possibly forming a government with Shas betrayed a core promise of the campaign, but I did not feel it was my place to second-guess Barak's judgment about what coalition was possible. He was in a tough spot. Barak organized multiple parliamentary teams to meet with the various parties, but he also had back channels and private talks with the various players. The press was not impressed with the process, describing it maliciously as "stuck, stuck, stuck."[89]

Barak met twice with Sharon to no avail. In one meeting, they opened a map of the West Bank and started arguing over where the roads would go around the various settlements. "This cooled Barak off a lot," a participant noted.[90] Barak's eyes were fully open to the consequences of this choice: "If I would join hands with Likud, we can have a major reform of inner life [of Israel]—at a price of putting an end to the peace process."

Shas leaders quickly indicated that their spiritual leader would welcome a meeting to negotiate reconciliation between Barak and Rabbi Ovadia, Barak really believing Shas "is a legitimate political and social movement."[91] Barak turned to Yitzhak Herzog, affectionately known as "Bougie," to negotiate with Shas and write a potential agreement. Bougie, a Barak insider, came from a lineage of rabbis, including his grandfather, Rabbi Isaac Levy, the first chief rabbi of Israel and his father, Chaim, its sixth president. Bougie was part of the Israeli elite who sought to keep the religious elements in society close to the center. On peace negotiations, Barak's number one priority, the Shas leaders were easy and pragmatic, knowing that any future agreement would go to a referendum. Rabbi Ovadia Yosef cared about only one issue, the draft of the Orthodox into the army, the issue that Barak used to challenge Netanyahu from his time in the wilderness. The negotiations were drawn out as Barak tried every formula to keep his promise. But Shas would only accept a committee from all sectors to review the issue, in effect keeping the status quo. Only at 5 A.M. the day before Barak was to present his government to the Knesset, did he say, fine, I'll sign it. He understood the consequences of bringing in Shas.

Barak was about to embark on a historic journey, but he knew how explosive the combination of parties was and how improbable its future. Shas, emboldened by its electoral gains and now the second largest party, was in an even stronger position to make demands on the budget. Yet Barak had given the Education Ministry to a left-wing secular party that was determined to keep Barak's promise and shift funds to the state schools and universities. To avoid a confrontation with the settlers Barak gave the National Religious Party, the settlers' party, control over settlements and housing construction in the territories. Finally, Sharansky joined the government to advance the Russian community's secular civic agenda, but he was deeply conservative and distrustful of the Palestinians. A unity government with Likud with economic and social priorities would have proved much more stable and effective, but Barak believed "I created the only coalition that was able to cross the bridge towards this historic settlement."

On July 6, 1999 Prime Minister Ehud Barak presented his government to the Knesset. He recognized that many wanted to place their hopes in him, including "the mothers who do not sleep at night and fathers tormented by anguish." He was genuine when he said "we will not close our eyes as long as is needed in the future so that mothers in Israel sleep peacefully in the coming years."[92]

He declared in the strongest possible terms that Israel was at a unique moment in history: "In the annals of the Knesset there are turning points, ends of eras and beginnings of new ones." This "will be chronicled" as such a moment: "We know that the victory of Zionism will not be complete until the achievement of genuine peace, full security, and relations of friendship, trust and cooperation with all our neighbors." His priority and bold ambition could not be clearer: "It is our duty to ourselves and our children to take decisive measures to strengthen Israel by ending the Arab-Israeli conflict."

Presumably that was what he told Chairman Arafat when he had his first official meeting with the Palestinian leadership at Erez Crossing five days after the speech, though the Palestinians were looking for something less bold, just the resumption of steps suspended by Netanyahu. The talks did not go well. Barak told President Clinton of his vision when he arrived in Washington four days later. In a three-hour private meeting in the Oval Office, a night with the two couples at Camp David, and no fewer than four dinners, Barak laid out his plan to achieve peace with both Syria and the Palestinians on all outstanding issues within fifteen months, by April 2000. He wanted to negotiate a short-term delay in the established agreements with the Palestinians so all the parties could agree to this bolder goal. He envisioned an extraordinary remaking of the Middle East, sorting out Lebanon, normalizing Israel's relations with the Arab states. While Clinton was concerned about some of Barak's thinking on Syria, overall he was "enthusiastic."[93]

The White House dinner hosted by the President and Mrs. Clinton for the new prime minister of Israel and his wife became a kind of reunion. James and Mary Matalin, Bob Shrum and his wife Marylouise Oates, a writer and former columnist for the *Los Angeles Times*, and Rosa and I were waiting together in the long queue that slowly worked its way through the parlor room on the second floor of the residence. Everyone spoke in hushed tones. When we arrived in front of the first couples, our wives pulled back and applauded and cheered as we hugged and laughed. The clamorous breach of decorum raised heads up and down the White House corridors. But for me, it was a serene night. We were conscious of the history Barak wanted to make, very far removed from the troubles at home.

The Israeli public did not like what it was seeing. While open in principle to agreements with Syria and the Palestinians, the pace seemed too fast and they thought Barak had his priorities badly wrong. In our first survey after the formation of the new government, three quarters of the country thought the government should be concentrating first on the domestic problems of his broad mandate, but nearly as many thought Barak's priority was the opposite, the peace process before anything else, producing "a massive disconnect with the public," I wrote with a sense of foreboding. Barak had fully intended to

To Stan — with deep appreciation & friendship
E. Barak

Barak and Clinton in the receiving line at the gala dinner at the White House during Barak's first visit to Washington right after his election, with Bob Shrum to their left and James Carville and myself to the right. [Author's collection]

pursue his broad mandate, but the public was right about his priorities. The cabinet had barely met yet, but less than half the country thought Barak was keeping his campaign commitments.[94]

Forming a government with Shas was deflating. To get a sense of public sentiment, Shas in our late November polls had a thermometer score of just 24.1 degrees among the Jewish public. That put Shas just a couple of degrees warmer and more popular than Arafat and Syria's Assad.[95]

The new government was a soap opera bordering on tragedy. It continuously threatened to fall and take Barak down with it. Barak had managed to achieve the approbation in three months that took Netanyahu three years to achieve. Before the end of summer, Shas, followed by United Torah Judaism, threatened to resign because the government had chosen to move a large turbine on the Sabbath. The austere budget introduced in September just left a smaller pie to fight over. It revealed the contradictions of his coalition. Prominent ministers attacked the budget for doing nothing about poverty. With the December 30 deadline approaching, there was a rising crisis between the secular education minister and Shas leaders over funding for the Shas school networks. A last-minute compromise allowed the government to save face but not Barak's education promises.

The economy and Barak's approach to it did not help as Barak tried to remake the Middle East. Even as he struggled to win the votes for his first budget, the unemployment rate rose to 9.1 percent, a seven-year high, with 213,000 people out of work. At the end of year, the government reported that one in six Israelis, over a million, were living in poverty, underscoring how large were the social gaps that Barak had promised to close.[96] The stories and reality increased the pressure on the government to make investments to relieve poverty, but Barak was self-consciously committed to "Third Way" economic policies of lower spending, inflation, and interest rates that produced such growth in the United States and Britain.

"The government I head will not spend irresponsibly," Barak declared, expressing his impatience with the politicians. I "will not pay for laziness and corruption and will not encourage whining and dependence." At the end of year, barely 40 percent of Israelis thought Barak cared about people like them.[97]

Also brewing during this period was an investigation by the state comptroller's office into the financing of the party campaigns in the last election, with the spotlight on the use of nonprofit organizations to organize rallies and mobilize voters. Using a loophole in the laws affecting financing for direct election for prime minister, the Barak campaign created a whirlwind of street-level activity, people holding signs at intersections and papering the country with waves of slogans and attacks. Many of Barak's top campaign advisors were distracted that fall, except perhaps Barak, but the "scandal" would get his attention after the first of the year when the state comptroller issued a damaging report and referred the matter to the police to see if criminal prosecutions were warranted. In time, nobody would be prosecuted, but the events eroded Barak's standing.

At the end of the year 1999, seven months after the formation of his government, voters were disappointed. Nevertheless, they had a lot invested in Ehud Barak and were not giving up. Two thirds said Barak could be trusted to protect Israel's security.[98]

SYRIA FIRST

On Friday, November 15, Barak called together at his home in Kochav Yair all his political, campaign, and media advisors who had dispersed after election night in May. Virtually none of them went into government with Barak and none advised him during these rocky first months. It was a cathartic meeting and it took three hours to get past the anger and bad feelings. Barak began the meeting by apologizing for turning to a new set of advisors, experienced in government, who he thought could best handle the current phase and issues. But that was the wrong choice. I appreciate your skills and need you with me, he said. Israel had the chance to do something very momentous, a comprehensive peace with Syria, but he acknowledged that he could not bring such a peace without their help.

When he was done, people spoke in turn as if at a Baptist revival. Who are these people in the prime minister's office? What do they know about your issues? How could you squander the goodwill from the election? When everyone had spoken, they agreed to put aside their anger and do what had to be done to tackle the issue of a Syrian peace. To their near universal amazement, there could be a referendum in six months on an agreement to return virtually all of the Golan to Syria.

Even with the aid of recent memoirs, it is not at all clear why Barak concluded that such a breakthrough was imminent. True, Assad gave early signals that he viewed Barak as "serious," but in that period Assad seemed to be backtracking and wearing a more traditional unrevealing Syrian mask. Over the same month, however, Barak grew deeply worried about Assad's health and pushed Clinton relentlessly to bring things to a head.[99] He also decided to prepare his own forces at home so he could bring things to a head in Israel as well. He asked the group to organize an urgent campaign, with research and messages, mobilizing at the street level, and all the communication activity that we would need to win public support and a referendum.

His reassembled team understood the urgency, but there was little enthusiasm among his own people for such an agreement. Like the rest of the public, they expected progress first on the Palestinian front, where Barak had promised to unfreeze the peace process and restore hope. That's what Rabin died for. On the other hand, what's the point of it? The Golan was peaceful, indeed idyllic; the settlers there were not religious extremists, but patriots, Zionists in the socialist mold of the Galilee, who had secured the north for Israel. Syria was one of the least lovable regimes and home for every rejectionist Arab group in the world, hardly a worthy and trusting partner for our first peace. I got a call in the States early the next morning from Tal Silberstein and Moshe Gaon: wake up, we have to get started urgently. While I had conducted a couple of polls in the six months since the election, I was basically monitoring things, not really advising, engaged, or speaking with Barak. Like the rest of his team, I was happy for the reunion but not particularly for the agreement. In one of my first trips to Israel with Rosa decades earlier, we drove up to the abandoned Syrian positions on the Golan, their rusting artillery and the bunkers along the cliffs. I remember looking down on the kibbutzim and saying, "I'd never give it back." It is for that kind of response that Israel has brought so many visitors to this spot. Near the end of this last campaign when I found myself in Israel on weekends, Moshe and Tal used the lull on Shabbat to drive up to the Golan, well past the Syrian bunkers, seeing the wineries and Mount Herman where Israelis have a clear view of the Syrian plain.

I was once again awed by Barak's boldness. In the survey, we were not looking at the various possible elements of an agreement, which in some combination might maximize public support. Instead, we were looking at a total agreement and total peace, reflecting Barak's approach to life and apparently to the peace process. I was learning through the survey instrument of Barak's "heroic instinct," what U.S. negotiators and President Clinton were coming to understand more directly. "He would conclude historic peace agreements whatever the political risk," Dennis Ross, the chief U.S. negotiator, wrote of Barak's approach. He would then outline the specifics of a final agreement and final bottom line, though without truly disclosing what was really final, and wanted to know "if the Syrians were prepared for this outcome." Barak was impatient with the give-and-take of talks, preferring "to leapfrog over it and make a deal rapidly on these terms."[100]

Well, that was where our first survey started. We asked first without elaboration whether people would vote yes or no to a "peace agreement" reached by Barak and Assad. But that was followed immediately by a second form of the referendum question, leapfrogging all the details: "Imagine that a settlement with the Syrians included an Israeli withdrawal from nearly all of the Golan. The agreement would provide for the demilitarization of the Golan Heights, an end to the conflict in Lebanon, and normal relations with Syria." In that case, will you vote yes or no? The rest of the survey was devoted, not to the specifics of the proposal, but to the benefits for Israel. That the Syrian agreement would "lead to the withdrawal of the IDF from Lebanon" and that it would allow "Israel to focus on challenges at home and to increase economic and educational opportunities" were the most convincing arguments for the Israeli public.

The public was unenthusiastic about reaching a peace accord with Syria. Nonetheless, in that first survey over 60 percent of the Jewish public supported a Syrian agreement in principle and a like number favored an agreement that returned the Golan for a total peace. Even after a battery of attacks, reminding voters that Israel would give up its "only natural water resources" for a cold peace with the Syrians, a majority of 57 percent continued to support an agreement.[101] That grudging majority was what Barak would take with him into the first public meetings with the Syrian foreign minister in mid-December.

Support would drop significantly with events, but Barak never doubted that if he could bring an agreement—one that allowed a withdrawal from Lebanon, that created a peace with a major Arab state, and one that was supported by the president of the United States—Israeli voters would support it, and in large numbers. He believed this was what Israeli leaders did. More-over, it was what the people wanted them to do, even if they were fearful of the consequences. Ben-Gurion was Barak's abiding reference point but in the context of the Syrian debate, Barak repeatedly reminded us of Menachem Begin's example: only a third of the country supported returning all of the Sinai to Egypt before Camp David. But afterward, two thirds did when it meant normalizing relations with Israel's most muscular enemy.

The problem for Barak was not whether he could pass an agreement in a referendum, but how to keep his government from collapsing before he got there and how to maintain public confidence in his leadership, which was under assault on many fronts, many self-created. There are not many leaders who would choose such a moment for greatness.

Just to add to his handicap, Barak was determined that an agreement that returned land to an Arab state and that changed Israel's borders forever be achieved with a majority of Jewish voters. Indeed, the Knesset was poised to require that in law.[102]

That is why the Russian immigrants were so central to the future. Equal in number to the Arabs, they could easily provide a large majority to the "no" side in a referendum. They had voted for Barak not because of hopes for peace but because he promised to address the economy and to reduce the influence of the ultra-Orthodox. Well, at this moment in December, unem-ployment hit a new high, yeshiva students got their exemption from the army, and Shas won its education funding. "Barak appears to be in the middle of an on-going collapse" among Russian voters, I wrote. Only a third thought he was keeping his campaign promises or cared about them. His standing in that community had fallen below that of Netanyahu and Sharon.[103]

Barak assumed the Jewish citizens of Israel would accept a historic com-promise, as they had in the past, but I was not sure it was true for these new immigrants. They came to Israel after the 1967 war when the Golan seemed like uncontested Israeli territory and all the Russian parties were against any return of land to Syria.[104]

This all took on greater urgency when President Assad informed Ross and U.S. Secretary of State Madeleine Albright in early December that he was ready for a representative of the Syrian government to meet formally with Ehud Barak. Ross, who had seen a lot, was genuinely stunned, observing that he had never seen Assad "in such an agreeable mood," which was all Barak needed to hear.

"From my military experience," he told Ross, "I know that when you have the initiative you must capitalize on it or lose the momentum and the opportunity." He wanted a meeting within a week, which would continue until there was an agreement. The United States, however, believed the first meetings must be shorter and more exploratory, followed by more meetings in January.[105]

"If we miss this opportunity," Barak warned a not-well-behaved Knesset, "it may cost us in blood." Sharon, disdaining Barak's proposed framework for a Syrian agreement, warned, "Never have I seen such a desire to capitulate." And when Barak put the issue to a vote of the Knesset, twenty-four members abstained, leaving Barak fourteen votes short of a majority.[106]

On December 15, Ehud Barak, prime minister of Israel, Farouk al-Shara, foreign minister of Syria, and Bill Clinton, the president of the United States, stepped into the Rose Garden of the White House to launch the first meeting between an Israeli head of state and a top representative of the Syrian government. They were each to make short statements about this propitious moment before adjourning to Blair House for two days of preliminary talks. The president and Barak both spoke crisply, given the cold weather, of putting old rivalries and the horrors of war behind and looking ahead to peace. But the Syrian foreign minister seized the moment to rehash the history of Syrian grievances, "the occupation, which is undoubtedly the source of all adversities and wars," Israel's responsibility for the flight of a half million Syrian people, whose suffering exceeds that a few thousand Golan settlers who seek "to muster international sympathy." The speech left the White House officials shifting from foot to foot. There was no Rose Garden handshake.[107]

When they returned to the Oval Office, the president was angry, exclaiming, "Shara has screwed us." Ross tried to salvage the talks by warning Shara that he had embarrassed the president and "created a problem for Barak, making him look weak and naive before his own public."[108] A problem?

The newspapers in Israel reacted almost instantaneously with these headlines: "Clinton and Barak Surprised at Ashara's Stern Speech"; "Golan Sources: It Was a Declaration of War, Not Peace"; "Every Beginning Is Difficult"; "A Cold Start"; "The Syrians Are the Same Syrians."

The scene in Washington confirmed their fears and produced, I wrote to Barak, "alarming results" that underscored "the deep caution of the Israeli public about any Syrian agreement." The public became immediately more fearful about the peace process and more doubtful about Barak's strength of leadership. Nearly half believed Barak was moving ahead "much too fast"—up a remarkable 25 points from before the White House meetings. Barak personally lost more than 10 points off the perception of him as "strong" and someone who "stands firm," the very qualities he would need to carry the country with him.[109]

There was a perceptible rise in sympathies for the Golan settlers, reflected in the campaign being organized under the banner, "Haam im Hagolan,"

"The People Are with the Golan." "You can see it in the streets everywhere you look—balconies, cars, in big junctions, on TV—everywhere," Ilan Goldstein, the campaign's media man, wrote me with alarm.[110]

For all that, the increasingly attentive public was not lost to a referendum. Indeed, Barak was even more confident he would win. Support for an agreement in principle dropped, but held at 55 percent for a pact that gave up the Golan for a total peace. After hearing the new arguments for and against an agreement, support rose rather than fell. "If we move effectively and the agreement produces the right outcomes," I wrote, "a real majority is possible."[111]

Barak's immediate response to his weakened position and the rising opposition was to build the capacity of his own forces. In my world, he wanted to see tracking polls every week and a clear strategy and message to win a referendum, which he said would happen in April. Given the events in Washington, that seemed surreal, but he must have known something.

Barak spoke with President Clinton on December 23 and talked about things he needed to make the "intensive" phase of talks taking place the following week in Shepherdstown, West Virginia, work, at least for him—a start to Lebanon negotiations, an upgrade of diplomatic relations with an Arab country, and U.S. commitment on economic investment and advanced military equipment for Israel, to name a few. At the end of the call, he said, one more thing, Stan Greenberg, your pollster, has done a survey, which shows what Israel needs to achieve if I am to win a referendum on giving up the Golan. What he did not say on the phone was that he wanted the politically astute Bill Clinton to see the political rubble and the price Barak paid for Syria's coldness in Washington; he wanted Clinton to understand the urgent need for public signs of progress on things that mattered to Israel. Lebanon. Normalization.

I had no idea at the time that Barak was using my polls—"tactically," as he described it—until I got a call to deliver a copy of the questionnaire and results to the president. Having been there in an earlier life, I could imagine him whipping through the survey, seeming just to scan each page, but really absorbing the results and the implications of each question. A few days later, I got a series of urgent e-mails from Moshe that "EB is looking for you" and that he wanted James and me "to brief Bill C on the ongoing poll results privately and directly." Be totally frank. "He is not concerned with the implications of the data. He wants him to know the whole truth," which we knew was pretty ugly. I reached the president that night through the White House operator, something I had not done in five years and even then, infrequently, and then, never on questions of war and peace. On the call, I underscored the immediate suddenness and scale of Barak's fall after the White House meeting, no doubt raising Clinton's ire with Shara. I was frank, as I had been with both of these leaders, but I also showed that Barak could win a referendum if he could bring a Lebanon withdrawal, normalization, and preserve Israel's control over the water. The president got it, as he later told the top negotiator, that with these elements, "the Israeli voters might just vote for it."[112] He clearly took great joy in getting an inside view into Barak's political challenge at home, which redoubled his efforts, according to Ross, to get some movement on diplomatic relations with Israel, World Bank activity, and Lebanon—none particularly successful.[113]

More than ever, Barak was now focused on the specifics of each question to make sure that we were getting the wording of each "accomplishment" right. He knew what he was trying to achieve for Israel in the negotiations, but he wanted to know which ones mattered the most to the public, particularly those that could mobilize the president of the United States. Among the things we tested, most important for Barak was "the United States committing to provide Israel with the most advanced weapons systems and make Israel the only superpower in the Middle East" and a new "Israeli-American military alliance, similar to NATO, committing America to defend Israel if attacked."[114] This last outcome probably had an audience of one. Indeed, after the poll was completed, I got an e-mail on New Year's Eve asking me to have another conversation with "the comeback kid," his code name in our communications.

The negotiations were to resume in a couple of days and I used New Year's Day at home in New Haven to review all the surveys and focus groups and to send Barak a note.[115] Support for an agreement had survived the formal launch and may even be recovering a couple of points. We began those first serious talks at a symbolic crossroads, with exactly 50 percent of Jewish voters supporting an agreement that took the Syrian border to the eastern coastline of the Sea of Galilee, the largest body of water in Israel. The Gallup polls conducted for the prime minister's office right before New Year's showed a slightly wider lead for the "yes." And in the month ahead they would show support right at that 50 percent mark for Jewish voters.[116]

Though I did not know it at the time, Barak had drawn his own red line—Israel's undisputed sovereignty over the Sea of Galilee. He told President Clinton of this absolute when they met after Barak formed his government and reiterated with U.S. negotiators at every point in the process. This has been described as his assessment of the limits of Israeli public opinion, or the limits of his electoral mandate, but that misreads him. For Barak, the waters of the Kinneret—the Sea of Galilee—were integral to Israel as a nation and central to the country's long-term security. From day one, he communicated that if Syria would acknowledge that, then all the rest would sort itself out. This was a central starting point and as bold a red line as returning to the June 4, 1967, border was for the Syrians.

From my New Year's vantage point in New Haven and without a personal history in the peace camp, I began to craft a message centered on security, rather than peace to take to Shepherdstown and the country. With the grim dark-suited Syrians—no hugs, no handshakes—it would be difficult to recapture the hopefulness of Oslo. One Israeli author who had always shared those hopes, Amos Oz, spoke of his country's lowered expectations for anything from the Syrians: they "think that we will give them the Golan and they will send us a receipt by fax."[117] So I proposed we settle on one very clear benefit, the end of conflict in Lebanon, and the reassurance would bring a new level of security from American military guarantees and Arab recognition.

I proposed that Barak—and President Clinton—speak about the goal of a Syrian agreement in new terms, to achieve a more secure Israel, and after it was recast by Bob Boorstin, formerly of the Clinton campaign and White House and now with our company, we proposed "a more secure future—one our children can depend on." This was a grudging message for a grudging peace.[118]

The Israeli-Syrian talks resumed on September 3, 2000, this time in the more remote location at Shepherdstown, 166 West Virginia, on the route to Antietam, America's Civil War battlefield. The participants spent eight frustrating days to no good end. In the arcane world of Middle East negotiations, Assad came to view Shepherdstown as a failure, a moment when his representatives were forthcoming on key issues, while Barak and his team offered nothing in return. Scarred by the Syrians' use of the first meeting to attack Israel and with Clinton only paying token visits each night, Barak was in no mood for the penultimate meeting at which the big issues would be settled. In this interval between meetings, he tried without success to get the United States, the Arab states, or Syria to send some signal that Barak was not on a fool's errand.

The United States and Syria had one common goal for the talks—getting Barak to accept what they believed Rabin had conceded and the Syrians had "pocketed": the June 4, 1967, border as the starting point for discussions, even if the parties disagreed on where the line actually ran. Barak did not accept that Rabin had conceded that point and certainly thought he should not concede at the outset of the negotiations what the Syrians most wanted, a principle that frustrated U.S. negotiators but a first principle for Barak who, earlier in his first ministerial position, had risked alienating Rabin when he abstained on the Oslo Accords because Israel gave up too much before negotiating the biggest issues. That should only happen at some final moment, when both sides went to their real bottom lines. With the talks coming to a close, the president asked permission to place a call to Assad to communicate his personal judgment that Rabin's pocket was now Barak's, but Barak refused. It was not the right moment.

I had no idea what was actually happening at Shepherdstown, though very conscious of the over 150,000 who assembled in Rabin Square on a drizzly night to stir the country, waving posters and banners in Hebrew and Russian, "The People Are with the Golan" and "The Golan Stays, Barak Goes." The opponents launched a new street-level campaign, depicting the future destruction of the Golan villages as they were returned to the Syrians who did not even offer "a human gesture." The speakers' program included two members of Barak's own cabinet who promised to withdraw their parties if Barak brought back an agreement.[119]

The rally was not necessary because Israel and Syria never reached agreement and there would be no referendum. There were many further meetings, including a meeting of Presidents Clinton and Assad in Geneva in March, but even a bold Israeli proposal left Assad "not interested." We continued to poll on a range of issues, even on the possible perimeter and border around the Sea of Galilee (four meters or four hundred meters) to understand whether that undermined for the public Barak's concept of Israeli sovereignty. But that was all irrelevant. What I now know is that those moments created facts, "pocketed" positions that become the starting points for future negotiations and understandings between peoples. Barak ultimately told his cabinet and thus the world what was previously whispered—that leaders from Rabin to Netanyahu accepted the return of virtually all the Golan to Syria; Barak also affirmed Israel's absolute sovereignty over the Sea of Galilee.

The moment was also fateful for me. Dennis Ross concluded that Syria and Israel could have reached an agreement in March or April had Assad's health and concerns about succession not stopped him, or they could have reached a deal in December or January had Barak not gotten cold feet. Reflecting later observations by Barak's own negotiator, as well as a former IDF chief of staff and Center Party leader, who were at Shepherdstown, Ross wrote "unbeknownst to us, Barak received the results of a poll that made doing the deal with Syria more problematic than he had thought." That poll persuaded Barak "to hold fast in Shepherdstown regardless of the Syrian moves" so that he could "show his public that he had made no concessions at Shepherdstown."[120] And Martin Indyk, appointed ambassador to work closely with Barak in this process, was stunned when Barak told him, "I can't do it." The reason, Indyk wrote: "Barak's pollsters were warning him that that kind of public support simply wasn't there yet and that he would have to find a way to reverse the negative mood."[121]

An Israeli journalist, Raviv Drucker, in a book highly critical of Barak's use of polling, used my leaked memos to draw a similar conclusion. The intensified Syrian track and the public reaction to the first Barak-Shara meeting triggered intensified polling, Drucker wrote, that showed a populace extremely worried about Barak's rush toward an agreement. Barak's negotiation strategy was affected by Greenberg's "warning flags" and assertions about Barak being in "a dangerous position," Drucker said. "Only Ehud Barak can explain the motives behind his negotiation strategy in Shepherdstown," Drucker concluded. "The polls and pessimistic analyses presented to him frequently during the summit, surely affected his decision-making."[122]

I have been haunted by Dennis Ross's conclusion since I read it—that the polling led the otherwise fearless Ehud Barak to get cold feet and miss the opportunity for a peace with Syria. In writing this book, there is no observation that bothered me as much as this one and, if true, no other finding will have as much impact on my own peace of mind and my own judgment about the character of my work for political leaders. A continued belligerency with Syria and all its implications for the Arab world and Iran is a heavy responsibility, and I take the issue seriously.

When I presented Ross's conclusion to Barak, he was contemptuous: "Bullshit."

Moshe Gaon, who was directly involved, reacted similarly: "Bullshit. Complete bullshit."

Still, the charge needs to be addressed.

Barak insists with me, as he did with Itamar Rabinovich, Israel's former ambassador to the United States and author of *Waging Peace*, that Syria would not budge from its starting principle, which called for Israel to accept withdrawal to the June 4, 1967, line, as a precondition for discussing all other issues. That insistence prevented movement at Shepherdstown. Barak was willing to make an abstract commitment but not a specific one until he saw whether Assad was flexible on the Sea of Galilee. Barak feared that an early commitment would surely be leaked to the press, probably by the Syrians, and bring down his government before he could get to the decisive stage of the negotiations. Partial understandings did indeed leak, shaped by both sides, and causing problems for both sides.[123]

By the time he got to Shepherdstown, after the disaster of the Blair House meeting, and with no new Syrian gestures, Barak likely downgraded what he thought was possible at that point, particularly since Clinton was not even present for the key meetings. But based on his planning for an April referendum and Lebanon withdrawal, Barak clearly intended to reach a total agreement. He viewed Shepherdstown as a step in the process, not as it turned out the last meeting when Assad would be open to a major deal. It is possible he miscalculated, but he was not delusional as everyone else drew the same conclusion. According to Indyk, Clinton did not press Barak harder because "he was operating under the faulty assumption that there would be another round of negotiations" and Barak had committed to him that he would accept the

Rabin pocket at that point. A week later, Indyk flew to Israel, "to help put the finishing on the agreement with Syria, never considering the process could crater again," while Prince Bandar of Syria met with Asad a few days later, who told him "he wanted to reach agreement in one 'decisive' round."[124]

Barak is amused by the idea that he would hesitate because of fear of political death at home. This is a fearless man already way out on a high wire. He believed he was using polling tactically in the negotiations, not as a vehicle to save himself at home. He wanted President Clinton to see "how complicated it is" to do certain things: "It was a way to signal to them [the White House] the same way that Assad indicated he has internal problems and can't afford to do some things." The more the president understood the ongoing political cost, the difficulties of winning a referendum, and the red lines, the more he would work for things that Barak and Israel needed. For that purpose, the actual results hardly had to be embellished, just promptly and fully shared with the president.

The idea that Barak got surprisingly "bad" news in a secret poll, "unbeknownst" to the negotiators, is almost silly. Barak crashed in the public polls within days of the Blair House meeting before Christmas, with support dropping to near 40 percent. The grim reality in Israel was the problem, not the polls. And all of our polls after Blair House were shared with the president.

Did unpromising poll results lead Barak to hesitate, thinking this would be harder to achieve than he imagined? For this, I go back to Barak's first principle: "I never questioned that I would win" a referendum. Indyk got an earful of it only two weeks after Shepherdstown when Barak told him the gaps between the sides were small and he "now believed that such a deal could produce a landslide victory in the referendum." Barak always believed that and the earlier impression was clearly tactical. His confidence was not based on our polls. It stemmed from his own reading of Israel's history and interests. "No outcome with due respect to polling," Barak declared, "no outcome of any polling could have changed my mind about what was needed for Israel."

In any case, my polling showed a Jewish majority for an agreement as Barak envisioned it and wrote Barak that we could win a referendum. Barak left the negotiators with a very different impression, leading Indyk to reflect that perhaps Clinton should have summoned his former pollster to Shepherdstown "on that last fateful evening to argue with their ultimate boss" about "what it would take to change Israeli public opinion." But no such visit to the woodshed was really needed.[125]

Barak is quite capable of making miscalculations—thinking he knows best, not helping the other side meet its goals, not empathizing with people, and having little patience with politics and politicians—but I do not doubt that he was doing what he believed was right for Israel, regardless of the political price.

I ask myself sometimes how many political leaders would be at such a meeting with so little domestic support, a government that could implode at the first signs of concessions, with a foreign leader who only shows contempt for your country, and an agreement that on any given day is opposed by half the country. There was clearly a different calculus at work for Barak, which takes you into a different realm of thinking.

But let me introduce a more conventional political calculus, even if Barak was disdainful of such things. What if Barak made a calculated decision after being humiliated at Blair House to emerge from Shepherdstown with greater legitimacy, more public trust, and politically strengthened so that his government would not fall and he could better make his case to the public? What if he concluded as Indyk reports that "I cannot look like a *freiers*," a sucker, "in front of my own people."[126] Had he succeeded, he faced an immediate judgment in a first-time referendum in Israel. That means "public opinion is as much his battlefield right now as the negotiating tables in the United States," *New York Times* reporter Deborah Sontag pointed out. From this perspective, the turning point or missed opportunity was not Shepherdstown but Blair House, when the Syrian foreign minister spurned Barak's hand and attacked Israel. "Such details may seem trifling within the larger context of two enemies making an effort to move from a state of hostility and belligerency to a state of peace," Rabinovich, the former ambassador to the United States, wrote, but they are packed with symbolism, in this case, producing a crash in confidence in Barak. Syria was using the moment to create a symbolic moment of its own, but it was Barak who would face the voters.[127]

Israelis were trying to make a judgment: could they trust Barak to get the balance right in reaching an irreversible compromise with their Arab enemies? They thought Rabin wanted to be feared, not loved by his enemies, and his reluctance to shake Arafat's hand was evidence that they could trust him to get the balance right. But what the voters took away from Blair House was a Barak rushing too fast, ready to give away too much. That conclusion, if it deepened, could have fundamentally undermined Barak's ability to win public support for a future accord. In my memo to Barak after Blair House I reminded him of the virtues that allowed Rabin to bring the public with him and say "there will be moments" when it seems "the process is stuck," but "these moments will serve you well. The public would like to see a tough negotiation and a careful approach discussing such delicate issues." I do not know whether that affected Barak's approach to Shepherdstown after the disaster of Blair House, but it would have been a reasonable thing to do, if you thought this is the middle, not the end, of the process.

Finally, these assessments miss how Barak used polling and perhaps a lesson to pundits and other leaders. Barak escalated his polling program, not to be more cautious in negotiations but to be more bold—as he had to face a "no" campaign that was organizing and "winning" in the street. His polls were heavily oriented toward developing a rationale for the agreement that could dominate the public debate and shift the momentum in the country. When on a daring mission, you want as much intelligence as possible so you can minimize risk at each step as you seek to achieve the improbable.

INTERLUDE

My father decided after the New Year that he would no longer allow the doctors and nurses to attach him to tubes to prolong his life. He was eighty-seven years old, itself improbable after a life of smoking two packs of cigarettes a day until he retired. His mind was as acute as ever, graduating from slide rule to computer in the last year so he could use an Excel spreadsheet to display the condominium's budget for the next year. But the arteries were not keeping up with the brain and he was in constant pain. My mother called to tell us that Dad would be released from the hospital the next day and that Rosa and I should fly down right away to Fort Lauderdale because he would be in the hands of the hospice nurses.

The cell phone service was not great in the apartment, so I was spending a lot of time right outside on the open walkway that looks down on the parking lot. The whole complex got to listen to my conversations. To my surprise, I got a call from Israel, "Can you hold on for the prime minister?" Ehud came on quickly to ask about my father. And then he told me to take the phone over to my father's bed, which sat alone in the sun room, except for the monitoring equipment, the IV for pain medicine, and the nurses. When I said "Dad," his eyes opened and he was very conscious. Ehud said, quite loud but slowly, "Tell your father that the prime minister of Israel gives you a big hug and wishes you L'chaim."

So I did not easily join those who asked, Haven't you given up on Barak yet?

Some political leaders, like Bill Clinton, live through big lows and big highs and if they are lucky, finish at the right time with high standing. That was Barak of the campaign period. But as prime minister, he had only lows—that is, his problems were cumulative, as he faced crisis after crisis. The word "crisis" becomes tired, but at each point you could not anticipate what choices Barak would make, the new risks he would take, and new political pain we all would experience.

Barak's questioning by the state comptroller, the finding of wrongdoing on campaign financing, and the attorney general's requesting a police investigation all concentrated the mind. Trapped in the condo in Fort Lauderdale going on ten days with only the prospect of the Super Bowl to keep us sane, I decided to concentrate my mind on the developing "crisis." The memo had been building up in my head as I watched the public's growing disillusionment with Barak and I wanted to shake him to become more conventionally political. His one-mission approach to being prime minister was losing voters in so many ways that it undermined his ability to achieve even that mission. "We are surely in the midst of a crisis of confidence, which is surely deepening." I presumed the two "surely's" would double my emphasis if "crisis" and "deepening" were not strong enough. Reflecting the anguished discussions in the focus groups, I wrote that voters saw a prime minister who "acts like a general or the head of Mossad." They saw him as "secretive and alone" and "never consults or really speaks with the people." And while Barak may have prioritized a grand peace, they had not forgotten that he "ran on a grand vision of domestic renewal." He had not made "even the slightest effort to keep his promises," which had broken an "electoral bond." Just a third thought he "cares about people like me," produced by people's more personal indictment: "he's missing a soul"; "he doesn't see me when I'm a meter away."[128]

The peace process was the least of the problems. There could well be a majority for a "cold peace," I wrote, but voters were desperate for something more from their leader. When we met weeks later to discuss that memo, I said I fully understood that he couldn't exactly bring people into his confidence when in the middle of protracted and secret diplomacy and negotiations, but voters think they live in a democracy. They want to know that you think what they think matters—the elemental start for a bond that enables you to take people with you on this journey.

THE PALESTINIAN TRACK

What voters had in mind when they turned to Barak to continue Rabin's way was a peace with the Palestinians, not the Syrians. Rabin gave his life seeking to resolve the Israeli-Palestinian conflict that is all too immediate for people: the violence and suicide bombers, instability, the Israeli occupation, huge costs, and the normal issues deferred. The Oslo Accords provided a way out and a path for mutual recognition, the exchange of land for peace and staged confidence-building actions on both sides, with the big issues, like Jerusalem and Palestinian refugees, deferred to some future, almost theoretical "final status" negotiations.

Netanyahu viewed the Oslo Accords as a betrayal. Only under the greatest international pressure did he grudgingly and partially implement its terms, and with continuing terrorist attacks, froze its implementation. The

United States and the Palestinian leadership were desperate for a thaw and some evidence of progress on the ground, to rebuild mutual trust and reduce the pressure for a Palestinian revolt. With the Palestinian track frozen, the security establishment by February was fearful the frustrations on the Palestinian street would boil over as violence.[129]

But almost 60 percent of the Jewish public in Israel supported an agreement with the Palestinians when we did our first test of it in January. There was never that kind of support for a Syrian agreement and support held at the level through February and March to May, and only then dropped to around 55 percent. On the Palestinian issue, unlike the Syrian, some very big issues had been settled, creating broad support for the process, at least in Israel. The great majority in the country believed the election reaffirmed the country's commitment to this process.

Barak never agreed with the Oslo concept because it meant Israel returning virtually all the occupied territories—and Israel's main bargaining chips—before even getting to the big issues, leaving Israel in a weakened bargaining position. Reading from Barak's attitude and impatience, I believe he thought Arafat and Peres were content to circumnavigate the world, be toasted in the best circles, negotiate in perpetuity for small progress, while never having to educate their own people on the historic compromises that a real agreement would require. But Barak believed Israel faces existential threats that require responsible leaders who would move boldly and rapidly to achieve a final settlement of the Israeli-Palestinian conflict. That is why he went to the White House after he formed his government, to tell them he intended to settle the outstanding issues within fifteen months. That is why he worked to suspend Oslo and change the timetable with the Palestinians—to delay or cancel certain "small" steps in the phased process, negotiate a new framework for an agreement by February 2000, and a final status agreement by September 2001. The boldness of it all excited President Clinton's imagination, but the contradictions were quickly evident to the Palestinians.

There was a logic and truth to Barak's bold gambit. With such a fragile coalition, why gamble scarce political capital to achieve small, intermediate steps—the return of 6.1 percent of the territory or three villages in the proximity of Jerusalem—when all of that would be subsumed by a comprehensive settlement giving the Palestinians 80 or 90 percent of the land? Why bring down the government prematurely on a small issue when, if we were all patient, we could get into a room to settle all the outstanding issues?

But that left the Palestinian leaders empty-handed, with a peace process that was still mostly frozen, delivering very little evidence of progress.

The three Palestinian villages—Abu Dis, Azariyeh, and Anata—dramatically illustrated both the fragility and logic in Barak's position but also the cost to the Palestinians. Arafat had personally asked Barak that the three villages near Jerusalem be included as part of the next transfer of territory. From Abu Dis one can see the Dome of the Rock, the oldest mosque in the world atop the Temple Mount at the heart of Jerusalem, and Arafat declared he would not accept future transfers without the villages. By April, Barak committed to President Clinton that he would transfer the villages and battled to win passage in the Knesset in May. He succeeded only by caving in to Shas in the latest struggle on education spending. On the very day of the Knesset vote, the macabre celebration of Israeli independence, Nakba Day for the Palestinians—the "Day of Catastrophe"—turned into the bloodiest confrontation in years, leaving twelve Israeli soldiers and almost two hundred Palestinians injured. The imagery of armed Palestinian police firing on Israeli soldiers shocked Israel and stopped Barak from completing the just approved transfer of the villages, even when pressed by President Clinton and the Palestinians.[130]

Each halting stage in the peace process was linked with Barak's growing domestic woes that brought him to new, unimaginable political lows. At the end of March, I received an e-mail from Moshe detailing the day-by-day, drip-by-drip travails, from a vote of no confidence and a doctors strike to a new tent city pitched by the employees of a poor bankrupt town. "That's it," Moshe signed off. "Looks good or what?" Not mentioned in Moshe's list was the continuing rise in unemployment, ten months after our election, accompanied by an austere Barak economic narrative. Our offer was pretty stark, I wrote: "a severe dose of responsibility with almost no promise of opportunity."[131]

For the first time, I believed and wrote that our approach to governing and negotiating left us "so weakened and isolated" that it could not be sustained. "The peace-minded but secular voters are no longer interested in Barak's form of peace," which depended on even more deals with Shas: only 15 percent of Barak's own voters favored any more compromises with Shas to keep the government alive. At the same time, "security-minded but more religiously traditional voters are losing interest in reaching an agreement with the Palestinians." The result was a "meltdown" of our own making.[132]

LEBANON

On May 24, a month before Barak's announced deadline, Barak oversaw the secret and sudden overnight withdrawal of all Israeli military forces from southern Lebanon, ending the eighteen-year involvement in that country. For Barak, it was a pledge that he felt honor-bound to fulfill, though the sudden overnight departure left many Israelis uneasy. On the one hand were images reminiscent of the U.S. Marines fleeing Saigon, with our local allies dangling from the helicopters. Here, the Lebanese fighters allied with Israel crowded at the fence, while the IDF was forced to bomb their bases and equipment, lest they fall in the hands of the Hezbollah. Lebanon declared a national holiday, as Hezbollah took full control along Israel's northern border. But that competed with images of Israeli soldiers depicted dead-center on the front page, smiling and proud, with the caption, "Mom, we're out of Lebanon," and with the announcement of the army chief of staff: "Today, May 24, 2000, we have brought our soldiers home."[133]

I was as surprised by the overnight evacuation as everybody else. It was a commitment that we had known he would keep, but not how or when. We barely ever polled on it and when we did, only a minority favored such a unilateral withdrawal without an agreement with Syria or Lebanon. Afterward, however, two thirds were immediately supportive, rising to over 80 percent in the coming months—meaning Barak no longer had to cite Begin's Sinai withdrawal to be assured of public support for an agreement. Support mixed with a great deal of ambivalence about the "humiliation" of the retreat, the perception of Israel not being strong, and wondering what lessons the Palestinians would take from the moment. Any political bounce for Barak was short-lived, but whenever we conducted focus groups in the future, somebody would say, "He got us out of Lebanon and for that he deserves our salute. He had the courage that no other leader had to take us out of Lebanon."[134]

TO CAMP DAVID

When I presented Barak with my note on his May "meltdown," he did not respond as a normal politician, seeking to regain his political footing or cautiously. Faced with growing trouble, Dennis Ross marveled at his "counterintuitive" response, almost propelled "toward the fast track." It will be harder for these parties to make parochial demands, Barak told Ross, if we were "on the brink of a historic breakthrough to peace." Thus, "we must move to an endgame in two weeks."[135]

But why should Arafat, who had seen Israel freeze its treaty commitments and the transfer of villages and quake at any mention of Jerusalem, want to go to a summit? The Palestinian leaders were deeply distrustful of Barak and pessimistic about any such grand meeting. Why should President Clinton risk a summit when so little had been achieved in the last six months?

As Barak headed down the fast track, he did the same with our polling on the Palestinian issue. Barak wanted an immediate survey, which he had to have by May 17. In an e-mail, Moshe indicated, "He has some very complex things he wants to know. This will take time to think on your part how to do it."[136] I was getting my first look at the very specific terms and complex issues that would be addressed in a final status negotiation.

Until May, our strongest framework for a Palestinian agreement reflected our established red lines and absolute commitments:

> No return to the 1967 borders.
> No foreign armies west of the Jordan.
> No right of return for Palestinian refugees.
> And no division of Jerusalem.[137]

I do not remember asking myself, "And why would the Palestinians accept this?"

The polling changed in character, specificity, and urgency from mid-May. Instead of testing the great majority of settlers remaining in Israel, we tested moving twenty thousand (mostly acceptable) and moving sixty thousand (not acceptable); instead of "most of the territory going to a Palestinian state," we looked at returning 80 percent of the land, a proposal that 47 percent opposed and 47 percent favored. There was still a near 55 percent majority for a Palestinian agreement in principle, but now we tested a much more robust agreement as Barak's best take on the final terms: a Palestinian state with the capital at Abu Dis, with 90 percent of the territory returned, demilitarized, fifty thousand settlers forced to move, and some arrangement with Palestinian neighborhoods in Jerusalem governed by a Palestinian municipal authority. Importantly, the agreement now said, "the conflict is declared over." The Jewish public split evenly on this agreement, which we thought was surprisingly positive.[138] We were fairly confident that a majority was moving toward accepting a full agreement, though again I did not ask myself, "And why would the Palestinians accept this?"

Jerusalem, I presumed, was a different matter. Beginning in May, people were speaking with growing anxiety about Jerusalem, and by June I wrote, "There is growing evidence of a public determination not to tamper with Jerusalem." Two thirds of the Jewish citizenry of Israel said it was unacceptable to allow a Palestinian capital in East Jerusalem.[139] It was hard to underestimate the emotional response to Jerusalem in the focus groups, the immediacy of three thousand years of history, and the worry that the one shared element of Judaism may be put at risk. In just raising the subject, you were tampering with things that were somehow not permitted.

"King David said, 'If I forget thee, O Jerusalem, let my right hand forget her cunning,'" one participant lamented, but "that message doesn't mean anything to Barak." One of the more secular observed that Jerusalem was "the only frame I have left for Judaism [and] we've had it for 3,000 years."

They spoke of Jerusalem as the "Jewish soul." Trying to divide it would violently divide the society. "Once you cut that soul," a Likud man observed, "it will bring about war amongst our own people."[140]

They continually drew on metaphors in which separation meant no existence: "It's like tearing the head off your body"; "It's like taking away your beloved child that you've nurtured and nursed"; "it's like robbing a person's amulet. You can't live without your amulet." The Shas men concluded categorically, "Jerusalem cannot be divided"; "Nobody will ever dare to divide Jerusalem."[141]

In an unexceptional observation, I wrote, "The inclusion of East Jerusalem in the final status agreement is a dead end."[142]

On July 6, 2000, the White House announced that Chairman Arafat and Prime Minister Barak would join with the president on July 10 for a summit meeting at Camp David to address the great issues, noting that while action on the talks had its perils, "so too does inaction."[143] Barak had already decided in mid-May that he had to go to the endgame. His goal was to hold all his cards until the summit, avoid spending any further capital, implement past agreements, and keep his government from crashing before July 10. It was not hard to convince the president that there was an opportunity there that might soon be gone. With the Democratic and Republican conventions convening in August, the window was small. Arafat thought he had no choice and accepted the invitation, as Ross describes it, "with a profound sense of gloom and suspicion."[144]

Everything Barak had done and endured since his election victory in May 1999 had been directed at getting him into a room with the president and the Palestinians with a mandate to settle their conflict.

To get into that room, Barak had to endure one final act of ignominy for his government that placed him in the Hall of Fame of the political daring. He had to cave in to Shas one more time on their education money, leading the left-wing Meretz Party to resign. But then, when Barak accepted the invitation to Camp David, Shas and two other right-wing parties opposed to the talks resigned in turn, leaving Barak with only forty-two seats in the 120-seat Knesset—and no government. The leader of the Likud opposition called for a vote of no-confidence because of Barak's "capitulation" to Arafat, forcing Barak to return from Egypt to confront his opponents in the Knesset. After a tumultuous four-and-a-half-hour debate, Barak lost a plurality of the Knesset votes but survived because the abstention of the Arab parties left the opposition short of a majority.[145]

Without a government, Barak turned to his Jewish and Zionist legacy for his legitimacy. In his departing speech to the Knesset, he first reminded the country of the leadership that braved political and parochial opposition to create a secure Israel: David Ben-Gurion when he "established the state in spite of the fierce internal opposition"; Menachem Begin when he "broke through the circle of enmity surrounding Israel and made peace, despite the strong opposition of the right wing"; and the Rabin government "when it paved the way towards [reconciliation with] our Palestinian neighbors, in spite of the bloody incitement in the streets."

And then in closing his remarks to the Knesset, he called upon the Talmud, "the prayer of peace of the Jewish people since time immemorial: 'Bestow peace, goodness and blessing, life, favor, kindness and mercy upon us and upon all Israel, Your people.'" He reminded the assembled how the prayer ends, "Blessed art Thou, Almighty God, who blesses His people Israel with peace."[146]

So, Barak got on his plane to Washington with no government and no prospect of forming one. The headlines that morning read: in *Yedioth Ahronoth*, "To the Summit—Alone"; in *Ma'ariv*, "To Camp David—Without a Government"; in *Haaretz*, "Barak to Summit Despite Losing Majority in Knesset." Though the prime minister was departing to meet with the leader of the free world and Israel's closest ally, a plurality of Knesset members voted to formally censure him. His foreign minister refused to go to Camp David and campaigned in the settlements against the negotiation; 200,000 protesters would soon assemble in Rabin Square to stop the peace process. Barak's job approval rating fell to just 25 percent. Quite a send-off. At least on arrival, he had the comfort of my memo, "The public has completely lost confidence in the current government on all fronts."[147]

Veteran journalist Nahum Barnea described Barak as a "crazed alpinist," courageous and foolhardy.[148] I am sure landing by dark of night in Beirut and killing the terrorists responsible for the Munich massacre demanded uncommon courage and fearlessness, but in my world, this seemed like fairly brave stuff.

Only slightly less remarkable than Barak's fearlessness was the wisdom of the Israeli citizenry, which understood this could be one of those fateful moments for their nation and was in the process of unlocking its thinking about the issues before the country. Barak's sinking political fortune was great sport but not the issues he was putting on the agenda. In the world I am used to, when a political leader loses standing and legitimacy, everything he touches turns to coal. But Israeli voters do not allow themselves that luxury. In the same memo that I wrote about the public's total loss of confidence in him, I noted that a different dynamic was at work on the issues surrounding the peace: "As some issues are debated, they gain acceptability with the Jewish public." Abu Dis—the village that nearly brought down the government two months earlier—was no longer seen as part of Jerusalem and was readily accepted as a Palestinian capital. A majority now agreed to giving 80 percent of the territories, and a near majority supported an agreement granting 90 percent of the territories to the Palestinians and displacing fifty thousand settlers—all up over the course of one month. On the eve of the summit, I underscored for Barak that "opinions are dynamic and we are witnessing changes as the debate progresses."[149]

THE PRESSURE COOKER

Barak and Arafat made no remarks and paused only for photographs as they walked arm-in-arm into Laurel Lodge at Camp David, the setting where Begin and Sadat agreed to create an enduring peace between Israel and Egypt. This time Barak worked out of Dogwood Cottage, Sadat's home at Camp David, while Arafat took Birch Cottage, Begin's earlier home in the woods. The goal, as the president said on departing for the talks, was to achieve "principled compromise" on the outstanding issues dividing these people, including Jerusalem.

They took no questions because of the blackout. Fearing that leaks would jeopardize the ability to address sensitive issues, the parties banned cell phones and allowed only limited access to landline telephones. Neither party was allowed to bring press spokespeople into the camp.

Barak, as it turned out, had his own ideas on how he would organize his activities and how he would work with his citizenry at home. He treated his communications and research as support operations, just as if he were on a military mission. He wanted daily polls so that he could test his progress in building support for specific terms and for a full agreement, and to test new ideas and formulas as they emerged in his thinking or the negotiations. These polls were for his eyes only—not for other members of the negotiating team and not for the Americans, who had Camp David fully wired. The IDF had installed a secure phone line to IDF central command based in Tel Aviv, on which Barak was able to have a nightly call with his team in Israel. He had also created a satellite base in an officer's fire school in Emmitsburg, Maryland, just five minutes from Camp David where Eldad Yaniv, political advisor to Barak, and two Israeli soldiers slept and worked. Eldad talked almost continuously with Barak at his cabin and with Tal in Tel Aviv, and he sent secure envelopes via an army secretary to Barak. All our polls were faxed to Eldad, who had them delivered to Barak. The time difference with Israel worked for us, allowing us to finish calling a poll at 9 P.M. Israel time and to have the processed results in Barak's hands by midnight in Camp David, when, as we knew, Barak did his most important work.

Moshe and Tal were the center of the operation in Israel. Their mission was to send up "trial balloons" every day on the emerging issues and shape of a total agreement, as Barak saw it. This was carefully worked through with

Barak and then worked with journalists, sometimes drawing on academics and experts who were asked to go public and speak about possible options, on Jerusalem, for example. Barak was trying to create a parallel public consideration of the new frontiers of thinking about how to achieve peace with the Palestinians. If we were successful, any peace agreement would also face a brutal test in either a referendum or new elections.

At the launch of the Camp David talks, I flew to Israel so that I could fully understand the issues we were testing with the public and also so I could listen and watch people in focus groups think about the choices facing Israel. These were complicated issues but people understood them, whether we interviewed them by phone or had a more extended conversation in focus groups. The details and nuances mattered here for the ages.

I needed to speak with Ehud directly, so my colleagues decided to sneak me into the IDF base in the middle of Tel Aviv, probably the most heavily secured military facility in Israel. We rejected the idea of hiding me in the trunk of one of the authorized cars and decided instead to be more direct. I would simply sit, mute and uninteresting, as my colleague showed his papers from the driver's window. We were waved through and walked quickly to an office where a special phone was installed to allow secure communication to Camp David. I drew on all my Hebrew vocabulary, which at that point included *"shalom"* (hello, goodbye), *"to da"* (thank you), *"to da roba"* (thank you very much), and all the numbers that I heard people repeat in their ratings of ads in focus groups, *"ehad l'chamesh"* [1 to 5], not to mention *"tekua, tekua, tekua."* We were in a room guarded by a young female soldier, who, like many of the women draftees, was practiced in wearing her uniform so tight that movement was not possible. I was worried that when Ehud called, people would hear my English, but unexpectedly, Tal went off with our guard, not to be seen again that night.

The next day, the secure phone was moved to an apartment of one of my Israeli colleagues in Tel Aviv, so that we could avoid sneaking into the base and spare Tal his responsibility.

It occurred to me that these elaborate arrangements were made to keep the Americans and my former boss from intercepting and knowing Barak's bottom line. For President Clinton and the United States, getting an Israeli-Palestinian peace was *an* issue, but for Barak and Israel, this was *the* issue and it never occurred to me to compromise the mission.

Barak brought his own philosophy and game plan to Camp David, which the Americans did not like very much. From Denis Ross's account we know that Barak thought they should do nothing for two days, struggle for two more, and only then after five days, set out ideas for an agreement. Barak believed he should develop a pressure cooker, with risk of explosion and failure, leading both sides to set out their bottom lines. He thought every Israeli concession before that point would only lead the talks to move closer to the Palestinian position, without any real new offers from the Palestinians.[150] At Day Five of the talks, Barak was still not giving his negotiating team any room because he thought the pressure was not great enough on the Palestinians, to the great anger of the president.

The Palestinians were contributing to the pressure cooker because, unknown to us at the time, they were trying to offer as little as possible. Arafat did not trust Barak and felt cornered by Barak's close relationship with President Clinton. His negotiators were divided on how to approach the talks, though united on their fear of a deal that would be rejected on the Palestinian street. Thus, at Day Five, they, too, were failing to negotiate, leaving the president to walk out of one meeting in anger.

JERUSALEM

When I was in New Haven for the July 4th weekend with my family and writing my pre–Camp David note for Ehud, Moshe called and said, "And by the way, Ehud wants to check this." For the first time, he wanted to ask about East Jerusalem, the Palestinian neighborhoods outside the Old City walls but very much in the heart of Jerusalem. He wanted to approach it as a kind of last resort: Could you "support East Jerusalem being part of a Palestinian state if it was the only way to achieve a final peace agreement" and avoid a descent into violence, a second intifada—or would you rather cut off your hand than ever divide Jerusalem?[151] Only a third of the Jewish public would entertain the idea when we got the results back, but I knew that if I could see him over the phone Moshe was shaking his head: "I don't know where he's going here." We were entering the world of never-never land. Wasn't this a real red line? Barak was holding on by a thread politically and about to entertain the impermissible.

By Day Five of the negotiations at Camp David, we had incorporated into our description of the total agreement the following clause: "Palestinian neighborhoods in East Jerusalem become part of the Palestinian capital, which they call, Al Quods." There were reassurances about Israel maintaining sovereignty over Jerusalem, but the red line had been crossed. When I got the results, I did not know which was the bigger shock—Barak actually saying yes on dividing Jerusalem or the fact that half the Jewish public said they would nonetheless vote yes in a referendum.[152]

Without pausing to take in that finding, I drafted, with careful guidance, by the end of Day Six, a new last question. One final thing the callers asked:

"Imagine that there was one last proposal with respect to the Old City to achieve an agreement: *Christian and Muslim areas would come under Palestinian sovereignty. The Armenian and Jewish areas, including the Western Wall, would come under Israeli sovereignty.* If that were the last thing to achieve a full final status agreement, would you accept it or not accept it?" "Autonomy" had become "sovereignty" and the Old City walls had been breached, with the support of about 45 percent of the Jewish public.[153]

Barak was developing and embellishing a new concept: by giving up the "highly concentrated Palestinian neighborhoods" and by annexing the large suburban Jewish settlements in the West Bank, he was expanding the borders of Jerusalem and creating a Greater Jerusalem with a deeper Jewish character and recognized by the world as the capital of Israel. The concept became more robust through each survey and by Day Eight at Camp David it was fully incorporated into the overall agreement that we were testing with the public. He had no doubt convinced himself that his plans strengthened rather than divided Jerusalem—an argument, amazingly, the public would soon come to accept.

I was in Israel when we rushed across that red line, and the whole Barak team was both astonished and unsettled, though there was little time to take stock. It was not just that we had crossed into unknown political territory; it was that we were personally unsettled about the choice. Our mantra, "no division of Jerusalem," allowed us like the rest of Israel to avoid examining the issue, but now we were without guidance, except our faith. Eldad could not believe we were only now looking at the issue; Tal said keep moving; Moshe was opposed; and I was troubled. With the imagery of Jerusalem reunited after the 1967 war, I was viscerally opposed to dividing Jerusalem, but had I really thought this through? I was more troubled by the breaking of the absolute pledge, a precondition to winning public trust and winning office, yet if the voters were willing to reopen the issue, who was I to be so literal? Sometimes you just have to trust the commander.

On Day Six at Camp David, Barak's negotiating team offered the first real new moves on Jerusalem, including sovereignty on some outer villages and some special arrangements on the inner ones, as well as for the Muslim and Christian quarters of the Old City. There was some dispute about whether they were operating with a mandate from Barak, but given our research, I found it hard to believe they were on a rogue mission. Later that day Barak reacted in "apocalyptic terms," according to Ross, and sent a long letter to President Clinton, clearly angry and dark, noting disagreements in his own delegation over this unauthorized offer, without any real negotiation, "without the Palestinians moving one inch." He concluded, "I do not intend to allow the Israeli state to fall apart physically or morally."

Ross could not decide whether Barak was in "personal crisis" or a "manipulation" to pressure the president to pressure Arafat.[154] I had no firsthand knowledge, but I favored the latter, which momentarily seemed to have the desired effect: Clinton pushed Arafat for some signs of movement and likely over-interpreted Arafat's willingness to move on some territorial questions. That bogged down the next day's talks as the Israelis met for thirteen hours while everyone else grew frustrated. At midnight, the president and Barak had an unpleasant meeting where Clinton expressed his frustration.

On Day Eight, the summit was on the verge of failure. In a last resort, Ross proposed a Jerusalem compromise that neither side responded to. The Palestinians were fractious and Arafat mute. Suddenly, Barak asked to see the president and finally made a real offer, what the president described as Barak's bottom lines, which he wanted the president to present as his own. Barak proposed 91 percent of the territory for the Palestinians and a swap of some land from Israel; a security arrangement; and on Jerusalem, Palestinian sovereignty over the neighborhoods in East Jerusalem and the Muslim and Christian quarters. The Americans concluded that Barak wanted a deal and the fear of failure had moved him to make an offer. I believe Barak had been waiting for this moment, his pressure cooker. I knew that he was indicating through our back channel to Emmitsburg and Tel Aviv that an agreement was possible.

The president now had to bring Arafat to conclude "this is a historic moment" for him. They met that night for a solemn meeting but the next day, Day Nine, the answer came back: No. This answer was explosive, with the president scheduled to leave that day for the G-8 meetings in Okinawa. Barak roared that Arafat was never serious; Arafat was off alone and emotional, and when pressed by U.S. mediators, responded by asking whether they wanted to "go to his funeral."

But neither side was ready to be blamed for a breakdown, and I believe Barak was determined to achieve an agreement, if there was any possibility. The two sides agreed to hold informal discussions on the status of the Temple Mount, or the Haram-esh-Sharif, as it is called by the Palestinians, but they could not even agree on the ground rules. They were on hold until the president returned.

On Day Nine the described agreement in our survey included a range of difficult things, including forty thousand settlers displaced, exchange of land in the Negev, but also for the first time proposed Palestinian "sovereignty over the Temple Mount."[155] We were now at the holiest of holies, and at that point had the support of about 40 percent of Barak's Jewish subjects. Who knew where Barak and the public would end up on this final point of contention?

But Barak now realized he had nobody on the other side who could say yes to his vision of settling the Israeli-Palestinian conflict. Ross reported that Barak was "extremely morose" at dinner and stopped whatever informal discussions were taking place: "He was shutting down."[156] Ross and others said they had never seen Barak "so depressed," which was almost certainly real, not manipulation. His mission's fate was finally determined when Arafat could not take the risk to make history. Every political choice and compromise, every contortion of his government, every political low was done to get him there with those actors for that decision. Now it appeared to be over.

It was not clear how far Barak was willing to go to achieve an agreement. Internationalization of the Temple Mount was an acceptable concept for the Israelis, we had found earlier, but Barak now understood that what the Palestinians wanted was sovereignty, which two thirds of the Israeli public opposed.[157] Nonetheless, he did test a full agreement during this interlude in the talks, including the Palestinian neighborhoods of East Jerusalem being incorporated in the Palestine capital of Al Quods, and with the Palestinians having *sovereignty* over the Muslim and Christian quarters *and the Temple Mount*. At that point a stunning 45 percent of the Jewish public supported such an agreement, which concluded with this brief sentence: "The Israeli-Palestinian conflict is over." I was absolutely sure Barak believed that he could win a Jewish majority for such a historic and final agreement.

Up until that point, Barak had not asked that I call President Clinton. Unlike in the Syrian agreement, he had not wanted the Americans to know what he was considering and what his real bottom lines were. But now he was insistent that I reach the president to share the results, I suspect because they were real bottom lines and a possible agreement. I tried to reach the president through the White House switchboard, which had to get the message to him at the G-8 meetings. I did not hear back for a day, but I did hear from Eldad four times because Barak was pressing him to find out whether I had reached President Clinton. When the president called, I heard "okay," "okay," "okay," businesslike, as he processed each result. We were no longer lingering over Barak's fascinating political troubles, but on this possible total agreement.

When President Clinton returned, there were intensive efforts to find a formula for an agreement but Arafat was not prepared to do it. The answer was still no. Over those fourteen days, the president concluded that historic things were put on the table, but Arafat had offered no substantive ideas. When Clinton and Barak met at 3:45 in the morning Barak was "very somber" according to Ross, and believed he would be forced to go to a national unity government, an end to negotiations and peacemaking, accompanied by a quick deterioration into violence.[158]

EDUCATING AND MOVING A NATION

The American team concluded that "something profound has happened at Camp David": "taboos" on the core issues of Jerusalem, borders, and refugees had been broken. Above all, Jerusalem, Ross wrote, was no longer a "slogan" for both sides, but "demystified." Even those who were more critical of Barak's role there grant him the insight that the days of "partial moves [are] over, and the parties [have] to move toward a comprehensive and final settlement."[159]

What was less appreciated was how much Ehud Barak moved, not just the negotiating process, but the whole country of Israel to a new understanding of how to achieve a final peace with its Palestinian neighbors. No such process happened on the Palestinian side, which helps explain the tragic result, not yet fully told.

The Barak team was negotiating inside, but outside it was trying to get the public to lower the predictable barriers and weigh the issues in all their seriousness and rethink Israel's choices. The "leaks" formed a parallel narrative. They began harmlessly on the third day with the story that Barak was reading a Ben-Gurion biography, setting off stories about the scale of Barak's thinking. On the same day, respected journalists wrote about the fantasy of the old maps, as Barak had all but accepted new parameters, including Israel giving up 95 percent of the land occupied in 1967, a territorial swap for the remainder and the return of refugees through family reunification. On Day Six the press noted that the new experts who were summoned to Camp David were directed to a document that laid out three big alternatives for Jerusalem, including the idea of a divided but greater Jerusalem. With an aspiration for a final agreement still alive, one journalist wrote that Barak thought "the willingness of the Palestinians to declare an end to the conflict would be an unparalleled landmark in history."[160]

After a month of public discussion of the choices, starting in late June, a near majority supported giving 90 percent of the territories to the Palestinians, up 10 points. A majority supported uprooting sixty thousand settlers, who would have to move or live under Palestinian sovereignty, up 13 points. A sizable majority supported thirty thousand Palestinian refugees returning for family reunification, up 15 points during the process.

At the end of Camp David, 45 percent of the Jewish population accepted a complete division of Jerusalem, with Palestinians having sovereignty over the Temple Mount; a majority supported it with the holiest sites internationalized. The idea of the Palestinian neighborhoods becoming part of a capital of Palestine and creating a Greater Jerusalem grew from a near majority idea when first raised during the talks to a large majority by the end.[161]

When the Israeli journalist Raviv Drucker looked at this process, he saw Barak, the "poll addict," whose obsession ended up setting his agenda and leading to flawed decision making. But Barak, from the weakest possible political position, was trying to move the country to a place it had never gone, facing popular judgment by referendum. The polling allowed him to monitor his progress in engaging and moving people on the key issues and how they might respond to things no one had yet imagined. He rarely opted for the popular over the less popular course; a "bad" result was more likely to spur him to a better formulation. And even at the low point in the negotiations, when he seemed depressed before the prospect of failure, he was testing an even bolder plan.

When we conducted focus groups among young Likud supporters near the end of the Camp David talks, most of the participants in the groups, presented with the full agreement, thought Barak should sign it. But that count was less important than the new thinking around Jerusalem, previously the flashpoint for emotions and the fear of Israel being torn asunder. Participants asked, So why would we want to maintain control of the Arab areas? "Part of Jerusalem belongs to the Palestinians—that's the big deal?" And another noted, "it's not like they're giving up Jewish parts." One person concluded as if it was all self-evident, "Jerusalem will be divided."[162]

Was this the same country that was in an emotional breakdown a month earlier at the thought of Jerusalem being severed from the body of Israel?

When George Tenet, head of the CIA, arrived during the G-8 pause in the negotiations, he was briefed on the state of the talks and immediately "wondered whether Barak could deliver what he had accepted, and asked incredulously," according to Ross, " 'Why hasn't Arafat accepted this?' " Other respected members of the Israeli delegation felt they were lucky Arafat said no because "we cannot do everything that was raised here."[163]

They were reflecting the conventional wisdom about where Israelis stood on the historic issues separating the Jewish state and the Palestinians, but we knew that Barak had taken people to a new place, from which it would not be easy to return to the old myths.

Why did Arafat say, "No, No, No, and No" again? There are the obvious and plausible reasons, including his distrust of Barak and fear of being cornered by Barak and Clinton. Arafat did not share Barak's post-Oslo vision that the time for partial agreements had passed. Given the rising discontent in the territories, small gains might just be fine, thank you. Nonetheless, he still might have seen, as Clinton argued, that a historic moment was upon him and he could make a decision for the ages.

I think Arafat was frozen because he knew that he had not prepared the

Palestinian public for such a moment. An agreement would have brought a violent upheaval, perhaps at the risk to his life. Unlike Barak, he had not created a parallel process of public education at Camp David, just as he had not created such a process since the Oslo Accords. His Palestinian subjects had accepted a number of important compromises, including recognition of Israel and renouncing terrorism, but a two-state solution and resolution of Jerusalem required much more.

When we eventually did research among the Palestinians of the West Bank and Gaza at the end of the year, it became apparent how well Arafat may have read his own people. When presented with the proposed full Camp David agreement, three quarters of the Palestinian public rejected it, half adamantly. They viewed it not as a historic compromise, but as "surrender by the Palestinians." Large majorities opposed the idea of a demilitarized state, internationalizing the holy sites, giving Jerusalem neighborhoods to Israel, and Israel having a recognized capital in Jerusalem. The very idea of "ending the conflict" was a betrayal that spurred them to a yet greater conflict.[164]

NIGHTMARE

With the failed talks at Camp David, the country and the world assumed that Barak as prime minister would have to form a unity government with Likud, thus closing that chapter of failed peacemaking. In our surveys, 60 percent of the Jewish public wanted exactly that, and a like number, no return to government with Shas. Barak forced the country to face the implications of the peace path, but now the public said enough: it overwhelmingly wanted the peace process pushed to a far back burner and "a domestic social and economic agenda" pushed to the front.[165]

The negotiations to form a new government would go on for four painful months, but worse was the nightmare of violence and continued negotiations that would take the country to new levels of despair. Despite the failed talks at Camp David, Barak never really stopped pursuing negotiations with the Palestinians. Despite the humiliation of it, for him, Israel still faced the looming threat of terrorists armed with nuclear weapons and the urgent need to achieve an Israeli-Palestinian peace. With Sharon insisting in coalition negotiations that Barak repudiate the lines drawn at Camp David, he faced a Hobson's choice.[166]

Sharon made it doubly difficult. Accompanied by a cadre of Likud MKs and a large security and police escort, Sharon asserted the right of Jews "to visit every place in the Land of Israel," a clear provocation at a time of great tension. It set off a stone-throwing clash that spread quickly to East Jerusalem and then grew to days of pitched battles, with stones and guns across the

West Bank and Gaza. In the first few days, fifty Palestinians were killed and five hundred injured as well as a handful of Israeli soldiers, leaving the "hopes for peace in the Middle East," one reporter wrote, "in bloody shambles." Each stage in this escalating battle was enflamed by tragic scenes played over and over again on television screens across Israel, the territories, and the world. A twelve-year-old boy was killed in a crossfire of Israeli soldiers in Gaza as his father pleaded for his life and tried to protect him; the Palestinians' ransacked Joseph's Tomb in Nablus; two Israeli soldiers retained in a Ramallah police station were beaten to death by a mob in the station and their bodies dragged through the streets hitched to a car. The peace in Israel was shattered when Israeli police fired on and kill thirteen Israeli Arab demonstrators—Israeli citizens—who joined the protest against Sharon's invasion of the Temple Mount and were now profoundly alienated from Israeli society. With the Palestinian death toll at three hundred by the end of the year, the conflict was spoken of as the "Second Intifada" or the "al-Aqsa intifada"; more accurately, "a limited Palestinian-Israeli war."[167]

Barak escalated the military response and issues, giving ultimatums to Arafat—end the fighting or the peace process will be declared dead—yet he extended the deadline repeatedly lest the process perish in the flames of the Second Intifada. The country had lived a lifetime with terrorism and hostage crises and formally would not "negotiate under fire," yet Barak was doing just that. Ross concluded that Arafat was using the Intifada to enhance his standing and bargaining position. Indeed, promises of a new openness on peace terms got him a White House meeting.[168]

Barak faced another fateful deadline, this time unmovable: November 28, with a majority of the Knesset ready to vote the end of his tenure. On Friday morning before that vote, Barak called Moshe, Tal, and Eldad to come to his house Friday evening. "I know it is Friday," Barak said on the phone, the beginning of the Jewish Sabbath, "but I'm going to take a serious decision." And that evening he told his advisors "I'm going to election." They were incredulous: "You can't win; you are not going to make it; you are going to lose the election," they told him in unison. But Barak insisted that he could win.

On the drive back from Jerusalem to Tel Aviv, Tal called me in Washington. "This is a very serious moment. You have to arrange a call first thing in the morning with James, Bob, and yourself to speak with Ehud."

"They will say the same thing," I said, but Tal responded, No, Barak has to hear it from all of you.

So Saturday morning the Israeli advisors drove back to Jerusalem for a conference call with Barak and Nava, Ehud's wife, and the political advisors. James, Bob, and I were standing around the speakerphone in my office. We all said hello, and Barak belted out, "Hello," stretching out the "o." He quickly moved to the topic, "Look, I am in a very bad political situation and there is no alternative to just call for election and let's hope that Ariel Sharon will be the leader of the Likud and not Bibi. I'm not sure that I can win this election."

And all three of us in turn shouted into the speakerphone to be heard in Jerusalem, "You are going to lose the election." And Barak came back to me, "Is there any chance to win the election?" and I told him, "Ten percent, that's all."

On November 28, 2000, Barak announced there would be early elections for prime minister. He accepted Tal's advice not to call simultaneous elections for the Knesset, which would surely produce a swing to the right-wing parties. Appearing in the Knesset during a riotous debate, Barak said, "You want elections? I'm prepared." That surprised and quieted the members. And then in typical Barak style, he challenged them to battle: "I've won every election I've ever run in to date."[169]

Barak's advisors were quieted, too, depressed by the prospect of a campaign in that environment. They would never quite understand his decision, but accepted his bravado in the Knesset that he believed he could win. I now think Barak concluded that elections were the only way to continue the negotiating process, now assured a sixty days' window to the end of Clinton's term. He preferred that tiny chance at a peace agreement to forming a government with Sharon that would survive to do what he considered ordinary things. When I later shared this conclusion with Eldad, he exclaimed, "My God. Then he's a hero."

In his speech to the nation ten days later setting the formal date for the election, he posed a question to himself: "What is your most urgent priority?" And he answered consistent with his mission: "In a world starring extremist terrorists like Bin Laden or Muslim fundamentalists, which extremist regimes hold nuclear options in their hands," I must press ahead to a political solution for these two nations, even in the face of violence. Barak said for the first time that he had made a mistake to delay his social and civic agenda for the sake of the Palestinian track, but his priorities remained unchanged.[170]

Not surprisingly, we conducted "big research," as it was referred to in the campaign, to see if there was any path to winning the election. There was not. The first polls showed us losing to Sharon by almost 20 points, and before the end of December, by 25 points, where it would stay. No messages were convincing and no amount of information produced any shift to Barak at the end of a survey. People were set in concrete.

People were also deeply fearful of the violence, which was immediate and personal and full of meaning. They saw Barak as indecisive, zigzagging, a puppet of the international community, which was hostile to Israel. He negotiated while Israelis died, which I confess offended me, too, with peace so remote. Voters thought Barak could not unite the political class or the people around him. A Sephardic man advised the politicians, "and if you can't do it then dismiss yourself from the position or get a grip and find someone that can."[171]

In some ways, the alienation of Israeli Arabs—who gave Barak 95 percent of their vote a year and a half earlier—was the most troubling. Despite their hate for Sharon, they seemed determined not to vote as an enduring statement on the government violence. When the "police will kill you," they said in focus groups, you become "enemies of the state, not citizens." Barak was only slightly more popular in the Arab community than Arafat in the Jewish.[172]

The results were not a surprise, but Moshe, Tal, and I drove up to Jerusalem to share them with Barak, sometime after midnight. We would make the case to Ehud that he withdraw as a candidate to preserve his reputation and future political options: "The country will come to see you as 'a hero' for sacrificing your career for the chance of peace." We were going to propose that the prime minister withdraw as a candidate and support Shimon Peres as the Labor nominee. Peres had been frantically maneuvering to challenge Barak. We assembled in Barak's study around his desk. We were joined by Nava and Doron, who had not been part of the discussion until that point. Moshe sat at the desk across from Barak and made the case, convincingly. Barak listened but waved his hand, dismissing the idea without a second's consideration. He had his own plans.

On December 22, President Clinton, not yet ready to give up, reassembled the negotiators from both sides in the Oval Office to hear him read what were described as the president's "ideas" for a final settlement. Barak encouraged such a moment, and Arafat implied he was open to it. The U.S. plan went a few steps beyond what was discussed on Day Twelve at Camp David, and included various options for separate sovereignty over the Haram, and the Western Wall and Holy of Holies. Finally, "The agreement clearly mark[s] the end of conflict and its implementation put[s] an end to all claims."

These "Clinton's ideas" were not for negotiation. They had to be accepted, yes or no, by December 27 and all future negotiations would take place within those parameters.

We tested in our survey the impact of Barak saying yes or no to President Clinton's ideas for a settlement. When he said no in this simulated exercise, "Israel cannot accept this breach of our red lines," the public cheered and, amazingly, the frozen race thawed and Sharon's lead fell significantly. Though this kind of survey exercise always exaggerates the impact, it was capturing a besieged public desperate for its leader to stand up to the Americans and outside world.[173]

I met privately with Barak to share this stunning result, though it was awkward in every way possible. As an American, should I be undermining my president's initiative for peace? And who am I anyway to be advising on such an issue for Israel? Wasn't Barak elected to make peace and carry on the Rabin legacy? And most of all, I was just not convinced that the frozen race could really be unfrozen. Barak had come to meet at my room because Moshe thought this was important enough to be discussed away from the campaign. Barak listened, clearly got it, and left me with the impression that he would recommend that the Security Cabinet reject Clinton's ideas that night, the deadline for a decision. He said very clearly, "This is all beside the point because Arafat will not be able to say yes to Clinton."

That night, the Security Cabinet, with Barak's support, voted to accept the Clinton ideas with reservations, though within its parameters, creating a new starting point for any future negotiations.

And of course Arafat missed the deadline and ultimately said no.[174]

During the death march to the February 6 election, a most unlikely negotiation began in the Egyptian town of Taba, near Israeli Eilat on the Red Sea, one day after President Clinton's term came to an end. The Israeli and Palestinian teams were negotiating directly, no longer with U.S. assistance, to see if they could reach an agreement before the election. With the election pending, many in the government questioned the legitimacy of such negotiations and any agreement, which would hardly bind the new prime minister. With the continuing Palestinian violence, including car bombs in Netanya at the New Year, the Israeli public wanted nothing of it. They were angry that Israeli leaders continued to negotiate with the Palestinians while ordinary citizens perished.

The talks recessed and resumed from January 21–27, 2001, in the midst of new acts of violence, leaving the participants with an uncertain mandate from both the Israeli and Palestinian sides. In trying to judge the possible electoral impact of Taba, I asked Barak what the chance was of success, and he said, without hesitation, "Zero."

At one point during the talks, Yossi Beilin, the Labor MK who played a role in the Oslo Accords and who was a driving force in Taba, came to my hotel room to talk to me about the sad state of the election in the Arab areas. He had the unenviable job of trying to recoup our losses there. But then he turned to Taba and said quietly, which is his way, "I want you to convince

Ehud that ceding Palestinian sovereignty over the Temple Mount will not pose a political problem for him. The public will accept it." I presumed he was there because this must be one of the sticking points that was blocking progress in the talks. With Barak's "zero" in my head, I said, "I can't say that." In any case, I would leave it to Barak to decide how Israel protected the Holiest of the Holies.

Oh my God, it happened. Arthur Finkelstein, Netanyahu's guru, sat at the King David Hotel, with a view of the Temple Mount and golden dome, receiving cabinet members seeking his support on particular policies. At the Dan, I only got to look at the Mediterranean. Time to exit.

END

We met in the broadcast center like it was a real campaign, but we all knew it was make-believe. One evening during the end of the advertising period, Bob Shrum, Moshe Gaon, and I had a late meeting with Ehud to talk about scripts, which he kept rejecting. We were in a small room in the basement down the hall from the studio, when Bob said, "Why don't we forget all this crap and you say whatever you want." Barak warmed to the idea of creating a record for history, rather than trying to win over voters. He began to dictate the ad, though it sounded more like a plan. He even got a map that he spread out on the table to show the lines and borders that might have been created—and that might have saved thousands of lives and funerals—only to come back to the same issues and same lines.

Barak began speaking directly to camera. "I know that it is not popular to speak about concessions that we made for peace." But on this election eve, "I intend to put in front of you" the principles, without which "we cannot have an agreement with the Palestinians." He then laid out the contours of what was agreed to at Camp David and put the spotlight on the Old City. In his last election, his ads included the mayor of Jerusalem saying Barak would never divide Jerusalem, but now he, Barak, was talking about passing "the control of the Muslim and Christian quarters" to the Palestinians. And he presented his new vision of a Jerusalem that "will be bigger than ever with a clear Jewish majority for generations."

If we do not reach a peace, there will be "another difficult battle." And tragically, "after we bury ours and they bury their many more, we will return to the same table to discuss the same exact issues." Those who tell you otherwise are "not telling you the truth."

Barak finished his ad at the end of this campaign by asking "every father and mother in Israel, what price are you ready to pay—the price of painful concessions or the price of many thousands of our children losing their lives in the next war?" For Barak, the choice was clear: "I prefer the price of peace over the price of war."[175]

After the election, everyone was angry with Ehud. Just 38 percent of the voters chose Barak over Sharon, who garnered 62 percent for his part. Only 15 percent of Arabs turned out to vote, contributing to the lowest turnout in Israel's history.[176] Barak lost the chance of peace and to address the social gaps. While he had avenged Rabin's murder, his failure in office allowed Ariel Sharon, infamous for his role in the Lebanon war and the Second Intifada, to become Israel's leader.

Everyone was angry because Ehud did not listen and consult, cultivated few political allies, and staffed his office with inept, even disloyal personnel.

I was more than frustrated, but I also watched an entire people set aside taboos and consider first questions about Israel's future and, as Barak said, after many more lives are lost, the two peoples will come back to the same issues and solutions. While all parties will continue to posture, everyone really knows what the final settlement will look like, even where the line gets drawn in Jerusalem. Barak's legacy, oddly, is the silence that allows the Israelis and Palestinians, even Lebanon and Syria, to consider a peaceful resolution of their long-standing conflicts.

I had other reasons not to be angry, starting with Ehud's phone call to my father. But even without an embrace, he had shaken me out of my deep ambivalence about my faith, though not my discomfort with synagogues. Helping elect the prime minister of Israel is a big thing in my world and has allowed me to become much more comfortable in my Jewishness and develop an instinctive identification with Israel.

Barak also taught me some things about my own work as pollster, perhaps more than any of the other leaders. In my frustration with his failure to bring people into his orbit, I came to appreciate even more how much strong political leaders require a special bond with people to succeed. God, I wished Barak had some of those skills, yet what would be the price of cultivating such sensibilities? How many leaders with bare popular support and no government would go off and make breathtaking and unpopular concessions to make a historic peace?

For all his indifference to popular opinion, Barak trusted the public to take seriously the issues facing Israel and I watched in awe as people weighed subjects and solutions that previously had been forbidden. Before he went to Camp David, I wrote him that "opinions are dynamic," but not on the emotional issue of dividing Jerusalem, a line he pledged not to cross. He taught me to be very careful before telling any political leader with bold goals that the public will not follow.

7

GONZALO "GONI" SÁNCHEZ DE LOZADA

EBRUARY 2003. ANTIGOVERNMENT riots have broken out in the streets of La Paz, Bolivia. Rioters break down the doors of a government ministry building and begin ransacking it. Desks, chairs, and files are stacked in the plaza and put to the torch. An effigy of the nation's president is burned.

Well-armed police move into the area, firing tear gas to disperse the crowds. Then gunshots ring out, followed by more. The rioters flee the plaza, running for cover. Left behind is a small boy apparently huddling against a pillar for protection. But he isn't huddling. He's lying on his side, red blood pooling around his feet.

"Is there someone injured there?" a demonstrator calls back. People begin shouting—"Ambulance," "Ambulance."

Then the grim verdict: "He's dead. Don't pick him up, he's dead."

A voice is heard, "Nearly eighty people have been killed in clashes between Bolivian troops and mostly poor, indigenous protesters." Fires engulf the government offices, as organizers chant, "Gringo asshole step down."

Far above the tumult, the president sits in a private airplane, quiet, seemingly alone.

And the voice again: "Following weeks of deadly protests, there are reports that Gonzalo Sánchez de Lozada, known as Goni, has resigned and has fled to the United States earlier today."

* * *

The scenes are from *Our Brand Is Crisis*, Rachel Boynton's documentary about the presidential campaign of Sánchez de Lozada and his eventual flight into exile.[1] Named "The Best Feature Documentary" of 2005 by the International Documentary Association, it was hailed by critics as "riveting" and "without peer." But the film isn't so much about Sánchez de Lozada as it is about his team of American consultants, people whom Boynton describes as sincere, even idealistic professionals, symbols for America and American assumptions, seeking to spread democracy.

For anyone unfamiliar with Bolivia and its politics, the film creates a uniform impression. Sánchez de Lozada is little more than a lug. While there is passing mention of his social agenda and political history, mostly he seems to be a multimillionaire businessman raised in America, speaking a heavily accented Spanish. "Clueless," "arrogant and aloof," and "little in common with his countrymen" are common remarks from film reviewers.

Bolivia was about to be engulfed by a populist violence and anger about America and multinational corporations, yet this pro-American leader, "the blinkered Goni," wrote one reviewer, "doesn't have the know-how to fix a stopped toilet, much less a country on the verge of economic collapse."[2]

To offset his failings as a candidate, Goni hires a team of American professionals who bring in their full array of American campaign weapons, from polls and focus groups to television advertisements. Reviewers seemed surprised that the American consultants actually seem to believe in their candidate and that his election would be good for the poor in Bolivia. But Boynton dispels that innocence. Soon it becomes obvious that the consultants only love the game and are determined to win at any cost. They "brand the crisis" for Goni, showing little interest in the real crisis.

Their methods are good enough to get Goni elected in a close contest, but "in selling a pro-globalization, pro-American candidate," they crash against the popular forces in Bolivia that are opposed to Goni's market reforms. The reviewers and the movie romanticize the enormously popular movement leader who leads the blockades and marches, who carries the country with him and topples the new president to become president himself. "Now," the *Guardian* reviewer observed, "that would have been a campaign worth running."[3]

In the end, the reviews conclude that the liberal impulse played out in Bolivia is no less arrogant than the neoconservative one playing out in Iraq.[4]

The documentary's first screening in the Washington, D.C., area was at the Silverdocs film festival in the close-in suburb of Silver Spring. It was held in the restored AFI Silver Theater, just a few blocks from my old high school, Montgomery Blair, and the theater of choice in my early driving and dating years. I was never conscious that it was 1930s Deco, but it is now much noticed and admired. The theater was packed with a Beltway crowd, leavened with a healthy number of loyal friends and employees who remained afterward for the intense commentary of the director, journalists, and our own Jeremy Rosner, vice president of the company and involved in campaigns around the world. As they left the theater there were no stones thrown, no protest signs. Mostly people left more intrigued than hostile.

I valued the reaction of one of my closest friends, Fabiana Jorge, who advises global companies. She found the movie "disturbing." It seemed all about "fame" and winning with whatever works. "There's a total disconnect between campaigning and governing, like it doesn't even matter what they would do in government." She added, "I know this is all in what the director chooses to show, but the Americans show no real interest in the country, the people. You don't see where anybody cares about the people."

How did it all go so wrong?

DAY TRIP TO BOLIVIA

It was Mark Feierstein's fault. For him, advising and helping someone like Gonzalo Sánchez de Lozada was the reason he came to work for our firm. At the beginning of 2001, while I was in London working for Labour's reelection, Mark wrote me an e-mail in his characteristic monotonic understatement. "I think this is something worth pursuing." He described Goni as "an effective, modern, centrist leader and very pro-American." Will you take a meeting?

Later, I got e-mails asking whether I would consider a one-day trip to Bolivia to meet with Goni? A one-day trip to Bolivia? This is where Butch Cassidy and the Sundance Kid fled to carry on robbing mining payrolls and where one third of the population lives twelve thousand feet above sea level. Planes take off from La Paz without refueling for fear they will be too heavy to lift off in the thin Andean air. Mark stepped up his lobbying: "I don't want to raise expectations—I'm still afraid we may not be in the running—but if we've got a shot, I think we should pursue aggressively. Besides, I hear La Paz is nice this time of year . . ." They asked me to hold time to speak with Goni on June 7, election day in Britain when you mostly hang around the campaign headquarters and pretend you have something important to do.

For some reason, the call with Goni was delayed until five days later. I expressed my condolences on the passing of Victor Paz Estenssoro, leader of the 1952 Bolivian revolution, who was elected president four times. He also founded the MNR (the National Revolutionary Movement in its English translation), the party Goni now led. I apologized for not being able to get together because of the work for Tony Blair, which I hoped he would understand. In the office talking points for the call, that was my launching pad: "Today's victory is a prime example of how we use research and strategic advice to help candidates and parties develop a message, strategy, and communication plan to transform themselves." Then I decided to let Blair's victory interpret itself: "We are very anxious to work for your election as president."[5]

A week later, I flew to La Paz for one day to show I cared enough about his race to pass the endurance test. If the primo pollster will do this, he must want this campaign and must be willing to stay personally involved. I first flew to Miami to catch the overnight flight to La Paz. To make the thing a touch crazier but worth it, I jumped in a cab for the thirty-minute trip to Joe's Stone Crabs in South Beach. I never tip a maître d', but I knew that at Joe's, a twenty-dollar bill makes all things possible. Just a big plate of the medium stone crab claws. Back to the airport with time to spare for the 11:30 P.M. American Airlines flight, business class of a sort. I slept through the view of the Cordillera Real mountains, though I saw enough to know the peaks give way in an instant to a flat expanse of land and runway, all perched on an escarpment at twelve thousand feet, the snow-capped peaks of the Andes visible in the distance.[6]

It was 7 A.M. in La Paz, although we were actually high above it on a plateau, the Altiplano, an elongated plain, five hundred miles long, reaching Lake Titicaca some fifty miles to the west and from there on to Peru. I was met by Goni's scheduler, Bea Bedoya, one of the many serious women in proximity to Latin American power who only rarely get authority or titles. A driver whisked us away on a paved road that quickly took us into El Alto, a poor city of a million people who have been moving here through multiple generations to escape the changes in the hinterland, once ruled by Indian civilizations. Many of the Aymaran women were wrapped in blankets and wearing these improbably round bowlers. The houses were small, adobe or brick with corrugated metal roofs, some with small gardens. But all was dusty and stark, with wide dirt streets like *High Noon*, with only the main crossroads paved to handle the fleets of minibuses.

These good folks live on this windswept plain where the air is thinnest and the least healthy. Everyone who has ever traveled in Bolivia tells you, as if they were all reading off the same warning label: take the altitude very seriously; no amount of global bravado will immunize you; sleep; don't jog; and absolutely don't do meetings on arrival.

Our SUV headed down into the canyon that protects La Paz from the mountain winds, giving us a grand view of the series of valleys that make up this city. We drove down to the city center, always down, a path that heavy rains find irresistible, taking a heavy toll below. The city center, too, is on an incline, with blocks of low office buildings as well as some ten- to twenty-story buildings, concentrated a few blocks from the main street. We proceeded

down for another fifteen minutes or so, reaching the more affluent Zona Sur
and the exclusive neighborhood three thousand feet below the Altiplano.
Here, the air was thicker, though still not healthy.

We were dropped at the Casa Grande Hotel, each with an apartment-size
suite. It was 2001 and, to my amazement, we had broadband in the room.

All I cared about at that point was the bed. I could grab a ninety-minute
nap at best before going to meet Goni at his house at noon for a three- or
four-hour meeting. The warnings must be right because I do not remember
much about the meeting. Showing up was the main test. I made it, albeit
with an oxygen-deprivation headache. Goni was amused, as are most Bolivians, by the discomfort of the foreigners.

The house was large and comfortable, stuffed full of furniture, personal
things, and portraits of patriarchs and matriarchs, all done in an old Spanish
colonial style I do not usually like, except this really *was* old Spanish colonial.
We sat in the large dining room, which was dominated by a wooden table, maybe
twenty-five feet long, surrounded by high-backed wooden chairs. Mark and I
sat on one side of the table and Goni was joined on the other by Mauricio
Balcazar, his son-in-law and closest campaign advisor, former minister of information and head of a very professional Bolivian survey firm. The meeting
started late and was interrupted frequently by calls and sidebar conversations. It ran on and eventually became a meal as the household staff emerged
from the kitchen and began circling the table with three courses of un-
adorned food. It reflected the house, very comfortable, not grand at all or
showy. In Bolivia, Goni frequently tells me, "the poor are very poor but the
rich are not so rich."

With Mark and I flying out at 9:20 that night, I started sending cues that
the meeting should draw to a close, including getting up and standing behind
my chair. Don't worry. With the clock approaching 8 P.M. I must have been
showing my panic. Mauricio and Bea exchanged knowing looks: "No problem." Stupid me. We were there with the former president of Bolivia. At
8:30, they turned us over to Goni's security detail, who threw our bags and
us into their Jeep Cherokee, with its oversized wheels and raised body and
eight-cylinder engine. We were transported into a scene from the movie ad-
aptation of Tom Clancy's *Clear and Present Danger*, turning abruptly off the
main road, jumping from one small side street to another, racing up the canyon as if we were trying to stay one step ahead of the Colombian drug lords.
Impressive, we thought, until Mark and I rushed up to the airline counter,
passports and tickets in hand. The flight was gone. You don't understand, I
said. The flight was gone. In an instant, I realized that Goni's legacy is not
universally admired.

We ran across the airport, bags in hand, to another airline, caught a flight to Santa Cruz in the tropical lowlands, where the air is heavier and all the international flights stop to fuel up. There, we dashed across the airport, caught up with our American Airlines flight, and slumped, exhausted, in our seats. Must have passed the test, I thought.

A DAY IN THE LIFE

It took six months for Goni to make his choice and settle on the details, but on October 29 we assembled at our office in Washington for an all-day meeting with Goni to launch our efforts. Goni wanted not just polling and strategy, but a full, integrated program. Thus, Jeremy Rosner, Mark Feierstein, and I were there for the research; Bob Shrum was there with Tad Devine, a partner in his media firm and manager of Al Gore's 2000 effort. Tal Silberstein, now part of our international collaboration, had flown in from Israel to deal with campaign organization. James Carville, who played the role of general strategist, could not be with us, but offered us a table at his restaurant, West 24, as a place to break for lunch. Goni was present with Mauricio Balcazar.

We met in the conference room for a good seven hours, surrounded on every wall by trophies of Greenberg's exploits: one wall with posed pictures of world leaders, Mandela, Clinton, Blair, "Thanks for your brilliant numbers"; on the opposite wall, an expanse of Greenberg book jackets, end to end, from *Politics and Poverty* to *The Two Americas*. One end wall was filled with an oversized Barak campaign poster; and in the last corner, a large neon sign, "Meltdown," for Clinton's worst moment after Gennifer Flowers and Vietnam draft stories in New Hampshire. If I were dead, this would be a shrine with candles; if my father were alive, this could be his rec room, a substitute for the room of varsity sports trophies only my brother won. More recently, Freda Amar, my personal assistant, had the good sense to depose Barak and create a wall of pictures for governors, U.S. senators, and members of congress that Al Quinlan—more quietly than me—helped elect as head of our U.S. campaign work; prompting Jeremy's team to jam his framed book covers and pictures into the only remaining space on the wall.

The meeting started with Goni's take on the state of the country and more importantly, according to the agenda, "What is Goni's vision for the country? What does he want to accomplish as president? What are the key policy initiatives he has in mind?" The starting point for this work always is the intersection of campaigning and governing.

As we sat around the conference table that morning with time to reflect, my first impression of Goni was his age: seventy-one. Would he have the energy for this race? Was he strong enough to dominate the forces that threatened to tear the country apart? Of course, Goni knew what we were thinking, and I got my first taste of his ready resort to irony and self-deprecating humor. "That's why I hired the best," he said, while looking around the room. "I need a team that can get an old fool elected."

My second impression was his ease in speaking in English, the nuance of language, even irony that few can achieve in anything but their first language. It made me realize how much we miss when we force a leader to explain his or her purpose in English or through the meat grinder of simultaneous translation. The other side of fluency for Goni, however, was his accented Spanish, characterized by his detractors as "Gringo Spanish."

While Goni had lived in Bolivia for the last half century, he was reared and educated in the United States, where his parents lived during long periods of diplomatic service or political exile. His parents were progressives in a society in which women and peasant farmers were denied the vote. His father came to teach political science at Williams College in the depth of the Great Depression. He knew Franklin Roosevelt and traveled in New Deal circles with the likes of Henry Wallace, Harry Hopkins, and Harold Ickes. Goni's mother was a feminist who became general secretary of the Inter-America Commission for Women, working with the president of the organization, Eleanor Roosevelt.[7]

From exile, his father joined the National Revolutionary Movement, the MNR, in 1950 when it announced for agrarian reforms and renounced any alliance with the armed forces to attain power. The redistribution of land, an end to serfdom and the system of unpaid work, and a universal vote was achieved only in 1952 with the Bolivian revolution. The MNR, like the PRI in Mexico, was a nationalizing party, guided by an ideology that presumed only the government can successfully create industries, direct the country's development, and achieve a more equitable society.[8]

After graduating from the University of Chicago, Goni returned first to Argentina in 1950 where he joined the MNR, then in conspiracy against the old order. Immediately after the revolution, at age twenty-one, he moved back permanently to Bolivia. While his father served the new democratic government as Bolivia's ambassador to Peru, Venezuela, and then the United States, Goni pursued a range of professions outside politics, from documentary film-making to starting a petroleum service to buying a tin mine that would ultimately create his fortune. It was a good thing because the new democracy survived little more than a decade before President Paz Estenssoro was deposed in a coup in 1964 that sent him into exile in Peru and Goni's father back into exile in the United States. The coup launched a chaotic, almost comic succession of military juntas, swinging between reform and reaction, extreme left and extreme right. The most enduring junta of this two-decade period of military governance was led by then Colonel Hugo

Banzer Suárez, who came to power in a bloody coup, the bloodiest political turnover since the revolution of 1952. In 1971, his tanks crushed the leftist army general Juan José Torres, who had received aid from the Soviet Union. Banzer crushed the unions and presided over an economic boom that allowed the junta to rule for seven years.[9]

In 1979, the generals allowed a free election, which the MNR won, but without the absolute majority necessary to gain the presidency. Goni ran for office for the first time and won a seat in the House of Deputies. With no democratic party willing to form a coalition with now General Banzer, there was an impasse that brought two more years of coups, tanks, and waves of executions, as corrupt military governments deep in the new cocaine trade divvied up the spoils.[10]

With the whole society arrayed against it, the military relinquished power to a coalition of left parties that held on for three years. But it could not handle the rising economic crisis and political turmoil and called early elections.

In 1985, Paz Estenssoro became president for the fourth time, after edging out General Banzer in the political maneuvering when nobody would form a coalition with the former junta leader.[11] Goni was elected for the first time to the Senate, the upper chamber, and became president of the Senate. The president appointed him the minister of planning with responsibility for tackling the economic crisis.

Goni was very clear in the meeting about how he would approach the election. He was a businessman who tackled each problem with as much information as possible, weighing the alternatives and probabilities, a kind of analytic thinking he associated with America. In his businesses, he always used American lawyers. And except for that impetuous decision to purchase a tin mine, he avoided impressionistic judgments. His method was to focus on one problem at a time, bore deeper and deeper into the problem and thus gain more and more confidence in the solution. That made him something of a technocrat and policy wonk in a world of politicians and street protesters.

When he ran as the surprise MNR candidate for president after tackling Bolivia's financial crisis, he was new to the world of campaigns. Indeed, up to that point Bolivia was more schooled in stealing or canceling elections than in running them. So in his first campaign in 1989, he avoided the Chilean firms with their "artistic" approach and instinctively turned to American professionals, to Mark Malloch Brown, later to an aide of Kofi Annan, and Ed Reilly of Sawyer Miller, one of the top U.S. political media firms with a history of work in Venezuela and Colombia.

I want people who are "confident and professional," he told us, enough to "give me bad news"—"the truth, whole truth, and nothing but the truth." You see, "I wanted to hire somebody I will listen to," Goni said, "being the disciplined politician I am."[12] I did not know him well enough yet to know whether he was playing with me.

In deciding whom to hire this time, Goni had immediately ruled out Penn & Schoen because they had worked for the election of General Banzer when no democratic party considered him a legitimate coalition partner. Mauricio met with Dick Morris, who ranted about finding "one idea" and only one idea on which the whole election would turn. Morris needed to be paid an obscene amount of money to figure out what that idea was. Goni and his team thought perhaps the election would be more complicated than that.[13]

Some of the veterans of Sawyer Miller did want to do Goni's campaign, but with Blair's victory fresh in mind, Goni asked himself, "Why hire old boxers that don't train anymore?" He is more indirect than Barak, but Goni wanted to win.

"I never thought I was God's choice, God's gift to popularity," Goni told us in the conference room and me later in an interview. "A heavy English accent, a great deal of idealism that made me stubborn, wanting to achieve things, I always thought I was a tough sell." At age seventy-one, running with a lot of history, "I am carrying a big load." That was why he was sitting with us. "And by accepting that fact," Goni said, "I accepted people who could sell me."

I always tense up when I hear anyone talk about "selling me." It reminds me of Joe McGinniss's provocative book *The Selling of the President 1968*, the first account of the new media elite that supposedly sell and brand candidates as if they are commercial products. That's why I have shunned the identity as pollster. Goni was actually serious, but mainly because he is what he is: an economist and businessman, a policy wonk who has broken a lot of dishes bringing change.[14]

Goni was running, he told us, to "consolidate my reforms." I am running "to salvage my legacy and to serve my country," but that did not do justice to his work. Goni was a fearless and radical social reformer who worked against long odds to transform a dysfunctional social order and reduce inequality in one of the poorest countries on earth. When Goni took charge of the country's finances in 1985, 60 to 70 percent of the country lived in poverty. Bolivia's per capita income was the lowest in South America, combined with the highest infant mortality rate and lowest life expectancy. While over half lived in urban areas, most had deep roots in the rural regions and were barely a generation removed from a near feudal peasant social order.[15] The poorest were almost all Aymara or Quechua, the indigenous Indian communities, to which over half the population traced its origins—the highest Amerindian proportion for any country in Latin America.[16]

"Crisis" understates what faced the government when the last general departed in 1982. The parade of right- and left-wing military governments stole and borrowed everything they could and the first democratic government failed to get finances under control while struggling to meet pent-up popular needs. Six economic packages were stopped by intense opposition, including general strikes in 1984 and 1985, broken by a temporary state of siege. It opted for a massive rise in seigniorage, that is, printing money.[17]

So when Paz Estenssoro was elected in 1985, Bolivia faced hyperinflation, by one calculation the seventh worst in the history of the world. An annual inflation rate of 3,000 percent means a 50 to 100 percent increase in prices each month, but the rate jumped to an unimaginable 60,000 percent as the new government took office. Unemployment was rising and incomes shrinking, indeed they had fallen for five years in a row. The international tin market collapsed so completely that sales stopped, with prices falling two thirds. The state-directed economy was failing the poor and pretty much everybody else, except the twenty-seven thousand militant tin miners with protected jobs and food allotments, government workers and teachers, and the peasant coca growers with the one cash crop whose price was rising in world markets.[18]

In 1985, it was not at all clear that a democratic government could address the crisis, even if it knew what to do. The military option was very real, with General Banzer the top vote getter at the last election.

Paz Estenssoro was determined to be bold and appointed Gonzalo Sánchez de Lozada to address the crisis. At a reception before the new government took over, Goni met Jeffrey Sachs, the young Harvard economist who came to Bolivia at the invitation of his students to witness the crisis and hyperinflation and offer a plan of action. Sachs recommended a package of policies—lifting controls on currency, capital, and prices—implemented immediately, simultaneously, and universally, thus the characterization "shock therapy." The goal was to change the rules, incentives, and psychology, which would only be possible with bold action. With the government stymied on even the simplest reforms, this all seemed rather improbable.

Yet Goni told Sachs his plans were too cautious: "No, no, you have to go much beyond that. You don't understand, we need so much more, and you're just going on the surface." With Sachs likely frozen in place, "Yes, it's one thing to stop hyperinflation, but this country needs a complete overhaul. We've got to get out of the mess we're in," Sachs asked himself, like nearly everyone who first meets Goni: is he being ironic, "just trying to provoke me?"[19]

Goni and a handful of policy advisors closeted themselves in Goni's dining room around the long table for three weeks to develop their plan of action, which they took to the president. Within a month of taking office, the president addressed the country on TV, calling for support for his new economic plan, declaring simply, either "we act or Bolivia dies." In a burst of activity, the government decontrolled prices, raised energy prices to increase government revenue, liberalized trade, removed all capital controls, froze private and public sector wages for six months, and put tin operations on an economic basis, buying out three quarters of the 27,000 workers. Within thirty days, the inflation rate fell to almost zero.[20]

The end of hyperinflation launched a new period of feverish work around Goni's dining room table, developing one reform after another: the tax system, the government and judiciary, and an emergency social fund to create projects and jobs in poorer areas. The United States was useless during the crisis and the IMF acted as an instrument of Citibank, demanding that Bolivia resume debt payments during the crisis, which Goni refused. The U.S. government suspended aid during the crisis until President Paz Estenssoro instituted a new anti-drug policy to eradicate the coca fields.[21]

The unemployment rate rose from 16 percent in 1985 to 21.5 percent in 1988, stabilized, and then dropped sharply in 1991. By the time of the 1989 elections, every major party from left to right accepted the new economic order, with Goni viewed as the man who led Bolivia out of the crisis.[22] That aura carried Goni to a surprise first-place finish in his first run for the presidency in 1989. But without an absolute majority, the Bolivian Congress selected the president and Goni lost out amid the post-election maneuvering.

Before that first meeting with Goni in our offices, I read and reread the accounts of Goni's assault on hyperinflation and the closed economic order in a country almost too impoverished to make any progress. Yet Jeffery Sachs carried the model to Poland and Russia, both of which soon followed Bolivia's example.

Bolivia?

Unlike many Democrats, I had been a supporter of economic reform and open trade going back to my time in academia. I know the theoretical arguments as well as the history of liberal presidents who fashioned the international economy and postwar economic growth. When I first came to Washington I worked for the Democratic Leadership Council, not the major unions, and was comfortable with the DLC's pro-trade posture. When candidate Bill Clinton had to decide whether to support NAFTA, just signed by the first President Bush, I presented my recommendations to an intense meeting of all the political and economic advisors. I could see Al Gore rising up in his chair, followed closely by Sandy Berger, when I began by describing how skeptical voters were of trade. But then I watched them slip back when I underscored poll findings that showed those same voters wanted a president who was outward-looking and not defensive on trade. Breaking with Paul Begala and George Stephanopoulos and Mrs. Clinton, I urged support for NAFTA. Thus I was prepared to believe that reformers could be successful politically.

When Goni ran for the presidency again four years later, in 1993, he was the presumptive favorite, clearly aided, rather than weighed down, by his reputation as an economic modernizer. During the campaign, Goni unveiled, in broad daylight for voters to see, his "capitalization" plan to transform state-owned industries, described as "a transforming shock" in his election manifesto, the "Plan de Todos," the Plan for Everyone.[23] Goni won the presidency in a landslide by Bolivian standards, with 36.2 percent of the vote among five competing parties, giving him the biggest margin since the restoration of democracy. The MNR also won two thirds of the seats in the Senate, putting Goni in a position to govern boldly in his presidency from 1993 to 1997.

As I read and reread the accounts of his presidency, I would stop and shake my head. I have worked for more than a few leaders who have chanced bold changes, but few have been as innovative in modernizing an economy, while simultaneously addressing the "great problem, which is the inequality of income distribution," in Goni's words.[24]

Capitalization was the most controversial part of his program but also the most innovative. Rather than simply privatizing the old and inefficient state industries at the heart of the economy, he created a framework for mostly foreign investors to make payments to attain 50 percent of the stock in a transparent and internationally supervised auction. It was called capitalization because the purpose was to attract capital—direct foreign investment in a place where few investors dared to tread. Unlike conventional privatization, none of the new money went to the government, avoiding the kind of profligacy and corruption that comes with newfound money. And 5 percent of the shares were reserved for sale to employees, thirty thousand of whom bought them. With capitalization, direct foreign investment rose almost 50 percent to comprise 20 percent of the economy—$8 billion of new investment. The investment in the gas and oil sector allowed the construction of a pipeline to Brazil and exports to this new export market; it brought new exploration, producing a ten-fold increase in Bolivia's gas reserves. That would make possible the new and embittered battle over Bolivia's gas.[25]

More innovative yet, and more important to Goni, was the unbreakable new link of capitalization to social provision for the aged. All the state-owned stock and future dividends were deposited in a capitalization fund to support a new state pension plan, called Bonosol, or Solidarity Bonus. The Bonosol is a powerful statement about the beneficiaries of reform—a $250 annual payment to all those over age sixty-five—equal to a quarter of the per capita income in the country and equal to half of the average income for those living in poverty. People received their first Bonosol in the last year of Goni's presidency, when the constitution did not allow him to succeed himself.[26]

Before Goni's presidency, money for public investment was distributed based on the number of taxpayers, not people, meaning all state funds went to the department capitals and virtually none to the rural areas—a system that suited the traditional elites. Goni made a simple but radical change in the formula, distributing the money for public works on a per capita basis. This reform, called "Popular Participation," doubled the portion of the national budget going to public works and schools. That produced the creation of 314 new municipalities in urban and rural areas and an explosion of new civic organizations, as the law required popular participation in planning and oversight. The law tripled spending on education.

His education reforms were met by a national teachers strike, joined by the largest union federation and tin miners, most of whose members up until then looked down on the indigenous population. Goni's reforms transferred power in the education system to the parents and municipalities, required bilingual education in Aymara and Quechua where appropriate, and the testing of teachers accompanied by merit-based pay increases.

Goni introduced universal prenatal and infant health insurance, which came into force in 1996. He then made health care free for all over age sixty-five.[27] Overall infant mortality was cut by a third; the mortality rate for infants under five years of age was cut by over 40 percent; the percentage of children in secondary schools rose from under a third to two thirds, and per capita income went up from $835 to $940 a year.[28]

With Goni unable to succeed himself, General Banzer won the election on August 6, 1997, recalling the better economic times under the military and promising to renationalize Bolivia's major industries. He did not follow through on that promise, fearing a breach with the United States, Brazil, and Spain and global financial institutions, but he vilified capitalization and canceled the Bonosol, breaking the so-called unbreakable link between economic reform and social insurance, and keeping Goni's most important legacy from becoming institutionalized.[29]

"When I saw how Banzer took apart what we had done," Goni told me later, running in 2004 "became a moral imperative." Goni believed he had "instituted revolutionary change," which for him meant "radical change that cannot be reversed." With all "my studies of dialectics and dialectical materialism . . . I forgot there is the counterrevolution."

So, Goni is running, he told us briefly in the conference room and later in an interview, under the "the absolute imperative" to "get back" and "restore the Bonosol." The vast revenues from the new gas can fund an ever increasing Bonosol, but also education and health care for the poorest, gas connections for most urban houses, and electric power for the rural areas. That was his vision.

After lunch at West 24, we reassembled to discuss the competition, divided between the traditional parties and various breakaway leaders on the one hand and the anti-system parties and movement leaders on the other. The two blocs shared nothing except their hatred of Goni and rejection of the "neoliberal model." Their critiques blended into a conventional wisdom that said Bolivia's key industrial treasures were sold off to foreigners, the jobs forever lost with the remaining positions given to foreigners over Bolivians; and that the new gas would be sold to foreigners rather than used in Bolivia for the benefit of Bolivians. The opposition parties, movement, and charismatic leaders can be arrayed in the degree of their hostility to capitalization and determination to renationalize key state industries.

While Goni felt it was the success of capitalization and the Bonosol that motivated his enemies on the right and left, the popular opposition had embraced powerful national symbols. Over Goni's objection, local officials in Cochabamba pushed ahead with a plan that increased water rates from the start to finance construction and that forced peasant users to pay for previously free water. Over a two-week period, pitched battles led by the coca growers left six people dead in what is now known as the "Water War."[30] The other symbol was the government's modest 18 percent royalty on new gas reserves, for the popular opposition a symbol of Bolivia's wholesale liquidation of a national asset and weakness before foreign capital.

But for Goni, none of these symbols took away from his mission now "to come back," turn out the counterrevolutionaries, "correct my mistakes, build on my successes."

At 8 P.M. the principals adjourned to a room to iron out the contract. The details had already been sorted, including the symbolic concessions on the size of the monthly fees and the written, not symbolic, guarantee that I would go to Bolivia each month. Goni reminded us, "you guys are very expensive," letting us know that we would be working for someone who spent as much time sorting one-thousand-dollar issues as one-million-dollar ones. The signing ceremony took place two days later on Halloween.

THE OTHER STRUGGLE

When I first called Goni from Britain, we did not speak of that other struggle that was competing to control Bolivia's future. In mid-June, the Banzer government sent six hundred heavily armed troops to reinforce the 750 that rushed in the previous week to Los Yungas, one hundred kilometers northeast of La Paz, to the valleys where coca was grown legally for traditional use, but also illegally for market. Faced with the expanding efforts of the Banzer government to eradicate 2,300 hectares (5,700 acres) of coca fields, the coca farmers set up dozens of roadblocks.

The roadblocks did not win much public sympathy and did not stop the government, determined to proceed with its plan to eliminate coca. But the peasant resistance leaders continued to talk of going into the mountains and resuming "the armed struggle." By the end of June, the government proceeded with charges of sedition against Felipe Quispe, known as El Mallku, leader of the Union Federation, who views himself as leader of the Aymara in the Altiplano and the rural areas beyond. It also moved to lift the parliamentary immunity of Congressman Evo Morales, head of the coca growers, so he could face charges over the violence on the highways.[31]

Two weeks before our meeting with Goni in Washington in October, Evo issued an ultimatum: the government must stop eradication of coca in the Chapare province or face a total confrontation. The threat was ominous, since security forces had lost control of that zone over the past two months, as peasant protesters blocked the soldiers from leaving their camps. Members of the Landless Movement took two soldiers hostage in an ambush, again bringing a rush of military and police reinforcements. "The government has declared war, the Chapare has been militarized," Morales claimed. The day after our Washington meetings, the government sent an additional four thousand police and armed forces into the Chapare, where the coca growers were poised to block the Santa Cruz–Cochabamba highway, the nation's most important all-weather route, which carries two thirds of Bolivia's commerce. The government was determined to proceed to "zero coca," a government spokesman declared. That day, Morales was in Havana heading up a delegation of coca growers. After the breakdown Cardinal Julio Terrazas called for a dialogue on eradication that led to a thirty-day moratorium. Nonetheless, the government declared that by next August 6, when it was to leave office, there would be no coca left in the Chapare, and Evo announced he would create an armed force to protect the farmers from the government.[32]

As if to preempt our work in Washington, the coca growers and landless peasant groups announced on the Friday before our meeting that they would form a unified party to contest the June 2002 elections, called MAS—in English, the Movement Toward Socialism. Later, they would join eighteen other parties, some minor, on the official electoral list, with Evo Morales as their candidate for president.[33]

What was the real story? In this impoverished country on the edge of the global market, coca is Bolivia's biggest cash crop, but also the illicit trade that makes it hard for Bolivia to build ties with and export other crops and goods to the United States and Europe. From 1998 to 2001, the government made an unprecedented effort to destroy coca crops under the U.S.-financed "Dignity Plan." The front line in this war was the Chapare where the government destroyed forty thousand hectares of coca crops, 85 percent of the total land under illegal cultivation. It was an earthquake for these small, relatively successful producers.[34]

Coca is a unique crop because it is dominated by small producers who spend little on inputs like pesticides. They harvest four or five crops a year and sell to a ready world market. The Chapare emerged as the center of coca production and the cocaine trade in the early 1980s, making the last junta leaders fabulously rich. While the rest of the country was in economic crisis, the Chapare was like gold rush country. Population in the farming region beyond the control of government exploded from 40,000 to 215,000 in just seven years from 1980. Many of the displaced miners, schooled in a Latin American Trotskyism and the use of blockades to press demands, moved to the Chapare, strengthening the militancy of these independent producers.[35]

So when the Banzer government in 1997 announced its Dignity Plan, it was set for a confrontation with entrenched peasant producers determined to battle for their livelihood. When it announced August 2002 as the deadline for total victory, one month after the election, the government ensured that there would be a parallel popular struggle. The coca growers moved to the lead in the anti-system forces in the election, as one movement leader observed, because "no one was bombarding my cows or eradicating my soy beans."[36]

On the day that El Mallku was charged with sedition and Evo moved one step closer to losing his parliamentary immunity, Moody's Investors Service gave foreign investments in Bolivia a positive B1 rating. "The promising future of gas exports to Brazil and other markets" would allow Bolivia to achieve a favored status compared to many of its neighbors. What Moody's understood was that there was real money on the table, elevating the stakes for many in and outside of politics on who controls the government. Two consortiums, British Gas and British Petroleum, with the Spanish energy group Repsol YPF, and TotalFina and Elf with Exxon, were competing to carry forward the project.[37] If the government succeeded in implementing the two liquefied natural gas projects to carry Bolivia's natural gas to North America, there would be $8 billion in new foreign investment, equal to the country's GNP. Newspaper editorials heralded the prospect that Bolivia would stand second only to Venezuela as an energy power in the region. The stories noted that landlocked Bolivia would likely be using a port in Chile, its historic enemy.[38]

President Ricardo Lagos of rival nation Chile indicated he was open to restoring diplomatic relations with Bolivia, as the presidents of the two countries met to discuss the prospect of a site on the Chilean coast for the export of natural gas.[39]

The new year of 2002 brought an agreement between Bolivia and the international consortium to export liquid natural gas to the United States and Mexico. With the government determined to eradicate the coca crop by August and take a lot of money off the table, it had just contracted to put a lot more on it. For his part, Goni hoped voters would acknowledge his responsibility and turn to him to lead since there would be no money but for capitalization. For the popular movements, all this just increased the urgency of decrying capitalization and reclaiming the gas and oil industries for Bolivia. For them, the election was merely one tactic for the pursuit of popular goals.[40]

THE SOLUTION TO THE CRISIS

Less than two weeks after our meeting in Washington—and before we had done any research in Bolivia or developed any strategy—Goni spoke before the American-Bolivian Chamber of Commerce and put down his marker: "Things are bad and getting worse" under General Banzer and now, after Banzer's illness and resignation, under his successor. The worst problem, he said, was "the economic crisis." Despite the effects of the Asian crisis, the Russian collapse, Argentine devaluation, and 9/11, the government refused to take action. "We need to take measures to protect the patient before it catches triple pneumonia." Fortunately, "I participated in a miracle during Victor Paz's government," Goni recalled immodestly, when we "turned around a situation of absolute economic, social and political collapse." He did not say that he was the only candidate who could save the patient, but that was the message.

The election, he concluded, "will be defined by capitalization; it will be defined by corruption and the economic crisis."[41]

About the same time, Tal Silberstein traveled to Bolivia to meet the people in the MNR and campaign and to prepare an assessment on the state of organization before developing a campaign plan. During one of the meetings, he asked everyone to write down why people would not vote for Goni. Tal wrote on a big sheet as they each read out in turn what they had written:

Too conservative.
He sold the country.

He is corrupt or allows corruption to occur.
He didn't deliver the 500,000 jobs he promised.
He's a technocrat.
He doesn't listen to people.
He's arrogant and elitist.
He doesn't care about people.
They don't understand capitalization.
He can't form alliances.
He brought too much change.

Their responses were hard on Goni and, without Goni in the room, very frank. Then Tal asked them to write down why people would vote for him. Again he wrote the answers on a big sheet:

He's the only solution to the crisis.
He needs to finish the job he started.
MNR is the party of change.
MNR is the party of qualified people.
He is patriotic.
He represents the hope of Bolivia.
He has courage, intelligence, is a leader.
Is serious, capable, and honest.
Goni is the best for people.
MNR is the right party at a critical time.

They, too, were edging toward a conclusion that Goni was the leader with the experience and qualities "at a critical time," the "only solution to the crisis." Goni was both the problem and the solution, even for his own team.

While he may have been the man for the moment, Goni seemed particularly tired during this round of party meetings with Tal, according to Amy Webber, our new person on the ground there every day, savvy and beautifully fluent in Spanish. Goni often closed his eyes in my meetings but, then again, when Tal presses a point relentlessly, you sometimes feel like you're in a dentist's chair.[42]

THE PARADOX

In mid-December I flew to La Paz. This time I made sure to wake up early enough on the flight to see the morning glow across the high plateau and distant mountains. Jeremy Rosner and I, but particularly Mark Feierstein, would be observing our first groups, eleven of them conducted in Mauricio Balcazar's facilities in La Paz and Santa Cruz, the rest in homes and hotels in Cocha-bamba, Potosí, and Chuquisaca. There did not appear to be any place too remote to gather people around a table to discuss their lives and politics. We were also to report on the national survey conducted face-to-face in all departments where we were pushing Mauricio's interviewers deep into the rural areas, unlike the conventional press surveys that stop at the cities' edge. With MNR's traditional strength with many older and rural voters, our sur-veys were more likely to get Goni's vote right.

So that I could get my head into this new world, the team organized a set of focus groups, starting at noon in Mauricio's research office ten blocks from our new hotel, now in the city center. I took a quick nap and then a taxi the few short blocks to his office, both concessions to the altitude. The taxi ended up stalled in traffic, stopped by marchers in front of the San Francisco church, a daily occurrence as conflicts continued between the Chapare coca growers and the government. I barely noticed that MAS that day chose five potential candidates, including both El Mallku and Evo Morales.

No amount of experience dulled my interest in watching these first groups before my mind was spoiled by all the insider strategizing and calculating.[43] These first groups, one mostly mestizo from La Paz and the other mostly poor Aymara from El Alto, were undecided voters still considering Goni, though you would not know it from the comments: "liar," "traitor," "the anti-Christ," "he's the one who ruined us with capitalization." Poor and wear-ing traditional attire, they were very different from the Israelis. But they, too, welcomed the artificial respite of the focus group room. As I watched from the dark, their comments seemed even more pointed. And they were para-doxical, so much anger and disappointment, yet a grinding reality that did not allow them to close the chapter on Goni.

Between groups, we adjourned for lunch to a small conference room filled by a round table. It was set with place mats, knives and forks, and a Big Mac in the center of each plate. Is this a joke? I asked. I thought we were about to have some empanadas stuffed with spicy beef or potatoes, but a Big Mac? I never eat at McDonald's, but if they are in Paris, why not La Paz? So, I ate my first Big Mac, with each bite confirming the critics' worst fears about global-ization.

In the evening, we went to the campaign to report in the large conference room, where James joined us after flying in from Brazil. Jeremy was present-ing the results on our first wave of research using a PowerPoint projector so he sat on one side of the room like a teacher. Goni and Mauricio and ten of his closest people in the MNR were spread around the large table to hear the

Up against the one-way glass, watching and listening to people from El Alto in the La Paz focus group facility, with Jeremy taking near verbatim notes from the English translation. [Christine Burrill]

report on the new crisis. Over 70 percent believed the country was on the wrong track, fueled above all by worries about unemployment, with considerable help from poverty and low salaries, as well as corruption—an ugly brew. Like no other place I have worked on elections, with the possible exception of South Africa, the responses were tinged with desperation, on the edge of life without anyone to turn to for help or support. "We are starving to death," said one person, speaking for the group. "There are no jobs." People talked about reducing from three to two meals because they didn't have the money for food: "There are days when one has to go through the day with bread and water or canned food." It put some perspective on our complaining focus groups in my own country.[44]

The political class had betrayed them. Corruption was rampant, even as people were starving. The politicians made big promises, but instead stole the money intended for the poor and enriched themselves. The elites in business, politics, the judiciary, and the military maneuvered for their own advantage—all exaggerated by market reforms, privatization, and gas or coca that rewarded private gain and brought more money into the mix. In their view, the economic crisis began with Goni's capitalization, when Bolivia's industries were sold to foreigners, the jobs taken by foreign workers, and the United States began making all the decisions. He had promised 500,000 jobs, but instead, they believed, Bolivia lost that many.

The people did not look to Goni because he did not look to them. Most of those in our focus groups described Goni and the MNR as for the rich, "the high society person," distant from them. His sarcastic tone was not seen as ironic or humorous, but as evidence of disdain for the campesinos. "I don't hate you," one of the participants observed. "But if you love us don't make fun of Bolivia."

Only a third said he cared about people, which seemed high under the circumstances.

But this was a survey in which voters expressed their disdain for all living politicians, the best known scorned by some 60 percent of the voters.[45] That held for Goni, with only 20 percent viewing him positively. But all the anger with Goni paled in comparison with their feelings about former President Hugo Banzer, with half as many positive responses and even more negative ones.

For all the contempt, we began this race at 20 percent of the vote and tied for first, but we knew that was not good enough; we were close to our ceiling, with very few additional voters—we estimated maybe 6 percent—open to supporting Goni. The top vote getter in the past has often garnered around 15 percent but that left you to the vagaries of the Congress. Goni won the popular vote once before and failed to win the presidency, so the MNR believed Goni must get to the high 20s or 30 percent mark to really win the presidency.

The great majority of the public did not want what we and the other traditional parties were selling. They wanted to vote for a candidate from outside the traditional parties who could bring change, but they were certainly not looking to the anti-globalization candidates. The populist union, peasant and indigenous candidates, all together, were just getting 7 percent of the vote, most of that for El Mallku. Evo was getting only 2 percent. Those two "popular leaders" were the two most unpopular leaders in the country, more unpopular than General Banzer.[46]

In the first poll, 40 percent were voting for an anti-system party or were so alienated they intended to leave their ballot blank. The strongest anti-system impulse was against corruption, pushing to the top of the pack Alberto Costa Obregón, a former judge with the courage to prosecute corrupt politicians, including investigating President Banzer for the murder of political dissidents during the junta. Costa Obregón was getting 13 percent of the vote and almost running even with Goni, and when we drafted for him a powerful message about corruption and poverty in a survey he nearly took an outright majority in the simulated election.

The danger ahead was that one of the candidates from the traditional parties would take up the "change banner" or that the anti-system voters would rally around a single candidate. Looking at Goni, Jeremy warned, "All of this creates a potential for a nonsystem candidate to capitalize on the public mood and surge to victory." Goni, who had a reputation for probity, would have to prioritize corruption if he was to confound that dynamic.

To emerge from this cauldron, Goni had to become a force for change himself, but defined on his terms. People were desperate about the crisis and granted that Goni had the qualities that made him right for the moment: almost 60 percent accepted that he was "capable" and a "strong leader." Goni was the one with the best ideas to address the economic crisis. Bringing together an understanding of the times and Goni's biography and basic instincts, now supported by poll data, Jeremy concluded, "We believe we need to define this election as a search for the person who can fix the crisis," thus crystallizing what Goni and his campaign team said before we ever arrived in La Paz.

But since 60 percent believed Goni was the cause of the crisis we faced a paradox right at the center of our campaign, one Jeremy delighted in explaining to Goni, which he in turn delighted in resolving. Why would people listen to him when they thought his capitalization had taken away jobs from Bolivians and made life harder? Later, when I talked to an American consultant for another candidate, he was amused by this strategy. Right, they were going to turn to this old guy who ruined the economy, who they hated, to solve the crisis.

For Goni, believing capitalization had been a success and had created jobs, there was no paradox, though he recognized this was not so simple for the public. I know what we accomplished, he told me, "but we don't want to get bogged down in Vietnam."

STAN'S 3-STEPS

Jeremy turned to me to talk about what would soon become known in the campaign as "Stan's 3-Steps"—the steps for getting people to listen again when a period of great hope has given way to a period of frustration, born of broken promises. I first faced this issue in South Africa after Mandela's victory and in Britain after Blair's triumph over the Tories. While both achieved important things in their first governments, voters despaired of progress on their core commitments. They were heard by voters when they spoke first of progress on things that people were ready to recognize (water and electricity in South Africa and economic stability and improved primary schools in Britain); second, they genuinely acknowledged that change had not gone far or fast enough and they, too, were personally frustrated, and third, when they took the unfinished agenda, the broken promise—jobs in South Africa and an improved health service in Britain—and made it their highest priority for the future. It had the virtue of being true.

When Jeremy raised the prospect of using the framework in Bolivia, I worried, as I always do, that it would be applied mechanically or invite insincere contrition by politicians who really had walked away from their promises. But the big surprise to me in listening in the groups was how voters who seemed to hate Goni and who thought he had little regard for them would readily and easily list his social accomplishments. When the moderator asked, "When you hear the name Goni, what positive things come to mind," one person after another around the table, group after group, came up with the same things—Bonosol for the elderly, children's health, prenatal care for the mothers, and education reform, popular participation, and school buildings. I know it is absurd, but I got teary each time I heard it. This wasn't just Goni's reconstructed history. His social policies touched some very poor people and now formed part of their complicated and informed relationship with this society and its former president.

So it was not difficult to get Goni to take up the first step in my approach, which was to speak of the most innovative areas where he tried to address poverty and inequality, much of it financed by capitalization. His promise to restore the Bonosol payment to 1,800 bolivianos a year led over half the voters in our survey to say they were more likely to vote for Goni.

Step three was not a problem. Goni had his tool kit and was ready to go to work to fix what was wrong with capitalization and bring forward his plan for jobs—to "start a massive road construction program to connect more communities and create jobs, including a new highway running from Bolivia's north to south, to be called the Victor Paz Estenssoro Highway," Jeremy's last contribution to Goni's New Deal vision. Goni may have been a market reformer, but he fully believed the government could create jobs with public works, and was offering plans, not rhetoric.[47]

Step two, however, was a dead end, at least for the moment. Goni believed capitalization was undermined by Banzer's counterrevolution, not by mistakes of conception, and he was mostly right. So saying, "I got some things wrong," caught in his throat. Jeremy tested in the focus groups and surveyed a kind of apology for not "doing enough to protect the poorest," but neither the voters nor Goni responded to the idea. I watched Jeremy sweat as he began to lose Goni.

Later, when we took Stan's 3-Steps from an interesting hypothesis and global musings to a formal message, we got our strongest result yet: 45 percent said they would be "much more likely" to support Goni after hearing this. No doubt the analytical Goni was grinding away, reflecting on this doubling of his vote.[48] Were we tempting him with an inauthentic and symbolic gesture to fool voters? I was a little uncomfortable, since he so strongly believed he had created jobs and that his work had been sabotaged. But no, what we were doing was puncturing the unreality among the most powerful. Almost teasing, I asked, how much do you think people's lives had really changed? Don't you think you learned anything that would lead you to do things differently?

THE FIELD OF DREAMS

While the campaign was slow to get organized, it had come quickly to a clear choice for the race, built on Goni's own sense of purpose and goal, to restore and fix his social and economic reforms without being trapped in the past. It had established priorities, to fix the crisis and stop the corruption that made Goni an agent of reform and change. Though weighed down by a lot of history, the campaign had a theory on how to get people to listen.

And to our surprise, it actually worked in practice.

The first test was the selection of a vice presidential candidate to run with Goni. He wanted to break new ground. With the help of a new survey, Jeremy and Tad Devine persuaded Goni to select not a politician, but Carlos Mesa, a well-respected and popular TV journalist who had crusaded against corruption. The party convention was electric as Goni introduced his young, charismatic running mate and their shared determination to battle corruption. Bob Shrum had written a spectacular speech that promised to "fully, completely and absolutely restore the Bonosol" and that attacked Banzer for stealing Bonosol's money for his pet projects.

Goni, however, did not give that speech, though at least he began by accepting the nomination "in the name of all the old people, the grandmothers and grandfathers, who with us will receive their Bonosol." Instead, he went off message to talk about free ID cards for campesinos and women to achieve a universal franchise but nobody noticed. The party activists were excited by the new team and new direction.[49]

After the convention, Goni and Mesa took the show on the road to Tarija in the south of Bolivia, Santa Cruz in the lowland, finishing in Cobija in the northern Amazon Basin. They drew good crowds mostly of MNR party activists at the airports and then at the center of town where they spoke. Mesa was a natural politician and dynamic speaker, which contrasted with Goni's plodding style. On the first two stops, Mesa spoke first, which exaggerated the contrast. Goni soon appreciated the problem and the order was reversed at Cobija. It did not stop the young women in the crowd from asking Goni to pass a paper and pencil to Mesa so they could get his autograph.

There was no mention of lessons learned, but both Goni and Carlos easily repeated that they would "eradicate the corruption and fix the crisis." Quite spontaneously, some people in the crowds were holding up both hands, one with the V, a symbol for the MNR, and the other an "open hand," becoming a symbol for clean hands promoted by Mesa.

Tad's starting point for our own first ads was the Bonosol, the link between economic reforms and social insurance and Goni's reason for running. This was Goni at his best, filmed in front of the closed ticket windows at the soccer stadium where the Bonosol used to be paid, with these very old men and women who, Amy reported, "just look like they have lived the toughest lives imaginable," moving her to tears. It got much more difficult when the ad required that Goni speak in crafted, straightforward talk and not add extra words. He spoke readily about the revolution, the crisis, and corruption, but "all very complex Goni talk," as Amy described it. He could not say, simply, "Today, Bolivia is in crisis." Nonetheless, the first campaign ad began with our framework. "Today, Bolivia is in crisis. . . . The collapse of our economy, the hypercorruption, has brought millions of Bolivians into desperation."[50]

In the groups, people were consumed first with the blockades and strikes that were making life that much tougher, particularly as shortages drove the price of food staples higher. There was a rising sense of crisis, elevated by the ads of another party attacking Goni because of the collapse of Enron, tangentially linked to the water problem in Bolivia. Yet voters still talked about Goni and Mesa signing their anti-corruption pact. There was a sense of possibility and relevance not evident before.

What really got heard in the groups were our test ads of Stan's 3-Steps, with Goni acknowledging the errors in capitalization or saying the change was not sufficient. People did a double take when Goni showed he was able to learn and grow. It was as if they were reluctant to give up their investment in him. His acknowledgment allowed them to recall the good social things. A woman in Santa Cruz went straight to step two: "I like the part where he says that he sees the negative things about what he did and that he's willing to fix that. He's looking at things from a different angle now, and he gives hope."[51]

Jeremy presented the findings to Goni at the campaign headquarters and Goni accepted the concept in principle. Of course, when he articulated the idea in his own voice, it was a pretty scrubbed version. "You want to say you learned a lot from that. When you're president this time, you are gonna obviously be much better at the job than you were," which a nanosecond later he took back, "but [you] want to acknowledge that you did some great things for Bolivia."[52] Still stuck at step one.

By early March people in the groups began quoting back our ads. Liberated by Goni's acknowledgment, some moved to step three, our unfinished agenda, and talked about him creating jobs, even though we never mentioned jobs in our ads.[53]

And remarkably, they came, as if we had just built a "field of dreams." By the end of February, our vote moved up from 20 to 25 percent, what we had thought was our full potential a few months ago and 10 points ahead of the next closest opponent. When Jeremy presented first at Goni's dining room table and then to the full campaign, there were compliments all around. Goni's personal standing was holding steady around the 36 percent mark, even as all but one of the other major candidates were falling. Three quarters had seen the advertising, and most liked what they saw. Carlos Mesa was very popular and we had gone from third place to first place on who would eradicate corruption. And above all, when people compared the field of major candidates, 35 percent choose Goni as the person with the "ideas to fix the crisis"—10 points above our vote.[54]

By the end of March, Goni's vote reached 27 percent, with the 30 percent mark in reach—the goal for achieving a certain and legitimate presidency.

THE "DIRTY WAR"

The problem is that someone else, Manfred Reyes Villa, was also building *his* field of dreams—with a candidacy centered on success as mayor in Cochabamba, his youth and attractiveness, his upbeat mood and message of change and hope. His ads began with a catchy song and a narration that rhymes: "Manfred Reyes is the man"; "a sensible heart for education and children"; "Bolivia needs a new heart"; "positive change." From the beginning, our background research warned that he had the potential to emerge as the candidate of change. Now he was the most popular of all the candidates and known universally as "Manfred" or "El Bon Bom," reflecting his good looks. His support was up 12 points in three months and stood at 22 percent of the vote, trailing Goni by just 5 points.[55]

We were not at all sanguine about the threat. In an early March memo, we described him as a "formidable opponent" and "we need to define" him "before he finishes defining himself." This would not be an easy task, as he had "an attractive, youthful, vigorous image, and a plausible case that he brought positive change." Voters wanted to be hopeful about the future and had started to invest in him. They would resist those who wanted to foreclose that option.[56]

Even as we were presenting our findings, Manfred Reyes Villa surged into a 6-point lead, 22 to 28 percent, rallying virtually all the anti-system voters, our worst nightmare.[57]

Manfred announced his "Plan for Positive Change," including the "four revolutions: economic, moral, social and municipal." His one hundred anti-crisis measures included 100 percent of children in school and construction of inexpensive homes for the poor. Though Manfred's history ran deep into the traditional parties and military, he called for a Constituent Assembly in six months with the power to change the constitution, something the anti-system candidates were demanding, and, most important, committed to renationalize the energy sector of the economy. Manfred was populist, nationalist, and full of promises for voters who wanted to believe things could be better.[58]

While we understood early on the threat posed by Manfred, we never thought he was the real thing, which is why we never questioned the necessity of "redefining him" for the public or, in campaign terms, "going negative." You did not have to look beyond the recent press clippings to know that as

Presenting one of our first message surveys to Goni at the party's headquarters, flanked by Jeremy on my right, who did the bulk of the analysis, and James on my left. Goni is sitting directly across from us, with Carlos Mesa, the vice presidential nominee on his left. [Christine Burrill]

mayor, he championed the water project, opposed by Goni, which raised water rates by 35 percent and triggered the Water War in which many died without producing any water. Manfred acknowledged holdings of $2 million in personal assets, but the papers were already reporting on his $5 million in properties, including an unknown number of houses in Miami, all acquired during a career as a soldier and elected official. The former military captain and aide to a military dictator promised to double the military budget. And rather than being grounded in anti-system politics, he opportunistically jumped from one traditional party to the next, his party resigning from the Banzer government in preparation for this race.[59]

Our task, we wrote in the memo, was to show that "he is not change, not new, just more of the same politics," which also happened to be true. But the campaign was squeamish about raising these issues, believing Goni and the MNR were in no position to throw stones. They had also moved into the lead, themselves riding a positive current on corruption and crisis.[60] In one of our meetings, Tal, in his usual blunt way, said, "We have to make him from a clean to a dirty candidate," though he assured the campaign it would "go through outside parties" and "it's not going to come from us." I know Tal. He lives and dies by giving individual reporters some angle, documents, or records that they can use to develop a story.[61]

With Manfred moving ahead of us in the polls and the campaign in near panic, we held urgent focus groups in La Paz to test our options. Manfred created hope. He would be a president who walked the streets. He wanted us to vote for our children because he would use the gas money for education, housing, and roads. Then we would poop on the party and play for them a rough ad on Manfred and the Water War. But they were protective of Manfred and did not want to believe what they were watching. Nonetheless, it was the best ad, and the campaign put it on the air two days later as two thirds of our media buy. The "Dirty War" had begun.[62]

Manfred responded immediately to Goni's desperate launch of the Dirty War, though not to the specific charges about the corrupt water project or sick children. Manfred promised to remain positive and hopeful. Indeed, a few days later, his campaign committed even further to his positive strategy, going up with a new ad and new song: "Bolivians, here is the change; Manfred . . . positive change; positive, with the young people, with new people; for the nation and of the heart."[63] Manfred's answer to the Dirty War was hope.

Virtually the strongest attack against Goni now was his waging a Dirty War against Manfred. It did not help that the Electoral Court had ruled that our ad was "defaming" of Manfred, though it did not rule against a replacement ad, which made the same points but relied more on newspaper reports.[64]

When politicians and campaign people smell failure, they begin to maneuver for position. As we approached the end of April, unknown to me, a parade of consultants was flown in by various internal sponsors to meet with Mauricio to tell him of a better way. The campaign was rife with criticism of Goni and the ads. He looked old; his voice was terrible; he rambled. The answer: fire the media team and put on positive spots, with a song. For a brief moment, they had not turned on the polling team, in hopes we would join the plotters: "The gringos need to discuss this with Goni."

A late-night meeting with Goni turned into "a mudslinging event," according to Amy. Virtually all the top party politicians turned on the Americans and the American way of doing things. It was also about being analytical versus intuitive, methodical versus spontaneous. And our approach was not exactly working, as far as they could see, while Manfred's "Latin song" ads were winning the Dirty War.[65] Carlos Mesa went to see Mauricio and told him "we must fire the Americans." Mauricio told him to feel free to talk to Goni. He was amused and never even entertained a change.

Manfred made a different judgment and joined the attack: "The dirty war is obviously thanks to the advising of foreign consultants. They are attacking him and Bolivians." He promised never to hire foreign consultants to come to Bolivia and "destroy Bolivians," perhaps not his first lie.[66]

Tad developed a potentially shattering spot that brought together the most powerful critiques with powerful imagery: Manfred, a man with a modest military career, acquired immodest houses, filmed from the sky, panning his multiple swimming pools and tennis courts, followed on the screen by a listing of homes with square footage in La Paz and Miami, which scrolled off the top. The narrator said, "An unexplainable fortune of millions that Manfred Reyes Villa made during his military and political career."[67] It left you to wonder: Captain Reyes Villa, a mayor who took care of himself but could not manage to get water to Cochabamba. When people saw it in the groups, they were stunned by the totality of it: "With what capacity can he govern if he did these things"; "You can't expect anything more from a captain in the army"; "But I hoped more of him, but now see he is like the rest"; "The spot is true: he lives like a king and people don't have water."

At the end of the group, they did not vote for Goni, but many cast blank ballots. We knew the spot had to air and, indeed, devoted 100 percent of our media buy to it. This was going to be painful.[68]

We had barely begun to tarnish Manfred's image, whose support continued to grow, both at our expense and that of reformist candidates, like Costa Obregon. We were down to 22 percent and would continue down to 20; Manfred was up to 28 percent and would continue up to 30 by the second week in May. A week later, at mid-month, six weeks before the election, Manfred led Goni by 11 points.

We knew that our ads risked hurting Goni more than Manfred, but there was no strategic alternative.[69] Jeremy got the job of flying to Bolivia to buy us a few days on the air and time for the powerful ad to get heard, even though we knew we were near the limit of what the campaign and the public would accept. How long? Jeremy asked the question everyone was posing. "The answer is that we need to stay with them until we bring Manfred down." He held Goni, if not the campaign, with a reassurance: "I want to stress that all of us—me, Tad, Bob Shrum, Stan, and James—are in complete agreement that this race remains winnable."[70]

We wanted to show a self-confident face, but we had serious doubts the strategy would succeed or that Goni could still win. We weren't worried that the ads were not "Latin" enough, because plenty of them had moved voters. But listening to the voters' passionate defense of Manfred and noting the lack of movement in our own polls, the MNR politicians could very well have been right. Mark was particularly skeptical. But we all agreed that there was no choice. Without raising doubts, the campaign was over.

James and I flew to La Paz to join Jeremy, Tad, and Tal, who were already there for days of meetings on how to make the turn away from the Dirty War. We proposed an ad that was simple and uncontestable, what Goni had done on infant and maternal health, with Carlos Mesa as the narrator. When we unveiled those positive spots in focus groups there was a visible sigh of relief, confirming that we had reached the end of the road on our attack strategy and raising some doubts in our own minds about the wisdom of what we had been doing. When Carlos Mesa and Goni unveiled the new ad at a press conference during our visit, the media declared that Goni had ended the "dirty war," and they pressed to know if he had fired his American advisors. In Goni fashion, he responded, "I haven't switched religions, I haven't left my wife, and I haven't changed advisors."[71]

Our plan was to return to "the crisis," as Tad rightly pointed out, "That's our brand."[72] The rising and cumulative doubts about Reyes Villa allowed us to create a new "message box" that voters found painfully believable. This was a serious moment and "Bolivia Cannot Afford to Make the Wrong Choice." While Goni and Carlos Mesa had "the experience and emergency plan to eradicate the corruption and revert the crisis," with Manfred, "the crisis could get even worse." Carlos Mesa almost chided them, ignore all those frivolous songs and bubbly ads. "We can't give ourselves the luxury of making a mistake."[73]

We all dispersed to our respective parts of the world, comfortable that we had made the turn and had a direction, but were people listening? Were they open to the diminished hopes implicit in our message? We were nervous, exacerbated by our new daily, global conference calls, ostensibly to help the campaign in this new phase, but more a sharing of anecdotes, waiting for signs of a turn. None of us was really sure Goni could come back.

But the signs began to emerge. A week after the press conference, the race stabilized, with Manfred at 30 percent and Goni 8 points back at 22 percent; Jaime Paz Zamora of the left-oriented MIR and relative to Victor Paz Estenssoro, was at 15 percent and Evo at 6 percent, in fourth place. Manfred's ascent had stopped and his image was tarnished, taking a toll on people's hopes as well.[74]

JOBS, JOBS, JOBS

"With one month to go in the race," we wrote, "Manfred Reyes Villa maintains a strong although not insurmountable advantage over Goni." But Jeremy was leaving a bigger opening then I really believed existed, and the memo was dominated by warnings that "time is very short" and "Goni's position is perilous" and "closing the gap will be challenging." Doubts about Manfred personally grew and doubts about his plans grew even more, but there were signs that the titanic battle between the top two and the lost hope was moving voters away from both of them. Each one of the four anti-system candidates gained, with Evo rising to 7 percent.[75] Voters had rushed to Manfred out of hope and he was a chimera, but their lives were too much on the edge to settle for a worse crisis averted. Better to gamble on some kind of change, even if it was phony or messianic.

I reread the transcripts from our focus groups in Cochabamba, La Paz, and Tiwanaku and sure, people accepted that things can go terribly wrong and grudgingly thought that Goni was the better choice, but it was such a diminished choice—not one to hold on to voters when they wanted so much more.

When Jeremy called in from some Eastern European country, I said, Jeremy, we can't get there. This diminished offer will be swamped by any hope of change. We have to throw long. Somewhere along this thought process I decided that we had to do the counterintuitive, the surprising, even if none of our polls said it would work. What did we have to lose? People wanted only one thing out of the election and that was jobs, some chance that they could work. I proposed, in effect, that we make our mission the one thing voters thought was our biggest failure, even though underneath there was a sense that Goni had some special way with economic things.

Jeremy got it immediately. Yes, yes. He was the man who threw out the idea of the Victor Paz Estenssoro Highway and now had the mission to execute our "emergency jobs plan." Our shared idea was to talk about jobs 100 percent of the time. James also was giving up on Goni's prospects and our earlier strategy. "Jeremy is just spending too much time in those coca fields." So, he was for throwing long, too.

Jeremy and I flew to Bolivia, talking back and forth, developing the new concept, arriving the morning of June 3, less than a month before the election, to meet with Goni and Carlos Mesa, face-to-face across the table, to lay out the idea. For the first time, we had no polling data on this new phase, just a belief that we were stuck and could not move without some big new idea. This one was grounded in what people wanted the most and Goni's history, but in all our research they just wouldn't listen to us. This was not Goni-land where analytic thinking was rewarded. But Goni understood where the race stood and he had pressed hard to run on the economy for a long time. He could not wait to go out and tell people, without apology, that he was a job creator, would fix capitalization, and had big plans for new jobs.

Can I tell them about the 500,000 jobs I created, he asked with irony. No, I answered without irony. Forget the past. The "crisis" was defined by one thing, lack of jobs, and we were now talking only about the future, our plan for creating jobs. This was the election he had wanted to run in the first place, though only in this compressed period would other campaigns and

Jeremy and I in the den in Goni's house, discussing his rally speech and his great reluctance to acknowledge mistakes on handling the economy and discussing the idea of totally jobs-centered campaign. [Michael Anderson]

media have allowed us to talk only about the future.[76] This probably should have been our closing strategy from the beginning.

Jeremy met immediately with Goni's economic advisors to talk through the policy options for the plan and that night we did a single focus group, recruited on an urgent basis, with eight women, all soft Manfred supporters. At the end the group broke 5 to 3 for Goni, and that was enough for Jeremy. The next day we affirmed the new approach in a memo, "The Emergency Plan for Jobs," with six elements, developed with the policy team, which we would test in the next poll. Along with the north–south highway, the 100,000 new units of affordable housing, and fifty thousand urban homes connected to the natural gas line were new commitments to require that 90 percent of capitalized company employees be Bolivian and the launching of a new Jobs Brigade for high school graduates. The ad team was ordered to produce a sixty-second ad in which Goni would tell the country of the plan. All the remaining advertising of the campaign would talk about different elements of the plan. We proposed to create a "jobs contract," a small card with six elements and a pledge to launch all six by Christmas.[77]

While Manfred had refused to debate one-on-one up until that point, Goni issued a new challenge for him to debate us on how to create jobs for Bolivia. In this new moment, Manfred accepted.

A week later, on June 12, we launched our plan for jobs and the new advertising. Goni had a whole new stump speech, which this time he delivered.

A week after that on June 17, just two weeks before election day, we got our one-on-one debate with Manfred, and Jeremy and Tad went off with Goni for debate camp in a remote village. By all accounts, Goni was "amazing," talking about learning from his experiences with CNN Español declaring Goni the winner within the first thirty minutes. Our team watched the debate itself along with forty-four focus group participants, almost all of whom switched to Goni after the debate. When asked what they remembered, they got right to jobs: "Goni did very well because he touched a point that affects all of us, and that is jobs. Because he said that once he is in office in the first 90 days, he'll start creating jobs." What made the undecided voters listen, amazingly, was Goni learning from his successes and most important, his mistakes: "It was good to know that someone learned. Good to hear him say he makes mistakes." Goni had found a way to be comfortable with step two of Stan's 3-Steps and people were now listening to him on jobs above all things.

Jeremy wrote in his post-midnight e-mail, "Goni is not dead."[78]

We got a lot of help from Manfred. He turned out to have an unregistered foreign business partner. When challenged by a candidate in a forum, he expressed contempt: "I never had partners, much less Germans," and there they go again, the Dirty War. But, as it turns out, he did have a partner, a German, one Rolf Reinhold Hacker Bielefeldt, holding 50 percent of the shares in their business. The German also turned out to be Manfred's father-in-law, who ended up as chief treasurer for the city of Cochabamba, leading one television channel to introduce the story, "Manfred lied about the German."[79] Atop the doubts raised earlier, the "lie" punctured Manfred.

A week later, again after official denials, the media was swept up in reports of Manfred's close ties to the Moonies, with the sect's center located in Cochabamba, as improbable as that seems. Manfred was forced to address the issue and before the campaign's close, he asked for an audience with the cardinal to deny any connections with the Moon sect and changed his advertising to show he was a Catholic.[80]

In the first poll after the launch of our jobs plan, we pulled within a point of Manfred, 24 to 25 percent. A week later and a week before the election, we edged back into first place for the first time since March, 24 to 23 percent, with the MIR candidate at 15 percent and Evo at 11 percent. But the trends were upward on everything, with Goni newly dominant as the candidate who would create jobs, eradicate corruption, and had new ideas to address the economic crisis. Jeremy noted that when the "blank" ballots were set aside, as they would be on election day, Goni was getting 26 points, and we could see him reaching 28 percent.[81]

THE OTHER WAR

The militant anti-system leaders and parties had a different calendar. The Banzer government over the past year had affirmed repeatedly to U.S. officials that they would eliminate 100 percent of the coca crop by August, one month after the election.[82] Ever disdainful of the constitutional authorities, Evo stepped up a nationwide campaign of protests and blockades in February that left the Altiplano looking like "a war zone." According to one account, "In the early morning, the roads are covered with rocks, like there was an avalanche." The military was there with tanks and soldiers in riot gear. The road to Oruro was blocked, keeping people from reaching the carnival celebrations. With expanding protests and a refusal to negotiate a pause, campesinos could not get their crops to market and were forced to sell near and cheap, while cooking gas and flour were scarce and dear in the urban areas.[83] Early in February, Evo grew a step more disreputable, with 70 percent of the country hostile to him. Only 3 percent supported him then in an election.[84]

Always sensitive, the United States issued a report critical of the government's recent efforts to eradicate coca. The government also faced an election described in the U.S. report as "unilateral," "erroneous," with a "lack of respect for Bolivia's sovereignty." That did not stop the U.S. ambassador, Manuel Rocha, from lecturing the government publicly for failing to meet the 100 percent goal. No doubt shaking his finger, he warned the candidates in the election that they would have to "take responsibility" after the election and maintain Bolivia's commitment to the Dignity Plan, which offered access to U.S. markets and money for substitute crops.[85]

The protests and the anti-system candidates were increasingly consumed with the idea of holding a Constituent Assembly—an assembly of delegates, animated by local popular participation, that could throw out the constitution and create a new national compact. For the campesinos, it took on a millennial quality that could bring a new land dispensation and renationalization of industry, especially gas. For the Aymara and other indigenous groups, it could bring a new national recognition of rights and claims.[86]

In mid-May, the anti-system groups launched indigenous marches from various parts of the country, demanding that the government call a Constituent Assembly, all to reach La Paz by June 15, two weeks before the election. Eventually, six groups of indigenous marchers numbering around three thousand arrived in La Paz, steeled by three weeks on the road, even more insistent on their demands. The marchers won a symbolic victory when their leaders reached an agreement with the government that some kind of "extraordinary Congress" would take place after the elections and indigenous leaders' ideas would get a hearing in the Congress.[87]

A second group of ten thousand marchers, backed by the national union federation, arrived separately in La Paz on the same day, disrupting the city center for three hours, demanding that Bolivia's natural gas not be exported through Chile, the reviled nation that seized Bolivia's only access to the sea in the War of the Pacific, which took place between 1879 and 1883. Evo joined his causes, saying," We must fight from the streets—defend our natural gas, and protect our sovereignty." And then he defined the election: "In this race, we're questioning the system." The election was just a part of another struggle. "It's like 1952—when the armed revolution kicked out the capitalist government."[88]

THE HONORABLE U.S. AMBASSADOR ROCHA

On June 11, the day the first indigenous marchers reached La Paz, the U.S. embassy made its first official comment on the election, with the director of the narcotics division observing that "Evo Morales is against the interest of Bolivia and its people" and "not the right choice for Bolivia." Evo welcomed the intervention and proposed that he debate not Goni or Manfred, but the

U.S. ambassador, Manual Rocha, because "the U.S. Embassy decided everything in Bolivia anyway and was the one that told all the traditional parties what to do."[89]

At that point Evo had emerged as the strongest of the anti-system candidates, but in single digits, 9 percent, and in fourth place in the race. His vote immediately bumped up to 11 percent where it stayed until the last week of the election.

With just four days before the election, the U.S. ambassador, not content to leave the matter to a functionary, signaled during a speech inaugurating an airport in the Chapare that he had "some clarifying comments," meaning nobody should miss this intervention: "I want to remind the Bolivian electorate that if they elect those that want Bolivia to go back to being an important exporter of cocaine, that the result will put in danger the future of the aid of the United States to Bolivia." That produced the banner headline, "US Will Suspend Aid if Evo Is Elected: Ambassador Rocha."

Goni and Manfred immediately condemned this intervention in the election, but Evo now had the stage, saying the United States "continues violating the sovereignty and dignity of the Bolivian people." Jeremy and I were even angrier than the candidates with this ham-handed attempt to help the traditional parties. The National Electoral Court, with responsibility for overseeing the elections, ruled on the Friday before the Sunday election that the ambassador's intervention violated Article 219 of the Constitution and Article 6 of the Electoral Code and called on the government to act to prevent future violations of Bolivian sovereignty.

Ten thousand Evo supporters gathered at the plaza at Cochabamba, chanting "Evo yes, Yankees no!" When some speakers were less than respectful, Evo intervened: "No comrades, don't boo the Ambassador, he is our best campaign manager. We owe him a lot. Please comrades, I ask for a strong applause for the ambassador," and the crowd happily cooperated.[90]

We were no longer polling but Tal watched all this from Bolivia and was deeply worried that the election had been turned on its head in the campaign's final moments by the Bush administration, supremely arrogant, indifferent to the crisis in Bolivia but self-satisfied when lecturing the people about doing what America thinks is right.

THE JUNE 30 ELECTION—AND MANDATE

When the 2.6 million Bolivians voted on Sunday, they managed to produce a virtual three-way tie for first place, with competing exit polls producing competing winners. BBC declared Goni the likely winner; CNN called it for Manfred. The hours after the polls closed at 6 P.M. were a kind of roller coaster for those in La Paz. James called every fifteen minutes that night as we got snippets from our man in La Paz. When the real votes started being counted, Goni and Manfred were in a dead heat, but as the rural vote came in, Goni moved into a lead that held, a result soon reflected in the exit polls, as they aligned and adjusted and did their magic. Within hours of the polls closing, Manfred declared he would form the new government. With visions of James Baker in Florida, Jeremy persuaded Goni and Carlos to do a press conference, lest the uncertainty become the stuff for popular conspiracies. At 11 P.M. Goni and Carlos held the press conference, confident they would form the new government, ahead in the count, ahead in the projections of all three stations—and the party with the most senators and deputies. By the next morning, there was a growing presumption that Goni, after a lot of horse-trading, would likely emerge as the next president.[91]

But this was a very close election. Goni's party got 22.5 percent of the vote, with Evo's—yes, Evo—in second place with 20.9 percent, less than a thousand votes ahead of Manfred, also with 20.9 percent, and the MIR's candidate at 16.3. The ambassador's intervention in the final days stopped short our rise but, more importantly, anointed Evo as the sole leader of the popular anti-system forces and prime combatant in the struggle against American influence, now put at the center of the election.[92] That nearly doubled his party's vote, taking him from a distant third or fourth place to finish within a percentage point of the lead and eligible to be chosen president by the Congress. It gave Evo a new national constituency of the poor, rural indigenous, and those with mixed ethnicity—united and ready to march with him.

In the days after the election, we were in celebratory spirits, though dispersed and unable to do much backslapping. While we thought Goni pulled ahead in the final weeks, we spent many more weeks believing we were on a death march. As James said, "there's always some scenario where somebody could win [if things fall into place perfectly] . . . but this is the only time where I've actually seen it happen."[93]

I called Goni to congratulate him and he was appreciative of all our efforts, but under no illusions about how hard the negotiations would be to form a government: "This is the time when Bolivia's politics is most dark," when the politicians barter ministries, gain patronage, control over areas of government, and set up toll stations for bribes. Goni said, "I'm not playing those games." And while I had no idea whether that was true, later his own MNR activists would riot and occupy government offices, demanding patronage jobs.

In the two days following the election, we conducted a nationwide post-election survey to understand what happened and what people intended by their vote. I was more than a little surprised by what happened in the election. Almost 40 percent said they were choosing a president who would act to reduce unemployment and those voters supported Goni by a wide margin over the other candidates. Apparently, we resolved the paradox for a brief moment. About a quarter of the voters said they chose a candidate who would tackle the corruption, and those voters, too, supported Goni by a wide margin. Goni set out a campaign to fix the jobs crisis and eradicate the corruption and that took him to his victory. The country was not celebrating, however. The election did not reduce the pessimism. The great majority still wanted a leader from outside the traditional parties and doubted Goni would keep his promises anyway.[94]

By the end of July, Goni signed an agreement with the MIR that gave them the majority to form a government and cabinet, and on August 6, Gonzalo Sánchez de Lozada became president of Bolivia for the second time.

HONEYMOON OF SORTS

That brought a precious period for Bolivia, lasting beyond Goni's first ninety days, indeed stretching almost to 180—a period when Goni worked to move his agenda and a discontented populace suspended judgment. Before Goni's swearing in, over 70 percent believed the country was on the wrong track, but the day after, it fell below 50 percent. In the grudging spirit of the time, optimism—actually believing the country is on the "right track"—remained at just 10 percent, rising not even a point. These wise voters were simply allowing for the possibility that things could be better, what we called in the memo to the new president, "a honeymoon of sorts."[95]

It was almost as if they knew that as soon as Goni settled into his office in the presidential palace that he would soon have a grim meeting on the public finances—the very same meeting that President-elect Clinton, President Mandela, Prime Minister Blair, and Prime Minister Barak sat through at virtually the same points in office. Each time it was worse than they thought, bordering on crisis. The previous government buried the bad news before the election and accelerated spending to aid its election. Rather than increase social spending, the new administration faced austerity, layoffs, and pay cuts.[96]

Like those leaders, Goni pressed ahead with his election agenda because that was why he ran and because his political life depended on it. He battled his own coalition partners to introduce and pass by the end of November the expansion of maternal and infant health care, now to be universal for all pregnant women and all children under five to take effect immediately. He reintroduced the Bonosol, restored to 1,800 bolivianos, guaranteed for the next seventy years with the first payments by the end of the year. For Goni, this was his first promise. He announced his Plan Bolivia, moving ahead with the Youth Brigade and public works to expand employment, mobilizing 50 million bolivianos for new road projects and seeking international support for the north–south highway. He submitted a plan for 250,000 gas connections, free of charge over the next five years.

So, at the end of his first ninety days, people were able to rattle off his promises with great specificity and, surprisingly, almost half said this "liar" was on the way to fulfilling his promises. Before the end of the year, almost 60 percent were giving him positive ratings on his social agenda.[97]

Goni readied himself to go to Washington for his meeting on November 14, 2002, with President George W. Bush at the White House. Before going, Goni upped the ante in a televised speech to the country: "I will be traveling to the USA to look for financing for all our needs," the programs for employment and economic stability.[98] When he got to the White House, the assistant secretary and the national security advisor for Western Hemisphere affairs warned him not to raise any specific money requests with the president. But Goni knew he was sitting on a powder keg. He asked for $150 million, saying, "I apologize for bringing it up at this meeting, but if I don't get this assistance now, I'll be asking you for asylum in a year's time."

Bush gave him nothing. The IMF and World Bank also said no.

The night before the meeting we hosted a dinner at Tosca, my favorite restaurant in Washington, for the new president and his family, our team, and some foreign policy glitterati. The toasts were not at all bittersweet. We were still in the middle of "the honeymoon of sorts" and did not know that Bush would stiff Goni. I had pulled back after the election, as Goni expected, so I did not even know of the budget problems. I had few regrets about our campaign and him and his mission, and my toast that night was full of admiration for Goni, the modernizing progressive leader.

What I did not realize was how isolated Goni was within his own society, within his own government and even his office. Goni now was seventy-two years old and did not have the same energy to push ahead with reforms and, in any case, his election did not bring the rush of professionals and advisors to fashion the next phase of reform. His party, the MNR, sixty years after the revolution, looked like a lot of older white guys, consumed with perquisites and patronage. They were forced to form a coalition with the MIR, joined a year later by Manfred's party—parties that were unpopular, uncooperative, opposed to Goni's ideas and uninterested in his mandate. In reality, the government was dependent on a coalition of traditional white, often corrupt politicians bent on protecting their privileges against the anti-system forces and the indigenous majority. With Evo back in the Congress with political immunity and heading the second largest party made up of supporters who believed he had really won the election, Goni's government had begun losing authority and support.

Goni's vision for modernizing Bolivia while addressing the acute inequality required exporting Bolivia's gas and creating a new unbreakable link with education and support for the poor. Without exporting and without that link, the new energy reserves created by his policies would be turned "into a big corruption game," he told me. He knew the traditional politicians and watched the experience of other energy-rich countries. His approach "enables Bolivia to become a normal, reasonable country"—the goal that infused all he did. Those who proposed building a pipeline over the Andes to Peru to reach the Pacific and the market in California knew nobody would finance such a scheme. Exporting through Chile was the only way for Bolivia to become a "reasonable country."

While Jeremy and our team shared Goni's view that populist politicians were fanning the nationalist fervor for their own purposes, we understood that the distrust of Goni on the gas issue grew deeper because the public thought that Goni was enamored of foreigners and could not protect the people or the nation's interests. They had no trust in the political class that would steal the new money, while ordinary Bolivians got higher prices for gas, no gas connections, only "tea and bread." "If he'll export our gas," one group participant observed about Goni, "maybe one day he'll export us."[99]

This was all the more volatile because Evo's supporters thought the election had legitimated popular struggle as much as democracy. Strikes and blockades had gained a new level of popular legitimacy, even if they were not actually popular. A large majority in the country saw them as "justifiable if the government moves too slowly to help the people" and an even larger majority opposed using the military to remove the blockades. That represented the ultimate coercive power of the state these humble people understood and a shift in the balance against them.[100]

THE NEW YEAR

Jeremy and Mark drove back with Goni after an event outside La Paz and used the moment to tell him "there is no way you can even start to get close to an acceptable level of support" on exporting gas through Chile and, more than that, to raise the alert level to red: "the reaction is going to be very hostile, possibly violent." While Jeremy and Mark did not see it as their role to say, "You can't do this," that was their implied message.

Goni was so passionate in his belief that this was right for the country and that conceding would leave him with no purpose that he reacted with an uncharacteristic outburst: "God damn it. I didn't get elected to sit on my ass.

This is important to the country. We need to convince people it is the right thing to do. And your job is to figure out how to sell it."[101]

With the new year, Evo and other militant leaders announced the resumption of blockades on key roads to stop coca eradication, despite efforts by Goni at year end to achieve "social peace through dialogue." The government offered some innovative ideas on "demilitarizing eradication," but Evo would only accept legalization of coca for domestic use and an end to U.S. efforts to eliminate coca. When the blockades resumed it was with a vengeance, requiring some twenty thousand troops to keep open Bolivia's main east–west highway. Thirteen died on both sides in the protests.[102]

On January 12, Goni addressed the nation, appealing for constructive dialogue, while deploring the violent blockades, which hurt the small producer and the nation. He offered talks in the government palace or to go out to the farmers, with the colonizadores. That one short wave of organized popular protest and the confrontation with the military also caused Evo's popularity to fall as much as Goni's, with over 60 percent viewing him negatively. But Evo was getting what he wanted, rising support for strikes, blockades, and violence; two thirds said they would support blockades to stop the tax increase and the export of gas through Chile.[103]

Goni then poured gasoline onto the flickering flames: he announced the austerity budget demanded by the IMF and necessitated by U.S. indifference. He told the nation that Bolivia could not go the way of Argentina and must choose "the way of seriousness, austerity, and responsibility." That included a new income tax of 12.5 percent for salaried workers, a 10 percent cut in government expenses, sharp limits on pay increases, and no new money for the universities. The police would have to settle for just a 2.2 percent increase. They responded by going on strike, abandoning their posts, and, in a breathtaking escalation of the violence, opening fire on the military guard at the presidential palace and spraying Goni's office with gunfire. Protesters rushed the Labor Ministry, burning furniture in the street, and set fire to the vice president's office and the offices of the MNR and MIR. It took eight hundred troops to secure the palace, but it was a mess, according to our new person on the ground, who returned to Bolivia a few days later. Tear gas lingered in the air and dried blood caked the floors both inside and outside the building.

Just three days after presenting his "IMF budget" to the nation, Goni withdrew it and the next night announced on TV that "calm and peace have been reestablished in all the national territory."[104]

Goni and Evo continued their spiral downward in popularity, though Goni was the president and the great majority of the country blamed him for the breakdown in order. The country was divided on whether he should re-sign. For his part, Evo was not so interested in his own poll numbers, as his goal was undermining confidence in the government and building support for popular resistance.[105]

Goni carried on, though he was at that point a much diminished leader with a diminished capacity to advance his agenda. He insisted on moving ahead with his plan to export gas through Chile, along with an intensive pro-gram of research to figure out "how to sell it." A discriminating public gave him high marks for his accelerated effort to bring gas to homes, but many more were "strongly" opposed to his export of gas, rising to 60 percent. In what Jeremy described as a "sobering result, survey respondents reject every argument we test to support exports."[106] We created simulated news stories using an actual newsroom set to see if people would react differently once it was a reality. They didn't.

On September 15, Evo launched a campaign to block the export of Bo-livia's gas through Chile. The one-day marches were minimally disruptive, but peasant groups in other areas threw up blockades in Caranavi and El Alto. Four days later, they were joined by the miners. Another group block-aded Sorata where many tourists go. When the buses with tourists and mili-tary escort passed through Warisata, they were fired upon. After the return fire, seven were left dead, leading to more widespread calls for the govern-ment to open negotiations. By the end of the month, protests intensified in El Alto, this time with new sectors—schoolteachers, bus drivers, and the retired—joining the peasants on the barricades.[107] Joining the blockades amid shouts of "Goni didn't deserve to be reelected," Evo picked up a bullhorn and declared, "We will overthrow the government."[108]

In early October, blockaders in El Alto stopped all food and gas from pass-ing through to Le Paz, and on October 12 Goni sent the army there to escort the fuel trucks to the city. But the confrontation involved violence on both sides and the rising fury left twenty-six dead. Violence the next day in La Paz killed twenty more. With those deaths, Vice President Carlos Mesa an-nounced that while still vice president, he no longer considered himself a member of the government. Goni reached agreement with his coalition part-ners for a freeze on the gas export plan and a promised referendum but it was too late. Concessions were elevating rather than diminishing the violence. The airport was closed and the marchers reached La Paz on October 15. The next day, 15,000 gathered in the Plaza San Francisco, two blocks away from the presidential palace, but there were also large marches in Cochabamba, Oruro, and Chuquisaca. With the intellectuals staging a hunger strike in churches until Goni resigned, it all looked more and more like a general strike. In La Paz, mini-blockades were popping up in the streets all over the city, the streets strewn with rocks and burning tires. Everything was closed and people were short of gas and chickens. The next day the most violent of the marchers, the miners, arrived in the city.[109]

Goni resigned on October 17 and flew out of the country, arriving in Miami the next morning and, two days later, in Washington, where he asked for asylum.

Underlying what I do in countries from Britain to Bolivia is an operating assumption that this is all on the level, that public opinion matters in so many ways, sometimes decisively, as with the export of gas from Bolivia. But as Goni pointed out, for all the brilliance, you "missed some of the big picture," as did he. "I was so damned dumb and you guys were dumb" thinking this was all about "public opinion" when there was another kind of war going on. Speaking eliptically and ironically, "You didn't realize that you had Russia arming the guerrillas and the U.S. arming the contras."

The coca growers waged war on the "neoliberal model" with barely a truce for the election because they faced extinction in a war financed by the United States. The cocaine cartels had more than a passing interest in the balance of forces there, just as the mafia networks in Pakistan, Iran, and Central Asia remain interested in the balance of forces in the southern provinces in Afghanistan where poppies are resurgent.[110] From the first time we met with Goni in Washington, Evo was meeting with Fidel Castro and Hugo Chávez about their approach to issues—leaders who are impatient with "public opinion" at the very least. And then there are those in Peru who have so much to lose if Bolivia exports its gas via a Chilean port. Goni believes, based on information available to him, that such interests financed the police rebellion, which inexplicably escalated the violence, shot up the president's office, ending with unidentified sharpshooters.[111]

Perhaps this is the fantasy world of political leaders living in exile with their conspiracies and unreal portraits of politics in their home countries. Or perhaps this is like Nelson Mandela's accusations about a "Third Force" that was financing and organizing "black-on-black" violence, which turned out to be true. Bolivia underscored something I have well understood: our efforts to convince and bring people with Goni on his project would not always be settled in the court of public opinion.

With Goni's resignation on October 17, 2003, Carlos Mesa became Bolivia's president and was a very popular leader during his year and a half in office, though nothing happened to alter the trajectory of events. He acceded to a future referendum on the gas issue and serious changes in the hydrocarbon laws regulating the ownership and sale of natural gas, but his popularity did not protect him from the protests and new waves of blockades led by Evo. Populist protests and blockades continued throughout the spring of 2005 and were coupled with dissatisfaction from both pro-business groups and legislators.[112] Carlos Mesa's resignation was accepted by the Congress very late at night on June 9 and a caretaker president called early elections for December 18, 2005.

In the campaign, Evo fused his battle against globalization and imperialism with the battle to achieve a historic settlement for the indigenous people of Bolivia. He elevated the stakes of the election with a warning, "If we don't win, neo-liberalism and colonialism will deepen." Those forces "robbed us of our national patrimony," he declared, with the commitment that the country "cannot continue to allow our most precious resources in the hands of foreigners."

After years of unrest, electing Evo was almost the only way to achieve social peace. But Evo gave voters more than that. He reassured middle-class and white voters with a credible vice president and TV ads with technocrats saying how they would govern. With Evo the only way to bring change against a corrupt political class indifferent to poverty, he won a sweeping victory, indeed, an improbable absolute majority. With excited crowds gathering in the Plaza Murillo for his inauguration, Evo began: "I want to say to all Aymaras, Quechuas, Guaranis and Chiquitanos: For the first time, we have the presidency." And with his inauguration, Evo celebrated with this tepid salute to democracy: "The 500 years of Indian resistance have not been in vain. From 500 years of resistance, we pass to another 500 years in power."

The corridors of the Congress are now decorated with posters of Che Guevara; cabinet members now chew coca leaf at cabinet meetings.[113]

With a deep sense of history and mission, the government on May Day decreed the nationalization of the gas industry and sent in the military to secure the installations for a future mandatory sale of assets to the government. While acrimonious negotiations with the oil companies would continue for two years, resulting in debates over royalties, contract wording, and levels of investment, the decree was clear on the new principle: "The state recovers title, possession and total and absolute control over these resources."[114]

GEORGE CLOONEY

Warner Brothers bought up the movie rights to remake *Our Brand Is Crisis*. It would be done as a "dark comedy." I was fairly certain that George Clooney would turn down the chance to play the pollster, preferring instead the role of James Carville, master of the "manipulation and orchestration involved in big-time political campaigning."[115] If only Jeremy and I had been more manipulative, we might have gotten the title role.

After the violence, the loss of life, the critical media commentary, and Evo's election, I have certainly paused to take stock. I did the same thing after the Democrats' defeat in 1994, Blair's decision to align with Bush on the Iraq War, and, most of all, after Mbeki's subsequent actions on AIDS and Zimbabwe. While Mbeki's actions occurred after my time with him, I have continued to ask in each case, What did I miss? I also have asked myself if our methods crossed the line into mere manipulation. But with Goni, the reflections have left me more certain, not less, of my course and his.

When Goni accepted too late a referendum on exporting gas through Chile, I asked myself then: Goni is deeply principled, but was it worth it if he was going to throw in the towel in the end? Should the powerful forces against him and the deep opposition of the public have won? Goni believed this was the only way Bolivia could become a "normal" country, and I can't answer my own question. Barak thought resolving Jerusalem was the only way Israel, too, could become normal, and I don't second-guess him now, even though I did at the time.

What I do know is none of my nerve endings are stimulated by the intellectual elite's hailing of Evo, "Now that would have been a campaign worth running," as the *Guardian* reviewer exclaimed. I am sure Evo was right in his critique of the traditional political parties and America's deeply exploitive and arrogant role in Bolivia, and I am sure he will get a better deal from the oil companies. But I am not fascinated by leaders who view democracy as a mere tactic and who manipulate national symbols to avoid tough national choices. Understanding how little the poor and democracy have ultimately benefited in other energy-rich countries, I come away from our work for Goni even more respectful of him and his bold efforts to help the poor in an enduring way.

At the risk of creating the biggest gap yet with elite judgments about the work of the "pollster-consultant industrial complex," I am proud of what we did to help Goni become president for the second time and help him bring people with him for his bold reforms.

CONCLUSION

V. O. KEY HAD BEEN dead four years when I arrived at Harvard for graduate work in 1967, but his unfinished manuscript, *The Responsible Electorate*, had just been published. As early as 1960 Key had been disdainful of the elites who were disdainful of ordinary voters and too ready to reduce politics to style and image, rather than to policy. "The perverse and unorthodox argument of this little book is that voters are not fools."[1] From his rich work on the states of the Deep South to that last book, Key was an empiricist. But I also came to realize how much of his argument and how much of my motivation as a pollster was grounded as well in the real world of politics and policy. Key knew that all regimes worry about public opinion, evidenced by the "persistent anxiety in the chronicled histories of the secret police." But he also knew that it is only in democratic societies that "public opinion in the long run must affect the course of public action." How that happens is a riddle that I hope is at least partially solved through this book. Clearly the translation of preferences is, at best, inexact. Yet the bottom line remains, as Key stated it, that the "preferences of the [governed] should be accorded weight by the governors constitutes the moral basis of popular government, an ethical imperative . . ."[2]

That is a difficult conclusion to reach if you believe that public opinion is the work of the masters of the "black arts." But my years of work in public opinion have convinced me more than ever that voters are very discerning indeed. I never fail to learn something surprising when I listen closely to people in focus groups thinking and talking through a problem. I recall in particular the African women and Zulu men who were undecided about their choice late in the ANC's first campaign. They were not ready to believe the promises of a better life and were desperate for assurance that Nelson Mandela would rein in the violent African youth. They were undecided for a reason, not because of lack of interest or knowledge. After Ehud Barak mused aloud that he might have joined a terrorist organization if he had been a Palestinian youth, it was the people in focus groups who upbraided him, not for the thought itself, but for the impermissibility of acknowledging it because it endangered Israeli lives. You have seen in the various accounts in this book how voters consistently brushed aside the spin and how these politicians quickly learned through our research that only the real thing would carry them. What was most striking in country after country was how remarkably sensitive and discriminating voters were about what was happening on issues important to their lives and how the main project had brought these leaders to power. I do not fully understand it but voters are just as discerning in impoverished Bolivia or South Africa, with their high rates of illiteracy and low rates of newspaper readership, as they are in Britain, the United States, and Israel with their higher education and literacy rates and more intensive media.

Despite an election that left Goni struggling for legitimacy amid popular protests from day one, people were immediately aware of the restoration of the Bonosol and spending on health care and gave Goni rising job approval ratings on those issues—but only on those. When Goni accelerated gas connections to people's lots in hopes of gaining greater space to advocate for gas exports, the government's approval went up on gas connections, but without any gain on handling natural gas overall. Following the announced austerity budget and the subsequent rioting, opinions about Goni crashed but not the regard for his work on social insurance.

In South Africa the political leaders grew frustrated when the new black majority, casting a discerning eye on the pace of real change, did not pause very long to relish their new freedom and the end to discrimination. When we polled three years into the new government, people were acutely aware that the government had extended electricity and water into deep rural areas with an immediate impact on the quality of people's lives, starting with the women who no longer had to walk miles with vases on their heads to fetch water. But these were not the big things that formed the core of what the voters believed to be a better life. There was the barest evidence of improvement in housing, though at least the government got modest marks for trying. That was not true for employment and crime. When the pace of new housing accelerated, voters acknowledged the improvement and gave the government a better grade there even as marks on jobs and crime continued to decline.

When ANC leaders spoke of progress too blithely, they looked out of touch and lost support. The facts were too real to be spun. Indeed, attempts at spin only increased the anger and broke bonds that often were never fully restored. The poor people of South Africa, as in Bolivia, had a big stake in the performance of their president and the government and they watched and judged with a subtlety that the leaders could not help but appreciate.

British voters, too, rebelled against the government's attempt to spin change in the public services where it was not real. That broken trust left them skeptical and discerning. In the second election, Labour won back these grudging voters, but only when the government poured huge amounts of money into health and education and when the Tories' promised tax cuts put that investment at risk.

With all his persuasive powers, voters would not give credit to Clinton on the economy before there was evidence of gains in income: no in 1994, but yes in 1996.

The fundamental lesson is that people matter because elections matter. You could only think otherwise if you haven't spent any time close to elected officials or candidates for office. Tightening poll numbers and the prospect of a hanging on election day increase the intensity and madness, but the consciousness of voters having their say in an election is evident from day one in every case. Perhaps candidates in safe legislative and congressional seats have more room for indifference, but not the ones I know. The antics of the Republicans in Washington over the past decade seemed to challenge that presumption when they ignored overwhelming public sentiment on Clinton's impeachment, taxes, and the Iraq War, and escaped accountability at the polls. They resorted to all manner of things, described by Jacob Hacker and Paul Pierson's *Off Center*, including the manipulation of language with the active help of the consultant class. When I read the book, I asked what happens when, after all the machinations to avoid accountability, they fall short and lose an election, as they did in 2006? What is the educative effect for the politicians of a public hanging they could not escape? A historic number of House and Senate members retired rather than face the voters again. And what is the educative effect of two hangings?[3]

In fact, in most of the stories that form this book, the voters would not wait for an election. They nearly crashed Britain's Labour government three years into office and voted in a Republican U.S. Congress in the off-year election essentially to punish the leaders for apparently not honoring the project as voters understood it. After the four-year wait for elections in South Africa and three years of limited change afterward, voters there became deeply angry and disillusioned, focused on the politicians who were riding a "gravy train." In the polls, the ANC dropped below a red line of 50 percent support and voters threatened to withdraw from the electorate, denying the ANC its legitimacy. That Israel's Ehud Barak pursued the peace process to the exclusion of his economic and social agenda and still catered to religious minorities also produced a crash in support and left him with no government. Bolivia's Goni was forced to flee the country.

Given those clear lessons, my first conclusion is that we would all be wiser if we began by granting voters their overdue respect.

LEADERS CONSIDERATE OF PUBLIC OPINION

My second lesson is even more unfashionable: that the leaders whose stories are the heart of this book deserve our respect precisely because they are consumed with people and popular support.

All the contemporary leaders I describe in this work had a special relationship with people and were considerate of public opinion, sometimes aligning themselves to gain strength to unite and move the country to a goal, and sometimes engaging and educating to make change possible. The relationship was sometimes empathetic and reciprocal, sometimes educative and directive, and sometimes both. These were strong-willed leaders, sometimes with a mission but certainly with a political project that required winning voters' support in an election and building a strategy for governing. All of them used polling and modern campaign techniques without apology, beginning with being elected in the right way with the right meaning so that afterward forces in society would gravitate to their work. They all sought with varying degrees of success and with different emphasis in different periods to become "popular," a term I use in the higher sense, to build a relationship or identity with people, maybe a bond, certainly to garner support and encourage loyalists who will be with them in tough times. Their leadership is not defined by defying the public or by being a "profile in courage" that attracts and entertains the media, but by aligning with and engaging and educating people.

Consider Nelson Mandela, the leader we can probably all agree did not put his finger to the wind to figure out his principles. I assumed that the scale of Mandela's place in history and the fundamental nature of the issues he faced would take him right past the soundings of public opinion and campaign techniques, but the opposite was true. He was deeply interested in public opinion and listened for hours to tedious reports on focus groups and surveys. Indeed, he even wanted to take charge of the research in the campaign. He attended a focus group during the protracted negotiations and saw how ordinary voters were coming to see the exile leaders and "Robben Islanders" as out of touch. Mandela thrived on the "People's Forum" in which he stood alone on his stage and any ordinary citizen could mount a platform of equal height to pose his or her question. That process clearly helped change the ANC as a party and Mandela as its leader.

Mandela was always conscious of his educative role. Because of his personal anger with de Klerk's failure to stop violence, he resisted in the debate, saying all parties, including the ANC, must take responsibility for ending the violence. But when Mandela's arrival at the ANC's final rally in Soweto was greeted with a burst of gunfire, a stern Mandela lectured his own people to take responsibility and stop the violence. He would do the same when leaving office before the parliament.

Bill Clinton experienced many highs and lows as a candidate and president, but he never could have survived without a bond with people, evident anytime he worked his way up the rope line, listening and talking to people, quoting them even weeks later during White House meetings. That is why the postcards people wrote to him at the end of focus groups were so important, a kind of unfiltered listening, circumventing all the trappings of the bubble that surrounds Washington. In a political and journalistic world, cynical and frenzied, he sought to connect directly, as in Keene, New Hampshire, where the "comeback kid" was carried up by his determination to fight for people. After the disastrous defeat in 1994, which gave Republicans control of Congress, a large majority of the country refused to give up on Clinton, providing a reservoir of hope that made it possible for him to come back. What people understood was that Bill Clinton loved politics and the whole process of winning people's affections and loyalty, reflected in the way he devoured polls. But they also saw another perspective, that he loved policy and the process, and threw himself into every line of the budget.

When Clinton lost his moorings for a period after the 1994 defeat, polling gravitated more deeply into the policy process, leading some observers to the conclusion that his appetite for polls had no limits. But I can only write about the Bill Clinton I know. He did not conduct a single poll during the year he was evolving his thinking about national affairs as head of the Democratic Leadership Council, nor before his announcement for the presidency, and not before he began his seminal New Covenant speeches that defined and distinguished his candidacy. There was just one set of focus groups in New Hampshire, a kind of gut check in the first primary state. Clinton did not poll on his free trade position, a central plank of his "New Democratic" platform, even when the main threat to his future, Ross Perot, was stealing votes with "America first" appeals. And most importantly, he agreed with his economic team right at the outset of his administration to a "deficit reduction target" that virtually eliminated his public investment program and affected everything else he did in his presidency because he accepted that it was the policy most likely to produce long-term economic growth—and what the public wanted most. He anguished and raged about each spending cut and who would be hurt by it, but never reopened the deficit target, even when told it might slow the economy in the short term.

Tony Blair never developed the kind of empathy with people or gained the kind of energy that Mandela and Clinton did from building their bond with people, but he was nonetheless consumed with public opinion and people's judgments mattered to him. That was the source of his passion to convince people of his course and to follow him. With great energy, he set out to convince the electorate that the "New Labour" was real and could be trusted on taxes, finances, the economy, and crime. After the election, he wanted to know if voters believed that Labour was delivering on his key promises. At each step, he redoubled his efforts to win people over. Blair had a high tolerance for Philip Gould's telephone calls after focus groups and for his sometimes hysterical overnight notes, but I never saw any evidence that immediate feedback moved Blair to do anything other than reevaluate how he could bring people to a different judgment.

When three years into Labour's first term the tight budgetary constraints came up hard against the promises and rhetoric about investment in the public services, voters were left feeling disillusioned and betrayed. Their trust in Blair and Labour crashed. That lost trust became a crisis for Blair, who realized he had breached a fundamental promise to people who were disengaging and reducing their investment in him. That was compounded by the Iraq War, the lack of weapons of mass destruction, and the intelligence dossier. Trust fell to such a level that Blair himself grew dark, contemplated ending his time as prime minister.

Sánchez de Lozada—Goni—was a bold economic reformer, a technocrat and policy wonk who hardly ever warmed to a crowd. But he was also a democrat at a time of economic crisis when the leading opponent was General Banzer, the longest serving of the junta leaders. He emerged with great popularity when, as an economic minister, he acted boldly to fix the crisis and ultimately won the presidency twice based on his ability to address economic issues linked to social reforms of the boldest kinds. But his relationship with people was transactional, based on his delivery of the goods, and therefore fragile. And because Bolivia was relatively new to modern elections and Goni was not a "natural" candidate of people, he hired the best American professionals he could find, as he did with the lawyers and accountants in his businesses. He deferred to their skills to get him elected so he could restore the reforms and, most important, export the newly discovered reserves of natural gas in order to fund education, completing the mission and his life's work. Maybe because of that, he was deeply and violently opposed by populist and nationalist forces whose relationship with democracy was transactional. When we said it could not be done, he pushed back: "We need to convince people it is the right thing to do. And your job is to figure out how to sell it."

For Ehud Barak, the former chief of the army, the mission was everything. Informed by a deep Jewish patriotism, he self-consciously followed the lead of Yitzhak Rabin and David Ben-Gurion—leaders who asked the people to embrace previously unacceptable compromises to secure a Jewish state and peace. Barak was trusted as a daring military person, but voters were not sure he cared much for people. Barak knew he needed a new unit, with top professionals both to win the election and to carry people with him on the mission. He stretched to embrace the issues that mattered to people, though he made clear he intended to carry on where the assassinated Rabin left off. For Barak, polling was like the intelligence that enabled him to contemplate impossible missions. If rescuing the hostages at Entebbe is imaginable, then why not defeat the "magician" Benjamin Netanyahu in an election and why not seek a peace with Israel's enemies and neighbors?

When he went to Camp David to negotiate a comprehensive peace with the Palestinians, he left with no government backing him and, if he succeeded, faced immediate elections or a referendum. In a matter of weeks, he forced a discussion of issues not previously discussable and moved people across red lines that every Israeli politician routinely affirmed they would never cross. As leader, he played an unprecedented educative role that changed what kind of peace was possible.

Goni and Barak knew they lacked the instinctive bond with people that a Clinton, Blair, or Mandela brought to politics, but they understood they had to move people, which is precisely why they turned to professionals like me. I was frustrated by the neglect of empathy and listening, yet had they paused like other politicians, would they have led across those red lines?

The stories I have recounted in this volume are essentially about contemporary politics. But it is worth recalling that Abraham Lincoln and Franklin Roosevelt viewed public opinion and their relationship with people as integral to their leadership, not an obstacle to it. They are the American presidents who took the country into "great" wars, conflicts that confronted transcendent issues and caused millions of deaths. They are the presidents responsible for virtually all of America's major periods of domestic reform, from ending slavery and grounding America in freeholding and free labor, to giving the federal government the authority to regulate markets and balance the big corporations, to the New Deal, the American version of the welfare state, including Social Security, union recognition, and heavy public investment. While pundits look at defiance of public opinion as the best measure of leadership, these presidents embraced public opinion as a precondition for their boldness.

Abraham Lincoln was a man of self-consciously moderate disposition, not inclined to break with precedent, even as he advanced his two nearly absolute goals: no spread of slavery and the defense of the American union. Though he believed slavery to be morally wrong and that slaves' humanity was recognized in the Declaration of Independence, he was extremely solicitous of long-standing popular opinion and the need to gain popular acceptance. During his debates with Stephen Douglas, Lincoln said that in "this and like communities, public sentiment is everything." Lincoln viewed it as his obligation to understand the limits of public opinion and to adapt his principles, indeed compromise them, to reflect the times so he could work with the disparate interests that he needed to hold together.[4]

Lincoln was a country lawyer, state representative, and Republican congressman in a state heavily populated by Southerners, 70 percent of whom voted in a referendum a decade earlier to bar Negroes from the state. Douglas attacked Lincoln in the debates as an "abolitionist" who favored the "amalgamation of the races." In order to even be heard on the slave question, Lincoln reassured voters that he was no abolitionist and had no interest in mixing black and white: "I am not, nor ever have been in favor of bringing about in any way the social and political equality of the white and black races."[5]

Lincoln knew how and when to hold his own counsel. Desperate to avoid triggering the breakup of the Union, he remained mostly silent between his election and inauguration. "I deem it due to myself and the whole country, in the present extraordinary conditions of the country and of public opinion, that I should wait and see the last development of public opinion before I give my views or express myself at the time of the inauguration." That extraordinary statement led the historian Richard Hofstadter to brand Lincoln a follower. Garry Wills had a more sympathetic take, crediting Lincoln for "leading by listening," recognizing "followers have a say in what they are being led to do."[6] In the White House, Lincoln followed the newspapers closely to understand what was going on in abolitionist New England, the border slave states that had not yet seceded, as well as the Confederacy. But he also said that "no hours of the day are better employed" than those that "bring me again within direct contact and atmosphere of the average of our whole people," what he called "promiscuous receptions" in the East Room in the White House where "each applicant takes his turn, as if waiting to be shaved in a barber's shop." Quite conscious of the importance of this to his whole project, he described them as "my 'public opinion' baths."[7]

Despite heavy pressure to move forward with the emancipation of the slaves, Lincoln worried that abolition would push the border slave states into the arms of the Confederacy. His reading of public opinion led him to conclude that he could better sustain support for the war and get recruits to the Union Army if the war's purpose was to save the Union, not to end slavery. He purposely delayed the issuance of his Emancipation Proclamation until the Union Army achieved a battlefield victory so its release would be interpreted as a sign of strength, not weakness. It was justified as "a fit and necessary military measure," not presented as just or morally right. "I made a promise to myself and to my Maker" and he kept it, but conditioned without apology by his own feelings of how to sustain the greatest amount of popular support and ensure that the Union could carry on after the war.[8]

Franklin Roosevelt's self-confidence and mastery of the White House are the starting point for any study of presidential power, though central to all this was his deep identification with the common people who almost picked him up and handed him the keys to the White House. He acted on their behalf and used their mandate and need to press entrenched interests in the Congress and the economy to give way. His popular identity was central to his power. With a possible challenge in 1936 from the populist left represented by Huey Long from Louisiana and growing business opposition to the New Deal, he decried the "resplendent economic royalists" who wanted control of the government and, during the campaign, warned that only "a people's government in Washington" could enable him to carry forward.[9] Roosevelt devoured newspaper polls and straw ballots from county fairs, measures of public opinion that predicted his landslide victory even as the *Literary Digest* readers' poll gave the election to Alf Landon in 1936.[10]

Events in Europe and Asia would put Roosevelt into a different battle in his second term, this time to join the Allies in defeating fascism and creating a postwar world that could sustain the peace and restore prosperity. This was not a battle that the country relished. Fully 60 percent of the country in 1938 opposed getting embroiled in any European war.[11]

During this pivotal period, Roosevelt welcomed the aid of Hadley Cantril, director of the Office of Public Opinion Research at Princeton and one of the early innovators in modern survey research, who gave FDR private access to Gallup's national polls. Roosevelt wanted to monitor levels of support for joining the war in Europe and, most importantly, support for the Lend-Lease program to supply Britain with vast amounts of military supplies. Cantril conducted polls on the impact of Roosevelt's fireside chats, comparing the results for those who did not listen and for those who did, looking at the shift in opinion afterward. The fireside chat on December 29, 1940, for example, produced a 6-point rise in support to "help Britain, even at the risk of getting into war." Roosevelt was determined to use all his capacities and his identity with people to move the country to a new place on a project that would consume his energies and the whole nation in his last five years. He sent Churchill a poem by Henry Wadsworth Longfellow—a poem that earlier had brought Lincoln to tears:

> *Sail on, Oh Ship of state!*
> *Sail on, Oh Union strong and great.*
> *Humanity with all its fears*
> *With all the hope of future years*
> *Is hanging breathless on thy fate.*

To which Churchill responded on radio, "Give us the tools and we will finish the job!"[12] Using his relationship with people, Roosevelt would get the Congress to do just that.

How different the character of some of our contemporary leaders who forswear such a connection with people. When journalist Martha Raddatz pointed out to Vice President Cheney in a one-on-one interview that "two-thirds of Americans say [the Iraq War's] not worth fighting," he offered a noticeable silence and then, "So?"

"So—you don't care what the American people think?"

"No," Cheney affirmed. "I think you cannot be blown off course by the fluctuations in the public opinion polls. Think about what would have happened if Abraham Lincoln had paid attention to polls, if they had had polls during the Civil War."[13] Perhaps had Cheney taken some of Lincoln's " 'public opinion' baths," he would have waged a different war to a better end for America.

POLITICS WITH A PURPOSE

In television and movie accounts, the pollster and captive politicians are sent into a frenzy with each drop in their approval rating or vote for reelection. The implication is that these are leaders with their fingers to the wind. But that depiction trivializes how important people are to these leaders in order for them to succeed and not just in the minimal sense of getting reelected. In reality, the leaders in this book all struggled to advance their project, and their ability to align with people gave them strength and special standing. What really got their attention was a poll indicator that was a measure of success on their main political project. For Blair, without trust, he could not move people to follow him; without trust, he could not convince people that Labour had honored its pledges; without it, Labour could not get people to take a chance on reform. I could tell from Blair's body language and eyes that what mattered most to him was whether he was trusted by people and, indeed, that was the topic of the special survey when he nearly passed the torch to a new leader.

For Clinton, the key measure was whether he was a "different kind of Democrat." For Barak, it was whether the people were "hopeful or doubtful about peace with the Syrians or the Palestinians." For Goni, during the election what mattered, in addition to his vote, was who could "fix the economic crisis."

Each used polling to determine if the people were with them, increasing the prospects for actually doing what they set out to do. And as they drove forward on the mission, they used polling to look back over their shoulder to see if the populace was following, if the battalions were marching with them. They were consumed with keeping or building support for the mission, particularly at the time of key legislative or parliamentary battles and as they faced the looming judgment of the voters in reelection.

All these leaders presumed that the public was with them on their principal agenda because they had mounted successful campaigns that made their issues the most important ones and they won. Thus, people were a resource to be engaged, not people to be fooled or manipulated with cleverly "crafted" language. When the new government in South Africa appointed a cabinet czar for its Reconstruction and Development Programme, it was looking for a way to say "These pledges matter." When Clinton devoted his first State of the Union address to the economy, he was acting on the popular mandate and, indeed, when he got off topic on issues such as "gays in the military," the public let him know. Goni used his first ninety days, as promised in the election, to restore the Bonosol and funding for infant and maternal health.

They all moved because they believed they had a mandate to move forward on a project that had been affirmed by the voters and keeping these promises was also a matter of honor that other politicians and power centers should defer to. But that was an illusion. All these leaders faced big political and economic forces that left them weak and struggling to honor the mandate.

The sense of triumph on election day almost always obscured political weakness. Clinton received only 43 percent of the vote. One in five voted for Ross Perot and his anti-establishment party. While Clinton defined the election on his terms, so did Perot. Goni received just 23 percent of the vote and his main anti-system opponent, Evo Morales, contested the outcome. Goni was forced to form a coalition with parties that had no interest in restoring the Bonosol or in his vision of economic reform. Barak took every minute of his transition to form a majority coalition that failed to provide a working majority for any part of his agenda, other than to hold on to office. His government was a soap opera, poised to fall every time it failed to give into the religious parties or contemplated some new step in the peace process. The ANC was a unity government with positions allocated based on proportion of the vote.

Only the Labour government in Britain had a large parliamentary majority in a country where power is centralized, yet Labour—out of power for eighteen years—came to office with no experience running anything and with a limited program of reform.

It was at such moments of post-election headiness that we should have picked up Richard Neustadt's *Presidential Power* and recalled his lesson: presidents come and go, but "weakness is still what I see: weakness in the sense of a great gap between what is expected of a man (or someday woman) and assured capacity to carry through."[14] In the American case where divided government was intended to project exactly these kinds of roadblocks, only about 40 percent of major presidential initiatives since Eisenhower took office have actually become law. Even with a unified government, as in Clinton's first two years, only about half of initiatives ended up passing the Congress.[15] At the outset, the political and economic advisors in the White House could not imagine that a Democratic Congress would fail to pass the budget and destroy the Clinton presidency, yet it took the vice president casting the tie-breaking vote to keep that from happening.

As serious as these political weaknesses seem, they pale before the impotence confronting each leader in the face of global market forces. Finances severely limited their ability to prioritize and deliver in the anticipated way on their main initiatives. They were elected in change elections, but the fiscal capacity of the government was part of the problem in every instance. All faced reports immediately after the election about the fiscal situation being worse than expected and requiring even stronger austerity measures to balance the budget. After intense internal debates and battles with the Congress, Clinton's economic plan proceeded with almost no new investments. Labour committed not to increase government spending in the first two years though the public expected something very different. The ANC stretched out its targets and, in some critical areas like new housing, few new houses were built halfway through the party's first term. Under pressure from the IMF, Goni tried to raise taxes and hold down public sector wage increases, mistakenly starting with the police, who rioted and shot up his office.

The moment the leaders in this book came to realize how inhospitable were the other policy centers, they turned to the public to rally to their agenda and utilized the public's support to elevate their power in the battles ahead. That invited some crude governing by the numbers—trying to raise the perception of the president's popularity to shift the balance of forces to these leaders. Sometimes it meant signaling that the project was in jeopardy or, more often, convincing voters the ANC, Labour, or Clinton really was advancing their election promises and needed voter support to succeed.

When the agendas evolved or were compromised under pressure, the leaders sometimes moved from convincing people to educating them, and I do not use the word "educate" as a euphemism for manipulation, persuading the public about something that is untrue. Bill Clinton relished his educative role, which was often on display in his addresses to the Congress. When Clinton showed the country in his Oval Office address the pie chart with every $10 of deficit reduction achieved with $5 in spending cuts, $4 in taxes on the wealthy, and $1 in taxes on the middle class, the press viewed it as just another politician selling soap. But it was the clearest explanation I could come up with for the goal of the economic plan, the distribution and shared responsibility. The speech contributed to the popular momentum in support of the plan in the final days before the House and Senate cast their last votes.

I remain in awe of what Barak attempted to do during the negotiations at Camp David. When the media reported that Israel was considering giving up over 90 percent of the territories—something no politician had ever said out loud—or that the Arab neighborhoods of East Jerusalem might form part of a Palestinian state—in effect, dividing Jerusalem—the public came to take these things seriously. The press began debating and considering issues that previously were walled off; columnists wrote of earlier agreements when Israel made historic compromises; no doubt, people discussed these things in a Jewish way with their families and co-workers. What we know was unimaginable at the beginning of the process became imaginable. In a matter of weeks, Jerusalem went from a no-go area that stirred the greatest emotions and warnings from me to something that brought much more considered reactions in which people weighed the benefits of separation from the Palestinians, a Greater Jewish Jerusalem, and an "end of conflict."

Were these leaders being educative or merely manipulative? V. O. Key reminds us, "Political leaders who shirk the task of popular education are misfits who do not understand the responsibilities of their jobs." He was reflecting the admonition of Thomas Jefferson and James Madison, who insisted that authority be subject to popular control but who also accepted the obligation for public opinion to be informed. In an ongoing debate with Alexander Hamilton in the period after the publication of the *Federalist Papers*, Madison argued for the sovereignty of public opinion but also for an intense process of deliberation and communication within communities.[16] All the leaders described in this book worked to keep people with them as they battled for their agenda and project, which required extensive work when the

subject shifted to deficit reduction instead of investment, Jerusalem, exporting natural gas, and WMD. I did not doubt, however, that these leaders believed they were persuading people to back politics good for the country.

I took great pride in my solution to the problem of trust and delivery and
democratic accountability—what got labeled in Bolivia as Stan's 3-Steps—
though was it a solution or merely a clever trick?

In South Africa, both the voters and Mandela acted as if they signed a
"promissory" note, as the political theorist Jane Mansbridge describes this
kind of representation, with a strong presumption and obligation that the
ANC would keep its promises or face the sanction of the upcoming election.
When leaders spoke about progress and the big changes in South Africa, the
citizenry would not settle for what citizens of any normal country get, like
access to schools and lavatories or the right to vote and sit in parliament.
They were not content with a good try. They expected delivery on the
pledges for a better life that ANC leaders both before and after the election
said was a matter of honor.

Voters only listened to the ANC when it began its narrative with areas of
indisputable changes, like the extension of water and electricity, that really
did change the conditions of life or when Mandela or Mbeki acknowledged
that they, too, were disappointed with the pace of change, saying it was not
enough. That only started to move voters back to the ANC when the ANC
showed it was battling against reactionary forces to achieve change on a key
promise—a million new houses—and as the houses were being finished in
large numbers four and a half years into office, it broke through to people's
consciousness. But the mood only went from grudging to hopeful when there
was a future offer—a commitment to prioritize the issue with a new mandate from the voters.

Mbeki, the new leader of the ANC, asked voters to support the party because it kept its original promises, acknowledging the "promissory" note, but
also asking them to trust him to honor the new pledges, a process what
Mansbridge calls "anticipatory representation." What is so important for my
work is that this kind of judgment requires voters to be "educable (or manip-
ulable)" to assess the past so they can make sound judgments about the future. While V. O. Key was focused on elections to keep politicians accountable,
what matters in this process is whether the deliberation is real or just political leaders manipulating perceptions of reality.

What I did in South Africa—as well as in Britain and Bolivia—was help
fashion a narrative that enabled voters to interpret the reality and project
what the future might bring. Did this narrative raise the quality of deliberation or was it a form of manipulation? What I do know is that the narrative

made it possible for people to acknowledge the 2.5 million households that got water, ending the need for millions of women to travel many kilometers each day; it allowed them to see the new houses as part of a story and to consider a new mandate with a future offer. Without the water and without the million new houses, voters would have trashed the narrative.

For Goni in Bolivia, there could be no new narrative without the reality of restoring the Bonosol payments for seniors; for Blair in Britain, there could be no new narrative until there were major increases in new public investment. If you believe the popular accounts of the consultant class, you would think there is no problem too great for them to solve, but I would suggest that real people have their say.

I fully appreciate the skepticism and wonder myself: when Republican politicians say they are cutting taxes for all taxpayers when in reality it is for the wealthiest and biggest corporations, do they wink at their advisors or do they really believe it?[17]

PICKING THE FIGHT

The key to understanding politics is knowing who picked the fight and what they are fighting about because that decides what issues are important and who gets engaged. My own politics was formed by Robert Kennedy's campaign when a young generation chose between competing public goals, issues, values, and voting coalitions. That was a Democratic primary election perhaps like America's 2008 presidential election, in which choosing a candidate was really a choice between different content and meaning.

Much of this I learned soon after the 1968 election when I devoured E. E. Schattschneider's *Semisovereign People* as my self-constructed wall between academia and politics began to crumble. That book helped dislodge more than a few bricks in my wall, especially his provocative concept that "Nothing attracts a crowd so quickly as a fight," his simple starting point. "Nothing is so contagious," with the "excitement of the conflict communicated to the crowd." For Schattschneider, as for me, "This is the basic pattern of politics." And for those ambitious in their politics, "He who determines what politics is about runs the country, because the definition of the alternatives is the choice of conflicts, and the choice of conflicts allocates power." When you succeed, you make your coalition of interests matter while at the same time condemning your opponent to the worst of political fates, irrelevance.[18]

That is what I have tried to do ever since. My experience has demonstrated repeatedly the enormous power of defining the conflict and the choice. The media and other campaigns took notice with Bill Clinton's victory—the "it's the economy, stupid" and "change versus more of the same," ripped off right from the survey and popularized by James. But it was not spin after the fact. The "choice" was taped up on a column in the war room and shaped what the campaign said and did and, in the process, made George H.W. Bush irrelevant. Bush tried to get the choice centered on character—trusted leader versus the untrustworthy—and leadership— winner of the Cold War versus "a failed governor of a small state." But those choices simply lost their force as we imposed our own definition of the battle. The election was the ultimate confirmation of the hypothesis. But as Schatt-schneider understood, the story did not end with the election: the major political and economic actors and media moved immediately to Clinton's economic plans and budget, accepting the agenda that followed from the election's choice. When Clinton began that first State of the Union address by telling the country he would devote his entire address to the economy, he was attempting to reaffirm what the battle was about and force everyone to accept his priorities and issues. Unfortunately, 1992 was a complicated three-way election in which Ross Perot competed to define the choice, mak-ing deficit reduction much more central.

When Clinton went to the country at various points—"going public" in the academic literature—it should be considered in the context of his project and the attempt to maintain control over the principal issues and choices lest he risk being displaced and disempowered. Clinton was trying to engage people in support of the project to raise popular support for him and his agenda and affect the balance of forces in Washington. He needed to educate people about the budget, remind them of the stakes, and build confidence in the president and his authority. The goal was at least to keep people with him and avoid collapse, but more to rally them to the cause.

Nearly lost in all the excitement about Labour's win in 1997 was the dis-engagement of voters, the sharp drop in turnout, at a time when voters were demanding change and the election was full of excitement. Traditionally, Britain's voters turned out in large numbers, even when Margaret Thatcher was at her strongest and humiliating Labour at the polls because this was a big fight: a battle for industrial Britain between a party of the working class and a party of capitalists. The choice produced a lot of voters but not a lot of votes for Labour, unfortunately, which suited the Tories fine. Blair's biggest change was to say that is not our battle: we are not drawing that line. The move from "Old Labour" to "New" was not just rhetorical; it was a choice of battles, a dif-ferent set of issues, and maybe even different coalitions of supporters.

But Labour under Blair displaced the old without substituting the new. Indeed, that was the main unresolved tension during all of Blair's ten years. The political team came back over and over again to a plank in the party's new stated principles, "a community in which power, wealth and opportunity are in the hands of the many not the few," that had been formulated after much debate and research. But Blair wanted to escape the divisiveness and the class language, instead aspiring to "One Nation," offering a choice between community and dissolution, unity and division, rooted deeply in his worldview and faith. The tension was never resolved, but as each election approached, created an operative choice—between Labour committed to investment in public services and the Tories, more interested in tax cuts than investment. After three successive defeats, the Tories accepted the terms of surrender, including abandoning tax cuts. But Labour failed to choose a new battle that would create a compelling new choice for the times that engaged people and made this new political dispensation sustainable. Labour's vote sank to 36 percent in an electorate that itself shrank to nearly the smallest since Britain achieved the franchise.

The choice for the ANC was between "now is the time" and "a better life for all." It was not a choice of slogans but a much more fundamental choice about the definition of the election, whether it was about blacks finally achieving their rightful control over government or about changing the life fortunes of the black majority. Mandela not only came to understand the difference but sought to impose the definition on the media and all the parties, including his own, making it the main standard for judging success. African voters came to the polls in near biblical scale in that first democratic election, a result with many fathers, but we should not forget that demoralization only gave way to hope after voters came to believe their lives would be better and peace restored. When, three years later, voters came to doubt this was real, the response was lost support for the ANC and disengagement, undermining the ANC's legitimacy.

What stood out in the Barak campaign was not the battle lines that worked but the ones that Barak himself, the Labor politicians, and Israeli elites suppressed. The truth is that Israeli elites around the two largest parties were satisfied to contest "security versus peace" in some variation, and the social gaps, though in practice both left and right accepted market-oriented economic policies. Barak was persuaded to make the economy and education central parts of his campaign, but not the bigger divide over religion. We were forced to abandon our most powerful choice—the country desperate for a leader who would unify the country and not give into the demands of Orthodox and settler extremists. Within that framework, we could change the budget priorities to fund secular education and pursue peace. When the concept appeared on our first billboards, Labor politicians decried it. Barak himself was uncomfortable since every government since independence including Ben-Gurion's invited religious parties to join the government, believing it was important to the Jewish character of the state. The politicians were worried not that the strategy would fail but that it would succeed, legitimating a public battle over how secular a society Israel should be and what role religion should play, potentially threatening Israeli society. Those were legitimate concerns, but understand it was an elite choice, as voters overwhelmingly wanted this battle and agenda and wanted the change that would come with every citizen serving in the army and getting equal access to education funding. With Schattschneider my bible and a respect for the popular judgment and myself uncharacteristically aligned with Jewish opinion, I felt it my mission to make sure Barak and the Labor politicians knew that there were other bold lines to draw.

On each election night when so many thousands went into the streets in an exhilarating release of joy joined by the millions who watched, every one of these leaders spoke of their aspiration for unity, to overcome the divisions of the election and the country's history. A joyous Bill Clinton declared, "and perhaps most important of all," the goal of uniting the country, "to bring our people together as never before so that our diversity can be a source of strength." Nelson Mandela reached out "a hand of friendship to the leaders of all parties . . . to join us in working together to tackle the problems we face as a nation." Tony Blair affirmed that Britain "will build a nation united with common purpose" now that we are finally "uniting to put the divisions of the past behind us"—"uniting at last as one nation." Ehud Barak began there, too. "We extend a courageous hand to all, to the secular and the religious," declaring, "everyone is part of Israel." Even Gonzalo Sánchez de Lozada declared his desire for Bolivians to be "responsible and united," without the night of celebrations in the street and a clear victory.[19]

The newly elected leaders all expressed a desire for unity, and in Mandela's case it was actually an extension of the election itself and the end to the history that gave South Africa its deeply divided and unequal society. Unity was an affirmation of the election's message and his own personal history for an inclusive politics open to black and white that brings just power to blacks but "a better life for people." And for all the leaders, the appeal to unity was simply an effort to go beyond the ugliness and divisiveness of the campaign and to reach out to groups, perhaps to increase the chance of governing successfully.

But for some of the leaders, "unity" had more content to it and reflected a competing personal mission. For Clinton, it was about the gulf between black and white that left America divided in its own unique ways. When he said "and perhaps most important of all," he was saying this is my primary concern and priority, very different from the line he drew during the campaign and ones the voters heard when they voted. The same was true for Blair, who wanted everyone to know that in addition to speaking up "for that decent hard-working majority of the British people," he intended to speak up for the values in community. On election night, Barak offered a hand of friendship to the ultra-Orthodox but actually much more, their inclusion in a government that could pursue peace at the expense of much of Barak's education and constitutional agenda.

It is understandable that the leaders made that call on election night, but across the countries, that switch also displaced the battles and issues on which the election was fought, thus playing down a politics for the "forgotten middle class" or "hard-working majority." When people criticized Clinton for bringing his campaign into the White House symbolized by the war room, the complaint was less about the techniques and more about the choices and dividing lines from the campaign. That blurring of the lines also blurred the politics and the agenda.

As the 2008 Democratic primary crystallized as a gargantuan battle between Barack Obama and Hillary Clinton, they each tried to draw bold lines that would define the choice and the primary electorate. Clinton began with an unassailable lead early in the race, but the battle for meaning changed the rules and the coalitions. She tried to make the race about being "ready on day one" versus untested change, but in a year when 90 percent of Democrats thought the country was on the wrong track, Obama became the candidate of change, the future, and hope. There was fascination with the idea of the first woman or first African American president—a stark contrast with the politics under George Bush's America. Their battle produced extraordinary interest and a doubling of Democratic primary turnout—up among all groups but particularly by younger and minority voters and independents. Clinton battled back on the economy and for the middle class, but in the end the candidate who defined the change and the choice set the rules that governed the primaries.

The Republican nominee John McCain watched Hillary Clinton fail to make experience a decisive choice and selected the outsider Sarah Palin as his running mate so that these "mavericks" could compete for the mantle of change. But the economic crisis nearly disqualified them and Obama finished the election as the dominant candidate of change in a change election that brought in millions of new voters and a breathtaking increase in turnout. Nonetheless, after Obama swears on the Bible to uphold the Constitution, I suspect we will hear a great deal about "unity."

POLITICAL PROJECT AND
PERSONAL MISSION

What was most surprising to me in reliving these campaigns and with the benefit of time and others' biographies and memoirs and reintroducing myself to these leaders was learning that the political project that attracted me to them was such an inexact measure of their life's personal mission, independent of politics. In the hothouse atmosphere of a campaign, I assumed their mission and politics were the same, the rest just details and tactics to be worked out. In fact, when the campaigns struggled to get Clinton, Mandela, Blair, Barak, and Goni to accept a particular definition of the election, a set of issues, or a message, I mostly assumed the explanation lay outside them—the influence of big donors, special interests, or the party politicians, or a reluctance to deal with the aggravation and the fallout. So, when Bill Clinton would hesitate on the middle class or talking about corporate excess, Frank Greer, his media advisor, would look at me and ask who is getting to him—the DLC, the donors? And when Clinton reworked the schedule for the last weekend of the campaign to go to African American churches, I would ask George Stephanopoulos who is getting to him—his Arkansas supporters, maybe his liberal Hollywood friends? But had I understood his life and purpose better—which applies to all these leaders—I certainly would have had different conversations, though I am not at all sure I would have offered better advice for his election and, importantly, I am not at all sure that Clinton or, in other circumstances, Blair or Barak, wanted me to divert my eyes and focus.

Mandela is likely the exception, but that has more to do with my academic career, which had immersed me in South African history and political economy, and the fact that this was a first-time, all-race democratic election—the culmination of Mandela's life's work. His goals in the election were contained within his mission, evident in how he shaped the ANC in the 1950s toward all-race politics and how he dealt with each generation of new black activists. He was as consumed with smashing and marginalizing the Pan-Africanist Congress in the first election in 1994 as he was when he battled the PAC for control of the ANC in his home neighborhood of Orlando in Soweto or ensuring the ANC's approach dominated in the antiapartheid movement inside and outside South Africa. He embraced "A Better Life for All" with a passion appropriate to his mission, as he understood, perhaps more than the other leaders, that it challenged the "Africanist" impulses of the younger generations and the strong temptation to view the election as the African majority finally winning control of government. For Mandela, the

Reconstruction and Development Programme and the campaign's pledges constituted a contract that specified "a better life for all." With the election, he not only danced with joy for the whole world, he lectured all the parties on their obligations to keep the pledges. His personal mission and political project were joined that night.

But that union of project and mission for Mandela only highlights his difference from the others. Clinton's political project that he embraced and articulated at the Cleveland DLC convention was a Democratic Party electable again, respectful of mainstream values, committed to the middle class that worked hard and played by the rules, no longer willing to indulge irresponsibility at either the bottom or top of the ladder, and prepared to radically change government to work for people. The test of seriousness was an economy that created jobs and raised middle-class living standards. Clinton embraced a political project that heavily overlapped with my own, indeed, one I presumed we both shared with Robert Kennedy, stopped suddenly by an assassin.

Clinton championed a reformist middle-class populist project when he first ran for Congress in 1974 and nearly upset the safe Republican incumbent, and when he ran for attorney general and governor, understanding this populist project's power in bringing together black and white behind a Democrat. But what I missed when I joined the Clinton effort in 1990 was the distinction between his political project and his personal mission. He was so engaged and so deeply political that I did not allow for the distinction, yet at so many points he sent signals: the hope to announce at Little Rock High, the scene of Governor Faubus's last stand against federally imposed integration, the contrasting passion for his speeches at the Pleasant Grove Baptist Church in Detroit and Macomb County Community College, his closing the campaign in an African American church, his election night speech on unity, and our meeting the day after when he expressed his desire for a more diverse inner political group. His mission was no small one—to take the South and the country beyond the deep racial divisions and the racial thinking and to make our diversity a national strength. I am sure he viewed the emerging political project as advancing that mission but they were not the same, and in 1992 being seen as a "racial liberal" was not the route to winning white middle-class voters. In that first presidential campaign, the mission more often than not yielded to the project, but in government, the opposite was frequently the case. The economic plan quickly lost its middle-class appeal and content as he decided to prioritize deficit reduction, but he fought to maintain those parts, like the earned income tax credit, whose beneficiaries were low-income workers and minorities. Poverty reduction, particular for African Americans and Hispanics, was a higher priority than raising middle-class incomes.

The tensions in this distinction got built into the campaign and the White House's decision making because Clinton designed it that way, reflecting a pattern evident for most of these leaders. They created a diverse group of insiders in their team, each of whom they empowered to create diversity of perspective and intense discussions, but also as a check on themselves and their own instincts, with shifting power in the group depending on the leader's changing sense of the needs. This certainly felt and looked like "chaos," as Bob Woodward described it, but there was more purpose than we all understood.

Clinton basically decided by the time of Cleveland to run a national campaign focused on the middle class with a populist edge and recruited a full-time team, all people who had championed and won with these ideas before joining him. But to set boundaries and to put a check on them and perhaps his own instincts, he empowered top DLC advisors more committed to reforming government, who better understood the South and were hostile to the old Democratic special interests. And then, he periodically introduced those who shared his Southern and Arkansas experience, people who insisted on more of a civil rights focus and larger role for African Americans and women. At the edge of the group were the economic and foreign policy advisors who periodically came to play key roles.

After the election and during the transition, President-elect Clinton disempowered the political people and empowered the new economic policy team, as well as those who prioritized cultural change and diversity. Actually, both of those dominated in his first two years, even though he worried that the White House would lose track of the middle class and lose sight of the election. I told the American Enterprise Institute conference after the president spoke to the political advisors at Camp David that he wanted people like myself in the White House "who bring a broader perspective, who remember the campaign, who remember the promises of the campaign, who remember the mission."[20] But there was never any doubt in retrospect who Clinton really empowered: he accepted the deficit targets and gave up nearly all the investments and even accepted the plan knowing it was front-loaded and might slow the economy in the lead-up to the 1994 midterm election. After the 1994 congressional defeat, Clinton empowered a new political team with a different perspective who dominated the policy advisors, but that was President Clinton's choice for different times.

In battling to save his wife's candidacy for the presidency in 2008, he focused like a laser on her election, with the impossible task for him of championing the first woman over the first African American candidate for president—a Solomon's choice that could not but undermine his personal mission and work. On the brink of defeat, he threw himself into the fray, determined for his wife to win and convinced biased media had failed to expose Obama's vulnerabilities. The resulting brawl nearly put all of them asunder. But when Clinton stilled the Democratic convention in Denver on August 27, 2008, and told the world, "Barack Obama is the man for the job" and "on the right side of history," he worked to make it all whole again. His personal path back and his final word on the choice for the election, "Barack Obama will lead us away from the division and fear of the last eight years back to unity and hope," took him back to his personal mission and legacy.

Tony Blair became passionate about social justice not in the university Labour club but in intense discussions with fellow students, some of whom considered Marx and Gramsci fashionable, but also a communitarian philosopher who underscored that the individual needs a strong community and increasingly, religious teachings that led him to be confirmed in the Anglican church. He later wrote about a Christian socialism that scorns the selfishness and acquisitiveness of the Conservatives and champions Christian values, a unity of individual and community, represented by the Holy Communion. The Labour Party was a vehicle for social action, one that ultimately had to be changed, but his thinking about society preceded his party involvement and was much broader. When he occasionally published his views on faith and politics, he got hammered internally and in the press, the Conservatives hitting him for putting God on Labour's side. "I could see nothing but trouble in talking about it," Alastair Campbell wrote in his dairy. "British people are nothing like Americans," and Blair promised him he would "never do it again."[21] Blair, however, maintained his close friendship with Peter Thomson, an Australian priest from Oxford days who returned to Britain with Blair's rise and continued their discussions, including a faith group that met regularly and privately even during the campaign.

Blair came to believe that the Labour Party could only win and only be a vehicle for his socialist values if it modernized in the way Clinton had changed the Democratic Party. Because of his use of the words "community" and "responsibility" and the appropriation of Clinton slogans and the war room concept, I assumed a commonality that was not fully justified, though from the outset I knew "community" was especially important to him. The main choice and narrative in Labour's first big victory centered on change and the economy, creating opportunities for "hard-working families," "the many, not the few," even though Blair worried it made Labour sound "old" and divisive, and might ultimately clash with his view of community.

I came to work for Blair at the point when the political project and his mission met in which the electoral task forced a kind of consistency, evident at the end in 1997, 2001, and 2005. At near dawn, when he claimed victory, however, he always pulled them apart, acknowledging the political project and his personal mission as powerful guides for governance. What became clear with 9/11 was that the mission was probably much more important for him, aligning his politics and values, giving new meaning to the "power of community" for home and among nations. But his belief that the fight against the evil of terrorism could only be fought arm-in-arm with George Bush, who believed in unbridled individualism not community, put him at odds with Britain, many of his advisors, and, painfully, me.

This all might have been smoother had Blair created a team or appointed advisors that aligned more with his mission, but the opposite was true: all the speechwriters, policy advisors, and campaign people, including myself, embraced the political project, even as we struggled to make it work with Blair's "One Nation" ideas and, even more difficult, his decision to go to war in Iraq. Blair met with his religious study group in the lead-up to the 1997 election precisely to make sure political goals did not trump his personal ones. And throughout his time in government, he despaired at the lack of support among his advisors, but it was his group, likely intended to bring him back to more conventional political goals.

Ehud Barak was not subtle about his mission. He was the super-smart, focused, and fearless leader with a passion for Zionism and Jewish traditions who came to lead Israel's elite commando unit and then the IDF before turning to politics. To lead in the tradition of Yitzhak Rabin really did bring together his mission and political project at the moment in time when a historic accommodation with the Arab world seemed possible. That unity of personal mission and the political task gave him clarity in direction that he worked to disguise. His victory night speech was written by the Rabin aide who read Rabin's blood-soaked note at his funeral, and when Barak formed a government, he was clear about how he intended to use the fateful period ahead.

But Barak knew he could not get this opportunity unless he made the Labor Party electable in the same way that Clinton and Blair modernized their parties. That meant facing Labor's elitist history of neglecting the new immigrants and providing reassurances about security and not giving in too readily to the Arabs. It also required a serious domestic vision that addressed the role of the ultra-Orthodox, the disunity, and the economy.

Barak moved to address the economy in the manner of both Clinton and Blair in their first two years, that is, an austerity that outlasted his government; his education agenda got lost in the never-ending battles with Shas. Along with others, I begged Barak to remember the whole of the political project, though his lack of a Knesset majority meant he had to choose—either a social and economic agenda or the pursuit of peace—and for him, that was no choice. Barak felt he had a higher obligation and, indeed, he believed that whatever people said, they expected him as a leader of Israel to make that choice.

Goni's family was part of the progressive elite that sought to reform education in an earlier time and joined with the MNR to reform land ownership, create the right to vote, and establish democratic governments. In that tradition and educated in economics, Goni ventured the boldest possible reforms, first to force Bolivia into the global economy and later to capitalize the state industries to create health care for women and children and a pension bonus; exporting the newly discovered gas reserves to fund education would have completed the story of reform and modernization, a life's mission. Sadly, the economic reforms were only intermittently popular and understood, more often seen as a betrayal of the nation's patrimony. He won support because of his success in fixing the crisis and got a second chance in a contested election where most wanted to vote against the established parties and nearly all opposed his plans for exporting the gas via Bolivia's historic enemy, Chile. He was clear about his plans, but with the support of only one in five voters, he did not have a political mandate for his personal mission and in this violent period, popular protests forced him from office and into exile.

From outside and often inside these circles, this disjunction between political project and personal mission variously looks like betrayed promises, dithering, internecine struggles, or lack of direction, but there is much more to it than I understood at the time.

"CLASS WARFARE DOESN'T WORK IN AMERICA"

I have been characterized as being ideological—an "unabashed liberal" associated with an "unreconstructed liberalism" that colors my advice. I work hard to guard against the last but the former is true in two important respects.[22] First, I do have a personal political project going back to Robert Kennedy of working to unite a bottom-up majority to win power to improve life broadly and offset inequality. That has affected for whom I have worked and for whom I have thrown in body and soul. And second, my experience in multiple campaigns and countries and understanding of these times has led me to believe that the idea of governing for the many makes center-left parties relevant. It is therefore an important hypothesis to consider in most races. That can take you to some crude choices, but also to elevated and expansive ones, like "A better life for all" or "One Nation, not a two-tier Britain."

In the 2008 primary campaign, Obama was intent on transcending the old partisan divisions and Hillary Clinton on cobbling together a coalition of groups and thus neither wanted to fly the banner of middle-class populism. But the intensity of the battle and the popular reality changed all that. Obama affirmed he is the one "who's taken on the oil companies, worked to strip away their tax breaks as they run up record profits, and demanded higher gas mileage standards." He was keeping up with Clinton, who declared, "The wealthy and the well connected have had a president. It's time the middle class had a president, who will stand up for you."[23] Even John McCain began to deplore the excess compensation to CEOs, and the greed on Wall Street that produced the economic crisis.

In my own work, I have been religious about getting the key players, the campaign, and the leader right up front to identify the alternative theories of the race so that I could test them in the most rigorous way possible. The language of the survey had to capture the different messages and choices to demonstrate which one was the most compelling and provide a basis for all the players to settle on the emerging message. Indeed, I was quick to give up on core messages that were not compelling, did not hold up under fire, or just gave way to others as the campaign reached new stages.

I found that if you are going to argue for a "populist" choice you had better have the data to deflect the incoming fire from some force that attempts to delegitimize efforts to give class meaning to the election. But also understand I have been subjected to at least as much fire from the left and old interests. I questioned liberal orthodoxy in my writing and established in my polls the power of reassuring voters on welfare, the power of unions, taxes, crime, and religious faith—steps that were strongly resisted by major groups in these coalitions.

I also learned from these leaders and the responses of voters and evolved my thinking in major ways. While I casually wrote of a larger role for government, Clinton insisted on skepticism about bureaucracy and on reinventing government in his DLC Cleveland address and the "New Covenant" speeches at Georgetown. He even rewrote my questionnaire to test the theme. He trained my ear to think "American" and I would make the critique of "failed government" our entry to investment. Later, joined by the DLC and other advisors, I worked both during the inaugural week and "Meltdown II" to get the president to return to reinventing government, and reforming welfare.

The political advisors and I were too slow to accept that Clinton's economic plan when stripped of its investments was really a deficit reduction plan, but when the research showed voters would rally to it, I moved and proposed a deficit-centric message, though one where a fair distribution of the burden was key to its power.

I have come to appreciate in virtually all these countries that there are forces at play, not always visible and direct, that work to preclude messages and strategies that highlight class, equity, or fairness; even when the survey tests well, "the facts," repeatedly take you to that message or choice. When elections are imminent, the survey findings often displace other considerations and usually win out: "people first" or "a better life for all," each with the implicit or explicit demand for greater equity. On the eve of a tough parliamentary or congressional vote, politicians again empower the survey research, but it is not easy to win the argument. Governance is replete with ideological blockages that greatly affect the battle lines and the issues that get highlighted, the language used, and what coalitions get formed. In ways that are not altogether visible in the country, the process works to preclude a class choice or argument for greater equity. As close as I got to the president and prime minister, I still felt there was another meeting I was not at.

After every one of these elections, these big, sometimes historic, leaders had a "come-to-Jesus" meeting with the principal managers of the economy. Without even being in the meeting, I knew the content: "That was all well and good for the campaign, but you need to understand that the economy is at great risk, deficits are out of control, investment will not be forthcoming, austerity and fiscal balance has to be your first priority." The Labour leaders knew the story and moved immediately to make the Bank of England independent, subjecting itself to a new discipline, a move widely applauded for its boldness and seriousness. Clinton sat with Fed chairman Alan Greenspan and the new team of economic advisors, Barak with the governor of the Bank of Israel, Goni with the IMF, and Mandela with the governor of the Reserve Bank and the finance minister. I am confident these leaders made the right choice for long-term growth, as evidenced in the later periods of growth in all these countries, though the choice produced immediate disillusionment that grew into a sense of betrayal. There were also real social consequences. The new governments were left with fewer tools and resources to make sure the growth expanded opportunity and shared the bounty more broadly.

In Britain, my first full-length message survey included a battery testing different ways to define the choice in the election. The strongest one used language adapted from the party's new statement of purpose, "Labour works for all the people. The Conservatives work for the privileged few." Tested along with ten other choices, it was dominant then and every time we conducted the exercise over many years, evolving into "working hard for Britain's hard-working families." And when Labour had lost its lead in 2004 over the Tories, I sat with Blair in his study at Chequers and dwelled on a single graph that illustrated the power of our message: "In a modern and uncertain world, hardworking people, *not just the few*, have the opportunity to make a better life." It was 15 points stronger with the added reference to the privileged. But he felt it smacked of old and not the new politics that had opened up Labour to so many former Tories, though the data did not support that conclusion.

The crash of the old class politics without a new choice and battle line led many voters, particularly blue-collar voters, to disengage altogether, while the political parties figured out their new identities and battle lines in a new politics. The fact is messages were consistently stronger when they recognized there were forms of inequality and grievance. A focus on "hard-working families," like the "forgotten middle class," contained a critique of the insufficient rewards for work and how modern Britain is organized. Only as the election approached—and the prospect of a hanging at the hands of the voters—did resistance to these messages weaken, but that only underscores the point.

Whether the focus of the Clinton economic plan was on investments or deficits, the strongest arguments always underscored the distribution of burden, clarity that the greatest burden would be borne by the very wealthiest, those who were enriched by the 1980s when the game was rigged, and that Clinton's passion was the middle class. It was a conclusion based on data and illustrated, sometimes dramatically, time after time in the Oval Office. Yet, the 1980s disappeared from his State of the Union address on the economy, except as a reference to a time when politicians failed to address the deficit. The term "middle class" disappeared, too, from his speeches during this period until the eve of the vote on his budget. After the passage of his economic plan, the president abruptly stopped speaking about distribution and shared burden.

After the president's Oval Office address in which he used some of the language of the campaign, the "commentariat" deemed the speech "not well received." But pundits reached that conclusion not by measuring public opinion through polls, but by the fact that the stock market slipped 83 points. The middle class was purged from the joint session address on the economy. Bob Rubin deplored the "class-laden" language and argued that using the term "wealthy" strongly implied their gains were ill-gotten. Given that implication and without evidence, he maintained that the "middle-class people don't respond well to disparagement of economic success" and that businesses may be less willing to invest. Rubin importantly was supportive of the progressive tax rates in the policies, just not the narrative and battle lines that enable a leader to engage and build support.

The ideological blockages provided an opportunity for consultant-advisors who lived off the assertion that ideology is dead, such as Dick Morris, who declared, "Class warfare doesn't work in America"—allowing him to dismiss with much authority and no testing the battle lines that the political advisors proposed to Clinton at the end of the very difficult 1994 campaign. Attempts to define the choice with reference to equity, class, or those at the "top" were de-legitimated. The blockage also created an audience for pollsters who identify their favorite swing or center group—"security moms," for example—that is supposed to be an elixir, the key to success in America's elections, usually without evidence that it is true, but with important consequences for the character of our politics.[24]

HOW DO YOU KNOW VOTERS WON'T GO THERE?

Ehud Barak surprised me the most and taught me the most, beginning with how far and how fast he was willing to go to pursue his Talmudic responsibility, "Blessed art Thou, Almighty God, who blesses His people Israel with peace." When we conducted our first surveys and focus groups, voters and our team were conscious of our red lines: "No return to the 1967 borders"; "No foreign armies west of the Jordan"; "No right of return for Palestinian refugees"; and "No division of Jerusalem." While I showed some modest movement on the key questions, there was no movement on Jerusalem; indeed, people nearly cried in the groups, "It's like taking away your beloved child that you've nurtured and nursed." My conclusion came easily: "The inclusion of East Jerusalem in the final status agreement is a dead end." After all, two thirds of the Jewish public said it was unacceptable to have a Palestinian state with its capital in East Jerusalem.

Over just a concentrated four-week period, Barak, with an approval rating below that of President George W. Bush after four years of the Iraq War, and with the support of only one third of the Knesset members and no government, got the country to go with him across those red lines. In the end 45 percent of the Jewish public supported a full settlement returning East Jerusalem, the non-Jewish quarters of the Old City, and Palestinian "sovereignty" over the Temple Mount, over half if internationalized.

If I cannot believe what people tell me is unacceptable in my surveys on Jerusalem, then what of my findings on other subjects? Why can't a determined leader change these too? Even before Barak went to Camp David I picked up a shift in attitudes and reactions to information and I wrote on the eve of the summit, "opinions are dynamic and we are witnessing changes as the debate progresses," but nothing like the scale of the shifts that came later on issues that previously could not be discussed but then became possible.

I can explain all this after the fact: an Israeli citizenry uniquely vulnerable and conscious of its Jewish history, unwilling even to think certain thoughts until they do, the result of a leader who uniquely understands Israel's security needs and devoted a lifetime to protecting them, like Zionist leaders before him, saying we have to do this for the sake of Israel. Barak reminded me repeatedly when looking at the data that this was true of Rabin when he accepted the creation of the Palestinian Authority, for Menachem Begin when he gave back the Sinai, and for Ben-Gurion when he accepted a Jewish state on a part of Palestine.

But it does not change the question I now must face whenever I see a survey result that sets such dramatic limits on what is possible. How do you know that people will not rethink their starting points? How do you know they will not be moved by a deliberative process that thinks about the problem in new ways? How do you know a strong leader—even one who seemed to have lost the public confidence—cannot bring people to a fundamentally new place on a cherished subject? How do you know you won't discourage a less fearless leader from chancing to be bold?

I do not have an answer to this question, other than to constantly remind myself that opinion is changeable, that I must always simulate changing circumstances, and that I should be wary of telling a leader the public will not join him or her in this. I think of Barak when I think about our team telling Goni that he could not win public support for exporting natural gas via Chile into international markets. I think that the subsequent violent events support the truth of our conclusion, but what if Goni had been able to marginalize the populist anti-democratic forces and the new exports brought a flow of funds into education? I have no doubt that the poor who scorn him now would have honored his work, as they did the Bonosol.

The most painful and serious critique of my work came in the assessment of the U.S. negotiators after Barak's efforts to achieve a comprehensive peace with President Assad of Syria failed. That failure was partially attributed by the U.S. officials to a "bad poll" I supposedly gave Barak that gave him "cold feet" and my advice that he could not win a referendum in Israel. If one considers subsequent events, including Syrian backing for Hezbollah and Hamas, the assassinations of anti-Syrian democratic leaders in Lebanon, and the Second Lebanon War and its consequences for Israel, that is a heavy responsibility. I have spent much time rehearsing in my head why I think it is not remotely true. The public polls had already documented Barak's crash but, despite that, our polls showed majority support for an agreement and I wrote that Barak could win a referendum. Barak himself deemed that tale "bullshit" and told me that his judgment, right or wrong, was that the time was not right. I did point out later that Barak would gain greater legitimacy to negotiate such an agreement if the public saw him not as head of the "peace camp" but more like Rabin, who only reluctantly embraced Arafat's hand. But that is not why he said no at that moment.

Barak was determined to reach an agreement with his red line, return of virtually all of the Golan with absolute Israeli sovereignty over the Sea of Galilee, and he was convinced whatever the poll numbers that the Israeli public would never reject an agreement supported by the prime minister and the president of the United States. But again, how many leaders are so firm in their mission that they would not get "cold feet" faced with a crash in the polls? The reason the lead U.S. negotiator Dennis Ross's conclusion is so disturbing is not because I believe it explains Barak's behavior, but because I believe it describes how most leaders, even bold ones, might reasonably respond to such information. Perhaps they were right to hesitate and give due consideration to how they would bring the public with them. It certainly places a premium on having leaders with clarity of mission as they deal with the many trade-offs and possibilities that could cause them to rein in their ambition for change.

MERE TACTICS

Maybe the political game is winning out. I risk sounding like every previous generation of elders lamenting the ways of youth, but the civil rights and antiwar struggles of the 1960s and early 1970s were a period of ferment not just for the public but also for the political activists who would soon make adult choices about their lives. For those who became consultants between 1966 and 1988, my generation, about 60 percent said they were motivated by their beliefs and ideology, with a handful more wanting to see their political party do better. That looks a lot like the other Democratic pollsters and media people I have worked with, who could each write his or her own book. But the primacy of belief and ideology drops with each new age cohort, to just 40 percent with the most recent generation of consultants. Almost half of the new generation says they are in it for the thrill of competition and the money.[25] That invites a focus on the game, the tactics and winning outside the idea of a political, partisan, or ideological project.

The politics of tactics centers on the rush and sense of cleverness—beating your opponent to the punch but better, getting around some substantial and frustrating roadblock by doing something surprising or breaking out of type. The problem is when the cleverness becomes a substitute for advancing the project or mission.

I was very excited when I figured out how to get heard on delivery of promises—Stan's 3-Steps: First, spotlighting progress in areas people believed really happened, second, acknowledging mistakes or change is not enough, and finally, committing to a future agenda. But it required that leaders humble themselves by admitting falling short and showing they learned. Voters needed to hear that the leader understood that the job was half done or that it took too long or was not yet felt by enough people. All the leaders fought against saying these things because they believed they had achieved considerable things despite great political odds and financial constraints. Voters would appreciate that had only their political advisors done a better job communicating the real story.

This all seemed pretty innocent to me because, of course, they had not fulfilled all their promises and had learned a lot in the process. Why not say it? But I respect those leaders who often have good reasons, besides arrogance, for saying, no to this advice. Take Goni. He believed that his economic program did create the 500,000 jobs that he promised, with studies to support him. He was proud of the reforms and his work on the economy and did not want to take the edge off his critique, even though voters tuned him out. Only months later, when Goni said in an advertisement and then in a debate, I've learned some things, was he able to break things open. It is hard to overstate the impact on voters of hearing a former president and one of the richest people in the world concede that, in effect, he had learned from them.

One of my most tension-filled presentations was to the full election committee of the National Executive Committee of the ANC three years into office, with the chief of staff from Mandela's and Mbeki's offices, and the previous and current campaign managers, the heads of research and communication for the party and government. These were people who lived through the many decades of struggle and exile and prison and who defeated the apartheid government. There I was telling them that voters thought they are out of touch and on a gravy train, that they were not keeping their promises on the important things and people's lives were no better. They glared at me, some disputing the data for the first time. It took one-on-one meetings with Mbeki and Mandela afterward for them to accept the findings, though they seemed more upset with the voters than me for not acknowledging the change. They soon began a "listening campaign" with members of parliament going back to local areas and eventually Mbeki spoke on the radio to the country right before the next election. I was convinced this was the right thing and wrote the script, but I understand the history that made them reluctant.

But while some in the ANC understood the problem, I did not know Mbeki well enough to know whether his acknowledgments on crime and jobs that I wrote for him were anything but a tactic. I was excited when I heard him on the radio acknowledging the need to do better, but with subsequent events, I also can't get those words out of my head.

It was the silence rather than the words on AIDS that rings in my head. In a society beginning to be ravaged by a disease that was only beginning to be acknowledged by the political class, I found an African public almost totally silent in my groups. This was near the end of my work there, but apparently people would only break through the sexual taboos when leaders spotlighted the issue and talked about sexual transmission. The issue would only top the polls when the leaders made it a priority. Former President Mandela would break with the government to do just that on AIDS, as well as in Zimbabwe, where life expectancy is now the lowest on earth and millions have fled to South Africa. On both issues as president, Mbeki's "Africanist" instincts would leave him silent or worse.

My starting point for helping make these parties electable was the need for reassurance, but in others' hands and over time that could become just a big play in a political game that contributes to the end of ideology. I urged on Blair and Clinton a "relentless reassurance" on issues that held people back from voting for the "New Democrats" and "New Labour." In Clinton's case, that included the death penalty, taxes, and welfare reform; in Blair's case, union influence, being tough on crime, economic stability, and interest rates and taxes. Mandela needed to show that his pledges were credible and achievable and that he would take responsibility for reducing the violence. Barak had to convince people that he could be trusted to protect Israel's security, and not to give too much to the Arabs, above all, Jerusalem. In each case, they were addressing the past, highlighting policies and a history that had made the party unelectable or disqualified or left voters unsettled, not sure whether to trust them with power.

There were two aspects that made this a strategy, rather than a tactic. The leaders believed in all these policies and, indeed, considered them essential to their project for change. Clinton supported the death penalty and led welfare reform as a governor; Blair emerged as a national leader because of his passion about crime and controlling the unions and because of Gordon Brown's passion to rein in spending and avoid tax increases; Barak ran and led in Rabin's way to make sure security was number one.

And second, and perhaps more important, the reassurance was a two-step process that liberated voters to embrace the main purpose of the project. With worries about taxes, spending, inflation, unions, crime, security, and the like greatly reduced, voters could give these parties a mandate to change government, invest in job creation, schools, and health care, even a bold peace. Once voters were confident of the reassurances, they relished the chance to support our priorities in government.

I began to have doubts about all this when the Republicans and Tories attacked Clinton and Blair for clever tactics, stealing their policies, winking and half admiring them for the trick. Indeed, some in our own team who were less focused on the larger political project relished the steal. That suited everyone because the consultants looked clever and it seemed like nothing happened ideologically, as policies were stolen simply to confound and confuse, creating a sense of no difference. That the leaders believed strongly in the policies and that they were advanced not for their own sake but as a way of advancing the larger project got lost in the new tit-for-tat game of "stealing issues."

As always, Dick Morris took the game more seriously than anyone else. His game plan was simple: "Fast-forward the Gingrich agenda so that the deficit is reduced, welfare is reformed, the size of government is cut, and regulations are reduced. This will make the Republican issues less appealing since they will be on their way to solution." The issues are raised not to advance the president's larger project, but simply and powerfully, to diminish the need for Republicans. That it reinforces the conservative ascendancy in ideas is of no great importance.[26]

Some members of the "pollster-consultant industrial complex" survey these machinations and see the "end of ideology"—the end of big political projects, big issues, or strong party affinities—as the new reality. For some, the scorn for ideology or political purpose creates a new mission and new rules. That is Frank Luntz's and Dick Morris's whole premise. The former's work is targeted at "the not-so-silent majority of Americans who reject ideological soundness in favor of the sound center." The latter asserts, "Voters do not want to topple establishments"; "just help children and families live better, the era of *the big issue* has left us." Ideology is not a big force: it "went the way of big government." That leaves us with a public agenda "of small bricks of progress, each a good idea, most of them stemming from consensus and all aimed in a positive direction to improve people's lives in specific but small ways."[27]

For Clinton, the 1994 defeat was a time for realism and new thinking, given the hard reality of new Republican majorities in both the House and

Senate. Morris, however, turned that realism into a reality of his own. Morris's advice was to think small; "there is a perfectly good and fine list right here of bite-size achievements that they can and will digest." And on what you want to do: "you print the menu of the things you want. Then I'll advise which dish to have for dinner tonight." Clinton's 1996 presidential campaign, journalist John Harris observes, advanced a group of "poll-tested initiatives, many deliberately small in scale," and Mark Penn, in the post-election debates, argued strongly for their importance and for the diminished role of ideology, despite the titanic battle between Clinton and the Gingrich Congress over Medicare, education, and the environment.[28]

The thrill for Morris apparently was the three weeks in July 1996 when he was the "secret intermediary" that "got bills passed into law and made history." He was excited about his role helping both current and former clients, one Democrat and one Republican, in an act of "post-ideological" transpartisanship, unembarrassed about the result. "It was this decision by [Trent] Lott that probably won the Senate, and likely the House too, for the GOP in the '96 election. Had the Republicans remained totally obstinate, the public would have rejected them decisively"—and finishing the sentence for him—"and would have given Democrats control of the Congress." But that project did not seem to interest him.[29]

A candidate "triangulating" against his own party "represents the ultimate extension of a campaign approach," political scientist Diane Heith argues, but in fact it is the opposite: the campaign approach is the consequence of triangulation—in this case a politics devoid of purpose with neither a big project nor partisanship. Primacy of polling, absent a project, is just a big menu of policies and just a big menu of groups, not derived from some goal, project, or ideological formation. "At its heart, triangulation lacks any ideology or goal beyond victory."[30] This is good news for the consultants. In the United States, Morris can work for both Democrats and Republicans. Globally, it means Luntz can work for the former communists in Italy; Penn for Berlusconi and the former junta leader General Banzer in Bolivia.

In the year before the 2008 election, Mark Penn, the lead strategist and pollster for Hillary Clinton's campaign, wrote a book, *Microtrends*, in which he dismissed the idea of "megaforces sweeping us all along." Instead, he told us, America and the world "are being pulled apart by an intricate maze of choices, accumulating in microtrends—small, under-the-radar forces that can involve as little as 1 percent of the population, but which are powerfully shaping our society." To understand then what is happening and have an impact, we need to get out our microscopes and magnifying glasses, "in sociological terms," get out our "polls, surveys, and statistics."[31] If I ever come to think of my work in such terms, then take me out and shoot me. In any event, the voters in 2006 and 2008 formed into the megaforce that swept away a lot of conventional wisdom, consultants, and politicians.

At the White House Correspondents Dinner in 1993, when the president was supposed to entertain with self-deprecating humor and slaps at the media, President Clinton read out an urgent telegram that he received from his pollster, Stan Greenberg: "I don't have a clue what you should do. Follow your instincts, but send the check anyway."[32] In fact, Clinton's one criticism of me, according to Morris, was that "he wouldn't tell me what to do."[33] Clinton, in fact, always went to that point: give me a plan. That was true in the campaign and in the White House during our fifteen-minute meetings and in the intense meetings on his budget and economic plan; and that was his main criticism of his political advisors, his campaign, and his White House senior staff. But that distorts Clinton to make the consultant look more powerful. When Clinton got the plans or the "to dos," however, he did not just start checking down the list; he scrutinized them, compared them with his other lists and priorities, with his own political project and personal mission; and he ran them by people, thinking through the consequences, bringing his own judgment—and only then acted on some and discarded the rest.

But there is some truth to the president's criticism. I was very conscious that my role as pollster to the president took place within the context of his election and the political project, which we shared. I told a panel of presidential pollsters at the American Enterprise Institute at the end of the president's first year, "at the center of any presidential campaign and any presidency, [is] a presidential idea that creates the moment that makes this presidency possible." I "use this opportunity [when I meet with the president] to talk about what is the mood in the country, how he's being understood and interpreted," though all within "a presidential idea that creates the moment." I did not use such meetings to offer some personal set of prescriptions and I could recall no moment where we sat there "to figure out what the initiatives of the administration would be," I told the panel. The policies and initiatives "are derived from the President's vision, from the campaign, what he set out to do."[34] Our work together was grounded in a politics with a purpose, indeed a big purpose.

What brought the president to politics and what brought me out of academia were the political and social upheaval of the 1960s and the 1968 choice between Eugene McCarthy and Robert Kennedy and the RFK presidency that never was. It inspired a generation here and many around the world who thought a politics for social justice and workers could unite the country. Through the campaigns of Clinton, Mandela, Blair, Barak, and Goni and others, I thought to build a diverse majority that would use government to check inequality and private excess and build community. Each of these leaders in their own way advanced along that path, though I have come to realize that what I do is not about the cumulative scorecard, but the choices we make at each political moment.

We are living through a period of tumult and change and I am confident a new generation is finding new purpose for its journey.

ACKNOWLEDGMENTS

This memoir/book was so much harder to write than anything I've tried before. Were I taking to pen to defend the virtue of pollsters and campaign consultants, the words would have come easy, but not only was I ambivalent, I wasn't sure where I would come out in the end. This violates my snarky advice to students and employees: you can only write well if you know what you are going to say. But in the process of writing this book, I continually was surprised by my changing conclusions about myself, my role, and about the leaders I thought I knew so well.

Also, when I write about numbers, public opinion, social trends, and venture advice, I bombard the page. I'm invested in the words, to be sure, but there is a certain distance as I throw them out there as interpretation or to provoke reactions. But when I wrote this book in first person about my own thinking and feelings at the time, and my observations about these leaders that I respected, it was totally different. I wrote like I owned every word, thought, and piece of history, and I ground out only two or three pages on my best days.

I compounded the problem by writing the first draft in present tense—to the dismay of Tom Dunne, master of this imprint at St. Martin's Press, who embraced this book as an idea and held on even when I showed up with some 750 pages. A little embarrassed to write a memoir, I used present tense to put myself in scenes, describe what I saw and felt at the time, and better capture the uncertainty and risk—as if I really didn't know the future and how these stories and campaigns would end.

If that draft manuscript morphed to a book, it was due to the work of Rob Kirkpatrick, my senior editor at St. Martin's Press who was intrigued by the book's bigger scope and who worked overtime to get all the gears turning. And it was due to Doug Sease—the first professional editor-writer I ever let rework my writing. Getting rid of present tense voice was the least of the changes as he made each story more inviting and accessible, ruthlessly discarded material I loved, tightened the narrative, loosened the prose, and forced me to really explain what I do as a pollster in a common-sense language. If you have got this far in the book, he must have succeeded.

Bob Barnett is a little unbelievable as my agent. He helped at every stage, making sure I stayed with the right publisher and right deal, brought out the right book at the right time and responding to e-mail in seconds off his Black-Berry as if he were working with no other authors. And he is responsible for getting Doug Sease and I together.

No one took more responsibility for this book than Jaclyn Macek who began as my project coordinator and quickly and gracefully emerged as the skilled manager of all the moving pieces, rigorous editor, master of the sources and research and protector of the book's quality right to the end. In the process, she not only emerged as a remarkably skilled professional, she developed a passion for the work of these leaders and politics and the work of our company.

Richard Wike and Mike Zini served successively and successfully as the senior researchers over three years, responsible for bringing together the extraordinary amount of material, much of it inaccessible or unreadable, and built the narrative and time line that made all my writing possible. While I wrote this book with few numbers, that conceals the shelves devoted to all my memorandum, notes, news clippings and articles, survey results, books of cross tabulations, and focus groups transcripts. They were aided in their work at Greenberg Quinlan Rosner by Tim Schmitz, David Garr, and Brandy Delahoussaye. Eric Senn, who directs the IT department, somehow brought all these surveys and memos in formats long forgotten by humankind on line, and in the process brought to life much of the company's history.

While writing this book, a pretty remarkable group of young people seasoned beyond their years—Sam Weston, Clark Jennings, Jaclyn and now Darryl Lockett—served as my project coordinators. They got the thankless job of keeping the book moving, while convincing everybody else that Stan really was doing his day job, even when I disappeared almost every morning from 4 A.M. until nearly 11, or for a week in some distant time zone to write. Sam also searched out material for the Blair chapter; Clark persuaded the Clinton Presidential Library to provide access to my meeting schedules; and Darryl helped finalize the book. Freda Amar, my executive assistant, is indefatigable, keeping the rest of my life from falling into chaos but having lived through my work for these leaders, emerged as an important resource for the team.

Because this is a memoir, you get permission to put yourself center stage, but it was Jeremy Rosner and Mark Feierstein who took the lead in Bolivia and often Jeremy in Britain. We are all part of a company that has grown bigger than us. Al Quinlan is the leader as president who, with Anna Greenberg and Mike Bocian, did groundbreaking work with so many major U.S. campaigns and advocacy groups. They tutor all of us on emerging campaign techniques and thinking, new polling methods, and our rapidly changing society. Ana Iparraguirre leads my team and she has taken all our work on U.S. national politics and issues to a new level, despite my being consumed with the book. Howard Briskin as chief operating officer created more than the illusion of a smooth operating company, and Edie Nardecchia shows that we're not just a company that fields an extraordinary amount of high quality research, but a company of people who value their work together.

I am awed by the number of people who offered to read and critique parts of the book, but particularly Doug Sosnik, Sam Popkin and Ed Greenberg, my brother, who offered extensive reactions to the original plan of the book and to most of the key chapters. Donna Brazille, Bob Dahl, David Dreyer, Paul Gewirtz, Pat Griffin, Bob Shrum, Mark Steitz, Rick Weiner, and Tina Weiner read individual chapters, providing invaluable suggestions, but also more general ones that sometimes gave me the confidence to barrel ahead and, sometimes, to step back and rethink. Larry Jacobs at the Hubert H. Humphrey School at the University of Minnesota brought his colleagues together, including Lisa Disch, who convinced me to abandon some of my simple-minded ideas about electoral mandates and how leaders relate to people.

Steve Bing reacted to my emerging ideas about leadership, including reading some of the key chapters in draft form and always provided me insights about Bill Clinton. His near decade-long support for Democracy Corps has created an incomparable resource for progressives, but inadvertently provided the data that enabled me to assess Clinton's legacy and the change in U.S. politics that made the 2008 election possible.

Bill Clinton was in many respects the starting point for the book, and I thank him for allowing me to play out my role. Almost everything else followed, even if it took some twists and turns. Part of my motivation for writing the book was to address the caricature of Bill Clinton as "poll driven" and just saying what people want to hear that diminished what he was trying to do and trivialized my own work. And, not unimportant to me, I wanted to write myself back into scenes where I had been erased in popular accounts, like *Primary Colors*.

Fortunately, I had my own diary for the campaign period, but I could not have written the Clinton chapters without the personal interviews of George Stephanopoulos, Paul Begala, Sidney Blumenthal, Gloria Cabe, James Carville, David Dreyer, Joe Goode, Marcia Hale, and Gene Sperling. Bob Woodward agreed to read the draft chapter and more, invited me to interview him so he could amend some of his conclusions about Clinton. Discussing with him the fate of the Clinton economic plan made me very aware of how this book will be coming out just as the next president copes with the troubled economy, rising deficits, and personal promises to bring change.

I wish I had kept a diary for my work with Nelson Mandela and the ANC campaigns, though I kept extensive notes and wrote my usual memos. Again, many of my collaborators agreed to be interviewed, including Pallo Jordan, Marcel Golding, and especially Ketso Gordhan and Roshene Singh, the effective campaign managers for these historic elections who welcomed my participation then and were helpful in manifold ways. Frank Greer's recollections from the inside were indispensible, as were Pat Keefer's from the outside. Jeremy Seekings and Matt Eldridge provided access to their interviews with the players, and Craig Charney to his surveys for the ANC and his superhuman recall of events and meetings. Halton Cheadle and Wilmot James read this materially closely and helped me get it right. The chapter would have been so much richer had my friends still in government been able to participate, but I wrote this history respectful of their work.

Tony Blair was open and reflective in our interview, even though he had just left office and was already pressed by events in the Middle East, which we also managed to discuss. This chapter was aided by timely interviews with Ed Balls, Sidney Blumenthal, Elaine Kamarck, Margaret McDonagh, Jonathan Powell, Bob Shrum, and close editing by Philip Kremen and Wendy Braverman.

I wrote the Barak chapter first because the history was so immediate, because it raised many personal issues for me as a Jew, and because it uncovered so many issues about the role of polling. Writing that chapter was cathartic and opened me up for the rest of the memoir. My colleagues, whatever their conflicting politics in the post-Barak era, agreed to long interviews, including James Carville, Doron Cohen, Moshe Gaon, Jim Gerstein, Yizhak Hertzog, Boris Krasny, Bob Shrum, Tal Silberstein, and Eldad Yaniv. Barak, too, agreed to an interview in which he showed great clarity about what he sought. Some of these agreed to the additional indignity of reading the long draft chapter to help me get it right.

The Goni chapter, and to some extent the book, gained its purpose in the reactions to Rachel Boynton's documentary, *Our Brand is Crisis*. My extended interview with Goni enabled me to gain insights into his motivation and interpretation of the campaign and subsequent events. Mauricio Balcazar and Bee Bedoya helped us be professionals in Bolivia and helped me get the book right, as did Jeremy Rosner and Mark Feierstein in their interviews. Amy Webber is my hero as someone who went to Bolivia, gained everyone's trust, kept her values intact, and offered the closest reading of all of my draft chapters, helping me get this complicated story right from the ground up.

I am grateful to my family for lots of things, but everyone—my children, Anna, Jonathan and Kathryn Greenberg, and my wife, Rosa DeLauro—read every chapter and not just the chapters where they figured. When Anna BlackBerryed me from a panel she was on in Texas, "Reading Barak. I love it. A page-turner," I began to feel this was not all too arcane. The same was true for Kathryn's reading, when she told me she stalled in the Blair chapter. I carried Rosa's pile of marked-up chapters with me to all corners of the globe. And when Jonathan, who works the mad hours of a chef, read the whole book through in days, I thought, maybe this is more than a group of stories.

Instead of devoting a chapter to how I got here, which would have put the spotlight uncomfortably on me rather than the leaders, I decided to weave my story into the story of each leader. That brought home to me, more than I realized, how central my family is to everything I have done and how much I depend on each one's support and love. And that story now ensnares Ari Zentner and John Delicath and my precious grandchildren.

Rosa and I are partners and soul mates in all this, though I'm not sure I kept up my end of the compact. Writing is so self-centered and this memoir was triply so. Yet with Democrats taking control of the Congress, she was doing the real stuff, battling and winning a major increase in food stamps, extension of the child tax credit to low income families, new authority to the FDA and Consumer Product Safety Commission, and amazingly, House passage of the bill assuring equal pay for equal work for women. And meanwhile she was still reading my chapters. So, I got a lot of work to do for my best friend and hero.

This book is dedicated to Rigby Maya Zentner, Sadie Liberty Delicath, and Teo Isaac Zentner, our grandchildren, who give us such joy, and time together with them trumps preparing for any committee hearing or writing any poll.

I hope this book is worthy of all of those who made it possible.

Stanley B. Greenberg
Washington, D.C.
June 7, 2008

NOTES

INTRODUCTION

1. Joe Klein, *Politics Lost: How American Democracy Was Trivialized by People Who Think You're Stupid* (New York: Doubleday, 2006), pp. 1, 13; *Election Unspun: Why Politicians Can't Tell the Truth*, BBC Channel 4, April 18, 2005.

2. George Bush, "Remarks by President Bush at 2007 President's Dinner," US Newswire, June 13, 2007; "Edwards Campaigning Against Poverty," *WCF Courier*, August 20, 2005; Fareed Zakaria and Newt Gingrich, Interview, *This Week with George Stephanopoulos*, ABC News, November 6, 2005; Peter C. Rollins and John E. O'Connor, *The West Wing: The American Presidency as Television Drama* (Syracuse: Syracuse University Press, 2003), pp. 42–62; "Myth and Reality in the Hollywood Campaign Film: *Primary Colors* (1998) and *The War Room* (1994)," Syracuse, New York: Syracuse University Press, 2003, pp. 288–305; Andrew Marr, "How Blair Put the Media in a Spin," BBC News, May 10, 2007; Jon Stewart, *The Daily Show*, New York: Comedy Central, April 19, 2005.

3. Tyler Smith, "No Doubt: Global Pollster is Sure Labastida Has a Key to the Mexican White House," *Marketplace* January 30, 2000; Sebastiano Messina, "An American Guru in Rome," *La Republica*, January 24, 2001; Elizabeth Kolbert, "A Pollster Conquers the World," *The New Yorker*, May 31, 1999; Editorial, *Akron Beacon Journal*, p. 75; Rory Carroll, "Italy's Left Banks on US-style Poll Blitz: Insults and Kisses Set Tone for Election Campaign," *The Guardian*, October 24, 2000; Maria Latella, "Guru Greenberg Introduces Himself," *Corriere della Sera*, January 24, 2001; Benjamin Ginsberg, *The Fatal Embrace: Jews and the State* (Chicago: University of Chicago Press, 1998), pp. 5–18; Stanley B. Greenberg, "A Strange Waltz in Vienna," *New York Times*, March 27, 2001.

4. Susan Herbst, *Numbered Voices: How Opinion Polling Has Shaped American Politics* (Chicago: University of Chicago Press, 1995), pp. 160–61; Benjamin Page, "The Semi-Sovereign Public," in Jeff Manza, Fay Lomax Cook, and Benjamin I. Page, eds., *Navigating Public Opinion: Polls, Policy, and the Future of American Democracy* (Oxford: Oxford University Press, 2002), pp. 326–32, 334; James A. Stimson et al., "Opinion and Policy: A Global View," *PS: Political Science and Politics* 27, no. 1 (March 1994), pp. 29–35; James A. Stimson et al., "Dynamic Representation,"

American Political Science Review 89, no. 3 (September 1995), pp. 543–45, 552–60; Jacob S. Hacker and Paul Pierson, *Off Center: The Republican Revolution and the Erosion of American Democracy* (New Haven: Yale University Press, 2005), pp. 25–29, 73, 75–80; Democracy Corps, "Time Series on Party Thermometer Scores, 2002–2006," Internal Document; Stanley B. Greenberg, "Conservative Failure Conference," Presentation to CAF Conference, May 3, 2007; Lawrence R. Jacobs and Robert Y. Shapiro, *Politicians Don't Pander: Political Manipulation and the Loss of Democratic Responsiveness* (Chicago: University of Chicago Press, 2000), pp. 28–38, 317.

5. Martin Gilens, "Inequality and Democratic Responsiveness," *Public Opinion Quarterly*, 69, no. 5 (2005), pp. 783–92; Lawrence R. Jacobs and Theda Skocpol, "American Democracy and an Era of Rising Inequality," in Lawrence R. Jacobs and Theda Skocpol, eds., *Inequality and American Democracy: What We Know and What We Need to Learn* (New York: Russell Sage Foundation, 2005), pp. 10–11; Jeffrey H. Birnbaum, "The Road to Riches Is Called K Street," *Washington Post*, June 22, 2005; Page, "The Semi-Sovereign Public," pp. 331–33, 338; Tom Rosenstiel, "Political Polling and the New Media Culture: A Case of More Being Less," *Public Opinion Quarterly* 69, no. 5 (2005), pp. 700–704; Thomas E. Patterson, "Of Polls, Mountains: U.S. Journalists and Their Use of Election Surveys," *Public Opinion Quarterly* 69, no. 5 (2005), pp. 722–23; Hacker and Pierson, *Off Center*, pp. 47–53, 177–78.

6. V. O. Key, *Public Opinion and American Democracy* (New York: Alfred A. Knopf, 1964), p. 547; Jacobs and Shapiro, *Politicians Don't Pander*, p. xvii, 7, 27, 102–10, 141, 151; Frank Luntz, Strategy document, *Luntz Playbook for Winning the Elections in 2006* (The Luntz Research Company, 2006); Douglas A. Lathrop, *The Campaign Continues: How Political, Consultants and Campaign Tactics Affect Public Policy* (Westport, Connecticut: Praeger, 2003), p. 64; John F. Harris, "A Clouded Mirror: Bill Clinton, Polls and the Politics of Survival," in Steve E. Schier, ed., *The Postmodern Presidency: Bill Clinton's Legacy in U.S. Politics* (Pittsburgh, University of Pittsburgh Press, 2000), pp. 93–97; Dick Morris, *The New Prince* (New York: St. Martin's Press, 1999), pp. 71–74.

7. Scott McClellan, *What Happened: Inside the Bush White House and Washington's Culture of Deception* (Philadelphia, PA: Public Affairs, 2008), pp. xiii, 62, 73–77; John McCain, Remarks at the Greater Columbus Convention Center, Columbus, OH, May 15, 2008.

1. BILL CLINTON: ACT I

1. Stanley B. Greenberg, "Focus Group Report: Strategic Considerations," Memo to Governor Bill Clinton, August 7, 1990; Bill Clinton, *My Life* (New York: Alfred A. Knopf, 2004); Eleanor Clift and Tom Brazaitis, *War Without Bloodshed: The Art of Politics* (New York: Scribner's, 1996), pp. 28–29.

2. Clinton, *My life* p. 370.

3. Together in this project was John Mollenkopf, Gary Oren, and myself—and as I recall, John wrote the paper.

4. Stanley B. Greenberg, *Politics and Poverty: Modernization and Response in Five Poor Neighborhoods* (New York: John Wiley & Sons, 1973).

5. Stanley B. Greenberg, *Middle Class Dreams: Politics and Power of the New American Majority* (New York: Times Books), 1995.

6. Clift and Brazaitis, *War Without Bloodshed*, p. 27.

7. Stanley B. Greenberg, "From Crisis to Working Majority," *The American Prospect* 2, no. 7 (September 1991).

8. Clinton, *My Life*, pp. 11–12, 27–30.

9. Ibid., pp. 37–39, 59–63; David Maraniss, *First in His Class: A Biography of Bill Clinton* (New York: Simon & Schuster, 1995), pp. 11–20.

10. Clinton, *My Life*, pp. 119–23, 175–77, 189–90.

11. This account of Clinton's electoral pursuits in Arkansas draws primarily on the account in my earlier book, *Middle Class Dreams*, pp. 182–203; it also draws on Clinton's recollections in his autobiography, *My Life*, pp. 210–25.

12. Clinton, *My Life*, p. 258.

13. Ibid., pp. 264–66.

14. Ibid., p. 258.

15. Ibid., pp. 283, 293–302.

16. Ibid., p. 122.

17. Peter Goldman, Thomas M. DeFrank, Mark Miller, Andrew Murr, and Tom Matthews, *Quest for the Presidency 1992* (College Station: Texas A&M Press, 1994), pp. 14–17; Greenberg, *Middle Class Dreams*, pp. 148, 341.

18. Greenberg, *Middle Class Dreams*, p. 312.

19. Much of this description draws from personal interviews with Frank Greer and Gloria Cabe.

20. Bill Clinton, Keynote Address, Democratic Leadership Council, Cleveland, Ohio, May 6, 1991.

21. David Broder, "Democratic Group Finds No Champion," *Washington Post*, May 9, 1991; Tom Baxter, "Gore to Gauge How Tax Plan Flies with Party," *Atlanta Journal-Constitution*, May 7, 1991; Jeffrey Stinson, "Clinton's Speech Brings Delegates to Their Feet," *Arkansas Democrat-Gazette*, May 7, 1991; John King, "Clinton's Star Rises, as Does Cleveland's," Associated Press, May 8, 1991.

22. Greenberg, *Middle Class Dreams*, p. 210.

23. Stanley B. Greenberg, "The Plan for Non-Candidacy," Memo to Governor Bill Clinton, August 6, 1991.

24. This account of the day-to-day activity of the campaign is based on a contemporary diary that I kept, starting August 30, 1991, through to election day 1992.

25. Stanley B. Greenberg, "Campaign Update and Process," Memo to Governor Bill Clinton and the Campaign, September 1, 1991.

26. While the Democratic Leadership Council's "Southern strategy" originally surfaced in September, Clinton later shared with me a memo from Al From in mid-November that was still arguing for a Southern strategy, and that "trying to outbid other candidates for the affection of the 'forgotten middle class' was a fool's errand." Al From, "Sharpening Your Edge," Memo to Bill Clinton, November 14, 1991.

27. Stanley B. Greenberg, presentation notes, Washington Court Hotel, September 13, 1991.

28. This report on comments by Galston and others is based on my handwritten notes during the meetings.

29. George Stephanopoulos, *All Too Human: A Political Education* (Boston: Little, Brown, 1999), pp. 28–30.

30. Stanley B. Greenberg, "Bill Clinton: New Hampshire," Exploratory focus group memo, Manchester, New Hampshire, September 27, 1991.

31. Ibid.

32. John Harris, *The Survivor: Bill Clinton in the White House* (New York: Random House, 2005), pp. x–xi.

33. Bill Clinton, "Announcement Speech," Old State House, Little Rock, Arkansas, October 3, 1991.

34. Stanley B. Greenberg, "Message Initiative," Memo to the Clinton Campaign, October 7, 1991; Stanley B. Greenberg, Personal Diary, October 7, 1991; Stanley B. Greenberg, meeting notes, "Message Initiative," October 11, 1991; Stanley B. Greenberg, "The Organizing Meeting," Memo to Bill Clinton and the Message Group, October 15, 1991.

35. Bill Clinton, "The New Covenant: Responsibility and Rebuilding the American Community," Speech at Georgetown University, October 23, 1991.

36. Stanley B. Greenberg, Personal Diary, October 13–15, 1991; Stanley B. Greenberg, "Update: The Economic Address," Memo to the Message Group, October 27, 1991.

37. Stanley B. Greenberg, "Update: The Economic Address," Memo to the Message Group, October 27, 1991.

38. Stanley B. Greenberg, Personal Diary, November 5, 1991.

39. Stanley B. Greenberg, Personal Diary, November 19–20, 1991.

40. Bill Clinton, "A New Covenant for Economic Change," Remarks to students at Georgetown University, November 20, 1991.

41. Stanley B. Greenberg and Celinda Lake, "The American Economy in the Public Mind," sponsored by the Center for National Policy, January 9, 1992; Stanley B. Greenberg and Celinda Lake, "Public Polling Results, October 1991–December 1992," Internal document.

42. Greenberg-Lake, Survey of New Hampshire primary voters, December 20, 1991.

43. Stanley B. Greenberg, "New Hampshire Update," Memo to the Clinton Campaign, December 26, 1991; Greenberg-Lake, Survey of New Hampshire voters, December 20, 1991.

44. Stanley B. Greenberg, Personal Diary, December 28–29, 1991.

45. Ibid., December 30, 1991–January 1, 1992.

46. Clinton Campaign Ad, "Plan for America's Future," January 2, 1992.

47. Stanley B. Greenberg. Personal Diary, January 12, 1992.

48. Ibid., January 17, 1992.

49. Goldman et al., *Quest for the Presidency 1992*, p. 90; Stanley B. Greenberg, Personal Diary, January 18, 1992.

50. Goldman et al., *Quest for the Presidency 1992*, pp. 116–33; Stanley B. Greenberg, Personal Diary, January 25–26, 1992, February 6–10, 1992, February 17–18, 1992.

51. Goldman et al., *Quest for the Presidency 1992*, pp. 111–12.

52. Ibid., 150–51; Clinton, *My Life*, pp. 390–91.

53. Stanley B. Greenberg, Personal Diary, February 20–22, 1992.

54. Goldman et al., *Quest for the Presidency 1992*, p. 156.

55. Ibid., pp. 156–57.

56. Ibid., pp. 159–60.

57. Stanley B. Greenberg, Personal Diary, March 1, 1992.

58. Goldman et al., *Quest for the Presidency 1992*, p. 159; Stanley B. Greenberg, Personal Diary, March 2, 1992.

59. Goldman et al., *Quest for the Presidency 1992*, p. 160.

60. Stanley B. Greenberg, "The Florida Baseline Survey," Memo to Bill Clinton and Campaign, March 2, 1992; Stanley B. Greenberg, Personal Diary, March 2, 1992.

61. Stanley B. Greenberg, Personal Diary, March 3, 1992.

62. Ibid., March 4, 1992.

63. Ibid., March 5, 1992.

64. Ibid., March 6, 1992.

65. Ibid., March 8–9, 1992.

66. Ibid., March 10, 1992.

67. Ibid., March 11, 1992; Goldman et al., *Quest for the Presidency 1992*, pp. 187–88.

68. Stanley B. Greenberg, Personal Diary, March 8, 1992.

69. Stanley B. Greenberg, "Macomb County: Speech Notes," Memo to Bill Clinton and Campaign, Paul Begala, and George Stephanopoulos, March 12, 1992.

70. Stanley B. Greenberg, Personal Diary, March 12, 1992, Greenberg, *Middle Class Dreams*, pp. 218–21.

71. Stanley B. Greenberg, Personal Diary, March 12, 1992; Goldman et al., *Quest for the Presidency 1992*, p. 188.

72. Greenberg, *Middle Class Dreams*, pp. 220–21.

73. Ibid., pp. 221–22.

74. Clinton nonetheless won the New York primary with 41 percent of the vote, and took Pennsylvania with 56 percent; Cathleen Decker, "Clinton, Bush Win Pennsylvania Vote," *Los Angeles Times*, April 29, 1992; A L. May, "'Very Queasy' About Clinton," *Atlanta Journal-Constitution*, April 29, 1992.

75. Greenberg-Lake, "Public Polls," October 1991–December 1992.

76. Stanley B. Greenberg, Personal Diary, June 4–5, 1992; Stanley B. Greenberg, "Moving the Campaign to the Next Stage," Memo to Bill Clinton and Company, George Stephanopoulos and the Message/Strategy Group, and Mickey Kantor, Eli Segal, and David Wilhelm, May 25, 1992.

77. Stanley B. Greenberg, Personal Diary, June 12, 1992.

78. Ibid., June 14–18, 1992.

79. Greenberg, *Middle Class Dreams*, pp. 225–27. Note that I use the description of the message from the book, though my diaries have enabled me to correct the dates for the various presentations.

80. Stanley B. Greenberg, Personal Diary, June 26–28, 1992.

81. Robert E. Rubin and Jacob Weisberg, *In an Uncertain World: Tough Choices from Wall Street to Washington* (New York: Random House, 2004), pp. 104–5.

82. Howard Kurtz and E J. Dionne, "Clinton Pushes Tax Cut in Debut Ad," *Washington Post*, January 10, 1992.

83. Bill Clinton and Al Gore, *Putting People First: How We Can All Change America* (New York: Times Books, 1992).

84. Stanley B. Greenberg, Personal Diary, July 15, 1992.

85. Greenberg-Lake, National survey of likely voters, July 21, 1992.

86. Stanley B. Greenberg, Personal Diary, October 24–25, 27, 29, 1992.

87. Ibid., October 26, 1992.

88. Ibid., October 27, 1992.

89. Ibid., October 29, 1992.

90. Ibid., October 30, 1992.

91. Ibid., November 1, 1992.

92. Ibid., November 2, 1992.

93. Ibid., November 3, 1992.

94. Ibid.

95. Ibid., November 5, 1992; Stanley B, Greenberg, "White House Strategic Operations: The Character of the Clinton Presidency," Memo to President-elect Bill Clinton, November 5, 1992.

2. BILL CLINTON: ACT II

1. Stanley B. Greenberg, "The Clinton Presidency: Political Goals: Post-Election Survey; Post-Election Thinking," Memo to President-elect Bill Clinton and others, November 18, 1992; Greenberg-Lake, Post-election national survey of 2,000 actual voters, November 4–8, 1992.

2. Ibid.

3. Bob Woodward, *The Agenda: Inside the Clinton White House* (New York: Simon & Schuster, 1994), p. 52–60, 66; Clinton, *My Life*, p. 451; Alan Greenspan, *The Age of Turbulence: Adventures in a New World* (New York: Penguin, 2007); Note: These descriptions are also informed by interviews I conducted with George Stephanopoulos, Gene Sperling, Paul Begala, and James Carville.

4. Gene Sperling, "Topics for Economy Conference," Memo to Mickey Kantor, Bob Reich, and John Emerson, November 25, 1992.

5. Seventy-two percent approve, ABC News/*Washington Post* national survey, 1,011 respondents, December 11–14, 1992; 77 percent approve, NBC News/*Wall Street Journal* national survey, 1,004 respondents, December 12–15, 1992; 67 percent approve, Gallup national survey, 1,004 respondents, December 18–20, 1992.

6. Joe Goode, "Georgia Groups," Memo to Stanley Greenberg, December 8, 1992; Woodward, *The Agenda*, p. 61.

7. Joseph E. Stiglitz, *The Roaring Nineties: A New History of the World's Most Prosperous Decade* (New York: W. W. Norton, 2004), pp. 41–44.

8. Rubin and Weisberg, *In an Uncertain World*, pp. 118–25; Clinton, *My Life*, pp. 458–61; Woodward, *The Agenda*, pp. 70–82.

9. Stanley B. Greenberg notes, "Budget Meeting," January 12, 1993; Woodward, *The Agenda*, pp. 83–84. Note that Woodward has this meeting on January 13, even though my notes say the 12.

10. Woodward, *The Agenda*, pp. 85–87.

11. Elizabeth Drew, *On the Edge: The Clinton Presidency* (New York: Simon & Schuster, 1994), pp. 59, 63–64.

12. Greenspan, *The Age of Turbulence*, p. 146.

13. Stanley Greenberg notes, "Message Objectives: Clinton Administration," Message Board Retreat, January 15, 1993.

14. Stanley Greenberg, presentation notes, "Economy/Budget Presentation," White House Retreat, January 23, 1993.

15. This account is based on my presentation notes for the meeting, which are quite detailed, though I have filled in verbs and transitions. Stanley B. Greenberg, presentation notes, meeting with President Bill Clinton, January 27, 1993.

16. Stanley B. Greenberg, "The Clinton Polling/Research Program," Memo to President-elect Bill Clinton, Eli Segal, George Stephanopoulos, and David Wilhelm, November 23, 1992.

17. Greenberg, presentation notes, meeting with President Bill Clinton, January 27, 1992.

18. Stanley B. Greenberg, "Clinton Economic Program," Memo to President Bill Clinton and others, January 26, 1993; Joe Goode, "Los Angeles and Chicago Suburban Focus Groups," Memo to Stanley Greenberg, January 27, 1993.

19. Stanley B. Greenberg, presentation notes, "Cabinet Retreat," Camp David, January 30, 1993; Woodward, *The Agenda*, pp. 99–106; Drew, *On the Edge*, pp. 47–50; Clinton, *My Life*, pp. 488–89.

20. Officially, the first address of the president is a joint session address, not State of the Union, but it's commonly referred to as State of the Union anyway.

21. Woodward, *The Agenda*, pp. 112–13, 118–19, 123; Clinton, *My Life*, pp. 491–95.

22. Stanley B. Greenberg, "Post-Inaugural: New Kind-of-Democrat?", Memo to President Bill Clinton and others, February 5, 1993; Greenberg-Lake, National survey of likely voters, February 1–2, 1993

23. Stanley B. Greenberg, meeting notes, February 8, 1993.

24. Stanley B. Greenberg, presentation notes, presidential meeting, February 10, 1993; Greenberg-Lake, National survey of likely voters, February 8–9, 1993.

25. Stanley Greenberg, presentation notes, meeting with President Bill Clinton, February 13, 1993.

26. Bill Clinton, Address from the Oval Office, February 15, 1993.

27. Woodward, *The Agenda*, pp. 128–29; Drew, *On the Edge*, pp. 76–77.

28. Rubin and Weisberg, *In an Uncertain World*, p. 120; Stanley B. Greenberg, drafts of Joint Session Address, 1993, with personal edits.

29. Drew, *On the Edge*, pp. 76–80; Dan Balz and Ruth Marcus, "The Windup for the Pitch: How Clinton's Team Drafted Game Plan to Sell Program," *Washington Post*, March 7, 1993; Woodward, *The Agenda*, pp. 130–32.

30. Bill Clinton, Address to the Joint Session on the State of the Union, February 17, 1993; Clinton, *My Life*, pp. 493–97; Woodward, *The Agenda*, pp. 131–35.

31. Woodward, *The Agenda*, pp. 136–37; Rubin and Weisberg, *In an Uncertain World*, pp. 120, 128–29.

32. Stanley B. Greenberg, meeting notes, "Planning Meeting," February 20, 1993.

33. Stanley B. Greenberg, presentation notes, President Bill Clinton, Oval Office, January 20, 1993; Greenberg-Lake, National survey of likely voters, February 18–20, 1993.

34. Greenberg-Lake, "Postcards to President Clinton," Dayton, Ohio, Dial Groups, February 17, 1993.

35. Woodward, *The Agenda*, pp. 144–45.

36. Ibid., pp. 144–47, 167–68.

37. Stanley B. Greenberg, presentation notes, meeting with President Bill Clinton, April 16, 1993.

38. Stanley B. Greenberg, presentation outline, President Bill Clinton, April 28, 1993.

39. Stanley B. Greenberg, presentation notes, DLC, New Orleans, Louisiana, April 30, 1993; Stanley B. Greenberg, "The Perot Voters and American Politics: Here to Stay?," in Democratic Leadership Council, *The Road to Realignment: The Democrats and the Perot Voter*, Washington, D.C., July 1, 1993.

40. Jim Lehrer, Peter Hart, and Linda Divall, "Analyzing President Clinton," *NewsHour with Jim Lehrer*, April 30, 1993.

41. Stanley Greenberg, Rahm Emanuel, George Stephanopoulos, Paul Begala, Mandy Grunwald, David Dreyer, Mark Gearan, Joan Baggett, and David Wilhelm, "*Manhattan II*," Memo to President Clinton and others, April 20, 1993; Al From, "The Next 100 Days," Memo to President Bill Clinton, April 16, 1993.

42. Woodward, *The Agenda*, pp. 168–71; Drew, *On the Edge*, pp. 126–27. Note that Woodward and my memo have this meeting occurring on April 20, while Drew has the meeting on the 21st.

43. Stanley B. Greenberg, "The Economic Campaign," Memo to President Bill Clinton and others, May 5, 1993.

44. Woodward, *The Agenda*, pp. 176–80.

45. Ibid., pp. 201–8.

46. Stanley B. Greenberg, presentation notes, "Presidential Presentation," June 9, 1993.

47. Stanley B. Greenberg, Mandy Grunwald, Paul Begala, and James Carville, "Strategic Rethinking," Memo to President Clinton and others, June 8, 1993.

48. Greenberg Research, National survey of 1,000 presidential year voters, June 6–8, 1993.

49. Stanley B. Greenberg, "Defining the Economic Plan: The June Surveys," Memo to President Bill Clinton and others, June 10, 1993.

50. Gene Sperling, "Reconciliation Message," Memo to David Gergen and others, June 11, 1993.

51. The assembled advisors, "Positioning for Conference," Memo to assembled advisors, June 24, 1993; political advisors, "Positioning for Conference," Memo to President Bill Clinton and others, June 25, 1993.

52. Paul Begala, "The Zero Option," Memo to President Bill Clinton, July 1, 1993; Stanley B. Greenberg, Mandy Grunwald, Paul Begala, and James Carville, "The Budget Conference: Turning Point on the Economy," July 2, 1993.

53. Woodward, *The Agenda*, pp. 246–57. I was interviewed for Woodward's book and was stunned when he described the full conversation, virtually in order, before he asked me any questions. His account was more accurate than mine at the time, so I defer to his here. Also see Drew, *On the Edge*, pp. 225–27.

54. Laura Tyson, Alan Blinder, and Joseph Stiglitz, "Deficit Reduction in FY1994," Memo to Thomas McLarty and Members of the Reconciliation Team, July 15, 1993.

55. Woodward, *The Agenda*, pp. 274–75; Stiglitz, *The Roaring Nineties*, pp. 41–44.

56. Drew, *On the Edge*, pp. 265–66.

57. Greenberg Research, "Survey Research on President's Oval Office Address on Economic Plan," Memo to Chairman David Wilhelm, August 4, 1993.

58. Greenberg-Lake, National survey of 1,000 likely voters, August 4–5, 1993.

59. Account of Rosa DeLauro, then deputy whip; Stephanopoulos, *All Too Human*, pp. 176–78; Woodward, *The Agenda*, pp. 307–9; Drew, *On the Edge*, pp. 267–69.

60. Mike Wallace, "The Agenda: Journalist Bob Woodward Writes About the Clinton White House, The Chaos, and Who is Really Running Administration," CBS News Transcripts, *60 Minutes*, June 4, 1994.

61. Andrew Smith, "'Absolute Chaos': Book Cites Rage, Indecision in Clinton White House," *Newsday*, June 4, 1994.

62. Bob Woodward, Interview with author, June 19, 2007.

63. Remarks by President Bill Clinton, DSCC Reception, Ritz-Carlton Hotel, Chicago, Illinois, September 23, 1994. Also see Remarks by President Bill Clinton, Bethel AME Church, Harlem, New York, September 25, 1994; Remarks by President Bill Clinton, Senator Robb Virginia Victory Rally, McLean Hilton Hotel, October 3, 1994; Remarks by President Bill Clinton, Ford Assembly Plant, Dearborn, Michigan, October 11, 1994; Remarks by President Bill Clinton, City Club, Cleveland, Ohio, October 24, 1994.

64. See Kenneth T. Walsh's fascinating account of the presidential plane, particularly its use by President Clinton: *Air Force One: A History of the Presidents and Their Planes* (New York: Hyperion, 2003), pp.176–204.

65. I traveled on a number of his campaign swings in this period, but do not have a schedule from that period, thus do not know the dates or the specific speech being discussed. The meetings and presentations that I describe here on Air Force One happened during this period.

66. National Economic Account data, Bureau of Economic Analysis, 1993–1995 <www.bea.gov/national>.

67. Rubin and Weisberg, *In an Uncertain World*, pp. 126–29; Greenberg Research, National survey of likely voters, September 27–28, 1994; Greenberg Research, National survey of likely voters, October 29–30, 1994.

68. Stanley B, Greenberg, "The First 1994 Survey," Memo to President Clinton and others, January 6, 1994.

69. Stanley B. Greenberg, "Understanding the Economy: America 1994: Report III," Memo to Senators George Mitchell and Tom Daschle and others, June 16, 1994; Stanley B. Greenberg, Michael Waldman, Gene Sperling and Many Grunwald, "The Clinton Economic Message," Memo to the economic team, June 30, 1994; Stanley B. Greenberg, "The Prime Time Press Conference: Thematic Issues," Memo to President Bill Clinton and others, August 8, 1994.

70. Stanley B. Greenberg, "The 1994 Race Defined: Party II," Memo to the Democratic Congressional Leadership, October 12, 1994; Greenberg Research, National survey of likely voters, October 16–17, 1994.

71. Stanley B. Greenberg, "The President and the Democratic Congress: America 1994: Report I," Memo to President Clinton and others, January 15, 1994; Stanley B. Greenberg, "Presidential Presentation: Speech Impact," presentation notes, January 27, 1994; Stanley B. Greenberg, Presidential Presentation, presentation notes, February 5, 1994.

72. Stanley B. Greenberg, "May 1994: Turning Point," Memo to President Bill Clinton and Hillary Rodham Clinton, May 17, 1994; Stanley B. Greenberg, "Democrats—1994: Part One," Memo to President Clinton and others, June 13, 1994.

73. Stanley B. Greenberg, "Democrats—1994: Part Two: Taking Charge of the Agenda,"

Memo to President Clinton and others, June 13, 1994; Stanley B. Greenberg, "An Issue Agenda for Democrats: America 1994: Report II," Memo to Senators George Mitchell and Tom Daschle and others, June 16, 1994.

74. Clinton, *My Life*, p. 628; Dick Morris, *Behind the Oval Office: Winning the Presidency in the Nineties* (New York: Random House, 1997), pp. 9–17.

75. Stanley B. Greenberg, "Mistaking a Moment for a Mandate," *New York Times*, March 9, 1995.

76. Dick Morris, *Behind the Oval Office*, p 14.

77. Douglas Jehl, "Clinton Stumps for Candidates but Watches Where He Goes," *New York Times*, November 3, 1994.

78. Stanley B. Greenberg, *The Two Americas: Our Current Political Deadlock and How to Break It* (New York: Thomas Dunne Books, 2004), pp. 81–90; Lawrence Mishel, Jared Bernstein, and Heather Boushey, *The State of Working America, 2002/03* (Ithaca: Cornell University Press, 2003), pp. 100, 124–26, 160–61.

79. Greenberg, *The Two Americas*, pp. 80–81; Bill Clinton, remarks at DLC Retreat, Hyde Park, New York; Elizabeth Drew, *Showdown: The Struggle Between the Gingrich Congress and the Clinton White House* (New York: Simon & Schuster, 1996), pp. 93–106; Michael Waldman, *POTUS Speaks: Finding the Words That Defined the Clinton Presidency* (New York: Simon & Schuster, 2000), pp. 154, 168–69; Stephanopoulos, *All Too Human*, pp. 371–75.

80. Democracy Corps/Campaign for America's Future, "Post-Election Survey," National survey of 2,000 likely voters, November 2–3, 2004.

81. "Black Leader to Bill Clinton: 'Chill,'" *CNN.com*, January 21, 2008; "Clyburn Feels Clinton Conduct Could Doom Dems' White House Chances," FoxNews.com, April 25, 2008.

82. Ashley Parker, "Bill Clinton Takes to the Churches," *New York Times*, February 10, 2008: David Gergen, *Eyewitness to Power: The Essence of Leadership, Nixon to Clinton* (New York: Simon and Schuster Paperbacks, 2000), p. 273; Mike Allen, "Bill Clinton Sounds Off on Backlash," *Politico*, January 12, 2008; Jonathan Alter, "Leading Democrats to Clinton: Pipe Down," *Newsweek*, January 19, 2008; Maureen Dowd, "Two Against One," *New York Times*, January 23, 2008; Ron Fournier, "Clinton Makes Race an Issue" *Associated Press*, January 23, 2008; Katherine Q. Seelye, "A Former President, Back in the Thick of Politics," *New York Times*, January 27, 2008; "Hillary Clinton Apologies to Black Voters" *CNN.com*, March 17, 2008; Todd S. Purdum, "The Comeback Id," *Vanity Fair*, July 2008; Bill Clinton, "Vanity Fair Article on President Clinton," Office of President Clinton, June 2, 2008.

83. Joshua Green, "The Front-Runner's Fall." *The Atlantic.com*, September 2008; Mark Penn, memo to Senator Hillary Clinton, "Weekly Strategic Review on Hillary Clinton for President Campaign," *Atlantic.com*, March 19, 2007; Note: These descriptions are also informed by interviews I conducted with George Stephanopoulos, Gene Sperling, Paul Begala, James Carville, Rahm Emanuel, and Marcia Hale.

3. NELSON MANDELA

1. Nelson Mandela, *Long Walk to Freedom: An Autobiography of Nelson Mandela* (Boston: Little, Brown, 1994), pp. 3–16; Anthony Sampson, *Mandela: The Authorized Biography* (London: Vintage, 1999), pp. 10–11.

2. Frank Greer, Interview with author, September 21, 2006; Craig Charney, Interview with author, October 24, 2006; Pallo Jordan, Interview with author, November 16, 2005.

3. Sampson, *Mandela*, pp. 423–24.

4. Shula Marks, *The Ambiguities of Dependence in South Africa: Class, Nationalism, and the State in Twentieth-Century Natal* (Johannesburg: Ravan Press, 1986), pp. 43–45, 69.

5. Robert A. Hill and Gregory A. Pirio, *The Politics of Race, Class and Nationalism in Twentieth Century South Africa* (London: Longman, 1987), pp. 209–15, 222–27, 231–43.

6. Robert Kennedy, Address Before the National Union of South African Students, University of Cape Town, June 6, 1966; Reuters, "Kennedy Denounces Apartheid as Evil," *New York Times*, June 7, 1966; Adam Kellett-Long, "South African Crowds Cheer Kennedy on Last Day of Visit," *Washington Post*, June 9, 1966.

7. Gail M. Gerhart, *Black Power in South Africa: The Evolution of an Ideology* (Berkeley: University of California Press, 1979), pp. 58–64, 70–84.

8. Stanley B. Greenberg, Hearings Before the Subcommittee on Africa of the Committee on Foreign Affairs, House of Representatives, September 14, 1983.

9. Pat Keefer, Interview with author, November 15, 2005. In our interview Keefer indicated that they waved a copy of *Time*, but it is the *Newsweek* issue that featured the consultants in its account of the election. See *Newsweek*'s Special Election Edition, November/December 1992 issue. It depicted Clinton on the cover, with the headline, "Exclusive: How He Won. The Untold Story."

10. Center for the Study of Foreign Affairs, "Black Labor Unions in South Africa: Report of a Symposium," Foreign Service Institute, U.S. Department of State, Washington, D.C., 1987.

11. Stanley B. Greenberg, "Open and Close Unionism in South Africa," *South African Labour Bulletin* (January–February 1985), pp. 5–23; Stanley B. Greenberg, *Legitimating the Illegitimate: State, Markets and Resistance in South Africa* (Berkeley: University of California Press, 1987).

12. R. W. Johnson and Lawrence Schlemmer, eds., *Launching Democracy in South Africa* (New Haven: Yale University Press, 1996).

13. Craig Charney, Interview with author, October 26, 2007. Charney was kind enough to provide copies of their baseline poll (Research Initiatives and Marketing and Media Research, "The First Election: Baseline Survey Report," October 1993).

14. This summary of events draws on Patti Waldmeir, *The Anatomy of a Miracle: The End of Apartheid and the Birth of the New South Africa* (New York: W. W. Norton, 1997); John Laredo, "End of the Beginning," Human Sciences Research Council, South Africa (1994), pp. 244–62; Allister Sparks, *Tomorrow Is Another Country: The Inside Story of South Africa's Negotiated Revolution* (Chicago: University of Chicago Press, 1996); Jeffrey Herbst, "Prospects for Elite-Driven Democracy in South Africa," *Political Science Quarterly*, 112, no. 4 (Winter 1997–98).

15. Sampson, *Mandela*, pp. 417–27, 458–59; Waldmeir, *The Anatomy of a Miracle*, pp. 214–18, 225–34; Sparks, *Tomorrow Is Another Country*, p. 139; Herbst, "Prospects for Elite-Driven Democracy in South Africa," *Political Science Quarterly*, 112, no. 4 pp. 598–600, 609–10; Martin Meredith, *South Africa's New Era: The 1994 Election* (London: Mandarin, 1994), pp. 23–25, 43–49.

16. Meredith, *South Africa's New Era*, pp. 48–50.

17. Waldmeir, *The Anatomy of a Miracle*, pp. 168–88, 206–18; Sampson, *Mandela*, pp. 430–37; Sparks, *Tomorrow Is Another Country*, pp. 139–40.

18. David Beresford, "Mandela Calls a Halt to Talks: ANC Leader Breaks Off Negotiations with 'Murdering' Government," *The Guardian* (London), June 22, 1992.

19. Waldmeir, *The Anatomy of a Miracle*, pp. 223–25.

20. Peter Malherbe, "Acclaim as South Africa's Nobel Duo Stand Firm in a Pledge for Peace," *Sunday Times* (South Africa), December 11, 1993.

21. Craig Charney and Susan Booysen, "The Minds and Feelings of the Swing Voters: Keys to Ensuring the Success of South Africa's First Democratic Election," Research Initiatives, December 1992; Analysis Group, "Project Hope" Frequency Questionnaire, October 1993.

22. This analysis of the public polls is greatly helped by Robert B. Mattes, "The Impact of Public Opinion Polling on South Africa's Transition to Democracy: A Report to the 'Investigation into Research Methodology Project' of the Human Sciences Research Council," Cape Town, 1995, pp. 30–36; John Lesage, "Can the ANC Win?", *New African* (London), December 1992, p. 11.

23. Greenberg Research, Frequency Questionnaire, October 1993.

24. Anton Harber, "Experienced Trio Lead Shrewd ANC Campaign," *Weekly Mail and Guardian*, November 26–December 2, 1993; Meredith, pp. 59–61.

25. Ketso Gordhan, Interview with author, November 19, 2005.

26. Pallo Jordan, "The African National Congress: From Illegality to the Corridors of Power," *Review of American Political Economy*, no. 100 (2004), pp. 208–10; Raymond Suttner, "The Character and Formation of Intellectuals Within the South African Liberation Movement," Paper presented to CODESRIA, 30th Anniversary Conference, Dakar, December 8–11, 2003, pp. 32–33; Adrian Hadland, "Nelson Mandela: A Life," in Kader Asmal, David Chidester, and Wilmot James eds., *Nelson Mandela: From Freedom to the Future: Tributes and Speeches* (Jepperstown, South Africa: Jonathan Ball, 2003); Mandela, *Long Walk to Freedom*, pp. 148–49.

27. Daniel Silke and Robert Schrire, "The Mass Media," in Andrew Reynolds, ed., *Election '94 South Africa: The Campaigns, Results and Future Prospects* (New York: St. Martin's Press, 1995), pp. 131–33.

28. Tom Lodge, *Politics in South Africa: From Mandela to Mbeki* (Bloomington: Indiana University Press, 2002), pp. 29–30; Ketso Gordhan, Interview with author, November 19, 2005.

29. Gerhart, *Black Power in South Africa*, pp. 58–64, 70–84.

30. Mandela, *Long Walk to Freedom*, pp. 110–19; Gerhart, *Black Power in South Africa*, pp. 88–90.

31. Mandela, *Long Walk to Freedom*, pp. 149–53; Sampson, *Mandela*, pp. 94–95; Gerhart, *Black Power in South Africa*, pp. 93–95, 146–49.

32. Sampson, *Mandela*, pp. 118–19.

33. Ibid., pp. 163–69.

34. Nelson Mandela, "Statement from the Dock, Rivonia Trial, Pretoria Supreme Court, April 20, 1964," in Asmal et al., eds., *Nelson Mandela*, pp. 27–42.

35. Sampson, *Mandela*, pp. 272–78

36. Herbst, "Prospects for Elite-Driven Democracy in South Africa," pp. 598–600.

37. Philip Jacobson, "Running Scared," *The Times* (London), March 26, 1994.
38. Matthew Eldridge, "In Retrospect: A Collection of Interviews with Strategists and Candidates from the African National Congress's 1994 Western Cape Campaign," paper, University of Cape Town, 1994.
39. Some of this is described in Johnston and Schlemmer, eds., *Launching Democracy in South Africa*, pp. 127–29. Also see interviews with Ketso Gordhan, Frank Greer, and Pallo Jordan.
40. Mark Orkin, "Second Elections Commission Workshop with CASE and RS," Memo to Stanley B. Greenberg, May 28, 1993. This portrayal draws on various news stories and speeches in 1993: Frederik Willem de Klerk, Speech Before Natal National Party Congress, August 11, 1993; Frederik Willem de Klerk, Speech Before Kempton Park rally, November 1993; *Sunday Times* (South Africa), advertisement, November 14, 1993.
41. Bill Keller, "Mandela and de Klerk Open Fire in Battle for Votes," *New York Times*, February 3, 1994; Bob Drogin, "South Africa Campaign Busts Wide Open: Nelson Mandela and Supporters Rally to Celebrate Freedom. President de Klerk's Party Takes Credit for It," *Los Angeles Times*, February 3, 1994; "ANC Hits 'New Nats' with Election Poster Power," *Weekend Argus*, February 5–6, 1994.
42. Stanley B. Greenberg, "Positioning the Campaign," Memo to ANC Election Team, February 16, 1994; Stanley B. Greenberg and Frank Greer, "Strategic Plan: ANC," Memo to President Nelson Mandela and the Election Team, February 16, 1994.
43. Matthew Eldridge, "Now Wasn't the Time: The ANC's 1994 Election Campaign in South Africa's Western Cape Province," MA thesis. Stanford University, April 1997, pp. 38–42.
44. Ibid., pp. 50–51, 65–66.
45. Robert Mattes, Hermann Giliomee, and Wilmot James, "The Election in the Western Cape," in Johnson and Schlemmer, eds., *Launching Democracy in South Africa*, pp. 121–23; Eldridge, "Now Wasn't the Time," pp. 66–69.
46. This account of the economic debate depends on two books with very different perspectives on the emerging economic policy: Alan Hirsch, *Season of Hope: Economic Reform Under Mandela and Mbeki* (Scottsville, South Africa: University of KwaZulu-Natal Press, 2005), pp. 51–53; and William Mervin Gumede, *Thabo Mbeki and the Battle for the Soul of the ANC* (Cape Town: Zebra Press, 2005), pp. 77–78.
47. Hirsch, *Season of Hope*, pp. 2, 20–25, 70–71; Gumede, *Thabo Mbeki and the Battle for the Soul of the ANC*, pp. 81–83.
48. Gumede, *Thabo Mbeki and the Battle for the Soul of the ANC*, pp. 81–83; Hirsch, *Season of Hope*, pp. 12, 16–21; Government of South Africa, "A New Housing Policy and Strategy for South Africa," White Paper, 1994; S. Klasen, "Poverty, Inequality and Deprivation in South Africa: An Analysis of the 1993 Saldru Survey," *Social Indicators Research*, 41 (1997).
49. Hirsch, *Season of Hope*, pp. 31, 48–54; Gumede, *Thabo Mbeki and the Battle for the Soul of the ANC*, pp.71–73.
50. Hirsch, *Season of Hope*, pp. 59–61; Gumede, *Thabo Mbeki and the Battle for the Soul of the ANC*, pp. 76–79.
51. Bob Drogin, "'Freedom Train' Kicks Off S. Africa Campaign: Elections: ANC Leaders Mandela Presents Party Platform after Rail Trip," *Los Angeles Times*, January 30, 1994; Monica Oosterbroek, "Mandela Unveils Election Wish List," *Sunday Times*

(South Africa), January 30, 1994; Liz Sly, "ANC's Tough Job: Aid Poor, Keep the Rich," *Chicago Tribune*, January 31, 1994.

52. Oosterbroek, "Mandela Unveils Election Wish List," *Sunday Times* (South Africa), January 30, 1994. See also Tom Lodge's judgment about the plan, "The African National Congress and Its Allies," pp. 30–32.

53. This commentary is based on my handwritten notes from the focus groups, March 3, 1994.

54. Stanley B. Greenberg, "Message Statement," Memo to President Nelson Mandela, the ANC Election Team, and ANC Media Team, March 4, 1994.

55. Advertising file, Greenberg Research, internal document.

56. Document with radio campaign, "Radio Campaign."

57. Final script, ANC, "Jobs—60 Seconds," March 20, 1994.

58. Stanley B. Greenberg and Frank Greer, "Strategic Plan: ANC," Memo to President Nelson Mandela and the Election Team, February 16, 1994; and a later memo, Greenberg, "Message Statement," March 4, 1994.

59. Stanley B. Greenberg and Frank Greer, Memo to the ANC Election Team, February 16, 1994.

60. Stanley B. Greenberg and Frank Greer, "Speech Points/The Basic Campaign Message," Memo to President Nelson Mandela, March 6, 1994.

61. "De Klerk to Rightists: Be Peaceful," *Chicago Tribune* wire service, March 1, 1994; Liz Sly, "Amid Violence, Homeland Joins S. Africa Ballot," *Chicago Tribune*, March 12, 1994; Bill Keller, "A Homeland Agony," *New York Times*, March 13, 1994; Liz Sly, "S. African Tells Bophuthatswana It's No Longer a Separate Country," *Chicago Tribune*, March 13, 1994; Paul Taylor, "S. African White Militants Split into Separate Factions," *Washington Post*, March 13, 1994.

62. Paul Taylor, "Zulus to Vote with Ballots or Bullets; South Africa's Election Intensifying Intra-Tribal Violence," *Washington Post*, March 28, 1994.

63. Michael Hamlyn, "Bloodbath as Johannesburg March Turns into Battlefield," *The Times* (London), March 29, 1994; Bob Drogin, "20 Die as Unrest Invades Urban South Africa," *Los Angeles Times*, March 29, 1994; Bob Drogin, "Unrest Won't Harm S. Africa Vote," *Los Angeles Times*, March 30, 1994.

64. Tony Trew, Memo to Stanley B. Greenberg, March 28, 1994.

65. Stanley B. Greenberg, "Late March Survey," Memo to the ANC Election Team, March 28, 1994.

66. Tony Trew, Memo to Stanley B. Greenberg and Frank Greer, March 30, 1994; Stanley B. Greenberg, "Reassurance," Memo to the ANC Election Team, March 30, 1994.

67. Liz Sly, "Clamping Down in S. Africa: Zulu Chief Objects, Others Welcome Steps," *Chicago Tribune*, April 1, 1994; Tom Masland and Joseph Contreras, "Ballots or Bullets," *Time*, April 11, 1994; Tos Wentzel, "The Election Must Go Ahead," *Argus*, April 6, 1994.

68. Draft print ad, "Reassurance Print Campaign," April 5, 1994.

69. I actually do not have a transcript of what Sparks said. I have pieced this together from my handwritten notes on the interactions and issues for the report of Project Opposition: "De Klerk: Analysis of Speeches—Arguments and Style," April 12, 1994, used by Sparks in preparing for this role; quoted material is from speeches by de Klerk, cited in the report.

70. Paul Taylor, "Mandela and the Fine Art of Debating," *Washington Post*, April 15, 1994.

71. These observations are based on my contemporaneous notes.

72. Shaun Johnson and Esther Waugh, "De Klerk, Mandela Pledge Cooperation," *Star*, (South Africa) April 15, 1994; Darryl Accone, "Great TV Battle a Lackluster Affair," *Star* (South Africa), April 15, 1994; Liz Sly, "De Klerk, Mandela Clash in Uneasy Opposition," *Chicago Tribune*, April 15, 1994; Bob Drogin, "Mandela, De Klerk Clash in South Africa TV Debate," *Los Angeles Times*, April 15, 1994; "Symbolism Wins Day for Mandela," *Weekend Star* (South Africa), April 16–17, 1994.

73. Scott Kraft, "Mandela Courts Zulu Vote in Tour of Natal," *Los Angeles Times*, April 17, 1994; Scott Kraft, "Zulu Leader Nears Deal to End South Africa Vote Boycott," *Los Angeles Times*, April 19, 1994; Liz Sly, "Mythic Past Fuels Zulus," *Chicago Tribune*, April 18, 1994; Liz Sly, "Zulu Leader Capitulates on Elections," *Chicago Tribune*, April 20, 1994; Bill Keller, "Zulu Party Ends Boycott of Vote in South Africa," *New York Times*, April 20, 1994; "Buthelezi Eagerly Begins Campaigning," Reuters, April 20, 1994; "Six Days Left, Zulus Kick Off Election Drive," Associated Press, April 21, 1994; "This New Day," *Cape Times*, April 20, 1994; Scott Kraft, "Elections Silence the Killing Fields," *Los Angeles Times*, April 23, 1994.

74. Robert Mattes, *The Election Book: Judgment and Choice in South Africa's 1994* Election, IDASA, Public Information Center, Cape Town, 1995, pp. 42–46.

75. Eldridge, "Now Wasn't the Time," p. 1; Norman West, "New ANC Tactics to Beat Nats," *Sunday Times* (Cape Metro); Mattes, Giliomee, and James, "The Election in the Western Cape," p. 129.

76. Derek Schrier, "April 15/16 poll—Western Cape Coloureds—Metro/Urban Only," Memo to Ketso Gordhan, Tony Trew, and Stanley B. Greenberg, April 19, 1994.

77. William Claiborne, "Mandela at Stock Exchange, Offers Assurances to Whites," *Washington Post*, April 23, 1994; "Mandela Tries to Assure S. African Business," *Chicago Tribune*, April 23, 1994; Bob Drogin, "High Stakes, High Hopes in S. Africa," *Los Angeles Times*, April 23, 1994.

78. Drogin, "High Stakes, High Hopes in S. Africa."

79. Sampson, *Mandela*, pp. 481–82; Bob Drogin, "Mandela Scolds Gun-Toting Supporters at Rally," *Los Angeles Times*, April 24, 1994.

80. William Claiborne and Michelle Singletary, "Bomb Kills 9 in S. Africa as Voting Nears," *Washington Post*, April 25, 1994; Bob Drogin, "Car Bomb Kills Nine as S. Africa Vote Nears," *Los Angeles Times*, April 25, 1994; Charmeela Bhagowat and Lee-Ann Alfreds, "Outrage as Nine Die in Bomb Blast," *Star* (South Africa), April 25, 1994.

81. Scott Kraft, "Mandela Urges Reconciliation as He Ends Historic Campaign," *Los Angeles Times*, April 25, 1994; Rich Lyman and Glenn Burkins, "Goal Is Near, Mandela Tells Throng," *Philadelphia Inquirer*, April 25, 1994.

82. David Beresford, "12 More Die in South Africa Bombing Campaign," *The Guardian*, April 16, 1994.

83. The reports on meetings are based on my contemporaneous notes. These are supplemented by the "Daily Media Monitor Briefing," produced multiple times during the day, summarizing reports from the field and press reports.

84. Liz Sly, Frank James, and *Chicago Tribune* staff writers, "South Africa Tastes Freedom,"

Chicago Tribune, April 27, 1994; Paul Taylor, "Historic Election Begins in S. Africa; Some Snags Reported in First Day," *Washington Post*, April 27, 1994.

85. R. W. Johnson, "The Election, the Count, and the Drama in KwaZulu-Natal (KZN)," in Johnson and Schlemmer, eds., *Launching Democracy*, pp. 278–81; ANC, Northern Natal Region, "ANC Northern Natal Report on Election Irregularities and Problem: 26th April 1994; Lynne Duke, "In S. Africa's Zulu Homeland, Snafus Bring Cries of Foul," *Washington Post*, April 28, 1994.

86. Sampson, *Mandela*, pp. 482–83; Paul Taylor, "S. African Vote Hits Snags on Second Day," *Washington Post*, April 28, 1994.

87. Francis X. Clines, "The South Africa Vote: 31 White Rightists Held in Bombings in South Africa," *New York Times*, April 28, 1994.

88. African National Congress, "ANC Statement on the Voting Process in Natal," Draft Statement, April 18, 1994.

89. Stephen Laufer, Gavin Evans, Gaye Davis, and Stefaans Brummer, "Monitors in IEC Palace Revolt," *Mail & Guardian* (South Africa), April 23, 1994.

90. Stanley B. Greenberg, Personal Notes; Khetso Gordhan, Interview with author, November 19, 2005.

91. Paul Taylor, "ANC Count Projects Election Landslide," *Washington Post*, May 1, 1994; Francis X. Clines, "Vote Count Starts Ever So Slowly in South Africa," *New York Times*, May 1, 1994; Bill Keller, "Mandela's Party Grasps Firm Lead in Early Results," *New York Times*, May 2, 1994.

92. R. W. Johnson, "The Election, the Count and the Drama in KwaZulu-Natal," pp. 288–95.

93. "Sounding Presidential, Mandela Tells Plan to 'Heal' South Africa," *Chicago Tribune*, April 30, 1994.

94. Stanley B. Greenberg, "Press Briefing on Incoming Data, 5:00 P.M.," May 1, 1994; Paul Taylor, "ANC Count Projects Election Landslide," *Washington Post*," May 2, 1994; Keller, "Mandela's Party Grasps Firm Lead in Early Results."

95. Liz Sly, "De Klerk's Party Wins a Place in New S. Africa," *Chicago Tribune*, May 2, 1994.

96. R. W. Johnson, "The Election, the Count and the Drama in KwaZulu-Natal," pp. 294–97.

97. Pat Keefer, Interview with author, November 15, 2005.

98. Nelson Mandela, "Speech Announcing the ANC Election Victory," Carlton Hotel, Johannesburg, May 2, 1994. Note that the news reports on the speech had additions not in the official text. See Helen Grange and Chris Whitfield, "It's President Mandela, Free at Last and a Toast to a New SA," *Star* (South Africa), May 2, 1994.

99. R. W. Johnson, "The 1994 Election: Outcome and Analysis," in Johnson and Schlemmer, eds., *Launching Democracy*.

100. Nelson Mandela, "Address to the People of Cape Town," Grand Parade, May 9, 1994; Nelson Mandela, "Address to the Nation at the Inauguration of Nelson Mandela as President of the Republic of South Africa," Union Buildings, May 10, 1994, in Asmal et al., eds., *Nelson Mandela*, p. 184.

101. Nelson Mandela, "Freedom Day 1995," Union Buildings, Pretoria, April 27, 1995; "Freedom Day 1996," Union Buildings, Pretoria, April 27, 1996; "Freedom Day

1997," Upington, April 27, 1997, in Kader Asmal, David Chidester, and Wilmot James, eds., *In His Own Words* (New York: Little, Brown, 2003), pp. 71–83.

102. South African Institute of Race Relations, "Watchdog on the South African Elections: 9," May 31, 1994; Lawrence Schlemmer, "South Africa's First Open Election and the Future of Its New Democracy," in Hermann Giliomee and Lawrence Schlemmer, eds., *The Bold Experiment: South Africa's New Democracy* (Johannesburg: Halfway House: Southern Publishers, 1994), p. 197.

103. Robert Mattes, *The Election Book: Judgement and Choice in South Africa's 1994 Election* (IDASA: Cape Town, 1995), pp. 21–23, 62–65, 91–94; R. W. Johnson and Lawrence Schlemmer, "Into the Brave New World," in Johnson and Schlemmer, eds., *Launching Democracy*, pp. 257–58.

104. Hirsch, *Season of Hope*, pp. 6, 69–70.

105. Gumede, *Thabo Mbeki and the Battle for the Soul of the ANC*, pp. 85–86.

106. Poll conducted by Greenberg Research for the U.S. Information Agency, "The New South Africa: A Promising Start, Though Problems Linger," USAID, September 29, 1994.

107. Lodge, *Politics in South Africa*, pp. 25–26; Gumede, *Thabo Mbeki and the Battle for the Soul of the ANC*, pp. 87–89; Hirsch, *Season of Hope*, pp. 97–101.

108. Based on the report on public polls by the ANC National Elections Unit, "Briefing on Research Results," November 1997.

109. Ketso Gordhan became the director general of transport and then city manager of Johannesburg; Pallo Jordan, minister of information; Gill Marcus, deputy minister of finance and then deputy governor of the Reserve Bank; Joel Netshitendze, head of the policy unit in the president's office; and Tony Trew, chief director of policy and research for the Government Communication and Information System.

110. Markinor Socio-Political Survey, National survey of 1,299 respondents, March 1998.

111. Stanley B. Greenberg, "Reclaiming the High Ground: Report on the ANC Baseline National Poll," Memo to the ANC Election Team, May 13, 1998. While I do not have my notes from this presentation, these quotes are drawn from the memo I wrote based on the notes. In addition, I do have the notes from a presentation four days later with Thabo Mbeki.

112. Allister Sparks, *Beyond the Miracle: Inside the New South Africa* (Chicago: University of Chicago Press, 2003), pp. 21–23, 46, 52.

113. Lodge, *Politics in South Africa*, pp. 57–59; Hirsch, *Season of Hope*, p. 69. In fact, 1,129,612 cheap houses were built by end of 2000, accommodating five million of the 12.5 million eligible.

114. Lodge, *Politics in South Africa*, pp. 27–29; Hirsch, *Season of Hope*, p. 173.

115. Stanley B. Greenberg, presentation and discussion notes, ANC Strategic Meeting, Shell House, October 28, 1998; Stanley B. Greenberg, focus group notes, "Project Alien," July 1998.

116. Based on accounts by Lodge, *Politics in South Africa*, pp. 257–61; Sparks, *Beyond the Miracle*, pp. 292–95; Gumede, *Thabo Mbeki and the Battle for the Soul of the ANC*, pp. 152, 156–57.

117. Daniel J. Wakin, "South Africa's No. 2 Leader Appeals for AIDS Action," Associated Press Worldstream, October 9, 1998.

118. Nelson Mandela, World Economic Forum, Session on AIDS, February 3, 1997; Gumede, *Thabo Mbeki and the Battle for the Soul of the ANC*, pp. 177–80. This account draws on Allister Sparks, *Beyond the Miracle*, pp. 285, 291–95; Lodge, *Politics in South Africa*, pp. 256–61; Gumede, *Thabo Mbeki and the Battle for the Soul of the ANC*, pp. 153–73.

119. Focus groups: African men, Johannesburg, August 25, 1988; African women, Untata, January 21, 1999.

120. Stanley B. Greenberg, presentation notes, Shell House, January 11, 1999.

121. Greenberg Quinlan Research, Survey of African respondents, 1,890 interviews, January 1999.

122. National survey of 64 Asian respondents, January 1999; national survey of 1,890 Coloured respondents, January 1999, national survey of 346 white respondents, January 1999.

123. Stanley B. Greenberg, "The ANC Message Focus," Memo to the ANC Team, January 14, 1999.

124. Stanley B. Greenberg, "Message/Slogan Research," E-mail to Melissa Levin, Jannie Hofmeyr, Tony Trew, and Phil Warf, February 3, 1999.

125. Stanley B. Greenberg, "Request for Your Input/Direction," E-mail, February 5, 1999; Stanley B. Greenberg, "The ANC Media Campaign," Memo to the ANC Media Team, April 26, 1999.

126. Stanley B. Greenberg, "The ANC Victory: 1999: Underlying Patterns of Support," Memo to the ANC Team, June 3, 1999.

127. Thabo Mbeki, "Statement on the ANC 1999 Elections Victory," Gallagher Estate, Johannesburg, June 3, 1999; Philippe Bernes-Lasserre, "Mbeki Vows to Move 'Forward, Faster,'" Agence France Presse, June 3, 1999.

128. Nelson Mandela, State of the Nation Address, Houses of Parliament, Cape Town, February 5, 1999, pp. 167–71.

4. TONY BLAIR: ACT I

1. Saatchi & Saatchi, Conservative Party Public Party Broadcasts, "Labour's Tax Bombshell," January 6, 1992; Anthony Seldon, *Blair* (New York: The Free Press, 2005), pp. 93–107, 119–23; Tudor Jones, *Remaking the Labour Party: From Gaitskell to Blair* (London: Routledge, 1996), pp. 20–24, 88–91, 110–12, 120–24; Philip Gould, *The Unfinished Revolution: How the Modernisers Saved the Labour Party* (London: Abacus, 1999), pp. 117–29; William Keegan, *The Prudence of Mr. Gordon Brown* (Chichester, West Sussex: John Wiley & Sons, 2004), pp. 5–6.

2. Andrew Rawnsley, *Servants of the People: The Inside Story of New Labour* (London: Penguin, 2000), p. xv.

3. Paul Routledge, *Gordon Brown: The Biography* (London: Pocket Books, 1998), pp. 172–73; Seldon, *Blair*, p. 662; Robert Peston, *Brown's Britain* (London: Short, 2005), pp. 40–42.

4. Seldon, *Blair*, pp. 147–48.

5. Seldon, *Blair*, pp. 93–107; John Prescott, *Prezza: My Story: Pulling No Punches* (London: Headline Review, 2008), pp. 186–87, 201.

6. Ivo Dawnay, "Labour Attacked on Clinton Focus," *Financial Times*, January 5, 1993; Colin Brown, "Labour to Learn the Lessons of Clinton," *The Independent*, January 4,

1993; John Rentoul, *Tony Blair: Prime Minister* (London: Warner Books, 2001), pp. 195–96.

7. Seldon, *Blair,* p. 124; Rentoul, *Tony Blair,* pp. 194–200.

8. Michael Jones, "Labour Agonises over Left-Wing Triumphs in US," *Sunday Times* (London), January 10, 1993; Alexander MacLeod, "Britain's Labour Party in Tumult over Advice from Clinton Strategists," *Christian Science Monitor,* January 20, 1993; Gould, *The Unfinished Revolution,* pp. 176–77; Seldon, *Blair,* pp. 122–24.

9. Gould, *The Unfinished Revolution,* pp. 175–76.

10. Ibid., pp. 171–75.

11. Anthony King et al., *New Labour Triumphs: Britain at the Polls* (Chatham, New Jersey: Chatham House, 1998), pp. 17–37; David Butler and Dennis Kavanagh, *The British General Election of 1997* (New York: St. Martin's Press, 1997), pp. 14–15; H. Kastgendick and R. Stimshaff, eds., *New Labour: Turning Point in British Politics* (Philo, 1999), pp. 4–5.

12. Anthony King, "Why Labour Won—At Last," in King et al., *New Labour Triumphs,* p. 195.

13. Rentoul, *Tony Blair,* pp. 227–47.

14. NOP Research Group Ltd., National Survey, October 1995.

15. Butler and Kavanagh, *The British General Election of 1997,* pp. 48–49; Jones, *Remaking the Labour Party,* pp. 120–25; Gerald Taylor, *Labour's Renewal* (London: Macmillan, 1997), pp. 104–5, 113–16.

16. Jones, *Remarking the Labour Party,* pp. 1–20, 41–51, 72–77, 110–11; Peter Mandelson and Roger Liddle, *The Blair Revolution: Can New Labour Deliver?* (London: Faber & Faber, 1996), pp. 51–52; Taylor, *Labour's Renewal,* pp. 168–71.

17. Seldon, *Blair,* pp. 223–28; Peter Riddell, *The Unfulfilled Prime Minister: Tony Blair's Quest for a Legacy* (London: Methuen, 2005), pp. 26–27; Mandelson and Liddle, *The Blair Revolution,* pp. 53–55; Gould, *The Unfinished Revolution,* pp. 227–30; King, *New Labour Triumphs,* pp. 17–37; Butler and Kavanagh, *The British General Election of 1997,* pp. 14–15; Kastgendick and Stimshaff, *New Labour,* pp. 4–5; *New Labour,* Seldon, *Blair,* p. 124; Sidney Blumenthal, Interview with author, April 14, 2007.

18. While my work for the White House ended in the spring, I did continue to poll for the DNC through the 1996 election.

19. Butler and Kavanagh, *The British General Election of 1997,* p. 12. The pattern of support for Edgware is also evident in Harrow West and Enfield Southgate and Enfield North, places where we would be conducting focus groups in North London. Election results have been compiled from the historical election tables available at www .election.demon.co.uk.

20. I incorporated these quotations into my presentation notes, Stanley B. Greenberg, "State of the Race," presentation notes, May 17, 1995.

21. Gould, *The Unfinished Revolution,* back cover.

22. I do not know whether I conducted this exercise at this first group, but Philip usually turned to me for a question when we collaborated on groups and I did use this exercise frequently.

23. Stanley B. Greenberg, presentation notes, Tony Blair, "State of the Race," May 17, 1995; Stanley B. Greenberg, "Strategic Observations on the British Elections: Notes from America," Memo to Tony Blair, MP, June 8, 1995.

24. NOP, National Survey of 1,364 likely voters, October 1995; Paul Eastham, "They Couldn't Be Closer to Blair," *Daily Mail*, February 13, 1999.

25. Anthony Seldon, *The Blair Effect: The Blair Government, 1997–2001* (London: Little, Brown, 2001), p. 228.

26. Stanley B. Greenberg, "Economic Messages," Memo to Philip Gould, June 27, 1995.

27. Philip Gould, "Governing for All Britain: Conference Strategy: 1995," PowerPoint presentation, July 31, 1995; see also Philip Gould, Memo to Stanley Greenberg, July 31, 1995.

28. Philip Gould, Memo to Stanley Greenberg, July 31, 1995.

29. Philip Gould, "Polling Report Summary," September 9, 1995.

30. Gould, *The Unfinished Revolution*, pp. 251–52; Philip Gould, "Polling Report Summary," September 9, 1995.

31. Alastair Campbell, *The Blair Years: The Alastair Campbell Diaries* (New York: Alfred A. Knopf, 2007), pp. 85–90.

32. Tony Blair, "My Vision of a New Britain," Speech to the Labour Party Conference, October 3, 1995.

33. "Blair Compared to JFK," *Daily Telegraph*, October 6, 1995; William Keegan, "Hits and Myths in Blair's Quest for Labour's Big Idea," *The Observer*, October 8, 1995; "A Very British Coup," *The Economist*, October 7, 1995.

34. Iain Macwhirter, "BMW Factor Behind the Real Debate in Brighton," *The Scotsman*, October 4, 1995; "Falling in Love at Last," *The Guardian*, October 4, 1995.

35. This is an accurate description of what I reported to Blair at this point and of the first time I met with Blair at his home and met Cherie, but it is not clear on which of my trips in July and October 1995 this occurred. Gould refers to a December meeting, but my calendar does not show me in London then.

36. Greenberg Research, National survey of 1,364 likely voters, September 1995; Stanley B. Greenberg, "The Pre-Conference National Survey," Memo to Tony Blair, November 20, 1995.

37. Seldon, *Blair*, pp. 4–5, 18–22; Philip Stephens, *Tony Blair: A Biography* (London: Penguin, 2004), pp. 1–5.

38. Stephens, *Tony Blair*, pp. 4–7.

39. Seldon, *Blair*, pp. 28–31; Stephens, *Tony Blair*, pp. 10–11.

40. Seldon, *Blair*, pp. 32–33; Stephens, *Tony Blair*, pp. 17–21.

41. Seldon, *Blair*, pp. 33–34; Stephens, *Tony Blair*, pp. 13–14.

42. Seldon, *Blair*, pp. 47–53.

43. Ibid., pp. 61–66.

44. Routledge, *Gordon Brown*, pp. 17–19, 36–39, 56–61, 67–79, 94–107; Peston, *Brown's Britain*, pp. 25–31; Keegan, *The Prudence of Mr. Gordon Brown*, pp. 19–35.

45. Routledge, *Gordon Brown*, pp. 114–19; Keegan, *The Prudence of Mr. Gordon Brown*, pp. 44–49; Peston, *Brown's Britain*, pp. 31–32, 37–39.

46. Routledge, *Gordon Brown*, pp. 136–37.

47. Seldon, *Blair*, p. 662.

48. Tony Blair, Foreword to "Reclaiming the Grand: Christianity and Socialism," in Paul Richards, ed., *Tony Blair: In His Own Words* (London: Politico's, 2004).

49. Greenberg Research, Watford focus groups, February 27, 1996; Greenberg Research, Total Time Series for U.K. Labour surveys, April 1995–April 1996.

50. Routledge, *Gordon Brown*, pp. 212–28.

51. Tony Blair, Interview with author, September 21, 2007; Cambell, *The Blair Years*, pp. 112.

52. Greenberg Research, National survey of 1,545 likely voters, January 1996; Stanley B. Greenberg, "The First 1996 National Survey: Strategic Observations," Memo to Tony Blair, February 16, 1996.

53. Philip Gould, "Focus Group: Watford," March 5, 1996; Philip Gould, "Getting Personal—Distilling the Essence of Tory Vulnerability: Developing a Populist Economic Message," March 6, 1996.

54. Campbell, *The Blair Years*, pp. 98–100.

55. Stanley B. Greenberg, Focus group observation notes, Watford, February 26, 1996.

56. Philip Gould, "Economic Message," Memo to Tony Blair and Gordon Brown, March 3, 1996.

57. Stanley B. Greenberg, "Labour's Economic Message," Memo to Philip Gould, March 8, 1996.

58. Stanley B. Greenberg, presentation notes, Tony Blair, March 14, 1996.

59. Stanley B. Greenberg, "Focusing the Labour Message," Memo to Tony Blair, May 9, 1996.

60. Stanley B. Greenberg, "The Labour Party Conference: Focusing the Labour Party Campaign," September 11, 1996; Greenberg Research, National survey of 1,473 likely voters, September 30–October 24, 1996.

61. Greenberg Research, Survey of 1,000 likely voters, September 30–October 24, 1996; Tony Blair, Labour Party Conference Speech, Blackpool, England, October 1, 1996.

62. Rentoul, *Tony Blair*, p. 286.

63. Gould, *The Unfinished Revolution*, pp. 267–68.

64. Butler and Kavanagh, *The British General Election of 1997*, pp. 52–54.

65. Greenberg Research, Survey, September 30–October 24; Greenberg Research, National survey of 1,512 likely voters, November 1996.

66. Butler and Kavanagh, *The British General Election of 1997*, pp. 52–54.

67. Gould, *The Unfinished Revolution*, p. 269.

68. Stanley B. Greenberg, "Signs of Life on the Other Side: Assessment of the October Survey," Memo to Tony Blair, November 17, 1996; Stanley B. Greenberg, "The First Message Poll," Memo to Tony Blair, December 5, 1996.

69. Gould, *The Unfinished Revolution*, pp. 288–89; Stanley B. Greenberg, "Signs of Life on the Other Side," November 17, 1996.

70. Campbell, *The Blair Years*, pp. 145, 148–49; Routledge, *Gordon Brown*, pp. 235–37.

71. Butler and Kavanagh, *The British General Election of 1997*, pp. 82–84; Gould, *The Unfinished Revolution*, p. 343.

72. Written comments to the question "What are your overall impressions of the election campaign today?" drawn from comments in focus groups conducted in Edgware on April 8, 1996, and focus groups in Watford on April 9, 1996.

73. Campbell, *The Blair Years*, pp. 166, 172–73.

74. Stanley B. Greenberg, "Labour Polling," Memo to Philip Gould, July 22, 1996.

75. Butler and Kavanagh, *The British General Election of 1997*, pp. 36–37, 44, 101; Routledge, *Gordon Brown*, p. 268.

76. Stanley B. Greenberg, "The Latest Tracking and Other Matters," Memo to Tony Blair, April 7, 1997.

77. Stanley B. Greenberg, "The Pre-Election Survey: The Economy and Europe," Memo to Philip Gould, March 18, 1997.

78. Stanley B. Greenberg, "The Changing Campaign: Campaign Poll 6 (April 17–19)," Memo to Tony Blair, April 21, 1997; Stanley B. Greenberg, "The New Plateau: Campaign Poll 7 (April 20–22)," Stanley B. Greenberg, Memo to Tony Blair, April 23, 1997; Routledge, *Gordon Brown*, pp. 280–81.

79. Stanley B. Greenberg, "An Increasingly Stable Labour Vote: Campaign Poll 8 (April 22–24)," Memo to Tony Blair, April 25, 1997; Stanley B. Greenberg, "A Stable Close to the Campaign with Some 'Chipping': Campaign Poll 9 (April 25–27)," Memo to Tony Blair, April 28, 1997.

80. Gould, *The Unfinished Revolution*, pp. 365, 383–85.

81. Ibid., pp. 388–89, 392.

82. Geoffrey Evans and Pippa Norris, *Critical Elections: British Parties and Voters in Long-Term Perspective* (London: Sage, 1999), pp. xix–xxiii.

83. Tony Blair, "Speech at Royal Festival Hall," May 2, 1997; Ben Macintyre and James Landale, "Jubilant Campaign Staff Make It a Night to Remember," *The Times* (London), May 2, 1997.

84. Maureen Dowd, "Liberties; Labour's Love Lost?," *New York Times*, April 23, 1997.

85. Butler and Kavanagh, *The British General Election of 1997*, p. 117.

86. Campbell, *The Blair Years*, pp. 197–99.

87. Evans and Norris, *Critical Elections*, pp. 67, 72–76,166, 172–74, 178; Butler and Kavanagh, *The British General Election of 1997*, p. 299.

88. This is when the high thermometer ratings for both Labour and Blair dropped and the vote lead narrowed.

89. Campbell, *The Blair Years*, pp. 209; Federal News Service, "News Conference with President Clinton and British Prime Minister Tony Blair, 10 Downing Street, London," May 29, 1997.

90. Tony Blair, "Speech by Rt. Hon Tony Blair, Prime Minister and Leader of the Labour Party to the Labour Party Annual Conference," Brighton, September 30, 1997.

91. Anthony Giddens, *Over to You, Mr. Brown* (Cambridge, U.K.: Polity Press, 2007), p. xi.

92. Seldon, *The Blair Effect*, pp. 186–93, 226–31.

93. Campbell, *The Blair Years*, pp. 247–48; Greenberg Research, Total Time Series for U.K. Labour surveys, January 1997–November 1997.

94. Greenberg Research, National survey of 1,005 likely voters, September 12–18, 1997.

95. Tony Blair, Conference Speech, Brighton, September 30, 1997.

96. Stanley B. Greenberg, "The Welfare Challenge," February 16, 1998; Greenberg Research, National survey of 1,012 likely voters, January 30–February 6, 1998.

97. Simon Henig and Lewis Baston, eds., *Politico's Guide to the General Election* (London: Politico's Publishing, 2000), pp. 1–30; Seldon, *The Blair Effect*, pp. 193–98.

98. Tony Blair, Speech to the Labour Party Conference, Blackpool, September 29, 1998.

99. David Miliband, "Delivery: Policy Progress," Memo to Prime Minister, January 19, 1999; Peter Hyman, "Delivery," Memo to Prime Minister, January 22, 1999.

100. Tony Blair, Untitled Memo to Jonathan Powell and others, January 23, 1999; Lance

Price, *The Spin Doctor's Diary: Inside Number 10 with New Labour* (London: Hodder & Stoughton, 2005), p. 76; Tony Blair, Untitled Memo to Jonathan Powell and others, May 30, 1999.

101. Stanley B. Greenberg, Labour presentation notes, July 23–26, 1999; Stanley B. Greenberg, PowerPoint presentation to Tony Blair, July 11, 1999; Greenberg Quinlan Research, National survey of 1,010 likely voters, July 6–11, 1999.

102. Tony Blair, Speech to the Labour Party Conference, Bournemouth, September 28, 1999.

103. Paul Johnson, "Yesterday Was a Sad Day," *Daily Mail*, September 29, 1999.

104. Tony Blair, Interview with author, September 17, 2007; Campbell, *The Blair Years*, p. 448.

105. Tony Blair, Conference Speech, Bournemouth, September 28, 1999.

106. Stanley B. Greenberg, "The New Strategic World: Opportunity for Hegemony," Memo to Tony Blair, November 3, 1999.

107. Philip Gould, E-mail to Stanley Greenberg, November 5, 1999; David Miliband, "The New Strategic World," Memo to Stanley Greenberg, November 9, 1999.

108. "Another Winter of Crisis for the NHS," *Daily Mail*, December 29, 1999; Colin Brown and Cherry Norton, "The NHS Crisis: Doctors Warn of 'Mayhem,'" *The Independent*, December 29, 1999; "The Unhealthy Truth," *Sunday Times* (London), January 9, 2000; Riddell, *The Unfulfilled Prime Minister*, p. 50.

109. Peston, *Brown's Britain*, pp. 267–68; Riddell, *The Unfulfilled Prime Minister*, p. 51.

110. Ian Katz, "The Inside Man," *The Guardian*, March 15, 2008; Interview with Andrew Marr, BBC News, March 16, 2008.

111. Stanley B. Greenberg, "Strengthening the Underlying Structures: Report on the February National Tracking Survey," Memo to Tony Blair and Gordon Brown, February 28, 2000; Stanley B. Greenberg, PowerPoint presentation to Tony Blair, February 28, 2000; Greenberg Quinlan Research, National survey of 1,012 likely voters, February 10–18, 2000.

112. Philip Gould, "Poll, NHS," E-mail to Stanley Greenberg, February 25, 2000; Philip Gould, "Timing and Money," E-mail to Stanley Greenberg, February 29, 2000; Gordon Brown, "Strategy Document—March," Memo, March 2000.

113. House of Commons debate transcript, March 15, 2000.

114. Stanley B. Greenberg, "NHS Presentation Notes: Brown and Blair," March 15, 2000; Stanley B. Greenberg, "Rebuilding Labour's Position," Memo to Tony Blair and Gordon Brown, March 22, 2000; Stanley B. Greenberg, PowerPoint presentation to Tony Blair, March 13, 2000; Greenberg Quinlan Research, National survey of 1,000 likely voters, March 3–13, 2000.

115. Gordon Brown, "Chancellor of the Exchequer's Budget Statement," March 21, 2000.

116. House of Commons debate transcript, March 22, 2000.

117. Seldon, *Blair's Britain*, p. 23.

118. Tony Blair, "Our Position," Memo to Jonathan Powell and others, April 9, 2000.

119. Price, *The Spin Doctor's Diary*, p. 211; Stanley B. Greenberg, "Sorting Out the Strategic Issues: Notes on the Post-Budget National Survey," Memo to Tony Blair and Gordon Brown, April 20, 2000.

120. Campbell, *The Blair Years*, p. 453.

121. Ibid; Philip Gould, "Poll," E-mail to Stanley Greenberg, May 20, 2000; Tony Blair, "Note," May 24, 2000; Philip Gould, "Message," E-mail to Stanley Greenberg, May 26, 2000; Tony Blair, Interview with author, September 21, 2007.

122. Stanley B. Greenberg, presentation notes, Chequers, June 1, 2000.

123. Tony Blair, Interview with author, September 21, 2007.

124. Stanley B. Greenberg, Labour presentation notes, June 1, 2000; Greenberg Quinlan Research, National survey of 1,001 likely voters, May 22–29, 2000.

125. Stanley B. Greenberg, meeting notes, June 1, 2000.

126. Price, *The Spin Doctor's Diary*, pp. 226–27; Campbell, *The Blair Years*, pp. 457, 460, 462–63, 466.

127. Stanley B. Greenberg, "Labour Poll Memo," E-mail to Philip Gould, July 28, 2000.

128. Stanley B. Greenberg, "The Message Structure," Memo to the Gore Team, August 14, 2000.

129. Robert Shrum, *No Excuses: Concessions of a Serial Campaigner* (New York: Simon & Schuster, 2007), pp. 336–340.

130. Stanley B. Greenberg, "The Conference Speech," E-mail to Philip Gould, September 22, 2000; Stanley B. Greenberg, PowerPoint presentation for Tony Blair, November 19, 2000; Greenberg Quinlan Research, National survey of 1,000 likely voters, November 14–19, 2000.

131. Stanley B. Greenberg, "2001," Memo to Labour Team, January 5, 2001; Greenberg Quinlan Research, National survey of 1,000 likely voters, January 24–28, 2001; Seldon, *The Blair Effect: 1997–2001*, pp. 228–32; Stanley B. Greenberg, "Kicking the Campaign Off Right or Kicking Off the Right Campaign: Reflections on Recent Polling and Focus Groups," Memo to Labour Team, March 12, 2001.

132. BBC commentary, Web, December 5, 2000; Pippa Norris, ed., *Britain Votes 2001* (New York: Oxford University Press, 2001), pp. 67–68.

133. Stanley B. Greenberg, PowerPoint presentation for Tony Blair, April 18, 2001; Greenberg Quinlan Research, National survey of 1,030 likely voters, April 17–18, 2001.

134. Philip Gould, "US/UK," E-mail to Stanley Greenberg, October 16, 2000; Price, *The Spin Doctor's Diary*, p. 263.

135. Price, *The Spin Doctor's Diary*, pp. 282–83.

136. "Labour Launches 'Ambitious' Manifesto," *The Guardian*, May 6, 2001; Price, *The Spin Doctor's Diary*, p. 323; Seldon, *Blair*, pp. 455, 463.

137. Greenberg, PowerPoint, April 18, 2001; Greenberg Quinlan Research, Survey, April 17–18, 2001; Greenberg, "Kicking the Campaign Off Right," March 12, 2001.

138. Paul Waugh, "Blair: Time for a Clean Break from Thatcher Legacy," *The Independent*, June 6, 2001.

139. Stanley B. Greenberg, "Dominating the Final 10 Days: The Election Dynamic and Consolidating the Vote for Labour," Memo to the Labour Campaign Group, May 24, 2001.

140. Pippa Norris, "Apathetic Landslide: The 2001 British General Election," in Norris, ed., *Britain Votes 2001*, pp. 1–6, 211.

141. Stanley B. Greenberg, "What Happened: Notes on the 2001 Election," Memo to Labour Team, July 12, 2001. This analysis was prepared with Greg Cook, based on the actual results, a combined database of surveys, and exit polls.

142. Seldon, *Blair*, pp. 466–67.

5. TONY BLAIR: ACT II

1. Campbell, *The Blair Years*, pp. 559–62.
2. Seldon, *Blair*, pp. 483–88; Peter Riddell, *Hug Them Close: Blair, Clinton, Bush and the "Special Relationship"* (London: Politico's Publishing, 2003), pp. 145–51.
3. Seldon, *Blair*, pp. 489–91.
4. Riddell, *Hug Them Close*, pp. 158–60; Seldon, *Blair*, pp. 496–98.
5. Blair had a mean thermometer score of 75.8, to Bush's 75.0, among likely American voters. Democracy Corps, National survey of 1,000 likely voters, October 30–November 1, 2001.
6. For this account, I use the version of Tony Blair, Labour Party Conference Speech, October 2, 2001 available at: http://politics.guardian.co.uk/speeches/story/0, ,590775,00.html; Seldon, *Blair*, pp. 499–501.
7. Michael White, "Let Us Reorder This World," *The Guardian*, October 3, 2001; Philip Stephens, *Tony Blair: The Price of Leadership* (London: Politico's Publishing, 2004), pp. 276–77.
8. Campbell, *The Blair Years*, pp. 392–93, 404–6.
9. Riddell, *Hug Them Close*, pp. 108–14; Stephens, *Tony Blair*, pp. 225–26; Seldon, *Blair*, pp. 391–405.
10. Anthony Seldon, *Blair Unbound* (London: Simon & Schuster, 2007), p. 57; Hugo Young, "Simple but Heartfelt Vision," *The Guardian*, October 3, 2001.
11. Stanley B. Greenberg, "Disengagement and the Power of Community: Beyond the Conference Speech," Memo to Tony Blair, October 21, 2001.
12. Ian Katz, "The Inside Man" *The Guardian*, March 15, 2008; Seldon, *Blair's Britain*, p. 57; Tony Blair, Interview with author, September 21, 2007.
13. Riddell, *Hug Them Close*, pp. 90, 92–93.
14. Campbell, *The Blair Years*, pp. 614–15.
15. Riddell, *Hug Them Close*, pp. 186, 199–200, 202; Seldon, *Blair*, pp. 572–75.
16. Robin Cook, *The Point of Departure: Diaries from the Front Bench* (London: Pocket Books, 2004), p. 206.
17. Ibid., pp. 130, 135.
18. Bob Woodward, *State of Denial: Bush at War, Part III* (New York: Simon & Schuster, 2006), p. 113.
19. Stanley B. Greenberg, "New Plateau," Memo to Prime Minister Blair, August 1, 2002.
20. Seldon, *Blair Unbound*, p. 112; Campbell, *The Blair Years*, pp. 623, 630–31.
21. Karl Agne, An Analysis of Public Polling, August 30, 2002; Dana Milbank, "Democrats Question Iraq Timing," *Washington Post*, September 16, 2002.
22. Campbell, *The Blair Years*, pp. 635–36; Seldon, *Blair*, pp. 577–79; Riddell, *Hug Them Close*, pp. 209–12; Bob Woodward, *Plan of Attack* (New York: Simon & Schuster, 2004), pp. 178–79.
23. Cook, *The Point of Departure*, p. 174; Seldon, *Blair*, p. 586.
24. Stanley B. Greenberg, James Carville, and Bob Shrum, "RE: Iraq," Democracy Corps Memo, October 3, 2002.
25. This conversation took place with Blair and I recall it at the reception. It might well have happened after a Number 10 meeting at his office where we often spoke afterward about developments in the United States.

26. Stephens, *Tony Blair*, p. 319; Riddell, *Hug Them Close*, p. 225; Cook, *The Point of Departure*, p. 292; Woodward, *Plan of Attack*, p. 297.

27. Greenberg Quinlan Rosner Research, National Survey of 1,000 likely voters, January 7–12, 2003; Stanley B. Greenberg, PowerPoint presentation to Tony Blair, January 16, 2003.

28. Greenberg Quinlan Rosner Research, National survey of 1,502 likely voters, February 21–27, 2003; Stanley B. Greenberg, PowerPoint presentation to Tony Blair, March 4, 2003; Seldon, *Blair Unbound*, p. 135.

29. Cook, *The Point of Departure*, p. 271.

30. Seldon, *Blair*, p. 620.

31. Stephens, *Tony Blair*, p. 322; Riddell, *Hug Them Close*, pp. 261–62, 267.

32. Seldon, *Blair Unbound*, pp. 164–65; Cherie Blair, *Speaking for Myself: The Autobiography* (London: Little Brown, 2008), p. 314; Prescott, *Prezza: My Story: Pulling No Punches*, p. 334.

33. Robert Worcester, Roger Mortimore, and Paul Baines, *Explaining Labour's Landslide* (London: Politico's Publishing, 2005), p. 84.

34. Riddell, *Hug Them Close*, pp. 213–14; Stephens, *Tony Blair*, p. 328–39.

35. Greenberg Quinlan Rosner Research, National survey of 950 likely voters, June 23--July 6, 2003. Other polls have the parties even from May, lasting until October 2004.

36. Stephens, *Tony Blair*, p. 331.

37. Stanley B. Greenberg, "The Upcoming Joint Session," E-mail to Jonathan Powell, July 14, 2003.

38. Tony Blair, Address to the Joint Session of Congress, July 17, 2003.

39. Seldon, *Blair Unbound*, p. 218; Campbell, *The Blair Years*, pp. 721–22.

40. Stephens, *Tony Blair*, pp. 329, 343–44.

41. Ibid., p. 357.

42. Greenberg Quinlan Rosner Research, National survey of 961 likely voters, November 9–16, 2003; Stanley B. Greenberg, PowerPoint presentation to Tony Blair, November 16, 2003; Stanley B. Greenberg, "Overcoming Tory Consolidation and Labour Demoralization," Memo to the New Labour Team, December 8, 2003.

43. Seldon, *Blair Unbound*, p. 269, 271–73, 294; Peston, *Brown's Britain*, p. 335; Prescott, *Prezza: My Story: Pulling No Punches*, pp. 305–15.

44. Stephens, *Tony Blair*, pp. 362–36, 368, 374; Peston, *Brown's Britain*, p. 336; Riddell, *Hug Them Close*, p. 217.

45. Seldon, *Blair Unbound*, pp. 269–71.

46. Peston, *Brown's Britain*, p. 337.

47. Greenberg Quinlan Rosner Research, National survey of 920 likely voters, March 9–20, 2004; Stanley B. Greenberg, PowerPoint presentation for Tony Blair, March 15, 2004.

48. Stanley B. Greenberg and Anna Greenberg, "Strategy for the Media Fund: Joining the Battle in March," Memo to the Media Fund, January 23, 2004.

49. Democracy Corps, National survey of 1,024 likely voters, April 19–22, 2004; Democracy Corps, PowerPoint presentation, April 26, 2004.

50. "President Bush Commends Israeli Prime Minister Sharon's Plan," Remarks by President Bush and Prime Minister Sharon, White House Press Release, April 14, 2004.

51. Thom Shanker and Jacques Steinberg, "The Struggle for Iraq: Captives; Bush Voices 'Disgust' at Abuse of Iraqi Prisoners," *New York Times*, May 1, 2004; "Patrick E. Ty-

ler, "The Struggle for Iraq: Britain; Blair Offers an Apology for Abuses by Soldiers," *New York Times*, May 10, 2004.

52. Seldon, *Blair Unbound*, pp. 269–73, 294; Cherie Blair, *Speaking for Myself: The Autobiography*, p. 370; Prescott, *Prezza: My Story: Pulling No Punches*, p. 320.

53. Peston, *Brown's Britain*, p. 343.

54. Greenberg Quinlan Rosner Research, National survey of 763 likely voters, July 6–14, 2004; Stanley B. Greenberg, PowerPoint presentation for Tony Blair, July 21, 2004.

55. Peston, *Brown's Britain*, p. 343; Prescott, *Prezza: My Story: Pulling No Punches*, p. 317.

56. Stanley B. Greenberg, "Iraq Note: Reflections on the Survey and Recent Focus Groups," Memo to the Kerry Campaign, September 17, 2004; John Kerry, Speech at New York University, September 21, 2004.

57. Tony Blair, Speech to the Labour Party Conference, Brighton, September 28, 2004.

58. Democracy Corps, National survey of 1,004 likely voters, September 26–28, 2004.

59. Stanley B. Greenberg, "Tax," E-mail to Philip Gould, May 12, 2004; Prescott, *Prezza: My Story: Pulling No Punches*, p. 309.

60. Stanley B. Greenberg, "Notes," E-mail to Philip Gould and Jonathan Powell, January 13, 2005; Stanley B. Greenberg, "Health Speech," E-mail to Gould, Campbell, Powell, and Morgan, March 7, 2005; Stanley B. Greenberg, "Changed Race: Voter Shifts Apparent in the Public Polls," Memo to Labour Team, April 7, 2005; Worcester et al., *Explaining Labour's Landslide*, p. 71; Greenberg Quinlan Rosner Research, "UK Labour Marginals Survey," National survey of 1,508 likely voters in 107 marginal constituencies, February 1–10, 2005.

61. Sam Weston, "Philip," E-mail to Stanley Greenberg, April 15, 2005.

62. "Blair Secures Historic Third Term," BBC News, May 6, 2004.

63. Ibid.

64. Stanley B. Greenberg and Jeremy Rosner, "Looking at the 2005 Vote and Labour's Diminished Standing: First Report on the 2005 Labour Campaign," Memo to Tony Blair and Gordon Brown, May 16, 2005; Stanley B. Greenberg and Jeremy Rosner, "Learning from the Marginals—New Audiences Going Forward: Second Report on the 2005 Labour Campaign," Memo to Tony Blair and Gordon Brown, May 18, 2005; Worcester et al., *Explain Labour's Landslide*, pp. 1–4, 216–17, 266–69.

65. This is the result for the United Kingdom, including Northern Ireland. If we look at Great Britain only, the share is 36.2 percent. The later analysis is based on Britain only.

66. This estimate is based on a computer simulation that takes the increased vote from all the other parties according to their share of the vote; a second more cautious simulation assumes that the Conservatives cannot be further eroded, so all additional Labour gains come from other parties.

67. Greenberg and Rosner, "Looking at the 2005 Vote and Labour's Diminished Standing: First Report on the 2005 Labour Campaign"; Greenberg and Rosner, "Learning from the Marginals—New Audiences Going Forward: Second Report on the 2005 Labour campaign"; Stanley B. Greenberg and Jeremy Rosner, "The Campaign's Research Design and Structure," Memo to Tony Blair and Gordon Brown, May 23, 2005.

68. Stanley B. Greenberg and Miranda Lewis, "Winning Hearts and Minds: Prospects for Progressivism," in Nick Pearce and Julia Margo, eds., *Politics for a New Generation: The Progressive Movement* (London: Palgrave Macmillan, 2007); Giddens, *Over to You, Mr. Brown*, pp. 6–13, 185–216.

69. Riddell, *The Unfulfilled Prime Minister*, pp. vii, 5–6, 20, 191, 196.
70. Greenberg and Lewis, "Winning Hearts and Minds," p. 47; Julia Margo, Sonia Sodha, and Robert Vance, "State of the Nation: Audit of Britain," in Pearce and Margo, eds., *Politics for a New Generation*, pp. 59–65; Giddens, *Over to You, Mr. Brown*, pp. 25–27; Polly Toynbee and David Walker, *Better or Worse? Has Labour Delivered?* (London: Bloomsbury, 2005), pp. 83–84.
71. Anthony Seldon and Dennis Kavanagh, *The Blair Effect: 2001–5* (Cambridge: Cambridge University Press, 2005), pp. 284–91, 294–97; Toynbee and Walker, *Better or Worse?*, pp. 11–18, 37; Giddens, *Over to You, Mr. Brown*, p. 87.
72. Seldon and Kavanagh, *The Blair Effect: 2001–5*, pp. 262–64; Toynbee and Walker, *Better or Worse?*, pp. 85–91,110–18.
73. Greenberg and Lewis, "Winning Hearts and Minds," p. 47–48; Margo et al., "State of the Nation," pp. 66–66, 68–70; Giddens, *Over to You, Mr. Brown*, pp. 28–31.
74. Tony Blair, Interview with author, September 21, 2007.

6. EHUD BARAK

1. Lee Hockstader, "A Campaign Spin in Tel Aviv," *Washington Post*, April 7, 1999.
2. There is in fact a long tradition in Israel of Jewish American consultants working for the major parties, including Zev Furst and David Garth for Menachem Begin in 1981.
3. The Social Democrats took 40.9 percent of the vote, for a total 45 percent of parliamentary seats. They were followed by the Christian Democrats, with 35.2 percent of the vote and 20 percent of the seats, and the Greens and Christian Social Union with 8 percent vote share and 7 percent of the seats each. Roger Boyes, "Kohl and Waigel Bow Out as Germany Enters New Era," *The Times* (London), September 28, 1998; Doron Cohen, Interview with author, October 30, 2005.
4. Lee Hockstader, "Brainstormer: After Many Campaigns, Israel's Next Leader Mulls His Next Move," *Washington Post*, July 20, 1999.
5. Leslie Susser, "The General's General," *Jerusalem Report*, August 26, 1993; Patrick Cockburn, "General on the Campaign Trail," *The Independent*, May 8, 1999; Larry Derfner, "Is He Up to the Job?" *Jerusalem Post*, May 14, 1999; Dina Kraft, "From Prankster to Politician," *Ottawa Citizen*, May 17, 1999; Lisa Beyer, "Warrior for Peace," *Time*, May 31, 1999; Charles M. Sennott, "On Street in Beirut, Pondering Barak as Warrior, Peacemaker," *Boston Globe*, June 16, 1999; David Horovitz, "The Observer Profile: Ehud Barak: Israel's Little Napoleon," *The Observer*, July 11, 1999; Deborah Sontag, "Peace, Period," *New York Times*, December 19, 1999; Connie Bruck, "The Commando: Ehud Barak Took Huge Risks and Trusted No One. Now He Is Alone," *The New Yorker*, April 17, 2000.
6. Bruck, "The Commando."
7. Ibid.
8. Derfner, "Is He Up to the Job?"
9. Hockstader, "Brainstormer."
10. Ehud Barak, Interview with author, October 30, 2005.
11. Dennis Ross, *The Missing Peace: The Inside Story of the Fight for Middle East Peace* (New York: Farrar, Straus & Giroux, 2005), p. 120.
12. Bruck, "The Commando."

13. Moshe Gaon, Interview with author, August 4, 2005.

14. Rebecca Trounson, "Military Hero Wins Vote to Lead Israel's Opposition Labor Party," *Los Angeles Times*, June 4, 1997.

15. We fielded a special survey of the immigrant Russian voters, as well as conducted focus groups of Sephardim and religiously traditional voters—all thought to be the key swing groups that must be reached to have any chance of significant gains. And within two months, we fielded a second message survey to sharpen our attacks on Netanyahu.

16. Serge Schmemann, "Bombers Kill 13 in Jerusalem Market," *New York Times*, July 31, 1997; "4 Die in Triple Suicide Bombing," *Jerusalem Post*, September 5, 1997; Serge Schmemann, "3 Bombers in Suicide Attack Kill 4 on Jerusalem Street in Another Blow to Peace," *New York Times*, September 4, 1997; Barbara Demick, "Israelis Shell-Shocked by Blasts, Failed Raid," *Philadelphia Inquirer*, September 6, 1997.

17. Verter Yossi, "PM Blames Labor for Chain of Disasters," *Haaretz*, September 9, 1997.

18. Greenberg Quinlan Research, National survey of 1,242 respondents, September 2–4, 1997. Note that this was the first survey conducted.

19. Ibid.; Nina Gilbert and Dan Izenberg, "Knesset Set to Repeal Direct Elections," *Jerusalem Post*, March 7, 2001. Note that the prime minister has historically been selected by the president as the party leader most able to form a government. In 1992 the Basic Law was amended, allowing the direct election of the prime minister, distinct from the Knesset election. May 1996, May 1999, and January 2001 are the only elections in which the prime minister was directly elected. The Basic Law was amended again in 2001, eliminating direct prime ministerial elections and returning to the original system.

20. Stanley B. Greenberg, "Positioning Barak and Labor: A Report on National Surveys and Focus Groups," Memo to Ehud Barak, October 14, 1997.

21. Much less important in the survey was Barak acknowledging that Labor lost touch with religious values and committing to respect Jewish traditions.

22. Janine Zacharia, "The Final Frontier," *Jerusalem Report*, May 1, 1997; Sarah Honig, "Peres Berates Barak Apology to Sephardim," *Jerusalem Post*, September 30, 1997.

23. Greenberg Quinlan Research, National Survey of 1,848 respondents, September 2–4, 1997.

24. Stanley B. Greenberg, "Strategic Issues: The Baseline Research," Memo to Ehud Barak, December 8, 1997.

25. Stanley B. Greenberg, "Positioning Barak and Labor: A Report on National Surveys and Focus Groups," Memo to Ehud Barak, October 14, 1997.

26. Christopher Walker, "Labour Leader 'Encouraging Arab Terrorism,'" *The Times* (London), March 7, 1998.

27. Sarah Honig and Arieh O'Sullivan, "Terrorist Creates Stir with Barak Quote," *Jerusalem Post*, March 11, 1998.

28. "Hebrew Press Review," *Jerusalem Post*, March 15, 1998; Margalit Dan, "The Failure of Terrorism," *Haaretz*, March 7, 1998.

29. Walker, "Labour Leader 'Encouraging Arab Terrorism'"; Gideon Alon, "A Remark Gone Severely Awry," *Haaretz*, March 17, 1998; John Daniszewski, "Remarks on Terror Become Fighting Words in Israel," *Los Angeles Times*, March 11, 1998.

30. Susan Hattis Rolef, "Barak and Hamas," *Jerusalem Post*, March 10, 1998.
31. We conducted eight focus groups, starting March 19 and finishing March 26, 1998.
32. This presentation is based on my memo to Ehud Barak, "The Rebuilding Phase: Report on the Third Message Survey," April 27, 1998.
33. Greenberg Quinlan Research, National survey of 1,200 respondents, November 17–23, 1998.
34. "A Step Toward Separating Religion and State," *Haaretz*, May 12, 1998; Michele Chabin, "From Yeshiva to Army? Haredi Draft Bill Underscores Religious-Secular Tension," *The Jewish Week*, May 29, 1998; Dan Ezenberg, "High Court Hears Plea to End Yeshiva Draft Deferments," *Jerusalem Post*, July 8, 1998; Liat Collins and Haim Shapiro, "Court Gives Knesset Deadline for Draft Deferments," *Jerusalem Post*, December 10, 1998.
35. Greenberg Quinlan Research, National survey of 803 respondents, March 26–April 1, 1998.
36. In 1998, 7.4 percent of draftees—28,000—were exempted because of attendance at a yeshiva.
37. Kim Hannah, "Barak's Sweet Defeat," *Haaretz*, July 10, 1998.
38. Stanley B. Greenberg, "The Center-Unity Project: Report on the July National Message Survey," Memo to Ehud Barak, August 10, 1998.
39. Stanley B. Greenberg, "The Unity Positioning: Government for All, Not Just the Extremists," Memo to Ehud Barak, November 13, 1998.
40. Herb Keinon, "Labor's Wounded Hero," *Jerusalem Post*, June 15, 1998; Michael Yudelman, "Barak: No Threat to My Leadership," *Jerusalem Post*, June 15, 1998; Daniel Bloch, "Barak Under Siege," *Jerusalem Post*, June 21, 1998.
41. Greenberg Quinlan Research, National survey of 1,200 respondents, November 17–23, 1998.
42. Liat Collins, "PM, Barak in Harsh Exchange. Trade Barbs, Telephone Numbers of Media Advisors During Knesset Debate," *Jerusalem Post*, July 7, 1998; Gideon Alon and Verter Yossi, "Barak Comes Out Swinging at Knesset Wakens," *Haaretz*, July 7, 1998; "Finkelstein and Greenberg by the Numbers," *New Jersey Jewish News*, July 16, 1998.
43. Doron Cohen, "Israel Trip," E-mail to author, November 30, 1998.
44. "Finkelstein and Greenberg by the Numbers."
45. Stanley B. Greenberg, *Race and State in Capitalist Development: Comparative Perspectives* (New Haven: Yale University Press, 1980).
46. Nina Gilbert, "Barak's US Spin Doctors Hold First Meeting with Labor Faction," *Jerusalem Post*, December 16, 1998; Osnat Cohen, "Netanyahu—Nice Guy, Failed Statesman," *Globes*, December 17, 1998; Larry Derfner, "Ehud Barak's Answer to Arthur Finkelstein," *Jerusalem Post*, December 18, 1998.
47. Segev Amira, "Carville and Co. Hold Forth on How to Spin and Win," *Haaretz*, December 12, 1998.
48. Lee Hockstader, "Barak File Taken in Break-in in DC," *Washington Post*, January 14, 1999.
49. Benjamin Netanyahu, "Statement to the Knesset," BBC Worldwide Monitoring, December 21, 1998.
50. Benjamin Netanyahu, "Address to Likud Central Committee, Tel Aviv," BBC Worldwide Monitoring, December 27, 1998.

51. Sven Nackstrand, "Troubled Netanyahu Launches Reelection Bid Amid Rare Good News," Agence France Presse, December 27, 1998; Ehud Barak, "Statement to the Knesset," BBC Worldwide Monitoring, December 21, 1998.

52. Nehama Duek, "Likud and Labor Open with Smear Campaigns," *Yedioth Ahronoth*, January 8, 1999.

53. Sharon Moshavi, "Israeli Political Debate Heats Up over Break-in," *Boston Globe*, January 14, 1999; Tracy Wilkinson, "Israel Candidate's Campaign a Victim of U.S. Break-in," *Los Angeles Times*, January 14, 1999; "U.S. Pollster for Opponent of Netanyahu Is Burglarized," *New York Times*, January 14, 1999.

54. Cheryl W. Thompson and Lee Hockstader, "Burglars at D.C. Polling Firm Left Clues, Sources Say," *Washington Post*, January 21, 1999.

55. David Zev Harris, "Netanyahu Says Washington Break-in 'Smells Bad,'" *Jerusalem Post*, January 21, 1999; Krau Nicole and Horowitz Nitzan, "Israeli Police Ready to Help D.C. on Fingerprints—If They're Asked," *Haaretz*, January 27, 1999.

56. Greenberg Quinlan Research, Focus groups, Ashkenazi men, January 13, 1999.

57. Stanley B. Greenberg, "Adjusting the Barak Positioning," Memo to the Barak Team, January 15, 1999; Stanley B. Greenberg, "Establishing Barak's Position in the Emerging Race," Memo to the Barak Team, January 26, 1999.

58. Marius Schattner, "Israel Starts 1998 Without a Budget," Agence France Presse, January 1, 1998; William A. Orme, Jr., "Economy at Risk as Israel Campaigns," *New York Times*, January 21, 1999.

59. "Voice of Israel Radio," BBC Worldwide Monitoring, April 15, 1999.

60. Glen Weiner, "Job Promise," E-mail to author, April 19, 1999.

61. Greenberg Quinlan Research, Focus groups, Ashkenazi men, January 13, 1999; Greenberg Quinlan Research, Focus groups, Russian men, Tel Aviv, January 14, 1999.

62. "Disgruntled Haredim Threaten to Win Netanyahu the Election," *Mideast Mirror*, February 10, 1999; Editorial, "Beyond the Pale," *Jerusalem Post*, February 11, 1999; Batsheva Tsur, Haim Shapiro, and Amy Klein, "Fearing Possible Bloodshed, Weizman Pleads to Cancel Rally," *Jerusalem Post*, February 12, 1999; Amy Klein, "A-G: Don't Probe Yosef," *Jerusalem Post*, February 22, 1999.

63. Eldar Akiva, "How to Win Friends and Influence People," *Haaretz*, February 25, 1999.

64. When specific, the critique raises serious doubts about Netanyahu for over 60 percent of the voters, but when made general, it proves 7 points less powerful.

65. Greenberg, "Adjusting the Barak Positioning"; Greenberg, "Establishing Barak's Positioning in the Emerging Race."

66. Zvi Alush, "Rabbi Ovadia: The Torah Is like a Thorn in the Eyes of the Secular Judges," *Yedioth Ahronoth*, March 19, 1999.

67. Greenberg Quinlan Research, National survey of 670 respondents, March 8–9, 1999; 675 respondents, April 4–5, 1999. As the campaign got into its final phases, we soon discovered that we were not alone in this space. In the battle for the Knesset, at least three parties—the left and secular Meretz, Natan Sharansky's party, the Israel B'Aliyah, and the new party, Shinui ("Change") were centering their argument on the haredim.

68. Greenberg, "Establishing Barak's Position in the Emerging Race."

69. Abraham Rabinovich, "Mothers' Cries Swell Chorus of Protest," *The Australian*, March 5, 1999; "No-Win South Lebanon War Claims Life of Army General," *Mideast Mirror*, March 1, 1999.

70. Greenberg Quinlan Research, National surveys: 690 respondents, April 13–14, 1999; 673 respondents, April 22–25, 1999; 670 respondents, April 26–27, 1999.

71. Greenberg Quinlan Research, National surveys: April 13–14, 1999; April 22–25, 1999.

72. Greenberg Quinlan Research, Report on Focus Groups conducted April 11–14, 1999.

73. The average viewership was 29.3 percent; an amazing 42 percent on the first day. Viewership then declined, rising to 26 percent on the last night. Eytan Gilboa and Yaron Katz, "The Media Campaign: The Shift to Alternative Media," *Middle East Review of International Affairs* 3, no. 4 (December 1999).

74. Each of these surveys had a sample size of three hundred respondents and took two nights to administer.

75. Greenberg Quinlan Research, National surveys: 670 respondents, March 8–9, 1999; April 26–27, 1999; 668 respondents, April 28–29, 1999; and 659 respondents, May 2–3, 1999.

76. This description is based on news accounts and commentary: Flore de Preneuf, "Fireworks over Rabin Square," *Salon.com*, May 18, 1999; Marc Carnegie, "Israelis Cheer Barak, Hail the End of Right-wing Government," Agence France Presse, May 18, 1999.

77. This account of Barak's speech is based on a CNN account, with Joie Chen and Wolf Blitzer providing commentary, CNN, "CNN Live Event Special," May 17, 1999, Transcript 99051703V54.

78. Ehud Barak, "CNN Live Event Special," May 17, 1999; Ehud Barak, "Ehud Barak Delivers Victory Speech," BBC Worldwide Monitoring, May 18, 1999; "Barak Promises Unity in Rabin Sq.," *Haaretz*, May 19, 1999.

79. Lee Hockstader, "Consultants Revel in Barak Victory; Strategists' U.S.-Style Campaign Reshapes Israeli Politicking," *Washington Post*, May 20, 1999.

80. Ibid. Also, this account is based on my handwritten notes from the seminar and from news accounts.

81. Overall, 53 percent said "peace" was the most important reason, followed by the "economy" (30 percent) and social issues, like poverty (11 percent); Stanley B. Greenberg, "The Barak Mandate," Memo to Ehud Barak, June 28, 1999.

82. James had left for home several days before the election, saying, "It was done."

83. Deborah Sontag, "Peace. Period," *New York Times Magazine*, December 19, 1999.

84. Yitzhak Herzog, Interview with author, October 29, 2005.

85. Sontag, "Peace. Period."

86. Avraham Avi-hai, *Ben Gurion State-Builder: Principles and Pragmatism, 1948–1963* (New York: John Wiley & Sons, 1974), pp. 32–36.

87. Ehud Barak, Interview with author, October 30, 2005.

88. Greenberg Quinlan Research, National survey of 735 respondents, May 25–26, 1999.

89. *Israel News Today*, June 11, 1999.

90. Yitzhak Herzog, Interview with author, October 29, 2005.

91. Schlomo Ceszana et al., "Messages from Shas to Barak," *Ma'ariv*, May 20, 1999;

Nahum Barnea, "Interview with Ehud Barak," *Yedioth Ahronoth*, May 20, 1999. Ehud Barak, Interview with author, October 30, 2005.

92. Israel Ministry of Foreign Affairs, Speech by Prime Minister Ehud Barak on the Presentation of the Government to the Knesset, Jerusalem, July 6, 1999; Ehud Barak, Interview with author, October 30, 2005.

93. Ross, *The Missing Peace*, pp. 497–500.

94. Greenberg Quinlan Research, national survey of 778 respondents, August 1–5, 1999; Stanley B. Greenberg, "Governance Report on the First National Baseline Survey," Memo to Prime Minister Ehud Barak, August 10, 1999.

95. Greenberg Quinlan Research, National survey of 1,335 respondents, November 30–December 2, 1999.

96. "Israeli Jobless Rate Hits Seven-Year High of 9.1 Percent," Agence France Presse, November 26, 1999; Lee Hockstader, "New Statistics on Poor Jar Israeli Complacency; One in Six Citizens Below Poverty Line," *Washington Post*, December 21, 1999.

97. Moshe Perl and Eli Kamir, "Interview with Prime Minister Ehud Barak," *Ma'ariv*, November 26, 1999; Rivka Freilich, "Ehud Barak: 'I Am Not God. I Cannot Work Miracles,'" *Ma'ariv*, December 3, 1999; Hemi Shalev, "Barak: 'Stopping the Peace Process Will Lead to Many New Graves,'" *Ma'ariv*, December 3, 1999; Greenberg Quinlan Research, National survey of 602 non-Russian Jewish respondents, December 20–22, 1999.

98. Greenberg Quinlan Research, National survey of 692 Jewish respondents, December 27–29, 1999.

99. Ross, *The Missing Peace*, pp. 529–32.

100. Ibid., p. 521.

101. Greenberg Quinlan Research, National survey of 1,335 veteran Jewish and Russian respondents, November 30–December 2, 1999.

102. Greenberg Quinlan Research, National survey of 696 Jewish respondents, December 27–29, 1999.

103. Stanley B. Greenberg, "The Referendum's First Challenge: The Russian Community," Memo to Martin Bunzl, the Russian Project, December 17, 1999.

104. Ibid.

105. Ross, *The Missing Peace*, pp. 536–39.

106. Hugh Dellios, "Israelis Jeer Barak Ahead of Syrian Talks," *Chicago Tribune*, December 14, 1999.

107. "In the Three Main Players' Words: A Sense of Their Moment in History," *New York Times*, December 16, 1999; Deborah Sontag, "Syria and Israel Begin Peace Talks After 4-Year Halt," *New York Times*, December 16, 1999.

108. Ross, *The Missing Peace*, pp. 540–42.

109. Stanley B. Greenberg, "Public Thinking on the Eve: Report on Public Attitudes after the White House Meetings," Memo to Ehud Barak, December 24, 1999.

110. Ilan Goldstein, E-mail to author, December 24, 1999.

111. Greenberg Quinlan Research, National surveys: 602 Hebrew-speaking respondents, December 20–22, 1999; 692 Jewish respondents, December 27–29, 1999; Greenberg, "Public Thinking on the Eve."

112. Martin Indyk, *Innocent Abroad: An Intimate History of American Peace Diplomacy in the Middle East* (New York: Simon & Schuster, 2009), p. 262.

113. Ross, *The Missing Peace*, pp. 546–48.

114. Moshe Gaon, "Important—Polling," E-mail to author, December 26, 1999.

115. Stanley B. Greenberg, "Creating a Rationale for Change: Report on the End of Year Survey of Public Opinion," Memo to Ehud Barak, January 1, 2000.

116. Yossi Venter, "Barak's Problem: Marketing a Product Which Doesn't Exist," *Haaretz*, January 4, 2000.

117. Ross, *The Missing Peace*, p. 570.

118. Stanley B. Greenberg, "Pause Improves Peace Prospects," Memo to Jim Gerstein, January 20, 2000.

119. Moshe Gaon, E-mail to author, January 7, 2000; Ilan Goldstein, E-mail to author, January 17, 2000; "Israeli Demonstrations Draw 100,000," Associated Press, January 10, 2000; Deborah Sontag, "Opponents of a Golan Heights Deal Rally in Tel Aviv," *New York Times*, January 11, 2000.

120. Ross, *The Missing Peace*, pp. 555, 589.

121. Indyk, *Innocent Abroad*, p. 251.

122. Raviv Drucker, *"Hara-kiri": Ehud Barak and the Moment of Truth*, trans. Jonathan Adiri (Tel Aviv: Yedioth Ahronoth Books, 2002), pp. 71–73, 75–86, 90–105.

123. Itamar Rabinovich, *Waging Peace: Israel and the Arabs, 1948–2003* (Princeton: Princeton University Press, 2004), pp. 133–35.

124. Indyk, *Innocent Abroad*, pp. 269, 272, 286.

125. Ibid., pp. 271, 285.

126. Ibid., p. 251.

127. Sontag, "Opponents of a Golan Heights Deal Rally in Tel Aviv"; Rabinovich, *Waging Peace*, pp. 131–32.

128. Stanley B. Greenberg, "The Leadership Issue: Report on the First Wave of Referendum Focus Groups," Memo to Jim Gerstein, January 28, 2000. Note that this memo was leaked and formed part of the book by Raviv Drucker, *"Hara-kiri."*

129. Ross, *The Missing Peace*, pp. 592–94.

130. Ibid., pp. 592, 598, 601–2, 617–22, 625; Yossi Beilin, *The Path to Geneva: The Quest for a Permanent Agreement, 1996–2004* (New York: RDV Books, 2004), pp. 141–43.

131. Stanley B. Greenberg, "The Barak Economic Discourse," Memo to Ehud Barak, March 27, 2000.

132. Stanley B. Greenberg, "Meltdown," Memo to Jim Gerstein, May 20, 2000.

133. *Israel News Today*, May 24–25, 2000.

134. Dahlia Scheindlin and Bob Boorstin, "Institute for Peace and Security: Report on Focus Groups (May 31–June 1, 2000)," June 7, 2000.

135. Ross, *The Missing Peace*, pp. 622–23, 626–28.

136. Moshe Gaon, "Important Poll," E-mail to author, May 6, 2000.

137. Stanley B. Greenberg, "Winning on the Palestinian Front," Memo to Jim Gerstein, March 3, 2000.

138. Stanley B. Greenberg, "The Fruits of Peace Project: Report on a National Survey and the State of the Peace Process," Memo to the Institute for Peace and Security, July 3, 2000.

139. Stanley B. Greenberg, "Regaining Standing in an On-going Battle," Memo to Jim Gerstein, June 14, 2000.

140. Scheindlin and Boorstin, "Institute for Peace and Security."

141. These Shas voters participated in focus groups in July after the announcement of the

summit. Michelle Koriant, "Summary: Shas Voters," Memo to Erika Schlachter, July 13, 2000.

142. Greenberg, "Regaining Standing in an On-going Battle."

143. Susan Milligan, "Clinton Calls a Summit on Mideast," *Boston Globe*, July 6, 2000.

144. Ross, *The Missing Peace*, pp. 646–49; Beilin, *The Path to Geneva*, pp. 147–51.

145. Deborah Sontag, "Barak's Coalition Crumbles on Eve of Summit Talks," *New York Times*, July 10, 2000; Suzanne Goldenberg, "Israeli Coalition Collapses on Eve of Peace Summit," *The Guardian*, July 10, 2000; Tracy Wilkinson, "Barak—Battered but Unbowed," *Los Angeles Times*, July 11, 2000.

146. Ehud Barak, "Address to the Knesset by the Prime Minister Ehud Barak on the Camp David Summit," BBC Worldwide Monitoring, July 10, 2000.

147. *Israel News Today*, July 10, 2000; Stanley B. Greenberg, "Issues for Camp David," Memo to Jim Gerstein, July 12, 2000.

148. Nahum Barnea, "To the Summit—Alone," *Yedioth Ahronoth*, July 10, 2000.

149. Greenberg, "Issues for Camp David."

150. Ross, *The Missing Peace*, pp. 653–54; Hussein Agha and Robert Malley, "Camp David: The Tragedy of Errors," *The New York Review of Books*, August 9, 2001; Benny Morris, "Camp David and After: An Exchange," *The New York Review of Books*, June 13, 2002.

151. The actual choice was this: "I would never support East Jerusalem being part of a Palestine state if it was the only way to achieve a final peace agreement." In that survey, we also added East Jerusalem as an item in a battery where we looked at other possible new elements, but at the end of the survey; Greenberg Quinlan Research, National survey of 676 respondents, July 6–10, 2000.

152. Greenberg Quinlan Research, National survey of 520 respondents, July 16–17, 2000.

153. Ibid.

154. Ross, *The Missing Peace*, pp. 677–81.

155. Greenberg Quinlan Research, National survey of 420 respondents, July 20, 2000.

156. Ross, *The Missing Peace*, pp. 696–98.

157. Greenberg Quinlan Research, National survey of 681 respondents, July 23, 2000.

158. Ross, *The Missing Peace*, p. 708.

159. Ibid., p. 711; Agha and Malley, "Camp David and After: An Exchange."

160. Herb Keinon, "In Ben-Gurion's Image?," *Jerusalem Post*, July 14, 2000; Hemi Shalev, "The Last Trump Card," *Ma'ariv*, July 14, 2000; Nahum Barnea and Shimon Shiffer, "Beginning to Talk About Jerusalem," *Yedioth Ahronoth*, July 17, 2000; Hemi Shalev, "The Irksome Burden of History," *Ma'ariv*, July 23, 2000.

161. Greenberg Quinlan Research, Total Time Series of national Israeli surveys, May 26, 1999–July 23, 2000.

162. Dahlia Scheindlin, "Focus Group Summary: Likud Voters," July 24, 2000.

163. Ross, *The Missing Peace*, pp. 699, 709.

164. Brian Katulis, "MEPIC Focus Groups: Palestinians in the West Bank and Gaza," Memo to Stanley Greenberg, December 6, 2000.

165. Greenberg Quinlan Research, National survey of 569 Jewish veteran respondents, July 27, 2000.

166. Ehud Barak, "Statement by PM Barak on His Return from Camp David Summit," Israel Ministry of Foreign Affairs, July 26, 2000.

167. Tracy Wilkinson, "12 Killed in Palestinian Battles with Israeli Forces," *Los Angeles Times*, October 1, 2000; Tony Allen Mills, Jon Swain, Uzi Mahnaimi, and Marie Colvin, "Wrath of Ages," *Sunday Times* (London), October 15, 2000; Middle East Policy Council, "Conflict Statistics, Sept. 29, 2000 to April 26, 2006"; Rabinovich, *Waging Peace*, pp. 153–55.

168. Charles M. Sennott, "Barak Issues an Ultimatum," *Boston Globe*, October 8, 2000; Ross, *The Missing Peace*, pp. 737–42.

169. Deborah Sontag, "Barak Declares Early Elections, in a Surprise Move," *New York Times*, November 29, 2000.

170. Ehud Barak, "Statement Announcing Resignation," trans. Dahlia Scheindlin, December 10, 2000.

171. Dahlia Scheindlin, "Focus Group Summary: Shas and Sephardi Voters, Bat Yam," Memo to Stanley B. Greenberg and Robert Boorstin, November 28, 2000; Dahlia Scheindlin, "MEPIC Focus Group Report: Veteran Jews and Russians," Memo to Stanley Greenberg, December 7, 2000.

172. Stanley B. Greenberg, "The Campaign Against Sharon," Memo to the Barak Team, December 22, 2000.

173. Greenberg Quinlan Research, National tracking survey, December 31, 2000.

174. Ross, *The Missing Peace*, pp. 748–56; Beilin, *The Path to Geneva*, pp. 220–23.

175. Barak campaign ad, "Principles."

176. Israel, Central Election Committee, "Final Results."

7. GONZALO "GONI" SÁNCHEZ DE LOZADA

1. *Our Brand Is Crisis*, DVD, Directed by Rachel Boynton, New York: Koch Lorber Films, 2006. Note that Boynton's depiction of the violence mixes images from events in February and October 2003, and thus mischaracterizes Goni's departure.

2. David Edelstein, "Our Men in Bolivia," *New York*, March 6, 2006; Ronnie Scheib, "Our Brand Is Crisis," *Variety*, April 11–17, 2005; Stephen Hunter, "Political Expert Exports Put Their 'Brand' on Bolivia," *Washington Post*, March 31, 2006.

3. Rupert Smith, "Political Consultants Pushed Bill Clinton into Office. But How Would Their Focus Groups and Branding Do in Bolivia?," *The Guardian*, March 22, 2006.

4. Owen Gleiberman, "Our Brand Is Crisis; Is the Democratic Process Exportable?," *Entertainment Weekly*, March 10, 2006; David Denby, "Candid Cameras," *The New Yorker*, March 6, 2006.

5. Mark Feierstein, "Bolivia?," E-mail to author, January 26, 2001; Mark Feierstein, "Bolivia Status," E-mail to author, April 6, 2001; "Talking Points for Call with Gonzalo Sánchez de Lozada," Internal office memo, June 11, 2001.

6. Lesley Gill, *Teetering on the Rim: Global Restructuring, Daily Life, and the Armed Retreat of the Bolivian State* (New York: Columbia University Press, 2000), pp. 1, 25–31.

7. Mauricio Balcazar, Interview with author, June 14, 2006; Note: this was also confirmed by Jorge "Tuto" Quiroga, who served as Banzer's vice president and became president upon Banzer's death.

8. Gonzalo Sánchez de Lozada, interview by *Commanding Heights*, PBS, 2002; Margaret Hollis Peirce, ed., *Capitalization: A Bolivian Model of Social and Economic Reform*,

(Washington, D.C.: The North South Center: Miami and The Woodrow Wilson Center, 1997), pp. 71–72, 87; Jeffrey Sachs and Juan Antonio Morales, "Bolivia: 1952–1986," *Country Studies*, no. 6 (San Francisco: International Center for Economic Growth, 1988), pp. 11–13.

9. Herbert S. Klein, *Bolivia: The Evolution of a Multi-Ethnic Society* (New York: Oxford University Press, 1993), pp. 247–58.

10. Kenneth D. Lehman, *Bolivia and the United States: A Limited Partnership* (Athens: University of Georgia Press, 1999), p. 191.

11. In the popular vote, Paz Estessoro placed second in a field of ten with 26.4 percent of the vote; Suárez received 28.6 percent; Jamie Paz Zamora of the MIR placed third with 8.8 percent. None of the other candidates cleared 5 percent.

12. Gonzalo Sánchez de Lozada, *Commanding Heights* interview. Note that quotes were edited for tense.

13. Mauricio Balcazar, Interview with author, June 14, 2006.

14. Joe McGinniss, *The Selling of the President 1968: The Classic Account of Packaging a Candidate* (New York: Penguin, 1969).

15. Peirce, *Capitalization*, p. 29; Paul Mosley, "Microfinance and Poverty in Bolivia," *Journal of Development Studies* (April 2001), pp. 101–33; Klein, *Bolivia*, p. 153; Elizabeth Jiménez Zamora and Marcelo Mercado Lora, "Economic Growth, Poverty, and Institutions: The Case Study of Bolivia," Global Development Network, 2005, pp. 8–10.

16. United States, Department of State, "Bolivia Series: Background Notes," March 2006.

17. Juan Antonio Morales and Jeffrey Sachs, "Bolivia's Economic Crisis," National Bureau of Economic Research, Cambridge, Massachusetts, Working Paper No. 2620 (June 1988), pp. 15–21, 24; Lehman, *Bolivia and the United States*, p. 193; Morales and Sachs, "Bolivia's Economic Crisis," pp. 21, 24.

18. Jeffrey Sachs, *The End of Poverty* (New York: Penguin, 2005), p. 93; Jeffrey Sachs, "The Bolivian Hyperinflation and Stabilization," *AEA Papers and Proceedings* (May 1987), p. 280; Gill, *Teetering on the Rim*, pp. 70–71; Klein, *Bolivia*, pp. 271–76.

19. Jeffrey Sachs, interview by *Commanding Heights*, PBS, 2002, pp. 6–7.

20. Gonzalo Sánchez de Lozada, *Commanding Heights* interview, pp. 8–10; Sachs, *The End of Poverty*, pp. 95–100; Felipe Larrain and Jeffrey Sachs, "Bolivia: On the Road to Development," Report prepared for the Ministry of Exports and Competitiveness, Bolivia (September 1993), pp. 3–6, 11.

21. Jeffrey Sachs, *Commanding Heights* interview, pp. 10–11; Sachs, *The End of Poverty*, pp. 102–3; Klein, *Bolivia*, pp. 200–201.

22. Larrain and Sachs, "Bolivia: On the Road to Development," p. 12.

23. Peirce, *Capitalization*, pp. 97–126.

24. Sánchez de Lozada, *Commanding Heights* interview, p. 4.

25. Grover Barja and Miguel Urquiola, "Capitalization and Privatization in Bolivia: An Approximation to an Evaluation," Center for Global Development Working Paper (February 2003), pp. 1–4.

26. Grover Barja and Miguel Urquiola, "Capitalization, Regulation and the Poor: Access to Basic Services in Bolivia," Discussion Paper No. 2001/34, World Institute for Development Economic Research, United Nations University (July 2001), pp. 4–6.

27. Peirce, *Capitalization*, pp. 71, 89.

28. Barja and Urquiola, "Capitalization, Regulation and the Poor," pp. 11, 28. Note that this study shows an improvement in electricity and phone coverage, though not only in urban areas, with poor neighborhoods benefiting equally.

29. Sebastian Martínez, "Pensions, Poverty and Household Investments in Bolivia," Working Paper, University of California, Berkeley (October 2004).

30. Geraldine Dalton, "Private Sector Finances for Water Sector Infrastructure: What Does Cochabamba Tell Us About Using This Instrument?," Occasional Paper No. 37, School of Oriental and African Studies, University of London (September 2001).

31. "Bolivian Government Dispatches More Troops to Coca-Growing Region," Agence France Presse, June 19, 2001; "Bolivia: Peasant Leader Quispe Says Willing to Resume Armed Struggle," BBC Monitoring Latin America, June 26, 2001; "Bolivia: Press Highlights," Cochabamba Los Tiempos, June 26, 2001.

32. "Coca Growers Give Ultimatum to Government," La Razón, October 15, 2001; "Protests: Bolivian 'Landless Workers' Hold Two Police, One Civilian Hostage," EFE News Service, October 15, 2001; "Government Will Not Declare State of Siege in Chapare," El Deber, October 30, 2001; "Bolivian Coca Producers Threaten to Defend Crops with Dynamite," EFE News Service, October 28, 2001; "Evo Morales Wants Dialogue with Government," La Razón, November 19, 2001; "Church Wants Cacaleros to Accept Government's Offer," El Deber and Nuevo Día, November 29, 2001.

33. "Coca Growers, Peasants Confirm Political Alliance," Cochabamba Los Tiempos, October 26, 2001.

34. Vanessa Arrington, "Colombian, Bolivian President Call for Open Markets for Andean Nations," Associated Press Worldstream, August 20, 2001; "Another Coca Farmer Death Intensifies Conflict in the Chapare," Associated Press Worldstream, October 17, 2001; "Coca: Seven Injured in Clashes Between Bolivian Army and Coca Growers," EFE News Service, October 18, 2001.

35. Klein, Bolivia, pp. 219, 278; Lehman, Bolivia and the United States, pp. 177–78, 185–86, 194–96. When Goni was elected president in 1993, he was not enthusiastic about the eradication plans, but was forced to honor prior agreements with the United States. He proposed a large increase in U.S. aid to achieve a "zero option," but U.S. aid declined instead. By the end of the 1990s, coca production was up 27 percent since the agreement signed with the United States in 1987.

36. Alma Guillermoprieto, "A New Bolivia?," The New York Review of Books, August 10, 2006; Ahmed Rashid, "Afghanistan: On the Brink," The New York Review of Books, June 22, 2006.

37. "California Confirms Interest in Bolivian Natural Gas," EFE News Service, October 22, 2001; "Foreign Firms Seek to Tap Vast New Gas Reserves," La Razón, November 1, 2001.

38. "Bolivia Gets Positive Rating from Moody's Investors," Cochamba Los Tiempos, June 26, 2001; "Bolivia Bets on Gas Exports," El Deber, September 26, 2001; Editorial, "The Opportunity Gas Offers," El Deber, Santa Cruz, October 26, 2001.

39. "Chile Open to Restoring Diplomatic Relations with Bolivia," La Prensa, November 26, 2001.

40. Los Tiempos Web site (Spanish), supplied by BBC Worldwide Monitoring, February 18, 2002.

41. Gonzalo Sánchez de Lozada, Speech at the American Bolivian Chamber of Commerce, November 8, 2001.

42. Amy Webber, "Tal's Bolivia Trip, November 10–13, 2001," observation notes.

43. Gonzalo Sánchez de Lozada, Interview with author, June 27, 2007.

44. Greenberg Quinlan Rosner Research, National survey of 1,503 respondents, November 27–December 4, 2001; Jeremy Rosner, presentation notes, November 27–December 4, 2001; Stanley B. Greenberg, Jeremy Rosner, and Mark Feierstein, "Goni Holds Narrow Lead but Must Escape an 'Electoral Box,'" Memo to Gonzalo Sánchez de Lozada, December 21, 2001; Greenberg Quinlan Rosner Research, Focus group summaries: Patacamaya, November 27, 2001; Sacaba, November 28, 2001; Warnes, November 29, 2001.

45. This is based on the thermometer question, with scores below 50 representing a "cool" or unfavorable response; scores above 50 on this 100-point scale are considered "warm" or favorable.

46. Greenberg Quinlan Rosner Research, Survey, November 27–Deccember 4, 2001.

47. Gonzalo Sánchez de Lozada, Interview with author, June 27, 2007.

48. Stanley B. Greenberg, Jeremy Rosner, and Mark Feierstein, "Nine Keys to Help Goni Escape from His Electoral Box," Memo to Gonzalo Sánchez de Lozada, January 28, 2002; Greenberg Quinlan Rosner Research, National survey of 1,002 respondents, January 10–14, 2002.

49. Gonzalo Sánchez de Lozada, "Acto de Proclamación a Candidato por La Presidencia de La República por El MNR," Speech to the MNR Convention, February 3, 2002.

50. "My Fellow Bolivians," Campaign ad, January 23, 2002.

51. Brian Katulis, "Focus Groups, El Alto and La Paz," E-mail to author, February 18, 2002; Jeremy Rosner, "Notes from Bolivia," E-mail to author, February 20, 2002.

52. *Our Brand Is Crisis*, DVD.

53. Jeremy Rosner, "Bolivia: Interesting Progress in FGs," E-mail to author, March 8, 2002.

54. Greenberg Quinlan Rosner Research, National survey of 3,498 respondents, February 17–27, 2002; Jeremy Rosner, presentation notes, La Paz, March 5–6, 2002; Stanley B. Greenberg, Jeremy Rosner, and Mark Feierstein, "Goni Makes Gains, Although Race Likely to Tighten Soon," Memo to Gonzalo Sánchez de Lozada, March 17, 2002.

55. Manfred Reyes Villa, "Bolivia Needs a New Heart," Ad transcript, April 4, 2002; Greenberg Quinlan Rosner Research, National survey of 1,500 respondents, March 20–25, 2002; Stanley B. Greenberg, Jeremy Rosner, and Mark Feierstein, "Goni Continues Gains, but Reyes Villa Poses Threat," Memo to Gonzalo Sánchez de Lozada, April 16, 2002.

56. Greenberg, Rosner, and Feierstein, "Goni Makes Gains"; Greenberg, Rosner, and Feierstein, "Goni Continues Gains."

57. Greenberg Quinlan Rosner Research, National survey of 3,503 respondents, April 23–30, 2002; Stanley Greenberg, Jeremy Rosner, and Mark Feierstein, "The Challenge of Overtaking Reyes Villa," Memo to Gonzalo Sánchez de Lozada, May 11, 2002.

58. Bolivia News Summary, *La Prensa, La Razón, El Diario*, April 7, 2002.

59. "Dollars and Votes: How Much Do You Have, How Much Are You Worth," *La Prensa*, April 8, 2002; "Manfred's Fortune Continues to Raise Questions," *La Prensa*, April 19, 2002; "What Does Manfred Reyes Really Have in Miami, and the Country?," *La Prensa*, April 20, 2002; "NFR Proposes to Double Military Budget,"

La Razón, April 30, 2002; "Manfred Has Three Homes in Miami," *La Prensa*, May 10, 2002; "Amidst Crisis, Armed Forces First Forum,"*La Prensa*, *La Razón*, June 15, 2002.

60. Jeremy Rosner, "Bolivia: Reyes Villa and Bonosol," E-mail to author, February 26, 2002.

61. *Our Brand Is Crisis*, DVD; "Manfred Reyes Villa's Opponents Have Files Ready on His Past," *La Razón*, April 14, 2002.

62. Focus groups, La Paz, April 10, 22, and 25, 2002; Rosner, Greenberg, and Feierstein, "The Challenge of Overtaking Reyes Villa," May 11, 2002.

63. Manfred Reyes Villa, "Another Song," Ad transcript, May 8, 2002.

64. Greenberg Quinlan Rosner Research, National survey of 1,542 respondents, April 23–30, 2002.

65. Amy Webber, "Conversation with Carolos Morales," E-mail to author, April 27, 2002.

66. "Manfred Says He Will Debate, Accuses MNR's 'Foreigners' of Dirty War," *La Razón*, May 5, 2002.

67. "MRV Mansion," Campaign ad, April 29, 2002.

68. Focus group transcripts: La Paz, April 29, 2002; Tarija, May 1, 2002.

69. Greenberg Quinlan Research, National survey of 1,498 respondents, May 10–12, 2002; National survey of 1,500 respondents, May 17–19, 2002.

70. Jeremy Rosner, presentation notes, May 13, 2002.

71. Jeremy Rosner, "Bolivia—Thoughts on Strategy, 43 Days Out," Memo to Greenberg Carville Shrom Team, May 17, 2002.

72. *Our Brand Is Crisis*, DVD.

73. Rosner, "Bolivia—Thoughts on Strategy"; Stanley B, Greenberg, Jeremy Rosner, and Mark Feierstein, "Reyes Villa Keeps Lead on Eve of Goni's New Strategic Phase," Memo to Gonzalo Sánchez de Lozada, May 22, 2002; Greenberg Quinlan Rosner Research, National survey of 1,500 respondents, May 17–19; Message Box, "Core Message—Bolivia Cannot Afford to Make the Wrong Choice," May 13, 2002.

74. Greenberg, Rosner, and Feierstein, "Reyes Villa Keeps Lead."

75. Greenberg Quinlan Rosner Research, National survey of 1,500 respondents, May 24–26, 2002; National survey of 3,500 respondents, June 1–3, 2002; Stanley B. Greenberg, Jeremy Rosner, and Mark Feierstein, "The Race Stabilizes: Report on the Third Tracking Survey, One Month Out," Memo to Gonzalo Sánchez de Lozada, May 31, 2002; Stanley Greenberg, Jeremy Rosner, and Mark Feierstein, "Waning Enthusiasm for Leading Candidates: Report on the Fourth Tracking Survey," Memo to Gonzalo Sánchez de Lozada, June 6, 2002.

76. Jeremy Rosner, "Emergency Plan for Jobs," E-mail to author, June 4, 2002.

77. GCS, "Action Plan for the Final Four Weeks."

78. Jeremy Rosner, "Bolivia Debate: Focus Group Verbatims," E-mail to author, June 17, 2002; Jeremy Rosner, "Next Steps," E-mail to author, June 17, 2002; GCS, "After the Debate: Winning the Final 12 Days," Memo to Gonzalo Sánchez de Lozada, June 17, 2002.

79. "Documents Put Reyes Villa in Trouble," *La Prensa*, *La Razón*, *El Diario*, June 7, 2002; *Daily Bolivia News*, *La Prensa*, June 12, June 13, 2002.

80. "Moon Sect Reveals That It Is Close to Manfred and Has Links," *La Prensa*, June 21,

2002; "In 17 Days Manfred Falls with 5 Lies," *La Razón*, June 20, 2002; "Manfred Will Visit the Cardinal to Deny Connections with the Moon Sect," *La Prensa*, June 24, 2002.

81. Greenberg Quinlan Rosner Research, National survey of 1,558 respondents, June 17–18, 2002; National survey of 1,635 respondents, June 21–24, 2002; Gonzalo Sánchez de Lozada, Interview with author.

82. This commitment was affirmed again during the campaign.

83. "Its Carnival . . . Lots of Carnival News," Bolivia News Summary, February 11, 2002; "Bloques Causing More Economic Problems," Bolivia News Summary, February 16, 2002.

84. Greenberg Quinlan Rosner Research, National survey of 3,498 respondents, February 19–27, 2002.

85. "US Critique of Quiroga's Fight Against Drugs," Bolivia News Summary, March 5, 2002; "President Tuto Quroga Rejected the United States Report on Its Drug Eradication Program," *La Razón*, *La Prensa*, *El Diario*, March 19, 2002.

86. "Constituyente," Bolivia News Summary, March 14–15, 2002; "Bolivia's Rocky Road to Reform," *International Crisis Group*, Latin America Report No. 18, July 3, 2006.

87. "Indigenous March Grows, Government Put in a Tight Spot," Bolivia News Summary, March 27, 2002; "Indigenous Marches Could Become Violent When They Enter La Paz," *La Prensa*, *La Razón*, *El Diario*, June 6, 2002; "The Conflicts Worry the Electoral Court, First Group of Marchers Arrive," *La Prensa*, *La Razón*, *El Diario*, June 8, 2002; "Pre-Agreement Reached with the Constituent Assembly, Indigenous Groups Divided," *La Prensa*, *La Razón*, *El Diario*, June 13, 2002.

88. "Ten Thousand People Ask That the Port for LNG be Peruvian and Not Chilean," *La Prensa*, *La Razón*, *El Diario*, June 13, 2002; *Our Brand Is Crisis*, DVD.

89. "US Puts Evo 'Under Observation,' the MAS Not Surprised," Bolivia News Summary, *La Prensa*, *La Razón*, *El Diario*, June 12, 2002; "Evo Morales Wants to Debate with US Ambassador," Bolivia News Summary, Channels 9, 7, 11, June 14, 2002.

90. "US Will Suspend Aid if Evo Is Elected: Ambassador Rocha," Bolivia News Summary, June 26, 2002; "US Ambassador Threatens to Boycott if Evo Elected or Allied With," Bolivia News Summary, June 27, 2002; "Electoral Court Criticizes Rocha and Asks Tuto to Stop the Ambassador," *La Prensa*, *La Razón*, *El Diario*, June 28, 2002.

91. Jeremy Rosner, "Bolivia Update," E-mail to author, July 1, 2002.

92. Our post-election poll showed voters deciding in the last week and last days to switch their votes to Evo from Goni and Manfred. Greenberg Quinlan Rosner Research, National post-election survey of 1,000 respondents, July 1–2, 2002.

93. *Our Brand Is Crisis*, DVD.

94. Greenberg Quinlan Rosner Research, National survey of 1,000 respondents, July 1–2, 2002; GCS, "A Narrow Victory Provides Clues for a Broader Mandate: Report on the Post-Election Survey," Memo to Gonzalo Sánchez de Lozada, July 11, 2002.

95. Greenberg Quinlan Rosner Research, National survey of 1,000 respondents, September 6–9, 2002.

96. Amy Webber, E-mail to author, September 10, 2002.

97. Jeremy Rosner, presentation notes to President Gonzalo Sánchez de Lozada, October 23, 2002: Greenberg Quinlan Rosner Research, National survey of 1,000 respondents, October 11–14, 2002.

98. Gonzalo Sánchez de Lozada, Speech, October 27, 2002; Gonzalo Sánchez de Lozada, Speech, November 9, 2002.

99. Stanley B. Greenberg, Jeremy Rosner, and Mark Feierstein, "Taking Back the Initiative and Connecting with the People: Report on the September 2002 Research," Memo to President Gonzalo Sánchez de Lozada, September 23, 2002.

100. It was clear that winning popular support for the export project would be difficult. A memo from December notes that "nearly two thirds, 63 percent, prefer exporting through Peru rather than Chile. When survey respondents are told that exporting the gas through Peru is not an option, the same share, 63 percent, says they would rather not export the gas at all." The only way to make headway would be to "radically reframe the issue," instead putting the stress on how the gas revenues will be used (education and social programs). At best, the memo warns, this has the "potential to blunt the intense opposition to exporting through Chile," but not to sell the program outright. Stanley B. Greenberg, Jeremy Rosner, and Mark Feierstein, "Investing the New Political Capital, Reframing the Gas Debate," Memo to President Gonzalo Sánchez de Lozada, December 20, 2002; Stanley B. Greenberg, Jeremy Rosner, and Mark Feierstein, "Launching the Second Sánchez de Lozada Administration: Report on the August 2002 National Survey and Focus Groups," Memo to President Gonzalo Sánchez de Lozada, August 23, 2002.

101. Jeremy Rosner, Interview with author, July 28, 2006.

102. Graham Gori, "Bolivian Authorities Clash with Farmers Demanding Right to Grow Coca," Associated Press Worldstream, January 13, 2003; "Coca Growers, Bolivian Government Meet to End Highway Siege," Agence France Presse, January 27, 2003.

103. Jeremy Rosner and Mark Feierstein, "Civil Unrest Badly Damages Government Standing," Memo to President Gonzalo Sánchez de Lozada and Mauricio Balcazar, January 25, 2003; Greenberg Quinlan Rosner Research, National survey of 1,000 respondents, February 21–24, 2003.

104. Gonzalo Sánchez de Lozada, Speech to the Nation, February 10, 2003; Jeremy Rosner, "Bolivia Violence," E-mail to author, February 12, 2003; Mark Feierstein, "Bolivia Violence," E-mail to author, February 12, 2003; Gonzalo Sánchez de Lozada, Speech to the Nation, February 12, 2003; Gonzalo Sánchez de Lozada, Speech to the Nation, February 13, 2003; Guillermoprieto, "A New Bolivia"; "Police Firing Near Bolivian Government HQ; President Leaves Building," Agence France Presse, February 12, 2003; Graham Gori, "Bolivia Hit by Wave of Violent Protests, Leaving at Least 17 Dead and 100 Injured," Associated Press, February 12, 2003.

105. Jeremy Rosner and Mark Feierstein, "Support Falls, but Reaction to Recent Steps Is Favorable," Memo to President Gonzalo Sánchez de Lozada, March 2, 2003.

106. Stanley B. Greenberg, Jeremy Rosner, and Mark Feierstein, "Opportunities for a Political Rebound: Report on the July 2003 Research," Memo to President Gonzalo Sánchez de Lozada, August 11, 2003; Jeremy Rosner and Mark Feierstein, "Over-

coming Opposition to Exporting Natural Gas: Report on the July 2003 Research,"
Memo to Minister Jorge Berindoague, August 12, 2003.

107. Willem Assies, "Bolivia: A Gasified Democracy," *Revista Europea de Estudios Latino-americanos y del Caribe* (April 2004), p. 30; Guillermoprieto, "A New Bolivia."

108. *Our Brand Is Crisis*, DVD.

109. Assies, "Bolivia," p. 30.

110. It is important to note that Evo Morales has never been accused of personally enriching himself in this process.

111. Gonzalo Sánchez de Lozada, Interview with author, June 27, 2007.

112. Kate Joynes, "President of Bolivia Offers to Leave Office as Protests Rage On," *World Markets Analysis*, June 7, 2005.

113. Assies, "Bolivia"; David Rieff, "Che's Second Coming?," *New York Times*, November 20, 2005; Dan Glaister, "Coca Farmer Turned Saviour of the Left Promises Wind of Change in Bolivia," *The Guardian*, December 8, 2005; Bill Faries, "After Win, Morales Faces Tough Task," *Christian Science Monitor*, December 20, 2005; Colin McMahon, "Morales Takes Reins, Slams Economic Elite," *Chicago Tribune*, January 23, 2006.

114. Patrick J. McDonnell, "Bolivian Leader Nationalizes Fuel Industry," *Los Angeles Times*, May 2, 2006; "Now It's the People's Gas," *The Economist*, May 6, 2006.

115. Adam Dawtrey, "Clooney, WB Get in 'Crisis' Mode: Documentary Re-imagined as a Dark Comedy," *Variety*, April 23, 2007; *Our Brand Is Crisis*, as described by Netflix, <http://www.netflix.com/Movie/Our_Brand_is_Crisis/>.

CONCLUSION

1. Key, *The Responsible Electorate: Rationality in Presidential Voting, 1936–1960* (Cambridge: Harvard University Press, 1961), pp. 4–7.

2. Key, *Public Opinion and American Democracy* (New York: Alfred A Knopf, 1961), pp. 3, 412, 547.

3. Hacker and Pierson, *Off Center*, p. 25.

4. George M. Frederickson, "A Man but Not a Brother: Abraham Lincoln and Racial Equality," *Journal of Southern History* (February 1975), p. 40.

5. David Herbert Donald, *Lincoln* (New York: Simon & Schuster, 1995), pp. 206–9, 216, 220–21, 226–27; John G. Geer, *From Tea Leaves to Opinion Polls: Politicians, Information and Leadership* (New York: Columbia University Press, 1996), p. 72; Frederickson, "A Man but Not a Brother," pp. 41–46.

6. Geer, *From Tea Leaves to Opinion Polls*, p. 73; Garry Wills, "What Makes a Good Leader?," *The Atlantic Monthly* (April 1994), pp. 64–69.

7. Geer, *From Tea Leaves to Opinion Polls*, p. 73.

8. Harry J. Maihafer, *War of Words: Abraham Lincoln and the Civil War Press* (Washington, D.C.: Brassey's, 2001); Donald, *Lincoln*, pp. 365–68; Geer, *From Tea Leaves to Opinion Polls*, p. 75.

9. Wills, "What Makes a Good Leader?," pp. 70–76.

10. Robert M. Eisenger, *The Evolution of Presidential Polling* (New York: Cambridge University Press, 2003), pp. 81–84.

11. Roper survey of 5,171 face-to-face interviews for *Fortune*, December 1938.

12. Eisinger, *The Evolution of Presidential Polling*, pp. 40–45; Hadley Cantril, various documents, Office of Public Opinion Research, Princeton University, reproduced from holdings of Franklin D. Roosevelt Library. Copies of the original documents were provided by Robert Eisinger, for which I am thankful.

13. Dan Froomkin, "Cheney Doesn't Care What You Think," *Washington Post*, March 20, 2008.

14. Richard E. Neustadt, *Presidential Power and the Modern Presidents: The Politics of Leadership from Roosevelt to Reagan* (New York: The Free Press, 1991), p. ix.

15. George C. Edwards III, *On Deaf Ears: The Limits of the Bully Pulpit* (New Haven: Yale University Press, 2003), pp. 9–10; Gilens, "Inequality and Democratic Responsiveness," pp. 784–76.

16. V.O. Key, *Public Opinion and American Democracy*, p. 555; Colleen A. Sheehan, "Madison v. Hamilton: The Battle over Republicanism and the Role of Public Opinion," *American Political Science Review* (August 2004), pp. 405–8, 414–19.

17. Jane Mansbridge, "Rethinking Representation," *American Political Science Review* (November 2003), pp. 515–20; Key, *Public Opinion and American Democracy*, p. 555; Jürgen Habermas, *The Structural Transformation of the Public Sphere*, 7 ed, (Cambridge, Massachusetts: The MIT Press), 1997, pp. 29–30, 218–22.

18. E. E. Schattschneider, *The Semisovereign People: A Realist's View of Democracy in America* (Fort Worth: Harcourt Brace Jovanovich College Publishers, 1975), pp. 1–3, 46–48, 62–75.

19. *Daily Bolivia News*, August 5, 2002.

20. Stanley B. Greenberg, Speech to the American Enterprise Institute, "Annual Policy Conference: Pollsters," Washington, D.C., December 8, 1993.

21. Campbell, *The Blair Years*, pp. 111–12.

22. Gwen Ifill, "The 1992 Campaign: Campaign Profile," *New York Times*, October 27, 1992; Jonathan Cohn, "Mr. Populism Returns," *The New Republic*, September 11, 2000.

23. Hillary Clinton for President, Press Release, "New Ad: Hillary Promises to Be a 'Partner' to Ohio's Working Families in a New TV Ad," March 3, 2008; "Adwatch: Obama Responds to Clinton Ad on Oil Industry Money," Associated Press, April 27, 2008.

24. Morris, *Behind the Oval Office*, pp. 14–15, 80–81; Ari Berman, "Hillary Inc.," *The Nation*, June 4, 2007; Mark Schmitt, "The Real Case Against Mark Penn," *Talking Points Memo*, May 9, 2007.

25. David A. Dulio, *For Better or Worse?: How Political Consultants Are Changing Elections in the United States* (New York: State University of New York Press, 2004), p. 56. Motivation of consultants: 53.5 percent beliefs or ideology plus 7.5 percent help party get majority; about 20 percent thrill; money 11.2 percent; power and influence 4.5 percent: pp. 61–66.

26. Morris, *Behind the Oval Office*, p. 37.

27. Morris, *The New Prince*, p. 58.

28. Harris, *The Survivor*, p. 163; Morris, *Behind the Oval Office*, pp. 9, 13.

29. Morris, *Behind the Oval Office*, 293, 297; Harris, *The Survivor*, p. 168.

30. Diane J. Heith, "Continuing to Campaign: Public Opinion and the White House" in Michael A. Genovese and Matthew J. Streb, eds., *Polls and Politics: The Dilemmas of Democracy* (Albany: State University of New York Press, 2004), pp. 63–67.

31. Mark J. Penn, *Microtrends: The Small Forces Behind Tomorrow's Big Changes* (New York: Twelve/Hachette Book Group USA, 2007), pp. xii–xviii.

32. Bill Clinton, Remarks at the Annual White House Correspondents' Dinner, Washington, D.C., May 1, 1993.

33. Morris, *Behind the Oval Office*, p. 41.

34. Stanley B. Greenberg, Speech to the American Enterprise Institute, December 8, 1993.

INDEX